170

The New York Times

SPORTS
of the
TIMES

A Day-by-Day Selection of the Most Important,
Thrilling, and Inspired Events of the
Past 150 Years

EDITED BY

WILLIAM TAAFFE *and* DAVID FISCHER

St. Martin's Press   New York

Book Design by Michael Collica

Library of Congress Cataloging-in-Publication Data

Sports of the Times: a day-by-day selection of the most important, thrilling, and inspired events of the past 150 years / edited by William Taaffe and David Fischer.—1st ed.
    p. cm.
ISBN 0-312-31232-6
1. Sports—United States—History. I. Taaffe, William. II. Fischer, David 1963– III. New York Times.
GV583.S69   2003
796'.0973—dc21

2003047028

First Edition: November 2003

10 9 8 7 6 5 4 3 2 1

To William P. Taaffe and Robert L. Fischer,

who in their stride showed two sons the

inherent romance of sports.

Introduction

For those who avidly follow sports, and even for those who don't, a series of momentous events begins to form over time in the mind's eye. It's a common repository, if you will. The fan who would think nothing of paying $250 for a ticket to the Super Bowl and the one who would rather spend it at the opera both remember or have heard of certain compelling moments in sports: The United States Olympic hockey team's "Miracle" on Ice in 1980. Babe Ruth's 60th home run in 1927. The night a young man with a big mouth from Louisville, Cassius Clay, did indeed become the greatest.

Over the years, these shared moments evolve into a kind of canon of sports. It's a beautiful, even romantic repository. Fans and casual followers alike know many of the elements. Jesse Owens winning in the Berlin Olympics while Hitler looked on is part of the canon. So is Joe Namath guaranteeing (and then delivering) a victory in the Super Bowl. The night Cal Ripken broke Lou Gehrig's "unbreakable" record for consecutive games played is also included. And yes, so is the achingly sad Munich Massacre, when 11 Israeli Olympic team members died at the hands of Palestinian terrorists in 1972.

The words and photographs you have in your hands catalog this memory book in a unique way—by calendar date, regardless of the year, directly from the pages of *The New York Times*. With certain concessions for balance and pace, we have chosen what in our judgment is the most important or compelling event on each date, along with the three next most significant events in ranking order. *The Times*, an international newspaper today, was distinctively New Yorkish for much of its 152-year history. Yet no special emphasis has been given to New York teams or events to the exclusion of events far from Manhattan.

A word about our procedure. Certain events—like the Super Bowl in January, the Masters in April, the Olympics in late summer and the World Series in October—dominate their respective seasons. In a volume of this size, just as on the sports pages, they can crowd out other events happening at the same time. And so to enhance the variety of *Sports of the Times*—to pitch the reader a slider, as it were—we've opted on occasion for a basketball headliner during a baseball week or an important tennis story in the midst of a fortnight of football.

Nevertheless, we've attempted to choose the top events and runners-up on all but a handful of dates. We accepted three premises: That news value is primary. That some events become more compelling when viewed with hindsight. And that the world of sports cannot be interpreted apart from the society and the era in which it exists. Hours of debate went into making the choices. And so difficult were some selections that on five dates top billing on a single day was shared by events from two different years. On one other day (Oct. 18, the most crowded in sports history) we saw no alternative to designating three headliners. Finally, we've selected 50 events as especially important or compelling. These have been designated on the respective dates by five stars down the side of the page.

This book would not have been possible without the creativity, sound judgment and tireless work of our collaborators, the photo editors Brad Smith and Francisco Bernasconi. Brad came late to the project after Francisco's deadline tasks at *The Times* compelled him to withdraw, but his imagination more than made up for his midstream arrival. The scope and appearance of the book was greatly enhanced by the imagination of Mike Levitas, former head of *The Times* book development program; we welcomed the deft editing and timely suggestions of Marc Resnick of St. Martin's Press. And the project in a real sense would have been next to impossible to accomplish without the understanding and support of our wives, Donna Taaffe and Carolyn Fischer.

Many others contributed ideas, time, advice and encouragement. They include Richard Barranger, Brent Bowers of *The Times*, Bob Ingham, Don Mennella, Rick Parker and Arnold Rabin. To all of them, and to numerous other friends and associates who shared our vision, our deep and abiding thanks.

—WILLIAM TAAFFE
Henderson, Nevada

—DAVID FISCHER
River Vale, New Jersey

JANUARY

January 1, 1929
Roy Riegels's Wrong-Way Run to Daylight

[Unsigned, *The New York Times*]

PASADENA, Cal.—In a thrilling football game before a capacity crowd of 70,000 in the Rose Bowl here today, the Golden Tornado of Georgia Tech defeated the University of California by a score of 8 to 7, the victors scoring on a safety and a touchdown. The Western eleven rallied in the fourth quarter on a straight march from its own 2-yard line.

The game was marked by an unusual play, which, it ultimately developed, was of great importance in the final score. It led to Georgia Tech's safety. Captain-elect Roy Riegels of the Golden Bears, playing center, snatched up a Tech fumble in the second quarter and started toward the Georgia Tech goal. Tech men sprang up in front of him and in eluding them Riegels cut back across the field. He turned again to escape and in so doing apparently became confused and started toward his own goal, sixty yards away. As he pounded down the side line both California and Tech players stood amazed in their tracks.

Benny Lom, halfback for the Golden Bears, sensed the situation almost immediately and sprang into action. Down the field he went after the flying Riegels, who only put on more speed as he heard feet pounding in the turf behind him. Finally Lom grabbed hold of his mate at the California 3-yard line and turned him around. Making interference for Riegels, Lom started back up the field, but a wave of Tech tacklers hit Riegels before he could more than turn around, hurtling him back to the 1-yard line.

California immediately took up the punt formation, but Riegels, at center, was nervous, and Lom, receiving the ball to kick, was little steadier. As the ball was snapped, Maree, Georgia Tech tackle, stormed through and blocked the punt. The ball rolled out of the end zone, but the officials ruled that the Breakenridge, Calif., quarterback had touched it and that a safety would be scored against California.

Lom was the outstanding hero for the losers. He played smart football, was in every play and carried the ball on sweeping end runs. He shot through tackle and over guard, hurled long passes to the ends, or short, snappy passes to the other backs. His kicking was excellent.

Roy Riegels centering for California in 1929. His notorious wrong-way run on New Year's Day helped Georgia Tech win the Rose Bowl and prompted the radio announcer Graham McNamee to exclaim: "What am I seeing? Am I crazy?" (Associated Press)

Runners-up

1979: With Notre Dame down by 22 points in the fourth quarter of the frigid Cotton Bowl in Dallas, Joe Montana staged his greatest collegiate comeback, coming off the bench and leading the Irish to a 35–34 victory over the University of Houston with a touchdown pass to Kris Haines with no time left on the clock.

1995: Coach Tom Osborne's Nebraska Cornhuskers, led by quarterback Tommie Frazier, won the national championship by defeating Miami, 24–17, with two fourth-quarter touchdown drives in the Orange Bowl after being down by 17–9. It was Osborne's first title after more than two decades as coach.

1938: Stanford University's Hank Luisetti, who revolutionized college basketball two seasons before by inverting the running one-hander in an age of the two-handed set shot (*see Dec. 30*), became the first collegian to score 50 points as Stanford defeated Duquesne, 92–27, in Cleveland.

January 2, 1982
A Prize Fight of a Football Game

By MALCOLM MORAN

MIAMI—At the end of the wildest, highest scoring playoff game in National Football League history, Kellen Winslow of the San Diego Chargers looked more like a boxer at the end of a fight. Winslow, a tight end who became an all-pro because of his ability to catch passes, displayed another skill that helped the Chargers advance to the American conference championship game for the second straight season today with a 41–38 victory over the Miami Dolphins.

The Chargers won when Rolf Benirschke, who missed a 27-yard attempt early in overtime, kicked a 29-yard field goal 13 minutes 52 seconds into the extra period. But if not for Winslow, the game may not have gone into overtime, and the Dolphins would have ended the sixth overtime game in playoff history with the greatest playoff comeback.

After rallying from a 24–0 deficit to tie the score, and after two more touchdowns by each team that made the score 38–38, the Dolphins drove to the San Diego 25. With four seconds to go in regulation time, Uwe von Schamann lined up for a 43-yard field-goal attempt. But the snap from center was high, and Winslow, who does not ordinarily play on the field-goal-blocking unit, was able to deflect the kick. "It was the biggest thrill of my life," Winslow said. "I felt like I scored three touchdowns."

A 34-yard attempt by von Schamann, 11:27 into overtime, was blocked by the defensive end Leroy Jones. That allowed Benirschke, who missed a 27-yard attempt in overtime, to make the kick that put the Chargers into the A.F.C. championship game. The Dolphins had come from behind on the play of Don Strock, who replaced David Woodley at quarterback in the second quarter, with Miami trailing by 24 points. Strock completed 28 of 42 passes for 397 yards and four touchdowns.

Dan Fouts, the Charger quarterback, completed 33 of 53 passes for 433 yards, a league playoff record, and three touchdowns. The Dolphins gained 466 net yards and San Diego 564, for a total of 1,030. The two teams surpassed the league record for most points in a playoff game, 73, which was established in a Detroit–Cleveland game in 1973 and Chicago's 73–0 victory over Washington in 1940 [see Dec. 8].

There were 11 team records set. And after the end of the fourth longest game in N.F.L. history, which ended in darkness four hours and three minutes after it began in the late-afternoon sunshine, there were two locker rooms full of players who had gone beyond themselves. In the 18th week of an emotionally draining season in San Diego, the Chargers have gone as far as they did last year. They are one game from the Super Bowl. "We've got some guys who are in that part of their career that it might be their last chance," Fouts said. "When you get a little desperate, you find something extra."

Rolf Benirschke kicking the 29-yard field goal that propelled the Chargers into the A.F.C. championship game by outlasting the Dolphins, 41-38, in Miami. The marathon ended 13 minutes 52 seconds into overtime. (Associated Press)

Runners-up

1984: With Bernie Kosar coolly slinging side-arm passes, the University of Miami defeated favored Nebraska, 31–30, in the Orange Bowl for the national title. To his credit according to most fans, Coach Tom Osborne went for a 2-point conversion after the Cornhuskers' final touchdown, but failed.

1987: Penn State intercepted Miami University's Heisman Trophy quarterback, Vinny Testaverde, five times in the Fiesta Bowl, giving the Nittany Lions and Coach Joe Paterno a 14–10 victory and their second national title in five seasons.

1965: Under the goal posts of the Orange Bowl, where he had performed superbly in a 21–17 loss to the University of Texas the day before, Alabama quarterback Joe Namath signed a three-year contract with Jets owner Sonny Werblin for an unheard-of $427,000. It was the highest salary of any professional athlete at the time.

January 3, 1973
Absentee Owner? Sure

By JOSEPH DURSO

George Steinbrenner, left, and Michael Burke, right, at a press conference announcing their acquisition of the Yankees from CBS. General Manager Gabe Paul is at center. "We plan absentee ownership," Steinbrenner said. (The New York Times)

NEW YORK—The Columbia Broadcasting System said today that it was selling the New York Yankees to a 12-man syndicate headed by Michael Burke, now president of the team, and George M. Steinbrenner 3d of Cleveland.

The price is $10 million in cash, which is $3.2 million less than CBS. paid for the franchise in 1964, the last year the Yankees won the American League pennant. Mr. Burke, who has been running the club for CBS, will continue to direct it for the self-styled "absentee owners," and the Yankees, he said, will remain in New York.

"We plan absentee ownership as far as running the Yankees is concerned," Steinbrenner said. "We're not going to pretend we're something we aren't. I'll stick to building ships."

The only partners in the syndicate who appeared at Yankee Stadium for the announcement were Mr. Burke and Mr. Steinbrenner, 42-year-old chairman of the American Ship Building Company and part-owner of the Chicago Bulls basketball team.

No other partners were identified—except as "prominent business executives and sportsmen"—though the Yankees said they would be introduced in person here next week.

The sale itself was no surprise, since Mr. Burke acknowledged last July that CBS was listening to offers. But two aspects of the sale did raise some eyebrows: the price, which was considered a bargain in today's professional sports market, and the fact that CBS sold so far below its original purchase price.

In its statement CBS said "the $10 million purchase price substantially recoups the original CBS investment of $13.2 million, taking into account consolidated financial results during the period of ownership. The purchase price is well in excess of the value carried on the CBS books."

Runners-up

2003: Ohio State, coached by Jim Tressel, won its first national football championship in 34 years with a 31–24 victory over Larry Coker's Miami squad. Maurice Clarett scored the winning touchdown and Buckeye linebacker Matt Wilhelm batted down a Ken Dorsey pass in double overtime in one of the most dramatic games in college history.

1993: In the biggest comeback in N.F.L. history, Buffalo Bills quarterback Frank Reich, spelling the injured Jim Kelly, overcame a 32-point third-quarter deficit and beat the Houston Oilers, 41–38 in overtime, in a wild-card playoff game. The Bills eventually lost in the Super Bowl to the Dallas Cowboys.

1983: The Dallas Cowboys' Tony Dorsett went 99 yards for a touchdown in a Monday night loss to the Minnesota Vikings in the Metrodome, setting an N.F.L. record that will never be beaten for the longest run from the line of scrimmage.

Make Way for Eric

By MICHAEL JANOFSKY

ANAHEIM, Calif.—If you ever wondered why they pay talented running backs all that money, you only needed to watch Eric Dickerson today in the Los Angeles Rams' 20–0 playoff victory over the Dallas Cowboys.

He not only ran 34 times for 248 yards, a National Football League playoff record, he scored two touchdowns and brightened up an otherwise dismal game. Thanks to his rushing, five sacks by the Rams' defense and excellent play by their special teams, the Rams advanced to the National Conference championship game Jan. 12, when they will play the winner of the game Sunday between the Chicago Bears and the Giants.

Dickerson, who missed the first game of the season because of a contract dispute, later signed an extension that will bring him more than $2.5 million after the 1986 season. From the looks of things today, the Rams got the better of the deal. Dickerson ran 55 yards on the first play from scrimmage in the second half to give the Rams a 10–0 lead and he scooted 40 yards for another touchdown on the third play of the fourth quarter for a 20–0 lead. On each, he got picture-perfect blocks from his teammates, and once he cleared the Dallas secondary, no one was able to get a hand on him.

"That was as good a game as I have ever seen a man play," said John Robinson, the Rams' coach. "Eric ran very, very hard. From the first play, I sensed that we would be able to be successful running the ball. We got great blocking, particularly on the right side. I don't think anybody could have had a better day."

Dickerson's yardage surpassed a playoff record that has stood for 22 years and

Eric Dickerson galloping through the Patriots' defense while with the Colts in 1987. Enigmatic though gifted, he racked up more than 13,000 yards, the fourth-highest total ever, during 11 years with the Rams and Colts. (Associated Press)

was the most ever given up by the Cowboys. It was also the most yards ever gained by a Ram running back. The playoff record had been held by Keith Lincoln of the San Diego Chargers, who ran for 206 yards in a game against the Boston Patriots. Jim Brown of the Cleveland Browns ran for 232 yards against the Cowboys in 1963. Willie Ellison held the Rams' rushing record, 247 yards in 1971.

"Dallas didn't think we could run on them," said Dickerson, mindful of the Cowboys' No. 4 ranking against the rush in the regular season. "But our strength is our running game, and we knew we could run on them."

That was most evident on his touchdown runs. On the first, he followed blocks by the center, Tony Slaton, and the right guard, Dennis Harrah, as Barry Redden, the fullback, knocked Mike Hegman, the left linebacker, out of the play. "It was a quick hit up the middle," Dickerson said. "For some reason, they were playing their safeties and cornerbacks up, maybe in a blitz. We knew if we could catch them in a blitz, we could burn them."

On the second scoring run, he took a pitch from Dieter Brock and raced round the right side. "Michael Downs tried to tackle me high," Dickerson said, referring to the Cowboys' free safety. "There was no way I was going to let him tackle me."

The Chicago Bears dominated the Rams, 24–0, in the National Football Conference championship game the following week at Soldier Field in Chicago, holding Eric Dickerson to 46 yards on the ground. The Bears then won the Super Bowl over the New England Patriots.

Runners-up

1996: Don Shula, the N.F.L.'s winningest coach, told a local television station on his 66th birthday that he had decided to retire from the Miami Dolphins. He left with a record of 347–173–6 with the Baltimore Colts and Miami. His teams appeared in six Super Bowls in his 33-year coaching career, winning twice.

2000: After 34 years, Coach Bobby Bowden finally completed an undefeated season as top-ranked Florida State University, led by wide receiver Peter Warrick's 20 points, captured its second national title in a decade with a 46–29 victory over

undefeated Virginia Tech in the Sugar Bowl.

1981: Trailing by 24–10 in the fourth quarter, the Dallas Cowboys made one of the N.F.L.'s most remarkable comebacks, scoring 20 points to beat the Atlanta Falcons, 30–27, in a divisional playoff game at Fulton County Stadium. The winning touchdown came with 52 seconds left when Danny White passed to Drew Pearson in the end zone. The Cowboys lost the next week to the Philadelphia Eagles in the N.F.C. championship game.

January 5, 1920
A Staggering (Then) Sum

[Unsigned, *The New York Times*]

NEW YORK—Babe Ruth of the Boston Red Sox, baseball's super-slugger, was purchased by the Yankees today for the largest cash sum ever paid for a player. The New York club paid Harry Frazee of Boston $125,000 for the sensational batsman who last season caused such a furor in the national game by batting out twenty-nine home runs, a new record in long-distance clouting.

Colonel Ruppert, President of the Yanks, said that he had taken over Ruth's Boston contract, which has two years more to run. This contract calls for a salary of $10,000 a year. Ruth recently announced that he would refuse to play for $10,000 next season, although the Boston Club has received no request for a raise in salary.

Manager Miller Huggins is now in Los Angeles negotiating with Ruth. It is believed that the Yankee manager will offer him a new contract which will be satisfactory to the Colossus of the bat. President Ruppert said yesterday Ruth would probably play right field for the Yankees. He played in left field for the Red Sox last season, and had the highest fielding average among the outfielders, making only two errors during the season. While he is on the Pacific Coast, Manager Huggins will also endeavor to sign Duffy Lewis, who will be one of Ruth's companions in the outfield at the Polo Grounds next season.

Mr. Frazee said tonight that he had sold Ruth to the New York Americans because he thought it was an "injustice" to keep him with the Red Sox, who "were fast becoming a one-man team." Mr. Frazee said he would use the money obtained from the New York Club for the purchase of other players and would try to develop the Red Sox into a winning team.

Ruth was told by The Associated Press in Los Angeles that Colonel Ruppert had announced the deal. "I am not surprised," he said. "When I made my demand on the Red Sox for $20,000 a year, I had an idea they would choose to sell me rather than pay the increase, and I knew the Yankees were the most probable purchasers in that event."

The acquisition of Ruth strengthens the Yankee club in its weakest department. With the added hitting power of Ruth, Bob Shawkey, one of the Yankee pitchers, said yesterday the New York club should be a pennant winner next season. For several seasons the Yankees have been experimenting with outfielders, but never have been able to land a consistent hitter. The short right field wall at the Polo Grounds should prove an easy target for Ruth next season and, playing seventy-seven games at home, it would not be surprising if Ruth surpassed his home-run record of twenty-nine circuit clouts next summer.

Ruth was such a sensation last season that he supplanted the great Ty Cobb as baseball's greatest attraction, and in obtaining the services of Ruth for next season the New York club made a ten-strike which will be received with the greatest enthusiasm by Manhattan baseball fans.

Ruth's crowning batting accomplishment came at the Polo Grounds last fall when he hammered one of the longest hits ever seen in Harlem over the right field grandstand for his twenty-eighth home run, smashing the home-run record of twenty-seven, made by Ed Williamson way back in 1884.

Jacob Ruppert's timing in the Babe Ruth deal was impeccable. Ruth went from 29 home runs in 1919 to 54 in 1920 and 59 in 1921 in the friendly Polo Grounds, dominating the game and making the 1919 Black Sox scandal (see Sept. 28) all but a distant memory.

Babe Ruth of the Red Sox in an undated photo, circa 1916. By selling him to the Yankees for an extravagant $125,000, the Sox parted ways with the best left-handed pitcher in their history. (Associated Press)

Runners-up

1957: Having been traded by the Brooklyn Dodgers to the crosstown New York Giants three weeks earlier for the journeyman pitcher Dick Littlefield and $35,000, Jackie Robinson announced his retirement from baseball at age 37.

2003: In the second-largest playoff collapse in N.F.L. history, the Giants surrendered a 24-point third-quarter lead and lost a wild-card game to the San Francisco 49ers, 39–38, at Candlestick Park. The N.F.L. announced the next day that the officials had erred in not calling a penalty on the game's last play that would have allowed the Giants another attempt to make a game-winning kick.

1971: The Harlem Globetrotters lost to the New Jersey Reds, 100–99, but then began an 8,829-game winning streak that did not end until Kareem Abdul-Jabbar's Legendary All-Stars defeated them in Vienna, 91–85, in September 1995. The Globetrotters' mostly scripted exhibitions have been an enduring part of sports since the promoter Abe Saperstein founded them in 1927.

January 6, 1994
Jealousy on Ice

By JERE LONGMAN

DETROIT [Thursday]—Nancy Kerrigan, the United States' best female figure skater and one of the gold-medal favorites for the 1994 Olympics, was attacked after practice today by an unidentified man who struck her on the right knee with a blunt object and escaped. The attack jeopardized Kerrigan's chances of qualifying for the Winter Games next month in Lillehammer, Norway.

Kerrigan, who is 24 and lives in Plymouth, Mass., had just completed a practice at Cobo Hall in preparation for tomorrow's competition at the United States championships. A witness said the attacker, described as a white man about 6 feet 2 inches and 200 pounds, hit Kerrigan with a club-like instrument resembling a tire iron, a crowbar or a nightstick. Kerrigan was taken to a local hospital for X-rays then released. No fracture was found, according to the doctor who treated her, who said she suffered a cut and a bruise and swelling but was able to walk with a limp. The doctor, Dr. Steven Plomaritis, said the attack appeared calculated.

"He was clearly trying to debilitate her," Plomaritis said.

Kerrigan's father, Dan, rushed to his sobbing daughter, lifted her and carried her into the locker room. "It hurts, it hurts so bad; I'm so scared," Kerrigan told her father.

It was not immediately known whether Kerrigan would be able to skate tomorrow in the short program. The right leg is the one that Kerrigan uses to land jumps during her skating routines. Competing in the

Tonya Harding and an attorney, entering Multnomah County Circuit Court in Portland, Ore., in March 1994. She pleaded guilty to a conspiracy charge in the attack on her figure-skating rival Nancy Kerrigan. (Associated Press)

two-and-half-minute program would not make the injury worse, Plomaritis said. Essentially, it would be a matter of how much pain she could withstand, he said. The women's competition concludes Saturday night at Joe Louis Arena.

Jerry Solomon, her agent, said late tonight that Kerrigan's knee continued to swell, forcing the cancellation of a planned practice. She will be examined again by doctors tomorrow morning. "She sustained quite a blow, physically and emotionally as well," Solomon said. Kerrigan told ABC Sports tonight that she would attempt to skate tomorrow. "It's not the most important thing, skating," Kerrigan said. "If I can't I'll have to deal with it. I'm O.K. It could have been a lot worse."

Today's attack was the third threatening incident recently that involved a figure skater. Tonya Harding, the 1991 national champion and a 1992 Olympian, reported a death threat on Nov. 4, which caused her to withdraw from the northwest regional championships in Portland, Ore. Harding said she has been traveling with a bodyguard. Katarina Witt of Germany was threatened by a man who sent her obscene mail and who was later ordered to spend 37 months in a psychiatric hospital and ordered not to contact Witt.

Tonya Harding pleaded guilty to conspiring to hinder prosecution in the attack on Nancy Kerrigan and was placed on three years' probation and fined $160,000. Jeff Gillooly, Harding's former husband, and three others, including her bodyguard, Shawn Eckhardt, accused of having hatched the plot, spent time in prison. Harding was permanently barred from all amateur skating competition.

Runners-up

1993: The N.F.L. consented to a new seven-year collective bargaining agreement that altered pro football by giving players much more freedom to move between teams. Owners were allowed to impose team salary caps, and players got the right to unrestricted free agency.

1985: Dan Marino had perhaps his greatest day as a pro, leading the Miami Dolphins into the Super Bowl by defeating the Pittsburgh Steelers, 45–28, in the American Football Conference title game at the Orange Bowl. He completed 21 of 32 passes for 421 yards and 4 touchdowns.

1976: Ted Turner, yachtsman and owner of WTBS, a satellite television station, bought the Atlanta Braves for a reported $12 million, quickly turning their games into prime-time programming and giving them national exposure. Partly because of cable television revenues, the perennial losers became a dominant team in 15 years, going from last place to first in 1991, though they lost to the Minnesota Twins in the World Series (see Oct. 27).

January 7, 1972
Dream Team

By THOMAS ROGERS

ATLANTA—The Los Angeles Lakers extended their record-shattering winning streak to 33 straight games tonight by routing the Atlanta Hawks, 134–90, in the National Basketball Association. Jim McMillian led the way early and Gail Goodrich late as the Lakers made the victory one of their easiest. They have not lost since Oct. 31.

By shooting 62.5 per cent in the first half and holding the Hawks to 35.8 per cent, Los Angeles turned the game into an early runaway. McMillian got 20 of his 26 points in the first half and Goodrich got 18 of his 23 in the second half. Wilt Chamberlain was the dominating factor under the boards.

Late in the third quarter, with the score 92–61, the Atlanta coach, Richie Guerin, benched his starters for a rookie-studded line-up. It was the Hawks' worst defeat in five years. "They kill you, demoralize you and take advantage of every break," Guerin said. "This is the sign of a great team."

"When we put it all together, we've got to be perhaps the greatest club ever," said Bill Sharman, the Laker coach who is in his first year at Los Angeles.

Wilt Chamberlain, employing his extraordinary rebounding and defensive talents to perfection, has made the Lakers a free-wheeling, offensive powerhouse.

With the 7-foot-1-inch center controlling the defensive board, the rest of the Lakers have been able to employ the fast break to advantage. Pacing the scoring are Jerry West, one of the league's all-time leaders in points and assists, and Goodrich, who in his seventh pro year has achieved the star stature predicted for him when he left the University of California, Los Angeles.

Jim McMillian, a second-year pro, and Happy Hairston, the forwards, have contributed at both ends of the court to round out the starting line-up. McMillian, an all-American selection at Columbia, received his chance to shine early this season when Elgin Baylor retired.

Jerry West (44) being fouled on a drive around teammate Wilt Chamberlain's screen in a December 1971 game against the Rockets. The Lakers won their 28th straight game en route to a record 33 in a row. (Associated Press)

Runners-up

1992: Tom Seaver, the franchise pitcher for the Mets who won 311 games in his 20-year career, was elected to the Hall of Fame with 98.8 percentage of the vote by the Baseball Writers' Association of America. It was the highest percentage ever earned in the history of the balloting—a sure sign of Seaver's enduring stature.

1990: The Giants lost a divisional playoff game to the Los Angeles Rams, 19–13, on Jim Everett's stunning 30-yard touchdown strike in overtime. Willie (Flipper) Anderson caught the pass in midstride and ran it straight into the Giants Stadium tunnel. The Rams lost in the N.F.C. title game to the San Francisco 49ers, who became the Super Bowl champions.

1889: Walter Camp, the Yale coach and father of football for having turned English rugby into the American game, named his first All-America football team, creating a tradition that has lasted for more than a century. Original All-Americas included two Yalies, end Amos Alonzo Stagg, later a famous coach, and guard William (Pudge) Heffelfinger, the first pro player (see Nov. 12).

Miracle in Music City

By THOMAS GEORGE

Frank Wycheck throwing a lateral to teammate Kevin Dyson, who ran 75 yards to complete a kickoff return for a touchdown with seconds remaining, giving the Titans a stunning A.F.C. wild-card playoff victory over the Bills. (Associated Press)

NASHVILLE—The play was the most familiar and folksy of backyard, old-school calls—the old across-the-field lateral on a kickoff with 16 seconds remaining—and it left the Buffalo Bills in shambles and lifted the Tennessee Titans to a dramatic, thumping, 22–16 wild-card playoff victory before 66,782 fans today at Adelphia Coliseum.

Many who saw it still cannot believe it. "What a play!" said Tennessee's Bruce Matthews. What a game. What a show. What a victory. What a loss. "What can you say?" asked Tennessee's Eddie George.

Plenty. Tennessee won the game with three seconds left on a 75-yard kickoff return for a touchdown by receiver Kevin Dyson. In a fourth quarter that featured four lead changes, Tennessee thought it had the game won when it kicked a 36-yard field goal with 1 minute 48 seconds left to lead by 15–13. Buffalo thought it had it won when Steve Christie made a 41-yard field goal with 16 seconds left to lead by 16–15.

But then Christie kicked off, Lorenzo

Neal gathered the short boot near the Tennessee 25, ran toward his right and then handed the ball off to teammate Frank Wycheck. Wycheck, a tight end, spun and threw the ball across the field to Dyson. Dyson caught the low toss and took off down the left sideline with a convoy of blockers. Buffalo was completely fooled, its players a few steps behind Dyson, and he raced 75 yards into the end zone. The play took 13 seconds, but the big question—did Wycheck throw a forward pass to Dyson?—would be answered by instant replay.

Referee Phil Luckett studied the play at his sideline replay booth while players and coaches from both teams stood and paced on the field, waiting. The clock said :03. It seemed as if Luckett was taking three days to decide. What would he rule? "I was talking to No. 25 on their team while we waited," said the Titans' Anthony Dorsett of Buffalo's Donovan Greer. "We both were saying: 'This is crazy. What if it's our way? What if it's your way?' Nobody knew what to expect."

The Bills' owner, Ralph Wilson, said he did. "When it went from the replay booth into the hands of the officials on the field, I knew we were through—and you can print that," Wilson said.

Luckett finally appeared and said the play stood as called. Touchdown. Tennessee (14–3) wins. Buffalo (11–6) loses. Tennessee marches on in the playoffs. The Buffalo season is finished.

Three weeks later in the Super Bowl in Atlanta, the Titans came from 16 points down to tie the Rams in the fourth quarter. But Kurt Warner connected with Isaac Bruce for a touchdown with 1 minute 54 seconds left for a 23–16 victory (see Jan. 30).

Runners-up

1955: Coach Adolph Rupp's top-ranked University of Kentucky basketball team was upset by Georgia Tech, 59–58. The loss snapped the Wildcats' 32-game winning streak and was their first defeat at Lexington in 130 home games over 12 years.

1978: Tracy Caulkins, a 14-year-old high school breaststroker from Nashville, set three individual United States swim records in a women's international meet at Brown University. She established marks in the 200-yard breaststroke and the

200- and 400-yard individual medleys. Caulkins won 48 United States national titles, the most ever, from 1978 to '84.

1995: Alberto Tomba, the matinee idol from Italy, clinched his first World Cup championship by winning the slalom at Kranjska Gora, Slovenia, for his fifth consecutive victory in the slalom or giant slalom. He had been the overall runner-up for the Cup title three straight times before the breakthrough.

January 9, 1958
'Big O' Scores Standing Oh!

By LOUIS EFFRAT

Oscar Robertson being carried off the court by his Cincinnati teammates after scoring 50 points to win the 1959 Holiday Festival at Madison Square Garden. He had scored 56 points there two seasons earlier. (Associated Press)

NEW YORK—"He's merely wonderful." That's how one college coach described Oscar Robertson, Cincinnati University's 19-year-old sophomore, who staged the greatest one-man show in Madison Square Garden basketball history tonight. No player, professional or amateur, ever had achieved so many points in a game as did Robertson in leading the Bearcats to a record-smashing 118–54 rout of Seton Hall.

The 56 points tallied by the 6-foot 5-inch star from Indianapolis set an individual scoring mark for the Eighth Avenue arena, where basketball has been played since 1934. Robertson left the game with 2 minutes 46 seconds remaining. He left with the cheers of 4,615 spectators ringing in his ears and with the knowledge that he had scored more points than the entire Seton Hall squad.

Coach George Smith's Bearcats captured the fancy of the fans easily. They simply overpowered Honey Russell's New Jersey Pirates and in doing so accounted for a college team scoring high at the Garden. Great as Robertson was, his Cincinnati quintet was hardly a one-man team. Connie Dierking was quite a performer. So were Ralph Davis, Wayne Stevens and Mike Mendenhall. Led by Robertson, the twice-beaten Bearcats averaged 56 per cent with their floor shots, making fifty of eighty-nine.

By half-time, when Cincinnati had soared to an incredible 58–20 advantage, virtually everyone in the Garden was singing the praises of the 196-pound Robertson, a smooth, stylish, sure-handed forward. With every move Robertson made it was obvious that he was the best collegian player seen here in many a season.

What made his performance all the more remarkable was the fact that he never attempted a shot from farther than twenty-five feet out and only three times did he do that, clicking each time. Most of the time, the lad drove in, hooked from the bucket, feinted his way in with lay-ups or tossed in short-range one-handers.

Robertson collected twenty-two field goals on thirty-two shots. He caged twelve straight fouls, grabbed fifteen rebounds and still found time to make a half-dozen assists. Against such an athlete, supported by so many strong Bearcats, Seton Hall never had a chance.

Runners-up

1903: The New York businessmen Frank Farrell and Bill Devery bought the Baltimore Orioles franchise of the American League for $18,000 and moved it to upper Manhattan, where it finished fourth as the Highlanders. The team was renamed the Yankees in 1913.

1963: Paul Brown, coach and general manager of the Cleveland Browns of the old All-America Football Conference and the N.F.L., the winner of seven league titles and the man after whom the very team was named, was fired by Art Modell, a former television and advertising executive who had bought the club two years before.

1972: Kareem Abdul-Jabbar's offensive brilliance for the Milwaukee Bucks and an impromptu "get back" defense devised by Bucks Coach Larry Costello brought an end to the Los Angeles Lakers' epic 33-game winning streak as Milwaukee scored a 120–104 victory before a national television audience (see Jan. 7).

January 10, 1982
'The Catch'

By DAVE ANDERSON

SAN FRANCISCO—Up on the scoreboard the clock showed only 58 seconds remaining in the National Conference Championship game today, but at the 49ers' sideline during their timeout, Coach Bill Walsh was talking to his quarterback, Joe Montana, as calmly as if it were the first day of training camp. And in a sense it was the first day of training camp.

"That play was nothing special," Bill Walsh would say later. "It's a play we practice from Day 1 in camp." Practice makes perfect. As the timeout was about to expire now, Joe Montana trotted out to the huddle. With a third-and-3 at the Dallas Cowboys' 6-yard line and trailing, 27–21, the 49ers could not afford any more turnovers. At the snap, Joe Montana moved out toward the right sideline. Quickly, he looked for Freddie Solomon, but then he noticed his other wide receiver, Dwight Clark, alone in the back of the end zone.

"I was getting pressured," Joe Montana said later, "but they weren't on top of me. I had a little room." But when Joe Montana threw the pass, he threw it "off the wrong foot," as coaches say, meaning off balance. It did not matter. The ball spiraled high into Dwight Clark's hands near the back line of the end zone. And when Ray Wersching added the extra point, the 49ers had a 28–27 victory that put them in Super Bowl XVI against the Cincinnati Bengals a week from Sunday at the Pontiac Silverdome.

"We're not overwhelmed by it," Joe Montana was saying now at his locker. "But we are excited about the honor of playing in the Super Bowl."

Joe Montana never appears to be overwhelmed by anything. And perhaps that's why he's been so successful so quickly. In only his third season, he has passed the National Football League's most frustrated franchise into an opportunity to "win it all" for the first time since the 49ers were founded in 1946 as a member of the All-America Conference.

Until today, the 49ers had never won more than a division title. And only three of those. But now they are the N.F.C. champions for the first time. And in two weeks they have a chance to win the N.F.L. title for the first time in Super Bowl XVI.

Nobody understood that any better today than two former 49ers—John Brodie, once their quarterback, and O.J. Simpson, who grew up here on Potrero Hill before emerging as a renowned running back with the Buffalo Bills and ending his career with the 49ers three seasons ago. Today they were sitting together when Joe Montana threw the pass for the winning touchdown. "John Brodie was crying," O.J. Simpson said later. "And he was raving about Joe Montana, saying that there isn't a quarterback in the league who can do what he can do, especially the way he throws off balance."

These are the 49ers of Joe Montana and Dwight Clark and Freddie Solomon and Bill Walsh, who is considered to be the N.F.L.'s newest "offensive genius." And week after week, Bill Walsh is justifying that description. "We drove 90 yards for a touchdown when we had to have it," the 49er coach said. "And to me, that is the vital essence of the National Football League."

Dwight Clark needs all 10 fingertips to snare a pass by Joe Montana, lifting the 49ers into a tie with the Cowboys in the final seconds of the N.F.C. title game. Ray Wersching's extra point sent the Niners to the Super Bowl. (Associated Press)

Runners-up

1991: Three days after Pete Rose was released from a federal prison camp after serving a five-month sentence for tax evasion, a special committee of baseball's Hall of Fame effectively barred him from election by recommending that people on the game's permanently ineligible list not be allowed on the ballot. Rose was made ineligible by the game's commissioner in 1989 (see Aug. 24), and as of July 2003 the Hall's controversial decision still stood.

1920: Playing in an era of shamefacedly open offensive hockey, Newsy Lalonde of the Montreal Canadiens set a National Hockey League single-game record with six goals as Montreal defeated the Toronto Maple Leafs, 14–7. Three weeks later, Joe Malone of the Quebec Bulldogs scored seven goals in a game against Toronto—a record that still stands.

1979: Daryl Moreau of De La Salle High School in New Orleans set a United States scholastic record by sinking his 126th consecutive free throw over two seasons. In 1978–79 he had set the national single-season percentage standard of 97.5 percent from the line (119 of 122 shots).

January 11, 1973
The Rule That Changed the Game

By JOSEPH DURSO

CHICAGO, Ill.—The owners of the 24 major-league baseball teams took a radical step today to put more punch into the game. They voted to allow the American League to use a "designated pinch-hitter," who may bat for the pitcher without forcing him from the game. The plan will be tried experimentally for the next three seasons by the American League, which has been hurt financially in recent years and has been searching for ways to energize baseball. But it will not be used in the National League, which has resisted the change.

The action was voted at a joint meeting of the major leagues in Chicago today, with Commissioner Bowie Kuhn breaking an impasse between the leagues. As a result, for the first time since the American League was organized in 1901, the two big leagues will play under differing rules.

The historic action of the seven-hour meeting of the owners concerned the "designated pinch-hitter," who would become the 10th man in the team's line-up, but whose only function would be to bat for the pitcher. By approving the experiment, which was tried in the high minor leagues three years ago, the club executives made the most basic change in the rules since 1903. That was when foul balls were ruled strikes. Since then, the spitball was banned in 1920, the "lively" ball was introduced in 1930, the strike zone was enlarged in 1962 and reduced again in 1969 and the pitcher's mound was lowered the same year.

But none of those changes revolutionized the rules that were essentially followed since the days of the old New York Knickerbockers baseball club a century and a quarter ago. "I hope it works," Commissioner Kuhn said after casting the vote that broke the stalemate between the two leagues. "I would have preferred that both leagues did it. But if it's successful in one, then I hope the National follows suit."

The National League's opposition to the change was bluntly expressed by league president Charles S. Feeney: "We like the game the way it is."

Designated hitter Ron Blomberg of the Yankees in June 1973. On opening day at Fenway Park that season he had become the first D.H. to appear in the major leagues, drawing a walk with the bases loaded. (Associated Press)

Runners-up

1987: "The Drive": Down by a touchdown with 5 minutes 34 seconds left in the A.F.C. title game against the Cleveland Browns in wind-whipped Municipal Stadium, John Elway marched the Denver Broncos 98 yards to tie the score with 37 seconds to go. Denver won in overtime, 23–20, and went to the Super Bowl for the first time in what most consider Elway's greatest single performance.

1970: Coach Hank Stram's Kansas City Chiefs became the second former A.F.L. team to win the Super Bowl, defeating the Minnesota Vikings, 23–7, at Tulane Stadium in New Orleans. Chiefs quarterback Len Dawson performed coolly after denying reports the previous week of his involvement in gambling improprieties.

1981: The Oakland Raiders, coached by Tom Flores and with Jim Plunkett at quarterback, defeated the San Diego Chargers, 34–27, in the A.F.C. championship game at Jack Murphy Stadium to become the first wild-card team to reach the Super Bowl. They beat the Philadelphia Eagles in that game, 27–10, in New Orleans.

January 12, 1969
'Broadway Joe' Guaranteed It

[Unsigned, *The New York Times*]

NEW YORK—People talk about Joe Namath. He excites comment. Today he is providing more than ever, because, after an all-America career at the University of Alabama and four years as the quarterback of the Jets, he sits supreme at the top of the hard-nosed world of professional football.

Namath, the ultra-publicized individualistic quarterback from Beaver Falls, Pa., today led the Jets to an astounding 16–7 victory over the Baltimore Colts in the Super Bowl game at Miami. He intended to do it and, last week, in preparation for the game, said he would do it. Few believed him. The victory, which elevated the American League to an equal level with the older National League, marks the high point of Namath's success-studded career.

"What we like about him is that he's a winner, he doesn't know about losing," commented Weeb Ewbank, the coach of the Jets, a few season ago.

Sonny Werblin, the former owner of the Jets, who signed Namath for a bonus of $387,000 and a Lincoln convertible, found another quality in Namath that he thought valuable. He said, on signing the sleepily handsome 6-foot-2-inch black-haired star: "Namath has the presence of a star. You know how a real star lights up a room when he comes in? Joe has that quality."

Joe Namath and Coach Weeb Ewbank during a tense moment of Super Bowl III. Namath's prediction of a Jets victory over the Baltimore Colts came true, propelling the A.F.L. to a merger with the N.F.L. (Barton Silverman/The New York Times)

Namath, who sparkled on the football field for Beaver Falls High School and at Alabama, has become a legendary figure since moving to New York in 1965. His penthouse apartment at 76th and First Avenue, with its famous white llama rug, is often the scene of get-togethers and parties. ("A get-together is when the guys come over to eat steaks and play cards; a party is when there are girls," he said.) Namath has pursued pleasure in the saloons and discotheques of the East Side, often in the company of beautiful young women. During one early-morning jaunt, he allegedly had a dispute with a sportswriter that is still awaiting legal adjudication.

Joseph William Namath, the fifth child of a Hungarian steelworker, was born in Beaver Falls on May 31, 1943, and started playing football with three older brothers when he was hardly able to hold the football. After a splendid career in high school, he was offered scholarships by 52 colleges and universities. He also was offered $50,000 to play baseball with the Chicago Cubs.

Under Paul (Bear) Bryant, Namath developed into one of the most sought-after passers in college football. Bryant called him "the greatest athlete I ever coached."

Runners-up

1958: Dolph Schayes, the dominant forward of the Syracuse Nationals, scored 23 points in a victory over the Detroit Pistons, surpassing George Mikan as the N.B.A.'s new career scoring leader with 11,770 points. Schayes played for 16 seasons and finished with 18,438 points.

1958: The National Collegiate Athletic Association adopted a new football rule, the 2-point conversion option after touchdowns, opening coaches to endless second-guessing but also giving teams another way to win. The N.F.L. waited for more than three decades before implementing the rule in 1994.

1975: The Pittsburgh Steelers, with Terry Bradshaw throwing passes, Lynn Swann catching them, Franco Harris running and Mean Joe Greene making tackles, won their first Super Bowl title after 42 years in the N.F.L., defeating the Minnesota Vikings, 16–6, at Tulane Stadium in New Orleans.

Nine Votes From Unanimous

By DAVE ANDERSON

NEW YORK—Nine has always been an important number in baseball. Nine players. Nine innings. And now another nine has emerged, the nine members of the Baseball Writers Association who did not vote for Henry Aaron on this year's Hall of Fame ballot.

Henry Aaron was elected, of course, along with Frank Robinson, but somehow the nine votes that Henry Aaron did not receive seem more significant than the 406 he did receive. To think that nine presumably responsible voters would deem Henry Aaron unworthy of the Hall of Fame is, in a word, preposterous. Almost scandalous. "I'd be lying if I said I didn't want to be unanimous," Henry Aaron was saying yesterday, "but I realized that nobody had ever been a unanimous choice. I was happy to come in second."

Henry Aaron meant second to Ty Cobb in the Hall of Fame election percentage. Back in 1936 when Ty Cobb, Babe Ruth, Honus Wagner, Christy Mathewson and Walter Johnson were chosen as the Cooperstown shrine's charter members, Ty Cobb collected 222 of a possible 226 votes, a 98.2 percentage. With 406 votes out of 415 ballots, Henry Aaron's percentage was 97.8.

But that still doesn't answer the question—how could nine voters not mark the square next to Henry Aaron's name on their ballot? "If a player deserves to be in the Hall of Fame by a unanimous vote," Henry Aaron said, "he should be rewarded with it."

Henry Aaron deserved it. Of all the players in more than 100 years of major-league baseball, he had the most home runs (755), the most runs batted in (2,297), the most total bases (6,856) and the most extra-base hits (1,477). He appeared in the most games (3,298), he accumulated the most official times at bat (12,364) and he had the most seasons with 100 or more games (22). But his home-run total is his monument. To put it in perspective, consider that if anyone is to approach it, he must average 35 homers for 20 years just to hit 700.

And yet nine voters chose to ignore Henry Aaron. Historically, of course, it wasn't surprising. Three years ago 23 voters chose to ignore Willie Mays; in 1966 there were 20 who ignored Ted Williams; in 1969 there were 23 who ignored Stan Musial; in 1955 there were 28 who ignored Joe DiMaggio. In this year's election there were 45 who ignored Frank Robinson, too. With 312 votes necessary for election, he received 370 votes, a landslide by Hall of Fame standards.

Jack Lang, a baseball writer for The New York Daily News and the secretary-treasurer of the B.B.W.A.A., would not divulge the names of the nine brethren in keeping with the tradition of a secret ballot. But he did describe some of the ballots, each of which permits a voter to select as many as 10 of the 42 candidates.

Henry Aaron as a 20-year-old rookie with the Milwaukee Braves, before a 1954 exhibition game at Ebbets Field in Brooklyn. He broke in that year, switched to uniform No. 44 and went on to hit 755 home runs. (Associated Press)

"One ballot was from a Latin-American writer who voted only for Luis Aparicio," Jack Lang said. "Another was from a writer in a Midwestern city who voted only for Juan Marichal."

One or two ballots omitting Henry Aaron would be understandable. Perhaps a member of the brethren was weary. Or hungover. Or in a hurry. Understandable, but not excusable. But nine votes? Never.

Runners-up

1999: Having led the Chicago Bulls to their sixth N.B.A. championship in eight years the previous summer, Michael Jordan, 35, announced his retirement for the second time. He returned to the N.B.A. with the Washington Wizards in 2001–2 but was not the Jordan of old and retired yet again in 2003.

1991: Bo Jackson of the Los Angeles Raiders hurt his hip in an A.F.C. divisional playoff game against the Cincinnati Bengals at the L.A. Coliseum. The injury led to a degenerative condition that forced his retirement from both football and baseball in 1994 following hip replacement surgery.

1968: Bill Masterson, a 30-year-old winger for the Minnesota North Stars, was fatally injured when he was checked heavily into the boards and hit his head on the ice in a game against the Oakland Seals. He died two days later of brain injuries.

January 14, 1973
First All the Way

By WILLIAM N. WALLACE

LOS ANGELES—The big scoreboard in the Coliseum flashed the message over and over, "The Dolphins Are Super," at the end of the Super Bowl contest today, and indeed the Miami team had played an almost perfect game in defeating the Washington Redskins, 14–7, for a perfect season and the championship. The game was watched by millions on national television. [Many television sets in the New York area were affected by atmospheric disturbances that interrupted the program.]

The score of the undefeated Dolphins' 17th victory could easily have been a more decisive 21–0 or 17–0 except for a single botched Miami play near the end of the game. That play featured little Garo Yepremian, the soccer-kicking specialist from Cyprus, attempting the skills of the big fellows, passing and tackling. Yepremian tried futilely to throw a pass after his 42-yard field-goal attempt had been blocked.

This pass was intercepted by Mike Bass, the cornerback, who ran 49 yards for the Redskins' only touchdown with 2 minutes 7 seconds left to play. The 155-pound Yepremian missed the tackle. This score put some suspense into a game that otherwise had generated little excitement because Miami was the dominant team from the start.

The Redskins had the ball one more time with 74 seconds remaining, but the Dolphin defense harassed Bill Kilmer, the Washington quarterback, and the final play was symbolic. Kilmer was dropped by Bill Stanfill and Vern Den Herder for a 9-yard loss on his 17-yard line.

Larry Csonka ran for 112 yards for Miami, 9 short of the Super Bowl record set by Matt Snell of the New York Jets in

Coach Don Shula riding high moments after the Dolphins achieved the only spotless season in N.F.L. history by defeating the Redskins, 14-7, in Super Bowl VII at the Los Angeles Coliseum. (Associated Press)

1969, while Larry Brown, the Redskins' No. 1 carrier, scratched out 72 in 22 carries. His average was 3.3 yards, a yard below his standard during the regular season. Brown's longest run was for 11 yards while Csonka had one for 49 yards, the most yards the Redskins' defense had given up on a single ground play all season.

Csonka's running mate, Jim Kiick, scored the second Miami touchdown on a 1-yard run in the second period and Howard Twilley, the wide receiver, made the first on a dazzling play in the opening quarter. Twilley, cutting inside and then outside, caught a pass from Bob Griese on the 5 and scored to complete a 28-yard play. Twilley turned the defending back,

Pat Fischer, all the way around on his fake.

Miami became the first team in the 53-year history of the National Football League to go through a season undefeated and untied. For the coach, Don Shula, a Super Bowl victory had been some time in coming. His two earlier qualifiers, the 1969 Baltimore Colts and last year's Dolphins, had lost, to the Jets and the Dallas Cowboys. "I'm 0–2," said Shula last week, "and on Sunday night I intend to be 1–2." He made it.

The closest any N.F.L. team has come to a perfect season since 1973 was when Mike Ditka's Chicago Bears went 18–1 in the regular and postseason in 1985 and January 1986. Don Shula's overall Super Bowl record was 2–4.

Runners-up

1968: The Green Bay Packers defeated the Oakland Raiders, 33–14, in Super Bowl II at the Orange Bowl. It was the final game on the sideline with the Packers for Vince Lombardi, who had recently announced he would step down as coach to become a front-office executive. One year later he was coaching the Washington Redskins.

2001: The Giants gained their third trip to a Super Bowl, thumping the Minnesota Vikings, 41–0, for the N.F.C. title. Quarterback Kerry Collins had by far his

finest day as a pro, passing for 381 yards and five touchdowns. New York lost Super Bowl XXXV to the Baltimore Ravens, 34–7 (see Jan. 28).

1954: Joe DiMaggio married Marilyn Monroe before a justice of the peace at San Francisco City Hall. Only one of his former Yankee teammates, Lefty O'Doul, attended. DiMaggio and Monroe lived together just nine months and the marriage ended in divorce in October 1955.

January 15, 1967
The Big Bang Bowl

By WILLIAM N. WALLACE

LOS ANGELES—Bryan Bartlett (Bart) Starr, the quarterback for the Green Bay Packers, led his team to a 35–10 victory over the Kansas City Chiefs today in the first professional football game between the champions of the National and American Leagues.

Doubt about the outcome disappeared in the third quarter when Starr's pretty passes made mere Indians out of the American League Chiefs and Green Bay scored twice. Those 14 points stretched Green Bay's lead to 28–10 and during the

final quarter many of the spectators in the crowd of 63,036 left Memorial Coliseum, which had been only two-thirds filled. The outcome served to settle the curiosity of the customers, who paid from $6 to $12 for tickets, and a television audience estimated at 60 million, regarding the worth of the Chiefs.

The final score was an honest one, meaning it correctly reflected what went on during the game. The great interest had led to naming the event the Super Bowl, but the contest was more ordinary than super.

Starr, methodical and unruffled as ever, completed 16 of 23 passes, six producing first downs on key third-down plays. Seven completions went to Max McGee, a 34-year-old substitute end who was in action only because Boyd Dowler, the regular, was hurt on the game's sixth play. McGee scored two of Green Bay's five touchdowns, the first one after an outstanding one-handed, hip-high catch of a pass thrown slightly behind him.

The Packers, who had been favored by two touchdowns, knew they were in a challenging game for at least half of the 2½-hour contest. But in the second half the mighty Packer defense shut out the Chiefs, who were in the Green Bay half of the field only once—for one play. And they were only four yards into Packer territory. The Packers changed their defensive tactics for the second half. They had not blitzed their linebackers during the first two periods and the four rushing lineman were unable to get at Dawson. But the blitz came in the third period and Dawson found himself harassed.

The Super Bowl games will now go on year after year, but it may be some time before an American League team will be good enough to win one, especially if the National League champion comes from Green Bay.

The American Football League completed its merger with the N.F.L. in 1970, as the Baltimore Colts, Cleveland Browns and Pittsburgh Steelers agreed to join former A.F.L. teams in a 13-team American Football Conference. The remaining N.F.L. teams composed a 13-team N.F.C. Roman numeral designation of Super Bowls began in 1969, when the Jets defeated the Baltimore Colts in Super Bowl III (see Jan. 12).

Max McGee, who wasn't expected to play, caught seven passes, including this one, as the Packers won the first N.F.L.-A.F.L. showdown. The crowd wasn't super: Memorial Coliseum was one-third empty. (Green Bay Packers)

Runners-up

1892: Rules for the new sport of basketball were published by Dr. James Naismith in Springfield, Mass. The first game was played with a soccer ball and peach baskets were nailed to the wall at either end of the gym. Metal rims were invented the following year so attendants would not have to fetch the ball by ladder after each basket.

1978: The Dallas Cowboys, behind Harvey Martin, Randy White and their "Doomsday

Defense," dominated the Broncos, 27–10, in Super Bowl XII at New Orleans. It was the first Super Bowl played indoors. Coach Tom Landry evened his Super Bowl record at 2–2.

1942: President Franklin D. Roosevelt issued what came to be known as the Green Light Letter, a message urging Commissioner Kenesaw Mountain Landis to "keep baseball going" during World War II to help maintain morale.

Challenging the Gospel

By LEONARD KOPPETT and GEORGE VECSEY

Curt Flood was more than content as a six-time Gold Glove center-fielder. But when he was traded to the Phillies, he sued baseball, arguing he shouldn't be shuttled between teams "like a slave." (Associated Press)

NEW YORK [Friday]—A suit charging baseball with violation of the antitrust laws was filed today in Federal Court here on behalf of Curt Flood, St. Louis Cardinal outfielder for the last 12 years. A hearing was set for Tuesday to consider the player's request for immediate release from the "reserve clause" restrictions that tie a player to one team indefinitely.

Named as defendants were the commissioner of baseball, the presidents of the National and American Leagues and the 24 major-league clubs. The case also can have an important effect on all major professional team sports.

Flood charged he would suffer "irreparable damage" if not allowed to play for a team of his choice in 1970. He sought an injunction that would prevent baseball from invoking the reserve clause rules against him. Under standard baseball practice, Flood's contract was traded to the Philadelphia Phillies last October by the Cardinals, who paid him $90,000 in salary for the 1969 season.

Flood was a regular with the Cardinals for 12 seasons with a cumulative batting average of .293. He was given the Golden Glove Award six times as the best outfielder in his league. Flood had resented being traded to the Phillies because he hated to leave "Cardinal-land," as he calls St. Louis, but also because he felt he had put too much time into his profession to be shuttled around "like a slave."

Out of this proud reaction, Flood is mounting one of the most serious challenges ever made on baseball's control of its hired hands. Several features of the Flood case distinguish it from previous challenges to the reserve clause. Flood is the most prominent, most successful and most highly paid player ever to challenge it and he is in the full flower of his career at the age of 31. Other famous cases have involved minor league players, fringe major leaguers or retired players.

And for the first time, a reserve clause challenger has the full backing of an official players' organization.

Curt Flood's challenge of the reserve clause was rejected by a United States District Court judge in August 1970, though the judge merely cited baseball's antitrust exemption and did not rule on the merits of the clause. The Supreme Court upheld the lower court by a 5–3 decision in 1972. Nevertheless, Flood had put the future of the reserve clause in question, and by 1976 a baseball arbitrator, working under the game's rules, established free agency for players (see Dec. 23).

Runners-up

1972: The Dallas Cowboys, led by Coach Tom Landry and quarterback Roger Staubach, dominated the Miami Dolphins in all facets of the game to win their first Super Bowl, 24–3, at Tulane Stadium in New Orleans. It was their first of five N.F.L. championships through 2003.

1974: Teammates on the field, in the nightclubs and apparently on the ballots of the nation's baseball writers, the Yankees' Mickey Mantle and Whitey Ford were elected to the Baseball Hall of Fame. Mantle, the storied center fielder, holds the World Series record for most career home runs, 18; the left-handed Ford holds the Series marks for victories, 10, and consecutive scoreless innings, 33 (see Oct. 8).

1905: Frank McGee scored 14 goals in the most lopsided Stanley Cup victory ever, 23–2, as the Ottawa Senators won the Cup title over Dawson City. Cup competition was a challenge series before the creation of the N.H.L., and Dawson City, Yukon Territory, traveled 23 days by dogsled, ship and train to face Ottawa in the best-of-three-game series.

January 17, 1988
Just Follow the Leader

By GERALD ESKENAZI

DENVER—A year later, the Browns fell nine feet short of creating their own heroics in the American Conference championship game. The Broncos again toppled them and once more will go to the Super Bowl. This one went even beyond the drama that was expected from these clubs as the Broncos won today by 38–33. The Broncos will suit up next on Jan. 31 for Super Bowl XXII in San Diego against the Washington Redskins.

For a while today, the Denver fans, bundled in their orange parkas, stopped rattling Mile High Stadium with their foot-stomping. The Browns recovered from a 21–3 halftime deficit, producing four touchdowns in just over 15 minutes. The crowd was looking at a distant mirror of last year's A.F.C. title game, with the images reversed. In that 1987 title game, the last time the clubs had met, John Elway led a much-remembered 98-yard drive in the last minutes of the fourth quarter to send the game into overtime, and Denver won, 23–20.

It took another Elway-engineered late drive today to put up what proved to be the winning points. With the score tied at 31–31 and with 5:14 remaining, Elway led a 75-yard march that ended with a dump-off screen pass to Sammy Winder, who drove 20 yards for a touchdown. On that drive, Elway connected with the rookie receiver Rick Nattiel for two receptions of 26 yards apiece. Nattiel was performing because Vance Johnson was hospitalized with a groin injury. "We got to win it here, in front of our fans," Elway said later. "I'm really relieved. I think that once I sit down and take a deep breath, I'll even more relaxed."

The Browns' quarterback, Bernie Kosar, nearly repeated the same improba-

ble act. He, too, started at his own 25, trying to launch a 75-yard scoring drive with 3:53 remaining. Cleveland got down to the 8, and visions of what Elway did last year surely cropped up in the minds of football fans. But today, the Browns' mirror cracked.

The versatile Earnest Byner took the ball on a play that was designed to send the runner inside. Instead, the middle was blocked and he ran to the outside, on his left, then cut back to the inside. He barreled to the 3, but was hit by Jeremiah Castille, a defensive back used in passing situations. Byner actually passed Castille, but the ball didn't. Castille stripped it, then pounced on Byner's fumble at the 3. Sixty-five seconds remained. Ironically, Byner was on his way to becoming the rushing and receiving star of the game. His seven receptions led both clubs and his 67 rushing yards were second best. He scored twice.

Unable to keep a drive going once they took over, the Broncos took a safety with 8 seconds remaining when Mike Horan, their punter, ran out of the end zone. The Browns took his subsequent free kick on a fair catch at their 24, still with the 8 seconds remaining. But Kosar's desperate pass at the gun sailed out of bounds in Denver territory.

"I just can't nail it down,"

said Art Modell, the Browns' owner, whose team hasn't been in a league championship game since 1969.

Despite their heroics in the A.F.C. championship game, the Broncos lost to Joe Gibbs's Washington Redskins in the Super Bowl, 42–10. This put the Broncos' Super Bowl record at 0–3. They won their first title against the Green Bay Packers in 1998 (see Jan. 25).

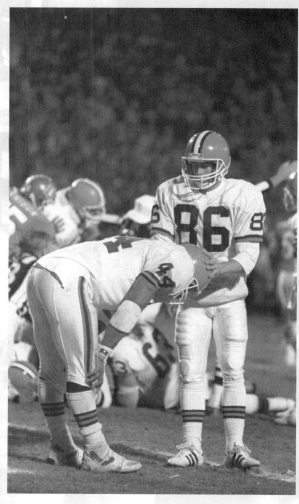

Earnest Byner (44) of the Browns being comforted after his fumble with 65 seconds left all but ended the A.F.C. title game. Minutes before, the Broncos' John Elway had staged a patented game-winning touchdown drive. (Associated Press)

Runners-up

1999: Up by 10–0 early, the Jets committed six turnovers, including four fumbles, and lost the A.F.C. championship game to the Denver Broncos, 23–10, at Mile High Stadium. It was the closest to the Super Bowl the Jets got under Coach Bill Parcells in his three seasons with the team.

1916: The Professional Golfers Association of America was formed at the Taplow Club in New York City. Rodman Wanamaker, a department store magnate,

donated the prize money for that year's P.G.A. Championship and the trophy that still bears his name.

1971: Jim O'Brien kicked a 32-yard field goal with five seconds left, leading the Baltimore Colts over the Dallas Cowboys, 16–13, at the Orange Bowl in Miami in the most sloppily played Super Bowl on record. There were a record 11 turnovers.

January 18, 1976
Dynamic Duo

By WILLIAM N. WALLACE

MIAMI, Fla.—The Super Bowl justified its existence today. The most heavily promoted and lavishly staged sports extravaganza of all presented to the 80,187 fans in the Orange Bowl and the vast television audience a well-played and exciting football game that was unresolved until the last play. The Pittsburgh Steelers won, 21–17.

The Dallas Cowboys were only 38 yards from the potential winning touchdown when the last play began. That final play wound up with Glen Edwards, the Steelers' safetyman, intercepting a pass by Roger Staubach, the Cowboy quarterback, in the Pittsburgh end zone, and it was typical of what had gone on in the 60 minutes of action. Super Bowl games have been characterized in the past by sluggishness and ennui, but not this one.

Tom Landry, the Dallas coach, said: "That Lynn Swann was really something. He made two big catches when he was covered." The coach thus cited the Pittsburgh wide receiver, who caught four passes for 161 yards, scored one touchdown, was given the game ball, the traditional symbol of victory, and also was voted the game's most outstanding player.

The first of Swann's two big catches came in the opening period on a pass from Terry Bradshaw, the play covering 32 yards and moving Pittsburgh to the Dallas 16. Three plays later Bradshaw passed 7 yards to Randy Grossman, the tight end, for a touchdown that tied the score, 7–7. Swann's second catch was the game's gem. It was a 64-yard touchdown play, Bradshaw's pass covering 59 yards in the air. That was the Steelers' final score, giving them a 21–10 lead. Swann certainly was covered well on both plays. Mark Washington, the cornerback, was right with Swann, but the second-year receiver from Southern California, who is now an all-pro performer, made remarkable, leaping catches of perfectly thrown passes.

Bradshaw was knocked silly on the 64-yard touchdown pass play by a safety blitz and did not play again. Terry Hanratty was the quarterback for the team's last offensive series, one in which the Steelers took a risk and got away with it. They had fourth down and 9 to go at the Dallas 41 with 88 seconds left. They chose not to punt and made 2 yards, turning the ball over to the Cowboys, who had just scored to trail by 21–17.

But Dallas had no more time-outs to stop the clock and the time did run out after five plays.

Lynn Swann of the Steelers corralling a pass from Terry Bradshaw against the Cowboys. Super Bowl X was the most riveting one to date. (Associated Press)

Runners-up

1983: Seventy years after the International Olympic Committee stripped Jim Thorpe of the decathlon and pentathlon gold medals he won in the 1912 Stockholm Games, they were returned to his children. He had been deprived of them when the I.O.C. learned that he had been paid $25 a week for playing semipro baseball.

1958: Willie O'Ree, a left wing, became the first black player in N.H.L. history when he was called up by the Boston Bruins and appeared in a shutout victory over the Montreal Canadiens. He played in 45 games over parts of two seasons, scoring four goals.

1959: Marian Ladewig of Grand Rapids, Mich., won her seventh national bowling All-Star Tournament (later renamed the United States Open). The best woman performer in the history of the sport, she won eight national opens in all and was voted Bowler of the Year nine times.

January 19, 1974
The Taste of Defeat

By GORDON S. WHITE Jr.

SOUTH BEND, Ind. [Saturday]— U.C.L.A.'s record 88-game basketball winning streak came to an end today on the same court where the Bruins had last lost three years ago. In a surprising and thrilling finish, unbeaten Notre Dame turned an 11-point deficit and apparent defeat in the last 3 minutes 32 seconds into a 71–70 victory.

Dwight Clay took a jump shot from the right corner and the ball went through for the winning points. With 29 seconds remaining, the Irish held on in a wild finale to beat the school that has been the National Collegiate champion for the last seven years and nine of the last 10. The crowd of 11,343 fans in Notre Dame's Athletic and Convocation Center was almost stunned. It was a few seconds before belief registered, apparently, and then the fans swarmed on the court, smothering the Irish players and Coach Digger Phelps with wild undergraduate enthusiasm.

The Irish will obviously move up from No. 2 to No. 1 in the weekly polls, replacing U.C.L.A., which has been No. 1 since the semifinals of the 1968 National Collegiate Athletic Association championship tournament. The victory came 20 days after Notre Dame's football team became the No. 1 team by beating Alabama in an equally exciting Sugar Bowl game. However, the basketball team will have to fight to retain its lofty spot because it meets U.C.L.A. in a return game a week from tonight at Pauley Pavilion in Los Angeles.

What made the victory more impressive was that the Irish beat the "Walton Gang," with Bill Walton playing the entire 40 minutes and playing very well. That U.C.L.A. could not get the ball to the big

redhead at the end was a telling factor after Clay's shot. Walton injured his back seriously in a fall during a game at Washington State last Monday, and had missed the last three U.C.L.A. victories. He played today with an elastic corset. He scored 24 points, had nine rebounds and intimidated Notre Dame throughout.

This was the first time that Walton or any of the other Bruins had tasted defeat as varsity players. Walton, Tommy Curtis and Keith Wilkes are the outstanding seniors who went a long time before losing. Phelps, in his third year as Notre Dame coach after leaving Fordham, said: "This was great for college basketball. I'm sure everyone was rooting for us the way they used to root against the New York Yankees. The win was special for Notre Dame, for the kids, for my staff, for my mother and father [who were present] and for us all."

This was only the sixth defeat for U.C.L.A. in the last eight seasons, during which Coach John Wooden's Bruins have won 218 games. Wooden said: "Once we got the game to break the record, it was relatively meaningless. We knew it would end sometime."

One week later at

Pauley Pavilion in Los Angeles, U.C.L.A. returned the favor, defeating Notre Dame by 94–75 and regaining the No. 1 position in the polls. In the N.C.A.A. tournament, the Bruins lost to David Thompson and North Carolina State in a classic semifinal (See March 23).

Bill Walton of U.C.L.A. hooking a shot over John Shumate of Notre Dame in South Bend, Ind. When the Irish won, snapping the Bruins' 88-game winning streak, Walton and his mates tasted defeat for the first time as varsity players. (Bettmann/Corbis)

Runners-up

2002: In heavy snow, New England's Adam Vinatieri kicked a field goal with 27 seconds left in regulation and another 8 minutes 29 seconds into overtime to defeat Oakland in a "Snow Bowl" divisional playoff game. The 16–13 victory put the Patriots in the A.F.C. title game against the Pittsburgh Steelers and inched them toward their first Super Bowl title.

1975: Johnny Miller, who had burst onto the golf stage by winning eight P.G.A. Tour events in 1974, continued his hot streak by capturing the Tucson (Ariz.) Open.

He defeated John Mahaffey by nine strokes with a record 25-under-par 263. The week before he had won the Phoenix Open by shooting 24-under-par 260.

1975: The former U.C.L.A. centers Kareem Abdul-Jabbar and Bill Walton faced off for the first time as professionals. Abdul-Jabbar, playing in his fourth N.B.A. season for the Milwaukee Bucks, easily got the best of it, scoring 50 points with 15 rebounds and 11 assists. Walton, in his first pro season for the Portland Trail Blazers, was held to 7 points.

The President Said Nyet

By TERENCE SMITH

WASHINGTON—President Carter proposed today that the Moscow Olympics be moved to another country or postponed or canceled if the Soviet Union failed to withdraw its troops from Afghanistan within a month. Declaring that "it's very important for the world to realize how serious a threat the Soviets' invasion of Afghanistan is," the President said that if the troops were not withdrawn in a month he would ask the United States Olympic Committee to urge the International Olympic Committee to transfer or cancel the Moscow games.

Failing that, the President said he would suggest to the U.S.O.C. that it formally withdraw American athletes from the games. Mr. Carter made his suggestion in a television interview and in a letter to Robert J. Kane, president of the U.S.O.C. Mr. Carter also endorsed the establishment of a permanent site for the quadrennial Games and mentioned Greece as an ideal location for the summer events.

Mr. Carter outlined his views on the Olympics in a letter to Mr. Kane that was released by the White House. He contended in the letter that the boycott was necessary to "make clear to the Soviet Union that it cannot trample upon an independent nation and at the same time do business as usual with the rest of the world." Moving the Olympics from Moscow, Mr. Carter said, would "reverberate around the globe" and could "deter future aggression." He said that if the International Olympic Committee rejected the suggestion to move the Games, athletes from the United States should boycott the Moscow competition and stage an alternative set of games elsewhere.

Although Mr. Carter lacks the authority to order a boycott, he told reporters after the broadcast of NBC's "Meet the Press" that he believed the United States Olympic Committee would support his proposal if the Soviet troops were not withdrawn.

Lord Killanin, the president of the International Olympic Committee, termed Mr. Carter's decision hasty and said it would be "legally and technically impossible" to move the Games from Moscow. In Moscow, the newspaper Sovetsky Sport said that the Soviet Union would send its athletes to Lake Placid for the Winter Olympics next month no matter what the United States did about the summer Games in Moscow. The reaction of American athletes to Mr. Carter's statement was mixed, although support seemed to be growing to stand behind any decision made by the Administration.

On April 12, after American hostages had been taken in Iran, an initially reluctant United States Olympic Committee voted to withdraw the United States team from the Moscow Games. Those Olympics, which opened in July, were not televised in the United States. Although the Soviet Union's team participated in the February 1980 Winter Games at Lake Placid, N.Y., the U.S.S.R. got a measure of revenge by boycotting the 1984 Summer Games in Los Angeles.

President Jimmy Carter calling for a U.S. boycott of the Moscow Olympics on NBC's "Meet the Press." He urged that the Games be moved to another country, postponed or canceled unless the Soviet Union withdrew its troops from Afghanistan. (United Press International)

Runners-up

1950: The N.F.L. Rules Committee voted to allow unlimited free substitution of players, quickly opening the way for the era of two-platoon football and specialization of positions such as field goal kickers. The new rule soon changed the face of the game; for one thing, the game became much faster as players performed for fewer minutes and had more time to rest.

1968: In one of college basketball's epic matchups, Elvin Hayes—to shouts of "E! E! E!"—scored 39 points to lead the second-ranked Cougars of Houston over Lew Alcindor and No. 1 U.C.L.A., 71–69, in a nationally televised game before 52,693 in the Astrodome.

1892: The first official game of basketball, invented the year before by Dr. James Naismith, a physical education teacher at Springfield College in Massachusetts, was played on a Y.M.C.A. court with peach baskets at either end. There were nine players to a side; by 1896, when the first collegiate game was played at the University of Iowa, sides numbered five men each.

January 21, 1990
Expletive Deleted

MELBOURNE, Australia (AP)—So much for Mr. Nice Guy. John McEnroe threw his racquet and a tantrum today at the Australian Open and became the first player to be disqualified from a Grand Slam event for misconduct since 1963, when a Colombian-born Spaniard, Willie Alvarez, was defaulted from the French Open.

McEnroe let himself get rattled by missed shots, close calls and a baby's cries. And after his default, with a 6–1, 4–6, 7–5, 2–4 lead against Mikael Pernfors, McEnroe admitted, "I don't really have anyone to blame but myself."

It was a sad and bizarre chapter in the career of one of the finest players in tennis, a 30-year-old former champion who came here determined to win his first major tournament since the 1984 United States Open. Only two days before, after winning his third match and playing his best tennis in years, McEnroe talked about how important it was for him to keep his temper under control. Yet all it took for McEnroe to revert to his old ways was a tough match against Pernfors, the Swedish-born two-time National Collegiate Athletic Association champion at Georgia.

McEnroe, composed and speaking softly a few minutes later, said his mistake was in not understanding the rules. He thought the rules of last year's Grand Slam tournaments—a four-step process to default—were in effect. Instead, a new three-step rule—warning, point, default—applied.

McEnroe won the first set easily, but as Pernfors picked up his game in the second set, McEnroe became increasingly agitated. He took a 2–1 lead after an exchange of breaks in the third set, but on the changeover he stood in front of a lineswoman he thought made a bad call. Bouncing a ball on his racquet and glaring at her in intimidating fashion, McEnroe was given a violation of the conduct code for unsportsmanlike conduct by the chair umpire, Gerry Armstrong. McEnroe argued with Armstrong, then returned to play, finally held service and went on to take the set.

In the final game of the fourth set, McEnroe fell behind, 15–30, on a wide forehand, then bounced his racquet on the court. At deuce, McEnroe hit another forehand wide, then smashed the court again with his racquet, cracking the head slightly. Armstrong called a code violation for racquet abuse, and McEnroe responded by swearing at him and asking for Ken Farrar, the Grand Slam chief of supervisors. Farrar came onto the court and talked with McEnroe, but the American continued complaining and swearing, his words clearly audible to nearby fans and television viewers.

Armstrong, with Farrar's approval, called, "Code violation, further abuse, default Mr. McEnroe. Game, set, match."

John McEnroe confronting an umpire during the 1991 U.S. Open. His boorish behavior in what had been a buttoned-down sport vexed officials and overshadowed his grand talent and feathery touch. *(Corbis)*

Farrar later described McEnroe's harangue as the most vile language he had ever heard in a tennis match. McEnroe stood with his hands on his hips while the crowd of 15,000 whistled, booed angrily and chanted, "We want McEnroe."

Runners-up

1979: Terry Bradshaw's four touchdown passes, including two to John Stallworth, led the Pittsburgh Steelers to a 35–31 victory over the Dallas Cowboys in Super Bowl XIII at the Orange Bowl in Miami. Pittsburgh, which had won titles against the Minnesota Vikings in 1975 and the Dallas Cowboys in '76, became the first team to win three Super Bowls.

1954: Bob Cousy of the Boston Celtics stole the show in perhaps the most exciting N.B.A. All-Star game, scoring 10 of the East's 14 points in overtime and dribbling out the clock for a 98–93 victory over the West at Madison Square Garden.

1986: Denis Potvin of the Islanders *(see Dec. 20)* tied Bobby Orr's N.H.L. record for defensemen by scoring the 270th goal of his career in a victory over the Philadelphia Flyers. Potvin retired in 1988 with 310 goals and currently stands fifth all-time among defensemen.

January 22, 1973
Down and Out in 4:35

By RED SMITH

KINGSTON, Jamaica—Under Caribbean skies that had never witnessed anything remotely like it, big George Foreman smashed Joe Frazier to the floor six times tonight and won the heavyweight championship of the world in 4 minutes 35 seconds. Arthur Mercante, the referee from New York, stopped the uneven match with Frazier on his feet but hardly in the contest.

A crowd of 36,000 saw one of the most startling upsets in two and a half centuries of heavyweight title matches. Frazier, in his 10th defense of the title New York State conferred on him in 1968 and his third since he whipped the former champion, Muhammad Ali, in 1971, had been favored at 1 to 3 in the betting shops here. Foreman, unbeaten in 37 fights and author of 34 knockouts since he won the Olympic heavyweight title in 1968, had been recognized as Joe's most formidable opponent since Ali but most boxing men doubted that he could stand up under the ceaseless pressure of a characteristic Frazier attack.

They'll never know now whether they were right or wrong, for Joe never got a chance to apply pressure. Looking rather thick in the middle at 214 pounds, the champion tried to "come out smoking," but Foreman used his greater size and longer reach to smother the fire. At 6 feet 3 inches, the challenger had three and a half inches in height and a five-inch advantage in reach. Reaching out with both hands, he fended off Frazier's early rushes, turning the challenge aside. Then he sank a hook deep into Joe's body, and the crowd had the first hint of what was in store. In a moment Foreman was moving forward, using both hands with authority. Even so, there was an instant of shocked silence

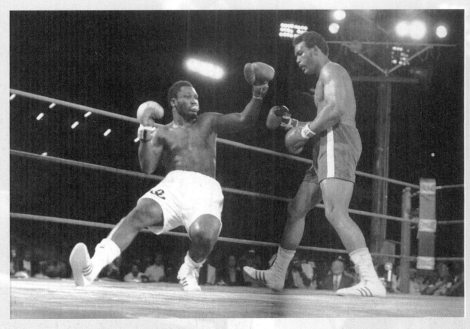

Joe Frazier, left, the heavyweight champion, heading to the canvas against George Foreman in Kingston, Jamaica. The stunning upset took six knockdowns and just 4 minutes 35 seconds. (Associated Press)

when an uppercut sent Joe sprawling.

The champion got to his feet immediately and resumed his jigging style, both hands high, as soon as Mercante completed the mandatory eight-count. By now there was bedlam in National Stadium. Sure of his power, Foreman forced Frazier into the champion's corner, brought up another uppercut to the chin, and Joe sank slowly to his knees. He rolled over, pushed himself up and took two or three staggering steps while Mercante continued the count. This time George was on him hungrily. The challenger pumped both hands to the head, and just as the bell ended the first round, a straight right put Frazier flat on his back.

The second round was barely under way when a short right sent Frazier on a little wobbly walk. He shuffled unsteadily to his right, hands down, and as he passed, Foreman nailed him on the left

ear. Down went the champion for a fourth time. Again he beat the count. He wobbled into the ropes where Foreman slugged to the head again and again. When Joe crumbled for the fifth time, it was a left that dropped him. A moment earlier, Mercante had pushed Foreman off and warned him for shoving Frazier. "But I was determined to keep chasing him," George said later, "no matter what."

He chased him. He caught him. He nailed him with one last right, and Mercante had had enough at 1:35 of the round. Talking a trifle thickly because of a cut under his lower lip, Frazier blamed his pride. He said he hadn't realized how strong Foreman was, should have tried to bob and move away but "my pride wouldn't let me." After the second knockdown, Joe said, the challenger simply overpowered him. He was beaten for the first time in 30 professional fights.

Runners-up

1989: In perhaps his greatest clutch performance as a pro, Joe Montana led the San Francisco 49ers on an 11-play, 92-yard touchdown drive with 34 seconds remaining to lift them to a 20–16 victory over the Cincinnati Bengals in the Super Bowl at Miami. It was the 49ers' third Super Bowl title in the decade, following their 1982 victory over the Cincinnati Bengals and their 1985 defeat of the Miami Dolphins.

1980: The P.G.A.'s Tournament Policy Board approved plans to create a new Senior P.G.A. Tour, immediately giving such stars as Miller Barber, Don January and Chi Chi Rodriguez a new lease on competitive life at the highest level.

1951: Fidel Castro, 24, who had been a star pitcher at the University of Havana and reportedly turned down a $5,000 bonus from the New York Giants to pursue a law degree, pitched as a civilian to one batter, the future major leaguer Don Hoak, in a Cuban winter league game. Castro began leading the Cuban guerrillas five years later and overthrew Fulgencio Batista in 1959.

January 23, 1983
A Swede for All Seasons

[Unsigned, *The New York Times*]

NEW YORK [Sunday]—Bjorn Borg has decided not to play a Grand Prix schedule or in any Grand Slam events this year, and has perhaps ended his tennis career. In a series of rapidly changing

Bjorn Borg beating Jimmy Connors in their semifinal match at Wimbledon in 1979. He won six French and five straight British titles, yet retired without a victory in four U.S. Open finals. (Bettmann/Corbis)

developments during the last 48 hours, Borg told a Swedish newspaper, Kvallposten of Malmo, that he did not have the proper motivation to regain the world's No. 1 ranking. "I cannot give 100 percent," the paper quoted him as having said, "and if I cannot do that, it would not be fair to myself to go on. Tennis has to be fun if you are to get to the top, and I don't feel that way anymore. That's why I quit."

The 26-year-old Swede has been playing exhibitions in Bangkok, Thailand. According to United Press International, when he was asked there what his plans were, he said, "I have no comment, except that I'm going to retire." Lennart Bergelin, his coach and adviser, said that Borg had "no real fighting spirit left."

Borg was to have left Bangkok today for a brief vacation in Nepal, then was scheduled to return to the United States later this week. Bergelin indicated that Borg had planned to wait until he arrived in New York to discuss his plans, but that he decided to move up the announcement because of the rumors that circulated last week about his retirement. With his decision, Borg has abandoned his previously stated intention of playing a reduced Grand Prix schedule in 1983 that would have

included Wimbledon and the United States Open.

Bob Kain, who represents him for the Cleveland-based International Management Group, said that Borg would probably play only one Grand Prix tournament this year, in Monte Carlo March 28. He resides there with his wife, Mariana, for tax purposes. Kain said he talked with Borg in Bangkok Friday night, and Borg then phoned a Swedish journalist friend to tell him of his plans. Asked whether Borg's announcement constituted retirement, Kain said: "I think the word retirement is too final. At age 26, he feels like he's expended all the energy he has to go for No. 1 in the world and win major titles. He doesn't feel he has any energy left toward that effort. He doesn't know if that may change in a year or two."

Borg joined the professional tour at age 16 in 1973, made steady progress and became the sport's dominant player. Through 1981 he had accumulated $3,597,641 from tournament prize money, bonuses and national team competition earnings. Highest among his achievements was his string of five straight Wimbledon titles, beginning in 1976, when he defeated Ilie Nastase of Rumania in the final.

He proceeded to win 41 consecutive matches at Wimbledon, a tournament record, finally losing in the 1981 final to John McEnroe. Along the way, he won finals against Connors twice (1977 and 1978), Roscoe Tanner (1979) and McEnroe (1980). The victory over McEnroe was considered one of the finest matches ever. It featured a 34-point tiebreaker in the fourth set that was won by McEnroe. But Borg recovered to win the fifth set and the match.

Runners-up

1983: The Jets' 14-year wait for an A.F.C. championship game ended dismally as the Miami Dolphins intercepted Richard Todd five times and the spongy Orange Bowl field limited Freeman McNeil's effectiveness and Miami advanced to the Super Bowl, 14–0. The Dolphins then lost to the Washington Redskins, 27–17, in Super Bowl XVII at the Rose Bowl in California.

1929: Jacob Ruppert, co-owner of the New York Yankees, announced that in the coming season the team would wear numerals on the backs of their uni-

forms—corresponding with their position in the batting order—to help fans identify the players. Babe Ruth got No. 3 and Lou Gehrig No. 4. Soon all teams had numbers on their uniforms.

1979: Willie Mays, the New York and San Francisco Giants' supreme center fielder who retired in 1973 with 660 home runs and 3,283 hits, was elected to the Hall of Fame. He was elected on the first ballot with 409 of a possible 432 votes.

January 24, 1995
Brawn, Sweat and Tears

By ROBIN FINN

Pete Sampras exulting during the Australian Open in 1997. Playing a match in the tournament two years earlier, his usual stoical demeanor gave way to a torrent of tears as he awaited word on his coach's failing health. (Associated Press)

MELBOURNE, Australia—Long before he won this tortured passion play that masqueraded as a quarterfinal match at the Australian Open, Pete Sampras, the event's defending champion and the world's No. 1 player, had already done the unthinkable. He broke down in tears under the spotlight on stadium court. And the instant this 3-hour-58-minute tear-jerker ended in a 6–7 (4–7), 6–7 (3–7), 6–3, 6–4, 6–3 post-midnight comeback against the ninth-seeded Jim Courier, the traditionally stoic Sampras was again overcome by sobs.

"I think we were both just playing our hearts out," said Courier, who suspected that his opponent's uncharacteristic histrionics might have something to do with his unease over going on with a title defense while his coach had been sent back to the United States for further treatment of a serious heart ailment.

Long before Sampras had resurrected himself from the ultimate in Grand Slam predicaments—a two-sets-to-none deficit—for the second match in a row, his opponent was coping in secret with a body-racking case of leg cramps. "I just physically gave out," said Courier, this Grand Slam event's champion in 1992 and 1993. "At 4–3 in the fifth, either one of us could have collapsed, but he was the one left standing. Pete's pretty determined, and certainly at a Grand Slam he's going to do whatever's in his power to win."

Sampras had worn himself into an emotional frazzle worrying about the health of his coach and best friend, Tim Gullikson, who spent the weekend undergoing tests in a private hospital after apparently suffering the latest in a series of strokes linked to a congenital heart ailment, which was first diagnosed in December.

Sampras was unable to talk about his crying jag, which began after he held serve in the opening game of the final set and then resumed intermittently throughout the set. "Hopefully I can recover from this whole experience," said Sampras, whose composure had reached the cracking point even before a spectator incited him to "win this one" for his coach. "I was really happy that I fought back; I didn't quit," said Sampras, who hurled 23 aces at Courier, two of them between sobs as he took a 2–1 lead in the final set.

It wasn't until Sampras took his first lead of the match by holding serve to start the fifth set that his emotions floored him. He sat down for the change-over and, with his shoulders heaving and his face buried in his towel, he burst into uncontrollable tears. He struggled through the next two games, then called the trainer over to help talk him through his distress.

Sampras had appeared on the verge of giving up the match, but instead he soldiered on, broke Courier in the eighth game, and converted his first match point when Courier's forehand return soared long. Up at the net, Sampras apologized to Courier and embraced him; Courier had, after all, been part of a group that, on the eve of this match, shared dinner with Gullikson before he flew home. Gullikson learned the results of the match while changing planes in Los Angeles en route to a doctor's appointment in Chicago.

Pete Sampras defeated Michael Chang in the semifinals and lost to Andre Agassi in the final (see Jan. 29). Tim Gullikson died of brain cancer in May 1996 at Wheaton, Ill. He was 44.

Runners-up

1987: Hana Mandlikova broke Martina Navratilova's 58-match winning streak, the third longest in history, with a 7–5, 7–6 upset in the finals of the Australian Open in Melbourne. Going into the match, Navratilova had not dropped a set in the tournament.

1980: The heirs of the original Mets owner Joan Whitney Payson, who had owned the team since its creation in 1962, sold the franchise to Nelson Doubleday of the book publishing family and Fred Wilpon, a Long Island real estate developer, for a reported $21.1 million, the most ever paid for a major-league franchise at the time.

1999: David Duval shot the third 59 in the history of P.G.A. Tour competition, at the Bobe Hope Chrysler Classic in La Quinta, Calif. The others were by Al Geiberger (1977, Colonial Country Club, Memphis) and Chip Beck (1991, Sunrise Country Club, Las Vegas).

January 25, 1924
The Olympics in Winter

The hockey final at the Chamonix Games, with the U.S. team working the puck near the Canadian goal. Canada won, 6-1, but only a handful of spectators watched. (Bettmann/Corbis)

CHAMONIX, France (AP)—The Winter sports of the eighth Olympic Games were officially opened today with the customary Olympic ceremonies, presided over by Gaston Vidal, Under Secretary of State for Physical Education. M. Vidal received the oaths of amateurism by the athletes entered for the competition. The teams of all the nations represented, bearing their national flags and emblems, then paraded from the City Hall to the skating rink, where the actual competitions will begin tomorrow.

On the arrival at the rink Under Secretary Vidal declared the official opening of the sports. His voice, caught up by enormous amplifiers on top of the grandstands, was sent reverberating up the sides of the high mountains which give the Chamonix Valley its magnificent setting. At the words, the 150 athletes, awaiting the announcement, clapped on their skates, jumped onto the immense sheet of ice before them, and the eighth Olympic Games, in their modern revival, were on.

Jewtraw, United States; Gorman, Canada; Thunberg, Finland; and Olsen, Norway, four of the fastest skaters here, hooked up in several turns around the rink in an impromptu race that brought the four or five thousand spectators to their feet cheering. The band of the Twenty-seventh Alpine "Blue Devils" played the national anthems of Austria, Belgium, Canada, Esthonia, the United States, Finland, France, Great Britain, Hungary, Italy, Latvia, Norway, Poland, Sweden, Switzerland and Czechoslovakia as the group of athletes passed in that order.

The athletes of Belgium, Canada, the United States and France received the most enthusiastic welcomes. Clarence J. Abel, St. Paul, of the American hockey team, was the bearer of the Stars and Stripes, and Harry Drury, Pittsburgh, carried the American emblem. They took the Olympic oath, administered by Vidal, on behalf of the American athletes. Both swore that the American athletes would be "loyal competitors, and respect the rules and regulations in a chivalrous spirit for the honor of our country and the greater glory of sport." Abel stumbled over his French a few times in repeating the oath, but he told M. Vidal that he would rather be tripped up in his French delivery than while shooting for a goal in the hockey competition. This brought a cordial laugh from the Under Secretary.

Thousands of visitors have gathered in this small Alpine town on the slopes of Mont Blanc, which today, for the first time in a week, threw off its blanket of thick clouds, the peak glistening in the bright sunshine and providing a wonderful setting for the Olympics.

Runners-up

1998: After four losses in the Super Bowl, the Denver Broncos finally won one, upsetting the Green Bay Packers, 31–24, at San Diego as Terrell Davis became the first player to rush for three touchdowns in the title game. It was quarterback John Elway's first victory after three disappointments in the Super Bowl.

1987: Bill Parcells's Giants, trailing the Denver Broncos by 10–9 at the half, erupted for 17 points in the third quarter on the passing of Phil Simms, who was 22 for 25 with three touchdown passes over all, and won their first Super Bowl, 39–20, in Pasadena, Calif.

2003: Serena Williams of Compton, Calif., defeated her big sister, Venus, 7–6, 3–6, 6–4, to win the Australian Open title in Melbourne for the first time and became the fifth woman in tennis history to hold all four Grand Slam championships—Australian and French Opens, Wimbledon and United States Open—at the same time.

January 26, 1986
Midway Monsters (With a Fridge)

By MICHAEL JANOFSKY

NEW ORLEANS—What happened here today in Super Bowl XX was shocking, even in the context of the Chicago Bears' merry dance through the 66th National Football League season. After winning 17 of 18 games to get here, the Bears demolished the New England Patriots by the almost mystical score of 46–10. For it was the Bears' frequent use of their "46 defense" and variations of it that caused six turnovers, four of them leading to 24 points, and a safety.

In the process of winning their first league championship since they beat the Giants for the 1963 title, the Bears set a number of Super Bowl records, including most points scored, the most decisive victory and the most sacks, seven. And not too surprisingly, a prominent member of the defense, the right end Richard Dent, who had led the league in sacks during the regular season, was named the most valuable player in the game, played before 73,818 at the Superdome. "It was a long way, but it was worth it," said Mike Ditka, the Bears' coach. "A lot of dreams were fulfilled. A lot of frustrations have been ended."

As it had throughout the season, the Bears' defense set the tone of play. Designed and directed by Buddy Ryan, Ditka's 51-year-old Merlin of a defensive coordinator, the Bears chased one quarterback out of the game, made the afternoon nearly as miserable for his replacement and almost shut down the Patriots' running game, which had been the strength of their offense throughout

William (The Refrigerator) Perry of the Bears, a defensive tackle who proved to be all the rage on offense, spiking the ball after rumbling for a touchdown against the Patriots. (Associated Press)

the season. Ryan was carried off the field by three of his charges, right behind Ditka.

Tony Eason, the Patriots' young quarterback, failed to complete any of the six passes he threw, was sacked three times and he fumbled once before he was—almost mercifully—replaced by Steve Grogan with slightly more than five minutes left in the first half. "I don't think the '63 defense would stand up to this one," said Ditka, who was a tight end on the 1963 Bears championship team. "This group is awesome."

Offensively, the Bears were nearly as creative, with Jim McMahon, the plucky quarterback, scoring twice on short runs and William (The Refrigerator) Perry lumbering for another touchdown. McMahon also completed 12 of 20 passes for 256 yards and had none intercepted. "I just

want to thank Coach Ditka for giving me the opportunity to play offense," The Refrigerator said. Referring to the score, he added, "Coach Ditka called it, and I was overwhelmed. I thought I was going in to block for Walter." Indeed, the one slightly disappointing note was that Walter Payton, the incomparable running back who had waited 11 years to play in a Super Bowl, did not score.

"They did a great job," Raymond Berry, the Patriots' coach, said. "Buddy Ryan does a great job getting them prepared. It's the best defense we have played all year. I wanted to come out throwing. I wanted to get their attention." The Patriots got the Bears' attention, all right. And then they got a dose of their defense that they are not likely to forget any time soon.

Runners-up

1960: Pete Rozelle, the 33-year-old general manager of the Los Angeles Rams, was elected commissioner of the N.F.L., succeeding Bert Bell. He was named on the 23rd ballot after Marshall G. Leahy, a San Francisco lawyer, and Austin H. Gunsel, a former F.B.I. man, among others, were considered and rejected.

1997: The Green Bay Packers, relying on the arm of Brett Favre and the kick returns of Desmond Howard, turned back the Patriots, 35–21, in Super Bowl XXXI in New Orleans. It was Green Bay's third Super Bowl victory; the Packers won

the first two that were played, defeating the Kansas City Chiefs in 1967 and the Oakland Raiders in 1968.

1983: Bear Bryant, who once said he would die if he ever quit coaching, succumbed to a heart attack in Tuscaloosa, Ala., 41 days after retiring as head football coach at the University of Alabama. Bryant, 69, stepped down with a record 323 victories and six national titles with the Crimson Tide (see Dec. 15).

January 27, 1991
Coach With a Plan, Always

By DAVE ANDERSON

TAMPA, Fla.—Shortly before noon, the Giants' locker room was empty except for one person. Already dressed in the blue-and-red sweater, red sports shirt and blue slacks that he would be wearing on the sideline more than six hours later, Bill Parcells was walking around, puffing occasionally on a cigarette, wondering if his game plan would work.

"I don't know what the time of possession was," the Giants' coach would say after the Giants' 20–19 victory over the Buffalo Bills in Super Bowl XXV. "But the whole plan was to try to shorten the game for them."

Bill Parcells always has a plan. Against the Chicago Bears in the playoff opener, it was four defensive linemen instead of three. Against the San Francisco 49ers in the National Conference championship game, it was contain Jerry Rice and the other wide receivers. And tonight it was control the ball so as to keep it away from the Bills' explosive no-huddle offense. As it turned out, the Giants had the ball almost twice as much as the Bills did: a Super Bowl record 40 minutes 33 seconds against 19 minutes 27 seconds.

"Bill Parcells," said Tim Mara, the Giants' co-owner, during the presentation of the Vince Lombardi Trophy, "is the best coach the Giants have ever had." Bill Parcells has also emerged as the National Football League's premier coach now as well as one of the best coaches in its history. Over the last five seasons, the Giants have earned two Super Bowl trophies, as many as have the 49ers, whom the Giants dethroned a week ago. Not that Parcells has done it alone. George Young has supplied him with blue-chip players who fulfill his plan. Wellington Mara and Tim

Scott Norwood of the Bills, 11, missing a potential game-winning 47-yard field-goal attempt with four seconds left against the Giants in the Super Bowl. "God . . . was on our side this time," said the Giants' Bill Parcells. (Associated Press)

Mara, the co-owners, have supplied their salaries.

But never before has an N.F.L. team earned a tray of Super Bowl rings with its backup quarterback as its starter. Back on Dec. 15, when Phil Simms suffered a severely sprained right foot in a 17–13 loss to the Bills in a raw rain at Giants Stadium, the Giants' chances of winning the Super Bowl appeared slim.

Other coaches and other teams might have surrendered to such adversity. Not this coach. Not this team. Parcells kept talking about how Jeff Hostetler "can do the job," about how this team built on defense and ball-control still had a chance to win. Parcells kept talking about how Hostetler didn't have to win any of the play-off games, that the 29-year-old quarterback had only to "play within" himself. Hostetler was unable to generate a touchdown against the 49ers as Matt Bahr kicked five field goals in a 15–13 triumph. But after trailing, 12–10, at halftime today, Hostetler found Stephen Baker for a 14-yard touchdown pass and Ottis Anderson, the 34-year-old running back, slashed into the end zone from the 1-yard line before Bahr's second field goal, a 21-yarder, provided the eventual winning point.

For all the Giants' success, they came within Scott Norwood's missed 47-yard field-goal attempt with four seconds left of losing last night's classic in Tampa Stadium. "God's playing in some of these games, but he was on our side this time," Parcells said. "If these two teams played again tomorrow, the Bills would probably win, 20–19." But these two teams don't play again tomorrow; they played tonight and the Giants won.

Runners-up

1996: Monica Seles won her first Grand Slam title since being stabbed in the back during a 1993 tournament *(see April 30),* defeating Anke Huber of Germany in the Australian Open. It was Seles's fourth Australian title, the third having come three months before the attack.

1984: Wayne Gretzky of the Edmonton Oilers scored a goal in the first period of a game against the New Jersey Devils, extending his point-scoring streak to 51 consecutive games, an N.H.L. record. Gretzky, at the apex of his talent, had 61 goals and 92 assists in those 51 remarkable games.

1973: Janet Lynn of Rockford, Ill., in second place after the short program at the United States figure-skating championships, staged a come-from-behind victory in the free-skating phase to edge Dorothy Hamill and win her fifth straight national title at Bloomington, Minn.

January 28, 1996
How to Buy a Super Bowl

By DAVE ANDERSON

TEMPE, Ariz.—In other years the Super Bowl was never for sale. But this time it's as if several months ago, Jerry Jones, the ostentatious owner of the Dallas Cowboys, strolled into Tiffany, only five midtown Manhattan blocks from the National Football League headquarters.

"That Lombardi Trophy in the window," he told the manager. "I'll take it."

"I'm sorry, sir," the manager said. "Yes, our silversmiths make that trophy, but it's merely on display here until the Super Bowl."

"You don't understand," Jones said. "It's already on my credit card. I'm here to pick it up."

"You can't pick it up," he was told. "Somebody from the N.F.L. office will pick it up, not you."

As it turned out, Jerry Jones really did buy the Lombardi Trophy. The price was $62 million, the amount in salaries and bonuses he paid his players this season in circumventing the N.F.L.'s $37.2 million salary cap. To create the cash flow for those bonuses, he defied the N.F.L. in signing multimillion-dollar deals with Nike, Pepsi-Cola and American Express.

And after the Cowboys' 27–17 victory over the Pittsburgh Steelers in Super Bowl XXX today, the Cowboys' owner really did pick up the Lombardi Trophy. In a ceremony on a hastily erected platform at the 10-yard line near the canopy to the locker rooms, Commissioner Paul Tagliabue presented the gleaming football-shaped trophy to Jones and Coach Barry Switzer. "We congratulate you," the commissioner said, "and your extraordinary group of players."

In the glow of the tightest Super Bowl since the Giants' 20–19 triumph over the Buffalo Bills in Tampa five years ago,

Tagliabue was being diplomatic. But on ABC television this morning the commissioner's true feelings surfaced. He described Jones's marketing deals as having "dishonored" the owners' agreement and having "appropriated" money that really didn't belong to the Cowboys. The N.F.L. has sued Jones for $300 million; he has counter-sued for $750 million.

Some of the Cowboys' marketing money went to pay the $12 million bonus cornerback Deion Sanders collected as part of the seven-year, $35 million contract he signed as a free agent early in the season. Jones also had been wise enough in other years to retain his three cornerstone players on offense with multimillion-dollar contracts that this season rewarded quarterback Troy Aikman with $3.5 million, running back Emmitt Smith with $2.4 million and wide receiver Michael Irvin with $5.5 million.

"Jerry has done a great job of keeping the nucleus together," Switzer said. "He believed in the coaching staff and was willing to write the check." But more than any other single player, Sanders proved to be the difference in this season's Super Bowl XXX outcome. The Cowboys had him while the San Francisco 49ers, who won the Super Bowl a year ago with him, no longer had him. And his mere presence influenced how other teams operated on offense. "When Deion's out there on his

Larry Brown, one of Jerry Jones's less expensive Cowboys, beginning a 44-yard interception return that set up Dallas's second touchdown against the Steelers. It was the first of two key picks for Brown. (Reuters)

corner," Switzer said, "other teams don't throw there that much. That's why our other cornerback, Larry Brown, got those two interceptions that turned this game."

Switzer's presence on the sideline represented another Jones decision: to hire him as coach after having split with Jimmy Johnson, the coach of the Cowboys that won the Super Bowl two and three years ago. And when these Cowboys arrived here a week ago, their owner, already looking ahead to tonight's celebration, was trying to make a decision for Arizona lawmakers. "I wonder if we can get a waiver," the Cowboys' owner said, "on the Arizona law that has a 1 A.M. last call for drinks."

Runners-up

1958: Roy Campanella, the three-time M.V.P. catcher of the Brooklyn Dodgers, was paralyzed from the neck down when his car overturned on an icy road in Glen Cove., N.Y. Inducted into the Hall of Fame in 1969, Campanella, one of the former Negro leaguers who helped integrate baseball, played on five pennant-winners during his 10-year career.

2001: Led by Ray Lewis, the Baltimore Ravens intercepted Kerry Collins four times

and dismantled the Giants, 34–7, in Super Bowl XXXV. It was the first Super Bowl loss for the Giants, who defeated the Denver Broncos in 1987 and the Buffalo Bills in 1991 in their first two trips.

1959: Vince Lombardi, the defensive coordinator of the Giants and one of Fordham University's "Seven Blocks of Granite" in the 1930's, was named head coach of the Green Bay Packers. He won five N.F.L. titles in his nine years with them.

The Treasure Down Under

By ROBIN FINN

MELBOURNE, Australia—Andre Agassi, reborn yet again this time as a balding pirate with a zealot's focus but a rational game plan, completed his Australian Open debut run with a flourish today, winning his second consecutive Grand Slam tournament and dethroning the top-ranked Pete Sampras at the same time. In scoring a 4–6, 6–1, 7–6 (8–6), 6–4 victory, the second-ranked Agassi performed the same baseline pyrotechnics that had hurtled him into the final without dropping a single set. His return of serve proved to be more than twice as reliable as that of Sampras's; he committed half the number of unforced mistakes made by the world's No. 1 player and he contributed 10 aces of his own, the last on match point.

Agassi, who now has raised a championship trophy at every Slam except the French Open, managed a calm yet impassioned recovery after surrendering the first set with a double fault on this sizzler of an afternoon. "Ironically, the one I haven't won yet is the one I felt I should have won first," said Agassi, twice a runner-up in Paris but previously unwilling to make the travel effort it took to compete here. "But I came here believing in myself, believing that I could win. It was the first time I ever came into a Grand Slam believing like that. And now, I'm not worried about winning all of them, I worry about winning each one."

Almost as acquisitive as the player himself, Agassi's latest mentor, Brad Gilbert, flashed his player the Paris signal the instant this Melbourne campaign had ended. Gilbert had predicted a seven-round, 21-set conquest and despite losing his first set of the tournament today, he came through in 21.3 sets thanks to Aaron Krickstein's semifinal injury default with Agassi ahead by 3–0 in the third.

In contrast, Sampras, who last year made a successful defense of five of six titles, for the second straight time found himself deprived of the honor of repeating as a Grand Slam champion. His 28 aces weren't sufficient artillery to thwart this colorful human backboard who, according to Sampras, "has the best return of serve in the world by far."

"I don't know how much room there is for improvement," Sampras said of Agassi. "If he stays fit, he's a threat to win every single major title of the year." At the United States Open, a physically wounded Sampras progressed only halfway through the tournament, then watched from the wings as the unseeded Agassi claimed the title. Here in Melbourne, Sampras's wounds were emotional as well as physical. "The matches I've played definitely took a toll, but that's not an excuse," Sampras said. "I did the best I could and lost to a better player. I'm not going to out-rally Andre. He's one of the best players in the world when it comes to ground-stroke confrontations, and although he's obviously always had all the talent in the world, he's put it all together in the last six months."

Andre Agassi gesturing to his coach, Brad Gilbert, after a four-set victory over Pete Sampras in the Australian Open. It was Agassi's second straight Grand Slam title. (Associated Press)

Runners-up

1995: Steve Young threw six touchdown passes, breaking Joe Montana's single-game Super Bowl record of five, as the San Francisco 49ers demolished the San Diego Chargers, 49–26, in Super Bowl XXIX at Miami.

1959: Adolph Rupp, who became basketball coach at Kentucky in 1930, won his 600th game there, then an N.C.A.A. record. He coached until 1972 and retired with 876 victories and four national titles. Dean Smith, the retired North Carolina coach, now holds the career record with 879 victories (*see Oct. 9*).

1961: Valeri Brumel of the Soviet Union broke the 1960 high jump record of John Thomas of the United States when he soared 7 feet 4½ inches in Leningrad. The news got to Thomas at a meet in Boston that his record of 7–2½ had been shattered. He jumped 7 feet 3 inches, better than his previous mark, but Brumel had become the new world champion.

'This Guy Is a Movie'

By BILL PENNINGTON

Kurt Warner of the Rams was sacked by the Titans here, but his inerrant passing, including a game-winning strike to Isaac Bruce with less than two minutes left, gave St. Louis the Super Bowl. (Associated Press)

ATLANTA—When Kurt Warner came onto the Georgia Dome field for the last time tonight, he wondered what happened to the game he thought his St. Louis Rams had had under control. "Here it was the Super Bowl, and we had been up 16 points," Warner said. "And now it's tied. And their fans are going nuts. Of course, I thought about some things. I wouldn't call them doubts, but you wonder."

Warner's last completion had been in the third quarter. The Rams had gained 2 yards in the fourth quarter. And the Tennessee Titans, who had been chasing the Rams for a half, had finally caught them. "It's moments like those when you draw back on your success through the whole year," Warner said.

What the Rams specialized in this season was attacking and throwing the ball downfield. And though the Titans had just tied the score, Warner went for it all on the next play, the Rams' first snap after the kickoff. Warner found wide receiver Isaac Bruce along the right sideline, using a technique that has been around football for decades but is very much in vogue again. Warner threw toward the back shoulder of Bruce—the pass was underthrown—who stopped and caught the pass as cornerback Denard Walker, unable to stop his momentum, drifted past him.

Bruce cut back and outraced a handful of defenders to the end zone with 1 minute 54 seconds left, scoring the stirring game-winning touchdown in the

Rams' 23–16 victory in Super Bowl XXXIV.

Although the Titans came within a yard of tying the score, a National Football League season that has seemed like a five-month victory tour for the Rams concluded with a very Rams-like championship game. In the center of it all was Warner, who was named the game's most valuable player after completing 24 of 45 passes for 414 yards. Warner, who also threw a third-quarter touchdown pass, set a Super Bowl record for passing yards. The old record was set by Joe Montana in 1989 with 357 yards. "It's a dream come true," Warner said. "It's everything you try to accomplish when you start playing football as a kid. I couldn't be happier."

Warner said the Bruce touchdown was actually a play the team had called earlier in the game. "I didn't get the ball in the right place then even though Isaac had him beat," Warner said. "I knew he could beat him again. I have a lot of confidence in him. I think our confidence had a lot to do with the way things ended. We were in the huddle saying, 'We got two minutes. That's plenty of time.'"

Although Warner was sacked just once, he was frequently under pressure from Tennessee's defensive line. "That young man has a lot of fortitude," said Rams Coach Dick Vermeil. "He's a great example of persistence. He is what we'd all like to be. This guy is a movie."

Kurt Warner was not a starting player in college until he was a fifth-year senior at Northern Iowa University. He was cut by the Green Bay Packers in 1994 and worked nights at $5.50 an hour at a Hy-Vee grocery store. He was picked up by the Rams after playing for the Iowa Barnstormers of the Arena Football League from 1995 to '97.

Runners-up

1983: John Riggins gained 166 yards on 38 carries as the Washington Redskins, behind their second-year coach, Joe Gibbs, upended Don Shula's Miami Dolphins, 21–17, in Super Bowl XVII at the Rose Bowl in California. It was the Redskins' first N.F.L. title since 1942.

1993: Monica Seles defeated Steffi Graf to win her third straight Australian Open and eighth Grand Slam singles title in the 14 such matches she had played. Three months later she was stabbed in the back by a spectator during a match in

Germany *(see April 30)*; although she won the 1996 Australian Open, she never regained her former dominance.

1999: Giants linebacker Lawrence Taylor, considered by many to be among the greatest football players ever, was elected to the Pro Football Hall of Fame in his first year of eligibility *(see Aug. 7)*, despite objections from some voters who felt his history of drug abuse should have kept him out.

January 31, 1970
Pistol Pete Lights Up the Night

By SAM GOLDAPER

BATON ROUGE, La.—Pistol Pete Maravich of Louisiana State broke Oscar Robertson's collegiate scoring record tonight with a 23-foot jump shot that gave him a career total of 2,974 points. The record came as L.S.U. routed Mississippi, 109–86, in the Southeastern Conference. He tallied 53 points in the game for a total of 2,987. He still has 13 games left in the regular season.

The slender Maravich, an all-America performer as a sophomore and junior, began this season 687 points behind Robertson and 14th on the scoring list. Robertson played at the University of Cincinnati from 1957–60.

An overflow crowd in the L.S.U. Coliseum went wild when Pete broke the record. About 1,100 students who couldn't get in saw the game on closed-circuit television in the nearby Student Union.

At the half, with L.S.U. leading by 53–40, Maravich had scored 25 points and needed only 15 more for the record. It took him nearly six minutes to break the mark. As the home capacity crowd of 11,000 chanted, "One more, one more," when he came close to the record, Maravich dazzled 'Ole Miss with his famous push-shot jumpers, head fakes and moving crossover dribbles under his legs. Maravich also had 12 assists.

The chant began when Maravich sank a 15-foot jumper with 7:57 remaining in the game. Almost three minutes later, after four futile tries for a basket, Pete hit on a 23-foot jumper for the record. The game was halted for five minutes as Maravich, hoisted to the shoulder of two teammates, Al Sanders and Bob Lang, was paraded round the coliseum and the crowd cheered.

"It's the greatest honor to come to me," said Maravich. "I think Oscar Robertson is probably the greatest basketball player ever and I think I'm fortunate to break his record."

Pete Maravich as a sophomore at Louisiana State. The son of a coach, he possessed ball-handling skills and a sixth sense on the court that astonished those who watched him. (Associated Press)

Runners-up

1993: The Dallas Cowboys won the first of their three N.F.L. titles in the 90's by overwhelming the Buffalo Bills, 52–17, in Super Bowl XXVII behind the passing of Troy Aikman, the running of Emmitt Smith and the defense of Charles Haley and Ken Norton Jr.

1988: Doug Williams, the first black quarterback to start in a Super Bowl, threw for four of his team's five touchdowns in the second quarter as the Washington Redskins exploded for 35 and routed the Denver Broncos, 42–10.

2000: Atlanta Braves closer John Rocker was suspended from spring training and the first 28 days of the season and fined $20,000 by Commissioner Bud Selig for remarks in a magazine interview that disparaged foreigners, gays and others. Rocker never returned to form after the suspension, losing his role with the Braves and bouncing from team to team.

FEBRUARY

February 1, 1984
The Incandescent King

By IRA BERKOW

NEW YORK [Wednesday]—Bernard King on the basketball court combines the late with the latest: His face is a study of concentration—eyes narrowed, goateed jaw set firm, like the portrait mask of a somber Pharaoh. When he walks, it is all hips and shoulders, the way a break-dancer on a street corner struts. He would be strictly comical if he weren't so sensational.

Tonight King scored 50 points in the Knicks' 105–98 victory over the Dallas Mavericks. It was his second straight 50-point game in consecutive nights. Tuesday night in San Antonio he scored 50 points, as he led the Knicks to a 117–113 victory over the Spurs. His point total was the most by any Knick in 16 years, or since Willis Reed scored 53 in 1967.

It is significant that King achieved that sum in a close game. "Bernard," said Dave DeBusschere, director of Knicks basketball operations, "is a big-shot person." King's two 50-point nights followed his performance Sunday in the National Basketball Association All-Star Game when he scored 18 points in 22 minutes and was instrumental in the East beating the West in overtime. And that followed the first half of his seventh N.B.A. season, a period in which he has unquestionably established himself as one of the best players in professional basketball.

The Knicks are on a hot streak, as reports describe it, winning four straight games and five of their last six, and they are eight games over .500, at 26–18. King might seem to be on a hot streak but he has been incandescent all season— remarkably enough, he has been even more glowing this week.

For the record, King, at age 27, is averaging more than 24 points, up from his career average of 21.9. He is near the top of the league in scoring. He plays what is known as small forward—he stands 6 feet 7 inches and weighs 205 pounds— and thus is not required to be a primary rebounder. That role falls to the muscleman on the opposite side of the court, Truck Robinson. Still, King has been pulling down 5.6 rebounds a game.

On defense, on occasion, he will get faked out, he might find himself out of position, and he might lose his man in a series of screens, but watching him fervently scramble to find his way would make even the hard-hearted begin to squeeze for him. On offense is where he is brightest. King is fast and strong and determined. He seeks a favorite spot on the baseline, urgently calls for the ball, and with his back to the basket, with two guys on him, two guys taller, he can still wheel and fake and, with a quick release on the way up, flip in a jump shot, or a jump hook, or whatever that odd shot is. Like bed sheets tied together for an escape out a window, the shot seems hastily constructed due to necessity, and eminently effective.

King has a theory, at least in regard to his drives. "I've got high hips and a sway back," he said, "and I wonder if that doesn't make me more flexible."

As with any exceptional athlete with longevity, however, there comes a certain degree of introspection. Bernard King rarely smiles on the court and rarely banters. "I know I've got this evil look," said King. "But in college it was worse."

Bernard King of the Knicks in Dallas on the night he scored 50 points in a game for the second evening in a row. "I know I've got this evil look," he allowed, "but in college it was worse." (Associated Press)

Runners-up

1968: After five N.F.L. titles and six conference championships in nine seasons, Vince Lombardi resigned as coach of the Green Bay Packers to become the team's general manager. He named Phil Bengtson as his successor. One year later Lombardi left the Packers to become coach of the Washington Redskins.

1984: David Stern, former chief legal counsel of the N.B.A., was named commissioner to succeed Larry O'Brien, a one-time aide to President John F. Kennedy. The league at the time was suffering financially, and Stern quickly restored its fortunes on the court, at the gate, among advertisers and in the public's consciousness.

1970: Terry Sawchuk, the Detroit Red Wings goalie acquired by the Rangers to give Eddie Giacomin a late-season rest, recorded the 103rd and final shutout of his career, at Madison Square Garden. The total is the N.H.L. record and, in an age of higher scoring, is not likely to be broken.

February 2, 1936
In a Class by Themselves

CHICAGO (AP)—Tyrus Raymond Cobb, fiery genius of the diamond for 24 years, will be the No. 1 immortal in baseball's permanent hall of fame. The famous Georgian, who shattered virtually all records known to baseball during his glorious era, won the distinction as the immortal of immortals today by outscoring even such diamond greats as Babe Ruth, Honus Wagner and Christy Mathewson in the nationwide poll to determine which 10 players of the modern era should be represented in the game's memorial hall in Cooperstown, N.Y.

Only Cobb, Ruth, Wagner, Mathewson and Walter Johnson, probably the speed ball king of them all, received the required majority to win places in the hall of fame, but Cobb had a margin of seven votes over his closest rivals, Ruth and Wagner. Of 226 ballots cast by players and writers, the Georgia Peach received 222, or four less than a unanimous vote. Ruth and Wagner received 215 each. Mathewson was fourth with 205 and Johnson fifth with 189. Seventy-five percent of the total votes, or 169, were needed.

Napoleon Lajoie, Tris Speaker, Cy Young, Rogers Hornsby and Mickey Cochrane ran in that order for the other five positions left for the moderns, players who starred from 1900 and on, but as none received 75 percent of the total vote their cases will be submitted to the Cooperstown committee in charge of the memorial to be erected in time for baseball's centennial in 1939. Their names will be submitted in another poll next year with five or seven places open.

The committee in charge of the vote tabulation, headed by Henry Edwards, secretary of the Baseball Writers Association, figured the struggle

The class of classes at the 1939 opening of the Hall of Fame. Standing, from left, are Honus Wagner, Grover Cleveland Alexander, Tris Speaker, Nap Lajoie, George Sisler and Walter Johnson. Seated are Eddie Collins, Babe Ruth, Connie Mack and Cy Young. (National Baseball Hall of Fame)

for ballots among the moderns would be a two-man battle between Cobb and Ruth. When the first 100 votes were counted, both Cobb and the home-run king were unanimous. Ruth was the first to fall out, losing a vote from a writer who had watched him hang up some of his greatest records. The committee was amazed. Vote counting stopped momentarily for a discussion on how anyone could leave the great Ruth off the list of immortals.

The same happened when Cobb missed his first vote. Too, there was some surprise when the usual vote of Cobb, Ruth and Speaker was broken up with a series of ballots for other outfielders.

George Sisler, whose great career with the St. Louis Browns was halted by impairment of vision, ranked 11th, with 77

votes. Fifty-one stars, past and present, were named, but few of the present ones received much support, for the reason that the voters figured that they would get their chances later, as one or two will be added to the list of immortals each year.

The Baseball Hall of Fame, the first of its kind in sports, initiated a movement in American culture to honor the memories and achievements of famous athletes. All major sports and even some minor ones have long since raised pantheons.

The hall was established in Cooperstown because legend had it that the first baseball game was played there 100 years before in 1836. In fact, most historians believe it was played at the Elysian Fields in Hoboken, N.J., in 1846.

Runners-up

1962: John Uelses, a 24-year-old Berlin-born Marine corporal using a new fiber-glass pole, became the world's first vaulter to crack 16 feet when he soared 16 feet ¼ inch in the Millrose Games at Madison Square Garden. The fiberglass pole eventually supplanted the wooden one, which had much less spring, and effectively rewrote the record books by allowing vaulters to soar higher.

1956: Tenley Albright of Newton Center, Mass., became the first U.S. woman to win a Winter Olympics gold medal when she captured the figure skating title at the Cortina Games in Italy. Two weeks before, she had fallen on the ice and severed a vein in her right ankle with her other skate blade; her father flew to Italy, performed surgery on her and she recovered to win the gold.

1949: The brilliant golfer Ben Hogan narrowly survived a head-on car crash with a bus in Texas. For a time it appeared he might never play again, but he recovered from his injuries and won the United States Open 16 months later at Merion Golf Club in Ardmore, Pennsylvania, defeating Lloyd Mangrum and George Fazio in an 18-hole playoff *(see June 11).*

February 3, 2002
As the Clock Ran Out

By THOMAS GEORGE

NEW ORLEANS—Adam Vinatieri's 48-yard field goal as time expired lifted the New England Patriots to the most dramatic finish in Super Bowl history tonight, a stunning, magical 20–17 upset victory over the St. Louis Rams in Super Bowl XXXVI before 72,922 fans at the Superdome.

In a city known for its reveling ways, this game and that kick rocked pro football. The Patriots felt that they had been given little chance to win this game, but that did not matter to them. They played solidly on offense, competently on special teams and excelled on defense, shutting down a potent Rams offense. Prolific? Stylish? Not today. Through three quarters the Rams managed 3 points. It took a flurried finish with two touchdowns in the final 10 minutes, the last one with 1 minute 37 seconds left, for St. Louis to tie the score at 17–17.

It was the New England defense, however, that gained the last yards and the last laugh, driving from its 17-yard line to the St. Louis 30 to set up Vinatieri's kick. The key play was Tom Brady's pass of 23 yards to Troy Brown to the St. Louis 36.

This Super Bowl was unlike any other in terms of the quality and depth of security after the Sept. 11 terrorist attacks. Eleven law enforcement agencies, led by the Secret Service, participated. The extra security was evident outside and inside the Superdome and even in the air, where helicopters and fighter planes patrolled. Fans—who were patted down from head to toe before entering the stadium—anticipated the extra security and arrived early. With the kickoff more than an hour away, Superdome officials announced that 95 percent of the capacity crowd was present.

Those fans were treated to a pregame concert that focused on freedom. Paul McCartney, Patti LaBelle, Marc Anthony, Mary J. Blige and Barry Manilow were among the performers. The national anthem was sung by Mariah Carey, and the fans in the three decks of the Superdome, from top to bottom, waved lights that were red, white and blue.

Once the game began, the Patriots quickly strutted their stuff. They jumped on top of St. Louis by 14–3 at halftime, scoring twice off Rams turnovers, and by 17–3 early in the fourth quarter. Bill Belichick, the Patriots coach, said: "We had to rush them with everything but the kitchen sink. We had to alternate our coverages. We disrupted them. Our players believe in themselves. They beat the No. 1 seed in the A.F.C. in Pittsburgh to get here, and now they have beaten the No. 1 seed in the N.F.C. in St. Louis."

Kurt Warner, the Rams' quarterback, struggled all game long. "To get this far and not finish it, that hurts," said Warner, who was 28 of 44 for 365 yards. "I made some mistakes today that cost us. They played aggressively, but we did too. They played a better game."

Warner's counterpart, Tom Brady, a 24-year-old second-year player who entered the season as a backup, ended it as the youngest quarterback to win a Super Bowl. He was also named the game's most valuable player for completing 16 of 27 passes for 145 yards and a touchdown but, more so, for managing the game superbly for the Patriots.

Brady won a Cadillac for the M.V.P. award, but the team he drove was more like a van. Emblematic of that were the introductions before the game. The Rams chose their offense to be introduced, but the Patriots chose to introduce neither their offense nor defense but their entire team as one unit. How prophetic.

Adam Vinatieri, celebrating after his 48-yard field goal as time ran out, lifted the Patriots to a 20-17 upset over the Rams. It was the most dramatic finish in Super Bowl history. (Barton Silverman/The New York Times)

Runners-up:

1990: Darryl Strawberry's career took a dramatic turn for the worse when the 27-year-old, five-time All-Star outfielder for the Mets entered a center for drug and alcohol abuse in Manhattan to treat what the team described as a drinking problem. He was traded to the Los Angeles Dodgers the following year and his career went into an irreversible decline.

1989: Forty-two years after Jackie Robinson broke the color line, Bill White, the former first baseman and Yankee broadcaster, was named president of the National League and became the highest-ranking black executive in professional sports history.

1990: Bill Shoemaker, 58, the greatest jockey in history, rode in his last race, finishing fourth at Santa Anita Park. He retired with 8,833 victories in 40,350 races.

February 4, 1987
Raise High the Broomstick

By BARBARA LLOYD

The crew of Stars & Stripes celebrates after sweeping the America's Cup series in Australia and returning the Cup to the U.S. after four years. Dennis Conner, the boat's skipper, gives a thumbs-up at far left. (Corbis/Sygma)

FREMANTLE, Australia—Dennis Conner avenged his 1983 loss of the America's Cup today, sailing a brilliant final race to win back yachting's most prestigious trophy for the United States. Conner's Stars & Stripes led the way around the 24.3-nautical-mile racing course to defeat Kookaburra III, Australia's defender, by 1 minute 59 seconds. That gave Stars & Stripes a 4–0 sweep in the four-of-seven series and touched off celebrations halfway round the world, particularly in San Diego, which will be the new home for the cherished yachting cup.

It took Conner nearly three years of dedication to reclaim the historic trophy after his bitter defeat in 1983. The Stars & Stripes team took command at the start today, allowing Iain Murray and his Kookaburra III team to chase him through the spectator fleet minutes before the start. More than 400 vessels filled with rooters waited eagerly for the race to begin. Overhead, 12 helicopters buzzed

the Indian Ocean racecourse. Conner edged his blue-hulled 12-Meter up to the start line, heading for the preferred left side of the course. Kookaburra was in hot pursuit, holding course to windward of Stars & Stripes in an effort to force Conner over the line early.

In the style the 44-year-old Conner has perfected through a decade of match-racing experience, he nudged the bow of Stars & Stripes up to the line just as the starting gun went off. Stars & Stripes crossed five seconds ahead of Kookaburra. The Australian boat headed to the right side of the course on port tack. Conner tacked over to close in on Kookaburra from the left. When the two met, Conner was not able to cross in front of Kookaburra. He tacked short of the Australian boat, which at that point split off to sail back to the right.

Several minutes later, the two boats converged again, but this time Stars & Stripes, with her superior speed, was able to cross two boat lengths ahead of

Kookaburra. A moderate sea breeze of 16 knots ushered the two boats through the first part of the race. By the first mark, the breeze was filling to 18 knots, the type of condition that the Stars & Stripes team likes best. At the first mark, Stars & Stripes was 26 seconds ahead. Murray sailed a faster downwind leg, gaining four seconds. But after the third leg—sailed upwind—Conner had stepped on the accelerator, rounding the third mark 42 seconds in front.

In the next two reaches, Stars & Stripes held a firm grip on the lead. At the fourth mark, the Kookaburra team flailed for nearly a minute as it tried to bring in the spinnaker that had broken free. At that mark, Stars & Stripes rounded with a 49-second advantage, its largest so far. In the fifth leg, Kookaburra managed to steal one second from Conner's leading margin. But in the sixth leg Conner lengthened his lead to 1 minute 11 seconds. After rounding the seventh mark with a lead of 1:16, Conner sailed up the final leg to his second America's Cup victory in the four times he has taken the helm of a 12-Meter in this international event.

Throughout their quest, Conner and his Stars & Stripes team agreed that they had nothing to fear by taking risks. From supercomputers to aerospace plastics, technology played a key role. The success of Conner's Sail America syndicate was attributable to large measures of hard work, creativity, thoroughness and experience.

The formula began paying off when Stars & Stripes began the four-month series of trial races in October. "Every call we made, we came up smelling like a rose," said Conner. Since then, it appears that little has changed.

Runners-up

1932: New York governor Franklin D. Roosevelt opened the third Winter Olympic Games at Lake Placid, the first Games held in the United States. Jack Shea, a native of Lake Placid and the patriarch of a family that produced three generations of Olympians, became the United States star of the Games, winning two gold medals in speed skating.

1969: Having fired former Air Force general William Eckert as commissioner, major-league baseball owners settled on Bowie Kuhn, their chief legal counsel, to replace him. Kuhn, the game's fifth commissioner, was given an initial one-year

term but eventually served 15 years, second in longevity to Kenesaw Mountain Landis (see Nov. 12).

1997: Unable to make a deal with the New England Patriots for the right to hire Bill Parcells as their head coach, the Jets pulled an end-around, hiring Parcells's top New England assistant, Bill Belichick, as "interim" coach and naming Parcells a "consultant." The strategem worked and Parcells soon took over as coach, much to the chagrin of the New England owner Robert Kraft.

February 5, 1943
The Puncher and the Dancer

DETROIT (AP)—Rugged Jacob La Motta, belting his foe through the ropes for a count of nine in the eighth round, handed Ray (Sugar) Robinson his first defeat in 130 fights by scoring a ten-round decision tonight before a record crowd of 18,930 spectators at Olympia Stadium. Both are New Yorkers. La Motta weighed 160½ for a 16-pound advantage.

In a fistic upset unequaled in many years, La Motta, a 3-to-1 underdog just up from preliminary ranks, gained the unanimous decision of Referee Sam Hennessy and the two judges. Where other foes had been floored or driven back by Robinson's punching power, La Motta kept wading in, scoring decisive body blows that softened the sugar boy for a tremendous assault in the late rounds. Late in the eighth round, La Motta hammered Robinson with a right to the body and followed with a left to the head that drove the previously undefeated pride of Harlem through the ropes onto the ring apron. The bell rang just as the knockdown timekeeper's hammer was coming down for ten.

The overflow crowd, the largest indoor turnout in Michigan boxing history, paid $50,000. Of this Robinson drew some $15,000 for a measure of consolation. Referee Hennessy's scorecard gave five rounds to La Motta, four to Robinson and called one even. Jolting Jacob won the last four by this accounting. Robinson's first defeat

came in his hometown, where he got his first training in the club that sent Joe Louis to the heavyweight title. But there was hardly an outcry against the decision.

At the start Robinson fought the battle according to well-laid plans. He kept dancing away from the rough La Motta who never has hit the deck, but his deadly left was in La Motta's face repeatedly. La Motta won the second, but the sugar boy piled up points as the fight wore on.

In the seventh, while Robinson was missing the target, La Motta started his grand slam finish. He hammered away with body punches mostly until he connected with the knockdown blow in the eighth. Then Jacob, who never lacks for confidence, waded in to take the ninth. In the tenth he had Robinson backed in a corner and was hitting him with everything he had. The victory squared their personal series at one fight each, Robinson having won a decision last October in New York.

Sugar Ray Robinson won 91 consecutive bouts over eight years after this loss. He relinquished his welterweight title in 1951 to fight Jake La Motta again for the middleweight crown and won on a knockout in the 13th round. Robinson, whose career record was 174–19–6, won the middleweight title five separate times between 1951 and '60.

Victorious in 129 successive fights, including 40 as a pro, Ray Robinson falls through the ropes of a Detroit ring, under the impact of Jake La Motta's fists. Robinson got back in the ring, but lost the decision in 10 rounds. (Bettmann/Corbis)

Runners-up:

1948: Dick Button of Englewood, New Jersey *(see Feb. 21)*, a freshman at Harvard University, won the first United States Olympic figure skating gold medal in history at the St. Moritz Games in Switzerland, wowing the judges with the first double axel ever performed in competition. Button later became the premier figure-skating commentator on television

1976: Hometown hero Franz Klammer, fast but forever on the edge of losing control, thrilled millions of worldwide television viewers by winning the men's downhill

on an icy course at the Innsbruck Olympics in Austria. He defeated the defending champion, Bernhard Russi of Switzerland by one-third of a second in a remarkable 1:45.73.

1960: Bill Russell of the Boston Celtics grabbed a record 51 rebounds to lead his team over the Syracuse Nationals, 124-100, at Boston Garden. Wilt Chamberlain of the Philadelphia Warriors broke the mark with 55 rebounds, the current record, nine months later against the Celtics.

February 6, 1993
A Man of Quality

By ROBIN FINN

NEW YORK—Arthur Ashe, a tennis champion who spent his years in the sport fighting discrimination and then spent the final year of his life seeking to broaden public awareness on the subject of AIDS, died today. He was 49. A New York Hospital administrator, Judith Lilavois, said Ashe died at 3:13 p.m. of pneumonia, a complication of AIDS. He was admitted to the hospital two days ago. "An additional statement will come from his family and the hospital tomorrow," she said.

Ashe was the only black man to win Wimbledon and the United States and Australian Opens. Militant in his conviction but mild in his manner, this slim, bookish and bespectacled athlete never thought himself a rebel and preferred information to insurrection. Since he believed his singular success carried inherent responsibilities, Ashe, during his decade-long professional tennis career and beyond it, dedicated himself to dismantling the barriers of poverty, privilege, racism and social stereotyping. Even the fact of his own mortality became a cause célèbre, and Ashe, in the headlines again, conducted his final campaign against the ravages of AIDS.

Ashe, who said he believed he contracted H.I.V., the virus that causes AIDS, through a transfusion of tainted blood during his second round of heart-bypass surgery in 1983, first learned of his infection after he entered New York Hospital for emergency brain surgery in September 1988. He was hospitalized after he suffered paralysis of his right arm, the one that served up 26 aces the day he became the 1968 United States Open champion. The surgery and a subsequent biopsy revealed the presence of toxoplasmosis, a parasitic infection linked to AIDS.

In recent weeks, Ashe had been hospitalized with pneumocystis pneumonia, according to an AIDS researcher. Two weeks ago he stayed in Manhattan, where he lived, rather than travel to Boston to receive an award. He appeared short of breath in a videotape that he made to be shown in the place of his appearance. But Ashe was as passionate as ever, speaking of a visit to South Africa he had made and how a young boy had told him that he was the first free black man he had ever seen.

Ashe chose not to publicize his condition, preferring to protect his family's privacy and being well aware of the inevitable demands such a disclosure would place on a man of his celebrity. He did not disclose his condition until April 8, 1992, and then only after being told that USA Today intended to publish an article about his illness as soon as it could confirm it. But after making his public admission, Ashe spent the rest of his days campaigning for public awareness, including a speech on the floor of the United Nations on World AIDS Day on Dec. 1.

When he made his reluctant admission, Ashe said: "I have good days and bad days. My ratio of good days to bad days is about six to one. I don't think anybody in my stage of this would be able to go through with no bad days. But I didn't want to go public now because I am not sick." Sick, in Ashe's terminology, meant being bedridden and nonfunctional. As an avid golfer, prominent speaker, occasional columnist for The Washington Post, television commentator for HBO and ABC Sports, author of a three-volume history of the black athlete in America, and a noted participant in countless civic projects and protests, Ashe hardly went into retreat in the four years that followed his AIDS diagnosis.

Arthur Ashe holds his Wimbledon trophy after defeating fellow American Jimmy Connors in the final match of the men's singles championship at Wimbledon, England, July 5, 1975. (Associated Press)

Runners-up

1972: On the opening day of competition at the Sapporo Games, the first Winter Olympics ever held in an Asian country, Japan's Yukio Kasaya, Akitsuga Konno and Seiji Aochi swept the medals in the 70-meter ski jump. In all its previous competition in the Winter Games, Japan had won just one lone medal.

1967: Shouting "What's my name?" throughout the fight, Muhammad Ali successfully defended his heavyweight title for the eighth time by severely battering Ernie Terrell in a 15-round unanimous decision. Terrell had insisted on calling Ali by his "slave name," Cassius Clay.

1971: Alan Shepard, having taken along golf balls and a makeshift 5-iron on the Apollo 14 mission, hit the longest golf shot in the sport's history on the surface of the moon—aided by its lack of atmosphere and gravity one-sixth that of Earth. Shepard reveled in how the balls flew "for miles and miles."

Seven Down, Seven to Go

By CLIFTON BROWN

Tiger Woods at Pebble Beach four months after his remarkable comeback in the National Pro-Am there. He teed off on No. 9 beside Carmel Beach in the U.S. Open, which he won by a stunning 15 strokes. (Associated Press)

PEBBLE BEACH, Calif.—The streak is alive, and so is the magic of Tiger Woods. In a comeback of epic proportions, on one of the world's great golf courses, Woods overcame a seven-stroke deficit with seven holes to play today to win the AT&T Pebble Beach National Pro-Am by two strokes over Matt Gogel and Vijay Singh. By winning his sixth consecutive start on the PGA Tour, Woods tied Ben Hogan, who won six consecutive starts in 1948, for the second-longest streak in professional golf history.

Byron Nelson holds the longest winning streak with 11 consecutive victories in 1945, a record that has long been considered untouchable. But the genius of Woods, who has already won 17 tournaments in three and a half years as a pro-

fessional, has allowed him to achieve remarkable feats, such as today's comeback, when he seemed hopelessly behind on Pebble Beach's picturesque back nine only to storm back for the victory.

It was a dramatic achievement, and fantastic even by Woods's high standards. Shooting a final-round eight-under-par 64, the best final round ever for a champion at Pebble Beach. Woods changed the momentum of the tournament with one brilliant shot—holing a wedge shot from 97 yards for an eagle at No. 15. When the ball landed about four feet right of the cup, then spun into the hole for eagle, Woods gave his signature fist pump, and it was almost like a knockout punch to everyone else on the leader board.

While Woods made three birdies and an eagle on the back nine, Gogel, a 28-year-old tour rookie looking for his first victory, collapsed with four bogeys on his final nine holes, squandering a commanding lead and becoming another of Woods's many victims. Woods finished at 15 under par for the tournament (273—68-73-68-64), two strokes ahead of Gogel, who shot a final-round 71, and Singh, who shot a 70. By succeeding the late Payne Stewart as the champion at Pebble Beach, and by winning on a course that he first played at age 12, Woods continued a streak of superb golf that has lasted almost six months. Since last August, Woods has won eight of his last nine starts on tour, including the P.G.A. Championship.

The more Woods continues to win, the more confident he seems to become. Though Woods was beaten in November in Taiwan, and at the Williams World Challenge in January, he has not lost an official PGA Tour event since the Sprint International last August. And today, when almost any chance to win seemed lost, Woods never lost faith. "I have the confidence to know I have done it before in the past, coming from behind, or edging someone out," said Woods, who won $720,000 to push his career earnings above $12.5 million, only about $31,000 behind Davis Love 3rd, the career Tour money leader. "I've had a pretty good run throughout my career of comebacks."

Runners-up

1949: Joe DiMaggio, the Yankee Clipper who previously had several contract battles with general managers Ed Barrow and George Weiss, became the first $100,000-a-year athlete when he signed with the Yankees. Next highest on the team's payroll at the time were Tommy Henrich and Phil Rizzuto at $40,000.

1882: In the last major bare-knuckle championship bout, John L. Sullivan knocked out Paddy Ryan in the ninth round at Mississippi City, Miss. Sullivan held the heavyweight title until 1892, when he lost to James J. Corbett under boxing's newly adopted Marquis of Queensbury rules (see Sept. 7).

1970: Louisiana State's Pete Maravich (see Jan. 31) scored 69 points in a 106-104 loss to the University of Alabama. It was the highest total ever by an N.C.A.A. Division I player in a single game, breaking the record of 68 points set by Niagara's Calvin Murphy 14 months earlier. Maravich's mark was surpassed by Kevin Bradshaw of U.S. International, who scored 72 points while helped by the 3-point shot rule in 1991.

February 8, 1980
Mary Decker Comes of Age

By FRANK LITSKY

Mary Decker, 21, winning the 1,500 meters in world-record time at Madison Square Garden. So dominant was her performance that her nearest competitor finished half a lap behind. (Associated Press)

NEW YORK—The largest crowd in indoor track history stood and stomped and screamed and clapped tonight at Madison Square Garden. The excitement was provoked by an astounding race by a record-breaking miler. No, Eamonn Coghlan was not the miler. The race was not even for men. The hero of the 73d annual Wanamaker Millrose Games was 21-year-old Mary Decker, who won the women's 1,500-meter run by 80 yards, half a lap, in 4 minutes 0.8 seconds, a world indoor record. This was her first New York appearance since 1974, when, as a pig-tailed schoolgirl, she won a Millrose title and a national championship.

Since then, she has quit track, undergone surgery on leg sheaths and come back. On Jan. 26, in Auckland, New Zealand, she set a world outdoor mile record of 4:21.7. Her time tonight translates to a 4:19 mile, remarkable because the tight turns of an 11-lap indoor track are more difficult to negotiate than the sweeping turns on a four-lap outdoor track.

Francie Larrieu, for years America's best runner at 1,500 meters and a mile, did not run because of illness. Her presence could not have made that much difference. Miss Decker ran the first quarter-mile in 60.3 seconds, faster than the first quarter of the Wanamaker Mile for men. She finished the half mile in 2:05.9, faster than any woman had run a half-mile race in the Garden. Two laps later, the crowd was standing and yelling encouragement. "The crowd helped tremendously," said Miss Decker. "I couldn't have set the record without it. I thought my pace was too fast, but this was a much stronger race than my mile record."

The meet was sold out nine days in advance. The crowd of 18,310 broke the indoor record of 18,307 for the 1964 Chicago Relays and the Games and Garden record of 18,301, set last year. The crowd was noisy because race after race provided records (world, American, Garden and meet) or tingling finishes or both.

Runners-up

1936: The first N.F.L. draft of collegiate players was held, creating a permanent talent stream for pro football. Jay Berwanger of the University of Chicago, winner of the 1935 Downtown Athletic Trophy—soon renamed the Heisman—was the first player selected, by the Philadelphia Eagles. He chose not to play and became a millionaire businessman in Chicago.

1998: N.H.L. stars arrived at the Winter Olympics in Nagano, Japan, removing restrictions against the participation of professionals in the Winter Games just as N.B.A. members of the United States "Dream Team" had done in the Summer Games at Barcelona almost six years before.

1981: Scott Hamilton, a 5-foot-3-inch, 115-pound jumping dynamo from Bowling Green, Ohio, received two perfect 6.0's in winning the first of four straight titles in both the national and world figure-skating championships as well as the gold medal at the 1984 Sarajevo Olympics in Yugoslavia. Hamilton almost died as a child of a rare digestive disorder and began skating at age 9 as therapy for it.

Satch Looks Back and Gains

By ARTHUR DALEY

NEW YORK—One of the more memorable of the many philosophical gems scattered over the years by Leroy (Satchel) Paige was this: "Don't look back. Something might be gaining on you." But Ol' Satch looked back today and was pleased to see that his reputation as an extraordinary pitcher had caught up with him. Formal notification was given this ageless marvel at a Toots Shor reception that a special committee had elected him to a special section of the baseball Hall of Fame at Cooperstown.

He will be formally inducted into the shrine next August at the same ceremonies and with the same éclat as the newest Hall of Famers who were named. But his plaque of recognition will hang in a new and different part of the National Baseball Museum, one that has been set aside for some of the fabled heroes of the old Negro leagues.

Satch is the first, "a historic first" in the words of Commissioner Bowie Kuhn. Hereafter, one ancient black campaigner will be elected each year and it is presumed that the next one will be Josh Gibson, the black Babe Ruth, just as Satch was the black Cy Young or Walter Johnson. Other victims of baseball's original color line will follow and resentment already has begun to stir in some quarters. Some observers are already regarding this as a pernicious form of segregation, keeping the Negro league stars apart from the other immortals.

Satchel showed little emotion when he stepped to the microphone to be interviewed. "I'm proud wherever they put me in the Hall of Fame," he said. Satch pitched for more than 40 years. He says he will be 65 years old in three months. "I

Leroy (Satchel) Paige of the Kansas City Monarchs preparing to take on the New York Cuban Stars in a Negro League game at Yankee Stadium in 1942. He played in the major leagues only in the twilight of his career. (Associated Press)

was born in August, no July, 1908," he says. That would make him 62. Disregard all Satch's statistics—except a few. He probably pitched somewhere between 2,000 and 2,500 games, winning 90 per cent of them. In a barnstorming game he struck out the deadly eyed Rogers Hornsby five times. In pitching against Babe Ruth's All-Stars he fanned 22 and also fanned 15 of Dizzy Dean's big league troupe. "Let 'em arguefy," once said Dean. "The best pitcher I ever seen is ol' Satchel Paige. My fastball looks like a change of pace alongside that li'l pistol-bullet Satch shoots up to the plate."

"The prewar Paige was the best pitcher I ever saw," said Bob Feller.

Throughout his baseball life, Satch heard one haunting refrain: "Too bad you ain't white." He unquestionably would have burned up the big leagues. Electing him to the Hall of Fame, therefore, is a belated acknowledgement of his extraordinary skills.

Satchel Paige is believed to have won more than 2,000 games in the Negro leagues between 1926 and '48, when he joined the Cleveland Indians. Among other black stars later admitted to the Hall were Josh Gibson, the power-hitting catcher for the Homestead Grays and Pittsburgh Crawfords from 1930 to '46; James (Cool Papa) Bell, the speedster who played in the Negro, Mexican and Dominican leagues from 1922 to '48; and Buck Leonard, first baseman and captain of the Grays from 1934 to '48.

Runners-up

1999: An ethics panel reported that to win the 2002 Winter Games, Salt Lake City Olympic officials showered Olympic delegates with cash payments and an array of gifts, from free trips to the Super Bowl to doorknobs and furniture. The scandal led to changes within the International Olympic Committee that prohibited delegates from visiting potential Olympic sites, much less receiving any gifts.

1983: Gunmen forced their way into the Aga Khan's stud farm in county Kildare, Ireland, and kidnapped Shergar, winner of the 1981 Epsom Derby and one of the world's top racehorses. The abductors demanded a $2.7 million ransom. A massive police search was mounted, no deadline for the ransom was ever set and the horse and assailants were never found.

1992: Magic Johnson of the Los Angeles Lakers, who retired from the N.B.A. three months earlier after testing positive for the H.I.V. virus, returned to play in the All-Star Game, scoring game highs of 25 points and 9 assists and winning his second most valuable player award in the classic.

The Ballerina on Skates

By LLOYD GARRISON

GRENOBLE, France—Peggy Fleming's victory in the Olympic figure skating tonight was not only a personal triumph, it was also a victory of the ballet over the Ice Follies approach to figure skating. For traditional aficionados, her victory had all the ingredients of a Good Guy whipping the Bad Guys in an Italian-made Western in which the film is no good unless the Good Guy guns down at least a posse of black-hatted hombres in the first reel. Tonight, the Colorado State college girl with a weakness for chocolate cake and whipped cream took on no fewer than 32 competitors and knocked them all dead.

Until Miss Fleming came along, the women's figure skating threatened to be dominated by skaters who are not unpretty to look at, but who resemble overgrown chorus girls with the legs of a Green Bay linebacker. The "Ice Follies" analogy was coined by Miss Fleming herself. "I primarily represent the ballet approach," she said. "That is, where the movements are more graceful and everything blends smoothly as you flow across the ice." Being polite, she describes the "Ice Follies" school as being merely more "athletic."

"Peggy," says Gebrielle Seyfert of East Germany, "has no weaknesses. I know I am the more athletic type and I'm trying to overcome it. Peggy lands softly and everything she does is connected. It's pure ballerina." At 5 feet 4 inches and currently weighing only 108 pounds, Peggy has occasionally gotten up to 112—with her penchant for desserts. But such rare lapses account for her breaks in discipline in a sport with incredible physical and psychological demands.

While at times exuding a sorority girl's impishness, on the ice she's all poise, a very worldly black-haired and dark-eyed beauty. At last year's world championships in Vienna, the Austrian press tried to pin down Miss Fleming's appeal both as a skater and as a young woman. Some described her as "classic." Others compared her to a Grecian beauty. The Express finally tabbed her as "America's Shy Bambi." Few would quibble with any of these descriptions. But Miss Fleming is refreshingly unconcerned about image-making. Before the finals here, she had her usual double-decker sandwich. After she had won and was finished with the interviews and the congratulations, she had her chocolate cake. And at last, with tonight's triumph, a few pounds more or less wouldn't matter.

Smooth, polished Peggy Fleming practicing a stag leap at the 1968 Grenoble Olympics. She was known for balletic grace before figure skating emphasized athleticism. (Associated Press)

Runners-up

1920: The major leagues outlawed doctored pitches, including the spitball, the shine ball and the emery ball—a move that brought more hitting into the game. The Brooklyn Dodgers' Burleigh Grimes and 16 others who used the forbidden pitches were allowed to do so for the rest of their careers under a grandfather clause.

1992: Bonnie Blair of Champaign, Ill., raced to a gold medal in the 500-meter speed skating final at the Albertville Games in France, beating 31 other finishers in 40.33 seconds and becoming the first American woman to win gold medals in an event in consecutive Winter Olympics.

1998: In one of its biggest soccer upsets, the United States defeated the world champion Brazilians, 1–0, advancing to the final of the Concacef Gold Cup tournament for the first time. Kasey Keller had the shutout, making four key saves on Romario, the 1994 World Cup hero. The United States had been 0–8 against Brazil and had been outscored, 19–0, by the Brazilians since an exhibition match in 1930.

They Almost Stole the Show

By SELENA ROBERTS

SALT LAKE CITY—There was outrage at the apparent sympathy vote tonight as the Olympic domination of the Russians went unbroken, with the calamitous journey of Yelena Berezhnaya and Anton Sikharulidze ending with a pairs gold medal, the 11th consecutive for the country. Few understood how 42 years of history was kept intact, though. The instant Jamie Salé drifted away from David Pelletier on the emotional final notes of the Canadian pair's "Love Story" routine, their reaction was that of winners. Pelletier kissed the ice, and Salé wiped happy tears from her eyes. The crowd inside the Salt Lake Ice Center chanted "Six! Six!" trying to coax the judges into delivering perfect scores for what appeared to be a flawless performance, or at least one better than that of Sikharulidze and Berezhnaya.

After all, Sikharulidze stumbled out of his double axel on the pair's second element. Even so, the international judges split their vote, 5–4. Russia, China, Ukraine, Poland and France still felt the presentation of the Russians deserved first place. Judges from the United States, Canada, Germany and Japan awarded first place to the Canadians. One official said there may have been politics within the sport that swayed the French judge to side with Russia. "What we can't control, we can't control," Pelletier said, choking with emotion. "It's tough."

One skating official privately called the result an embarrassment, and the choreographer for the Canadian pair, Lori Nichol, said Salé and Pelletier had clearly won, adding that the questionable scoring "hurt the sport." The Russians' coach, Tamara Moskvina, defended her team. "What decision? What controver-

The ice-skating judge Marie Reine Le Gougne of France at the Salt Lake City Games. The International Skating Union blacklisted her after the Olympics for colluding to fix the pairs competition in favor of the Russians. (Associated Press)

sy?" said Moskvina, who has coached four Russian teams to gold in her career. "There was applause for silver, gold and bronze."

It was not equal, though. The Canadians transfixed the audience, pulling off the polish of a Hollywood love scene. No clumsiness, just one clean line. "Our silver is worth gold to us," Salé said.

Two days later, Didier Gailhaguet, head of the French Olympic team, said that the figure-skating judge from his country, Marie Reine Le Gougne, was pressured to "act in a certain way" before

she voted to award the gold medal to the Russian team.

On Feb. 15, the International Skating Union, in an unprecedented move made under pressure from the International Olympic Committee, awarded a second set of gold medals to the Canadian team and suspended Le Gougne for misconduct. Le Gougne and Gailhaguet were suspended from any involvement in international skating on April 30 after the I.S.U. ruled that they had colluded to fix the event. They were also excluded from any skating participation in the 2006 Turin Games.

Runners-up

1990: Taking the world heavyweight title away from a boxer who had been declared all but unbeatable, James (Buster) Douglas rebounded from a nearly devastating eighth-round knockdown to pummel Mike Tyson into a knockout 1 minute 23 seconds into the 10th round of their fight in Tokyo.

1949: Willie Pep regained the world featherweight title in a savage 15-round upset over Sandy Saddler at Madison Square Garden. Pep outpointed Saddler, who had knocked him out in four rounds the previous October. In their memorable

four-fight series, Saddler, who had a lifetime record of 144–16–2, knocked out Pep (229–11–1) three times.

1973: Arnold Palmer, aged 43, won his 60th and final P.G.A. tournament by scoring a two-stroke victory over Jack Nicklaus and Johnny Miller at the Bob Hope Desert Classic at Bermuda Dunes in Palm Springs, Calif. Palmer won this tournament five times.

The Eagle Has Landed—and Hard

By PETER ALFANO

CALGARY, Alberta [Friday]—The red and white warm-ups identify Fast Eddie Edwards as a member of Her Majesty's Olympic team. He's an unlikely-looking athlete, though, at 5 feet 8 inches, peering though glasses with milk bottle lenses. Still, there are several countries that have an avid interest in the British ski jumper, a waif who has become Nordic skiing's adopted son.

Edwards, 24 years old, has been jumping for only two years, a mere beginner by Olympic standards. He is the only ski jumper in England, which means he spends most of the year away from home, training in places like Switzerland and Steamboat Springs, Colo. He became interested in the sport while on a skiing trip to Lake Placid, N.Y., when the cost of downhill equipment and lift tickets became too expensive. Edwards is a part-time plasterer from North Cheltenham, England, who has done such odd jobs as shoveling snow and babysitting in order to earn money so he can continue to jump.

At Lake Placid, he bought a used pair of skis for $60, was given a used helmet—fastened around his neck by a string—and borrowed boots that were so big he had to wear six pairs of socks. "I just went out to the ski jump at Lake Placid, introduced myself and said I wanted to jump," Edwards said. "They said, 'Fine.' There was this old gentleman, a man who I think was in the 1932 Olympics, who came to watch me, to make sure nothing went wrong."

In just 18 months, Edwards progressed from novice to World Cup performer, not an Olympic medal contender by any means, but a success story in his own right. He was told it would take eight or nine years. In a sport in which style counts as much as distance—the best ski jumpers soar through the air posing like hood ornaments on an automobile—Fast Eddie has wobbled his way to a personal best of jumping 91 meters from the 90-meter jump. When he arrived in Calgary late Wednesday night, several Canadians greeted him at the airport, holding a banner that read "Welcome Eddie the Eagle Edwards."

The perils of Eddie Edwards have made him a cult figure back home. Fast Eddie began skiing when he was 11 years old and went on a class trip to a ski resort in Italy. He skied on simulated trails in England, his goal to one day make the Olympic team. He did not anticipate that it would eventually be as a ski jumper, a pursuit that still causes him trepidation. "I used to get very scared at the top of the jump, thinking of a million reasons not to go down there," he said. "You have to fight the fear that your next jump could be your last."

It does not help that Edwards's thick lenses tend to fog when he places his goggles over them just before taking off. He has made some jumps virtually blind. "Usually, though," he said, "my glasses clear up enough for me to see where I'll land and on which part of my body." He has strained knee ligaments and broken his jaw, tying a scarf around the jaw and continuing to compete because he could not afford to pay for medical treatment. Now, Edwards is ready for his Olympic experience, modestly hoping to avoid finishing last. "That would be bigger news in Finland than a Finnish jumper winning the event," he said. "My girlfriend gave me a lucky gold boot that I'll hold just before the jump. And I'll say to myself, 'May I survive.'"

Eddie (The Eagle) Edwards receiving a hero's welcome at his hometown of North Cheltenham, England, following his Olympic ski jumping exploits at the Calgary Games. (Associated Press)

Runners-up

2000: Tom Landry, the taciturn snap-brimmed Texan who coached the Dallas Cowboys for their first 29 seasons, led them to five Super Bowl championships and had 20 consecutive winning seasons, an N.F.L. record, died of leukemia at 75.

1908: The first "around the world" auto race began in Manhattan, with ship connections tying together 13,341 miles in the United States, Siberia, Europe and points between. A four-man American team won, defeating units from Germany, Italy and France when they arrived at the finish line in Paris on July 30—169 days later.

1878: Inspired by the mask fencers used, Frederick Thayer of Massachusetts, captain of the Harvard Baseball Club, received United States Patent No. 200,358 for an invention to reduce cuts and bruises: a wire catcher's mask to be worn during baseball games, strapped over the head and cushioned against the chin.

February 13, 1995
Dodgers Look East

By CLAIRE SMITH

Hideo Nomo, a former five-time all-star in the Japanese leagues, signed with the Los Angeles Dodgers on this date, becoming the first Japanese major leaguer since Masonori Murakami, who played for the Giants in 1964–65. *The following article by Ms. Smith appeared in* The Times *on May 24.*

NEW YORK—Hideo Nomo of the Los Angeles Dodgers is known as the Tornado because of a unique pitching delivery in which he twists his body so much it looks like an unsprung piece of licorice. The nickname, it turns out, could also apply to the breath of fresh air brought to baseball by Nomo, the major league's first import from Japan in three decades.

True, Nomo has yet to earn a decision in five starts. And yes, he squandered a three-run lead against the Mets last night at Shea Stadium in his first start on the East Coast. Still, the 26-year-old contortionist from Osaka is causing a refreshing flutter of genuine interest in baseball. That is a welcome occurrence in a troubled sport too long preoc-cupied with depressing news about drugs, spousal abuse, strikes and lockouts.

What Nomo is creating is similar to the groundswell of curiosity that built up around another rookie Dodger pitcher, Fernando Valenzuela, 14 years ago. Valenzuela, whose instant stardom is still unequaled, came from another land

The Dodgers rookie Hideo Nomo starting the 1995 All-Star Game for the National League at The Ballpark in Arlington in Texas. He sparkled, striking out three and allow-ing one hit in two innings. (Associated Press)

(Mexico), too. And he applied a salve to a strike-torn game, something all of baseball has to hope Nomo can duplicate.

Nomo, who won 78 games in five years in the Japanese professional leagues, is turning heads not only on both coasts but across the Pacific, as the presence of more than 100 Japanese reporters at last night's

game shows. If Nomo is becoming quite the phenome-non here, he is all that and more in Japan. The NHK public television network, the BBC of Japan, broadcasts his games live. Therefore, last night's game was to start at 11:40 this morning in Tokyo. Some games broadcast from the West Coast begin at 3 or 4 in the morning on Tokyo televi-sion. And people watch.

Japanese players have tra-ditionally been content to stay at home. Until now. Nomo has an agent, all but unheard of in Japan. And the agent made a great effort to get him to the Dodgers, thanks in part to a $2 million signing bonus. But the money alone didn't make Nomo's decision any easier. He was earning more than a mil-lion dollars a year in Japan and is now just another minimum-wage rookie many, many miles away from home. Nevertheless, other Japanese players may well be on the way. If and when they come, maybe they, too, can help a game and its disgruntled fans remember what once made them think major league base-ball here is special. Just the way Fernando Valen-zuela reminded them a decade and a half ago.

Hideo Nomo became Rookie of the Year and the National League strikeout king in 1995. In 2001 he became the fourth pitcher in major league history to throw a no-hitter in both leagues.

Runners-up

1976: Dorothy Hamill of Riverside, Conn., won the women's figure-skating gold medal at the Innsbruck Winter Olympics, wowing judges with her signature spin dubbed the Hamill Camel and creating a new American hairstyle almost overnight. Life magazine called Hamill's "wedge" hairstyle "one of the most important fashion statements of the last 50 years."

1954: Eight years before Wilt Chamberlain scored 100 points in an N.B.A. game (*see March 2*), Frank Selvy of Furman University did it in a 149–95 victory over Newberry College in South Carolina. It was not considered a Division I collegiate record, however, because Newberry was not a Division I school.

1971: Vice President Spiro T. Agnew clipped three spectators with his first two shots, upstaging Arnold Palmer and other golf pros in the Bob Hope Desert Classic in California. One woman was taken to a hospital for ankle X-rays before being released. Mr. Agnew apologized profusely.

February 14, 1988
'It Slipped Out From Under Me'

By DAVE ANDERSON

CALGARY, Alberta—The ice is smooth now, glazed by a Zamboni machine. But for more than an hour tonight, the white smear leading to the red base of the padded gray wall resembled the skid marks of an automobile accident. And in the years to come, spectators at the indoor Speed-Skating Oval will point to the ice on that first turn. "Over there," they will say. "That's where Dan Jansen fell." That's where Dan Jansen lost his balance. And that's where he lost his chance for the gold medal he had dedicated to his 27-year-old sister, Jane Beres, the mother of three young daughters, whom he had lost to leukemia in the morning, only five hours after their last telephone conversation.

"She was still alive, she could understand me but she couldn't talk back to me," he recalled tonight. "She did understand what I said and I'm very happy about that, but I would like to keep the rest private." His sister had been ill for about 13 months. When the square-jawed 22-year-old Olympian was asked two days ago about her condition, he said: "She's not real good, they can't seem to get her into remission. She's having another round of chemotherapy. She'll watch my race in the hospital." But hours before the race, she died. "I had always planned on staying," he said tonight, hinting that he knew her condition was more critical than he had acknowledged. "That's what Jane would've wanted."

And about 8 seconds after his race started, for Dan Jansen, it was over. Sprawling across the ice in his skin-tight red-and-turquoise USA racing suit, he crashed into Yasushi Kuroiwa, a Japanese skater who started in the outside lane. "It felt like it slipped out from under me," he would say. "The next thing I knew, I

was in the pads."

Dan is the youngest of the nine Jansen children, many of whom had traveled to Calgary in two vans from their West Allis, Wis., home. But the mother had remained with Jane, and the father, who is retired, had returned home yesterday when Jane's condition worsened. Her widower, Richard, is a West Allis fireman with daughters ages 4, 3 and 1. "I talked to my family before the race," Dan said later, "and they said to just go out there and do the best I could. Try to put as much out of my mind as I could. I tried to do that and I did it pretty well."

While the other skaters raced, Jansen's fiancée, Natalie Greiner, a Canadian speed-skater, consoled him. But now he must try to prepare for the 1,000-meter sprint in four days. His sister's funeral has been delayed until after that race.

Four nights later in the 1,000 meters, Dan Jansen was on pace for a world record when he fell again at 600 meters and did not finish. Jansen did win gold and set a world record in the 1,500 at the 1994 Lillehammer Olympics in Norway, taking a victory lap while carrying his 8-month-old daughter, Jane, who was named after his sister.

Dan Jansen starting a race in the U.S. Olympic Trials in 1994. He competed in three Olympics before finally winning a gold in the 1,000 meters at the '94 Lillehammer Games in Norway. (Associated Press)

Runners-up

1984: Jayne Torvill and Christopher Dean of Britain won the ice-dancing gold medal for their slow, sensuous interpretation of Ravel's "Bolero" at the Sarajevo Games in Yugoslavia. All nine judges gave them perfect 6.0 scores for artistic impression, an unprecedented achievement in ice dancing.

1988: Bobby Allison, aged 50, held off a challenge from his son Davey, 26, to take the Daytona 500, becoming the oldest driver ever to win Nascar's most pres-

tigious event. Four months later on Lap 1 of a race at Pocono Raceway in Pennsylvania, Bobby was involved in a near-fatal crash that ended his career.

1993: Former Redskins Coach Joe Gibbs, who guided Washington to four Super Bowl appearances and three championships in 12 years before shifting careers to Nascar racing, won his first Daytona 500 as an owner with Dale Jarrett behind the wheel.

February 15, 1998
Never at Daytona, Until Now

By TARIK EL-BASHIR

DAYTONA BEACH, Fla.—Dale Earnhardt ended two decades of frustration at the Daytona 500 today the same way he had won so many races in the past: by being too tough to beat at the end of the race. Then he emerged from his black Chevrolet Monte Carlo and did something new: let his emotions take over. "My eyes watered up on that lap coming to get the checkered," Earnhardt said after winning Nascar's most prestigious race for the first time on his 20th attempt.

Earnhardt's victory, the 71st of his career but his first in 59 races, was not assured until he beat the pole sitter Bobby Labonte's Pontiac and Jeremy Mayfield's Ford to a yellow caution flag during the next-to-last lap. The three cars had just broken away from the lead group when a wreck involving John Andretti and Lake Speed brought out the third yellow flag of a very clean race. "That's when I realized I was going to win the race," said the 46-year-old Earnhardt, who pumped his fist as his car roared down the front stretch. His reputation for being too tough to beat when leading late in a race finally held up in the Daytona 500.

The 185,000 fans, a record crowd at Daytona International Speedway, were on their feet for the last 10 laps screaming for Earnhardt, whose failures here had made him the sentimental favorite. Their roar drowned out the sound of the cars as he led past the start-finish line on the 199th lap. One lap remained, but the waving flags meant there would be no more racing. Labonte and Mayfield held their positions to finish second and third. "I don't know what would have happened with another lap," Labonte said. "I've got to congratulate him. I had a feeling all winter he was going to win it. I guess I should have gone out and bet on him."

Earnhardt's average speed of 172.712 miles an hour was the third fastest in the history of the Daytona 500, which was run for the 40th time. As Earnhardt drove slowly down pit road on his way to the winner's circle, dozens of members of other pit crews climbed over the retaining wall to congratulate him. Earnhardt then steered his No. 3 car onto the neatly painted grass between the grandstand and the infield and punctuated his victory with a tire-spinning doughnut over the word "Daytona." "It was pretty awesome with all of them congratulating me," said Earnhardt, whose victory was worth a Nascar record $1,059,105. "I came down pit road and all those race teams out there gave me high-fives and were shaking my hand. It was just unbelievable."

Exactly three years and three days later, on the same Daytona track, Dale Earnhardt was killed on the final lap of the race that took him a career to win. He lost control of his black No. 3 Chevrolet and slammed into a wall almost head-on after being tapped from behind by Sterling Marlin. A nation of racing fans mourned for him.

Dale Earnhardt inching his familiar black No. 3 Chevrolet down pit road toward victory lane after winning the Daytona 500 in his 20th try. Known for his steeliness, he admitted his eyes watered up. (Reuters)

Runners-up

2002: In an unprecedented move for the Olympics, the Canadian figure skaters David Pelletier and Jamie Salé were awarded duplicate gold medals with the Russian pairs team. A French judge who had favored the Russian skaters four days before was suspended and her scoring was thrown out (see Feb. 11).

1936: Sonja Henie of Norway, the world queen of figure skating, won an unprecedented and never equaled third straight Olympic gold medal at the fourth Winter Olympics at Garmisch-Partenkirchen, Germany, edging Cecilia Colledge of England. Henie was a prodigy; in the 1924 Games, Sonja, 12, finished last over all, though one judge graded her first place in the free-skating phase of competition.

1981: Richard Petty, driving a No. 43 Buick, won his record seventh Daytona 500, beating Bobby Allison by 3.5 seconds. Petty, whose first 500 victory came in 1964, went from fifth place to first when he stopped for only fuel with 25 laps to go. Allison pitted for fuel and tires, and that was the difference.

February 16, 1926
Two Queens at Cannes

CANNES, France (AP)—Suzanne Lenglen of France remains undisputed tennis champion of the world by virtue of her 6–3, 8–6 victory today over Helen Wills of the United States after one of the most dramatic matches in the history of tennis, ending with both very near collapse.

Both seemed conscious of the responsibility resting on them, and for once the emotions of the California girl were not entirely held in check. Care and caution dominated the play, but as the fight became more bitter extra driving power was put into the strokes. When finally Mlle. Lenglen had achieved victory she threw her racquet in the air and leaped for very joy. Surrounded with flowers and showered with congratulations from many of the great of the world, Suzanne was given an ovation. The reaction made the tears flow down her face, but the cheers of the multitude soon brought back the smile of the victor.

Miss Wills took a 2–1 lead in the first set, but the French champion, playing with skill and finesse, won the fourth, fifth and sixth games. Helen took the next game, but Suzanne finished the set with careful placements. The second set was most dramatic. Miss Wills started by winning the first three games. Suzanne began to cough, placed a hand over her heart and stepped to the side lines, where she took a long draught of cognac with water.

Spurred by the stimulant, the French girl won the next three games, evening the count. Miss Wills took the seventh, the French girl evened it again, and then Helen made it 5–4. She had run the score up to 40–15 when, with one point to go for the set, an unaccountable decision by the linesman completely upset her. Suzanne's return struck several inches outside the line, and Helen made no attempt to strike at it. Nevertheless, it was allowed as a point for Mlle. Lenglen. Helen threw up both hands in a gesture of despair, while thousands of spectators at her end of the court shouted: "Out!"

From then on the American girl put up a spiritless fight and allowed Mlle. Lenglen to take the initiative. She fell behind, 6–5, and then tied the set at 6-all, but, although she brought the last two games to deuce, the old spirit was missing.

Suzanne Lenglen of France in 1926. Her storied victory over Helen Wills of the U.S. in a challenge match featured both a controversial call and a coughing fit remedied by a draft of cognac. (Associated Press)

Runners-up

1992: Martina Navratilova broke Chris Evert's all-time tennis singles record of 157 championships when she defeated Jana Novotna in three sets for her 158th title at the Virginia Slims tournament in Chicago. Evert had retired in 1989.

1997: Jeff Gordon, aided by a crash that took out Dale Earnhardt 10 laps from the finish while Gordon was running third, won the Daytona 500. At age 25 he became the youngest champion in the 39 years of the race and went on to win the season's Winston Cup title, his second in three years.

1984: Bill Johnson, 23, of Van Nuys, Calif., raced to a gold medal in the men's downhill at the Sarajevo Games in Yugoslavia, becoming the first American ever to win an Olympic downhill and toppling the more highly favored European powerhouses of Alpine skiing such as Franz Klammer of Austria and Peter Mueller of Switzerland.

February 17, 1968
Downhill Magic

By FRED TUPPER

The French hero Jean-Claude Killy racing to his second gold medal in the final heat of the giant slalom at the Grenoble Games. He won his third gold, and lasting fame, by winning the slalom in an icy fog. (Associated Press)

GRENOBLE, France—Jean-Claude Killy won the triple crown of Alpine skiing at the Winter Olympics today, but it took a jury's decision to make it official.

In the slalom race the idol of France, who had previously won the downhill and giant slalom, plunged through 131 gates on the 1,040-meter course in dense, icy fog for a two-heat time of 99.75 seconds. He had the fastest time in the first heat, from which he had started in the 15th position. In the second he was the first man down. Now all he could do was wait. It was agonizing. Haakon Mjoen of Norway had better times, but was disqualified for having missed gates. The other men who might have beaten Killy had

come and gone, and the thousands of fans peering through the mists were waiting for the seasoned Karl Schranz of Austria. Killy could be in danger.

Schranz had been third in the first heat. A spectator interfered on his second run and Schranz pulled off the course. He sidestepped back to the top and was given permission to go again. This time he was spectacular, darting and swiveling through the flags with such controlled abandon that his two-heat time was 99.22. That should have been it. The Austrian had won. But had he?

He was reported for missing a gate before the interference by the spectator. If so he would automatically be disqualified,

and that was the way the jury ruled in the end. The bulletin was flashed two hours after the race. So Killy, the darkly handsome customs officer from Val D'Isère, has brought all those magazine covers back to life. He has won the triple, a memorable feat achieved only by Toni Sailer of Austria in 1956 at Cortina.

Asked during a postcompetition news conference whether he had missed a gate before the incident with the spectator, Karl Schranz said, "It is possible, but if I did I didn't realize it." He said he was distracted by the spectator's shadow: "I was hypnotized by the dark shadow I saw ahead. It is possible that for the moment I missed a gate to avoid it."

Runners-up

1955: Mike Souchak set a P.G.A. Tour nine-hole record by shooting 27 on the back side of Bracken Ridge Park Golf Course in San Antonio in the Texas Open. He finished with a 60 for the round and then a 72-hole record total of 257 for the tournament.

1985: John Walker, the great New Zealand middle-distance runner, broke the four-minute mile for the 100th time in his career at a meet in Auckland. Walker held the mile record for nearly four years between 1975 and '79. Only Walker,

Steve Scott of the United States and Marcus O'Sullivan of Ireland have run as many as 100 sub-four-minute miles.

1985: Laffit Pincay Jr. rode four winners at Santa Anita Park in California, becoming the third jockey, behind Johnny Longden and Bill Shoemaker, to win at least 6,000 Thoroughbred races. He broke Shoemaker's record of 8,833 victories in 1999 (see Dec. 10) and reached the 9,000 mark in 2000.

February 18, 1979
Richard the Lion Hearted

By JAMES TUITE

DAYTONA BEACH, Fla.—There was Richard Petty in victory lane, king of all he surveyed, including a scoreboard that proclaimed him the winner for the sixth time of the Daytona 500-mile race. And on the backstretch there were Cale Yarborough and Bobby Allison flailing at each other after a crash took Yarborough and Bobby's brother, Donnie, out of the lead and out of the race.

Petty took the lead on the last lap, when the first two cars, driven by Donnie Allison and Yarborough, engaged in their fender-bending duel. Nothing could have been more satisfying to the 125,000 fans who jammed this saucer of sound and automotive fury than to see King Richard, driving against doctor's orders and with only a third of a stomach remaining after an ulcer operation, score a length victory over Darrell Waltrip. It was like Arnold Palmer winning another Masters, Joe Namath winning another Super Bowl, Willis Reed scoring the game-winning basket.

"We won! We won!" Petty screamed as he steered his Oldsmobile to the victory lane, a winner for the first time in 46 races. His fan club, the largest in auto racing, exulted with him, still tingling over the way he held off Waltrip's Olds in a thrilling stretch run. Petty, who was unaware of the fisticuffs going on on the backstretch, admitted that but for the backstretch crash he probably would have finished third. "If I had been as lucky as I was today I would have won two-thirds of my last races," he said after breaking his 45-race losing streak.

Petty had lost the 1976 Daytona because of a crash yards from the finish line, when David Pearson limped home the winner. He also survived some hairy moments in today's accident-packed race. Seven times, for 57 laps, the caution flag was waved. "I'm pretty dad-gummed glad this race is over," said Petty. "It's the worst I've ever seen for changing positions."

Thirteen drivers were involved in 36 lead changes in the race, won with an average speed of 143.977 miles an hour. "My car could have run better," Petty admitted, "so I was content to lay back most of the way." Three times the North Carolinian was in front, for a total of 12 laps. The $73,500 payoff raised his career earnings to $3,180,596.

Richard Petty beside his blue-anc-red No. 43 at Daytona in 1975. He coolly won his sixth Daytona 500 four years later when Cale Yarborough and Donnie Allison crashed while leading on the final lap. (Associated Press)

Runners-up

1951: The biggest point-shaving scandal in college basketball history began when three players from City College of New York, the defending national champion, were charged with accepting bribes to fix games. They eventually admitted their involvement, as did 29 other players from six schools, including the powerhouse University of Kentucky.

1999: In their most significant deal since they acquired Babe Ruth 79 years earlier, the Yankees traded for the five-time Cy Young Award winner Roger Clemens of the Toronto Blue Jays. New York sent David Wells, who pitched a perfect game the previous May, and two others to Toronto.

1978: A gun sounded for the first Ironman Triathlon on Waikiki Beach, in Hawaii. John Collins, a Navy commander, created and named the event—a 2.4 ocean swim, followed immediately by a 112-mile bike race and a full 26.2-mile marathon. There were 15 starters and 12 finishers; Gordon Haller, a Honolulu cabdriver, was the winner in 11 hours 46 minutes.

February 19, 1966
The Legend of Happy Valley

UNIVERSITY PARK, Pa. (UPI)—Joe Paterno, who passed up a chance to study law to develop outstanding quarterbacks as an associate football coach at Penn State, was named today as head coach at the university. He will succeed Charles R. (Rip) Engle, who announced his retirement, to take effect July 1. The 39-year-old Brooklyn-born Paterno was a quarterback at Brown University and his skill so impressed his head coach, Engle, that when Engle signed as head coach of Penn State in 1950 he persuaded Paterno to forsake law and join him as an assistant.

Engle's faith in his protégé was rewarded. Richie Lucas, an all-American; Tony Rados; Milt Plum; Dick Hoak; Galen Hall; Pete Liske and Jack White gained stardom as quarterbacks under Paterno's tutelage. Paterno was a star in football, basketball and baseball at Brooklyn Prep. From the 1946 through the 1949 seasons, Paterno was the Brown quarterback and was co-captain in his senior year. He also played varsity basketball three seasons. He and his brother, George, were teammates in the Brown backfield.

Seventy-five-year-old Joe Paterno on the Penn State sideline in 2002. He is said to still be firmly in control, but has gradually accepted new ideas that have kept his program flourishing. (Michael R. Sisak for The New York Times)

Paterno said he regarded his new assignment "as the best coaching job in the country." He added: "We are all part of a great football tradition. A winning tradition started 27 years ago by Coach Bob Higgins and continued under Engle. We have a great responsibility to carry on this legacy of success."

When the 60-year-old Engle announced his retirement last week, it was a foregone conclusion that Paterno would succeed him. During their 16-year partnership, Penn State never had a losing season. Their best season was in 1962 when the Lions won nine and lost one. The Nittany Lions have not had a losing season since 1938. Paterno voiced his appreciation for the years he spent with Engle as a player and an assistant. "I can't thank Rip enough for what he has done for me personally and for Penn State," he said. "It will be an impossible task to replace his inspiration and leadership. However, if hard work and dedication can succeed, then I'm certain our staff will develop good and exciting teams."

Joe Paterno's teams won two national titles, in 1982 and 1986, and went undefeated but uncrowned four other times through 2002. Playing as difficult a schedule as any in the nation, his teams had only two losing seasons in 37 years in Happy Valley through 2002.

Runners-up

1984: Phil and Steve Mahre, twins from Yakima, Wash., ended a season-long slump in a burst of skiing power by finishing first and second in the men's slalom on the final day of the Winter Olympics in Sarajevo, Yugoslavia.

1953: Ted Williams, the four-time American League batting champion from the Boston Red Sox and a Marine pilot since 1951, escaped with his life after crash-landing his burning F-9 Marine Panther that was nearly shot down during a bombing run in Korea. He crash-landed and climbed from the cockpit shortly before the plane exploded.

1989: Darrell Waltrip's calculated gamble not to make a final pit stop to take on more fuel with three laps remaining paid off as he crossed the finish line on fumes to win his first Daytona 500 after 16 tries. It was a chance that Ken Schrader and Dale Earnhardt, who finished second and third, were not willing to take.

February 20, 1988
Leap of Faith

By MICHAEL JANOFSKY

Brian Boitano of the U.S. in a signature leap during his impeccable freestyle program in the men's figure skating finals at the Calgary Olympics. He defeated Brian Orser of Canada in a tense duel. (Associated Press)

CALGARY, Alberta—With the performance of his life tonight, Brian Boitano won the gold medal in figure skating, the first gold won by the United States in the XV Olympic Winter Games.

Brian Orser of Canada, the world champion, came in second for a second consecutive time in Olympic competition. Four years ago in Sarejevo, Yugoslavia, Scott Hamilton won the gold for the United States, even though Orser won the short and long programs. Orser's undoing then was a seventh-place finish in the compulsories. This time, there was no such turn of events. Boitano, the four-time national champion and 1986 world champion, had placed second in compulsories and led the field after the short program night before last. Tonight, he skated a brilliant freestyle, winning superior marks from five of the nine international judges. Two of them, from Denmark and Switzerland, had the skaters tied in points but gave Boitano the victory on better technical marks. Under the current system of judging, introduced in 1981, this was the first tiebreaker decided on technical merit for an Olympic gold medal.

Boitano was nearly flawless in his execution. His jumps, including eight triples, were crisp, his movements energized, in part because of a wildly appreciative capacity crowd in the Saddledome. In the final seconds, his clenched fists at his heart and rink-sized smile were the surest signs he was satisfied with his 4-minute-40-second performance. He received a long standing ovation. "All I really wanted to do—and this is the truth—was skate my best," he told a television interviewer. "I didn't care what color medal I got. I was just trying so hard to take one thing at a time and not get excited."

His scores were good reason for excitement: five 5.9's and four 5.8's for technical merit and a range of one 5.7 to three 5.9's for presentation, the low score coming from the judge from Denmark. High as they were, however, the scores left room for Orser, who needed a virtually perfect program to beat him. Aleksandr Fadeyev of the Soviet Union skated next. His scores were well below Boitano's, and in the end below those of Viktor Petrenko, his younger countryman, who won the bronze. For all the acclaim, Orser fell into trouble within the first 90 seconds of his 4:41 program, nearly falling on a triple flip jump. "I am disappointed," he said in a television interview after he skated. "I knew to win, I had to stay on my feet and not have any falls at all."

His scores were unusual: eight 5.8's and one 5.9 for technical merit and three 5.8's, five 5.9's and one perfect score of 6.0 from the Czechoslovak judge for artistic impression. The final difference was created by the combination of higher scores for Boitano from the judges from the United States, Denmark, the Soviet Union, Switzerland and Japan. Orser carried West Germany, East Germany, Canada and Czechoslovakia. Boitano was appreciative of the audience reaction. "I felt so much support from Americans," he said. "It was overwhelming. I consider this medal for all America. This is your medal, too."

Runners-up

1952: Andrea Mead Lawrence of Rutland, Vt., won the women's Olympic slalom at the Oslo Games, becoming the first American to win two skiing gold medals in a winter competition. She had earlier won the giant slalom.

1971: At the World Weightlifting Championships in Columbus, Ohio, Vasili Alexeyev of the Soviet Union became the first man to lift at least 500 pounds in competition. Alexeyev, who had won two Olympic gold medals and eight world titles during the 70's, lifted 501¼ pounds in the clean and jerk.

1981: The legendary fisherman Roland Martin caught 21 bass during a three-day tournament at Toledo Bend, La., setting the seven-bass limit record of 84 pounds 11 ounces. He has been named angler of the year by the Bass Anglers Sportsman Society nine times since 1971.

February 21, 2002
As Cool as the Ice Below

By SELENA ROBERTS

SALT LAKE CITY—Against all Ouija board predictions and sentimental expectations, Sarah Hughes, a porcelain-faced 16-year-old from Great Neck, N.Y., won the Olympic women's figure skating gold medal tonight. Displaying the nerves usually reserved for matadors, Hughes flirted with danger to become the latest teenager to upend Michelle Kwan's Olympic moment. Hughes unleashed two triple-triple jump combinations on her way to the medal. After two amazing leaps of faith in herself, Hughes, a high school junior, went from fourth after the short program night before last to first place after the free skate tonight. Kwan, who was first after the short program, won the bronze medal, behind Irina Slutskaya of Russia.

"I didn't think it was possible after the short program, being fourth," Hughes said. "It's wonderful. It's something I've always dreamed of. There was no pressure on me to win. I skated for pure enjoyment. That's how I wanted my Olympic moment to be." And so it was. Not since 1992, when the format changed, had anyone reached up to grab gold from her position. But defying gravity was Hughes's strength tonight. It was the ruin of Kwan, who won a silver medal at the Nagano Games in 1998. Tonight she was crestfallen, half crying and half smiling, as she skated out to accept the bronze.

Slutskaya, who needed only to skate cleanly to win, sabotaged herself with a clumsy program. She thought she had done enough but was sunk by presentation marks that hovered at 5.7. She had four first-place votes, but Hughes had five. "It's upsetting," Slutskaya said, before alluding to the Russian Olympic Committee's threat to pull out of the

Hail and farewell: The 16-year-old American Sarah Hughes, flowers in her fist and a gold medal around her neck, acknowledges the cheers after her surprising victory at the Salt Lake City Games. (Ruth Fremson/The New York Times)

Games based on its belief that Russian athletes have been treated unfairly. "I lost over the second mark, as if I'm not artistic. But apparently, that's life. Interesting thing about these Olympic Games. I'm obviously not the only Russian to have suffered here."

Kwan was not betrayed by a judging controversy, but one unforgettable mistake. She was working through her nerves, maneuvering through the tricky turns around the pressure of having to overcome her past Olympic pain, when she fell out of a triple flip. The crowd groaned as she came to a stop with her hand bracing her fall. Suddenly, the

Olympics that seemed to belong to Kwan were over. Gamely, she added a triple jump at the end, but her glaring error had cost her.

With her father holding her hand, Kwan watched the marks cross the boards. Instantly, the life drained out of her body. There was no redemption, no happy ending. "I heard the audience try to lift my spirits when they started clapping in the middle of my program," said Kwan, who has four world titles and six national championships but no Olympic gold medal. "I made a few mistakes, but I kept on going strong. It just wasn't meant to be."

Runners-up

1982: The Islanders' N.H.L. record regular-season consecutive-game winning streak ended at 15 games when they were defeated by the Pittsburgh Penguins, 4–3. As the last seconds ticked off, the Pittsburgh Civic Center organist played "Taps." In 1993 the Penguins broke the mark by winning 17 games in a row.

1952: Dick Button, a Harvard senior, won his second straight Olympic figure-skating gold medal at the Oslo Games, defeating Hellmut Seibt of Austria

(see Feb. 5). Performing in Bislett Stadium to Enesco's "Rumanian Rhapsody," Button became the first skater to complete three consecutive double axels.

1992: Distaining acrobatic leaps, Kristi Yamaguchi completed a yearlong rise from runner-up United States national champion in 1991 to win the gold medal at the Albertville Games in France. She was the first American since Dorothy Hamill in 1976 to win the women's Olympic title.

February 22, 1980
Who Would Believe It?

By GERALD ESKENAZI

LAKE PLACID, N.Y.—In one of the most startling and dramatic upsets in Olympic history, the underdog United States hockey team, composed in great part of collegians, defeated the defending champion Soviet squad by 4–3 tonight. The victory brought a congratulatory phone call to the dressing room from President Carter and set off fireworks over this tiny Adirondack village. The triumph also put the Americans in a commanding position to take the gold medal in the XIII Olympic Winter Games, which will end the day after tomorrow.

The American goal that broke a 3–3 tie tonight was scored midway through the final period by a player who typifies the makeup of the United States team. His name is Mike Eruzione, he is from Winthrop, Mass., he is the American team's captain, and he was plucked from the obscurity of the Toledo Blades of the International League. His opponents tonight included world-renowned stars, some of them performing in the Olympics for a third time.

The Soviet team has captured the previous four Olympic hockey tournaments, going back to 1964, and five of the last six. The only club to defeat them since 1956 was the United States team of 1960, which won the gold medal at Squaw Valley, Calif. Few victories in American Olympic play have provoked reaction comparable to tonight's decision at the red-seated, small-ish Olympic Field House. At the final buzzer, after the fans had chanted the seconds away, fathers and mothers and friends of the United States players dashed onto the ice, hugging anyone they could find in red, white and blue uniforms.

Before the game, Coach Herb Brooks, from the University of Minnesota, had told his players: "You were born to be a player. You were meant to be here." Though only one of the 20 players in the room ever had competed in an Olympics before, they proved him right. From the opening minutes fans and players fed off one another

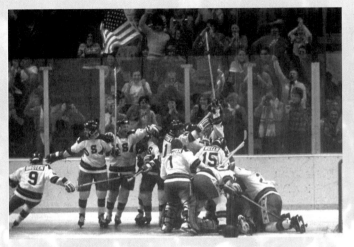

Members of the U.S. hockey team mobbing goalie Jim Craig after their stunning come-from-behind 4-3 victory over the Soviet Union before a jubilant crowd at the Lake Placid Olympics. (Assocciated Press)

in the festive atmosphere at the arena. The tempo and emotion of the game was established early, when a longtime Soviet star, Valery Kharlamov, wearing the traditional lipstick-red uniform, was sandwiched between two Americans. Suddenly, he was lifted between them and, looking like a squirt of ketchup, sailed into the air and then flopped to the ice. Beyond the constant pressure of intimidating body checks, though, were the intricate passing patterns of the Americans, who have derived many of their techniques from the Russians. The Soviet system is based on attack. The Russians more than doubled the shots on goal of the Americans, 39–16, but almost every one that the Russians took was stopped, often dramatically, by Jim Craig, a former goalie for Boston University.

No hockey game is played nonstop for 60 minutes, but this one came close. The Russians have been famed for their conditioning techniques. They also were considered the finest hockey team in the world.

The Americans struggled until the final period, never leading until Eruzione's goal. They trailed by 3–2 going into the last 20-minute period. In the last period, Mark Johnson swatted home a shot that David Silk had gotten off while being hauled down, and the puck eluded Vladimir Myshkin to tie the score. About a minute and a half later, with exactly half of the period over, Eruzione picked up a loose puck in the Soviet zone, skated to a point between the faceoff circles and fired a screened, 30-foot shot through the pads of Myshkin for the winning score.

The goal set off cheering that lasted through the remainder of the game, as the youngest team of all the American squads, average age 22, put itself in a position to win only the second gold medal for an American hockey team.

The United States team defeated Finland, 4–2, two nights later to win the gold medal. Rob McClanahan scored the winning goal in the third period and Jim Craig starred in the nets. Afterward, draped in an American flag, Craig skated around the rink, looking in the stands for his widowed father.

Runners-up

1959: The inaugural Daytona 500 was held, with Johnny Beauchamp declared by Nascar founder Bill France the winner in a photo finish. Three days later moving pictures showed that Lee Petty had won by three feet, and the decision was reversed. The name of Petty's son, Richard, would later become synonymous with Daytona.

1988: Bonnie Blair, of Champaign, Ill., set a world record of 39.10 seconds in the women's 500-meter sprint at the Calgary Games, becoming the first United States woman to win an Olympic speed-skating gold medal since Sheila Young at Innsbruck, Austria, in 1976.

1936: Sonja Henie of Norway, the reigning queen of international sports, won her 10th consecutive world figure-skating championship. Henie, who was 14 when she won her first title in 1927, later achieved financial success as both a professional skater in shows and a motion picture actress.

February 23, 1980
The Man in the Golden Suit

By GERALD ESKENAZI

Eric Heiden burning his way to a world record in the 1,500 meters and his fourth gold medal at the Lake Placid Games. He earned an unprecedented fifth gold two days later in the 10,000. (Associated Press)

LAKE PLACID, N.Y. [Saturday]—His left arm ached, but his legs did not betray him today as Eric Heiden earned a record fifth gold medal at the XIII Olympic Winter Games. In at least one way, this was the most remarkable of the five speed skating triumphs for the 21-year-old American, the first athlete to win five gold medals at one Winter Games. Today Heiden had to skate 10,000 meters—about 6.2 miles—after having raced at four different distances, demanding different stresses, in the previous eight days.

Yet, he shattered the world mark by more than six seconds—the equivalent of about 80 meters—and he was almost eight seconds faster than anyone else. The victory marked the fifth straight one in which Heiden smashed an Olympic mark. The world record gave him three such marks—at 1,000 meters, 1,500 and now 10,000. But even more than his medals or times it is the scope of Heiden's accomplishments that has dominated the Games. He won the 500-meter sprint a week ago Friday, he followed with the 5,000 victory last Saturday, the 1,000 on Tuesday, the 1,500 on Thursday and the 10,000 today. "It would be like a road racer winning sprints at 200 meters and 400 meters, the middle distances at 600 and 800, and then the mile," said Peter

Schotting, one of the United States speed skating coaches. Yet, it is not precisely like that because speed skating demands both endurance and strength.

The only person who has won even four gold medals at a Winter Games was Lydya Skoblikova of the Soviet Union, with four in speed skating in 1964. What will he do with his five golds? Heiden was asked. "They'll probably sit in my mom's dresser where the rest of them are," he said.

Although the winning time was imposing, Heiden was worried about winning that final gold medal, which he contends "will probably gather dust." With almost two miles to go he suffered the telltale sign of fatigue. His left arm dropped slightly. Normally, it is at his side during the glide position, when he is hunched over parallel to the ice, to create an aerodynamic line. "I said to myself, 'It's too early.'" If he was worried at that stage, the crowd did not know it. The fans saw Viktor Leskin of the Soviet Union, who held the world record of 14 minutes 34.33 seconds, hunched as if gasping in a vain attempt to stay with Heiden. Heiden's coach, Diane Holum, had called for a pace that projected a 14:30 finish. He did even better—14:28.13, eclipsing the Olympic mark by 22.46 seconds and shattering Leskin's world mark as well.

Heiden's latest victory evoked a standing ovation, and then some fans started to sing "God Bless America."

Eric Heiden of the 32-inch waist and 27-inch thighs retired from speed skating after the Lake Placid Games. He pursued bicycle racing and television announcing for a number of years and eventually earned a doctorate at Stanford Medical School, following in his father's footsteps as an orthopedic surgeon.

Runners-up

1983: Herschel Walker, the junior running back from the University of Georgia, signed with Donald Trump's New Jersey Generals of the new United States Football League for an estimated $1.5 million a year, making him by far the highest-paid player in football history at the time.

1960: The wrecking ball began demolition of Ebbets Field in Brooklyn, the storied home of the Dodgers from the 1913 to 1957 seasons, after which they left Flatbush for supposedly greener pastures in Los Angeles.

1985: Indiana University basketball coach Bobby Knight, angered by a foul call against one of his players and a technical against himself for yelling an obscenity, was ejected from a game against Purdue for hurling a chair from the bench area across the court during a game in Bloomington.

February 24, 1982
How Gretzky Got Great

By JAMES F. CLARITY

BUFFALO—The first seven times that Wayne Gretzky of the Edmonton Oilers shot the puck tonight, Don Edwards, the Buffalo Sabres' goalie, blocked it. Then, with less than seven minutes remaining and the score tied, 3–3, Gretzky did what more than 17,000 spectators, about 100 reporters and Phil Esposito had come to Memorial Auditorium to see him do: He scored his 77th goal of the season, breaking the record Esposito set in 1970–71, a 78-game season.

The record goal came at 13 minutes 24 seconds of the last period, an unassisted score on Gretzky's eighth shot of the game. His ninth and 10th shots also went past Edwards, at 18:16 and 19:43, to give him a total of 79 goals in 64 games. The crowd gave him a loud, but not uproarious ovation, because the record goals had put their team behind. Gretzky's three goals, and two assists recorded earlier, led the Oilers to a 6–3 victory. If he were to continue scoring at his present rate, Gretzky would have 98 goals by the end of the 80-game season. Gil Perrault scored the Sabres' three goals.

President Reagan and his wife, Nancy, sent a telegram of congratulations, but the praise that Gretzky, who is 21 years old, seemed to appreciate the most was given by Edwards, who skated the length of the ice to shake Gretzky's hand at the end of the game. Until tonight, Edwards had been Gretzky's nemesis, allowing him only one goal in nine games over three seasons.

"The first thing that came into my head," Gretzky said of the record-breaking goal, "was that it put us up, 4–3. Then there was relief and a sense of satisfaction and it took a lot of pressure off me." The

goal came after Gretzky took the puck from Steve Patrick, a Buffalo forward, just inside the Sabres' blue line. "The ice is chippier here, the puck skipped up," Gretzky said. He then carried it into the slot, where Richie Dunn, a defenseman, hooked his stick across Gretzky's arms. But Gretzky brushed the stick away, then got both hands back on his own stick and shot the puck low, from about 12 feet out. It went under Edwards's legs, and the record was broken.

The 78th and 79th goals seemed to awe the crowd and stun the Sabres. On No. 78, Gretzky took passes from Jari Kurri and Mark Messier and slapped a high shot from the slot. The 79th was a slap shot from the left circle, after passes from Risto Siltanen and Pat Hughes. Gretzky, who played about 29 minutes, said he was tired in the third period but not concerned that he might fail to get the record goal. "I got so tired," he said, "that I got my second wind." He said he was not now thinking of scoring 100 this season, but of his team winning the Stanley Cup. "The only thing I felt nervous about," he said, "was that

Phil had to be here, and I wanted him to get back to the things he had to do. That created all the pressure."

By season's end, Wayne Gretzky had set an N.H.L. record for goals (92), assists (120) and points (212) in a single season. The goals record still stands; Gretzky broke his own marks for both assists and points in the 1985–86 season with 163 and 215, respectively (see March 25).

The young Wayne Gretzky at the height of his powers in the early 1980's. His scoring records spoke for themselves, but his on-ice presence and sense of timing was also other-worldly. (Getty Images)

Runners-up

1994: Proving that figure skating sometimes is a contact sport, Oksana Baiul of Ukraine injured her back when she crashed into a German skater during a practice session at the Lillehammer Games in Norway. Two days later Baiul beat Nancy Kerrigan of the United States for the gold medal when two judges gave her higher technical marks.

1988: Matti Nykanen of Finland became the first ski jumper to win three gold medals in an Olympics when he captured a 90-meter team competition gold at the Calgary Games. He had already won the individual titles in the 70- and 90-meter ski jumps.

1979: Mike Bossy, the superb right wing of the Islanders *(see March 3),* reached the 50-goal mark for the second consecutive season when he knocked in his second goal of the night in a 3–1 victory over the Detroit Red Wings at Nassau Coliseum. Bossy scored 50 or more goals in each of his first nine seasons, a mark that Wayne Gretzky later equaled.

February 25, 1964
'Eat Your Words'

By ROBERT LIPSYTE

MIAMI BEACH—Incredibly, the loud-mouthed, bragging, insulting youngster had been telling the truth all along. Cassius Clay won the heavyweight title tonight when a bleeding Sonny Liston, his left shoulder injured, was unable to answer the bell for the seventh round. Immediately after he had been announced as the new heavyweight champion of the world, Clay yelled to the newsmen covering the fight: "Eat your words." Only 3 of 46 sports writers covering the fight had picked him to win.

A crowd of 8,297, on its feet through the early rounds at Convention Hall, sat stunned during the one-minute rest period between the sixth and seventh rounds. Only Clay seemed to know what had happened: he threw up his hands and danced a little jig in the center of the ring. The victory was scored as a technical knockout in the seventh round, one round less than Clay had predicted. Liston had seemingly injured the shoulder in the first round while swinging at and missing the elusive 22-year-old.

The fight was Clay's from the start. The tall, swift youngster, his hands carelessly low, backed away from Liston's jabs, circled around Liston's dangerous left hook and opened a nasty gash under Liston's left eye. From the beginning, it was hard to believe. All those interminable refrains of "float like a butterfly, sting like a bee," had been more than foolish songs. The kid was floating. He leaned back from Liston's jabs and hooks, backed into the ropes, then spun out and away. He moved clockwise around Liston, taunting that terrible left hook, his hands still low. Then he stung, late in the first round, sticking his left in Liston's face and following with a quick barrage to Liston's head. They con-

Cassius Clay reacting to the signal moment of his career: the realization that he had become heavyweight champion of the world when Sonny Liston failed to answer the bell for Round 7 in Miami Beach. (Associated Press)

tinued for long seconds after the bell, unable to hear the inadequate ring above the roar of the crowd.

For a moment, in the second round, Liston pummeled Clay against the ropes, but again Cassius spun out and away. Then the young man began to rumble as he had promised. His quick left jabs penetrated Liston's defenses, and he followed with right hands. He leaned forward as he fired rights and lefts at Liston's expressionless face. Liston began to bleed from a crescent-shaped cut high on the left cheekbone. Like a bull hurt and maddened by the picadors' lances, Liston charged forward. The heavy muscles worked under his smooth, broad back as he virtually hurled his 218 pounds at the dodging, bobbing, dancing Clay. His heavy arms swiped forward and he threw illegal backhand punches in his bear-like lunges. Once, Clay leaned the wrong way and Liston tagged him with a long left. Cassius was staggered, but Liston was hurt and

tired. He could not move in to press his advantage.

And now, a strange murmur began to ripple through the half-empty arena and people on blue metal chairs began to look at one another. Something like human electricity danced and flowed as the spectators suddenly realized that even if Cassius lost, he was no fraud. His style was unorthodox, but...

There was little action in the fourth, as Cassius continued to circle. Once he opened his eyes wide as a Liston jab fell short, and it seemed as if he were mocking the heavy-footed hunter. As it turned out, Cassius could barely see. He began complaining to Angelo Dundee, his trainer, at the end of the round. Something had gotten into his eyes from Liston's glove, from the sponge, somewhere. But he went out for the fifth anyway, and all Dundee could do was shout, "Stay away from him, stay away." Clay tried to stay away. Sensing something, Liston bulled forward, slamming Cassius with a left hook in the nose and lefts and rights to the body. Blinking furiously, Clay kept circling away. He never hit back. But Liston seemed the more tired in the sixth as Clay's eyes cleared and the younger man bore in, then leaped away, jabbing and hooking and landing a solid right to Liston's jaw. Clay's jabs were slipping through at will now, bouncing off that rock-like face, opening the cut under the left eye.

Liston walked heavily back to his corner at the end of the sixth. He did not sit down immediately. Then as Liston did sit down, Clay came dancing out to the center of the ring, waving his arms, all alone. It seemed like a long time before Drew (Bundini) Brown, his assistant trainer, was hugging him.

Runners-up

1989: After 29 seasons and two Super Bowl rings as the Dallas Cowboys' only coach, Tom Landry was dumped by Jerry Jones, an Arkansas oilman who had purchased the Cowboys and Texas Stadium for a reported $135 million. Jones hired Jimmy Johnson, his roomate on Arkansas' undefeated 1964 football team, as Landry's replacement.

1987: The National Collegiate Athletic Association levied the "death penalty" against Southern Methodist's football program, suspending it for one year and limiting

it to seven road games in 1988 because athletic officials improperly paid $61,000 to players.

1994: Phil Rizzuto, the long-ago Yankee shortstop and longtime Yankee broadcaster, was elected to the Baseball Hall of Fame at age 76 after 28 years of waiting. "I said 'Holy Cow' and almost fell to the floor," Rizzuto recalled about hearing the news.

February 26, 1935
Ruth Gets His Wish

By JAMES P. DAWSON

Babe Ruth, a Boston Braves vice president and right-fielder, before a game with the Cubs at Wrigley Field in Chicago in 1935. His vice presidency amounted to window dressing and he batted .181. (Associated Press)

NEW YORK—Babe Ruth terminated his fifteen-year career with the Yankees today to become an executive of the Boston Braves as well as assistant manager and an active player. The home run monarch closed the deal, by which he leaves the American League to join the National League, with Judge Emil Fuchs, president of the Boston club. A three-year contract has been agreed upon. Colonel Jacob Ruppert, owner of the Yankees, presented Ruth with his unconditional release and was instrumental in inducing American League club owners to waive on the Babe, making possible his transfer to the National. He returns to the scene of

his big league baseball start, to the scene of earlier triumphs, thrilled and supremely satisfied with the turn of events which so snugly fits him into an advantageous position just when baseball fans, chroniclers and associates were beginning to wonder what would happen to him.

Ruth was emphatic in his declaration that he would play with the Braves as well as help manage them. He doesn't know how many games he will figure in. All he knows is that he intends to keep active as a player until his days are definitely over, when he will turn his attention to executive baseball work. The acquisition of Ruth by the National League occasioned

some surprise, but it found no opposition among American League club owners, notwithstanding the loss of the league's undisputed drawing card. The transfer of the glamorous Ruth from one league to the other was accepted, not as a specific gain for the National League, but as a beneficial move for baseball generally. This was particularly true of Boston, where fans have been supporting the Red Sox more than the Braves.

Ruth proclaimed to the world last October, while attending the World Series, that he would not again sign a player contract, insisting that because of his years of service, his age and the ever-present danger of injury that might permanently incapacitate him he would sign only as a player-manager. Judge Fuchs reached out for the hitting monarch. There were reports that Ruth would be engaged by other clubs as manager. One report said that Colonel Ruppert would insist on retaining his owner's interest in Ruth, with the view, ultimately, of installing him as manager of the Yankees. "It would have been unsportsmanlike of me if I didn't grant Ruth's request," said Ruppert. "Opportunity knocks but once at the door of any man, and I saw here the greatest opportunity Ruth ever had. It would not have been fair to stand in his way. There are no strings on the release I give him. I get not a penny in return, not a promise, nothing. Ruth is a free man."

Babe Ruth never managed the Boston Braves or any other team, though managing was one of his fondest desires. He played in 28 games for the Braves in 1935, his last season, hitting .181. He coached at first base for the Brooklyn Dodgers in 1938 and then left the game altogether.

Runners-up

1960: David Jenkins of Colorado Springs won the men's figure-skating gold medal at the Squaw Valley Olympics in California. The audience gasped when Jenkins performed a spectacular "sit spin," fearing he was falling. Jenkins followed in the footsteps of his brother, Hayes, who won the men's singles gold medal in the 1956 Cortina Games in Italy.

1972: President Richard M. Nixon and Premier Zhou Enlai attended a Chinese table tennis exhibition among other events during the president's historic trip to China. What came to be called Ping-Pong diplomacy resulted in the restoration

of relations between the two countries and the end of the 21-year-old United States embargo against China.

1959: In one of the biggest trades in N.F.L. history, Pete Rozelle, the Los Angeles Rams' general manager, dealt nine players to the Chicago Cardinals for the star running back and former Olympic medalist Ollie Matson. The trade benefited neither team, each of which had a losing record until after Matson retired more than four years later.

Hell for Leather

By NEIL AMDUR

EAST RUTHERFORD, N.J.—On a track he helped design, Eamonn Coghlan ran the first sub-3:50 indoor mile—3 minutes 49.78 seconds—today during the Vitalis/U.S. Olympic Invitational meet. Aided by a brisk early pace, a competitive field and his determined desire for a permanent place in the record books, the 30-year-old Coghlan led the last half-mile of the 10-lap race as if on a mission.

Perhaps he was. Earlier in the month, Coghlan's father, Bill Coghlan, died of a heart attack during a visit here from Ireland to watch his son run in two meets—the Wanamaker Millrose Games at Madison Square Garden and this meet. Today, while recounting the race, Coghlan said he thought of his long-time Irish coach, Gerry Farnam, who died last year, and his father, and said to himself on the last lap, "This is for you guys."

"I never doubted it at all," he said of his record performance. "At least, I tried not to doubt it in my mental preparations." The two-time Olympian had set the previous indoor mark, 3:50.6, two years ago in San Diego. "I just went hell for leather," said Coghlan, who crossed the finish line with arms raised, glanced up at the "3:49" on the scoreboard clock, at first in disbelief, and broke out into an Irish jig on his victory lap.

Besides the spiritual rewards, it was a satisfying personal triumph for Coghlan, who missed the entire 1982 season with injuries and at times wondered about his long-range future in the sport. Coghlan was aware of the significance of his barrier-breaking performance, which he ranked with Roger Bannister's first sub-4-minute outdoor mile, in 1954, and John Walker's first sub-3:50, outdoors in 1975.

"That's something they can't take away," Coghlan said.

Coghlan again demonstrated why his stocky frame, short, efficient strides and explosive kick are perfectly suited for banked board tracks and why he is called "the chairman of the boards."

"He takes the turns so well," said runner-up Ray Flynn of Ireland, describing Coghlan's style. "He has a lower center of gravity, so he wastes less energy on the turns and gets more power coming off, like a race car."

Eamonn Coghlan pointing skyward after winning the masters mile in the Millrose Games in 1993. He had shattered the 3:50 barrier for the indoor mile 10 years earlier, shortly after burying his father. (Associated Press)

Runners-up

1988: Leading on the final night of competition, Debi Thomas, of San Jose, Calif., lost the women's figure-skating gold medal of the Calgary Olympics to Katarina Witt of East Germany when she fell on her first combination jump and skated a flat, flawed program under pressure. It was Witt's second straight Olympic gold medal; Thomas finished with the bronze.

1992: Tiger Woods, a 16-year-old amateur, became the youngest player to compete in a P.G.A. Tour event when he was invited to play in the Nissan Los Angeles Open. He posted a one-over-par 72 over the 6,946-yard Riviera Country Club Course but had a 75 in the second round and missed the cut.

1982: Earl Anthony, the smooth left-hander from Dublin, Calif., became the first million-dollar winner in the history of the Professional Bowlers Association when he overcame a slow start and rolled five straight strikes to defeat Charlie Tapp of South St. Paul, Minn., to win the Toledo Trust–P.B.A. National Championship in Ohio.

February 28, 1971
Nicklaus Outdoes Himself

By LINCOLN A. WERDEN

Jack Nicklaus studying a chip in the opening round of the P.G.A. Championship in Florida. He won his second P.G.A. title, giving him at least two victories in each of the world's four major tournaments. (Associated Press)

NORTH PALM BEACH, Fla.—Jack Nicklaus, as one of the game's great players, today achieved what no other golfer had done. With a final round of 73 for an aggregate of 281, the 31-year-old bomber won the Professional Golfers Association championship for the second time. In doing so he completed the cycle of having captured each of the world's four major golfing titles twice. He had won the Masters title three times, the British Open twice and the United States Open twice.

When he holed the final putt at the P.G.A. National Golf Club course, he clinched this championship by two strokes. He had won it previously in 1963. He had led here at the end of each round. Nicklaus won $40,000 of the $200,000 purse and the victory increased his major triumphs to 11. In addition to his nine championships in professional golf, Nicklaus won the United States Amateur title twice before joining the pros. He is one of four golfers who have carried off the world's four major championships,

the others being Ben Hogan, Gene Sarazen and Gary Player.

One of the pleasing sidelights to this victory for Nicklaus was that it was registered on his wife's birthday. Mrs. Barbara Nicklaus and their son, 9-year-old Jackie, were in his gallery. "I feel great," said Nicklaus after being surrounded by well wishers. "I pointed for this tournament. I was setting my sights for it, and when you do and have it happen, that's when you feel great." What lies ahead? "My goal has always been to win more tournaments than anyone. I think we all try to do something in life that separates us from someone else."

At the 16th, Nicklaus's tee shot at this par 3 landed on a spectator's blanket. After a free lift from it, Nicklaus chipped to the green and holed an impor-

tant five-footer for his par. Then at the long 17th, when he was ahead by one stroke over Billy Casper, he ran in another crucial five-footer, but this time it was for a birdie that gave him a two-stroke edge. At the 18th, he chipped up to within a yard of the cup and then holed his par 4 for the incoming 35 and 73. It was a great putting tournament for Nicklaus, who had a total of 30 one-putt greens, six of them today as he etched out his rounds of 69, 69, 70 and 73.

Runners-up

1986: Commissioner Peter Ueberroth issued one-year suspensions or heavy fines that amounted to 10 percent of their pay against Keith Hernandez of the Mets, Dave Parker of the Pittsburgh Pirates and five other players for cocaine use in the largest drug abuse scandal in major-league history. Twenty-one players in all were penalized.

1960: The United States, coached by Jack Riley of the United States Military Academy and led by Roger Christian, who scored four goals, won its first

Olympic gold medal in hockey with a 9–4 victory over Czechoslovakia at the Squaw Valley Games in California.

1940: The first live telecast of a basketball game occurred when a college matchup between Fordham University and Pittsburgh at Madison Square Garden was broadcast by the experimental station W2XBS to several hundred homes in New York. There was a 20-minute blackout due to technical problems.

MARCH

March 1, 1969
He Knew When to Quit

By GEORGE VECSEY

FORT LAUDERDALE, Fla.—Mickey Mantle, one of baseball's greatest stars for the last 18 years, announced his retirement today at the spring training base of the New York Yankees. "I can't hit any more," the 37-year-old Mantle said at a news conference at the Yankee Clipper Motel in a room overlooking the Atlantic Ocean. He also said his business interests were demanding more of his time and he would not be with the Yankees this year in any capacity.

Mantle is baseball's third leading home run hitter with 536, behind Babe Ruth's 714 and Willie Mays' 587. He led the American League in home runs four times and was voted most valuable player three times. He batted as high as .365 in 1957, but his average slipped in the last four years. He batted only .237 last year and his career average slipped to .298. "I feel bad that I didn't hit .300," he said in an unemotional 15-minute talk. "But there's no way I could go back and get it over .300 again. I can't hit when I need to. I can't go from first to third when I need to. There's no use trying."

The club management expressed sorrow at the retirement of one of the greatest of Yankees. "He's one of a kind," said the Yankees' president, Michael Burke, who added that Mantle's uniform number, 7, would be retired "of course." Burke and Manager Ralph Houk also gave strong indication they had not pressured Mantle into playing one more season. "This is Mickey's future," Burke said, "and he has agonized over this major decision. We want him to do what is right for him."

Mantle had fostered rumors of his retirement last winter in private talks with friends. However, he told the press

Mickey Mantle in the Yankee Stadium clubhouse on June 8, 1969. The team celebrated Mickey Mantle Day by retiring his No. 7 in an emotional on-field ceremony. (Associated Press)

over and over again that he would not make up his mind until spring training, probably after having worked out for several weeks. Mantle reported here from his home in Dallas last night, three days after other regulars had reported. He spoke with Houk on the phone last night, he said, and then had a long talk with Burke at breakfast this morning.

"I really hadn't made up my mind,"

Mantle said, "but I think I was just kidding myself. I told Ralph how I felt and he said if he was me he'd make up his mind as fast as possible. I'm really glad I decided to do it. I don't know how I'll feel not playing ball. I've been playing ball for 20 years and I'll probably miss it like crazy. I don't know how my four boys feel about it, but my wife has been after me to quit for three years. I know she's happy."

Runners-up

1949: Joe Louis (see June 22), who had held the world heavyweight title for 11½ years, longer than anyone else in history, announced his retirement at age 34. Having defeated Jersey Joe Walcott in his last fight the previous year (see June 25), he finished with a record of 63–3, which included 25 successful title defenses and 49 knockouts.

1990: Agreeing to television deals that eventually furnished the league about $3.3 billion over the next four years ($30 million a team each year), the N.F.L.

added two wild-card teams to its playoff format, introducing another round of playoff games and extending the season from the first week of September to the last week of January.

1984: Tamara McKinney of Lexington, Ky., won the giant slalom in Vail, Colo., becoming the first American woman to win a single season's World Cup skiing championship. Picabo Street of Sun Valley, Idaho, won season World Cup titles in 1995 and '96.

March 2, 1962
The Night of the Century

HERSHEY, Pa., (AP)— Wilt Chamberlain set a National Basketball Association scoring record of 100 points tonight as the Philadelphia Warriors defeated the New York Knickerbockers, 169–147. The combined score was an association record, too. Chamberlain topped many records with his awesome display. The 7-foot-1-inch Warrior center set a league record for field goals (36), free throws (28 of 32), most points for a quarter (31), and most points for a half (59).

Wilt said, "I wasn't even thinking of hitting 100, but after putting in nine straight free throws I was thinking about a foul-shooting record. It was my greatest game."

Wilt Chamberlain of the Philadelphia Warriors summing up his evening after scoring his N.B.A.-record 100th point against the Knicks at Hershey, Pa. He had 36 field goals and 28 free throws. (Associated Press)

The 316 points by the two teams surpassed the record of 312 made in Boston's victory over Minneapolis on Feb. 27, 1959, at Boston. The Celtics set a single-team record in that game, when they beat the Lakers, 173–139.

The crowd of 4,124 shrieked, "Give it to Wilt, give it to Wilt," as the Philadelphian scored again and again on his fall-away shots. The Warriors realized early that Chamberlain was hot. So they fed him the ball repeatedly. The Knicks tried to stall and then tried to mob Chamberlain with defense in an effort to slow his scoring. In the final period, Darrall Imhoff, who had been assigned to guard Chamberlain most of the night, fouled out. When Wilt hit 100, a few seconds before the end, the fans swarmed onto the court. The game was held up until they were removed.

The Warriors seemed determined to run away with the game, scrambling to a 19–3 advantage. However, with Richie Guerin hitting, the Knicks drew closer and it was 79–68 at the half. But Guerin, with 39 points, Cleveland Buckner (33) and Willie Naulls (31) couldn't overcome the lift given the Warriors by Wilt. Chamberlain had 25 rebounds.

Chamberlain's effort broke the league scoring record of 78 points, a mark he had set earlier this season. The recognized collegiate scoring record also is 100, set by Frank Selvy for Furman against Newberry in 1954. Selvy now plays for the Los Angeles Lakers. Two over-100 efforts—by Paul Arizin of Villanova and Bevo Francis of Rio Grande (Ohio) College—are not recognized by the National Collegiate Athletic Association because they were made against junior-college teams.

Among records set tonight was one by the Knickerbockers. Their 147 points was the most ever scored by a losing team, topping the previous mark of 139 by Minneapolis against Boston in 1959.

That Wilt Chamberlain hit the 100-point mark at the Hershey Arena, a field house that seated 7,225, and not at Convention Hall in Philadelphia (9,200) testified to the N.B.A.'s attendance woes at the time. The N.B.A. was small-time in 1962. Teams farmed out some home games each year to remote outposts of their fan base.

Runners-up

1969: Boston Bruins center Phil Esposito became the first N.H.L. player to score 100 or more points in a season when he slapped in two goals in Boston's 4–0 victory over the Pittsburgh Penguins at Boston Garden. He finished the season with 126 points. In the 1992–93 season, 21 players scored 100 or more points as offense predominated.

1970: Pete Maravich of Louisiana State University scored 55 points against Mississippi State to bring his season total to 1,263, breaking Elvin Hayes's single-season scoring record for the University of Houston in 1967–68. Maravich's total, still a Division I record, reached 1,381 points.

1951: The first N.B.A. All-Star Game was played before a crowd of 10,094 at Boston Garden as Ed McCauley of the Boston Celtics led the East to a 111–94 victory over the West. The star game, created by Haskell Cohen, a league publicity man, and Celtics founder Walter Brown, became a winter institution.

March 3, 1992
The Numbers Don't Lie

By GEORGE VECSEY

Mike Bossy celebrating a hat trick against the Penguins in January 1981. The Islanders winger retired in 1987 with 39 three-goal games, ranking third in N.H.L. history behind Wayne Gretzky and Mario Lemieux. (Associated Press)

UNIONDALE, L.I.—Mike Bossy was a wing the way Tom Seaver was a pitcher, the way Walt Frazier was a guard. He played for the finest New York team in the past quarter century. It makes no sense at all to throw tickertape off the roof of a suburban ranch house, or the arches of a fast-food stand, but there are rafters at the Nassau Coliseum, and tonight Mike Bossy's No. 22 was retired, hoisted into the eaves, alongside the No. 5 of Denis Potvin that was retired a month ago.

Forget the Yankees of Reggie, the Giants of Taylor, the Mets of Carter and Hernandez, even the Knicks of Reed and DeBusschere. The Islanders won like the old, old New York Yankees and they charmed like the old, old Brooklyn Dodgers, and Bossy often had the best statistics and the best insights on a glorious team. We need number-retirement ceremonies for players like Mike Bossy because they enable us to maintain standards, to keep some perspective, before we get too excited about the pheenom of the week. There is talk of the Rangers trying to win their first Stanley Cup since the famous year of 1940! 1940! 1940! as in the Long Island jeer of the same name. Let the Rangers win one. Then let them win three more.

It was a very nice thing for the Islanders to retire Bossy's number with the Montreal Canadiens in town, because it meant the writers from Bossy's hometown would be in attendance, and he could give interviews in both French and English. In his home province of Quebec, and in all of Canada, Bossy is a hockey legend, who retired five years ago, at the age of 31, because of a bad back. He knows the sport is still a minority taste south of the border, but he looked forward to returning to the Coliseum, which is rarely filled these days, nearly a decade after the great years.

Even while the Islanders were winning four straight Stanley Cups from 1980 through 1983, he was wise enough to know how wonderful it was. He made good money for that time, he respected the franchise, he fit in well with the quiet suburbs, he admired his teammates, and he had a best friend named Bryan Trottier sticking elbows into people and flipping him passes.

"I always said we went into games one or two goals ahead," Bossy said today. "The game was ours to lose. You could see it in the other team's faces. Once we won the first Stanley Cup, we knew how to win." That is what separated the Islanders from every other team in New York since the American League knuckled under to the Yankees in the first half of the 60's. The Islanders just kept winning, and very often Bossy was the ultimate weapon, the coup de grâce. He could have done without the back pain, but Mike Bossy does not mind the quick, neat career of 10 seasons, 575 goals, four Stanley Cups. For a career like that, they hang your number from the rafters.

Runners-up

1984: Peter Ueberroth, president of the Los Angeles Olympic Organizing Committee, was elected the sixth commissioner of baseball, to succeed Bowie Kuhn in October. Ueberroth, who served through March 1989, was given broad power to fine clubs, which Kuhn never had during his 16-year term.

1975: Francie Larrieu, a 22-year-old Californian who remained the premier American women's miler until the advent of Mary Decker in the early 1980's, set world indoor records in the mile (4:28.5) and the 1,500 meters (4:09.8) in the annual United States–Soviet track and field meet at Richmond, Va.

1968: Jean Beliveau of the Montreal Canadiens (see April 14) became the second N.H.L. player to score 1,000 career points when he netted a goal in a 5–2 loss by Montreal to Detroit at Joe Louis Arena. Gordie Howe of the Red Wings was the first to reach 1,000 points, in 1960 (see Nov. 27).

March 4, 1990
Too Young to Die

Hank Gathers of Loyola Marymount University demonstrating a thunderous slam-dunk in 1989, a season in which he was the N.C.A.A.'s leading scorer and rebounder. (Caryn Levy)

LOS ANGELES (AP)—Hank Gathers of Loyola Marymount University, one of the leading scorers in National Collegiate Athletic Association history, died tonight after collapsing on the court during Loyola Marymount's game against Portland. He was 23 years old. Gathers was pronounced dead at Daniel Freeman Marina Hospital, where he was taken after collapsing in the first half of the West Coast Conference tournament game. He died at 6:55 P.M. Pacific time, a school spokesman said. That was 1 hour 41 minutes after he collapsed. Mason Weiss, a cardiologist at the hospital, said the cause of death was unknown and an autopsy would be performed but mentioned that

Gathers had had another spell in a game less than three months ago.

As a junior last season, Gathers became only the second player in N.C.A.A. history to lead the nation in scoring and rebounding, averaging 32.7 points and 13.7 rebounds a game. Gathers, who was averaging 28.8 points this season, was the leading career scorer in the West Coast Conference. A 6-foot-7-inch, 210-pound center from Philadelphia, Gathers was projected as a first-round selection in this year's National Basketball Association draft.

It was the second time this season Gathers had collapsed on his home court during a game. On Dec. 9 against the University of California–Santa Barbara, Gathers went to the foul line with 13 minutes 56 seconds left in the second half, missed his first free throw, stepped away from the foul line and went down. He underwent several days of tests in a local hospital and returned after missing two games. Gathers began taking medication to regulate his heartbeat. Tonight, Dr. Weiss said that Gathers's previous condition "had been determined to be caused by a heart arrythmia, which was treated medically" and that he had been "released to participate in all athletic events."

Gathers persuaded the doctors to cut back on his medication, after which he felt his body strength improving. His play

improved and in the first week of February he scored 44 points against St. Mary's. Brian Quinn, the Loyola Marymount athletic director, said three physicians worked on Gathers while he was put into an ambulance and taken to the hospital. Gathers had given his team a 25–13 lead with a thunderous slam-dunk moments before collapsing near midcourt during a stoppage in play with 13:34 left in the first half. He appeared to be suffering convulsions for a few seconds. His mother and sister rushed out of the stands in front of a hushed crowd at Gersten Pavilion.

"I first noticed that Hank was in trouble just as he went to the floor," Coach Larry Steele of Portland said after sending his players back to the team's hotel. "It all happened so fast. Within two seconds, everybody realized that Hank needed help. Right now, we're not even having a thought." Gathers was carried off the court on a stretcher and taken outside, a short distance from the arena, and given cardiopulmonary resuscitation with his coach, Paul Westhead, standing just a few feet away. He was then transported to the hospital by ambulance.

In July 1997, in a tragedy similar to Gathers's, Boston Celtics captain Reggie Lewis, who had collapsed with a heart ailment during a playoff game three months before, died while shooting baskets at the team's training center in Waltham, Mass.

In a different yet traumatic basketball death, the all-American Len Bias, the second selection over all and the first by the Celtics in the N.B.A. draft two days before, collapsed and died of a cocaine overdose in his University of Maryland dorm room in June 1986.

Runners-up

1968: Joe Frazier (see March 8) knocked out Buster Mathis in 11 rounds at Madison Square Garden, staking claim to the world heavyweight title vacated by Muhammad Ali after his 1967 draft conviction (see April 28). Frazier was fully recognized as champion after defeating Jimmy Ellis in 1970.

1973: Chris Evert, a 19-year-old who had learned tennis as a child at the foot of her father, Jimmy, a teaching pro, won her first professional tournament, defeat-

ing Virginia Wade of Britain in the S&H Green Stamps event in Fort Lauderdale, Fla., Evert's hometown.

2000: Karrie Webb, a 25-year-old golf sensation from Australia, won her fourth title of the year in as many tournaments. She defeated Annika Sorenstam (see March 16), then of Sweden, in a sudden-death playoff in the Takefuji Classic in Hawaii.

March 5, 1966
The Union Goes to Bat

By DAVID R. JONES

WASHINGTON—Marvin J. Miller, a steel union official selected today as executive director of the Major League Baseball Players Association, said that the course he would chart for the organization would depend on the wishes of the players. "I'm very anxious to get the views of the players and find out what they would like this association to become," Miller said. "I'll have to feel my way and I'll be dependent on what they think." Miller said it would be premature for him to outline a course for the association because he had yet to talk to the players. "This all remains to be done in the future," he said.

Miller was elected by player representatives of the 20 major-league baseball teams to the $50,000-a-year job. He will represent the players in dealings with club owners and Commissioner William Eckert. He will begin his job on July 1, but his selection remains to be ratified by a majority of the players. He hopes to meet with the 20 teams during the next month before each votes on the ratification. The office is a new one and will be financed from proceeds of the All-Star baseball game. The players previously were counseled by Judge Robert Cannon of the Milwaukee Circuit Court, who held a similar job on a part-time but unpaid basis.

"I'm obviously pleased at the selection," Miller said. "I think it ought to be an interesting and challenging job, and I'm looking forward to it." Miller, 48 years old, has been assistant to the president of the United Steelworkers of America, the nation's third-largest labor union, since 1960. He is an intelligent, articulate and creative labor official who has played a major role in some of the more interesting labor relations developments of recent years. He was the union's chief architect of a plan, developed with Kaiser Steel Corporation in 1963, designed to serve as a self-adjusting labor agreement that would provide workers with equitable benefit gains without repeated strike threats. The plan has been widely hailed for its creativeness by labor relations experts.

Miller is a slight and soft-spoken, distinguished-looking man with gray hair and a mustache. He is a glutton for work and relaxes on the tennis court, where he plays a fierce game.

Despite his intention to "feel my way," Marvin Miller quickly became an active and forceful leader of the major-league baseball players' union. The average salary for a player when he started was $19,000. By the time he retired in 1984 the average was $240,000, and today it exceeds $2 million.

Marvin Miller, executive director of the baseball players' union, at a New York press conference on April 3, 1972. Four days earlier, the players had voted to strike for the first time in the game's history. (Associated Press)

Runners-up

1924: Frank Caruana of Buffalo bowled two perfect 300 games in a row in official competition. Unlike today, perfect games were uncommon in the 20's because of uneven lanes and equipment. Only 11 were rolled in 1924, making Caruana's double 300 the bowling equivalent of Johnny Vander Meer's consecutive no-hitters in 1938 (see June 15).

1993: After three Super Bowl championships with three different quarterbacks and after 12 years as the Washington Redskins' head coach, Joe Gibbs announced his retirement from football. He soon reestablished himself as a racing team owner in Nascar.

1973: In the strangest trade in baseball history, as well as a sign of the social times, Yankee left-handed pitchers Fritz Peterson and Mike Kekich arrived at spring training and announced that they had recently and permanently swapped wives, children and dogs. Within two years, both players had been dealt to other teams.

March 6, 1990
A Fairy Tale Beginning

By ROBIN FINN

BOCA RATON, Fla.—Her mother developed a stiff neck from nervous tension. Her father's eyes were bloodshot after a sleepless night. But Jennifer Capriati, the 13-year-old tennis phenomenon who finally made her professional debut this afternoon, experienced no debilitating jitters. After a massage and a couple of hours of luxurious relaxing at the Boca Raton home owned by her idol, Chris Evert, Capriati galloped into the first match of what is anticipated to be a historic career and emerged with a 7–6, 6–1 victory over Mary Lou Daniels.

Capriati's opponent, a 28-year-old circuit journeywoman, described herself as "on the way out." The teen-ager, serving aces at 95 miles an hour and crackling her double-fisted backhand into unreachable corners, proved that she deserves the chance to compete among women instead of girls. Last year, Capriati won the junior titles at the French and the United States Opens. When she skipped, grinning, onto the stadium court at the Polo Club today, she was engulfed by photographers. The crush of portrait-seekers was so great and so demanding that the crowd of 5,400 baking in the sun-filled stands booed for their removal.

Daniels, a gracious loser, described the reception as "mind-boggling." "But I think the only time I thought it was getting ridiculous was when someone told us to shake hands before the match," said Daniels, who is ranked 110th. "I couldn't do that.

"I'm not going to say that if we'd played on Court 23 with nobody around that I would have beaten her," Daniels said of the intrusions that accompany Capriati.

"She told me 'good luck' for my future," Capriati said. "I thought I played good for my first professional match." Capriati shook aside comparisons to Steffi Graf as being premature. "After all," she said, "I've only played one match." Capriati said she had been waiting for this match, the one that marked her rite of passage from the junior to the professional ranks, since September. The countdown for this coming-out party commenced in January, and Capriati was assigned the task of slamming her way past several male pros at Saddlebrook's Harry Hopman Tennis Academy in order to be adjudged fit to compete at the elite level.

She said she could not be sure she had the requisite mental toughness until she had extricated herself from her first-set difficulties. "I thought, 'I'm gonna play it tough,'" she said. "I'm going out there as a different player: I'm not a junior anymore, I'm a pro."

Having turned 14 by May, Jennifer Capriati made the semifinals of the French Open. She left the tour to concentrate on high school late in 1993 and was arrested separately for shoplift-ing and drug use. She returned to tennis in 1996 and won the Australian Open in 2001 and '02 and the French Open in 2001.

Thirteen-year-old Jennifer Capriati during a match in her first pro tournament, the Virginia Slims of Florida. She punctuated her debut by reaching the singles final, losing to Gabriela Sabatini, 6-4, 7-5. (Associated Press)

Runners-up

1983: The United States Football League played its opening games with Herschel Walker *(see Nov. 29)*, the New Jersey Generals' $5 million running back, gaining 65 yards. The league lasted three years in its ill-fated attempt to piggyback on the N.F.L.'s success.

1923: The extraordinary Johnny Weissmuller *(see Aug. 10)* of the Illinois Athletic Club set his 47th world swimming record. Completing the 440-yard freestyle in 4 minutes 58 seconds at a meet in New Haven, Conn., he broke his own record by 11 seconds and became the first to cover the distance in less than five minutes.

1966: Bob Seagren, a sophomore from Glendale City College in California, became the first athlete to pole-vault 17 or more feet indoors when he soared 17 feet ¼ inch with a fiberglass pole at the national Amateur Athletic Union championships in Albuquerque, N.M. The height bettered the 16–10 indoor mark of John Pennel *(see Aug. 24)*, his college apartment-mate.

March 7, 1982
Boring, But It Worked

By GORDON S. WHITE Jr.

GREENSBORO, N.C.—The Atlantic Coast Conference championship basketball game started as a thriller between two fine teams today, but became a bore when North Carolina used its four-corner stall in the last eight minutes to preserve a 1-point lead and beat Virginia, 47–45. By winning the title, North Carolina, ranked No. 1 in the nation in the weekly wire-service polls, earned an automatic bid to the National Collegiate Athletic Association tournament that starts this week.

Coach Dean Smith, whose trademark is the four-corner setup he favors as a means of holding a lead, said: "You saw a great game until eight minutes to play. It could have been great if they came out and chased us, and then we shot some layups." But Virginia did not go out, and the Tar Heels, in possession with a 44–43 lead and 7:34 remaining, called time and went into their stall. They did not shoot for 7 minutes 6 seconds.

The four-corner stall was once called the four-corner offense, but no offense appeared to be intended today. James Worthy, Mike Jordan, Jimmy Black, Matt Doherty and Sam Perkins played catch until Virginia committed its seventh foul of the half, which sent Doherty to the line with 28 seconds left. He made the first shot and missed the second in a one-and-one situation, putting the Tar Heels up by 45–43. Virginia then went upcourt with time to tie the game. But the Cavaliers lost their last chance when the freshman Jim Miller, pressured by Black, lost the ball out of bounds. Doherty was then fouled again and hit both free throws. Ralph Sampson, Virginia's 7-foot-4-inch center, made an uncontested stuff at the buzzer.

Doherty did not mind the four corners,

Michael Jordan, aged 19, driving around the Wake Forest defense in February 1982. Coach Dean Smith's tactic was to forge ahead, then hold the ball until time expired. Fans abhorred the strategy, but the Tar Heels won the N.C.A.A. title. (Associated Press)

saying: "I don't care about the image of the sport. It was good for Carolina basketball because we won the game." When asked about the tactic, Terry Holland, Virginia's coach, said: "I'm not getting involved in that controversy. North Carolina did what it thought it had to do to win."

The finish was in stark contrast to the start. Worthy, the all-America forward, set the pace when he took the opening tip and went in for a stuff basket. Carolina quickly ran off 8 straight points. Worthy was a terror on offense, scoring 14 of his 16 points in the first seven and a half minutes. Virginia, which had started so poorly, finally got the lead, 35–34, at 1:21 of the second half when Tim Mullen broke in for a backdoor basket. A few minutes later, Jordan,

the freshman forward, hit four long shots to give the Tar Heels a 44–41 edge. Jeff Jones's 25-footer cut the lead to 44–43.

It was then that Smith called time and installed the four corners. "A coach thinks to win a game under the rules," he said afterward. "We were just trying to win, and did. They have a 7–4 guy you want to get out from under the basket, and he won't come out. If Sampson had come out, it might have been different. When I use the four corners and win, I'm a genius. When I use it and we lose, I'm all wrong."

To thwart the stall, the N.C.A.A. adopted a 45-second shot clock for all men's games for the 1985–86 season. The time was reduced to 35 seconds beginning in 1993–94.

Runners-up

1954: The fast-checking, hard-skating Soviet Union, playing in its first international tournament, routed a heavily favored but highly nervous Canadian team, 7–2, to win the world ice hockey championships in Stockholm.

1983: By winning a World Cup giant slalom on Aspen Mountain in Colorado, the American Phil Mahre (see Feb. 19) clinched his third straight overall Cup title. Only Gustavo Thoeni of Italy (1971–73) and Ingemar Stenmark of Sweden

(1976–78) were able to achieve such a feat before Mahre.

1970: Austin Carr, a 6-foot-3-inch junior guard from Notre Dame, scored 61 points in an N.C.A.A. tournament game against Ohio University, setting a one-game record for the tourney that still stands. He broke Bill Bradley's mark of 58 for Princeton in 1968 (see March 20).

March 8, 1971
Frazier Earns the Crown

By DAVE ANDERSON

NEW YORK—In a classic 15-round battle, Joe Frazier broke the wings of the butterfly and smashed the stinger of the bee tonight in winning a unanimous 15-round decision over Muhammad Ali at Madison Square Garden. Defying an anonymous "lose or else" death threat, Frazier settled the controversy over the world heavyweight championship by handing Ali his first defeat with a savage attack that culminated in a thudding knockdown of the deposed titleholder from a hammer-like left hook in the final round.

During the classic brawl, one man in the sellout throng of 20,455 died of a heart attack. When the verdict was announced,

Ali, also known as Cassius Clay, accepted it stoically. Hurried to his dressing room rather than the postfight interview area, Ali remained there for about half an hour. Suddenly, he departed for Flower Fifth Avenue Hospital for X-rays of his severely swollen jaw. He was released from the hospital after 40 minutes and left unbandaged.

But even before Ali's jaw began to bloat, the unbeaten Frazier had dulled the vaunted weapons of his rival in recording his 27th victory, although he failed in his quest for his 24th knockout. Ali's defeat ended his winning streak after 31 triumphs, with 25 knockouts. "I always knew who the champion was," Frazier, his brow swollen above each eye, said later with a smile. The officials agreed with the Philadelphia slugger. Judge Bill Recht awarded him 11 rounds to four for Ali, while the other judge, Artie Aidala, had Frazier ahead by 9–6. Referee Arthur Mercante had it the closest, 8–6 for Frazier with one round even.

During his uncharacteristic postfight silence, Ali sent this word to newsmen through Drew (Bundini) Brown, his assistant trainer: "Don't worry, we'll be back, we ain't through yet." But regarding a possible return bout, Frazier said, "I don't think Clay will want one." Ali had predicted Frazier would fall

"in six rounds" and he had maintained that there was "no way" the recognized champion could outpoint him. But the swarming Philadelphia brawler, battering his Cherry Hill, N.J., neighbor, ended the 29-year-old Ali's credibility as a prophet.

Claiming exemption as a Muslim minister, Ali refused induction in the armed forces on April 28, 1967. He promptly was stripped of his title and license to box by the New York State Athletic Commission and the World Boxing Association, which governs boxing in most of the other states. Not long after that, Ali was convicted of draft evasion (see April 28). His sentence was five years in prison, plus a $10,000 fine, but an appeal is currently before the Supreme Court. While his exile matured Ali's physique, it sabotaged his speed. Ali remained unscratched, except for a slightly bloodied nose, but his jaw began to swell on both sides in the late rounds from Frazier's persistent hammering.

In the final round, Frazier landed a wild left hook that sent Ali sprawling onto his back in a corer. But the 6-to-5 betting underdog was up almost instantly and took the mandatory eight-count on unsteady feet. It was only the third time Ali had been knocked down in a decade of competition. Sonny Banks floored him in 1962 during his 11th bout and Henry Cooper flattened him in 1963 during his 19th bout. But the knockdown by Frazier was the final embarrassment for the deposed champion, the sixth ex–heavyweight champion to fail in an attempt to regain his title. The others were Joe Louis, Jack Dempsey, Jim Jeffries, Bob Fitzsimmons and James J. Corbett. Only Floyd Patterson has succeeded in regaining it. In his failure, Ali not only lost, but more embarrassing, he was silenced.

Joe Frazier, right, knocking down Muhammad Ali with a left hook in the 15th round of their heavyweight title fight. Frazier won a unanimous decision over Ali, who had returned from a four-year banishment for draft evasion. (Getty Images)

Runners-up

1999: Joe DiMaggio (see July 17), the flawless center-fielder who along with Babe Ruth and Mickey Mantle symbolized the Yankees' dynastic success across the 20th century, died at his home in Hollywood, Fla. He was 84.

1930: Babe Ruth signed a new contract with the Yankees for $160,000 over two years—by far a record for the time. When someone observed that his salary now surpassed President Herbert Hoover's, Ruth supposedly said, "I had a better year." Yankee General Manager Ed Barrow said, "No one will ever be paid more."

1937: Howie Morenz, the Montreal Canadiens' star center and three-time N.H.L. most valuable player, died at age 34 in a hospital of a heart attack after suffering complications from a broken leg he sustained in a game against the Chicago Blackhawks five weeks before.

March 9, 1935
Jesse Owens: First and Always

Jesse Owens of Ohio State University arrived on the national stage in this track meet by breaking a sprint record that had stood for seven years. From this moment on, the 21-year-old Owens dominated track and field, his career reaching its zenith when he won four gold medals at the 1936 Berlin Olympics (see Aug. 4). Those performances were historically significant because he disproved on the field Hitler's doctrine of Aryan supremacy.

CHICAGO (AP)—Jesse Owens, Ohio State sophomore Negro sprinter, raced to a spectacular world record in the finals of the 60-yard dash tonight in the twenty-fifth annual Western Conference indoor track and field meet. His time was 6.1 seconds, one-tenth of a second faster than the world mark set by Loren Murchison in 1928. The Buckeye Comet, off like a flash, was unable to shake off his chief challengers, the Michigan pair of Sam Stoller and Willis Ward, the latter the defending champion, until the last five yards. His finishing burst, however, gave him a yard margin over Stoller, who beat Ward for second by inches.

George Simpson, another Ohio State dash man, was the first Big Ten athlete to equal Murchison's time, taking the event in that time in 1929. Judd Timm, Illinois; Eddie Tolan, Don Renwick and Ward of Michigan and Don Bennett of Ohio since tied the mark that Owens broke today.

Michigan retained its team title, collecting points in every event except the shot-put to establish a new meet record total of 49½ points, 27 points better than its nearest rival, Ohio State. The best previous total was 45 points by Illinois in 1921.

Clayton Brelsford, Michigan sophomore, scored an unexpected victory in the one-mile run over his team-mate, Captain Harvey Smith, in 4 minutes 25.7 seconds. Claude Moore of Purdue, who set most of the early pace, was third. Brelsford took the lead in the middle of the next to last lap and pulled away to a 10-yard lead over Smith, the favorite. John Moore of Ohio was fourth, with another Wolverine runner, Harry O'Connell, fifth. The 70-yard high hurdles also went to a Michigan star, Robert Osgood.

Jesse Owens of Ohio State crossing the finish line in world-record time in the 220-yard dash at the Big Ten championships in Ann Arbor, Mich., in May 1935. Owens broke world marks in two other events—the broad jump and the 220-yard hurdles—and tied yet another in the 100-yard dash all in roughly an hour. (Associated Press)

Runners-up

1948: N.H.L. president Clarence Campbell imposed lifetime bans on centers Billy Taylor of the Rangers and Don Gallinger of the Boston Bruins for betting on their own teams in league games. No evidence was ever shown that they bet against their clubs or threw games.

1994: Bill Koch, who successfully defended the America's Cup in 1992, announced that the first all-female crew in the history of the competition would sail his yacht, America 3, in the defender trials in January 1995. Koch later reneged, using a man as the starter and tactician, and America³ lost to Black Magic of New Zealand, which won the Cup.

1958: George Yardley of the Detroit Pistons became the first N.B.A. player to score at least 2,000 points in a season when he collected 26 points in a loss to the Syracuse Nationals. Wilt Chamberlain of the Philadelphia Warriors (*see March 2*) holds the record of 4,029 points, set in 1961–62.

March 10, 1986
What's Next for Marvelous Marvin?

By DAVE ANDERSON

LAS VEGAS, Nev.—During the sixth round, Marvelous Marvin Hagler hit John Mugabi with everything but a blackjack table. The world middleweight champion had the Ugandan challenger wobbling against the ropes on three sides of the ring. When the bell finally rang, Marvelous Marvin Hagler plopped down on the stool in his corner. But instead of looking up at his trainer Goody Petronelli for instructions, he stared across the ring, as if wondering how the boxer known as The Beast had survived that round.

As it developed, John Mugabi somehow survived into the 11th round when Marvelous Marvin Hagler's barrage of right hands put him down for the count. And so Marvelous Marvin Hagler, his left eye puffed into a slit, retained his title with the 52d knockout in his 62–2–2 record, apparently creating a September rematch with Thomas Hearns of their eight marvelous minutes of nearly a year ago. Quickly, sharply, Thomas Hearns had finished James Shuler in 73 seconds of the first round.

But the middleweight champion's next fight apparently will be with himself. In a television interview in the ring moments after his triumph, Marvelous Marvin Hagler spoke about how "I have to give it a little thought, but this might be my last fight." Those might have been the words of a weary warrior's natural reaction to a brutal battle. Or they might have been a true and thoughtful reaction. Whatever they turn out to be, Bob Arum, the Top Rank promoter, sounded tonight as if he were still planning a Hagler–Hearns rematch in September. But the champion wouldn't confirm it. "Give me a little time to go home and think about it," the middleweight champion would say later in the

Marvelous Marvin Hagler, right, stalking John Mugabi during their 1986 middleweight title bout in Las Vegas. Hagler successfully defended his title for the 13th time, knocking out Mugabi in the 11th round. (Bettmann/Corbis)

interview area. "I'll know more then."

John Mugabi, meanwhile, had stirred the crowd of 15,553 in the outdoor arena atop the Caesars Palace tennis courts. In both the seventh and the 10th rounds, a chant of "Beast...Beast" drifted through the chill of the 51-degree weather, damp from showers in the hours before the bouts began. "In that sixth round," the African's manager, Mickey Duff, said, "he hurt the top of his right thumb, he probably has a hairline fracture. When he came back to the corner, he told me 'My hand is very bad.' I told him he couldn't quit now, not that he ever mentioned quitting, but he had to show Hagler the right hand, then hit him in the body where it wouldn't hurt so much. And he never mentioned his hand again."

Among the spectators was another possible future foe for the middleweight champion—Donald Curry. From the folding chair where he was sitting across the stage yesterday morning, Donald Curry, the world welterweight champion, watched Marvelous Marvin Hagler weigh in at 159½ pounds for tonight's title bout. But instead of just being an onlooker, Donald Curry was inspecting the middleweight champion as a future opponent. According to the timetable of Bob Arum, the Top Rank promoter, Curry looms as Marvelous Marvin Hagler's farewell opponent a year from September.

Marvelous Marvin Hagler, of course, might not want to continue that long—a factor even Bob Arum realizes. "Nothing is ever sure in boxing," the promoter said. "Marvin might say, 'What do I need Curry for?'"

Marvelous Marvin Hagler, who had his named legally changed to include the modifier, lost the middleweight title in a disputed split decision to Sugar Ray Leonard in 1987 (see April 6). Hagler retired to Italy with a record of 63–3–2, including 52 knockouts, and has lived quietly there ever since.

Runners-up

1992: With a 5–2 victory over the Philadelphia Flyers at Nassau Coliseum, the Islanders' Al Arbour became the second coach in N.H.L. history, after Scotty Bowman, to total 700 or more victories. Arbour led the Islanders to four consecutive Stanley Cup titles from 1980–83 (*see May 17*).

1974: Bobby Unser, the older brother, held off Al, the equally if not more successful brother, by 58-hundreths of a second and won the California 500 at Ontario. It was the closest 500-mile race the United States Auto Club had ever held.

Bobby Unser won three Indianapolis 500's (1968, '75, '81); Al Unser won four (1970, '71, '78 and '87).

1996: Arkansas' record run of 12 N.C.A.A. indoor track championships ended when Coach John McDonnell's squad lost to George Mason University at Indianapolis. McDonnell is the winningest track coach in United States history, with 36 national titles in cross-country, indoor and outdoor events. After their loss to G.M.U., the Razorbacks won four of the next six titles through 2002.

March 11, 1995
A Free Spirit Rules the Downhill

By CHISTOPHER CLAREY

LENZERHEIDE, Switzerland (AP)— Before this season she had never won a World Cup race, but with a victory here today Picabo Street became the first American to clinch a World Cup downhill championship. Street, the 23-year-old native of Sun Valley, Idaho, and the Olympic silver medalist in the downhill last year, won her fourth straight race and fifth over all in a time of 1 minute 50.57 seconds.

The following article by Christopher Clarey appeared in The Times *four days before Picabo Street won the title.*

SAALBACH, Austria—Even if Picabo Street had not begun dominating the World Cup downhill circuit, she would have turned her share of Tyrolean heads. In a discipline where the difference between fabulous and fair is usually too small to be counted aloud, camaraderie is not always part of the tight-lipped proceedings. But Street, the free-spirited daughter of free spirits, has never been one for quietly toeing the party line. Seldom has she met a topic she didn't want to exhaust, a stranger she didn't want to befriend or a facade she didn't want to bring crashing down. She has drawn a smile from the imperious Katja Seizinger by yanking on her ski jacket. She has moved young Austrian rivals to shout "morning!" at the top of their lungs from a passing chairlift. She has partied with fellow Norwegian speed demons until well after the midnight sun has called it an evening.

At the same time, she has wreaked havoc on the pecking order. Until Street burst onto the scene with her braided, red ponytail protruding from her crash hel-

met, no American had won four World Cup downhills in a career. Not Cindy Nelson. Not Hilary Lindh, Street's current teammate and polar opposite. Not even Bill Johnson, the mouth that roared loudest in 1984. But little more than a year since her Olympic silver medal in Norway, Street has managed to win four downhills in a single season, including the last three in a row. She would have won another last month if Michaela Gerg-Leitner hadn't come up with an improbable run from the 30th start position to snatch victory away in Cortina d'Ampezzo, Italy.

Five days before that, Florence Masnada conjured up the same sort of magic with bib No. 29 to keep Street from winning her first World Cup Super G. But that about sums up Street's list of recent disappointments, unless you count breaking up with her longtime boyfriend, Mike Makar, and being separated from her new dog, Dugan, a Christmas gift from her parents, Stubby and Dee.

"The last couple years as my results got better, I got more hungry," said Street, who earned few compliments for her work ethic before joining the World Cup circuit in 1992 and was sent home from a training camp in 1990 for burning the candle too much at one end. "I just

started chomping at the bit a little bit more," she said. "I started reaping and sowing, reaping and sowing. And I figured the more I sowed, the more I would reap. Now it's got to the point where I want to go for the World Cup overall."

Picabo Street won another World Cup downhill championship in 1996. She was the gold medalist in the Super G competition at the 1998 Winter Olympics at Nagano, Japan.

Picabo Street of Sun Valley, Idaho, speeding through the air on her way to becoming the first U.S. woman to win the gold medal in the downhill at the 1996 world championships in Sierra Nevada, Spain. (Associated Press)

Runners-up

1945: Byron Nelson began a P.G.A.-record 11-tournament winning streak as he teamed with Jug McSpaden in the Miami Four-Ball tournament at Miami Springs Golf Club. Nelson carried the streak solo through the Canadian Open at Thornhill Country Club in Toronto on Aug. 4.

1996: N.F.L. owners voted to allow the Cleveland Browns owner Art Modell to move his team to Baltimore, where they were renamed the Ravens. Outraged Browns fans finally received a replacement franchise, with the team's

distinctive brown-and-white uniforms and caramel-colored helmets, in 1999.

1989: Vreni Schneider of Switzerland, who became a three-time Olympic gold medalist, ended the annual skiing campaign by winning the women's slalom at Shigakogen, Japan, giving her 14 World Cup victories for the season, a record that still stands. Ingemar Stenmark of Sweden won 13 Cup races in 1977–78, the most ever by a man.

March 12, 1966
Bobby Hull Streaks Past 50

[Unsigned, *The New York Times*]

Bobby Hull of the Blackhawks, he of the jagged-tooth grin and 100-mile-an-hour slap shot, posing at Boston Garden the day after scoring a single-season record 51st goal against the Rangers in New York. (Associated Press)

NEW YORK—His blond hair contrasting with his blood-red Blackhawks jersey, his thick, gloved hands curled around the stick, Bobby Hull is electrifying as he skates down the ice faster than any man in hockey. He shoots at 120 miles an hour—the hardest slapshot in the sport. There is little doubt among his opponents and fans that the 5-foot-10-inch 195-pounder Robert Marvin Hull is the most exciting player in the National Hockey League. With a goal tonight against the Rangers in Chicago, he surpassed Maurice (The Rocket) Richard and Bernie (Boom Boom) Geoffrion as the greatest goal scorer in a single N.H.L. season.

Hull's record goal came on a deliberate 40-foot, straight-on slap shot at 5:34 of the final period, tying the game at 2–2. The Blackhawks, who went on to win by 4–2, had just caught fire on the first of Chico Maki's two goals and were on the prowl with a power play. Red Hay and Lou Angotti got assists on the historic score. Cesare Maniago, the lanky Ranger goalie, was partially screened by Eric Nesternko when Hull shot. His 51st goal broke the record he had shared with the former great stars of the Montreal Canadiens. Hull, however, did it against defenses rigged especially for him and against the game's toughest players who were given only one job each time they faced the Chicago left wing: Stop Hull.

Hull is frank about his life's ambition. He says in his biography, "Bobby Hull," which will be published March 31, "I want to make a million dollars and retire to a ranch." From the loneliness of a 14-year-old living 150 miles away from home to play junior hockey, Hull has traveled the long road to acclaim, wealth and stardom. His public image carefully nurtured, he speaks graciously to his fans and accommodates screaming teen-agers after each game with his autograph. He even speaks publicly as if he were a storybook hero, which to Chicagoans he is. He describes his house as "nine rooms, resting on top of a knoll overlooking a lagoon." Hull, now 27, lives on an island in southeastern Ontario with his wife, Joanne, and their three children—Bobby Jr., 5; Blake, 4, and Brett, 20 months. The island is not far from his 600-acre ranch, which he reaches in an 18-foot runabout.

As a youngster, he had the same ambition as every other boy in Point Anne, Ont.—to play hockey. He was barely into his teens when he went away for a junior team. He would cry nights and look forward to the weekends when his parents would be able to visit him. Four years later Hull was on the Blackhawks. By the time he was 20 he led the league in scoring and two years later he scored 50 goals in a season. Now in his ninth N.H.L. campaign, Hull already holds the Hawks' record for career goals. Many have zipped past opposing goaltenders because of his custom-made stick, which he uses much like a jai alai player uses a cesta. Hull curves the blade of the stick, and it gives him more whip (at one time he used to bend the blades under a door, but now he has convinced manufacturers to make them curved).

Runners-up

1983: Mike Bossy *(see March 3)*, the Islanders' right wing, connected for a pair of goals against the Washington Capitals at Nassau Coliseum, including his 50th of the season, making him the first N.H.L. player to reach the 50-goal level in each of his first six seasons.

1996: Mahmoud Abdul-Rauf of the Denver Nuggets, formerly Chris Jackson, was suspended without pay by the N.B.A. after refusing to stand during the national anthem before games. A compromise was reached when he said he would stand and pray during the anthem; the flag, he said, was a "symbol of tyranny and oppression" and thus his Muslim faith would not allow him to pay respect to it.

1966: The 59-year-old jockey Johnny Longden won the 6,032nd and final race of his career by riding George Royal to victory in the San Juan Capistrano Invitation Handicap at Santa Anita in Arcadia, Calif.

March 13, 2000
A Bittersweet End

By CHARLIE NOBLES and MIKE FREEEMAN

DAVIE, Fla.—As Dan Marino, the National Football League's most prolific passer, gave his farewell speech today after 17 years with the Miami Dolphins, he tried not to make eye contact with his wife, Claire, who sat sobbing nearby. "I kept telling Claire that I can't cry during this thing," Marino said after announcing his retirement at the Dolphins' training facility at Nova Southeastern University. "I felt many a time like crying, but I was able to hold back. Tried to make a few jokes and keep it loose."

Marino, whose career records include most touchdown passes (420), most passing yards (61,361) and most completions (4,967), said he decided to end his playing career at age 38 mostly because of his health. He has had six knee operations, ruptured an Achilles' tendon and, last season, sustained a neck injury that sidelined him for five games. "There are physical limitations I would have had to deal with," he said. "It kept coming back to how my legs felt during last season, going through the neck injury and not knowing whether I was going to be able to throw the football."

After the Dolphins indicated by their long, awkward silence that their interest in Marino had waned, he was temporarily invigorated by an offer from the Minnesota Vikings. Coach Dennis Green was so interested in Marino that he offered to let him fly home after every Sunday game and not return until Wednesday. Marino said he had gone through a number of emotional swings before deciding last week to pass on Minnesota's offer. "There were times I told Claire we were going and two hours later I'd say, 'No, I don't think I can go,'" he said. "It is the toughest thing I've had to deal with professionally in my life."

A person close to Marino said that if the Dolphins had shown as much enthusiasm for his continuing to play as the Vikings had, he would most likely still be a Dolphin. "He probably would have gone to training camp, to see how he felt physically, and then take it from there," the person said.

Marino came in a Dolphin, and he will leave one. That, by itself, is a remarkable achievement. When Marino is eligible for the Hall of Fame in five years, it may be the easiest decision voters ever had. Marino threw more passes for more completions for more yards and more touchdowns than anyone else. His 33,508 passing yards in the 1990's are the most in a decade for any quarterback. "It is hard to imagine another quarterback duplicating the kind of success Dan had," Don Shula, his former coach, said. "I know I won't see it in my lifetime."

Dan Marino running for a first down against the Patriots during the first quarter of a 1994 game in Miami. The Dolphins quarterback gained large chunks of yardage with his laser-like right arm, retiring as the N.F.L.'s all-time leading passer. (Agence France-Presse)

Runners-up

1961: Floyd Patterson, floored twice in Round 1 for counts of 2, knocked out Ingemar Johansson of Sweden at 2 minutes 45 seconds of the sixth round at Miami Beach, Fla., to retain his world heavyweight title. It was the third and final match between the two *(see June 20).*

1982: Ushering in an age of greater athleticism that was at odds with the balletic approach to figure skating, Elaine Zayak, a 16-year-old from Paramus, N.J., who was seventh after the short program, landed six triple jumps in the long program to win the women's world figure-skating title in Copenhagen.

1960: N.F.L. owners approved the move of the Chicago Cardinals, who had played on the South Side for 41 years with only one league championship to show for it, to St. Louis. In 1988, still looking for another title, they became the Phoenix Cardinals. They were renamed the Arizona Cardinals in 1994.

March 14, 1990
Susan Butcher's Alaskan Huskies

Musher Susan Butcher giving her sled dogs a rest during a 1991 training run in Koyuk, Alaska. Her team, consisting mostly of Siberian and Alaskan huskies, could withstand temperatures as low as 60 degrees below zero. (Corbis)

NOME, Alaska (AP)—Greeted by sirens, banners and shouts, Susan Butcher mushed into Nome in record time today to win her fourth Iditarod Trail Sled Dog Race in the past five years. Butcher was running about two hours ahead of Joe Runyan, the defending champion, in a reversal from the 1989 finish. Runyan won that race with a 65-minute cushion over Butcher.

Butcher had to drop three of her veteran dogs, including two leaders. She gave credit for the victory to her team, which she said had been "absolutely incredible." "I've never had a team go as strong as

this," she added. "I don't know what's in that team that could do it, but it must be the combination working together. There's been no strong dog to emerge from this group."

Butcher and Rick Swenson are the only four-time winners of the Iditarod, a 1,158-mile race from Anchorage to Nome. Her official time was 11 days 1 hour 53 minutes 23 seconds, more than 10 minutes better than her 1987 mark of 11 days 2 hours 5 minutes, which was set on another route. The previous record for the northern route, set by Butcher in 1986, was 11 days 15 hours 6 minutes. She won

$50,000 in first-place money plus $25,000 from Purina Pro Plan, one of her sponsors. The rest of the $200,000 purse will be split among the next 19 finishers.

The winning time came as something of a surprise this year. The 70 mushers who began the race March 3 in Anchorage had to contend with the deepest snow in a quarter-century, ash from a volcano, some unseasonably warm days, buffalo on the trail and marauding moose. Forced to forage in shoulder-deep snow, moose were especially aggressive this winter. At least two mushers had run-ins with the huge animals, who tangled their lines and stomped their dogs.

Swenson, who was leading out of McGrath near the halfway point, had to turn back and have his team checked by a veterinarian after one such encounter. That cost him the race. People emptied out of bars and stores as Butcher headed down Front Street to cross the finish line for her fourth victory. She has finished second three times and among the top 10 four other times.

The grueling Iditarod Trail Sled Dog Race has been held annually since 1973 but did not become widely recognized throughout the United States until it drew television coverage after Libby Riddles became the first woman to win it in 1985. Rick Swenson holds the record with five victories between 1977 and 1991.

Runners-up

1967: Less than two months after the first Super Bowl, the Baltimore Colts selected defensive end Bubba Smith of Michigan State as the No. 1 pick in the first combined A.F.L.-N.F.L. draft. Other top draft choices that year were quarterbacks Steve Spurrier of Florida, No. 3 by the San Francisco 49ers, and Bob Griese of Purdue, No. 4 by the Miami Dolphins.

1976: Bill Shoemaker, already the winningest jockey in horse racing history, rode Royal Derby II to victory at Santa Anita, becoming the first to win 7,000 races.

Shoemaker was passed for most career victories by Laffit Pincay Jr. with 8,834 in 1999 (see Dec. 10).

1953: Walter Dukes scored 21 points and grabbed 20 rebounds to lead Seton Hall over St. John's, 58–46, for the National Invitation Tournament championship at Madison Square Garden. Dukes, a huge star in the years before Bill Russell, had set the collegiate single-season record for rebounds (734), which still stands.

March 15, 1997
Smith Stands Alone

By MALCOLM MORAN

WINSTON-SALEM, N.C.—The buzzer sounded, an achievement Dean Smith called his "so-called record" was secured and Serge Zwikker took off across the basketball court. An instant after North Carolina's 73–56 victory over Colorado today increased Smith's career total to 877, one more than Adolph Rupp of Kentucky, Zwikker, the Tar Heels' 7-foot-3-inch center, took the basketball from the hands of a Colorado guard, held it over his head and carried it into history—until he was stopped by security. It was the first time the Tar Heels were stopped all day.

North Carolina had advanced to the round of 16 of the National Collegiate Athletic Association tournament for the 15th time in 17 years. It had overcome a first-half groin injury to Vince Carter, its third-leading scorer. It had held Colorado's dangerous Chauncey Billups to 11 points. It was energized, once more, by Ed Cota, the freshman who has become the latest in Smith's succession of New York point guards.

Before March 7, Cota had made two 3-point shots this season. He made 2 of 2 today, including one that started a 13–2 Carolina spurt after Colorado remained

within a point early in the second half. With Cota's calm direction, the Tar Heels continued to move forward until their tallest player started to leave the floor with the historic ball. A tournament official stood in his path. "She wanted the ball pretty bad," Zwikker said. "She said, 'We're going to give it to him later.' We said, 'We're going to give it to him now'."

An achievement even Smith once thought was unreachable this season—an opinion that was not disputed when the Tar Heels lost their first three Atlantic Coast Conference games—was followed by an understated presentation in a small dressing room. "I just said, 'Coach, here's the ball,'" Zwikker remembered. "He said, 'Thank you very much. This ball represents a lot of history.'"

The sense of history tonight could be felt throughout Joel Coliseum. A collection of former Tar Heels, which included stars such as Bobby Jones and role players such as Warren Martin, sat near the Carolina bench. "And there were a lot more who wanted to come," said Bill Guthridge, Smith's longtime assistant. "But we couldn't get tickets for them." Smith carefully listed nine assistants, from Ken Rosemond and Larry Brown through his current staff members Dave Hammers and Phil Ford. "I've named all the assistants," he said. "I can't name all the players. I could, but it would take me a while."

Dean Smith retired in 1997 (see Oct. 9) with a record 879 victories and a 36-year legacy that transcended triumphs and defeats. Because of the coaches and players they trained or taught, he and John Wooden of U.C.L.A. are widely considered the greatest coaches in their sport in the past half-century.

Dean Smith chastising a referee during his record-breaking 877th victory in the second round of the N.C.A.A. tournament in North Carolina. (Associated Press)

Runners-up

1869: The Cincinnati Red Stockings, the first baseball team composed completely of professionals, played their initial game, routing Antioch College, 41–7. The Red Stockings, paid an average annual salary of $950, and a total payroll of $11,000 finished the year 51–0–1.

1991: Sergei Bubka of the Soviet Union *(see Aug. 5)* became the first athlete to pole-vault 20 feet when he cleared 20 feet ¼ inch in an international meet in San Sebastián, Spain. The vault bettered the world indoor record of 19 feet 11¼

inches he set one month before. He soared to an outdoor record of 20–1¾ in 1994.

1970: Bobby Orr of the Boston Bruins became the first defenseman in the N.H.L. to score 100 points in a season when he collected two goals and two assists in a 5–5 tie against the Detroit Red Wings at Boston Garden. Orr changed the game by becoming the first truly offensive-minded defenseman. He led the league in scoring twice, which was unprecedented for a back-of-the-ice player.

March 16, 2001
Make Way for Annika

Annika Sorenstam of Sweden after becoming the first woman to shoot just that at Moon Valley Country Club in Phoenix. She had shared the lowest previous score by a woman, 61, with Karrie Webb and Se Ri Pak. (Associated Press)

PHOENIX (AP)—On the 17th hole, the only sound was the cooing of a dove in a pine tree. Annika Sorenstam tapped her putter on the ground, lined up the shot, then paced off the 25 feet to the hole and walked to the other side of the green. Ready at last, she stood over the ball and broke the silence by running the putt through a swale to within 8 inches of the cup, setting up a birdie. After a tap-in for par on the final hole, Sorenstam leapt into the arms of her caddie and kissed her husband, celebrating the first 59 in women's golf.

A day after saying she goes for a birdie on every hole, Sorenstam almost did just that, birdieing her first eight holes and 12 of her first 13 while shooting 13 under in the second round of the Standard Register Ping. "I'm overwhelmed," she said. "I can't

believe what I just did. It was an incredible day. I had a lot of thoughts in my head. I was trying to stay calm and hit good shots, trying to hit it straight every time." Her round included 13 birdies, no bogeys and 25 putts on the 6,459-yard Moon Valley Country Club course. She reached every green in regulation and her longest par putt was 3½ feet.

"You can use all the words you want—impressive, simple," Sorenstam's playing partner, Meg Mallon, said. "She had two tap-ins and one putt from about 6 feet. The rest were 10 to 25 feet. She put on a putting display, especially on the front side. She hit the right shots. It was the kind of round everyone dreams of playing."

On a sunny, warm, windless day, Sorenstam, 30, a native of Sweden, broke every Ladies Professional Golf Associa-

tion scoring record for one or two rounds. Her 59 was two shots better than the 18-hole record of 61 she shared with Karrie Webb and Se Ri Pak. Her 20-under 124 at the midpoint was three strokes better than the 17 under Webb shot at East Lansing, Mich., last year. Pak's low round was on a par-71 course, while Webb and Sorenstam shot their 61's on par-72 courses.

Sorenstam started her round on the back nine and birdied the first eight holes—second-best in L.P.G.A. history behind the nine in a row by Beth Daniel during a tournament in 1999—and finished her first nine in 28 strokes. She birdied the next four before three straight pars and the history-making birdie on No. 8, her 17th hole. She closed with a 31 with a final putt from 6 inches. "It was one of the longest putts I had all day—maybe not distance-wise, but it really felt like it," she said. "I was trying to count quickly if I counted right, because I didn't want to jump up and down when I thought it was 59, when it really was 60."

Either score would have been a record, but Sorenstam wanted to equal the PGA record shared by Al Geiberger, David Duval and Chip Beck. "It shows that we can play," Sorenstam said.

Sorenstam became the first woman in 58 years to compete in a PGA Tour event when she teed off at Colonial Country Club in Fort Worth in 2003 (see May 22).

Runners-up

1910: Barney Oldfield set a speed record of 131.275 miles an hour for the measured mile in a German Blitzen Benz at Daytona, Fla. Oldfield, the speed king of the horseless carriage world who twice raced in the Indy 500 at the end of his career, began driving for Henry Ford in 1902 and helped Ford win financial backing to start his motorcar company.

1970: The N.B.A. expanded from 14 to 17 teams by adding the Cleveland Cavaliers, Buffalo Braves (later moved to San Diego and then Los Angeles as the

Clippers) and Portland Trail Blazers. The league also realigned itself into Atlantic, Central, South and Pacific divisions.

1938: The first National Invitation Tournament, invented by the promoter Ned Irish of Madison Square Garden as the first major postseason tourney, ended with Temple University defeating Colorado, 60–36, in the championship game at the Garden. The N.C.A.A. tournament, which eventually eclipsed the N.I.T., was organized in 1939.

March 17, 1955
Leave Our Richard Alone!

MONTREAL (AP)—Thousands of spectators took over the Forum tonight in a frenzied demonstration against Clarence Campbell, president of the National Hockey League. They were furious over the suspension of their idol, Maurice (Rocket) Richard. Campbell was assaulted and pelted with fruit and overshoes before the game between Montreal and Detroit was forfeited to the visiting Red Wings. Throughout the riot, Richard sat in a seat at the end of the Forum. The Montreal team's high-scoring star was set down today for the rest of the regular league season and the post-season Stanley Cup playoffs.

Campbell arrived midway in the first period of the game. He was greeted by catcalls and assorted epithets by the crowd, which was getting out of hand even then. For the next quarter-hour the fans' pent-up emotions grew louder until they reached a fever pitch. At the intermission, with the Red Wings ahead by 4–1, a smoke bomb exploded and hundreds of the spectators, along with Campbell, made their way to the exits. Many were coughing. It was at this point that Fire Chief Armand Pare ordered the game halted for the "protection of the people." Fearful of a full-scale panic, Pare ordered his men from the building, explaining that the sight of firemen by the 14,000 persons might lead to a stampede.

Campbell was greeted with a barrage of programs, peanuts and eggs when he arrived at the home rink of the Canadiens' sextet. But he kept his composure through violent threats until the bomb went off. He was pelted with overshoes, rubbers and oranges all through his stay and finally was assaulted by a man who slipped through police lines on the pretext of being a friend of the league head. Campbell did not appear to be injured, but he made his way from the arena. Police said the man walked up to Campbell and offered his hand before punching him.

Richard was suspended by the league president for a fight with Hal Laycoe of Boston last Sunday night. Laycoe suffered a cut on the head, as did Richard. The Montreal ace also punched Linesman Cliff Thompson twice. Tonight, the spectators poured from the Forum after the bomb went off. They fell over one another. Outside, demonstrators who were equally furious as the ones inside threw rocks, frozen snow and bottles at police, streetcars and automobiles. Some overhead wires of the trolley lines were pulled down, too. Even in the afternoon there were indications of trouble, for Campbell received many threatening telephone calls. But he announced he would be at the game.

Montreal is perhaps the most rabid hockey city in North America. The suspension of Richard would be the equivalent of Baseball Commissioner Ford Frick suspending Willie Mays of the New York Giants in the middle of the pennant drive and adding that he couldn't play in the world series, either.

N.H.L. President Clarence Campbell, right, being approached by an angry fan at the Montreal Forum. Thousands were irate over his suspension of the Canadiens' Maurice (Rocket) Richard. (Associated Press)

Runners-up

1990: Julio César Chávez knocked out Meldrick Taylor in the final seconds of their 12-round world junior welterweight title fight in Las Vegas, raising his record to 69–0. He remained undefeated and untied until a draw against Pernell Whitaker in 1993.

1897: Bob Fitzsimmons, a 167-pound middleweight, knocked out James (Gentleman Jim) Corbett in the 14th round of their heavyweight fight in Carson City, Nev., claiming the world title. Afterward, Fitzsimmons said of the 183-pound Corbett, "The bigger they are, the harder they fall."

1973: The Philadelphia 76ers set an N.B.A. record for futility, losing their 68th game of the season. The Sixers finished with a 9–73 record and remain the only team in league history not to reach double figures in victories. The 1997–98 Denver Nuggets were the next most inept (11–71).

March 18, 1953
The Braves' New World

By LOUIS EFFRAT

ST. PETERSBURG, Fla.—Unlike Bill Veeck, who had failed to effect an American League transfer of his Browns from St. Louis to Baltimore two days ago, Lou Perini succeeded today in shifting his National League baseball franchise from Boston to Milwaukee. After a meeting of senior circuit club owners, Warren Giles, the league president, announced the unanimous approval of Perini's plan. Although the discussions lasted three and a half hours, Giles said "there was no real opposition" to the first shift of a major-league baseball franchise in half a century.

Before today the last change in the major-league map occurred in 1903, when the Baltimore Orioles became the New York Highlanders, now the Yankees. Minor details remain for the Boston-to-Milwaukee move, but the package was wrapped, sealed and delivered to Perini. To gain his point, the contractor-sportsman, a native New Englander, had to receive all eight votes of the National League club owners. One negative ballot would have brought rejection, but once Walter O'Malley of the Dodgers had moved for approval of the Braves' transfer and Horace Stoneham of the Giants had seconded the motion, every hand, including Perini's, went up in approval in the open vote.

Some observers thought Perini's success was almost as great a surprise as was Veeck's failure. It had been felt that the American League had set the precedent, when the Browns' plea was turned down. But Perini never lost confidence and Giles later declared that "the fine standing and prestige of Perini in our league was a great factor." Perini was congratulated by all of the baseball men present. O'Malley said he was "dubious at first, but I have high regard for Perini's judgment and went with him." Stoneham said, "I was with him all the way."

For the first time since 1901, when the Red Sox set up American League business at the Hub, Boston became a one-team city. At Milwaukee, the Braves' new home will be in County Stadium, a $5,000,000 structure that at the moment has 28,011 grandstand seats and 7,900 bleachers. The nickname of the team will continue to be the "Braves."

The Boston Braves' move to Milwaukee was the first in a series of moves that altered the major-league map.

The St. Louis Browns moved to Baltimore and became the Orioles in 1954, and the Philadelphia Athletics moved to Kansas City in 1955 (before shifting to Oakland in 1968).

In 1958, major-league baseball reached the West Coast when the Brooklyn Dodgers moved to Los Angeles and the New York Giants transferred to San Francisco. The Washington Senators moved to Bloomington, Minn., as the Minnesota Twins in 1961 and were replaced in Washington by an expansion franchise. That Senators franchise became the Texas Rangers in 1972.

Warren Spahn at the Polo Grounds in New York in the mid-1950's. A four-time 20-game winner with the Boston Braves, he had an M for Milwaukee on his cap after 1952. (Associated Press)

Runners-up

1945: Maurice (Rocket) Richard, in his third season at right wing with the Montreal Canadiens at age 23, became the first N.H.L. player to score 50 goals in a season in a 4–2 victory over the Boston Bruins. In Richard's day, when the regular season consisted of just 50 games, 50 goals was the standard for superstardom. Today, with an 82-game season, 50-goal scorers are disappearing.

1990: Ending a 32-day lockout of players from spring training camps, major-league baseball owners and players agreed to a new labor agreement to extend through the 1993 season. Continuing labor trouble, however, resulted in the cancellation of the World Series in 1994 (see Sept. 14).

1995: Janet Evans, the three-time Olympian from Placentia, Calif., won her 45th and final national swimming title, the 1,500-meter freestyle in the indoor championships at Minneapolis. Evans won three gold medals in the 1988 Seoul Olympics and one in the 1992 Barcelona Games. Tracy Caulkins won 48 national swim titles (see Jan. 8).

March 19, 1966
An Equal Opportunity Upset

By GORDON S. WHITE Jr.

This game for the national collegiate basketball championship represented a college basketball landmark: It was the first time that a single team, Texas Western, started an all-black lineup in an N.C.A.A. title game.

COLLEGE PARK, Md.—Texas Western, overlooked in preseason ratings last December, became the collegiate basketball champion for the first time by whipping long-time powerful Kentucky, 72–65, tonight in the final of the National Collegiate Athletic Association tournament. The Miners never lost their poise in the face of a strong comeback attempt by the team rated No. 1 in the nation. Their rebounding strength and fine shooting kept them ahead from after 9 minutes 40 seconds of the first half until the end of the game.

It was a glorious moment for the flashy players of Coach Don Haskins. The El Paso college got its first taste of the glory that Kentucky had fed upon four times in the past. The Wildcats have won more National Collegiate basketball championships than any other team. Kentucky never before went as far as the final of this tournament without winning. But, before 14,253 fans at the University of Maryland's Cole Field House, Coach Adolph Rupp's little men, who had done so well against taller teams all season, failed in their biggest game.

Nevil Shed, a New York boy, sank the free throw that put Texas Western into the lead it never relinquished. Few in the capacity crowd believed that this was the beginning of the end for the Wildcats. But the Texans, rated No. 3, believed in themselves and kept a tight grip on the situation. Dave Lattin, a strong 240-pounder

Texas Western rebounding against Kentucky en route to victory in the N.C.A.A. final. Don Haskins fielded an all-black lineup against Adolf Rupp's white squad, which included Pat Riley (foreground, right). (NCAA Photos)

from Houston, had too much power under the boards for Kentucky to cope with. Yet it was a little man who filled the hero's assignment for Texas Western. He was Bobby Joe Hill, who used his cut-and-go skills to run around and through Kentucky. The 5-foot-10-inch junior from Detroit dropped in some of the fanciest shots of the tourney and scored 20 points. He also was a demon on defense, often taking the ball away from Kentucky players.

As the Texans seemed sure of victory in the last minute, their fans began chanting, "We're No. 1." And as they left the arena, many were yelling, "We won this one for L.B.J." Rupp gave Hill credit for the inevitable "turning point of the game." The Baron referred to Hill's stealing the ball twice within 10 seconds for layups just after Shed sank the foul shot to give the Miners the lead they never lost.

Years later, Don Haskins, when asked if he had a racial quota, said, "No. No one I worked for has ever mentioned it. I guess I really didn't give much thought to it....I just thought about beating them. I really didn't know until after the game, and I got bushelsful of hate mail, how important that game was. All I did was play my best people. It was that simple."

Runners-up

1991: N.F.L. owners voted to take the '93 Super Bowl away from Sun Devil Stadium in Tempe and give it to the Rose Bowl because Arizona did not approve a ballot proposition to recognize Martin Luther King Day as a national holiday. After another ballot initiative passed in '92 following national criticism of the state, the league delivered the '96 Super Bowl to Tempe.

1995: One day after issuing a press release saying "I'm back" from his 1993 retirement, Michael Jordan, wearing No. 45 instead of his usual 23, scored 19 points for the Bulls in a 103–96 overtime loss to the Indiana Pacers.

1950: City College of New York, coached by Nat Holman, defeated Bradley, 69–61, to win the National Invitation Tournament at Madison Square Garden. Ten days later the same teams met there in the then-less-important N.C.A.A. tournament, with C.C.N.Y. winning by 71–68. The cheers were short-lived because of C.C.N.Y.'s coming involvement in a point-shaving scandal (see Feb. 18).

March 20, 1973
A Rare Honor for Clemente

By JOSEPH DURSO

ST. PETERSBURG, Fla.— Eleven weeks after he was killed on a mercy mission, Roberto Clemente was voted into baseball's Hall of Fame today in an extraordinary special election. The longtime outfielder for the Pittsburgh Pirates and folk hero in Puerto Rico thereby became the first Latin-American player picked for the museum at Cooperstown, N.Y. He also became the first player in baseball history to be elected in a special mail poll without the normal five-year wait, though Lou Gehrig of the New York Yankees was chosen by acclamation in 1939 when fatally ill.

Clemente made it by receiving 93 per cent of the 424 ballots cast. They were asked to decide on his immediate election with these results: 393 voted yes, two abstained and 29 voted no—most of them explaining that they simply opposed waiving the five-year rule. The results were announced at a brief and solemn ceremony here in the heart of baseball's spring training area on the West Coast of Florida. It was one year after Clemente had opened his 18th season in the major leagues and 79 days after he was lost in a plane crash into the sea off San Juan while taking relief supplies from Puerto Rico to victims of Nicaragua's earthquake.

Acknowledging the vote were the baseball commissioner, Bowie Kuhn; officials

Roberto Clemente in March 1972, just before his final season. He died in a plane crash on a mercy mission to Nicaraguan earthquake victims the following December. (Associated Press)

of the Pirates, led by General Manager Joe L. Brown, and Vera Clemente, whom Roberto married in 1964 after a chance meeting in her father's drugstore. Mrs. Clemente, fighting back tears, said only, "Thank you for everything." But later, in

an interview, she noted that it was the first time since the accident on New Year's Eve that she had left her three sons: Roberto, who is 8 years old; Luis, 7, and Enrique, 4.

A memorial was dedicated to Clemente today: the trophy given by the commissioner each year to a ballplayer of high reputation was named the Roberto Clemente Award. It was given tonight at the annual Governor's Dinner to Al Kaline, 38-year-old outfielder for the Detroit Tigers. Clemente's plaque at Cooperstown will be unveiled Aug. 6 when five other baseball figures enter the Hall of Fame in the annual induction. They are Warren Spahn, the pitcher; Monte Irvin, who was elected by the special committee on the old Negro leagues, and Billy Evans, George Kelly and Mickey Welch, voted in by the Veterans Committee.

During 18 seasons with Pittsburgh, Clemente became one of the great defensive stars of the game and batted .317 with 240 home runs and 3,000 hits. The last hit, a double off John Matlack of the Mets on Sept. 30, made him the 11th player in history to reach 3,000. He was 38 years old when he said good-bye to his wife at the airport on New Year's Eve and took off with a plane-load of relief supplies for Nicaragua.

Runners-up
1965: Bill Bradley of Princeton University, Rhodes Scholar, later a Knicks star, a United States senator and a presidential contender, scored 58 points in his college finale, a 118–82 victory over Wichita State in an N.C.A.A. title consolation game at Portland, Ore.

1954: Bobby Plumb sank a last-second shot to give Milan High School (enrollment 161) a 32–30 victory over Muncie Central in the final game of the Indiana High School basketball championships. It was the most famous high school basketball game of all time. Milan Coach Marvin Wood and others became central figures in the celebrated 1986 film "Hoosiers."

1992: Kenny Bernstein, the National Hot Rod Association champion in the top fuel division, the fastest class in the sport, became the first dragster to exceed 300 miles an hour when he was clocked at 301.70 m.p.h. in a qualifying heat at the N.H.R.A. Gatornationals at the Gainesville (Fla.) Raceway.

March 21, 1999
A Speck in the Sky

By MALCOLM W. BROWNE

Dr. Bertrand Piccard, a Swiss psychiatrist, and Brian Jones, his British co-pilot, became the first balloonists to circle the world nonstop on this date when they completed their 19-day odyssey over an invisible finish line in Mauritania. The following article appeared in The Times *two days later.*

GENEVA—As Dr. Bertrand Piccard and Brian Jones stepped from a plane in Cairo today, a trumpeter played the "Triumphal March" from "Aida" and a thunderous cheer rose from the dignitaries and well-wishers who had gathered at Geneva International Airport. In their dark blue flight suits, the champion pilots raised their arms in a victory salute and beamed at the crowd under a cold drizzle and overcast sky that included children who had the day off from school.

In a brief welcoming speech, Vice President Adolphe Ogi referred to Antoine de Saint-Éxupéry's famous children's book, saying, "Our little prince came down from the sky and landed in the desert among us." On Saturday, Dr. Piccard, 41, and Mr. Jones, who will be 52 next Saturday, completed a historic 19-day trip around the world in their Brietling Orbiter 3 balloon when they flew over an invisible finish line at 9 degrees 27 minutes west longitude in Mauritania. More than a score of pilots had tried to go around the world in a balloon before. All failed.

Among the crowd that met the two pilots here was Richard Branson, the billionaire balloonist who was one of Dr. Piccards's main rivals in round-the-world attempts. The most recent of those ended on Dec. 25 with a ditching in the ocean near Hawaii.

Dr. Piccard and Mr. Jones spoke of a "mysterious invisible hand" that had seemingly opened their way. After the craft had passed Puerto Rico, he related, calculations suggested that their slow speed would leave them out of fuel well short of their destination. "And then," Mr. Jones said, "suddenly the speed started to increase very rapidly, up to 150 miles an hour, and I just threw all my calculations away."

Bertrand Piccard comes from a family famous for daring, inventiveness and breaking altitude records in the air and depth records at sea. His grandfather, Dr. Auguste Piccard, also a medical doctor, invented the pressurized balloon crew gondola, allowing flights to very high altitudes. He became the first human to ascend into the stratosphere, at more than 50,000 feet, and also invented a deep-diving immersible called the Bathyscaphe. Auguste's son, Jacques Piccard, Bertrand's father, used the Bathyscaphe to descend to the deepest place on earth—the Marianas Trench, 35,815 feet below the surface of the Pacific Ocean.

The British millionaire Richard Branson

has made four unsuccessful attempts to circle the globe. In July 2002 Steve Fossett of Chicago became the first balloonist to do it alone.

The nine-ton Brietling Orbiter 3 balloon, with Dr. Bertrand Piccard and Brian Jones in the gordoa, passing eastward over the Swiss Alps at the start of their historic 19-day round-the-world journey. (Reuters)

Runners-up

1964: Coach John Wooden won the first of his 10 N.C.A.A. titles at U.C.L.A. as the Bruins defeated Duke University, coached by Vic Bubas, 98–83. U.C.L.A.'s Gail Goodrich scored 27 points and Kenny Washington had 26 points and 12 rebounds.

1946: One year before Jackie Robinson reached the major leagues with the Brooklyn Dodgers, halfback Kenny Washington signed with the Los Angeles Rams,

becoming the first black player in the N.F.L. He played until 1948.

1970: Vinko Bogataj, a little-known ski jumper from Yugoslavia, tumbled down a ramp at the Internationa Ski Flying Championship in Oberstdorf, West Germany. His fall became perhaps the most frequently viewed scene in sports history when ABC-TV's "Wide World of Sports" for many years made it part of its videotaped opener to illustrate the "agony of defeat."

March 22, 1989
The Commissioner's Secret

By THOMAS GEORGE

PALM DESERT, Calif.—Pete Rozelle announced today that after 29 years as commissioner of the National Football League he would resign as soon as a new commissioner was found.

"I decided in October, but I didn't want to become a lame-duck commissioner," Rozelle told a news conference here, where league owners are meeting. "My health is no problem except for the 20 pounds I gained from quitting smoking. It's just a matter of wanting to enjoy my free time. Even my close personal friends did not know. It's going to be a shock to them and that hurts me. I just think you only go through life once. I just think it is the overall period of time that has accumulated." Rozelle turned 63 years old on March 1.

Wellington Mara, the New York Giants' co-owner, and Lamar Hunt, the Kansas City Chiefs' owner, were to form a committee to search for Rozelle's replacement. A news conference is scheduled for tomorrow at which Rozelle will again talk about his resignation and Mara and Hunt, presidents of the National and American Football conferences, respectively, will announce the members of the search committee. Hunt said a replacement would probably be named before the beginning of the season.

Among the first names to surface in speculation about a successor were those of Tex Schramm of the Dallas Cowboys and Jack Kemp, the Secretary of Housing and Urban Development, who is a former professional quarterback. "Well," said Schramm, "it has to be someone younger than me and somebody willing to go 20 or 30 years again. I think that's important. It is a role that has to be filled for several years." Schramm is 68 years old. Bill Bidwill, the Phoenix Cardinals' owner, said: "I, nor anyone else, has even had time to give a thought about his replacement. But soon, we all will. We'll have to."

Rozelle said the court cases between the Los Angeles Raiders and the league beginning in 1980 and the N.F.L.–United States Football League trial in 1986 helped him make his decision. "When you talk about three trials in five years, it seemed for a while they were never going to end," he said. "And we had to do our job on top of that. These have not been pleasant times for the owners, myself or a lot of people close to football.

"I wanted everything solved on a high note with no outstanding litigation," he added. "But in October I just realized it's not going to be like that anymore. There is always going to be something. The next 30 years we'll see as much growth and change as ever before. I don't think the last 30 will compare to the next 30 years."

Rozelle, who was elected commissioner in January 1960, left the news conference teary-eyed. His announcement, which he conveyed privately to the owners of the league's 28 teams only minutes before the news conference, caught the owners completely off guard. Art Modell, the Cleveland Browns' owner, said: "He went I'm sure the only way he felt he could go. But he's been terrific, phenomenal."

Pete Rozelle died at age 70 of brain cancer at his home in Rancho Santa Fe, Calif., in December 1996.

Commissioner Pete Rozelle in 1985. The merger of the N.F.L. and the A.F.L., the creation of the Super Bowl and pro football's rise as the dominant spectator sport all occurred on his 30-year watch. (Associated Press)

Runners-up

1968: U.C.L.A., behind junior Lew Alcindor, snapped the University of Houston's 32-game winning streak with a 101–69 victory in the N.C.A.A. semifinals at Los Angeles. The next day the Bruins defeated North Carolina for their second straight national title and fourth in five years under Coach John Wooden.

1994: The N.F.L. made its first scoring rules change in 75 years, allowing the option of a 2-point conversion after touchdowns. The revision, which all college divisions had adopted in 1958, brought more strategy to the game—as well as strife, when coaches played safe for a tie instead of risking defeat for victory.

1973: Chris Evert played Martina Navratilova of Czechoslovakia for the first time in what became a storied rivalry (*see June 2*), defeating her by 7–6, 6–3, in Akron, Ohio. Evert won 21 of the first 25 matches they played, though Navratilova later firmly turned the tide. In their 80 head-to-head matches over all, Martina prevailed, 43–37.

March 23, 1957
Little Guys Win Big

Wilt Chamberlain of Kansas putting up a shot against North Carolina in their triple-overtime N.C.A.A. final. The great Chamberlain was thwarted at the end by a Tar Heel named Joe Quigg. (Rich Clarkson)

KANSAS CITY (UP)—North Carolina defeated Kansas, 54–53, in three overtime periods tonight to win the National Collegiate basketball tournament. Joe Quigg won the game for the unbeaten Tar Heels with two foul shots in the final six seconds and then blocked a pass to Wilt Chamberlain to foil a Jayhawk scoring bid. Quigg's jumping one-hand block kept Chamberlain from attempting one desperate shot in the last five seconds of the third extra period. It was the first time a national championship game went into overtime. The Tar Heels' victory extended their unbeaten streak to thirty-two games.

The final, frantic fifteen minutes of play produced two heated incidents on the court. In the first one Pete Brennan of North Carolina clamped his arms around Chamberlain's waist and began to wrestle. The second occurred when Tommy Kearns of North Carolina swung aside Gene Elstun of Kansas.

The dramatic finish of the title game occurred after a tight battle that was close except for the opening ten minutes, when North Carolina racked up a 19–7 margin. It was North Carolina by 29–22 at the half, and Kansas did not catch up until it took the lead at 36–35 with 16:40 left. Kansas was on top, 40–37, with ten minutes left and the score was 46–46 at the end of regulation play. The score was twice tied and the lead changed twice before the 46–46 deadlock.

The two teams scored only 2 points each in the first overtime. Chamberlain hit for Kansas and Bob Young, a substitute, tallied for North Carolina. The second overtime was scoreless. Kearns and Quigg then won the game for North Carolina, hitting for all the Tar Heel points in the third extra session. Kearns had a field goal and two free throws to match Chamberlain's overtime production. Elstun added another free throw to send Kansas ahead, 53–52, with twenty seconds left. Chamberlain blocked Kearns' shot but fouled Quigg, who hit for the 2 winning points. Kansas took time out with five seconds left and tried to feed the ball to Chamberlain, but Quigg made the game-saving block.

Chamberlain was the top scorer with 23 points. North Carolina's All-America, Lennie Rosenbluth, had 20. Rosenbluth fouled out with 1:45 remaining in standard playing time and did not play in the extra periods, which were mostly displays of stalling and ball control. The pattern of stalling began as soon as Kansas got its 3-point lead. North Carolina started slowing it down and Kansas followed suit. From ten minutes left in regulation time to five minutes, not a shot was fired. Both teams continued the stalling in the first two overtimes.

Third place in the championship went to San Francisco, the defending champion. The Dons defeated Michigan State, 68–60.

Runners-up

1994: Wayne Gretzky of the Los Angeles Kings tipped a pass from Marty McSorley into an open goal against the Vancouver Canucks, passing Gordie Howe of the Detroit Red Wings as the N.H.L.'s career goals scorer with 802. Gretzky went on to extend the record, which still stands, to 894 goals.

1974: North Carolina State, behind high-soaring David Thompson, ended U.C.L.A.'s seven-year reign as national champion with an 80–77 double-overtime victory in the N.C.A.A. semifinals at Greensboro, N.C. Coach Norm Sloan won the first of The Wolfpack's two national titles two nights later by defeating Marquette University, 76–64, as Thompson scored 21 points.

2002: Cael Sanderson, a 197-pound senior from Iowa State University, won an unprecedented fourth straight weight class title at the N.C.A.A. wrestling championships at Albany, N.Y., and finished his collegiate career undefeated. He received nearly a five-minute ovation from the 12,000 fans after he put Lehigh sophomore Jon Trenge on his back with a double-leg takedown.

March 24, 1962
Twenty-five Deadly Blows

By ROBERT L. TEAGUE

Benny (Kid) Paret slumps in a corner as Referee Ruby Goldstein clutches Emile Griffith, stopping their welterweight title fight. Paret, who never regained consciousness, died 10 days later. (Associated Press)

NEW YORK—Emile Griffith of New York regained the world welterweight boxing championship from Benny (Kid) Paret tonight at Madison Square Garden. Paret was knocked unconscious and underwent brain surgery at Roosevelt Hospital. Griffith stopped Paret after 2 minutes 9 seconds of the twelfth round. Paret was out on his feet. When he failed to regain consciousness in the ring, he was taken to his dressing room on a stretcher and later removed to the hospital by ambulance.

At the hospital, Dr. Harry Kleiman reported that the 25-year-old Paret was in serious condition. Dr. Lawrence Schick, a neurosurgeon, then performed surgery to relieve pressure on the brain. Another doctor at the hospital said Paret's chances to recover were "poor." In a waiting room downstairs from the operating room, about fifteen fans and friends quietly awaited word of Paret's condition. This group included Garden officials. Griffith was among those in the waiting room and said: "I'm sorry it happened. I hope everything is being done for him." Griffith left before the

operation began. Before Paret left the Garden, the last rites of the Roman Catholic Church were administered.

Although Griffith had been down for an 8-count in the sixth, his triumph was anything but surprising. He had been in command most of the way, and there had been times when the punishment he inflicted on Paret seemed much more than any normal human could withstand. What finally ended the stubborn Cuban's reign was a two-handed flurry that started with ten consecutive right uppercuts to the chin. The 23-year-old Griffith punched faster than most observers could count. All told, his winning assault consisted of twenty-five blows.

Long before Griffith had completed this cyclonic sortie, many in the crowd of 7,600 were begging Referee Ruby Goldstein to intervene. Goldstein was not moved to pity until one fact became obvious: The only reason Paret still was on his feet was that Griffith's pile-driving fists were keeping him there, pinned against the post in a neutral corner. Paret's eyes were closed. His hands dropped at his sides. His head snapped to the left and to the right as Griffith pounded away. The fact that Paret would not fall seemed to arouse the New Yorker to new heights of fury.

Perhaps he was remembering the split decision he lost to Paret here last Sept. 30. That was the bout in which Paret regained

the crown he had lost to Emile on April 1, 1960, at Miami Beach. That fight ended in a thirteenth-round knockout. Whatever it was that Griffith was thinking about tonight, it certainly was translated into something akin to savagery. After the ten rights to the face had failed to do the job, he began alternating the rights with left hooks. All these blows were thrown from behind Emile's back, it seemed. Paret sagged but still would not go down.

Goldstein finally made his move but had difficulty restraining Griffith. When the referee finally pulled the attacker away, Paret slid slowly down the ropes and to the canvas. He lay on his back unconscious for about eight minutes while physicians worked on him. He still was unconscious when carted to his dressing room. In a sense, it was something of a miracle that Paret had reached the twelfth round. Had he not possessed more courage than skill, he would have been knocked out in the tenth. Griffith punched faster and harder than his opponent. Paret frequently made the mistake of allowing his foe to bore in under slow-motion jabs and pump both hands hard to the body. And at close quarters, Griffith invariably was the man who managed to work a hand free to throw a stiff uppercut.

Griffith weighed 144 pounds and Paret 146¼ for the scheduled fifteen-round bout. Paret was guaranteed $50,000, and Griffith's purse was about $17,000. Griffith was a heavy favorite. The knockout was the fourth of Paret's professional career. His record now shows thirty-four victories, twelve losses and three draws. Griffith has won twenty-five bouts and has lost three.

Kid Paret remained in a coma until his death in a New York City hospital on April 3. Emile Griffith fought until 1977.

Runners-up

1956: The senior Bill Russell led the University of San Francisco to its second straight N.C.A.A. title with an 83–71 victory over Iowa. Russell scored 26 points and pulled down 27 rebounds as the Dons won their 55th straight game, the collegiate record at the time. The current record is 88 straight by U.C.L.A. from 1971 to '74 (see Jan. 19).

1936: In the longest N.H.L. game ever played, the Detroit Red Wings and the Montreal Maroons went six overtime periods at the Montreal Forum in Game 1 of the Stanley Cup semifinals before the Wings won on the game's only goal, scored by Mud Bruneteau. The time of game was 2 hours 56 minutes 30 seconds.

1978: O.J. Simpson, the N.F.L.'s single-season leading ground gainer (see Dec. 16), was traded by the Buffalo Bills at age 30 to the San Francisco 49ers for five draft choices. Simpson played two final seasons for the Niners, the favorite team of his boyhood, and retired to a career of hurtling over airport check-in counters for Hertz.

March 25, 1934
The First Master

[Unsigned, *The New York Times*]

AUGUSTA, Ga.—There was a long roar late today as a four-foot putt dropped on the home green at the Augusta National Club for a par 72 and Horton Smith stood up and grinned. He had won the Masters' invitation golf tournament and the $1,500 first prize with a score of 284 for seventy-two holes. The tall Missourian, pro at the Oak Park Club at Chicago, drove in this tournament better than ever before in his career. He was using a club strange to him, a Bobby Jones model driver borrowed from third-place finisher Paul Runyan the day the tournament began.

In a tie for thirteenth place was Jones himself, grand-slam champion of 1930, who returned to competition for this tournament. Jones finished with a total of 294, ten strokes behind the winner. Jones, finishing the tournament, congratulated the winner, who was the last man to defeat him in open competition, and then announced that he was not returning to competition in any national event. "I have no idea of returning to open competition," he said. "I hope to have this masters' tournament an annual affair and I will limit my competition to playing in it for the fun I get out of it."

The tournament was a tremendous success. The course, modeled after several in England, tested the players very well. Tremendous crowds tramped after Bobby on each round, with scores advising him, slapping his back, asking questions, urging him on. It was a wonder the Georgian was able to play as well as he did. Smith knew what he had to do to win today and his performance, under this pressure, was highly creditable. His chances appeared to be lost on the seventeenth when a seventy-five-yard approach pitch on the third

shot failed to run as far as he expected and left him with a ten-foot putt. But he rammed it home for a birdie 4. It was a dramatic moment.

The eighteenth saw him blast a long shot from the tee, a tremendous wallop, and then pitch to within twenty-five feet of the pin. He was a bit short with his putt and left himself a four-footer. It meant the

difference between victory and a tie. But Smith, after studying the lie coolly, dropped it in for the 284, which gave him a 1-stroke margin over Craig Wood. "I feel that I am back on my game after three years of trying," said Smith when it was over. Smith never has won a major tournament. His victory today probably is his greatest one.

Horton Smith during a Masters practice round in 1936. Two years earlier he had defeated, among others, Bobby Jones, who mentioned that he hoped to keep the tournament "an annual affair." (Associated Press)

Runners-up

1958: Sugar Ray Robinson, aged 37, gained a 15-round split decision over Carmen Basilio, 31, the New York State onion farmer, at Chicago Stadium to become the world middleweight champion for a record fifth time.

1896: James B. Connolly, a student at Harvard, won the "hop, skip and jump" competition—soon renamed the triple jump—to claim the initial gold medal of the first modern Olympic Games in Athens.

1982: Wayne Gretzky, the N.H.L.'s new 21-year-old scoring machine, knocked in two goals and assisted on two more in leading the Edmonton Oilers to a 7–2 victory over the Calgary Flames. The 6 points gave him 203 and made him the first player in the history of the league to score that many in a season. No other player has reached 200 in one year; Gretzky did so four times.

March 26, 1979
A Glimpse of the Future

By GORDON S. WHITE Jr.

SALT LAKE CITY—Michigan State grounded The Bird with a touch of Magic and a magnificent zone defense tonight to win its first National Collegiate basketball championship and end Indiana State's chance to achieve an unbeaten season. Despite a heavy load of personal fouls that created serious problems down the stretch, the Spartans held fast to an early lead and beat the Sycamores, 75–64, in the final of the 41st National Collegiate Athletic Association tournament before 15,410 persons in the Special Events Center of the University of Utah. The loss was the only one for Indiana State in 34 games this season. Michigan State finished with a 26–6 record.

Earvin (Magic) Johnson, who played the entire second half with three personal fouls, was his usual spectacular self, scoring 24 points for the winners. Larry Bird, the big man for Indiana State with a three-year career average of more than 30 points a game, was kept to only 19 points, his lowest scoring game in five N.C.A.A. tournament contests. There was no beating the Michigan State defense during this tournament and there was little any team could do to stop the fast offense triggered by the magic of Johnson's passing.

This defense stopped Bird after no other team could do so in this tourney. The 6–9 senior had scored 22, 29, 31 and 35 points in his four previous tourney games. What's more, Michigan State closed down the Indiana State passing lanes, and held Bird to only two assists. "We defended him with an adjustment and a prayer," said Jud Heathcote, the Michigan State coach. But while Heathcote was praying on the bench, Johnson, Greg Kelser, Ron Charles, Jay Vincent and Terry Donnelly shared the work of defending inside at the baseline. They crowded Bird like a flock of vultures every time he approached the baseline on offense. Bird's mates just could not get the ball to him very often and when they did, Bird would hesitate, something he rarely does.

Indiana State's man-to-man defense

Larry Bird of Indiana State helping Magic Johnson of Michigan State up from the floor in the N.C.A.A. championship final. The matchup of the two stars took the tournament to a new level. (Associated Press)

didn't appear to bother Johnson. He made one of the game's most exciting moves when he drove the baseline around Alex Gilbert only to be facing Bird, standing his ground under the basket. Kelser was coming down the lane to Johnson's left and the Michigan State sophomore faked a pass to Kelser. Bird took the fake and moved just a bit to defend Kelser coming into the basket. Johnson kept the ball and made an easy layup. Such spectacular play may have been Johnson's last for Michigan State. It is expected the Lansing, Mich., athlete who stayed home to play college ball will declare hardship and be drafted into the pros for next season.

March 26, 1973
Nearly Perfect Is Good Enough

By GORDON S. WHITE Jr.

ST. LOUIS—Bill Walton put on one of the greatest performances in college basketball tournament history tonight leading his University of California, Los Angeles team to its seventh straight National Collegiate Athletic Association championship. His record 44 points was only part of his total effort as U.C.L.A. defeated an exciting Memphis State team, 87–66, for its 75th consecutive victory over 2½ seasons and its ninth N.C.A.A. title in the last ten years.

But Walton's amazing work was toned down when, with 2 minutes 51 seconds remaining, the 6-foot 11-inch red-haired Bruin fell hard to the floor and hurt his left knee and ankle. He limped off the floor to an ovation from the 19,301 fans. This most mobile of the present college basketball big men has always played with pain in his knees. He tapes them before every game.

Walton's outstanding effort, hitting on 21 of 22 field goal shots, taking 13 rebounds and controlling both boards, was even more noteworthy because he played with three personal fouls from the start of the second half and picked up his fourth after 10 minutes and 33 seconds more. The fouls didn't hamper his motion in beating Memphis State's big men. He continued to play physically hard and in constant contact with the Tigers' who were trying their best to draw that fifth personal and send Walton to the bench. When he was hurt, U.C.L.A. had finally taken command of the game and was leading, 75–62.

But earlier, when Walton drew his third personal with 4:14 to go in the first half and U.C.L.A. led at 37–31, Wooden benched him for the remainder of the first half. Memphis State suddenly was playing a normal team of mortals and gained a 39–39 tie at intermission. Wooden, however did not remove his big junior hero after he drew that fourth personal. The coach didn't dare do that. U.C.L.A. could easily have lost its slim lead—61–55—at the time. Without Walton, this U.C.L.A. team is just another good team—maybe not even good enough to beat Memphis State.

Ronnie Robinson, Larry Kenon and Wes Westfall, Memphis State's tall men who worked on Walton in pairs and relays, just couldn't handle the big fellow from La Mesa, Calif., who zipped back and forth across the lane at the low post as if he was under 6 feet tall. He took in high and low passes from Greg Lee, Keith Wilkes, Larry Hollyfield and others and scored by out-reaching his defenders. He took rebounds jumping over the Tigers. Gene Bartow, Memphis State coach, said: "We couldn't contain Walton. I've never seen a player so dominating as Walton."

Bill Walton's 44 points broke the previous individual scoring mark of 42 points in an N.C.A.A. title game, which had been set by Gail Goodrich, also of U.C.L.A., against Michigan in 1965. Bill Bradley of Princeton (see March 20) and Austin Carr of Notre Dame (see March 7) scored more points in nonchampionship games of the tournament.

Bill Walton of U.C.L.A. hitting for 2 of his record 44 points in the Bruins' national title victory over Memphis State. It was U.C.L.A.'s 75th straight triumph and ninth championship in 10 years. (Associated Press)

Runners-up

1944: St. John's University, coached by Joe Lapchick, upended DePaul, 47–39, at Madison Square Garden to become the first back-to-back winner of the National Invitation Tournament. The Redmen, as they then were called, won a third N.I.T. title by defeating Bradley in 1959.

1917: The Seattle Metropolitans of the Pacific Coast Hockey Association became the first United States team to win the Stanley Cup in the pre-N.H.L. days by beating the Montreal Canadiens, three games to one. It was the first time the Cup went south of the Canadian border since being donated in 1893 (see March 27).

1946: Hank Iba's Oklahoma A&M team defeated the University of North Carolina, 43–40, for the Aggies' second straight N.C.A.A. title. Bob Kurland, the first dominant 7-footer in basketball, scored 23 points as A&M became the tournament's first two-time champion.

March 27, 1996
That's a Horse in the Desert

By DOUGLAS JEHL

DUBAI, United Arab Emirates—Cigar, the great American thoroughbred who traveled more than 6,000 miles to race here, held off a breathtaking stretch challenge tonight to win the $4 million Dubai World Cup by half a length and collect racing's richest prize. It was the 14th straight victory by the extraordinary 6-year-old bay, but it also was by far the narrowest of that streak. Soul of the Matter closed from the outside to run eye to eye with Cigar with just three-sixteenths of a mile to go, and the jockey Jerry Bailey had to ask the horse for more than he had ever asked before.

The triumph left Cigar just 2 victories short of the legendary Citation's record of 16 consecutive victories, vaulted Cigar past Alysheba as racing's career leading

money winner and swelled his international reputation. Still, Cigar's trainer, Bill Mott, said his horse was not at his best, underscoring just how risky and unusual an undertaking the race was for such a valuable horse. Mott said that as Cigar and Soul of the Matter thundered side by side down the stretch, he was counting the 11 training days that Cigar had lost after sustaining a bruised right foot only five weeks ago. "Tonight you saw him reach down and find something he hasn't had to use every time he's run," Mott said. "It was just sure grit, and it's really good to see that he's got it in him."

Gambling is not permitted in the Persian Gulf emirate of Dubai, where the eclectic scene at tonight's six-card race included foreigners in miniskirts,

Sudanese workers in turbans and members of the ruling family in royal robes. But for those who placed their bets outside the country, Ladbrokes, the British odds-making firm, had Cigar as the heavy even-money favorite. Soul of the Matter, a 5-year-old bay, was listed by British bookmakers at 25–1.

Cigar, who started from the eighth position in an 11-horse field, was the last one loaded into the starting gate for the mile-and-a-quarter race on the sandy Nad al-Sheba track. He slipped on the way out, leaving him in the middle of the pack with five furlongs to go. Cigar took the lead from the pacesetter, L'Carriere, on the final turn into the long three-furlong homestretch, but then Burt Bacharach's Soul of the Matter roared from last place to make the final challenge. "I was a bit worried," said Bailey, who wore the red, white and blue silks of Cigar's owner, Allen Paulson.

But Bailey responded with hands and whip to urge Cigar first a nose, then a shoulder and finally a half-length ahead in a race that the jockey, speaking of his mount, said was "not his best performance, but it was his best effort." Gary Stevens, who rode Soul of the Matter, said he believed his horse had actually nosed in front for a moment. "I think it's been quite some time since anybody's got past Cigar," he said. But Bailey, North America's 1995 Jockey of the Year riding the 1995 Horse of the Year, said, "Nobody was going by me, even if we went around again."

Cigar tied Citation's American record for consecutive victories with his 16th straight four months later (see July 13). Cigar won 19 of his 33 career races and was named Horse of the Year in 1995 and '96.

Cigar, along the rail, with Jerry Bailey up, toughing it out against Soul of the Matter in the Dubai World Cup. The victory was Cigar's 14th in a row, two short of the legendary Citation's record. (Getty Images)

Runners-up

1978: Forward Jack (Goose) Givens scored 41 points to lead the University of Kentucky over Duke, 94–88, at the Checkerdome in St. Louis for the Wildcats' fifth N.C.A.A. basketball title but their first in 20 years. It was the first national title for Coach Joe B. Hall.

1939: The first N.C.A.A. championship game, overshadowed by that of the National Invitation Tournament, was played at Northwestern University in Evanston, Ill., as Oregon defeated Ohio State, 46–33. The N.C.A.A. tournament gained

wider popularity than the N.I.T. in the mid-1950's.

1893: The Stanley Cup, a silver bowl that cost its owner 10 guineas ($50), was donated as an annual award for Canada's amateur hockey champions by Frederick Arthur, Lord Stanley of Preston. However, the pro National Hockey Association, forerunner of the N.H.L., took possession of the Cup in 1910 as the symbol of true hockey supremacy.

March 28, 1995
It Doesn't Get Better Than This

By DAVE ANDERSON

NEW YORK—Some nights, the Madison Square Garden electricians don't have to turn on the lights. Some nights, the athletes do it themselves. But tonight, one athlete turned on the lights.

Michael Jordan was that one athlete, soaring and swerving, slicing and spinning to 55 points, then whipping a pass to Bill Wennington, once of St. John's, for the decisive basket in the Bulls' 113–111 victory over the Knicks, the most magnetic regular-season theater in New York sports history. Usually the most memorable games anywhere occur in the World Series or the Super Bowl or the National Basketball Association playoffs or the Stanley Cup playoffs or a championship fight. But tonight was just a regular-season game. Sort of. In a sense, if the Knicks and the Bulls continue on their paths toward becoming opponents in the first round of the N.B.A. playoffs, tonight's game was really the opener of that three-of-five-game series, even though it won't count.

Looking to that series, Michael Jordan gave the Knicks something to remember him and the Bulls by. Old-timers might argue for Johnny Vander Meer's second consecutive no-hitter at Ebbets Field during the 1938 season or

for the Yankees snatching the American League pennant from the Red Sox in the final game of the 1949 season. But the

Michael Jordan of the Bulls soaring above the Knicks' John Starks in a personal 55-point explosion at Madison Square Garden. It was the fifth game back for Jordan after a two-year layoff. (Barton Silverman/The New York Times)

Cincinnati Reds' left-hander never possessed Jordan's luster. And the Yankees' triumph was a team effort. Jordan was

performing a virtual solo tonight.

Hours earlier, this was obviously an event: Jordan's return to the Garden nearly two years after wrecking the Knicks' championship hopes in the 1993 Eastern Conference playoff final, after a season of minor league baseball as a .202 hitter for the Birmingham Barons, after rejoining the Bulls only 10 days ago. By late afternoon, nearly a dozen television trucks were parked on West 33d Street, contributing to the traffic jam that had horns honking. Fans were in their seats earlier than usual.

Whatever the scalpers were getting was worth it. In more than a quarter of a century in what is still considered the new Garden, Jordan's 55 points were the most by an opposing player. Bernard King scored 60 there for the Knicks on Christmas 1984 against the Nets. But the Jordan numbers weren't as dazzling as the number he did on the Knicks in only the fifth game since his comeback began.

Michael Jordan and the Bulls, who had won three N.B.A. titles at this point and would win another three straight in 1996–98, lost to Shaquille O'Neal and the Orlando Magic in six games in the Eastern Conference semifinals the following May.

Runners-up

1992: Christian Laettner of Duke released a 17-foot jump shot barely before the final buzzer for a 104–103 overtime victory over Kentucky to win the N.C.A.A. East Regional basketball title at Philadelphia. The Blue Devils became the first team in 19 years to repeat as national champions with a victory over Michigan nine days later.

1999: With Fidel Castro watching for all 11 innings in a seat next to Commissioner Bud Selig, the Baltimore Orioles outlasted the Cuban national team, 3–2, in

Havana in the first game between a United States major league team and one manned by Cubans in 40 years.

1970: Dan Gable, probably the most storied figure in United States amateur wrestling, lost his only collegiate match after 98 victories while seeking his final N.C.A.A. title in the national championships at Evanston, Ill. Gable competed at Iowa State, became a gold medalist in the 1972 Olympics and then coached at Iowa, winning 12 national titles between 1976 and '93.

Twelve Vans to Indianapolis

By DAVE ANDERSON

A moving van carrying Colts equipment leaves Owings Mills, Md., for Indianapolis in the dark of night. Robert Irsay, the team's owner, was forever scorned for sneaking his team out of Baltimore. (Associated Press)

NEW YORK—At the opening of the Baltimore Colts' new suburban offices and training complex four years ago, Robert Irsay addressed the small audience that had gathered in Owings Mills, Md. "This building," the Colts' owner said, "is a symbol of our dedication to bring winning football back to our fans. We want our team to match the standards set by this building."

Dedication and standards—words to remember Robert Irsay by now that he has shown he understands neither. But in trying to sneak his National Football League club's belongings to Indianapolis in the dark of night this morning in 12 moving vans, he did show what a grimy business so much of sports has become. He also showed that the Supreme Court must rule on the legality of "free-agent franchises," as created in the N.F.L. by Al Davis in winning his Federal antitrust case that permitted the Raiders to go to Los Angeles from Oakland in 1982.

By moving the Colts' franchise in such a murky manner, Robert Irsay almost makes Al Davis look like a silver-and-black knight. Almost. But at least Al Davis went to court. In baseball, Walter O'Malley and Horace Stoneham at least had the permission of the other National League club owners before taking the Dodgers and Giants to California for the 1958 season. Without the necessity of N.F.L. approval, Robert Irsay moved his club's shoulder pads and film projectors in the middle of the night after a decent average of 40,923 ticket sales in Memorial Stadium last season, including a regular-season club record of 60,559 for one game. If the Colts can be moved that way, any other franchise area in any sport can wake up some morning to find itself without a team.

The offices and training complex in Owings Mills are now as empty as Robert Irsay's promise to notify Mayor William Donald Schaefer of Baltimore of his decision before he moved the franchise. From now on, when people think of Robert Irsay, they will remember the television film-clips of big yellow moving vans rumbling along dark rain-slicked roads after the Colts' offices and locker rooms had been evacuated.

Moving vans usually project a sense of success—a new home or a new job. And the movers always arrive early in the morning. But these movers resembled kidnappers or burglars using darkness to avoid detection. The yellow Mayflower vans had been gathered yesterday afternoon from as far north as New Jersey and as far south as Virginia, along with a busload of 45 movers and a truckload of packing material. The vans arrived at the Colts' complex about 10 that evening. Shortly before dawn today, the vans had been loaded and were on their way to Indianapolis.

The vans had been arranged by Mayor William Hudnut of Indianapolis with his neighbor, John B. Smith, the president of the Mayflower Corporation, as part of that city's offer to snatch the Colts. When the Colts' office staff arrived this morning at the empty complex, they were paid through the remainder of the week with checks drawn on an Indianapolis bank. The coaches, trainers and equipment men needed to accompany the team had been alerted to the move quietly late last night. Not that they were surprised. Robert Irsay also had shopped the franchise to city officials in Phoenix, Memphis and Jacksonville in recent years.

As with almost all the other teams that have moved since World War II, beginning with the football Rams going to Los Angeles from Cleveland in 1946, the new Indianapolis franchise will steal the nickname, too. That's always the cheapest trick in any franchise move.

Runners-up

1982: Apparently mistaking North Carolina's James Worthy for a teammate, Georgetown University's Fred Brown made a bad pass to him with five seconds left in the N.C.A.A. championship game at New Orleans to give the Tar Heels a 63–62 victory and their first national title under Dean Smith. Michael Jordan scored the winning basket.

1976: Bobby Knight's Indiana team, led by Scott May, Kent Benson, Bobby Wilkerson and Quinn Buckner, defeated the University of Michigan, 86–68, for the national title at the Spectrum in Philadelphia. The victory capped a 32–0 season for the Hoosiers.

2000: Major-league baseball played its first regular-season game outside North America when the Mets and the Chicago Cubs opened in the Tokyo Dome before a crowd announced at an even 55,000. The Cubs won, 5–3, 13 time zones ahead of the near North Side.

March 30, 1968
Open Tennis Comes of Age

By FRED TUPPER

PARIS—In a historic decision, the International Lawn Tennis Federation voted unanimously today for open tennis. That means that professionals will be allowed to compete against amateurs in a limited number of tournaments. Not one dissenting voice was heard as the entire agenda was approved with resounding applause at this extraordinary general meeting, fittingly enough held in the Place de la Concorde.

"It was an incredible result achieved here," said Bob Kelleher, president of the United States Lawn Tennis Association, "in a spirit of highest cooperation and friendliness." Until today, the federation had adamantly voted down over the years all attempts to introduce open tennis. In 1967 at Luxembourg, the open proposal was defeated, 139 votes to 83.

The British had made approval possible. In an unparalleled decision, they announced last October they would make the 1968 Wimbledon tournament an open. They said that in the future all players in Britain would be simply "players," not amateurs or professionals. And the British said they were ready to risk expulsion from the federation to make open tennis possible. Country after country fell into line, and today the world agreed.

What the federation is prepared to recognize is the following categories of tennis players: the "amateur," who is not paid; the "registered" player, who can profit from the game while not making tennis his profession, and the "professional," who makes his money from teaching or playing in events not organized by the national association. Everybody seemed happy. "It's a wonderful thing," said 70-year-old Jean Borotra, who had won Wimbledon as long ago as 1924.

"Amateurism is preserved."

The British were pleased. They continue their own interpretation of "players" as just that, neither amateurs nor pros, but they recognize the rights of other nations to call them what they want. The United States voted for open tennis in February and had worked here solidly behind the scenes all week for its success. Under the new conditions, the open tourney would logically be held in Forest Hills, Queens, the site of the national amateur championships, in early September. "I don't know whether Forest Hills wants an open," said Kelleher. "You have to creep before you can crawl, and the evolutionary process will take time."

The first United States Open was held in September 1968 (see Sept. 9). The tournament moved from Forest Hills to the National Tennis Center in Flushing Meadows in 1978.

Virginia Wade of Britain an amateur, in the semifinals of the first U.S. Open at Forest Hills, N.Y., in September 1968. She defeated Billie Jean King of the U.S., a professional, in the final. (Associated Press)

Runners-up

1987: Keith Smart popped in a 17-foot jumper from the corner with four seconds left to lift Indiana University to a 74–73 victory over Syracuse at the Superdome in New Orleans and give the Hoosiers their third N.C.A.A. title in the turbulent reign of Coach Bobby Knight.

1966: Sandy Koufax (*see Sept. 9*) and Don Drysdale, the star pitching tandem of the world champion Los Angeles Dodgers, ended a 32-day double holdout, signing with the club. Each received an estimated $135,000. Koufax went 27–9 with a 1.73 earned run average in his last season but was forced to retire with arthritis in his remarkable left arm (*see Nov. 18*).

1991: Led by Christian Laettner with 18 points, Duke University upset defending champion Nevada–Las Vegas, 79–77, in the semifinals of the N.C.A.A. tournament at the Hoosier Dome in Indianapolis. The loss snapped a 45-game winning streak for the Runnin' Rebels. Two days later Duke beat Kansas to win its first title in nine trips to the Final Four.

March 31, 1975
The Wizard Walks Off a Winner

By GORDON S. WHITE Jr.

SAN DIEGO—The University of California, Los Angeles won the National Collegiate basketball championship tonight for the 10th and last time under the direction of Coach John Wooden. The Bruins, proving speed more valuable than muscle, raced up and down court from start to finish to beat a powerful University of Kentucky team, 92–85, in Wooden's final game before retirement. When it was done, the crowd of 15,153 at the San Diego Arena remained to give Wooden, the Wizard of Westwood, a standing ovation for about four minutes.

In increasing their record of national basketball titles to 10 in the last 12 years and 8 in the last 9, the Bruins beat the school closest to them in national titles. The Wildcats have four. Although he would not admit it, this victory in his final game of 27 seasons as the U.C.L.A. coach may have been Wooden's most satisfying. This was a team not as strong as many of his former national champions—one not rated certain of the crown when the season began.

Wooden said following the thrilling triumph, "To say I thought we would win [the title] back then would be stretching a point." But Dave Meyers, the senior star of the team, said: "I wanted to do it for Coach all season. He's done a masterful job with the team that lost [Bill] Walton and [Keith] Wilkes," stars of the three preceding seasons.

Most unexpected of all, however, was the fact that U.C.L.A. beat Kentucky using only six players. This was the first time

John Wooden wearing a net as well as a smile after his U.C.L.A. Bruins defeated Kentucky for their 10th and final national collegiate title under his direction. (Associated Press)

Wooden used only six players in a national championship game. It paid off as the half-dozen slim, tall men kept up an unusually fast pace and achieved what U.C.L.A. teams in 1964 and 1965, and from 1967 through 1973, had achieved. And those teams had such star players as Walt Hazzard, Lew Alcindor, Sidney Wicks and Bill Walton. The mighty six who won this year's crown were Meyers, Marques Johnson, Rich Washington, Pete Trgovich, Andre McCarter and Ralph Drollinger, the man who came off the bench and had the finest game of his career.

Drollinger, the 7-foot-1 junior who has been criticized because he was not an Alcindor or Walton, was unusually strong under the boards. The frail Drollinger stood in there for 16½ minutes and beat off the Kentucky rebounders Coach Joe Hall kept fresh by sending them into the game in relays.

Trgovich, a 6–4 senior guard, had an excellent night on defense and scored 16 points. Washington, the 6–9 sophomore who was voted the outstanding player of the tournament, paced U.C.L.A.'s scoring with 28 points. Meyers had 24 points, Drollinger 10, McCarter 8 and Johnson 6. It just didn't matter that Kevin Grevey, Kentucky's leading scorer, had 34.

Runners-up

1931: Knute Rockne, the 43-year-old Notre Dame football coach, was killed with seven others when the commercial airplane in which they were flying lost its engines and crashed in a pasture in Kansas. The three-time national champion coach was en route from Kansas City to Los Angeles, where he was going to make a football movie.

1980: Jesse Owens, the legendary sprinter and long jumper whose four gold medal victories in the 1936 Berlin Olympics (*see Aug. 4*) undercut Hitler's doctrine of Aryan racial supremacy, died of lung cancer at age 66 in Tucson, Ariz.

1993: The N.H.L. changed the face of its divisions, discarding names like "Prince of Wales" and "Smythe," realigning teams and adopting a new playoff format in which qualifiers are seeded according to their records, N.B.A.-style. The move was an attempt to simplify the league's structure and increase its popularity, though it continued to trail pro basketball in attendance and television exposure by the end of the decade.

APRIL

April 1, 1985
They Shot the Lights Out

By ROY S. JOHNSON

LEXINGTON, Ky.—This was supposed to be a coronation, a celebration of the mighty Georgetown Hoyas as one of college basketball's greatest teams. Instead, the crowning was spoiled by a new and unlikely champion, the Villanova Wildcats. In what will surely be remembered as one of the most improbable outcomes in the history of the National Collegiate Athletic Association tournament, the Wildcats, who failed to finish in the nation's Top 40 in any poll this season, completed their emotion-filled postseason by playing the elusive "perfect game" at the perfect time.

They upset the favored Hoyas, 66–64, to win the school's first basketball championship ever before a national television audience and a capacity crowd of 23,124 shocked spectators at Rupp Arena. In Georgetown, Villanova was facing a team that had harassed opponents into shooting 39 percent from the field this season, the lowest in the country. But the Wildcats were not intimidated, and shot a tournament-record 79 percent from the field in the contest. They made 22 of 28 shots overall, including an incredible 9 of 10 in the second half. In addition, they made 22 of 27 free throws.

"I had no idea we were shooting the ball that well," said the Wildcat forward Dwayne McClain, who led all scorers with 17 points while adding 3 assists. "But we were taking our time and taking good shots." In the final precious seconds McClain lay sprawled on the court, clutching the ball and extending his fist upward in triumph. Indeed, the victory culminated a heart-wrenching joyride for the Wildcats, who finished at 25–10. After finishing the season with a Big East record that left them only tied for third in the

conference—behind Georgetown and St. John's—they strung together six straight victories buoyed by a moving togetherness that became their trademark.

Charged by their trio of seniors—McClain; the point guard Gary McLain, the emotional leader and unsung hero; and the 6-foot-9½-inch center Ed Pinckney—they eliminated second-ranked Michigan, fifth-ranked Memphis State and seventh-ranked North Carolina. And tonight they dethroned the talent-laden defending champions, who came into the contest with a 17-game winning streak and every intention of becoming the first team in 12 seasons to earn two successive titles.

But it was not to be. The Wildcats' fighting spirit overcame the Hoyas' talent. Pinckney outscored and outrebounded Georgetown's 7-foot center, Patrick Ewing—16 points to 14 and 6 rebounds to 5. That earned Pinckney honors as the most valuable player of the Final Four. The Hoyas, who ended their season with a record of 35–3, were gracious in defeat. As each of the Villanova players walked to the podium at center court and received his commemorative gold

watch, the Hoyas stood and applauded. "They taught college basketball how to win this season," Dave Gavitt, the proud commissioner of the Big East, said of the Hoyas. "Tonight, they taught college basketball how to lose."

Dwayne McClain, sprawled on the court, punches the air for emphasis and clutches the ball as the final seconds tick away, clinching Villanova's shocking upset over Georgetown in the N.C.A.A. title game. (Associated Press)

Runners-up

1987: The Mets were informed by major league baseball that Dwight Gooden (see Sept. 12), their 22-year-old pitching ace who went 24–5 in 1985 and helped them to the world championship in 1986, had tested positive for cocaine. He missed the first two months of the season in a rehabilitation center and was never as overpowering again.

1991: After five trips to the Final Four under Coach Mike Krzyzewski since 1986, Duke finally won its first N.C.A.A. championship, methodically defeating Kansas, 72–65, in the title game at Indianapolis.

1972: Major leaguers walked out at the end of spring training, beginning the first general players' strike in sports history. The walkout lasted until April 13. None of the 86 regular-season games that were canceled were made up—a move that affected the American League East Division when the Detroit Tigers, who played one game more than the Boston Red Sox, finished a half-game ahead of them.

April 2, 1986
Moving the Campus Downtown

DALLAS (AP)—The National Collegiate Athletic Association adopted the 3-point field goal in men's basketball today and decided to use instant replays to check scoring and timing errors. Dr. Edward S. Steitz, the secretary-editor of the association's rules committee, said the 3-point goal, which has become popular in the professional game, was adopted by the 12-member committee after five years of experimentation among 20 conferences.

The committee decided on a 19-foot-9-inch distance for the 3-point shot. The National Basketball Association awards 3 points for a shot made from a distance of 23–9, in an arc across the top of the key, or slightly less from the corners. "It's going to force teams to play more defense away from the basket," said Steitz. "People will say, 'You are putting the little man back in the game' and that's good."

Steitz, who is the athletic director at Springfield College in Massachusetts, pointed out that conferences had experimented with different distances for the 3-point goal. "Some

Ronnie Carr of Western Carolina on Nov. 29, 1980, when he hit college basketball's first 3-pointer, against Middle Tennessee State. The Southern Conference had been permitted to experiment with the shot that season. The N.C.A.A. adopted the rule five and a half years later. (Western Carolina University)

conferences used the pro distance and didn't find that desirable," Steitz said. "As a result of a questionnaire, most of the coaches preferred 19–9." Steve Alford, Indiana's all-America guard, gave the change a hearty endorsement, saying, "My jump shot's worth one more point now." But his enthusiasm was not shared by everyone.

Mike Krzyzewski, the Duke coach, said: "This is a revolutionary change, and I don't think it's good for the game right now. There are a lot of major coaches shocked by this. If we're shocked, then you know there hasn't been a lot of discussion about it, and certainly there has been no public outcry to implement a 3-point shot."

Larry Brown, the Kansas coach, said: "I think the 3-pointer has merit. I'm a little confused about the distance. I don't want it to be such an easy shot that it really becomes more important than anything, because I don't think that's the purpose. I do think it'll open the game up a little more and we probably won't see as many zones."

Runners-up
2001: Roger Clemens of the Yankees broke Walter Johnson's 74-year-old American League record of 3,508 career strikeouts on opening day in the Bronx. Clemens struck out five Kansas City Royals in a 7–3 New York victory, getting Joe Randa on a forkball for his 3,509th strikeout.

1972: Mets Manager Gil Hodges, the former Brooklyn Dodger first-baseman who managed the eight-year-old Mets to the world championship in 1969 (see Oct. 16), died of a heart attack while on a golf course in West Palm Beach, Fla.,

shortly before the team broke camp to head north.

1995: The University of Connecticut women's basketball team, led by the all-Americas Rebecca Lobo and Jen Rizzotti, defeated Tennessee, 70–64, and won the N.C.A.A. title at the Target Center in Minneapolis. UConn's 35–0 record was the best in women's Division I history until surpassed by the 2002 Huskies, who went 39–0.

April 3, 1989
Breaking in at the Top

By THOMAS GEORGE and MALCOLM MORAN

SEATTLE—Darryl Walker's desperation shot skidded hard off the backboard and into Glen Rice's hands, and moments later Rice was lugging more than just a basketball. Rumeal Robinson, the crafty Michigan point guard, knew how to start the celebration. He leaped into Rice's arms, and with their fists raised, both players chanted, "We're No. 1! We're the national champions!"

The Michigan Wolverines had finished third in the Big Ten Conference. They had entered the National Collegiate Athletic Association tournament with an interim coach and a reputation of losing early with powerful teams in the 1980's. And now here they were, indeed No. 1, beating Seton Hall in overtime tonight on two foul shots by Robinson, 80-79, for the national title.

So many hard times turned to shimmering moments here. From Steve Fisher, the interim coach who replaced Bill Frieder after Frieder accepted the Arizona State coaching job just before the tournament, to Sean Higgins, the Los Angeles prep all-American who attended Michigan only after the N.C.A.A. intervened to void his forced signing with U.C.L.A. "Coach Fisher told us in the huddle between regulation and overtime," said Mark Hughes, the Michigan forward, "that a friend of his from San Francisco said we were going to win by 1 point in overtime and that I should be in the game at the end. It turned out right, didn't it?"

Michigan Coach Steve Fisher, a mere two weeks on the job, barking instructions like a veteran tactician during the 1989 N.C.A.A. title game. His friend's pregame premonition of a 1-point overtime victory over Seton Hall was right on. (Associated Press)

Rice was brilliant, scoring 31 points, grabbing 11 rebounds and setting tournament marks for most points, field goals and 4-point field goals. But Seton Hall's John Morton was nearly his equal on this night, scoring 35 points, the most in his career. Morton poured in 17 of Seton Hall's final 20 points in regulation time, including the 3-point shot that tied the score at 71–71 with 25 seconds to play. His skills had persuaded P.J. Carlesimo, the Pirate coach, to direct his offense toward Morton with a 3-point lead in the final 100 seconds of overtime. But it was Morton's second missed shot in the closing minute and a half, an airball from 6 feet away with 9 seconds to go in the game, that created the Michigan opportunity that led to Robinson's winning foul shots with 3 seconds left.

Afterward, Seton Hall's Gerald Greene sat in the dressing room and inspected the box he had received. Inside the box was a small brown wood case, and inside the case was a silver ring with a black stone. On the stone were the letters N.C.A.A. Instead of being tempted to dwell on how close Seton Hall came, Greene preferred to think about how far the Pirates had come. "A lot of people don't have anything like this," he said as he looked at his ring. "This is something I'm going to remember. I've been here. I've played here. We were in the Final Four."

Runners-up

1985: Baseball owners and players agreed to expand the post-season championship series in each league from a best-of-five-game format to a best-of-seven. The following fall, the St. Louis Cardinals defeated the Los Angeles Dodgers, four games to two, and the Kansas City Royals beat the Toronto Blue Jays, four games to three.

1995: With forward Ed O'Bannon scoring 30 points and pulling down 17 rebounds, the U.C.L.A. Bruins, coached by Jim Harrick, won their first N.C.A.A. title in 20 years, defeating Arkansas, 89–78, in the final at the Kingdome in Seattle.

1993: Sheryl Swoopes a 6-foot senior forward, scored 47 points, a championship game record for women and men, to lead Texas Tech University over Ohio State, 84–82, in the N.C.A.A. women's basketball final in Atlanta. Bill Walton of U.C.L.A. scored 44 points in the 1973 men's final against Memphis State (see March 26).

April 4, 1983
Desperation, Then Bedlam

By DAVE ANDERSON

ALBUQUERQUE, N.M. [Monday]—From the moment Jim Valvano watched Houston slam dunk Louisville, 94–81, in Saturday's semifinals of the national collegiate basketball tournament, the North Carolina State coach knew what his Wolfpack had to do in tonight's championship game against the Phi Slama Jama fraternity. "We've got to control the game and put ourselves in position to win the game," Jim Valvano said. "Going down the stretch, we want to have a chance to win the game."

Seldom has a coach been more prophetic about the "tempo" of a game. As the final seconds flashed away tonight, North Carolina State won the title, 54–52, when the sophomore forward Lorenzo Charles soared up to grab Derek Whittenburg's long one-hander that was short and to the right of the basket and jammed it down with only one second showing on the clock.

Not only had the Wolfpack been in position to win, but Jim Valvano had virtually predicted the score. "If the score is 100-to-something, we're not going to win the game," he said yesterday, "but if it's in the 50's..." As it developed, the score was in the 50's, and North Carolina State, which had a relatively mediocre 20–10 record until it swept to six tournament victories, again holds the national championship it won in 1974 with David Thompson as its jumping jack and Norm Sloan as its coach.

"It's a dream," Jim Valvano was saying now after the presentation ceremony.

N.C. State Coach Jim Valvano waving the net in triumph after his undersized Wolfpack squad shocked Houston in the N.C.A.A. championship game. Only moments earlier he was rushing around the court searching for someone to hug. (Associated Press)

"That's what I told the players at halftime, that they were 20 minutes away from the dream. I had the dream for 16 years as a coach, and they had it all their years in college."

But what is now a dream for North Carolina State will be a nightmare for Houston and its 61-year-old coach, Guy Lewis, who was unable to hold onto what he had called "the big carrot hanging out there on a stick." Going into the last three minutes, Houston had a 52–46 lead after Clyde Drexler made two foul shots in a one-and-one situation. But the Phi Slama Jama fraternity never scored again. Two of the Phi Slama Jama fraternity brothers, Michael Young and Alvin Franklin, were fouled and went to the line in a one-and-one situation. But each missed his first free throw. "The whole thing came down to what everybody had been predicting all year," Guy Lewis said later, "that we'd miss a couple of free throws at the end of the game and it would cost us, and that's exactly what happened."

Jim Valvano knew that for all their spectacular slam dunks, Houston had been less than spectacular from the foul line, shooting only 61 percent. "They're not a particularly good foul-shooting team," the Wolfpack coach said. "So we figured we'd try to make 'em beat us at the foul line if they could. As soon as Drexler made his two shots, I told my players not to foul him, so we fouled Young and Franklin, but not Drexler again. Not the guy who made 'em. Make sure it's somebody else. Put the pressure on somebody else, an old Italian trick my father taught me in high school."

"It feels awful," the 61-year-old Lewis said. "I've never lost a game that I didn't feel awful, but this one was terrible. But in basketball, you throw the ball up and you take your chances." That's exactly what happened when Derek Whittenburg threw the ball up and Lorenzo Charles stuffed it Phi Slama Jama's face.

Jim Valvano coached at North Carolina State from 1980 to 1990, when he resigned because of accusations that he was involved in recruiting violations. He died of cancer at age 47 in 1993.

Runners-up

1974: Henry Aaron of the Atlanta Braves tied Babe Ruth's record of 714 career home runs with a shot into the left-field stands off Cincinnati Reds right-hander Jack Billingham in the season opener at Riverfront Stadium in Cincinnati. Commissioner Bowie Kuhn had ruled that Aaron should play at Cincinnati, although Aaron and the team preferred that he tie and break the record (*see April 8*) in Atlanta.

1937: Byron Nelson of Fort Worth, Tex., made up six shots within two holes in the final round of the Masters to overtake Ralph Guldahl of Dallas and win by two strokes. Nelson played Nos. 12 and 13 in 2 and 3, respectively, while Guldahl scored 5 and 6 there. The bridge over Rae's Creek on No. 13 is now called the Nelson Bridge in honor of his feat.

1988: Danny Manning grabbed 18 rebounds and scored 31 points, including the last 4 points of the game from the free-throw line in the final seconds, as the University of Kansas, under Coach Larry Brown, upset Oklahoma, 83–79, for its second N.C.A.A. title. Its first came under Coach Phog Allen in 1952.

April 5, 1915
Race and the Ring

HAVANA (AP)—Jack Johnson, exile from his own country, today lost the heavyweight championship of the world to Jess Willard, the Kansas cowboy, the biggest man who ever entered the prize ring and a "White Hope" who at last has made good. The Negro was knocked out in the twenty-sixth round with a smashing swing to the point of the jaw.

For twenty rounds Johnson punched and pounded Willard at will, but his blows grew perceptibly less powerful as the fight progressed, until at last he seemed unable or unwilling to go on. Johnson stopped leading and for three or four rounds the battle was little more than a series of plastic poses of the white and black gladiators. So it was until the twenty-fifth round, when Willard got one of his wildly swinging windmill right-hand smashes to Johnson's heart. This was the beginning of the end.

When the round closed, Johnson sent word to his wife that he was all in, and told her to start for home. She was on the way out and was passing the ring in the twenty-sixth round when a cyclonic right to the jaw caused Johnson to crumple on the floor of the ring, where he lay, partly outside the ropes, until after the referee had counted ten and held up Willard's hand in token of the cowboy's newly won laurels.

Johnson was slow in responding to the gong for what proved to be the final round, while Willard seemed fresh. Willard delivered four blows in this round—a left to the face, a right to the stomach, a left to the body, and the final right swing to the jaw that stretched the Negro out for the count. Johnson seemed powerless to make any defense. He was shaky from the start of the round.

There is much discussion tonight as to whether Johnson really was knocked out. In the sense of being smashed into unconsciousness, he certainly was not put out. The consensus of opinion is that Johnson felt that there was no possibility of his winning and when knocked down chose to take the count rather than rise and stand further punishment. Johnson often has stated that fighting is a business, and that he would not foolishly submit to repeated knockdowns when he found he had met his master.

A second or two after Jack Welch, the referee, had counted ten Johnson quickly got up. A moment later a rush of spectators to the fighting platform all but smothered the pugilists. Some fifty or more of the several hundred soldiers stationed about the fight arena jumped into the ring and under escort of the soldiers Willard and Johnson went to their dressing rooms. Willard was escorted half way to the city from the Marianão race track, where the fight was held, by a troop of Cuban cavalry. Crowds lined the streets and narrow roadways, and the new white champion was loudly cheered. He was decidedly the favorite all through the fight and tonight is the hero of the island.

Jack Johnson won the heavyweight title in 1908 (see Dec. 26). He was controversial in that day for twice marrying white women, and in 1912 he was convicted of violating the Mann Act and sentenced to a year in prison for taking his wife across state lines. Free on appeal, he fled the country. He had defended his title three times abroad (see July 4) before losing to Jess Willard.

Jess Willard standing near the fallen Jack Johnson in the 26th round of their heavyweight title bout in Havana. Johnson, almost outside the ropes, appears to be shading his eyes from the sun as Referee Jack Welch counts him out. (Bettmann/Corbis)

Runners-up

1896: The first Olympic Games of the modern era were opened by King George of Greece in Athens. Baron Pierre de Coubertin of France, founder of the modern movement, saw his dream come true as 311 athletes from 14 nations assembled at the foot of the Acropolis. There were no gold medals; each winner received a silver medal and a crown of olive branches.

1984: Kareem Abdul-Jabbar of the Los Angeles Lakers broke Wilt Chamberlain's 11-year-old N.B.A. record of 31,419 career points when he poured in 22 against the Utah Jazz in Las Vegas. Jabbar, the extraordinary 7-foot-2-inch center, whose record still stands, retired with 38,387 points in 1988.

1993: Trailing by 73–71 with 11 seconds left in the N.C.A.A. title game in the Superdome at New Orleans, the University of Michigan's Chris Webber called a timeout his team didn't have. The Wolverines were assessed a technical foul because of the blunder, and North Carolina won its third national championship and second under Coach Dean Smith, 77–71.

April 6, 1958
A New Kind of Hero

[Unsigned, *The New York Times*]

AUGUSTA, Ga.—One of the game's young stars, Arnold Palmer, earned the Masters title today with a closing 73 at the Augusta National Golf Club. The husky 28-year-old athlete, who won the National Amateur crown in 1954 two months before he joined the pro ranks, finished with a total of 284. Then he waited two hours for assurance that victory was his. The pivotal hole for Palmer turned out to be the 475-yard, par-5 13th, where he turned in a prodigious 3 for an eagle. He walloped a No. 3 wood to the green over the meandering creek and sank a twenty-foot putt.

Ken Venturi of California, who was paired with Palmer, was still in contention at that point, but his putting difficulties at the fourteenth smashed his hopes. He missed two-footers at the fourteenth and fifteenth. When Doug Ford, the 1957 Masters winner, and Fred Hawkins, the slim star from El Paso, failed to bag birdies at the home green that would have forced a deadlock, Palmer was safely in.

The new Masters champion has nerves of steel. Appropriately enough he comes from the steel area of Latrobe, Pa. It was at Latrobe, where his dad, M.J. (Deacon) Palmer, is the professional at the Latrobe Country Club, that Arnold first saw a golf club. He began to swing one of the objects he saw in his dad's shop when he was about 8 years old. Arnold always was a sturdy youngster and took to the game readily. But the atmosphere of steel still marks his demeanor and style of play.

He worked during one Christmas vacation from Wake Forest College in the Latrobe steel mill. "But I was a bricklayer when I was there," Arnold said tonight, looking far from a millman in his natty green jacket, denoting that he was now a Masters champion. At 5 feet 11 inches the 180-pound Palmer has been a determined fellow most of his life. At least regarding golf, he has had a positive attitude. He has strict regulations, too, for his training as a player. He reports: "I never stay out late. I always try to get at least ten or eleven hours sleep."

Palmer, as one of the "young guard" in golf, has been highly successful since he became a professional in November of 1954. This afternoon he became the youngest winner (at 28) since Byron Nelson, then 24, triumphed in 1937. Palmer received a compliment before he started the last round. Said Ford, the runner-up, "If I don't win today, Palmer will. He's strong enough for this big course. He'll never tire. He's got a game like steel."

Partly because of his personal magnetism and partly because his rise coincided with that of national television, Arnold Palmer was largely responsible for turning golf into a mass spectator sport. He won 60 professional tournaments, including four Masters titles, two British Opens and one United States Open.

Arnold Palmer reacting to a birdie putt that refused to drop in the 1963 Cleveland Open. Palmer's ability, obvious after the '58 Masters, and transparent emotions made golf a TV sport and won him a legion of admirers called "Arnie's Army." (Associated Press)

Runners-up

1987: In one of the greatest comebacks in boxing history, Sugar Ray Leonard *(see Nov. 25)*, fighting for just the second time since retina surgery in 1982, scored a stunning victory by split decision to wrest the world middleweight title from Marvelous Marvin Hagler, who had held it for 11 years. Hagler retired to Italy after the bout.

1973: The American League launched its "experiment" with the designated hitter rule *(see Jan. 11)*. Ron Blomberg of the Yankees became the first DH when he drew a bases-loaded walk in the opening inning at Fenway Park in a 15–5 Red Sox victory.

1980: Gordie Howe's remarkable 26-year N.H.L. career *(see Nov. 27)* came to an end when at age 52 he played his last game for the Hartford Whalers and scored his 801st and final career goal against his former team, the Detroit Red Wings. Howe played in all 80 regular-season games this season.

April 7, 1935
The Shot of a Lifetime

AUGUSTA, Ga. (AP)—Gene Sarazen, long famous for his spectacular finishes, fired the golfing shot of a lifetime today to tie Craig Wood, the belting blond from Deal, N.J., for first place in the Augusta National Golf Club's $5,000 invitation tournament. Each finished the seventy-two holes in 282, six under par. Trailing Wood by two strokes in a seemingly hopeless pursuit, with only four holes to go and sub-par golf necessary to have a chance, Sarazen blasted a 220-yard spoon shot that carried true all the way and rolled into the cup for a 2 on the 485-yard par 5 fifteenth hole.

The astounding "double eagle," as rare as a hole in one, electrified a gallery of 2,000, pulled Sarazen up to even terms with Wood, who had bagged a birdie on the fifteenth, and enabled Gene to keep deadlocked with his rival by playing par golf over the last three holes in one of the most exciting finishes any tournament has seen in years.

Sarazen started the final round three shots behind Wood, who had taken over the pace-setting position yesterday, and made them all up by negotiating the rain-soaked course in near-freezing weather with a 70, two under par, while Wood was finishing with a 73. Gene scored successive rounds of 68, 71, 73, 70, while Craig produced scores of 69, 72, 68, 73 for a total of 282. A birdie 3 at the fourteenth, thanks to a twelve-foot putt, gave Wood a two-stroke margin and set the stage for the shot of the tournament on the fifteenth. Craig got his birdie 4 on this 485-yarder, with the aid of two fine shots to the green, but Gene hit the bull's-eye with his spoon second shot for the deuce that echoed over the rolling countryside in the gallery's wild shouts.

"What was your first thought when you saw the ball roll into the cup?" someone asked Gene. "I started figuring," he replied. "It was the greatest thrill I have ever had on a golf course. I realized all I needed was par to tie."

Sarazen was actually in front when he got the first of his pars, a 3 on the short sixteenth, where Craig three-putted, and still a stroke in front with a 4 at the seventeenth, matching Wood's performance. But Craig had dropped a 16-footer for a birdie 3 on the eighteenth to make the target tougher to find, and Gene was satisfied to get a final 4. They will play off for first-place money of $1,500 at thirty-six holes tomorrow, starting at 10 A.M. and 2:30 P.M., Eastern Standard Time.

Sarazen and Wood are well matched for the play-off. Both are terrific hitters. Gene is a more consistent iron player, especially with the niblick, but Wood has the edge on the greens, based on their performances so far. Sarazen hasn't won a big tournament since 1933, when he last captured the National P.G.A. championship, while Wood has never won a title event.

Gene Sarazen won the next day's 36-hole playoff, shooting 144 to Craig Wood's 149.

Gene Sarazen, right, waiting for his winning putt to drop at the end of a two-round playoff in the 1935 Masters at Augusta National. Sarazen holed a double eagle on No. 15 to tie Craig Wood, left, in the final round of regulation a day earlier. (Associated Press)

Runners-up

1943: Seeking to better protect its players, the N.F.L. made wearing helmets mandatory for the following season. The helmets were flimsy leather jobs at first, which would hardly have been sufficient for the vicious hits of today. In 1948, Fred Gehrke, a Los Angeles Rams running back, began painting rams' horns on the team's helmets for $1 apiece and team logos were born.

1928: With his goalie injured in Game 2 of the Stanley Cup finals, Coach Lester Patrick put on the pads himself and led the Rangers to a 2–1 victory over the Montreal Maroons at the Montreal Forum. The Rangers went on to win the N.H.L. title in five games.

1968: The Formula One star Jim Clark of Scotland, the Grand Prix world champion in 1963 and '65 and the Indianapolis 500 champion in '65, was killed in the Hockenheim Formula 2 race in West Germany when his Lotus-Ford left the track and crashed into a stand of trees. He was 32 years old.

April 8, 1974
All Hail Hank

By JOSEPH DURSO

ATLANTA—Henry Aaron ended the great chase tonight and passed Babe Ruth as the leading home-run hitter in baseball history as he hit No. 715 before a national television audience and 53,775 persons in Atlanta Stadium. The 40-year-old outfielder for the Atlanta Braves broke the record on his second time at bat, but on his first swing of a clamorous evening. It was a soaring drive in the fourth inning off Al Downing of the Los Angeles Dodgers, and it cleared the fence in left-center field, 385 feet from home plate.

Skyrockets arched over the jammed stadium in the rain as the man from Mobile trotted around the bases for the 715th time in a career that began a quarter of a century ago with the Indianapolis Clowns of the old Negro leagues. It was 9:07 o'clock, 39 years after Ruth had hit his 714th and four days after Aaron had hit his 714th on his first swing of the bat in the opening game of the season. The history-making home run carried into the Atlanta bull pen, where a relief pitcher named Tom House made a dazzling one-handed catch against the auxiliary scoreboard. He clutched it against the boards, far below the grandstand seats, where the customers in "Home Run Alley" were massed, waiting to retrieve a cowhide ball that in recent days had been valued as high as $25,000 on the auction market.

So Aaron ended the great home-run derby, but also ended the controversy that had surrounded it. His employers had wanted him to hit No. 715 in Atlanta, and had even benched him on alien soil in Cincinnati. The commissioner of baseball, Bowie Kuhn, ordered the Braves to start their star yesterday or face "serious penalties." And tonight the commissioner was missing, pleading that a "previous commitment" required his presence tomorrow in Cleveland. His emissary, Monte Irvin, the former star of the Negro leagues and the New York Giants, was roundly booed when he mentioned Kuhn's name.

The first time Aaron batted, leading off the second inning, he never got the bat off his shoulder. Downing, wearing No. 44, threw a ball and a called strike and then three more balls. Then came the fourth inning, with the Dodgers leading by 3–1 and the rain falling, with colored umbrellas raised in the stands and the crowd roaring every time Aaron appeared. Darrell Evans led off for Atlanta with a grounder behind second base that the shortstop, Bill Russell, juggled long enough for an error. And up came Henry for the eighth time this season and the second this evening.

Downing pitched ball one inside, and Aaron watched impassively. Then came the second pitch, and this time Henry took his first cut of the night. The ball rose high toward left-center as the crowd came to its feet shouting, and as it dropped over the inside fence separating the outfield from the bull pen area, the skyrockets were fired and the scoreboard lights flashed in six-foot numerals: "715." Aaron, head slightly bowed and elbows turned out, slowly circled the bases as the uproar grew. At second base he received a handshake from Dave Lopes of the Dodgers, and between second and third from Russell.

By now two young men from the seats had joined Aaron, but did not interfere

Henry Aaron tracking the flight of his record 715th home run, off Dodgers left-hander Al Downing in Atlanta. Aaron, proving it's all about the wrists, averaged nearly 33 homers a season for the Braves from 1954 to '76. (Associated Press)

with his 360-foot trip around the bases into the record books. As he neared home plate, the rest of the Atlanta team had already massed beyond it as a welcoming delegation. But Aaron's 65-year-old father, Herbert Aaron Sr., had jumped out of the family's special field-level box and outraced everybody to the man who had broken Babe Ruth's record.

Henry Aaron finished his career with 755 home runs in 1975 as a designated hitter for the Brewers of the American League. Milwaukee was where he began his major-league career and where he elected to end it.

Runners-up

1955: Cary Middlecoff made what is generally considered the longest pivotal putt in major tournament history, rolling an 82-foot eagle putt into the hole on No. 13 in the second round of the Masters at Augusta, Ga. The former dentist defeated Ben Hogan by seven strokes two days later.

2001: Tiger Woods won his second Masters title, defeating David Duval by two shots. The victory gave him a "Straight Slam"—the Masters, the U.S. Open, the British Open and the P.G.A. in succession, though not in a single year.

1987: Al Campanis, a Los Angeles Dodgers vice president, resigned under pressure after suggesting on Ted Koppel's "Nightline" news program that blacks "may not have some of the necessities" to be managers or hold executive positions in baseball. The remarks, on the eve of the 40th anniversary of Jackie Robinson's playing his first major league game, created a firestorm of criticism.

April 9, 1995
Honor Thy Mentor

By LARRY DORMAN

Ben Crenshaw wearing the customary green jacket of the new Masters champion. Playing with a heavy heart after the recent death of Harvey Penick, his mentor, Crenshaw kept his emotions in check and his game under control. (Associated Press)

AUGUSTA, Ga.—The most mystical Masters of all came to a fitting conclusion today when Ben Crenshaw put the last lesson to good use. He did exactly what his teacher, Harvey Penick, told him to do, just before he passed away at age 90 last week. He took dead aim, to use Penick's best-known phrase, and putted his way to victory. In a final round fraught with emotion and with the kind of breaks and bounces, good and bad, that Augusta National always provides, Crenshaw prevailed. He did it by making every big putt he had to make and by shooting a final-round 68 for a 14-under 274 to beat his friend David Love 3d, who shot 66, by one stroke.

Throughout the brilliantly lit, warm afternoon, Crenshaw, 43, fought to keep his emotions in check and his game under control. He did both, right up to the end. There were many taut moments, but from the time he took the lead with a birdie at the second hole, he never relinquished it. He had many opportunities to do just that, but something wouldn't allow it. And when the final putt fell at the 18th, putting an end to his arduous climb to his second Masters title, Crenshaw bent over at the waist and wept, his tears falling on the green and on his hat, which had tumbled from his head. His caddie, Carl Jackson, rushed over to embrace him, and there were tears in many eyes in the throng at the green that rose as one to cheer him.

"So many times here at Augusta, you feel blessed," Crenshaw said. "I felt that way this week. I had a 15th club in the bag this week. That was Harvey." It had been a trying week for Crenshaw, on and off the course. On Wednesday, he and Tom Kite flew to Austin, Tex., for Penick's funeral. Love, whose late father also was one of Penick's students and played for him at the University of Texas, was thinking about going, too, but Crenshaw called him to advise against it. Crenshaw told Love, who had to win the Freeport McMoRan Classic in New Orleans last week just to get into the Masters, that he should save his energy, that Mr. Penick would understand.

"That's the kind of guy Ben Crenshaw is," Love said after play was over, "and that's why I'm really happy for him." Crenshaw said: "When you're 43, you don't know how many chances you're going to get. It was like somebody put their hand on my shoulder this week and guided me through it. He was here with me. I could feel it." So could everyone else. It was meant to be.

Runners-up

1965: The first indoor baseball game between major league teams was played when the Yankees and Houston Astros opened the Astrodome, which some called the Eighth Wonder of the World, with an exhibition game. Mickey Mantle hit the first indoor home run, though it did not count in the records.

1947: Commissioner A.B. (Happy) Chandler suspended Brooklyn Dodgers Manager Leo Durocher for the season, citing "conduct detrimental to baseball" related to his association with gamblers. Brooklyn went on to win the pennant under Burt Shotton. Durocher returned to the Dodgers the following year but jumped to the rival New York Giants in midseason.

1974: A college student named Ted Giannoulas, who answered a radio station ad for someone to wear a chicken suit at a San Diego Padres game, skittered onto the field at Jack Murphy Stadium. Despite a public protest by Ray Kroc, the team's owner, the San Diego Chicken became an institution, and the age of major league mascots had dawned.

Of Skill and Courage

By LOUIS EFFRAT

NEW YORK [Thursday]—Jackie Robinson, 28-year-old infielder, today became the first Negro to achieve major-league baseball status in modern times. His contract was purchased from the Montreal Royals of the International League by the Dodgers and he will be in a Brooklyn uniform at Ebbets Field tomorrow, when the Brooks oppose the Yankees in the first of three exhibition games over the week-end.

A native of Georgia, Robinson won fame in baseball, football, basketball and track at the University of California at Los Angeles before entering the armed service as a private. He emerged a lieutenant in 1945 and in October of that year was signed to a Montreal contract. Robinson's performances in the International League, which he led in batting last season with an average of .349, prompted President Branch Rickey of the Dodgers to promote Jackie.

The decision was made while Robinson was playing first base for Montreal against the Dodgers at Ebbets Field. Jackie was blanked at the plate and contributed little to his team's 4–3 victory before 14,282 fans, but it was nevertheless a history-making day for the well-proportioned lad. Jackie had just popped into a double-play, attempting to bunt in the fifth inning, when Arthur Mann, assistant to Rickey, appeared in the press box. He handed out a brief, typed announcement: "The Brooklyn Dodgers today purchased the contract of Jackie Roosevelt Robinson from the Montreal Royals." Robinson will appear at the Brooklyn offices tomorrow morning to sign a contract. Rickey does not anticipate any difficulty over terms.

According to the records, the last

Jackie Robinson, left, and Dodgers president Branch Rickey putting the final touches on Robinson's 1950 contract in the team offices in Brooklyn. Three years earlier Robinson broke the color barrier, changing the face of baseball. (Associated Press)

Negro to play in the majors was one Moses Fleetwood Walker, who caught for Toledo of the American Association when that circuit enjoyed major-league classification back in 1884 [see May 1].

The call for Robinson was no surprise. Most baseball persons had been expecting it. After all, he had proved his right to the opportunity by his extraordinary work in the AAA minor league, where he stole 40 bases and was the best defensive second baseman. He sparked the Royals to the pennant and the team went on to annex the little world series.

Robinson's path in the immediate future may not be too smooth, however. He may run into antipathy from Southerners who form about 60 percent of the league's playing strength. In fact, it is rumored that a number of Dodgers expressed themselves unhappy at the possibility of having to play with Jackie. Robinson, himself, expects no trouble. He said he was "thrilled and it's what I've been waiting for." When his Montreal mates congratulated him and wished him luck, Robinson said: "Thanks, I'll need it." Rickey, in answer to a direct query, declared he did not expect trouble from other players because of Robinson. "We are all agreed," he said, "that Jackie is ready for the chance."

Jackie Robinson was chosen by Branch Rickey to break the color barrier because Rickey knew he had the strength of character, not just the talent, to overcome the taunts that would come. Robinson won the Rookie of the Year award in 1947 and helped lead the Dodgers to seven pennants in the 10 years he played for them. He was elected to the Hall of Fame in 1962.

Runners-up

1896: In Athens, Spiridon Louis, a Greek, won the first modern Olympic marathon gold medal in 2 hours 58 minutes 50 seconds. According to the historian David Wallechinsky, merchants showered Louis with gifts, including clothes, jewelry, wine and free haircuts.

1960: Arnold Palmer staged one of his patented major-tournament comebacks *(see June 18)*, scoring birdies on the 17th and 18th holes at Augusta National to beat Ken Venturi by one stroke and win his second Masters title.

1975: Lee Elder of Dallas became the first African-American to compete in the Masters after the Augusta National club changed its policies to allow all P.G.A. Tour winners of the previous year to qualify. Elder, aged 40, shot 74 and 78 in the first two rounds and missed the cut.

April 11, 1962
Those Lovable Losers

By LOUIS EFFRAT

ST. LOUIS—History was made tonight by the New York Mets. They broke into the expanded National League at long last, but wound up on the short end of an 11–4 score, beaten conclusively by the St. Louis Cardinals at Busch Stadium. In their first official effort, the Mets unfortunately did much to beat themselves. Despite the sixteen hits the Cardinals collected, four ineffective New York pitchers, backed by a loose defense, hurt the Mets immeasureably.

The season opener here before 16,147 half-frozen fans saw the Mets commit three errors and permit three stolen bases. Adding to manager Casey Stengel's miseries, Roger Craig, the starter and loser, committed a balk that led to one of two St. Louis runs in the first inning. Also, the Mets bounced into two double plays. Homers by Gil Hodges and Charlie Neal were wasted. Neal, who also drove in a run with a single in the third, singled in vain in the seventh. Larry Jackson permitted eight hits in all.

Yet, a misplay by Neal proved the crusher. The second-baseman's failure to field a grounder in the sixth opened the gates for four runs that wrapped up the decision. Three of the runs off Bob Moorhead, making his big-league debut, thus were unearned. There were some good plays by the Mets though. Gus Bell made three excellent throws from right field that eliminated three St. Louis runners. On one of the plays, Hobie Landrith's block and tag of Bill White at the plate was outstanding.

The 42-year-old Stan (The Man) Musial, starting his twenty-second season with the Redbirds, made two singles and a double, drove in two runs and scored one. His tally in the third was the 1,859th of his career, tying him with the late Mel Ott for the National League record. Hodges's homer was his 362d, moving him ahead of Joe DiMaggio and putting him eleventh among major-league home run hitters.

The New York Mets went 40–120 in 1962, finishing 60 1/2 games behind the pennant-winning San Francisco Giants and prompting Manager Casey Stengel to cry, "Can't anybody here play this game?" Seven years, Marv Throneberry and a thousand mistakes later, they were world champions (see Oct. 16).

National League baseball returns to New York after a four-year hiatus as the expansion Mets, losers of the franchise opener in St. Louis two days earlier, fall in an encore at the Polo Grounds. An amazin' 118 more losses followed. (The New York Times)

Runners-up

1965: Twenty-five-year-old Jack Nicklaus won his second Masters title in stunning fashion, scoring a 16-under-par 271 and defeating his closest rivals, Arnold Palmer and the South African Gary Player, by nine strokes. The 280 of Palmer and Player would have won all but five of the previous 28 Masters.

1907: New York Giants catcher Roger Bresnahan, his legs bruised by foul tips, wore a set of cricket leg pants against Philadelphia, becoming the first catcher to don shin guards. Despite one manager's complaint that they posed a danger to sliding runners, baseball owners approved them as standard issue.

1912: The New York Highlanders, who played at Hilltop Park in the Washington Heights section of Manhattan, high above the Hudson River, adopted pin-striped home uniforms. The Highlanders, who were moved to New York from Baltimore in 1903, were renamed the Yankees in 1913.

April 12, 1954
Two Giants at Work

By LINCOLN A. WERDEN

AUGUSTA, Ga.—Sam Snead beat the champion today to win the Masters golf title for the third time. In the eighteen-hole playoff, necessitated because he and Ben Hogan deadlocked after seventy-two holes at 289, Sam was the winner, 70 to 71. "Those two players are the two finest golfers in the world—and that is a statement you can prove," commented Bob Jones, president of the Augusta National Golf Club where the extra-round test decided the tourney's eighteenth winner.

Some 6,500 were in attendance on a warm, sunny day as Snead overcame a putting lapse that had marred his rounds during the tournament proper. The long-hitting White Sulphur Springs, W. Va., professional had thirty-two putts during the round. He didn't need any at the tenth, where he chipped in from the back of the green for a birdie 3. This shot of approximately sixty-five feet came at a crucial time. Hogan and Snead had played the first nine on an even basis, since both were out in 35, one under par. The spectacular chip put Snead ahead. Earlier, Hogan, seeking to retain his Masters crown, had taken the lead at the fourth where Snead three-putted. Then Sam drew even at the sixth where he dropped a seven-footer for a deuce.

Hogan came back, however, at the twelfth with a par 3, where a bogey by Snead made them all square in strokes once more. However, the thirteenth—the azalea hole—that had proved so vital throughout the first four rounds, once more became a turning point. Snead was able to bag a birdie 4 at the thirteenth, while Hogan, the British and United States Open champion, played safe and took a par 5. After Hogan used a No. 4 iron and played short of the creek on this 470-yard hole, Snead walloped a No. 2 iron that flew the ball over the ditch and onto the green. Sam's resulting birdie 4 to Ben's 5 gave him a lead he never relinquished. Three holes later, Hogan, regarded as one of the steadiest putters in the game, failed to sink a three-footer for a par 3.

Hogan was meeting Snead for the first time since the Los Angeles Open playoff of 1950, which was Ben's first tournament following his almost fatal automobile crash of 1949. Hogan today tried desperately to beat Snead. When he didn't, he smiled and said, "I met Sam in 1950 and the outcome was the same as it was today. I'm a little younger than Sam (Hogan and Snead were both born in 1912, but Hogan is three months younger) and if I keep trying, maybe I'm going to win against him."

Sam Snead teeing off during his 18-hole Masters playoff against Ben Hogan in Augusta, as Hogan, second from left in immediate background, watches. Snead won by a stroke for his third Masters title. (Associated Press)

Runners-up

1954: The Minneapolis Lakers, coached by Johnny Kundla and led by the 6-foot-10-inch center George Mikan, defeated the Syracuse Nationals, 87–80, in Game 7 of the N.B.A. finals to win their third straight league championship and fifth in six years.

1987: On the second hole of a three-way sudden-death playoff in the Masters, Larry Mize, a native of Augusta, chipped into the cup on the 11th hole for birdie from 140 feet away, defeating Greg Norman for the title. Seve Ballesteros had been eliminated the hole before.

1981: Joe Louis (see June 22), who held the heavyweight boxing title of the world for almost 12 years and the affection of the American public for most of his adult life, died of cardiac arrest at his home in Las Vegas. He was 66 years old.

Older, Bolder and Still Golden

By DAVE ANDERSON

AUGUSTA, Ga.—Even some golf people who cherished Jack Nicklaus thought he would never win another tournament, much less a Masters. At 46, he was simply too old. He couldn't make the short putts anymore. He wouldn't wear contact lenses. He didn't compete in enough tournaments, and when he did, he sometimes missed the cut. He was too busy designing golf courses instead of playing them. He was too involved with his Golden Bear Inc. business responsibilities.

But today Jack Nicklaus reminded the world he was still Jack Nicklaus, the best golfer in history. He shot 65 and put on the Masters green jacket for the sixth time. He turned Augusta National into a theater in the pines. He heard the cheers. He felt the tears. "Walking up the fairways on the last few holes, I had tears in my eyes four or five times, I just welled up," he later acknowledged, referring to the cheers that resounded with his every shot. "But then I told myself, 'Hey, you've got golf to play.'"

And play golf he did, as only he can, as only he has. In assessing the exalted in other sports, debates always develop. Pete Rose or Ty Cobb, Muhammad Ali or Joe Louis. Walter Payton or Jim Brown. John McEnroe or Bill Tilden. Wayne Gretzky or Gordie Howe. Larry Bird or Oscar Robertson. And in golf, a few old-timers still prefer Bobby Jones or Ben Hogan to any of the modern golfers with all their modern equipment. But now Jack Nicklaus has ended all the golf debates, if any still existed. Now he has won 20 major tournaments, a nice round number that in the decades to come no one is likely to approach.

To appreciate what Nicklaus has accomplished, consider that he won his six Masters titles over a span of 23 years. Consider that he won his 20 major titles over a span of more than a quarter of a century, beginning with the 1959 and 1961 United States Amateurs and extending through a record-sharing four United States Opens, three British Opens, five Professional Golfers Association championships and now the six Masters green jackets, two more than Arnold Palmer, the king he dethroned two decades ago.

Back then Nicklaus was resented by the Masters galleries who adored Palmer, but today many of those same people cheered him, lived him, wept with him. "On the 17th tee, I was standing over my ball when I heard this large roar," he would recall. "Ballesteros had hit his ball in the water on 15, but I didn't know that at the time. It was a funny sound. It wasn't a sound of cheers, but yet it was a sound of cheers. As soon as I hit my tee shot, everybody told me Ballesteros was in the water."

Minutes later, another roar erupted on the 17th green. Nicklaus had holed an 11-foot birdie putt to take the lead. At the start of the round, he had been four strokes behind Greg Norman, and as he played the ninth hole, he had been four strokes behind Seve Ballesteros. But now he was leading. And when he parred the 18th hole after a 40-foot uphill putt to within 4 inches of the cup, his 279 total would win by one stroke.

Jack Nicklaus taking the Masters lead with a birdie putt on the 17th hole at Augusta National. Aged 46, he scored a tournament-record 30 on the back nine to finish with a 65, capturing his sixth and most satisfying Masters. (Associated Press)

Runners-up

1997: Tiger Woods *(see Feb. 7)*, 21, became the youngest golfer in history to win the Masters. He did so with the lowest score—18-under-par 270—in the 61-year history of the event, and his margin of victory, 12 strokes, was the widest of any major championship ever held in the United States.

1957: The Boston Celtics, led by two rookies, Tom Heinsohn, with 37 points, and Bill Russell, with 32, won their first N.B.A. title by defeating the St. Louis Hawks in double overtime, 125–123, in Game 7 of the finals at Boston Garden.

1984: Pete Rose of the Montreal Expos doubled to right field against the Philadelphia Phillies' Jerry Koosman at Olympic Stadium in Montreal for the 4,000th hit of his remarkable career. Only Rose, who retired with 4,256 hits, and Ty Cobb, with 4,191, have reached the 4,000 mark.

Their Cup Runneth Over

TORONTO (UPI)—Led by Jean Beliveau, the Montreal Canadiens swept to their fifth consecutive Stanley Cup tonight with a 4–0 triumph over the Toronto Maple Leafs. This was the first time that any National Hockey League team had won the cup five times in a row. Beliveau, a center, scored twice. Henri (Pocket Rocket) Richard and Doug Harvey counted one apiece as the Canadiens completed a four-game sweep. The Flying Frenchmen also needed only four games to knock off the Chicago Black Hawks in the semi-final round of cup play.

The 1951–52 Detroit Red Wings were the only other squad to win the cup in eight games since the league was founded forty-two years ago. Immediately following the game, the league president, Clarence Campbell, handed the cup to the Montreal captain, Maurice (Rocket) Richard.

The Canadiens dominated the action despite the Leafs' frantic efforts to make a contest of it. As they had in the three previous games, the Habs skated to a quick lead and then coasted. Bernie (Boom Boom) Geoffrion did not score, but the Montreal right winger collected three assists to tie a teammate, Henri Richard, and Red Kelly of Toronto in the race for the individual point title.

Montreal wheeled in front to stay in the first period, scoring twice on long screened shots from the points. Beliveau clicked at 8:16, with Junior Langlois and Geoffrion assisting. Then at 8:45, Harvey drove home a long shot that Toronto's goalie, Johnny Bower, could not see. Again, Langlois and Geoffrion assisted.

The Leafs had three great chances in the middle period; Dickie Duff picked a

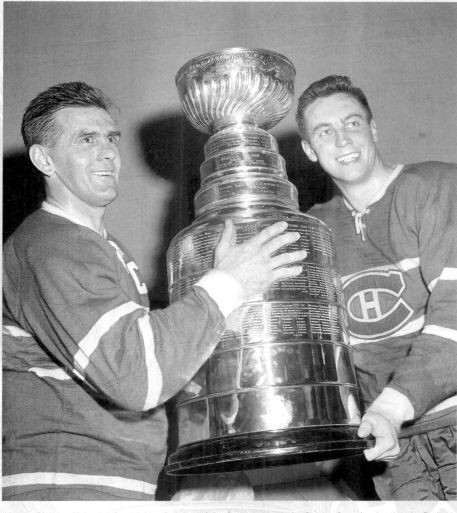

Déjà vu: Maurice Richard, left, and Jean Beliveau of the Canadiens with the Stanley Cup after beating the Bruins in 1958. Beliveau played on 10 Cup-winning teams and Richard was a force on eight during the team's dynasty years. (Associated Press)

post and Carl Brewer hit the crossbar behind Jacques Plante, the Montreal goalie. But it was the Canadiens who scored. The Pocket Rocket took the Rocket's pass, worked in close and fooled Bower. The final period was less than two minutes old when Montreal made it 4–0 on Beliveau's second counter of the game. The husky center took a relay from Geoffrion and Marcel Bonin to beat Bower

with an angled shot from 20 feet out.

The Montreal Canadiens, one of the original four teams in the N.H.L.'s first season, 1917–18, have won 23 Stanley Cup titles. Besides the five straight from 1956 to '60, the Canadiens won four consecutive titles in 1976–79 (see May 21). The Toronto Maple Leafs are the next most successful Cup team with 13 championships, though none since 1967.

Runners-up

1996: Greg Norman, leading the Masters by six strokes at the start of the final round, suffered perhaps the most humiliating collapse in major golf tournament history. He splashed his tee shot into Rae's Creek at No. 12, then fell like a rock before a national television audience, surrendering shot after shot to finish 12 strokes behind the winner, Nick Faldo of Britain.

1968: Roberto de Vicenzo, having apparently shot a 65 in the final round of the Masters to tie Bob Goalby, signed a scorecard filled out by his playing partner that mistakenly gave him a 4 on No. 17 instead of a birdie 3. The error cost

de Vicenzo possible victory in a playoff. The incorrect scorecard he signed became official and Goalby was declared the winner.

1910: President William Howard Taft threw out the first ball while attending the Washington Senators' home opener against the Philadelphia Athletics at American League Park in Washington, beginning a tradition always observed in the capital and frequently observed in nearby Baltimore to this day. The Senators, behind their ace, Walter Johnson, won by 3–0.

April 15, 1965
'Havlicek Stole the Ball!'

By GORDON S. WHITE Jr.

BOSTON—The Boston Celtics, forced tonight to put on one of their strongest battles in years, just managed to beat the Philadelphia 76ers, 110–109, and win the Eastern Division championship of the National Basketball Association for the ninth straight season. There was nothing easy to the triumph before the 13,909 fans who filled the Boston Garden for the seventh and deciding game of the playoff finals. Each team botched up a routine toss-in from out of bounds during the last five seconds of play. The failure by the 76ers was the more costly of the bad plays.

As a result, Coach Red Auerbach's Celtics will be going after their seventh consecutive league title when they meet the Los Angeles Lakers in the N.B.A. final playoffs here.

It was a wild finish tonight. With the score at 110–107 and the Celtics apparently assured of victory—only five seconds remained—Wilt Chamberlain easily made a layup as all the Celtics stepped out of his way to make sure they didn't foul the big man. This made the count 110–109, Boston. Then Bill Russell tossed the ball inbounds over Chamberlain's outstretched hands. But the ball hit the guidewire supporting the backboard and the 76ers were given the ball out of bounds. Now they had one last chance for a winning shot. Hal Greer

John Havlicek (17) during the N.B.A. playoffs in 1974. Relying on guile and agility, he was a member of eight championship Celtic teams. His defensive tenacity led, appropriately, to his legacy — a clutch steal to win the Eastern Division title in '65. (Associated Press)

stepped out of bounds and tossed in toward Chet Walker 30 feet away. John Havlicek of the Celtics rushed between Walker and the ball, slapped it down, took it over and the crowd went wild. Havlicek tossed the ball high in the air, and the Celtics were carried off along with Auerbach on the shoulders of happy fans storming the court. Boston had won the series, 4 games to 3.

It was a particularly sad moment for Chamberlain, the league's leading scorer, who has failed to pace a team to an N.B.A. title in six great years of professional basketball. He worked hard tonight, possibly harder than he did in any of the three victories the 76ers gained in this series. Sam Jones, the fancy shooter from outside, made 37 points. Havlicek, the Buckeye from Ohio State, got 26 and that important steal late in the game. Chamberlain managed to get 32 rebounds to 29 for Russell tonight, but Russell was credited with a most unusual nine assists. Chamberlain made 30 points, Russell 15.

The raspy radio call "Havlicek stole the ball! Havlicek stole the ball!" by the Boston Celtics' announcer Johnny Most became one of the most famous sports broadcasts of all time. The Celtics went on to defeat the Lakers and win their seventh of eight consecutive titles.

Runners-up

1947: Having signed a major league contract with the Brooklyn Dodgers within the week *(see April 10)* with the team's president, Branch Rickey, looking over his shoulder, Jackie Robinson played first base for the team in the season opener against the Boston Braves at Ebbets Field. He went 0 for 3 before a crowd of 25,623.

1985: Marvelous Marvin Hagler retained his world middleweight title in an unusually fierce fight against Thomas Hearns in Las Vegas. Hardly a second passed that

one of the boxers wasn't landing a stunning blow. Hagler, his face bloodied, was awarded a technical K.O. over the wobbling Hearns at 2:01 of Round 3.

1958: The first regular-season major league game was played on the West Coast when the San Francisco Giants defeated the Los Angeles Dodgers, 8–0, at Seals Stadium, the downtown minor-league field the Giants used until they moved to windy Candlestick Park in 1960.

April 16, 1940
An Opening Day Jewel

Bob Feller of the Indians working against the Boston Braves in the 1948 World Series. The Nolan Ryan of his day, Feller threw three no-hitters but lost almost four years of his prime in World War II. (Associated Press)

CHICAGO (AP)—Bob Feller of the Indians carved a niche for himself in baseball's hall of fame as the American League season opened today, pitching an amazing no-hit game to defeat the White Sox, 1 to 0, before 14,000 roaring fans. It was the first opening day no-hit contest in modern major-league history. It ended after 2 hours and 24 minutes of play as Ray Mack, Cleveland second sacker, made a great knockdown of Taft Wright's grounder and tossed him out at first by a step.

Feller, who struck out eight batsmen and walked five, earned the decision on two timely Indian safeties in the fourth inning. Jeff Heath singled to left with one out, and after Ken Keltner had flied out, Heath scored on a triple to right by Feller's catcher and friend, Rollie Hemsley. It was Feller's first no-hitter, although he has had three one-hit performances in his brilliant major league career. The 21-year-old star won twenty-four games last season.

The White Sox, even though they enjoyed six-hit pitching by the southpaw Edgar Smith, threatened seriously only once. In the second they had the bases filled with two out. Feller, using his blazing fast ball, then struck out rookie Bob Kennedy. Feller, who put on his great show before his parents, Mr. and Mrs. William Feller, and his sister, Marguerite, retired fifteen men in a row from the fourth inning through the eighth.

He got the first two men in the ninth easily, but Luke Appling, White Sox shortstop, gave him and the cheering fans several anxious moments. Appling drove four foul smashes to right before drawing a walk on the tenth pitch. Then Mack made his fine play on Wright's drive on the ground. The ball was to Mack's left and the infielder, with a fine stab, knocked it to the ground, picked up the rolling ball and shot it to First Baseman Hal Trotsky for the putout.

Bob Feller pitched three no-hitters and 12 one-hitters in an 18-year major-league career. He won 266 games and led the American League seven straight years in strikeouts while with the Indians. But he lost nearly four full seasons at the peak of his career while earning eight battle stars in World War II as an antiaircraft gunner aboard the battleship Alabama.

Runners-up

1952: Sugar Ray Robinson of Detroit came off the canvas in the third round and knocked out Rocky Graziano of New York City moments later in their world middleweight title fight at Chicago Stadium. Graziano fought once more and retired with a record of 67–10–6, including 52 knockouts.

1999: Wayne Gretzky, widely recognized as the greatest player in the history of hockey *(see Feb. 24),* announced his retirement from the Rangers. He played 21 years, one season in the World Hockey Association, the others in the N.H.L., and changed the way the game was played with his passing, vision and scoring skills.

1983: Steve Garvey of the San Diego Padres played in his 1,118th consecutive major league game, breaking the National League record held by Billy Williams of the Chicago Cubs. Garvey, who played most of his career with the Los Angeles Dodgers, extended the record to 1,207 games before retiring in 1987.

April 17, 1953
Tale of the Tape Measure

By LOUIS EFFRAT

Mickey Mantle of the Yankees being greeted by Yogi Berra after his 565-foot home run, the longest on record, at Griffith Stadium in Washington. A boy in a backyard showed an official where the ball landed. (Associated Press)

WASHINGTON—Unless and until contrary evidence is presented, recognition for the longest ball ever hit by anyone except Babe Ruth in the history of major league baseball belongs to Mickey Mantle of the Yankees. The 21-year-old athlete today walloped one over the fifty-five-foot high left-field wall at Griffith Stadium. That ball, scuffed in two spots, finally stopped in the backyard of a house, about 565 feet away from home plate.

This remarkable homer, which helped the Yankees register a 7–3 victory over the Senators, was Mickey's first of the season, but he will have to go some, as will any-

one else, to match it. Chuck Stobbs, the Nat southpaw, had just walked Yogi Berra after two out in the fifth, when Mantle strode to the plate. Batting right-handed, Mickey blasted the ball toward left center, where the base of the front bleachers wall is 391 feet from the plate. The distance to the back of the wall is sixty-nine feet more and then the back wall is fifty feet high. Atop that wall is a football scoreboard. The ball struck about five feet above the end of the wall, caromed off the right and flew out of sight. There was no telling how much farther it would have flown had the football board not been there.

Before Mantle, who had cleared the right-field roof while batting left-handed in an exhibition game at Pittsburgh last week (only Babe Ruth and Ted Beard had ever done that), had completed running out the two-run homer, Arthur Patterson of the Yankees' front-office staff was on his way to investigate the measure. Patterson returned with the following news: A 10-year-old lad had picked up the ball. He directed Patterson to the back-yard of 434 Oakdale Street and pointed to the place where he had found it, across the street from the park. The boy, Donald Dunaway of 343 Elm Street N.W., accepted an undisclosed sum of money for the prize, which was turned over to Mantle. The Yankee was to send a substitute ball, suitably autographed, to the boy.

Until today, when Mantle made it more or less easy for Lefty Ed Lopat to gain his first triumph, no other batter had cleared the left-field wall here. Some years ago, Joe DiMaggio bounced a ball over, but Mickey's accomplishment was on the fly. It is true that a strong wind might have helped Mantle, but if the A.A.U. will not recognize the homer, all of baseball will.

Runners-up

1963: Paul Hornung (see Dec. 12), the former Heisman Trophy winner and Green Bay Packers star, and Alex Karras, a Pro Bowl tackle for the Detroit Lions, were suspended from the N.F.L. by Commissioner Pete Rozelle for betting on N.F.L. games. Both sat out a full season before being reinstated. Both later became TV commentators, with Karras appearing on "Monday Night Football" from 1974 to '76.

1972: The Boston Marathon acknowledged women's competition for the first time in its 76-year history. Women had run in the race before, but their times and ranking had not been listed separately. Nina Kuscsik of Huntington, N.Y., became the first official women's winner, though she had run there three times before.

1976: Mike Schmidt of the Philadelphia Phillies became the 10th major leaguer to hit four home runs in a game. All the shots, at Wrigley Field, were consecutive as the Phillies overcame a 13–2 deficit to beat the Chicago Cubs, 18–16, in 10 innings.

April 18, 1923
And the Bronx Cheered

[Unsigned, *The New York Times*]

NEW YORK—Governors, generals, colonels, politicians and baseball officials gathered together solemnly today to dedicate the biggest stadium in baseball, but it was a ball player who did the real dedicating. In the third inning, with two teammates on the base lines, Babe Ruth smashed a savage home run into the right-field bleachers, and that was the real baptism of the new Yankee Stadium. That also won the game for the Yankees, and all the ceremony which had gone before was only a trifling preliminary.

The greatest crowd that ever saw a baseball game sat and stood in this biggest of all baseball stadia. Inside the grounds, by official count, were 74,200 people. Outside the park, flattened against doors that had long since closed, were 25,000 more fans, who finally turned around and went home, convinced that baseball parks are not nearly as large as they should be. The dream of a 100,000 crowd at a baseball game could easily have been realized today if the Yankee Colonels had only piled more concrete on concrete, more steel on steel, and thus provided the necessary space for the overflow. In the face of this tremendous outpouring all baseball attendance records went down with a dull thud. Back in 1916, at a world's series game in Boston, some 42,000 were present, and wise men marveled. But there were that many people in the Yankee Stadium by 2 o'clock today, and when the gates were finally closed to all but ticket holders at 3 o'clock the Boston record had been exceeded by more than 30,000.

It was an opening game without a flaw. The Yankees easily defeated the Boston Red Sox, 4 to 1. Bob Shawkey, war veteran and oldest Yankee player in point of service, pitched the finest game of his career, letting the Boston batters down with three scattered hits. The Yankees raised their American League championship emblem to the top of the flagpole—the chief feature of an opening-day program that went off perfectly. Governor "Al" Smith, throwing out the first ball of

Yankee Stadium on the day it opened in 1923. Cars had easy parking, 74,200 fans packed themselves inside and John Phillip Sousa and the Seventh Regiment Band raised the Stars and Stripes in deep center field. (Bettmann/Corbis)

the season, tossed it straight into Wally Schang's glove, thus setting another record. The weather was favorable and the big crowd was handled flawlessly.

Only one more thing was in demand, and Babe Ruth supplied that. The big slugger is a keen student of the dramatic, in addition to being the greatest home run hitter. He was playing a new role today—

not the accustomed one of a renowned slugger, but that of a penitent, trying to "come back" after a poor season and a poorer World's Series. Before the game he said that he would give a year of his life if he could hit a home run in his first game in the new stadium. The Babe was on trial, and he knew it better than anybody else.

He could hardly have picked a better time and place for the drive that he hammered into the bleachers in the third inning. The Yankees had just broken a scoreless tie by pushing Shawkey over the plate with one run. Witt was on third base, Dugan on first, when Ruth appeared at the plate to face Howard Ehmke, the Boston pitcher. Ruth worked the count to two and two, and then Ehmke tried to fool him with one of those slow balls that the Giants used successfully in the last world's series.

The ball came in slowly, but it went out quite rapidly, rising on a line and then dipping suddenly from the force behind it. It struck well inside the foul line, eight or ten rows above the low railing in front of the bleachers, and as Ruth circled the bases he received probably the greatest ovation of his career. The biggest crowd in baseball history rose to its feet and let loose the biggest shout in baseball history. Ruth, jogging over the home plate, grinned broadly, lifted his cap at arm's length and waved it at the multitude.

Runners-up

1962: The Boston Celtics, coached by Red Auerbach, won a then-record fourth straight N.B.A. title, defeating the Los Angeles Lakers, 110–107, in Game 7 of the finals behind a 44-rebound, 30-point performance by Bill Russell. The mark of three straight championships had been held by the 1952–54 Minneapolis Lakers.

1995: Joe Montana, arguably the finest quarterback in N.F.L. history *(see Jan. 10)*, retired at age 38 at a ceremony attended by 20,000 people in San Francisco.

He played 16 pro seasons, all but two of them with the 49ers, and left with four Super Bowl championship rings.

1942: The Toronto Maple Leafs, coached by Hap Day and led by goaltender Turk Broda, completed the greatest comeback in N.H.L. finals history, rebounding from a 3–0 series deficit and winning the Stanley Cup by defeating the Red Wings, 3–1, in Game 7 at Maple Leaf Gardens.

April 19, 1987
The Seventh, Eighth and Deciding Game

By ROBIN FINN

LANDOVER, Md. (Sunday)—It was hockey, but as the skaters skimmed slowly into quadruple overtime, the scene resembled the gradual disintegration of a marathon dance contest. The pace slowed, and the progression up and down the ice toward goals that suddenly loomed imposing as brick walls looked almost surreal. Even the ice seemed to respire, as if in weariness, and long glaring puddles formed at random on its surface.

This was hockey history, a classic game of two perfectly matched and equally unyielding opponents. Each came so close to reading each other's mind that their duel took on epic proportions. In fact, its resolution required all of Saturday night and a portion of this morning as the Islanders and the Washington Capitals laid siege to each other's goal. It ended, finally, in the steamy Capital Centre nearly seven hours after the game began. The Islanders beat the Capitals, 3–2, in the fourth overtime period in the seventh and deciding game of their opening-round playoff series.

"It didn't feel real anymore," said Pat LaFontaine, who scored the winning goal at 8 minutes 47 seconds of the fourth overtime, "and for the longest time it felt like no one was going to score." The same players who spent a prolonged evening immersed in the rigorous and ritual hitting, bumping, grinding and grabbing that are synonymous for body contact in their sport virtually collapsed in one another's arms when it was over. By then, the fifth longest game in National Hockey League history—the longest since Toronto defeated Detroit, 3–2, at 10:18 of the fourth overtime in a 1943 semifinal—no longer felt like a game.

The standard 60 minutes of hockey, in which the go-ahead goals by Washington's Mike Gartner and Grant Martin were countered by goals from Patrick Flatley and Bryan Trottier, seemed part of the distant past. As the overtime persisted and last night became this morning, only the moment mattered, and time seemed to slow. The skaters battled to survive each shift, abbreviated to 20 seconds instead of the normal one to two minutes, the goalies to somehow prod their bodies to block the next shot.

The face of Kelly Hrudey, the Islander goalie who made 73 saves, was mottled by the rash that signals heat prostration. Inside the players' gloves, their hands began to blister. All the participants figured their exertions had cost them 10 pounds each in fluid loss. "This feels like surviving a war and living to tell about it," Flatley said. "When it got to the third overtime and they played the theme from 'Twilight Zone,' I felt like taking a bow. That's the place we all were by then."

Islanders swarming Pat LaFontaine, hidden from view, after his goal in the fourth overtime period beat the Capitals in Game 7 of their playoff series. "It didn't feel real anymore," he said of the epic game. (Bruce Bennett Studios)

Runners-up

1998: Michael Jordan scored 44 points to lead the Chicago Bulls over the Knicks, 111–109, in the final game of the regular season, securing his record 10th N.B.A. scoring title with a 28.7 points-per-game average.

1897: The first Boston Marathon, with all of 15 participants, was held between Ashland, Mass., and Copley Square in downtown Boston. The racecourse has changed significantly over the years. John J. McDermott of New York was the winner in 2 hours 55 minutes 10 seconds.

1981: The longest pro baseball game ever played, between Pawtucket (R.I.) and Rochester of the International League, was suspended after 32 innings, 8 hours and 7 minutes with the score tied, 2–2, at 4:07 A.M. The future Hall of Famers Cal Ripken Jr. of Rochester and Wade Boggs of Pawtucket played in the game. Two months later Pawtucket won in the 33rd inning.

April 20, 1986
Not Quite Ready for Prime Time

By SAM GOLDAPER

BOSTON—Michael Jordan came, he scored but he did not conquer. The Chicago Bulls' exciting point guard scored a playoff-record 63 points today, 2 more than the mark set by Elgin Baylor of the Los Angeles Lakers on April 14, 1962, against the Celtics in the championship series. But the heroics of Jordan, who played 53 of the 58 minutes of today's double-overtime game, hitting 22 of 41 shots from the field, weren't enough.

The Celtics survived with a 135–131 victory at the Boston Garden that gave them a 2–0 advantage in their opening round three-of-five-game series. Today's game took 3 hours 5 minutes to play. It was a physical encounter, in which 66 fouls sent the two teams to the free-throw line for a total of 88 shots. Jordan made 19 of his 21 attempts. The game also produced an unlikely hero, the Celtics' Jerry Sichting, whose basket won the game. Sichting's clincher came while Bill Walton, who had 15 rebounds, and Dennis Johnson, who had been guarding Jordan, were on the bench with six fouls each.

With the Celtics enjoying a 116–113 advantage on a Kevin McHale layup with 48 seconds left in regulation, Charles Oakley, the Bulls' rookie, cut Boston's lead to 2 points 14 seconds later by hitting on one of two free throws. Then with nine seconds remaining and the Celtics seemingly headed to victory, Jordan stole the ball from center Robert Parish.

After a Bulls timeout, John Paxon inbounded the ball to Jordan, who launched a 3-point attempt that hit the iron and bounced off as the buzzer sounded. Just as the noisy, partisan crowd of 14,890 was claiming victory, Ed Middleton, one of the three officials, called a pushing foul against McHale.

After several minutes of loud booing from the fans had subsided, Jordan calmly hit both free throws, his 53rd and 54th points of the game.

Larry Bird called the performance by Jordan, who missed 64 games during the regular season because of a broken foot, "probably one of the greatest in the Boston Garden, on national TV and in the playoffs." Jordan's play was different and far more dramatic than the 49 points he had scored in the series opener. In that game, he seemed to try to do it all alone and tired after a 30-point first half. Today, most everything he did came within the flow of the game. When asked about the record, he said: "Forget the record. I'd give all the points back if we could win."

Michael Jordan, left, after forcing a first-round playoff game against the Celtics into overtime. He scored 63 points but lost and would have to wait five more years before carrying the Bulls to the N.B.A. title. (Associated Press)

Runners-up

1912: Five days after the sinking of the Titanic, the Boston Red Sox played their season opener at new Fenway Park, defeating the New York Highlanders (soon to be renamed the Yankees), 7–6, in extra innings. The Sox had moved from the Huntington Avenue Grounds, now part of the Northeastern University campus.

1916: After playing at the West Side Grounds for a number of years, the Chicago Cubs defeated the Cincinnati Reds, 7–6, in their opening game at new Weeghman Park, named after their new owner Charles Weeghman, formerly of the Federal League (see Dec. 22). In 1926 the park was renamed Wrigley Field, after William Wrigley, the chewing gum magnate who bought the team in 1919.

1993: Commodore Explorer, an 85-foot French catamaran skippered by Bruno Peyron of France, won the Jules Verne Trophy by breaking the 80-day round-the-world sailing barrier in 79 days 6 hours 16 minutes. He started at Lizard Point on the southwestern coast of England, sailed via the Cape of Good Hope, Cape Leewin and Cape Horn and docked at Ushant, France.

April 21, 1980
Who Is Rosie Ruiz?

By NEIL AMDUR

Rosie Ruiz being crowned the women's champion of the Boston Marathon by Massachusetts Gov. Edward J. King, at left. The laurel wreath upon her head quickly turned to ashes. (Associated Press)

BOSTON—Exclaiming "today my body was whipped," Bill Rodgers became the first runner in 56 years to capture three consecutive Boston Marathon titles when he won with a time of 2 hours 12 minutes 11 seconds. But while Rodgers's fourth Boston crown over all was expected in the field of 5,364 starters, the 84th race produced a stunning development when an unheralded 26-year-old runner from New York City, Rosie Ruiz, crossed the finish line ahead of 448 other women entries.

Running in only her second marathon and unnoticed by rival women, race statisticians or television cameras for almost all of the 26-mile-385-yard race, Miss Ruiz, wearing No. W50, staggered past the tape at the Prudential Center in 2:31.56. Her time was 147th over all and third-fastest in a marathon by a woman, surpassed only by the 2:27.33 turned in by Grete Waitz of Norway in last year's New York Marathon, and the 2:32.23 by Joan Benoit earlier this year.

Miss Ruiz, an administrative assistant for Metal Trading Inc. in Manhattan, received the traditional laurel wreath, a medal and a silver bowl for her victory. But as late as three hours after she had been interviewed by newsmen and photographed with Rodgers, Will Cloney, the race director, acknowledged that "there is an obvious problem with the determination of the women's winner." Cloney said officials of the sponsoring Boston Athletic Association would study a videotape of the race. But pinpointing Miss Ruiz's exact position may be impossible because only the first 100 runners were timed at each of the six official checkpoints and none were women.

Later this evening, during an interview in her hotel room, Miss Ruiz, noticeably shaken by the unexpected attention thrust upon her, insisted: "I ran the race. I really did."

"It is kind of hard to figure out," she had said after the race of her dramatic improvement of 25 minutes since her first marathon in New York last October. "When I got up this morning, I had so much energy." Miss Ruiz said she was prepared to take a lie-detector test. "I would take anything," she said. "I don't want to cause a commotion," she added, noting that her short hair and tall frame might have caused her to be mistaken for a male runner during the race. "I feel bad because I ran the race. I guess it all boils down to just not being known."

After marathon officials reviewed photographs and conducted interviews, Rosie Ruiz was stripped of the women's title on April 29 for entering the race near the end. Jacqueline Gareau of Canada was declared the winner.

Runners-up

1995: The Boston Celtics played their final regular-season game at Boston Garden, their home since 1946. Soon afterward, the Garden was razed and replaced by the Fleet Center next door. The Garden's famous parquet floor was used there until 1999, when it was replaced by a replica.

1935: First baseman Lou Gehrig was named captain of the New York Yankees, one of the few teams in the major leagues that have resorted to the custom. Following his death in 1941, the Yankees went without a captain until catcher Thurman Munson was given the title in 1976.

1951: The New York Knickerbockers lost the decisive Game 7 of the N.B.A. finals to the Rochester Royals, 79–75, at Rochester when Royals guard Bob Davies sank two free throws for the winning points. The Royals, led by Davies and Arnie Risen, won the first three games; the Knicks won three straight behind Vince Boryla and Harry Gallatin to force a Game 7.

April 22, 1954
The Clock Starts Ticking

By CHARLES PAIKERT

Danny Biasone, inventor of the 24-second shot-clock rule, in 1992. Biasone, who owned the Syracuse Nationals of the N.B.A. in the 50's, came up with the idea to speed up the game — and unknowingly may have saved it. (Associated Press)

The N.B.A. on this date adopted the 24-second shot clock, ushering in the modern era of pro basketball. The game radically changed when the season began the following October (see Oct. 30) as players forced the ball downcourt, concentrating on speed and offense. The rule was championed by Danny Biasone, owner of the Syracuse Nationals, then one of the league's nine teams. The following article appeared in The Times *on Oct. 30, 1984.*

NEW YORK—As the National Basketball Association games get under way this season, short, bald, 75-year-old Danny Biasone will be watching as many of them as he can on a battered television that's stuck inside the tiny, cramped office of his bowling alley in Eastwood, a blue-collar neighborhood in Syracuse. Surrounded by faded black-and-white team pictures of his old N.B.A. team, the Syracuse Nationals, Biasone will put his feet on his desk and hope the Philadelphia 76ers are on, because that's the team the Nats became when he sold them in 1963.

For Biasone, and for the N.B.A., this season will have a special meaning. It's the 30th anniversary of the year that Danny Biasone saved professional basketball, when he came up with the idea of the 24-second clock. The clock, and the speed, high scores and excitement that it generates, is taken for granted by today's fan, but it wasn't always so.

By the end of the 1953–54 season, a plague was infesting the N.B.A. Slow, boring, foul-riddled, low-scoring games became commonplace as teams sat on the ball. Such talented guards as Bob Cousy would, if their team had a lead in the fourth quarter, simply kill time by dribbling in the backcourt until they were fouled. It was not uncommon for at least five minutes to pass without a shot being taken from the field.

The solution, Danny Biasone was convinced, was a limit on the time each team had to shoot. "So I went to those fellas in the league and said I'm having a tough time selling something here," he recalled. "There's one thing basketball needs, I said. It needs a time. I don't care what the time is. Put in a time!"

On April 22, 1954, at the N.B.A.'s annual owners' meeting in New York, Biasone proposed a rule that would force each team to take a shot within 24 seconds of gaining possession. Why 24 seconds? "I figured out we were averaging about 60 shots a game per team," he said. "Twenty-four fits into the sixty, so if each team used up 24 seconds for a shot, they would average 60 shots. But the exact number wasn't important. My idea was to keep the game going, to speed it up."

Biasone was not a millionaire from a large city. He was, in fact, an Italian immigrant who owned a bowling alley and restaurant in Syracuse and had somehow acquired a franchise in the old N.B.L. [the National Basketball League, which merged with the Basketball Association of America in 1949 to become the N.B.A.] for $1,000.

When the Rochester Royals played the Boston Celtics to open the season on Oct. 30, the 24-second clock was an official N.B.A. rule. These days, "the most important man in the N.B.A." still goes into the bowling alley he has owned for forty years, the Eastwood Sports Center, every day. He still plays golf, he's still a "sports nut," and he still wishes he was in pro basketball. Although he has received a "special citation," he is not, shamefully, an official member of basketball's Hall of Fame.

Runners-up

1970: Tom Seaver of the Mets pitched himself into the record books by striking out 19 San Diego Padres—including the last 10 batters in a row—in a two-hit 2–1 victory at Shea Stadium. The performance tied the major league mark set by Steve Carlton of the St. Louis Cardinals in 1969 (*see Sept. 15*). Roger Clemens of the Boston Red Sox broke the record with 20 strikeouts in 1986 (*see April 29*).

1947: Joe Fulks scored 34 points to lead the Philadelphia Warriors over the Chicago Stags, 83–80, for the first Basketball Association of America title. The B.A.A. merged with the National Basketball League to become the N.B.A. in 1949.

1876: The first official National League baseball game was played, with the visiting Boston Red Stockings defeating the Philadelphia Athletics, 6–5, with two runs in the ninth inning. Boston's Jim O'Rourke got the first N.L. hit and Joe Borden became the league's first winning pitcher.

April 23, 1950
Basketball's First Dynasty

MINNEAPOLIS (AP)—Mr. Basketball—George Mikan of the Minneapolis Lakers—tonight paced his team to a 110–95 victory over Syracuse and the National Basketball Association championship. The Lakers took the best-of-seven series, 4–2. Mikan registered 40 points in leading the Lakers, hitting on thirteen field goals and sinking fourteen fouls.

Three fights spiced the game, which marked the third consecutive league championship for the Lakers. Police, in fact, had to interrupt a first-quarter set-to between Paul Seymour of Syracuse and Jim Pollard of Minneapolis. Billy Gabor of Syracuse and Swede Carlson also tangled, and Gabor also took on Slater Martin of the Lakers in the wild second period. Player-coach Al Cervi was banished from the game midway in the third quarter when he complained too loudly at a foul.

Minneapolis lost four players on fouls after it had extended its margin to 81–56 at the three-quarter mark. The Lakers were able to score their 100th point with three minutes to go in the game, marking the eighth time of the year they had reached the century mark. A crowd of 9,812, largest ever to see a pro basketball game in Minneapolis, saw the contest.

This was the first championship of the new N.B.A., which had been formed out of the demise of old National Basketball League. The N.B.L. folded when George Mikan and the Lakers left it after the 1947–48 season to join the stronger Basketball Association of America, which then renamed itself the N.B.A.

George Mikan (99) of the Minneapolis Lakers blocking a shot by the Harlem Globetrotters' Sweetwater Clifton in an exhibition game at Chicago in 1949. Two years later the N.B.A. paid Mikan, its first big man, unique homage: it widened the lane from 6 feet to 12 to keep him farther from the basket. (Associated Press)

Runners-up

1950: The Rangers, forced to play two "home" games of the finals at Olympia Stadium in Detroit because the circus was booked at Madison Square Garden, lost the Stanley Cup series to the Red Wings in a 4–3 double-overtime defeat in Game 7 at the Olympia.

1989: Kareem Abdul-Jabbar of the Los Angeles Lakers, the all-time N.B.A. scoring leader, played his final game against the Seattle SuperSonics at the Forum in Inglewood, Calif. It was his 1,560th league game, and he scored 10 points in a 121–117 victory. His teammates gave him a white Rolls-Royce.

1991: Christophe Auguin, a 31-year-old yachtsman from France, won the 27,000-mile BOC solo race around the world aboard the 60-foot sailboat Groupe Sceta. His victory capped a race marked by icebergs, whales, capsizings and even a suicide. The race took eight months; Auguin's chief rival, Alain Gautier, stalled just 212 miles from the finish.

April 24, 1963
What a Way to Go!

By ARTHUR DALEY

LOS ANGELES—The buzzer sounded and Bob Cousy flung the ball skyward in sheer exultation. He was entitled to the gesture. A glorious career on the court had reached a glorious end. With a farewell performance of supreme virtuosity Cooz the Magnificent had led his Boston Celtics to their fifth straight championship of the National Basketball Association. Thus did the Celtic captain complete his playing days on the triumphant note he deserved, still a champion among champions.

In a game against the Los Angeles Lakers that ended early this morning on television screens along the Eastern Seaboard, the Celtics defeated their foes, 112 to 109, in an electrifying contest of high dramatic content. The star of the production, naturally, was Cooz. The doddering ancient of 34 was bidding adieu to professional basketball to become the coach next season at Boston College. But in typical Cousy fashion he was able to reach back to his youth for another of his masterly clutch efforts.

It was a thrill to watch this artist make so blazing a departure and yet it brought with it jumbled emotions, an inescapable feeling of sadness. It was like watching Ted Williams hit his farewell home run, the sense of loss one experiences with the realization that we may never see his like again. Cooz was extra special. He was a little guy in a big man's sport and he inexorably cut down the giants to his size. There is an overwhelming tendency to regard him as the greatest of all basketball players. Maybe he was. At least he was not far from it.

The Holy Cross alumnus retired after 13 years of superlative effort. If this caused any erosion of his talents, it was not evident the final night. Cooz was always something of a breathtaking operative and again he had the fans gasping. He was comparatively new to the Angelenos and yet they recognized that he was the Houdini of the dribble art. He moved in from the start and took charge. He triggered the fast break. He found openings where no openings existed and threaded them with his passes. He surreptitiously handed off underneath like a three-card monte artist. He dribbled in and out like a minnow flashing among salmon.

Although there is no recollection of him dribbling behind his back in this game, he can do that without breaking stride. When he was forced to do so, he shot and picked up 18 points. But it was his quarterbacking that left the strongest impression. Basketball just isn't going to be the same without Cooz.

Bob Cousy, left, hugging Bill Russell after the Celtics defeated the Lakers for their fifth straight N.B.A. championship. Cousy, the supreme playmaker of his era, had said his 13th season would be his last. (Associated Press)

Runners-up

1967: The Philadelphia 76ers, led by Wilt Chamberlain, became the first team other than the Celtics to win the N.B.A. title since 1958 when they defeated the San Francisco Warriors, 125–122, in Game 7 of the finals at San Francisco's Cow Palace. Coached by Alex Hannum, the Sixers had a 68–13 regular-season record, best at the time in league history.

1945: A.B. (Happy) Chandler, a United States senator from Kentucky, was appointed baseball's second commissioner after the death of Judge Kenesaw Mountain Landis (see Nov. 12). Chandler played an instrumental role in Jackie Robinson's breaking the color line with the Brooklyn Dodgers in 1947 (see April 10).

1901: The first official game of the American League, organized and promoted by the former sportswriter Ban Johnson as a rival to the established National League (see Nov. 21), was played. The Chicago White Stockings defeated the Cleveland Blues, 8–2, before a crowd of more than 10,000 in Chicago.

April 25, 1995
The Man in the Yellow Blazer

By ROBERT McG. THOMAS Jr.

NEW YORK—Howard Cosell, who delighted and infuriated listeners during a 30-year career as the nation's best-known and most outspoken sports broadcaster, died today at the Hospital for Joint Diseases in Manhattan. He was 77. Mr. Cosell, who had been in failing health, died of a heart embolism, said his grandson, Justin Cohane. He had undergone surgery in June 1991 for the removal of a cancerous chest tumor.

From his first days on radio in the 1950's to the peak of his fame during his 14 years on "Monday Night Football," Cosell—once simultaneously voted the most popular and the most disliked sportscaster in America—tended to be loved and loathed for the same undisputed characteristics: his cocksure manner and his ebullient, unqualified immodesty. "Arrogant, pompous, obnoxious, vain, cruel, verbose, a showoff," Cosell once said. "I have been called all of these. Of course, I am."

Partly because he entered sports broadcasting in the mid-1950's, when the predominant style was unabashed adulation, Mr. Cosell offered a brassy counterpoint that was first ridiculed, then copied until it became the dominant note of sports broadcasting. "I tell it like it is," was the way he put it in a signature remark that was often challenged but never to the point where Cosell would back down. When the tape of a football game established that Cosell had referred to a black player as "that little monkey," Cosell, whose civil rights credentials were secure in any event, simply denied it. And if there were those who were shocked when he likened the autocratic International Olympic Committee chairman Avery Brundage to "William of

Howard Cosell, right, with Roone Arledge in a scene from a 1974 episode of "The Odd Couple." Arledge, the executive producer of ABC Sports, gave Cosell a career platform on "Monday Night Football." (ABC)

Orange" or offended when he suggested that most baseball players were "afflicted with tobacco-chewing mind," their complaints were music to Mr. Cosell's ears.

Mr. Cosell owed his position on "Monday Night Football" to his outspoken ways. Roone Arledge, the ABC executive who hired him in 1969, had made it a point that his broadcasters on his new program would be independent of the National Football League. Hiring Mr. Cosell drove the point home. To Mr. Cosell, criticism was another form of homage. If the criticism came from other broadcasters, he always considered the source: "There's one thing about this business," he once said, "there is no place for talent. That's why I don't belong. I lack mediocrity."

He spoke in a clutched-throat, high-pitched Brooklyn twang with a stately staccato that tended to put equal stress on each syllable of every word, infusing even

the most mundane event with high drama.

Howard William Cohen was born on March 25, 1918, in Winston-Salem, N.C., to Isadore and Nellie Cohen. His father, an accountant for a chain of clothing stores, eventually moved the family to Brooklyn, where Mr. Cosell played varsity basketball at Alexander Hamilton High School before attending New York University. During his college years he changed his name to Cosell, which gave rise to a famous put-down later: "Howard Cosell, a man who changed his name, wears a toupee and tells it like it is."

Mr. Cosell had so little vanity that he used to hang his toupee on a hatrack when he was off camera. But he was stung by the implication he changed his name from Cohen to disguise his Jewish heritage. He chose Cosell, he said, because it was close to the original spelling of his family's Polish name.

Runners-up

1976: Chicago Cubs outfielder Rick Monday became a national hero of sorts—and received a bicentennial commendation from President Gerald Ford—when he rescued an American flag that two protesters were attempting to burn in center field at Dodger Stadium in Los Angeles.

1974: The N.F.L. both popularized its product for television and "lengthened" the playing field by adopting two rule changes: It allowed for a 15-minute sudden-death overtime period in regular-season games and moved the goal posts to

the back of the end zones instead of over the goal lines, thereby making boring field goal attempts more difficult.

1964: The Toronto Maple Leafs, coached by Punch Imlach and led by Dave Keon, defeated the Detroit Red Wings, 4–0, in Game 7 of the finals at Maple Leaf Gardens to win their third straight Stanley Cup title. Toronto's Johnny Bower had 33 saves. The Maple Leafs also won three consecutive championships in 1947–49.

April 26, 1952
'I Wouldn't Sell This Putter'

RICHMOND, Calif. (UP)—Patty Berg of Minneapolis set a world record for women golfers today as she toured the Richmond Country Club in 30, 34–64. Playing from the regulation tees on the 6,339-yard course in the $3,000 Richmond Open, Miss Berg posted ten birdies and had two bogeys. Par for the course is 35, 37–72. Women's par is 36, 39–75. The former world record was 66 and was shared by Mrs. Babe Didrikson Zaharias and Opal Hill.

Miss Berg's key to success was a brand-new hammerhead putter, which she bought yesterday from the host professional, Pat Markovich. She took only eleven putts on the first nine holes for her five-under-par 30. On the return journey she had four birdies and one bogey, the latter coming when she three-putted from thirty feet away. She sank a 31-footer on the sixteenth for a birdie; she had a 25-footer on the sixth, a 15-footer on the ninth, and a 12-footer on the eighteenth. "It was the greatest round of golf I have ever played," Miss Berg said. "I wouldn't sell this putter for $100."

The stocky, redheaded star, now playing out of St. Andrews, Ill., said her game had improved "a lot" in the past month. "I'm hitting the ball twenty yards farther off the tee since taking some lessons this spring from Sam Snead," she said. "Now if this new putter continues to be as hot, everything should be all right."

Miss Berg was playing with young Marlene Bauer, who was overshadowed despite the fact she broke men's par also with a 71. That was the course record for women until Patty dropped her final putt for the gallery of 500 fans. Miss Berg not only set a world record for women and a new course record for women, but she also tied the men's record on this course set by E.J. (Dutch) Harrison four years ago.

Patty Berg was the winner of the first United States Women's Open in 1946 (see Sept. 1). Although she retired in 1980, she remains the all-time women's leader in major titles won with 16. She was a founder of the Ladies Professional Golf Association, or L.P.G.A., and served as its president from 1949 to '52.

Patty Berg in an undated photo at a tournament in Chicago. Berg was not only a brilliant golfer, but her willingness to ply the back roads for modest purses also helped open the door for women in sports. (Associated Press)

Runners-up

1999: Underlining the influence of money in sports, a group headed by Daniel Snyder, a young communications company owner, paid $800 million to buy the Redskins from the estate of Jack Kent Cooke. The price tag was by far the largest for a franchise in sports history.

1984: The New Jersey Nets, led by Buck Williams and Micheal Ray Richardson, stunned the defending N.B.A. champion Philadelphia 76ers in the first round of the playoffs, winning decisive Game 5, 101–98. It was the highest the star-crossed team rose in the post-season until they lost to the Los Angeles Lakers in the 2002 finals.

1988: After 45 years of frustration in their division playoffs and 18 straight post-season series losses, the Boston Bruins, led by Steve Kasper and coached by Terry O'Reilly, defeated the Canadiens in Game 5 at the Montreal Forum to win the Adams Division finals. The Bruins were later swept by the Edmonton Oilers in the Stanley Cup finals.

April 27, 1956
The Undefeated Champion

By WILLIAM R. CONKLIN

NEW YORK—Rocky Marciano, iron-fisted son of a New England shoe factory worker, retired today as undefeated world heavyweight boxing champion at the age of 31 to devote more time to his family.

The comeback trail, Marciano said, will never feel the weight of his feet so long as his present prosperity continues. To a boxing world that has seen numerous retirements-followed-by-comebacks,

Marciano said: "I thought it was a mistake when Joe Louis tried a comeback. No man can say what he will do in the future. But, barring poverty, the ring has seen the last of me. I am comfortably fixed, and I am not afraid of the future. Barring a complete and dire emergency, you will never see Rocky Marciano make a comeback."

Nicknamed "The Brockton Blockbuster" after his hometown of Brockton,

Mass., the black-maned Rocky will be 32 on Sept. 1. He broke into professional boxing on Feb. 21, 1947, with a three-round knockout victory. In a string of forty-nine fights he has been all-victorious. He has forty-three knockouts and six decisions to his credit. He has worn the heavyweight crown since he defeated Jersey Joe Walcott by a knockout in the thirteenth round in Philadelphia on Sept. 23, 1952.

Rocky, born Rocco Marchegiano, remembers the first Walcott fight as the toughest contest. "The first Walcott fight had to the toughest," he recalled in a Hotel Shelton press conference. "I was knocked down, bleeding and really hurt." In the second Walcott fight in Chicago on May 15, 1953, Rocky won by a first-round knockout. Earlier, he had blasted Louis' comeback hopes by knocking out the former champion in eight rounds in New York Oct. 26, 1951. "I didn't get hurt physically while fighting," Rocky said. "My physical condition has nothing to do with my retirement. My lonesome family convinced me that I should quit while I'm still in good shape."

One of the greatest take-a-punch artists in the ring, Marciano was sometimes criticized by boxing writers as awkward and inept. No one, however, minimized his aggressiveness and courage.

Rocky Marciano, born Rocco Francis Marchegiano, retired with unofficial career winnings of $1.7 million—a hefty sum for the era in which he fought. He was killed in 1969 when the small plane in which he was riding crashed in Newton, Iowa, near Des Moines. In 1985 Larry Holmes came within one victory of equaling Marciano's undefeated heavyweight record.

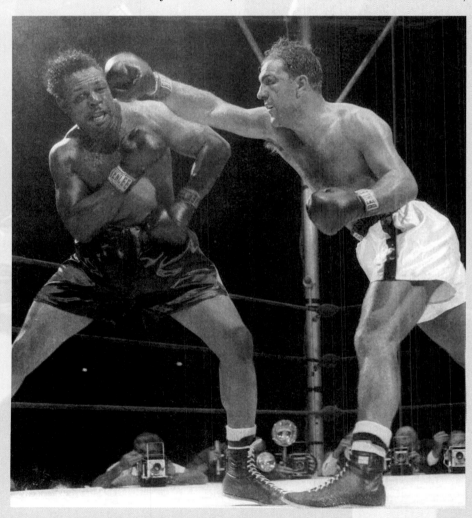

Rocky Marciano setting up Archie Moore, left, for a wicked left hook that instantly ended their September 1955 title fight in the ninth round at Yankee Stadium. It proved to be Marciano's farewell. (Associated Press)

Runners-up

1981: The rookie left-hander Fernando Valenzuela of the Los Angeles Dodgers became a national sensation almost overnight by pitching his fourth shutout of the young season, 5–0, over the San Francisco Giants and lowering his earned run average to 0.20. Valenzuela, whose listed age was 20, went on to help lead the Dodgers to the world championship over the Yankees.

1983: Nolan Ryan (*see May 1*) of the Houston Astros fanned Brad Mills of the Montreal Expos at Olympic Stadium in Quebec for his 3,509th career

strikeout, passing Walter Johnson for first place on the all-time list. Ryan retired in 1993 with 5,714 strikeouts.

1960: Two years after the Los Angeles Dodgers and San Francisco Giants successfully brought major league baseball to the West Coast, the N.B.A. voted to allow the Minneapolis Lakers to move to Los Angeles, where there were few lakes but millions of potential fans

April 28, 1967
Politics Wins in the Ring

By ROBERT LIPSYTE

HOUSTON—Cassius Clay refused today, as expected, to take the one step forward that would have constituted induction into the armed forces. There was no immediate Government action. Although Government authorities here foresaw several months of preliminary moves before Clay would be arrested and charged with a felony, boxing organizations instantly stripped the 25-year-old fighter of his world heavyweight championship.

"It will take at least 30 days for Clay to be indicted and it probably will be another year and a half before he could be sent to prison since there undoubtedly will be appeals through the courts," United States Attorney Morton Susman said. Clay, in a statement, distributed a few minutes after the announcement of his refusal, said: "I have searched my conscience and I find I cannot be true to my belief in my religion by accepting such a call."

Clay has maintained throughout recent unsuccessful civil litigation that he is entitled to draft exemption as an appointed minister of the Lost-Found Nation of Islam, the so-called Black Muslim sect. Clay, who prefers his Muslim name of Muhammad Ali, anticipated the moves against his title in his statement, calling them a "continuation of the same artificially induced prejudice and discrimination" that had led to the defeat of his various suits and appeals in Federal courts, including the Supreme Court.

Hayden C. Covington of New York, Clay's lawyer, said that further civil action to stay criminal proceedings would be initiated. If convicted of refusal to submit to induction, Clay is subject to a maximum sentence of five years imprisonment and a $10,000 fine. Mr. Covington, who has defended many Jehovah's Witnesses in similar cases, has repeatedly told Clay during the last few days, "You'll be unhappy in the fiery furnace of criminal proceedings, but you'll come out unsinged."

As a plaintiff in civil action, the Negro fighter has touched on such politically and socially explosive areas as alleged racial imbalance on local Texas draft boards, alleged discriminatory action by the Government in response to public pressure, and the rights of a minority religion to appoint clergymen. As a prospective defendant in criminal proceedings, Clay is expected to attempt to establish that "preaching and teaching" the tenets of the Muslims is a full-time occupation and that boxing is the "avocation" that financially supports his unpaid ministerial duties.

Cassius Clay, who changed his name to Muhammad Ali in 1965, was convicted of draft evasion in June and sentenced to five years in prison and a $10,000 fine. The United States Supreme Court overturned the verdict, 8–0, with Justice Thurgood Marshall abstaining, in 1971. Ali by then was back in the ring, having knocked out Jerry Quarry in 1970.

Cassius Clay being escorted by authorities in Houston after refusing to be inducted into the Army. Clay was a recent convert to Islam. He said, "I cannot be true to my belief in my religion by accepting such a call." (Associated Press)

Runners-up

1966: Coach Red Auerbach's Boston Celtics, led by Bill Russell, Sam Jones and John Havlicek on offense and by Tom Sanders and Don Nelson on defense, won a record eighth straight N.B.A. title, defeating the Los Angeles Lakers and Elgin Baylor in seven games. The closest any teams have come to the mark are three straight titles by the Chicago Bulls (1991–93 and 1996–98) and the Lakers (2000–2002).

1961: Warren Spahn, 40, pitched his second career no-hitter and 52nd shutout as the Milwaukee Braves beat the San Francisco Giants, 1–0. He retired in 1965 with 365 victories, most ever by a left-hander, and 63 shutouts. Only Eddie Plank of the Philadelphia Athletics, who pitched in the dead-ball era, when shutouts were common, had more from the left side, 69.

1988: The Baltimore Orioles' record at the start of the season reached 0–21, a fitting standard for futility, in a 4–2 loss to the Minnesota Twins at the Metrodome. The defeat was the 15th straight for Manager Frank Robinson after he replaced Cal Ripken Sr. six games into the season.

Flame Thrower for a New Era

By IRA BERKOW

BOSTON (AP)—Roger Clemens of the Red Sox set a major league record tonight by striking out 20 batters in a 3–1 victory over the Seattle Mariners. Clemens broke the nine-inning record of 19 strikeouts set by Steve Carlton for the St. Louis Cardinals in 1969, and equaled by Tom Seaver for the Mets in 1970 and Nolan Ryan for the California Angels in 1974.

The following article, by Mr. Berkow, appeared in The Times *on May 1.*

BOSTON—At first, only the catcher's mitt was loud. Roger Clemens began cracking his swift fastball and cunning curves into Rich Gedman's thick glove, and the Seattle batters swung and missed and swung and missed. Clemens struck out the side in the first inning, and quickly the fans on this cool New England night perked up. "It was a small crowd," Clemens would recall, "but it was a noisy one." And, as the game proceeded, every time he got two strikes on a batter, most of the crowd of 13,414 in Fenway Park Tuesday night was screaming.

"I wasn't sure what they were screaming about," Clemens said, "until Nip came over to me." He meant Al Nipper, also a pitcher for the Red Sox. "He said, 'Man, Rocket, you got a chance for an all-time record.'" It was the bottom of the eighth,

Roger Clemens posing with the game ball the day after his 20-strikeout performance. "I was challenging them," he said. "I was throwing the ball right down the heart of the plate." (Associated Press)

and Nipper had just seen the Fenway Park scoreboard flash the information that Clemens had 18 strikeouts, and was 2 short of breaking the major-league record.

The fans were on their feet and stayed that way throughout the ninth. Clemens struck out Spike Owens, swinging, to tie the record, and then got Phil Bradley, looking, for No. 20. "I was pitching on adrenaline all the time," said Clemens, "and challenging them. I was throwing the ball right down the heart of the plate." When the third baseman, Wade Boggs, came over to him after the Bradley strikeout and shook his hand, Clemens thought, "Hey, the game is over!"

Not yet. Ken Phelps, the next batter, was intent on not striking out for the fourth time in the game, and he succeeded. But all he could do was hit a ball weakly to the shortstop for the final out. "It just didn't sink it, what it all meant," said Clemens. "But my teammates were all excited, and when I got home I got calls from a lot of my family. And my brothers were crying, and my mother was crying, and they said, 'You're in the Hall of Fame.' Well, I didn't sleep a wink last night. I'm not a drinking man, but I think I should have had a few beers to relax me. I tried counting sheep, I tried everything."

While still a member of the Red Sox, Roger Clemens struck out 20 for a second time at age 34 in September 1996 in a 4–0 victory over the Tigers in Detroit. He entered the home ninth with 19 strikeouts and got Travis Fryman swinging for the final out.

Runners-up

1961: ABC's "Wide World of Sports," an anthology show produced by Roone Arledge, made its debut on national television with Jim McKay as host. The program, which covered such fare as auto racing in Monte Carlo and cliff diving in Acapulco, whetted Americans' tastes for nontraditional sports and also helped popularize the Olympics in the United States.

1970: Jerry West of the Los Angeles Lakers sank a 63-foot shot with one second left to tie the score against the Knicks in Game 3 of the N.B.A. finals in California,

but the Knicks won in overtime to take a two-games-to-one lead in the best-of-seven-game series. The Knicks won the title in seven games *(see May 8).*

1981: Steve Carlton *(see Sept. 15)* of the Philadelphia Phillies became the first left-hander to strike out 3,000 batters in his career when he fanned nine Montreal Expos in a 6–2 victory. He retired in 1988 with 4,136 strikeouts and ranks second on the all-time list. The left-hander Randy Johnson of the Arizona Diamondbacks had 3,746 strikeouts through 2002.

Knifed at Center Court

By IAN THOMSEN, Special to *The New York Times*

Monica Seles being aided by attendants after she was stabbed in the back by a fan during a changeover in a match at Hamburg, Germany. It took her two years to regain top form. (Associated Press)

Monica Seles, the world's No. 1 women's tennis player (see June 6), *was attacked by an assailant on this date as she sat with her back to the grandstand during a changeover in a tournament in Germany. The following article appeared in* The Times *on May 2.*

HAMBURG, Germany—This morning Monica Seles greeted Steffi Graf—the sad, solitary idol of her assailant. They did not know what to say to each other. "I said to her how I felt, how it also hurt me in a way," Graf recalled quietly. "We both could hardly speak. I don't want to say we were moved, we *were* moved, but we both were feeling what had happened very much in the moment. I told her that I was very sorry and that we are all thinking about her. She is very depressed. It came back to her more this morning than last night."

A hospital report said "the psychological condition of the patient has been attacked."

A 38-year-old German lathe operator told police he stabbed Seles, the world's No. 1 tennis player, in the back during her match Friday so that Graf, the current No. 2, could surpass her in the rankings. Identified by the police only as Gunter P.,

from the eastern German state of Thuringia, he said he had been planning his attack for some time before stalking Seles all week at the $375,000 Citizen Cup here.

The attacker walked to the bottom row of the grandstand, in front of where Seles sat during a changeover in her quarterfinal against Magdalena Maleeva. From behind her he turned suddenly and pulled a serrated steak knife with a 12-centimeter blade from a bag hidden under his clothing. Leaning over a short spectators' fence, he stabbed Seles once between the shoulder blades. She suffered a wound about one-half inch deep. He was apprehended by a security guard and two spectators.

"He said about his motive that he is a fan of Steffi Graf and he could not bear Monica Seles being the momentary No. 1 in the world," a police spokesman said. "He said several times that he did not plan to kill Monica Seles, he only wanted to make her unable to continue playing." Seles was expected to spend tonight at University Hospital. It was not known when she would leave the hospital or return to tennis. She is expected to miss the French Open, where she is a three-time defending champion. Most threatening to her, though, might be the psychological effect of being attacked on the court.

Monica Seles did not return to competition until August 1995. She never regained the No. 1 ranking and won only one more major tournament, the Australian Open in 1996. Her assailant, Günter Parche, was convicted of inflicting "grievous bodily harm," but a judge ruled him emotionally retarded and he served no time in prison.

Runners-up

1971: The Milwaukee Bucks, led by Oscar Robertson and the 24-year-old Lew Alcindor and coached by Larry Costello, swept the Baltimore Bullets in the N.B.A. finals, winning Game 4, 118–106, at the Baltimore Civic Center. The "Big O," in his 11th pro season, scored 30 points and had 9 assists.

1961: Using Joey Amalfitano's bat, Willie Mays of the San Francisco Giants became the ninth player in history to hit four home runs in a game as San Francisco routed the Braves, 14–4, at Milwaukee County Stadium.

1994: Bruce Baumgartner of Edinboro, Pa., the most decorated American wrestler in history, won his 15th national heavyweight title at the United States championships in Las Vegas. He went on to collect 17 national freestyle championships, including 14 in a row from 1983 to '96.

MAY

May 1, 1991
The Ageless Wonder

By JACK CURRY

Nolan Ryan, the biggest star in Texas, waves to the Arlington Stadium crowd after pitching the seventh no-hitter of his career, three more than any other pitcher. He was 44 at the time, and worked out on a bicycle immediately afterward. (Associated Press)

Nolan Ryan of the Texas Rangers pitched his seventh and final no-hitter on this date. The following article appeared in The Times *two days later.*

NEW YORK—He is John Wayne with a baseball cap. He is Betty Grable with a magnificent arm. Because he throws the ball so hard and has done it for 25 years, Nolan Ryan makes people stop what they are doing and watch him. And baseball fans, it seems, can never get enough of this wondrous 44-year-old pitcher.

On an evening when the Texas Rangers right-hander upstaged even Rickey Henderson's base-stealing heroics with a record seventh no-hitter, Ryan's nationally televised exploits heightened his stature to almost mythic proportions. They are already naming a portion of Route 288 near his hometown, Alvin, Tex., "The Nolan Ryan Expressway." After another no-hitter, maybe they will rename the town.

"No contest, it's Ryan," said Frank Robinson, a former teammate of Ryan and the manager of the Baltimore Orioles, when asked what was the bigger baseball story on a historic Wednesday in May. "The thing that I admire most is that he's a complete pitcher, 150 percent better than he was at any other time in his career. Hitters go up there, now, with hardly a chance."

Dozens of Texas Ranger fans belatedly raced to Arlington Stadium after Ryan held the Toronto Blue Jays without a hit for seven innings because they wanted to witness the remnants of a slice of baseball history. They wanted tickets for a game that was almost over so they could see Ryan go for it one more time. The loyal fans were not alone in their adulation for this athlete for the ages. Everyone wanted to see Ryan at his finest, whether it was Ryan's next-door neighbor, who listened to the game on the radio in his pickup truck because it offered the keenest reception, or Reid Ryan, who stopped writing a college book report to watch his father pitch the last two innings of the game on cable television, or the San Diego Padres and the New York Mets, who put postgame buffets on hold to crowd around television sets in clubhouses at Shea Stadium.

When ESPN zoomed Ryan into living rooms, taverns and baseball stadiums throughout the country for the eighth inning of the unfolding masterpiece, the spontaneity gave the event added significance. With the emergence of cable television, more people are treated to out-of-town baseball games, and Ryan looks bigger than life. Maybe he is.

"There's always one guy that defies the odds," said Joe Carter of the Blue Jays. "He's the guy."

Ryan did not disappoint the late-comers at Arlington who gambled that the no-hitter would remain intact. His strikeout of Roberto Alomar to end the game came on a 93-mile-per-hour fastball and was his 16th. Afterward, as usual, he rode an exercise bicycle for a half-hour with his right arm packed in ice. "I haven't gotten bored with no-hitters yet," Ryan said.

Runners-up

1991: Rickey Henderson of the Oakland A's passed Lou Brock of the St. Louis Cardinals as baseball's all-time leader with 939 stolen bases when he swiped third in a game against the Yankees at Oakland Coliseum. The game was halted for eight minutes as Brock came onto the field and toasted Henderson as "the greatest competitor that ever ran the bases."

1884: Moses Fleetwood Walker, a catcher, made his debut with the Toledo Blue Stockings of the American Association, then a major league, becoming the first black player in major league history. Walker, who batted .263 in 42 games in his only season, predated Jackie Robinson (*see April 10*), the first modern African-American major leaguer, by 63 years.

1999: Charismatic, a 31–1 long shot trained by D. Wayne Lukas and ridden by Chris Antley, won the 125th running of the Kentucky Derby by a neck over Menifee before a Churchill Downs crowd of 151,051. Charismatic returned $64.60 on a $2 bet to win, the third-largest payoff in Derby history.

2,130 Games, and Gehrig Sits Down

By JAMES P. DAWSON

DETROIT [Tuesday]—Lou Gehrig's matchless record of uninterrupted play in American League championship games, stretched over fifteen years and through 2,130 straight contests, came to an end today. The mighty iron man, who at his peak had hit forty-nine home runs in a single season five years ago, took himself out of action before the Yanks marched on Briggs Stadium for their first game against the Tigers this year.

With the consent of Manager Joe McCarthy, Gehrig removed himself because he, better than anybody else, perhaps, recognized his competitive decline and was frankly aware of the fact he was doing the Yankees no good defensively or on the attack. He last played Sunday in

Lou Gehrig gently encouraging Babe Dahlgren in the dugout before Dahlgren replaced him as the Yankees' first baseman in Detroit. Gehrig removed himself from the lineup, snapping his consecutive-games-played streak at 2,130. (Associated Press)

New York against the Senators. When Gehrig will start another game is undetermined. He will not be used as a pinch-hitter. The present plan is to keep him on the bench. Relaxing and shaking off the mental hazards he admittedly has encountered this season, he may swing into action in the hot weather, which should have a beneficial effect upon his tired muscles.

Meanwhile Ellsworth (Babe) Dahlgren, until today baseball's greatest figure of frustration, will continue at first base. Manager McCarthy said he had no present intention of transferring Tommy Henrich, the youthful outfielder whom he tried at first base at the Florida training camp. Dahlgren had been awaiting the summons for three years.

It was coincidental that Gehrig's string was broken almost in the presence of the man he succeeded as Yankee first baseman. At that time, Wally Pipp, now a businessman of Grand Rapids, Mich., was benched by the late Miller Huggins to make room for the strapping youth fresh from the Hartford Eastern League club to which the Yankees had farmed him for two seasons, following his departure from Columbia University. Pipp was in the lobby of the Book Cadillac Hotel at noon when the withdrawal of Gehrig was effected. "I don't feel equal to getting back in there," Pipp said on June 2, 1925, the day Lou replaced him at first.

Lou had started his phenomenal streak the day before as a pinch-hitter for Peewee Wanninger, then the Yankee shortstop.

This latest momentous development in baseball was not unexpected. There had been signs for the past two years that Gehrig was slowing up. Even when a sick man, however, he gamely stuck to his chores, not particularly in pursuit of his all-time record of consecutive play, although that was a big consideration, but out of a driving desire to help the Yankees, always his first consideration.

What Lou had thought was lumbago last season when he suffered pains in the back that more than once forced his early withdrawal from games he had started was diagnosed as a gall bladder condition for which Gehrig underwent treatment all last winter, after rejecting a recommendation that he submit to an operation. The signs of his approaching fadeout were unmistakable this spring at St. Petersburg, Fla., yet the announcement from Manager McCarthy was something of a shock. It came at the end of a conference Gehrig arranged immediately after McCarthy's arrival by plane from his native Buffalo.

"Lou just told me he felt it would be best for the club if he took himself out of the line-up," McCarthy said following their private talk. "I asked him if he really felt that way. He told me he was serious. He feels blue. He is dejected. I told him it would be as he wished. Like everybody else I'm sorry to see it happen. I told him not to worry. Maybe the warm weather will bring him around."

Lou Gehrig's illness was amyotrophic lateral sclerosis, to this day an incurable disease of the nervous system. After a moving 1939 farewell at Yankee Stadium (see July 4), he died in 1941 (see June 2).

Runners-up

1954: Stan Musial of the St. Louis Cardinals set a major league record of five home runs in a doubleheader against the New York Giants at Sportsman's Park in St. Louis. Nate Colbert of the San Diego Padres duplicated the feat in a twin bill against the Atlanta Braves in 1972.

1999: John Elway of the Denver Broncos announced his retirement after 16 N.F.L. seasons. He left after winning two straight N.F.L. titles, becoming the only

quarterback besides Otto Graham of the Cleveland Browns in 1955 to retire as a consecutive title winner.

1964: Bill Hartack rode Northern Dancer to victory in the one-and-a-quarter-mile Kentucky Derby in 2 minutes flat, breaking the mark of 2:00⅖ set by Decidedly in 1962. Secretariat (see May 5), the fastest ever in the Run for the Roses, shattered the two-minute barrier with 1:59⅖ in 1964.

May 3, 1986
Kentucky's Most Sentimental Derby

By STEVEN CRIST

LOUISVILLE, Ky.—A horse from California was supposed to win the 112th Kentucky Derby today, but hardly anybody expected it to be Ferdinand, a 17–1 shot ridden by a 54-year-old jockey and saddled by a 73-year-old trainer. But at the finish of a slow and roughly run Derby, it was Ferdinand, ridden by Bill Shoemaker and trained by Charlie Whittingham, drawing away to a 2¼-length victory over Bold Arrangement and Broad Brush, with the favored Californians, Snow Chief and Badger Land, off the board.

Shoemaker steered Ferdinand, a son of the English triple crown winner Nijinsky II, through heavy traffic from last place to first while covering the mile and a quarter in a dull 2:02⅕. Bold Arrangement, an English colt, won a three-way duel for second place, finishing three-quarters of a length in front of Broad Brush. Snow Chief, the 2–1 favorite, tired badly to finish 11th after taking a brief lead round the far turn. Ferdinand paid $37.40 for $2 to win, the highest Derby payoff since Gato del Sol, also a Californian, also rallied to win from last place and returned $41.40 in 1982.

The race was a sentimental triumph for Shoemaker, who became by far the oldest rider ever to win the race while scoring his fourth Derby triumph, and for Whittingham, a Hall of Fame trainer who had never won a Derby. Artistically, though, it was a less successful Derby run before a crowd of 123,891. The winner's time over a fast track was the slowest in 12 years, and more horses had rough trips than honest ones today.

Ferdinand, a handsome, chestnut-colored son of Nijinsky II and the Double Jay mare Banja Luka, was bred and is owned

by Howard and Elizabeth Keck of Los Angeles. Keck, who owned the cars that won the 1953 and 1954 Indianapolis 500's, is the Superior Oil heir who sold the company to Mobil for $5.7 billion in 1984. The colt came into the race with skimpy credentials and probably would have been lumped with the long shots in the mutuel field were it not for the popularity of Whittingham and Shoemaker. He had won only two of nine previous starts, and had been beaten by Snow Chief twice, by seven lengths in the Santa Anita Derby and by 6½ lengths in the Hollywood Futurity.

"This Derby win is the best," said Shoemaker, who was scoring his 8,537th victory and 942d stakes victory in a career that began in 1949. Shoemaker won earli-er Derbies on Swaps in 1955, Tomy Lee in 1959 and Lucky Debonair in 1965. Only Eddie Arcaro and Bill Hartack, each with five victories, have won the race more often.

Whittingham, who turned 73 last month, had only his third Derby starter in Ferdinand. After sending out a pair of overmatched long shots in 1959 and 1960, he vowed not to come back until he thought he had a chance. "The Kentucky Derby is probably the most important race," he said after winning it today. "You go anywhere in the United States and people hear you are a horse trainer and they ask if you ever won the Derby. When they find out I didn't, they say to themselves, 'Where does this guy train anyway?'"

Kentucky Derby winner Ferdinand takes a playful nip at jockey Bill Shoemaker's arm the day before the Preakness Stakes in 1986 as trainer Charlie Whittingham looks on. Ferdinand finished second to Snow Chief. (Associated Press)

Runners-up

1980: Genuine Risk, ridden by Jacinto Vásquez and trained by LeRoy Jolley, became only the second filly to win the Kentucky Derby and the first since Regret in 1915. She came from well back on the home stretch, holding off fast-closing Rumbo for a one-length victory.

1981: With Larry Bird making the winning basket on a 16-foot bank shot off a fast break with 1 minute 3 seconds left, the Celtics defeated the Philadelphia 76ers, 91–90, to win the N.B.A. Eastern Conference finals in seven games at the Boston Garden after being down by three games to one. The Celtics beat the Houston Rockets in six games in the finals and won their 14th league title.

1952: Eddie Arcaro, aged 36, rode Hill Gail to a two-length victory over Sub Fleet in the 77th running of the Kentucky Derby, becoming the first jockey to win the race five times. Bill Hartack tied Arcaro's record aboard Majestic Prince in 1969.

May 4, 1965
Go West, Young Man

By ROBERT LIPSYTE

NEW YORK—Lew Alcindor, the nation's most sought-after high school basketball player, announced today his intention to attend the University of California, Los Angeles next fall. Poised and articulate during his first news conference, the 7-foot-¾-inch, 18-year-old Power Memorial High senior said he chose the West Coast school "because it has the atmosphere I wanted and because the people out there were very nice to me."

Alcindor visited the U.C.L.A. campus a month ago, soon after the Bruin basketball team won its second straight National Collegiate championship. In Los Angeles today J.D. Morgan, the university's athletic director, said "we are tremendously pleased." He added: "Of course, this is the boy's announcement. By the rules of our conference we are not permitted to announce such enrollments."

Ferdinand Lewis Alcindor Jr.'s announcement, made in the Manhattan parochial school's gymnasium, ended several years of secrecy and speculation. He had never spoken publicly before, but always through his coach, Jack Donohue. The coach installed himself as a buffer between Alcindor and the 60-odd colleges who seriously bid for his enrollment and any interviewers and newspapermen who wanted to talk to him. As the boy's fame increased (he led Power to 71 straight victories and set the city record for scoring, 2,067 points, and for rebounds, 2,002), the pressure mounted. Alcindor's father, a Transit Authority patrolman, got an unlisted telephone number and his 5-foot-10-inch mother, as late as this morning, said, "Can't talk anymore, Mr. Donohue said not to say anything."

The gym was hung with banners cele-brating Power's winning Catholic High Schools Athletic Association teams (1939, 1963, 1964, 1965), its national high school championships ('63–'64 and '64–'65), and its six tournament victories, five of them during Alcindor's career. By 12:33 P.M., when Alcindor arrived in the gym from the cafeteria, several hundred reporters, photographers, television crewmen, radio broadcasters and students lined the room. Alcindor, wearing a dress shirt, jacket and tie, as does every student in the Irish Christian Brothers' school, stepped to the microphone and said: "I have an announcement to make. This fall I'll be attending U.C.L.A. in Los Angeles."

Surrounded by cables and electronic equipment, Alcindor carefully explained that his decision had been delayed because he was "very confused" on whether he wanted to stay home or go out of town. He expects to take a liberal arts course. His particular interests are music, journalism, and television. A B student, Alcindor is sports editor of the school's newspaper. He never lost his composure, even when someone seriously asked him if there were any liabilities in being tall in basketball. "None that I can think of," said Alcindor.

Lew Alcindor, the 7-foot-¾-inch senior from Power Memorial High School in Manhattan, announcing his intention to attend U.C.L.A. in the fall of 1965. Alcindor changed his name to Kareem Abdul-Jabbar in 1971. (Bettmann/Corbis)

Runners-up

1957: Bill Shoemaker stood in the stirrups aboard Gallant Man in the Kentucky Derby and misjudged the finish line, checking his horse by a fraction of a second and allowing Iron Liege to win by a nose in a photo finish. "I confused the sixteenth pole with the finish pole," said Shoemaker, who won four Derbies during his 42-year career, in 1955, '59, '65 and '86 (see May 3).

1965: Willie Mays of the San Francisco Giants established a new National League record for career home runs, hitting his 512th in a game against the Los Angeles Dodgers and surpassing the mark set by the New York Giants' Mel Ott 19 years before. The blast, off the left-hander Claude Osteen, put the "Say Hey Kid" in fourth place on the all-time list.

1989: One day after defecting from the Soviet Union, the 20-year-old hockey prodigy Alexander Mogilny signed with the Buffalo Sabres of the N.H.L. Mogilny had slipped away from a banquet in Stockholm during a celebration for the U.S.S.R.'s 21st world championship.

May 5, 1969
Winning Looked Easy

By LEONARD KOPPETT

Bill Russell (6), the Celtics' player-coach, hooking a shot over Wilt Chamberlain of the Lakers in Game 6 of the N.B.A. finals. When Boston won Game 7 two days later, it meant that Russell had been the center of 11 Celtics championship teams in 13 years. (Associated Press)

INGLEWOOD, Calif.—In a game whose complexion shifted more wildly than a schizophrenic chameleon, the Boston Celtics added another championship to their collection by beating the Los Angeles Lakers tonight, 108–106, in the seventh and deciding contest of the National Basketball Association final playoffs.

It was Boston's 11th title in the 13 years that Bill Russell has been its center, and its second in the last three seasons, during which Russell has also been the coach. In six of those finals the Celtics defeated a Laker team anchored by Jerry West and Elgin Baylor, but this time Los Angeles also had Wilt Chamberlain, who was supposed to make it invincible. Instead the amazing Celtics, written off as "aging" by many experts and only fourth in the Eastern Division during the regular sea-

son, produced the smart, opportunistic, team-minded basketball that has characterized them for years, and also had that little bit of good fortune that every champion needs.

Wilt hurt his right knee coming down with a rebound with 5 minutes 45 seconds to go and Boston's lead at 103–94. He hobbled around the court for a couple of plays, but finally had to sit down at 5:19 with the margin down to 7 points. Now, the all-but-exhausted Celtics were on the defensive, West was hot and with 3:07 still to play it was anybody's game with Boston leading by only 103–102.

The capacity crowd of 17,568 was screaming endlessly as both sides missed a couple of scoring opportunities, but that bit of luck came Boston's way at 1:17. John Havlicek, caught on the right side with time for a shot running out, had the ball deflected out of his hands by Keith Erickson. But it went to Don Nelson, at the foul line, and his shot hit the rim, went straight up and fell through for 105–102. Two free throws by Larry Siegfried wrapped it up, 107–102, and the last 4 Laker points during the last seconds meant nothing.

West, his movement hampered by a leg injury but his shooting touch unimpaired, scored 42 points. He set a playoff record by accumulating 556 in the 18 games the Lakers had gone through, surpassing the mark of 521 set by Rick Barry for San Francisco two years before. West also won the automobile presented by *Sport* magazine to the outstanding player of the series. But that symbolized, as clearly as anything, the difference between the teams. The Lakers had brilliant individuals, the Celtics played as a unit with five parts.

Runners-up

1973: Secretariat, trained by Lucien Laurin and with Ron Turcotte in the saddle, won the Kentucky Derby in 1 minute 59⅖ seconds, which today stands as the fastest time in the 129-year history of the race, breaking the record set by Northern Dancer in 1964 *(see May 2)*.

2002: The New Jersey Nets advanced to the N.B.A. Eastern Conference finals by defeating the Indiana Pacers, 120–109, in a climactic double-overtime Game 5 of the semifinals. Indiana's Reggie Miller sank a 35-foot bank shot at the buzzer to force overtime, only to have Jason Kidd take over the game in the second OT. The Nets defeated the Boston Celtics for the conference title but were swept by the Los Angeles Lakers in the league finals.

1904: Pitching for the Boston Pilgrims against the visiting Philadelphia Athletics, the 37-year-old right-hander Cy Young *(see June 30)* completed the first perfect game in the modern era, with the pitcher's rubber at the current 60 feet 6 inches from home plate. The game came in the midst of a record 23-inning hitless streak for Young.

May 6, 1954
He Beat the Clock

By DREW MIDDLETON

Roger Bannister, a 25-year-old British medical student, breaking the tape and the four-minute mile barrier, once thought to be a human impossibility, on the Iffley Road track at Oxford University in England. (Associated Press)

LONDON—Roger Gilbert Bannister ran a mile in 3 minutes 59.4 seconds tonight to reach one of man's hitherto unattainable goals. The 4-minute time sought by every great miler for twenty years was beaten by the slim, sandy-haired medical student in a dual meet at Oxford University. Running on the four-lap Iffley Road track, Bannister swept through the first quarter in 57.5 seconds. The middle quarters of the race were run in 0:60.7 and 0.62.3. Then with a final explosive burst, Bannister raced to the record with 0:58.9 for the last quarter.

The 25-year-old miler ran under exceedingly unfavorable conditions. There was a fifteen-mile-an-hour cross wind during the race and gusts touched twenty-five miles an hour just before the event began. Track authorities said they thought Bannister would have come close to 3:58 had there been no wind. But out of long experience with English weather, Bannister said later, there "comes a moment when you have to accept the weather and have an all-out effort and I decided today was the day."

Bannister's mile smashed the world record of Gunder Haegg of Sweden, who ran the distance in 4:01.4 at Malmo, Sweden, on July 17, 1945. The English runner's time at 1,500 meters, taken unofficially, was 3:43, equaling the world record held jointly by Haegg, Lennart Strand of Sweden and Werner Lueg of Germany. Bannister was running in a meet between Oxford University and a British Amateur Athletic Association team of which he is a member. Bannister had trained intensively for the event in an effort to better 4 minutes before Wes Santee of the United States and John Landy of Australia could do it.

After the race, Bannister praised Chris Brasher and Chris Chataway, his teammates who set the pace for most of the race, with Brasher doing the first quarter in just under 60 seconds. "We were under evens, so to speak, at the half-mile," Bannister said, "and then Chataway took over for the third lap and we reached the three-quarters in a shade over three minutes. So I had to take over then and try to do the last lap in about 59 seconds."

Bannister seemed particularly pleased to have set the record at Oxford. He recalled he had run his first race here as an Oxford freshman and that his time then was over 5 minutes. Bannister said casually he thought that "the 4-minute mile has been overestimated. Naturally, we wanted to achieve the honor of doing it first, but the main essence of sport is a race against opponents rather than against clocks."

Chataway, who ran for Cambridge in the past, was just ahead of Bannister after three-quarters of a mile and he continued to hold the lead until the two runners were about 300 yards from the finish. Then Bannister, who runs with a conventional style, effortlessly went ahead and sped down the final stretch. "I felt pretty tired at the end," Bannister remarked, "but I knew that I would just about make it."

Runners-up

1978: Affirmed, with Steve Cauthen up, held off Alydar, ridden by Jorge Velásquez, to win the Kentucky Derby by a length and a half, establishing their storied Triple Crown rivalry. Affirmed was trained by Laz Barrera and Alydar by John Veitch. Affirmed's time was 2:01½; no Derby winner in the next 20 years came close.

1998: The Chicago Cubs right-hander Kerry Wood, making his fifth major league start at age 20, set a National League record and tied Roger Clemens's major league record for most strikeouts in a game, 20, in a 2–0 one-hitter over the Houston Astros at Wrigley Field.

1982: Gaylord Perry won the 300th game of his career as the Seattle Mariners defeated the Yankees, 7–3, in the Kingdome. Perry, the self-confessed spitballer, was the first pitcher to win Cy Young awards in both the American and National leagues, taking the honors with the Cleveland Indians in 1972 and the San Diego Padres in 1978.

May 7, 1957
'If There Is a Doctor in the Stands...'

By LOUIS EFFRAT

CLEVELAND—Of tremendously greater concern to the Indians than the 2–1 decision they took from the Yankees tonight was an accident that befell Herb Score, their million-dollar southpaw. Felled by a line drive from the bat of Gil McDougald in the first inning, Score, the sight in his right eye endangered and his nose fractured, was removed on a stretcher and taken to Lakeside Hospital. Dr. C.W. Thomas, a local and prominent eye specialist, examined Score. The physician reported hemorrhaging in the eye so severe that it would be several days before the exact nature or the extent of the injury to the eye could be determined.

Nothing, including the seventh-and-eighth-inning runs that the Tribe scored to beat Tom Sturdivant, could make anyone forget what had happened in the first three minutes of the ball game. Even the Yankees, who were to see their six-game winning streak snapped by two unearned runs, were upset by the misfortune that befell Score.

The popular pitcher had disposed of Hank Bauer, the first Yankee he faced, on a grounder to Al Smith at third base. A moment later, McDougald, the second man, slashed a drive directly toward Score. Unable to get his glove up in time, Herb was hit squarely on the right eye. The ball caromed toward Smith, who threw out McDougald. Score, who had dropped as though hit by a bullet, lay on the mound. Members of both teams rushed to Score's side. Ice packs were applied and a stretcher brought out. The public address announcer requested: "If there is a doctor in the stands, will he please report to the playing field."

His eye closed and bleeding from the

Herb Score during a 16-strikeout performance against the Red Sox at Cleveland in 1955. His unlimited career was effectively ruined two years later when a line drive off the bat of the Yankees' Gil McDougald hit him near the right eye. (Associated Press)

nose and mouth, Score was carried off on the stretcher and taken to the hospital. At no time did Score lose consciousness. In fact, while in the clubhouse, awaiting the ambulance, Herb joked: "I wonder if Gene Fullmer felt this way." He referred to the recent knockout Fullmer suffered in his title bout with Ray Robinson.

The 23-year-old Score is rated by most experts the best pitcher in the majors. He was a ten-game winner in 1955, his first

year in the big show, and last season he captured twenty. His 245 strikeouts in 1955 and 263 in 1956 were the most by any hurler in either circuit. He had fanned thirty-nine in thirty-six innings this campaign before the accident.

Herb Score never recovered his brilliant form, winning 17 more games over five years with the Indians and the Chicago White Sox. He broadcast Indians baseball for more than 30 years.

Runners-up

1972: The Los Angeles Lakers, having won 33 straight games in the regular season (*see Jan. 7*), steamrolled the Knicks in five games for their first N.B.A. title since moving to California from Minneapolis in 1960. The Lakers, coached by Bill Sharman and with new players like Jim McMillian and Gail Goodrich emerging, erased a run of eight failures in the league finals.

1968: Dancer's Image, winner of the Kentucky Derby three days earlier, was disqualified after urine tests revealed he had run with phenylbutazone, a painkiller

used to alleviate inflammation of joints. Horses could use "Bute" at some tracks, but not Churchill Downs. Forward Pass was awarded the victory.

1959: The largest crowd in baseball history, 93,103, filled the Los Angeles Coliseum for a Dodgers–Yankees exhibition game dedicated to Roy Campanella, the All-Star catcher and power hitter who had been paralyzed from the neck down the year before (*see Jan. 28*). He received some $75,000 of the gate receipts.

May 8, 1970
Their Finest Hour

By LEONARD KOPPETT

NEW YORK [Friday]—The New York Knickerbockers, displaying their finest qualities with the limited physical but important spiritual aid of a limping Willis Reed, won the championship of the National Basketball Association tonight by routing the Los Angeles Lakers, 113–99, at Madison Square Garden.

Darlings of the basketball world and a subject of national sports interest since November, when they set a league record by winning 18 games in a row, the Knicks finally achieved the first title in their 24-year history by winning the seventh game of the final round of the playoffs. It was their 101st game this season. Walt Frazier, with 36 points and 19 assists, was the most brilliant individual, but this, like most Knick successes, was basically a team enterprise. By winning, the Knicks gave New York's happy sports fans their third professional world championship in 16 months. The football Jets won the Super Bowl game in January, 1969, and the baseball Mets took the World Series last fall.

For the 19,500 screaming spectators, the Knicks produced a staggeringly effective defense, their trademark throughout the season. In addition, their shooting was deadly in the first quarter as they built a 38–24 lead. Soon they had a 51–31 margin and it didn't dip below 20 points until the closing minutes.

Reed, as always, was an indispensable element, but in an unusual fashion. He had

Willis Reed celebrating after Game 7 of the N.B.A. finals in New York. A limping Reed scored only 4 points after injuring a thigh muscle in Game 5, but his presence inspired the Knicks to a 113–99 victory and their first league title. (Associated Press)

injured a muscle in his right leg that runs from the pelvis to below the knee early in the fifth game of the series, when the series was tied in games, 2–2. His injury seemed to doom the Knicks to defeat, because it left them with no counterweapon to Wilt Chamberlain, the 7-foot-2-inch giant who is the Laker center and the greatest scorer in basketball history. But the Knicks rallied to win that game which meant they were still alive when Chamberlain and the Lakers crushed them in Los Angeles on Wednesday night, while Reed sat on the bench. If Reed had been unable to play tonight, the Knicks would not have been expected to win.

As it turned out, after a late-afternoon examination by Dr. James Parkes, some painkilling injections, a few minutes of shooting practice and another injection just before the game began, Reed was able to start. He took the first shot at the basket, with the game 18 seconds old, and made it. A minute later, he hit another, making the score 5–2, and the effect on his teammates was electric.

As the game wore on, Reed felt more pain, and moved more slowly, even though he had another shot of painkiller at halftime. But the early momentum he helped give the Knicks was enough. "He gave us a tremendous lift, just going out there," said Coach Red Holtzman afterward. "He couldn't play his normal game, but he did a lot of things out there and he means a lot to the spirit of the other players." When it was over, Reed's line in the box score was unimpressive: just those two baskets in five shots, no free-throw attempts, three rebounds, four personal fouls. But his seasonlong contribution was taken into consideration and he was given the car that *Sport* magazine awards to the outstanding player of the final round of the playoffs.

Runners-up

1984: The Soviet Union, reacting to the United States boycott of the 1980 Moscow Olympics because of the U.S.S.R.'s 1979 invasion of Afghanistan (see Jan. 20), announced it would not attend the 1984 Los Angeles Games. Soon afterward, 13 other Communist bloc countries issued announcements that they, too, would stay home.

1968: Jim (Catfish) Hunter (see Dec. 15) of the Oakland Athletics pitched a 4–0 perfect game against the Minnesota Twins at Oakland Coliseum. There were no difficult plays behind him, but he went to three balls on a batter seven times.

It was the first perfect game in the American League since Charlie Robertson's for the Chicago White Sox in 1922.

1936: After falling from his mount and being trampled by four horses at Bay Meadows in California, the jockey Ralph Neves was declared dead and his body was taken to a cold storage facility. He somehow "revived," The San Francisco Chronicle reported, took a cab back to the track and rode again the following day.

May 9, 1930
From Worst to First

By BRYAN FIELD

BALTIMORE—William Woodward won his first Preakness and Earl Sande rode his first Preakness winner when Gallant Fox captured Maryland's greatest turf classic before 40,000 persons at Pimlico today. The son of Sir Galahad III and Marguerite came from next to last position at the half-mile mark to the heels of pace-making Crack Brigade at the mile. Three-sixteenths further, the end of the race, and Gallant Fox was the winner by three-quarters of a length and had earned $51,925. The time was 2:00⅘.

At the break Gallant Fox, from his No. 1 post position, next to the rail, broke smartly. But he lacked early foot and was securely pocketed on the fence. Going around the clubhouse turn, Sande lost more ground keeping his horse out of trouble and when all straightened out in the backstretch there was only one horse back of him. Then began the most electrifying dash that has been seen in Maryland in many a day. Finding a hole here and a gap there, Sande snaked his way through the field and was third at the far turn. At the top of the stretch Gallant Fox was now second, but there still was daylight between his nose and Crack Brigade's heels.

Coming to the outside, Sande let Gallant Fox run on his own courage. George Ellis, on Crack Brigade, went to the whip and Crack Brigade held Gallant Fox even. Again it looked as if Gallant Fox was beaten despite his courageous dash. But Sande called on his mount at the exact moment and on he came, never faltering a stride. Crack Brigade could not stand the strain and gave, just a trifle. That was right in front of the stand and hats, programs and people were in the air. The two horses swept over the line lapped on each other, only three-quarters of a length apart, but the winner was going away and Crack Brigade was a gallant and tired second.

Sande was sweat-streaked and dust-covered when he got to the jockey room after the race, the mixture making a fudge-like covering over his face. He praised Gallant Fox. "I didn't call on him until we hit the furlong pole," he said. "Then he came on with a rush and hung it on Crack Brigade."

Governor Albert C. Ritchie of Maryland presented the Woodlawn vase to Mr. Woodward, and among others present were Vice President Charles Curtis, Governor Larson of New Jersey, Senator Millard Tydings of Maryland and Mayor William Broening of Baltimore. Mr. Woodward was warmly congratulated in the clubhouse on the victory and because he bred Gallant Fox here in Maryland at his Belair stud in Prince George's County.

Gallant Fox joined Sir Barton (1919) as the second winner of the Triple Crown on June 7, scoring a four-length victory in the Belmont over Whichone. Gallant Fox is the only Triple Crown winner to sire another one: Omaha in 1935.

Gallant Fox, with Earl Sande in the saddle, wearing the roses after winning the Kentucky Derby on May 17, 1930. That year the Preakness was the first leg of the Triple Crown, followed by the Derby eight days later. (Associated Press)

Runners-up

1982: Sugar Ray Leonard, the 25-year-old world welterweight champion, underwent two hours of surgery at Johns Hopkins University to repair a partially detached retina in his left eye. He announced his retirement in November but returned to the ring in May 1984, scoring a victory over Kevin Howard.

1961: Baltimore Orioles first baseman Jim Gentile set a major league record by hitting grand slams in consecutive innings, one off Fedro Ramos in the first inning, the other off Paul Giel in the second, in a game against the Minnesota Twins in Bloomington. In 1999 Fernando Tatis of the St. Louis Cardinals hit two grand slams in one inning off Chan Ho Park of the Los Angeles Dodgers.

1975: Houston McTear, a high school junior from Baker County, Fla., streaked to a 9.0 clocking in the 100-yard dash, tying the record that Ivory Crockett of the Philadelphia A.A.U. club set the year before. Crockett had broken the great Bob Hayes's 1963 record by a tenth of a second.

May 10, 1970
Orr Owns the Stanley Cup

By GERALD ESKENAZI

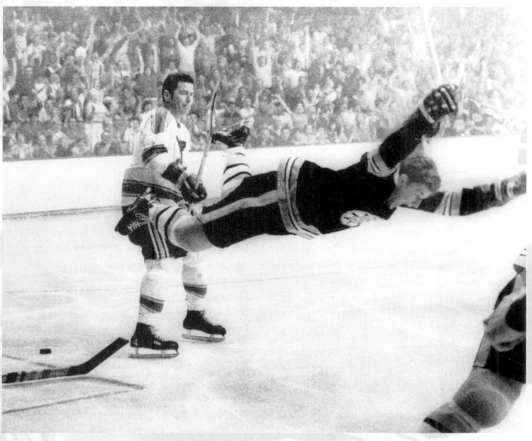

Bobby Orr of the Bruins scoring the Stanley Cup–winning goal against the St. Louis Blues while airborne 40 seconds into overtime at Boston Garden. Orr flicked in a pass from Derek Sanderson after being knocked off his feet by a defender. (Associated Press)

BOSTON—Although unable to leap over buildings with a single bound, Bobby Orr flew through the air in over-time today, rapped home Derek Sanderson's pass and gave the Bruins their first Stanley Cup since 1941. The symbolism was perfect. The goal was scored by the young man who made the Bruins the offensive threat that they are, and the pass came from the pug-nosed scrapper who helped to make them one of the National Hockey League's most fero-cious teams.

Orr's goal, after 40 seconds of the sud-den-death period, lifted the Bostonians to a 4–3 victory over the St. Louis Blues and completed a sweep of the four-of-seven-game series. The obligatory champagne splattered over the dressing-room walls. The players tapped one another over the head with the three-foot-high Stanley Cup. They chug-a-lugged champagne from the chalice, and Coach Harry Sinden got into a squirting match with John McKenzie.

The Bruins began their new era in 1967—for seven of the previous eight years they had finished last. Then Milt Schmidt, the general manager, told the scouts looking for promising players: "If

they can fit through the door, I don't want them."

Scoring in today's game, the only close one in this series, started with Rick Smith of the Bruins getting a rising shot past Glenn Hall, underneath a sign that read, "Happy Mother's Day Mrs. Orr." This was for Bobby's mother, who had come from their home in Canada. Red Berenson tied the score late in the opening period. Gary Sabourin of St. Louis and Phil Esposito traded goals in the second session. Esposito's was his 13th, breaking the playoff series record set by Maurice Richard of Montreal in 1944 (in nine games) and tied by Jean Beliveau of the Canadiens in 1956 (in 10 games). This was Esposito's 14th playoff game.

The pressure was on the Bruins in the waning minutes of the third period, after Larry Keenan gave the Blues a 3–2 edge in the first minute. The Bostonians wanted to win it at home, before 14,835 fans and a national television audience. It was John Bucyk, who has been with the Bruins since 1957, longer than any of his team-mates, who forced the game into overtime with a tip-in at 13:28.

As soon as Orr took Sanderson's pass in the overtime period he was rapped by Keenan and went sailing. But he knocked the disk past Hall. Then a crepe paper shower started, and because of the heat the colors ran, tinting the ice orange, yel-low and blue.

Runners-up

1973: With the center Willis Reed scoring 18 points, grabbing 12 rebounds and dishing out 7 assists in the decisive Game 5, the Knicks won their second and last N.B.A. title. They defeated Wilt Chamberlain, Jerry West and the Lakers, 102–93, at the Los Angeles Forum, winning the finals by four games to one.

1969: The merger of the A.F.L. and N.F.L. now official, the Pittsburgh Steelers, Cleveland Browns and Baltimore Colts agreed to become part of the American Football Conference for $3 million each by 1970. Two 13-team conferences were formed that season: the A.F.C. (including 10 ex-A.F.L. teams) and the National Football Conference.

1974: Julius Erving led the New York Nets to the first of their two American Basketball Association titles (see May 13), helping defeat the Utah Stars, 111–100, in the decisive Game 5 of the best-of-seven-game finals at Nassau Coliseum. Erving flew high for 20 points and pulled down 16 rebounds.

May 11, 1968
Hockey's Gallic Dynasty

By GERALD ESKENAZI

MONTREAL—The Montreal Canadiens, with their controlled madness, unleashed a final-period drive that enabled them to catch, and defeat, the St. Louis Blues, 3–2, today and win the Stanley Cup in four straight games. A goal by J.C. Tremblay that rattled off the posts gave the Frenchmen their 15th cup, and their eighth in the last 13 years they have played under the volatile coach, Hector (Toe) Blake. Minutes after the victory, Blake, who had said this was the "toughest and longest of them all," went on Canadian television and announced his retirement.

So the first series played between an expansion team and an established club ended under conditions more dramatic than had ever been expected. In sweeping the four-of-seven-game National Hockey League series, the Frenchmen never won a game by more than one goal and were forced into overtime twice.

The Canadiens bolted out of the opening face-off with their classic forward-motion attack, bringing guttural French cries from the 15,505 fans at the Forum. But after a few opening minutes of electricity they disappointed the crowd as they were continuously hamstrung by the prodding sticks and heavier blocks thrown by the Blues. But the Canadiens know the route to the 3-foot-high Cup by heart, and in the final 20 minutes they were perfect. Tremblay, who plays the game "cute," almost poked fun at the futilities of opponents who tried to stick-handle past him. He played his defensive position so perfectly and got off passes to forwards so deftly that the Canadiens began driving.

They hit St. Louis's goalie, Glenn Hall, eight times in the first five minutes, and the great 37-year-old goaltender began to juggle some of the shots. Tremblay finally spotted Henri Richard, and the small chunky center pushed the disk past Hall. Fewer than five minutes later, Tremblay rocketed in a 30-footer. Now the Canadiens were in full control and the Blues began to show their age and inexperience. They had been bulwarked on the road to the finals by the play of 43-year-old Doug Harvey on defense, and 37-year-old Dickie Moore. Both are former Canadiens stars.

The final buzzer sounded and the air was filled with flying newspapers, balloons and hats. A red carpet was rolled onto the ice and the Cup was hauled out, followed by Jean Beliveau, the Canadiens' captain. His right foot was in a cast and he hobbled on crutches (he broke an ankle bone last week). The Cup continues to be more than a symbol of hockey supremacy for the predominantly French-Canadian fans. It helps solidify their Gallic feelings and when Beliveau addressed them in French, they applauded wildly.

Hector (Toe) Blake, rookie coach of the Canadiens, receiving the star treatment from his players after they dispatched the Red Wings in the 1956 Stanley Cup finals. Blake coached Montreal for 12 more seasons, winning 7 more Cup titles. (Corbis)

Runners-up

1984: Sparky Anderson's Detroit Tigers defeated the California Angels at Tiger Stadium to lift their record to 26-4, the best start in major league history before or since. Detroit breezed through the regular season and post-season, steamrolling the San Diego Padres in the World Series, four games to one.

1972: The Boston Bruins, coached by Tom Johnson, won their second Stanley Cup title in three years, defeating the Rangers by four games to two when they took the finale, 3–0, at Madison Square Garden. Bobby Orr (see May 10) once again received the Conn Smythe Trophy as the tournament's most valuable player.

1977: Ted Turner, owner of the Atlanta Braves, took over as manager with his team in the midst of a 16-game losing streak but lost to the Pittsburgh Pirates, 2–1. The next day National League president Charles (Chub) Feeney ruled that Turner, forever 0–1, had violated a rule against managers having a financial stake in their team, and reinstated Dave Bristol as the skipper.

May 12, 1985
Luck of the Draw

By DAVE ANDERSON

NEW YORK—Until today, Dave DeBusschere had never won anything in a drawing. "At least nothing big," he would recall. "I think I got a set of club head covers at a golf tournament once, that's all."

And when he arrived at the Starlight Room of the Waldorf Astoria he was presented with a Knick button that had a blue-dyed rabbit's foot attached to it, but he shrugged and handed it to an onlooker. At the National Basketball Association Draft Lottery that would determine Patrick Ewing's future, if not his own future, Dave DeBusschere preferred to

depend on the power of a small prayer he had said at the 9:15 Mass this morning at St. Joseph's Church, not far from his Garden City, L.I., home.

"I said some prayers, like I always do," the Knicks' head of basketball operations was saying now about five hours later, "and then I thought, I'll be a little selfish and ask for Patrick Ewing in the lottery."

Dave DeBusschere had finally won something big—7 feet big. His prayer had been answered. So had the prayers of Knick fans everywhere, some of whom had booed Patrick Ewing when he appeared at Madison Square Garden with

the Georgetown team in recent years in Big East Conference games. But yesterday God was a Knick fan. And now Patrick Ewing will be cheered at the Garden as few basketball players ever have.

Cheered, but also scrutinized and criticized, as so-called saviors always are. Don't assume that the Knicks will be instant champions with Patrick Ewing at center. But even as the Boston Celtics and Philadelphia 76ers go to it in the Eastern Conference playoff final, they have begun to hear Patrick Ewing's sneakersteps. "He puts us on another level, but that's all," Dave DeBusschere said. "Don't forget that Ralph Sampson and Akeem Olajuwon didn't win the title for Houston in their first year. But now we've got a guy to build a team around."

When next season begins, Patrick Ewing will be at center, surrounded by Bernard King at small forward (although he will be returning from serious knee surgery), by Bill Cartwright and Pat Cummings at power forward, and by Rory Sparrow, Darrell Walker, Trent Tucker and Butch Carter at guard.

As he spoke, Dave DeBusschere was still bubbling from finally having won something big in a drawing. He was holding a white Knicks' jersey with Ewing's name and No. 33, his Georgetown number, on it. Each of the other six teams in the drawing had made up a jersey, too, but only Dave DeBusschere was holding a jersey now, holding a jersey that represented the privilege of bestowing millions on the 22-year-old Jamaican-born resident of Cambridge, Mass.

Patrick Ewing became the 1986 Rookie of the Year and led the Knicks to the playoffs in 13 of his 15 seasons with the team. But he was unable to lead them to an N.B.A. title.

Patrick Ewing, sizing up his future as the Knicks' franchise player, accepts a new jersey from general manager Dave DeBusschere, right, on the N.B.A.'s draft day in June 1985. David Stern, the league's commissioner, looks on. (Associated Press)

Runners-up

1926: Walter Johnson of the Washington Senators joined Cy Young as the only 400-game winners in baseball history when he defeated the St. Louis Browns, 7–4, at Griffith Stadium. Young won 511 games and Johnson 417; Grover Cleveland Alexander and Christy Mathewson are next on the all-time list with 373.

1985: Kathy Whitworth won the United Virginia Bank Classic in Suffolk, Va., for her

88th and final victory on the L.P.G.A. Tour. She holds the record for most titles of any golfer, male or female. Sam Snead, with 81, won the most among men.

1970: Ernie Banks, the Chicago Cubs' peerless shortstop–turned–first baseman, hit his 500th career home run off Pat Jarvis of the Atlanta Braves at Wrigley Field. Banks retired in 1971 with 512 homers, becoming the ninth major leaguer in the exclusive 500 club.

May 13, 1976
In a League of His Own

By PAUL L. MONTGOMERY

The brilliant Julius Erving defying gravity against the St. Louis Spirits in 1975. Dr. J guided the New York Nets to two American Basketball Association championships in three years before the N.B.A. merger. (Associated Press)

UNIONDALE, L.I.—In an astonishing comeback from a 22-point deficit with 17 minutes left in the game, the New York Nets defeated the Denver Nuggets, 112–106, tonight and won the championship of the American Basketball Association for the second time in three seasons.

The sixth game of what may have been the league's last championship series appeared to belong to Denver midway through the third quarter. But the Nets put on a slashing, clawing, full-court press and, point by point, scrambled their way back. Denver, losing more of its composure with each reduction of the lead, went five minutes without scoring during one stretch and looked like a defeated team long before the end. In the fourth quarter, the Nuggets committed an encyclopedia full of dribbling, passing and shooting errors and were outscored, 34–14.

"My guys showed tonight that they're not only great players but good people," said Kevin Loughery, the victorious coach. "We put it all together when we had to, and that's what's it all about." It was the second championship for the Nets, who began life as the New Jersey Americans when the A.B.A. was founded in 1967. They won in 1973–74, Loughery's rookie season as coach, and tonight's title was the first won by a New York team in a major sport since then.

It was a team effort. Julius Erving, who was brilliant throughout the series and was the unanimous choice for most valuable player, scored 31 points and had five steals during the Nets' surge. John Williamson got 24 of his 28 points in the second half and was a scoring demon, seemingly putting in a basket every time his team needed one.

Brian Taylor had 24 points and broke up Denver's defense with his drives down the middle. The backup center Jim Eakins played 34 minutes in place of the injured Kim Hughes and had a 3-point play near the end that was pure determination. Even Rich Jones, a seven-year A.B.A. veteran, survived an awful shooting night (1 for 12) and contributed four steals and nine rebounds to the comeback.

"This is my first championship, man, and it's so beautiful I don't know what to say," Jones said. "I don't know what the future is going to bring for this league, but I want to enjoy this night."

This was the last A.B.A. game played, with four of its seven remaining teams—the Nets, Denver Nuggets, San Antonio Spurs and Indiana Pacers—being absorbed by the N.B.A. Nets owner Roy Boe, who faced financial problems, sold Julius Erving's contract to the Philadelphia 76ers during the following preseason.

Runners-up

1958: Thirty-seven-year-old Stan Musial of the St. Louis Cardinals became the eighth major leaguer to collect 3,000 hits when he doubled as a pinch-hitter against Moe Drabowsky of the Chicago Cubs in a game at Wrigley Field.

1955: Mickey Mantle of the Yankees had the lone three–homer game game of his career, connecting for two clouts off the right-hander Steve Gromeck and one against the left-hander Bob Miller in a victory over the Detroit Tigers at Yankee Stadium.

1904: Charlotte (Lottie) Dod of England, already an international field hockey player, a champion figure skater, an Olympic silver medalist in archery and the youngest-ever Wimbledon tennis champion at age 15 in 1887, defeated May Hezlet, 1-up, to win the British Ladies' Open golf tournament at Troon, Scotland.

Out of Control

By CLIFTON BROWN

MIAMI [Wednesday]—It got wild in Miami tonight. And suddenly, a series that the Knicks looked as though they controlled had spun out of control. A melee with less than two minutes left in the game turned a 96–81 Miami victory into a controversy. There will be fines. There could be suspensions.

After the game, one of the referees, Dick Bavetta, said in a statement that all but two Knick reserves left the bench during the melee, making all of those players subject to a possible one-game suspension. Bavetta added that none of the Heat players left the bench. "We will review the tape," Bavetta said. "There were two players from New York who did not come off. We're not sure which two, but we will see that from the tape."

Nobody can predict how the Game 5 madness in the Eastern Conference semifinals will affect Game 6 Friday night, when the Knicks and Heat resume their battle at Madison Square Garden. But while the Knicks still lead the four-of-seven-game series, 3–2, it is clear that they could be severely shorthanded for Game 6.

This is why it pays to end a series as quickly as possible. Wild things happen in the playoffs. If the Knicks had won Game 5, they could have moved on right away and prepared for the Chicago Bulls in the conference finals. Instead, Miami remains a serious problem. Pat Riley is actually looking forward to making a return trip to the Garden, boos and all.

"It's a pressure game for them, they've got to win it," Riley said after tonight's game. "We're going up there to win."

But there will be more talk about what happened near the end of the game than

Heat Coach Pat Riley trying to push away John Wallace of the Knicks, center, in the midst of a bench-clearing scuffle in Game 5 of the N.B.A. Eastern Conference semifinals. The brawl changed the course of the series between the teams. (Associated Press)

about basketball. With 1 minute 53 seconds to play, Charlie Ward of the Knicks and P.J. Brown of the Heat tangled with each other as Tim Hardaway was taking a free throw, Brown picked up Ward and threw him out of bounds like a rag doll, John Wallace of the Knicks jumped on Brown, and the melee started, with players on both teams piling out of bounds trying to separate each other for nearly a minute.

Rod Thorn, the National Basketball

Association's vice president in charge of handing out discipline, will be watching this tape very closely. Asked if he was concerned about the possibility of any of his players being suspended, Knicks Coach Jeff Van Gundy said: "Certainly, we will be very concerned."

John Starks was ejected after the melee for making an obscene gesture to the crowd. As security officers led Starks to the locker room, spectators threw debris at him, but fortunately he continued on his way to the locker room.

So a series that was already physical took on a truly nasty tone. Even before the final melee, Charles Oakley was ejected with 1:55 left for needlessly shoving Alonzo Mourning. It was one of the few times in the series that the Knicks showed frustration, realizing that the series would not end in Game 5. And the Knicks had no one to blame for that but themselves.

The N.B.A.'s review of the game tape showed that Patrick Ewing, Allan Houston and three others left the Knicks' bench to join the melee. Jeff Van Gundy himself was nearly trampled trying to keep his players off the floor. With Ewing, Houston and Charlie Ward suspended from Game 6, New York lost, 95–90. Back at Miami Arena on May 18, the Knicks, who once led the series, three games to one, were eliminated under a deluge of Tim Hardaway 3-pointers.

Runners-up

1967: Mickey Mantle became the sixth player in history to hit 500 home runs, driving a pitch from Stu Miller of the Baltimore Orioles into the right-field stands at Yankee Stadium. Mantle finished his career after the 1968 season *(see March 1)* with 536 career homers. He was 10th on the all-time list after 2002.

1996: In his seventh start for the Yankees, 31-year-old Dwight Gooden revived the magic of his early Mets years *(see Sept. 12)* by pitching his only no-hitter, 2–0,

against the Seattle Mariners at Yankee Stadium. Paul Sorrento popped out to Derek Jeter for the final out.

1874: Harvard defeated McGill University of Montreal, 3–0, at Cambridge, Mass., in an 11-man-per-side game that resembled soccer but permitted running with the ball when pursued—"Boston rules." It was arguably the first rudimentary football game ever played.

May 15, 1948
Master Eddie and His Mount

By JAMES ROACH

BALTIMORE—Citation did it again today. In command from the instant the doors of the starting gate popped open, the Calumet Farm's great 3-year-old colt won as he pleased—or as Jockey Eddie Arcaro pleased—in the seventy-second edition of the $134,870 Preakness Stakes at old Pimlico.

It was Master Eddie's pleasure to mark this one up by half a dozen lengths. The Kentucky Derby winner was in front every foot of the mile-and-three-sixteenths journey—by a neck the first time under the wire, by close to a length going into the clubhouse bend, by two in the backstretch and by three as he entered the payoff lane.

At no point was he threatened by the three others in the line-up, though he was flicked with the whip twice. Arcaro decided he was loafing a bit at the entrance to the stretch and tapped him there; he did it again just outside the eighth pole. Citation got the idea, and kept pulling away from the others through the final yards. Second money went to the 30-to-1 outsider, Vulcan's Forge, owned by C.V. Whitney, in the only surprise of the race.

Citation, as expected, was a 1-to-10 shot, the shortest-priced favorite in Preakness history since the 1889 running. The "heavy track" condition after yesterday's downpour, plus the fact that Citation wasn't pressed, resulted in a time of 2:02 ⅗— the slowest since the

Preakness was made a mile-and-three-sixteenths event in 1925.

In making his score 2 up with one to go in his bid for racing's triple crown, Citation topped off a record-wrecking racing day for Calumet Farm, the remarkable establishment owned by Warren Wright of Chicago, which has headquarters on the Versailles Pike, Lexington, Ky. Citation netted $91,870. Including the jackpot hit by Calumet's Faultless and Fervent in the Gallant Fox Handicap at Jamaica, Calumet collected $169,670 this afternoon—a record single-day haul on the race tracks.

A bit damp around the withers, but otherwise showing little sign of having taken some exercise, Citation returned to the unsaddling enclosure to the acclaim of the crowd of 32,244. There, with owner Wright and trainer Horace Allyn (Jimmy) Jones beaming at all hands, Citation was draped with a blanket of black-eyed Susans, for which he displayed no great liking.

On June 12 in the Belmont Stakes, Citation defeated Better Self by eight lengths and became the eighth Triple Crown winner. His time for the one and a half miles matched the fastest to that point—the 2:28 ⅕ run by Count Fleet, the Triple Crown champion in 1943.

Citation, ridden by Eddie Arcaro, leading the Preakness by a length approaching the clubhouse turn at Pimlico. Citation beat Vulcan's Forge, running second above, by six lengths. (Associated Press)

Runners-up

1991: Bill Parcells, coach of the two-time Super Bowl champion Giants, resigned, citing heart problems. He was replaced by his aide, Ray Handley, who failed in three seasons. Parcells, however, was hardly finished, later coaching the New England Patriots and the Jets with notable success and the Dallas Cowboys in 2003.

1990: Petr Klima scored in the third sudden-death overtime period to give the Edmonton Oilers a 3–2 victory over the Boston Bruins in Game 1 of the Stanley Cup finals at Boston Garden. At 1 hour 55 minutes 13 seconds of playing time (5 hours 32 minutes over all), it was the longest game in finals history. The Oilers went on to win the Cup, four games to one.

1941: Joe DiMaggio went 1 for 4 with a single against the left-hander Eddie Smith of the Chicago White Sox in a 13–1 loss for the Bombers at Yankee Stadium, beginning his record 56-game hitting streak.

May 16, 1957
Yanks Play the Copa

[Unsigned, *The New York Times*]

Hank Bauer, second from right, with his wife and teammate Mickey Mantle, left, and ex-teammate Billy Martin a month after the Copacabana row. A New York grand jury had just cleared Bauer of possible charges. (Associated Press)

NEW YORK—Six members of the world champion New York Yankees were involved in a postmidnight disturbance tonight during a party at the Copacabana nightclub in Manhattan. The Yankees, who were at the club to celebrate Billy Martin's 29th birthday, included Mickey Mantle, Yogi Berra, Hank Bauer, Whitey Ford, Johnny Kucks and Martin. The disturbance stemmed from an argument between the players and members of a bowling club who also were celebrating at the club.

The party, at which all the players except Martin were accompanied by their wives, was planned long in advance. It was not immediately clear how the disturbance occurred or whether the police were called to the club, which is at 10 East 60th Street. Words apparently were exchanged between the players and members of a bowling club who also were celebrating at the Copacabana. One of the members of the bowling club, Edwin Jones, accused Bauer of striking him.

On June 4, The Times *carried the following unsigned article about fines levied against the players.*

Mantle, Berra, Bauer, Ford and Martin were fined $1,000 each and Kucks, a young pitcher in a lower salary bracket than the others, was fined $500. The fines were deducted from the checks the players received at the Yankee Stadium two days ago.

There were published statements yesterday that the disciplinary action had caused a rift between Casey Stengel, the manager of the team, and George M. Weiss, the general manager of the Yankees. Weiss issued this statement denying that a rift existed: "As for the reported friction between Casey Stengel and myself, this is wholly untrue. We have always consulted and agreed on all moves involving the team on and off the field, with the complete approval of Dan Topping and Del Webb (the co-owner of the Yanks).

Stengel appeared in a bitter mood when he was interviewed at Grand Central Station, where the Yankees departed for a trip to Cleveland and a three-game series with the Indians. Said Stengel: "I know of no rift between me and Mr. Weiss. Mr. Weiss hasn't lost a game all year. I have, me, the manager. Can't understand the big fuss. This [the nightclub incident] all happened three weeks ago. They're trying to make a big scandal over this because we're the Yanks."

Berra, Bauer and Kucks confirmed the fines. Ford insisted, "I wasn't fined." When pressed, he said: "I was told what to say. They haven't announced it, so why should I?"

As for the Bauer incident, the police refused to take action in the matter and Jones had Bauer taken into custody by a citizen's arrest on May 21. Bauer, 34, faces a hearing on charges of felonious assault. In the case of a citizen's arrest, the way is open for a suit for false arrest should Bauer be found not guilty. Bauer denied that he struck Jones. He was supported in this contention by other members of the party. However, the story was published and the fines were a result.

The Yankees went on to win the American League pennant by eight games and lose the World Series to the Milwaukee Braves in seven. Four weeks later, Billy Martin was traded to the Kansas City A's in an eight-player deal generally acknowledged to have stemmed from the brawl.

Runners-up

1980: The Los Angeles Lakers defeated the Philadelphia 76ers, 123–107, at the Spectrum in Philadelphia to win the N.B.A. title in six games. The rookie Earvin (Magic) Johnson, normally a guard, took over for the injured Kareem Abdul-Jabbar at center and scored 42 points.

1982: Coach Al Arbour's Islanders won their third straight Stanley Cup with a 3–1 victory over the Vancouver Canucks in British Columbia to complete a four-game sweep. Mike Bossy, who scored two power-play goals in the second period, was named the most valuable player of the post-season.

1987: Alysheba, ridden by Chris McCarron and trained by Jack Van Berg, duplicated his Kentucky Derby victory with a half-length triumph over Bet Twice in the Preakness Stakes. But Alysheba, sired by the great Alydar, lost to Bet Twice in the Belmont Stakes while attempting to win the Triple Crown.

May 17, 1983
Four for the Islanders

By KEVIN DUPONT

UNIONDALE, L.I.—Quickly and efficiently, the Islanders swept to their fourth consecutive Stanley Cup tonight with a 4–2 victory over the Edmonton Oilers and moved into the National Hockey League record book next to the Montreal Canadiens. Only the Canadiens have ever had similarly impressive streaks in Stanley Cup play with the record for five consecutive championships, from 1956 through 1960, and four consecutive titles from 1976 through 1979.

The Islanders, however, despite their Stanley Cup fortunes, have not experienced the recognition that the Canadiens had, even in the New York region. "We're not the New York Yankees," said Butch Goring, the Islander center who has been on all four of the club's championship teams. "We don't go running around telling everyone how great we are. We just go out on the ice every night and show how good we are."

The Islanders, backed by first-period goals from Bryan Trottier, John Tonelli and Mike Bossy, clung to a 3–0 lead that the Oilers cut to 3–2 by the end of the second period. Jari Kurri and Mark Messier were the scorers for Edmonton, a team that collected 424 goals during the regular season but managed only 6 against the Islanders, who swept the series in 4 games. "There's no question, Smitty was making the key saves," said Bob Bourne. "But I think we also showed that we've got the best defense in the game. Go down the list and look at some of these guys: Gord Lane, Denis Potvin, Stefan Persson, Tomas Jonsson, Ken Morrow, Dave Langevin. They did an amazing job."

Billy Smith, himself, continually said the same during the series. The Oilers never scored more than three goals in a game and three times were limited to two goals or less. The Islanders won the first two games in Edmonton by 2–0 and by 6–3, and then took Game 3 at home, 5–1. Again, in the final game, Smith was sharp, blanking the Oilers in the first and final periods. In all, he held the Oilers scoreless in 7 of the 12 periods, and tonight he turned away 24 of Edmonton's 26 shots. Smith turned away all seven Edmonton shots in the final period. He finished the playoffs with a 13–3 record, recording all but two of the Islanders' postseason victories, and finished with a 2.68 goals-against average for the playoffs against the Washington Capitals, the Rangers, the Bruins and the Oilers.

As the game ended, the sellout crowd of 15,317 heard the song "We Are the Champions of the World" blaring over the public-address system. Smith, with the Stanley Cup barely on the ice, was skating with a can of beer.

Islanders goalie Billy Smith turning away a shot by Kevin Lowe of the Oilers in Game 4 of the Stanley Cup finals. The Isles swept to their fourth straight title as Smith allowed no goals in 7 of 12 periods. (Associated Press)

Runners-up

1998: David Wells of the Yankees pitched the 13th perfect game in modern major league history, defeating the Minnesota Twins, 4–0, at Yankee Stadium. The other perfect games at the Stadium were by Don Larson in the 1956 World Series (see Oct. 8) and David Cone in 1999 (see July 18).

1939: In the first baseball game ever televised, Princeton University defeated Columbia, 2–1, in 10 innings at Baker Field in New York. The game, carried by W2XBS, an experimental station in Manhattan, reached a hardful of viewers in New York City. "It is difficult to see how this sort of thing can catch the public fancy," The Times sniffed in a review the next day.

1970: Henry Aaron of the Atlanta Braves singled against Wayne Simpson in the first inning of a game against the Cincinnati Reds at Crosley Field for his 3,000th major league hit. Later in the game Aaron walloped his 570th home run off Simpson. Willie Mays and Eddie Murray are the only other players with 3,000 hits and 500 home runs.

May 18, 1912
The Bad News Tigers

[Unsigned, *The New York Times*]

PHILADELPHIA—Nineteen baseball players, comprising the regular team of the Detroit Tigers, three-time champions of the American League, made baseball history at Shibe Park this afternoon by going on strike and refusing to play the Athletics, following the refusal of B.B. Johnson, president of the league, to lift the suspension against Tyrus Raymond Cobb, the Detroit's star outfielder, who, last Wednesday, climbed into the grand stand during the game with the New York Highlanders and mauled a spectator who had said things reflecting upon the player.

Just as if they were freight handlers, New England millworkers, striking longshoremen, or belonging to any of the disaffected class of craftsmen who have wage troubles, the athletes paraded off the field just before the hour for calling play—literally a walk-out. "Hughey" Jennings, manager of the Tigers, recruited a team on the field, played the Athletics with these "misfits" and thus avoided the imposition of a $1,000 fine, as prescribed by the rules of the league. The score was: Athletics, 24; Detroit, 2.

As the regular Detroit players left the field, the Saturday half-holiday crowd of more than 15,000 spectators arose and cheered. A few hissed, but their hisses were drowned in the roar of cheers and handclapping. The spectators had an inkling of conditions, and when the players started from the field, the occupants of the stands knew what had taken place. Jennings had said that his sympathies were with his players, but he had promised President Navin of the Detroit Club that he would have nine men on the field to meet the Athletics, and he made good this promise.

Through the stands was carried the rumor that Jennings wanted volunteers. By the dozens, amateurs, semi-professionals, and college athletes left their seats and swarmed around the Detroit bench trying to look like real ball players. Jennings sorted over the bunch and picked out six likely-looking young men. They were hustled into the dressing rooms under the grandstand and told to jump into the Detroit traveling uniforms. They put on a broad grin with their suits, for Jennings announced that each would receive $50 for his services for the afternoon. Then out on the field trotted the "misfits."

What the final outcome of the controversy will be no person seems willing tonight to predict. The players are forecasting that it means an upheaval in organized baseball, and the final triumph of the players over the officers of the League.

When American League president Ban Johnson threatened the real Tigers with lifetime bans from baseball, they played, with Ty Cobb's approval and thanks, in Detroit's next game. Cobb received a 10-day suspension and a $50 fine.

The great Ty Cobb with the Tigers in 1914. Fierce, hard and relentless, he hit .420 the year of the strike and finished with a lifetime average of .366 at age 41 in 1928. (Corbis)

Runners-up

1971: Rookie goaltender Ken Dryden, the most valuable player of the N.H.L. playoffs, made 31 saves as the Montreal Canadiens defeated the Chicago Blackhawks, 3–2, at Chicago Stadium in Game 7 of the finals. It was the Canadiens' 11th Stanley Cup in 19 years and 16th over all. Henri (Pocket Rocket) Richard, playing on his 10th Cup winner, scored the tying and winning goals.

1962: Al Oerter of Queens, N.Y., became the first athlete in history to throw the discus 200 feet, with a heave of 200 feet 5 inches, at a meet in Los Angeles. Oerter would go on to win discus gold medals at four straight Olympics: 1964 (Tokyo), '68 (Mexico City), '72 (Munich) and '76 (Montreal).

1963: Ernie Davis, the star running back at the University of Syracuse and the 1961 Heisman Trophy winner, died at age 23 after a 10-month battle with leukemia. He led the Orangemen to the 1959 national title as a sophomore, breaking many of Jim Brown's school records.

May 19, 1974
Kate Smith and the Broad St. Bullies

By PARTON KEESE

PHILADELPHIA—The Philadelphia Flyers arrived today. With a remarkable 1–0 shutout of the Boston Bruins at the Spectrum, the National Hockey League's West Division champions turned back the East Division champions, 4 games to 2, and became the first expansion team to win the Stanley Cup and the league title.

Nothing better typified a championship victory for the Flyers in their seventh season of existence than a shutout, a tribute to Bernie Parent, their goalie. Although it was the first time he held the high-scoring Bruins scoreless, Parent's sensational performances in the six games earned him the Conn Smythe Trophy as the outstanding player in the series.

The deciding goal today was scored by Rick MacLeish in the first period. MacLeish scored 13 goals in the playoffs to lead all players. However, none could have been more important to him and his team than the last one, on which he barely saw the puck and had little to do except to be in the right spot at the right time. André (Moose) Dupont, a Flyer defenseman, had received the puck at his position on the right point from MacLeish, who won the face-off from Gregg Sheppard on Philadelphia's first and only power play in the opening period. Dupont skated inside the blue line to the center and let go a soft shot at Gilles Gilbert, the Boston goalie. MacLeish, in the meantime, was battling Dallas Smith and Carol Vadnais, Boston defensemen, for position in front of the net. The puck struck Rick in the upper leg, deflected off his stick and slithered past Gilbert into the goal.

"Aw, I saw that lousy shot by Dupont," said the 24-year-old Gilbert. "But when a puck bounces off somebody on the way, you don't know if it's going high or low, right or left."

When Bobby Orr, Boston's superstar, was sent off the ice by Referee Art Skov for tackling Bobby Clarke on a breakaway with just 2 minutes 22 seconds left, it signaled the end of the game for all intents and purposes. Orr sat disconsolately in the penalty box and watched the Flyer fans create bedlam until the final buzzer sounded.

Then, with Parent and Clarke leading the way, the Flyers skated round the rink carrying the Stanley Cup as hundreds of fans swarmed on the ice. Those in the stands clapped and yelled and cried. The ending was almost as emotional as the beginning. First the rink crew wheeled in an organ, then they laid down a 30-foot carpet. And out stepped Kate Smith, in person, the good-luck "charm" of the Flyers. A recording of "God Bless America" by her had been "good luck," for the Flyers had won 36 of the 40 games at which it was played.

Kate gave it everything she had. She waved passionately to the roaring crowd. She threw punches in the air, and the fans screamed louder. With a spotlight on her, she aimed her hand pistol-like at the Bruins, and then started singing "God Bless America."

The rafters resounded, everybody joined in, and when she finished, the famous singer left in a tumult. But not before Orr and Phil Esposito stopped her to shake hands, hoping, perhaps, some of the luck would rub off.

Team symbol, crowd-pleaser, good-luck charm: Kate Smith singing "God Bless America" before the Stanley Cup playoffs between the Islanders and the Flyers in Philadelphia in 1975. (Associated Press)

Runners-up

1984: The Edmonton Oilers, featuring one of the highest-scoring offenses in N.H.L. history, ended the Islanders' four-year Stanley Cup reign (see May 17) with a 5–2 victory in Game 5 at Northlands Coliseum. Wayne Gretzky showed the way with two goals in the opening period.

1973: Secretariat, who had won the Kentucky Derby two weeks before (see May 5), made a bold move in the backstretch and thundered home ahead of Sham to win the Preakness Stakes by two and a half lengths in 1 minute 54⅘

seconds. The time was two-fifths of a second off the track record and made Secretariat the prohibitive favorite to win the Triple Crown in the Belmont Stakes (see June 9).

1989: The N.C.A.A., whose investigation had led to the resignations of Coach Eddie Sutton and Athletic Director Cliff Hagan months earlier, placed the University of Kentucky's storied basketball program on probation for three years for widespread recruiting and academic violations.

May 20, 1989
Saturday Thrill

By STEVEN CRIST

BALTIMORE—Sunday Silence, who raised more questions than he answered when he beat Easy Goer by two and a half lengths in the Kentucky Derby two weeks ago, proved himself a worthy Triple Crown contender today by winning the 114th and closest Preakness Stakes ever at Pimlico Race Course. The blackish colt from California raced head and head with Easy Goer for the length of the stretch before regaining the lead in the final yards to win by a long nose.

The last time a Preakness was decided in a photo finish was when Affirmed held off Alydar by a neck in 1978. Now Sunday Silence is one victory away from becoming racing's first Triple Crown winner since Affirmed, and his rivalry with Easy Goer, a son of Alydar, is the tightest Triple Crown battle since then. The two colts will hook up again in the Belmont Stakes at Belmont Park on June 10.

The winner had to survive a claim of foul from Pat Day, Easy Goer's rider, who alleged interference by Pat Valenzuela and Sunday Silence through their stretch duel. After reviewing the films for seven minutes, the stewards let the order of finish stand. The bettors in a record Pimlico crowd of 90,145, unconvinced by Sunday Silence's weaving Derby finish and the slow final time of that race, made Easy Goer the 3-to-5 favorite today and let Sunday Silence off as the second choice at 2 to 1. Sunday Silence paid $6.20 for $2 to win after running the mile and three-sixteenths in 1:53⅗, the third fast-est Preakness ever. Sunday Silence, a son of Halo and the Understanding mare Wishing Well, is owned by Arthur B. Hancock 3d, Ernest Gaillard and Charlie Whittingham and trained by Whittingham. The colt has won six of

Sunday Silence, foreground, and Easy Goer battling head and head down the stretch in the Preakness. Sunday Silence inched ahead in the final yards, earning a shot at the Triple Crown. (Associated Press)

eight career starts and is undefeated in five races this year.

The tight finish capped a race in which the two principals both looked as if they would win easily at some point. Each appeared to fire his best shot, and while there will be plenty of interest in a rematch, and some excuses made for the loser, the race seemed more genuine than the Derby. "I think this puts to rest the talk that Easy Goer is the better horse," Valenzuela said.

Shug McGaughey, Easy Goer's trainer, said within moments of the finish that he was eager to try Sunday Silence one more

time in the Belmont. But McGaughey seemed even more dispirited today than he was after the Derby, which he had hoped was a fluke. "We'll just try again," McGaughey said. "I guess I'm going to start hearing a whole lot about Affirmed and Alydar now, but I hope we can put that to rest in the Belmont."

Easy Goer finally lived up to his promise of early spring in the Belmont Stakes in June, roaring past Sunday Silence on the turn for home and winning by eight lengths. Sunday Silence thereby lost his chance to become racing's 12th Triple Crown winner.

Runners-up

1990: Sixteen-year-old Monica Seles ended the second-longest winning streak in tennis history when she defeated Steffi Graf, 6–4, 6–3, in the German Open in Berlin. It was Graf's first defeat after 66 straight victories, eight short of Martina Navratilova's record in 1984.

1900: The second modern Olympics opened in Paris, home of Baron Pierre de Coubertin, the movement's founder. Named the International Meeting of Physical Training and Sport, the Games were a failure. They were held as a

sideshow to the Universal Paris Exhibition, lasted more than four months and featured such long-since discarded events as cricket, croquet and tug of war.

1977: A two-year-old gelding named John Henry, owned by Harold Snowden Jr. and trained by Phil Marino, won his first start, a four-furlong maiden race at Jefferson Downs in Kenner, La. When he was retired in 1984 after 83 starts, he had won 39 races, finished in the money 63 times, received seven Eclipse Awards and earned more than $6 million.

May 21, 1977
Winning Fast and Easy

By JOSEPH DURSO

BALTIMORE—Some of the best-paid athletes in America spent the better part of two minutes trying to catch Seattle Slew aboard other horses today and, when the 102d Preakness Stakes was over, they joined the public in tossing bouquets at the undefeated 3-year-old colt. "He's got to be a good horse," said Willie Shoemaker, who has won 7,000 races in his career but who finished fifth today on the English champion J.O. Tobin. "He wins every time he runs."

"My horse ran O.K., but that other horse is too much for anybody," said Angel Cordero Jr., who won two of the last four Kentucky Derbies but who ran sixth today aboard Hey Hey J.P. Chris McCarron, who finished last with Regal Sir, said, "I never got a close enough view of Seattle Slew because the pace was too fast for my horse." And this report came from Danny Wright, who had the best view of all for the first blistering mile because Cormorant raced stride for stride with Seattle Slew and his French jockey, Jean Cruguet: "We were leading him down the backstretch and going into the far turn, but then he asked his horse to move and he did. I thought to myself: oh-oh. Then the bubble kind of busted. We just couldn't beat him."

In the Kentucky Derby, the favored Seattle Slew had been literally left at the gate but then overcame all kinds of adversity to finish in front of 14 challengers. That was his seventh straight victory and this afternoon at 5:40 o'clock he moved into the eighth position in the starting gate looking for No. 8.

Cormorant was in the race from the moment the gates sprang open. "He gave everything he had," Wright reported, "but he couldn't outfoot Seattle Slew today. We were actually leading him for almost a mile, and I thought I still had a lot of horse under me. But then..."

When that bubble "busted" for Wright, it expanded for Jorge Velásquez aboard Iron Constitution. By the time they headed into the stretch, he replaced Cormorant as the "chaser." "My instructions were to make one run at him," Velásquez related. "And we did make one run at him in the stretch." But as they flashed past the finish, Iron Constitution was still a length and a half behind "him"—Seattle Slew. And if any question was left unanswered, it was this: Could Iron Constitution or anybody else catch him if the race was longer?

The Belmont is five-sixteenths of a mile longer, but Velasquez was making no claims: "I thought I was gaining a little on him. But if the race was longer? My horse was trying his best, but I can't say that he would catch Seattle Slew." And that's what it came down to: Could anybody ever catch the undefeated Seattle Slew?

Seattle Slew went on to win the Belmont Stakes in June by four lengths over Run Dusty Run. He remains the only undefeated Triple Crown winner. Slew won 14 of 17 races in his three-year career.

Two weeks before his victory in the Preakness, Seattle Slew broke late from the gate in the 103rd running of the Kentucky Derby but wound up leading the field toward the finish line. (Associated Press)

Runners-up

1881: The United States National Lawn Tennis Association, composed of 33 clubs, was formed in a New York City hotel room as the national ruling body of the sport. Now simply the U.S.T.A., it assumed control over all rules—from the height of nets to the sanctioning of tournaments.

1979: The Montreal Canadiens, led by goalie Ken Dryden and right wing Guy Lafleur, defeated the Rangers, 4–1, in Game 5 at the Montreal Forum to win their fourth straight Stanley Cup. It was Les Habitants' 21st Cup in their 61 years in the N.H.L. and their 18th since the Rangers had last won in 1940.

1981: With center Butch Goring scoring two goals and being named the post season's most valuable player, the Islanders defeated the Minnesota North Stars, 5–1, at Nassau Coliseum to win their second straight Stanley Cup in five games. The Islanders went on to win four straight titles under Coach Al Arbour (see May 17).

'Gentlemen and Lady, Start Your Engines'

The Associated Press

Janet Guthrie before the Firecracker 400 at Daytona in 1977. Two months earlier she became the first woman to qualify for the Indianapolis 500. She competed there twice, finishing as high as ninth. (Bettmann/Corbis)

INDIANAPOLIS (AP) [Sunday]—Janet Guthrie became today the first woman to qualify for the Indianapolis 500 auto race. Her average speed was 188.403 miles an hour on this last day of qualification for the race next Sunday.

The 39-year-old Miss Guthrie was first in line for a qualification attempt today. Driving the No. 27 Lightning-Offenhauser for Rolla Vollstedt, she turned in successive laps of 187.500, 188.363, 188.798 and 188.957 m.p.h. She had the fastest speed on the opening day of practice two weeks ago, 185.6, then raised her own best to more than 191 before ramming the wall on

May 10. Her car was never the same after that. But more than a week of fine tuning and testing by her teammate, Dick Simon, brought the racer back up to competitive speeds.

Miss Guthrie did not make an official qualification attempt last year because her Vollstedt simply was not fast enough. At the time, she was unable to get above 173 m.p.h. in her own racer, but she proved her ability to many of the doubters by later practicing above 181 in A.J. Foyt's backup car. However, her debut at the Speedway last year still marked a number of firsts. She was the first woman to enter

officially the Indy 500, the world's richest automobile race. And she was the first woman to drive around the track in actual practice, as well as the first to complete the mandatory rookie test.

Her return to Indianapolis this year was greeted with somewhat less fanfare, but the crowds of spectators and newsmen continued to watch her every move. "I want to thank my folks for not bringing me up thinking I couldn't do something because I was a woman," she said, still shaking but beaming after today's qualification. "I've given a lot of thought to the symbolism of being the first woman here. I think it's important to credit the women's movement with creating the climate that made this possible."

Her best lap in practice this week was 183 m.p.h. But she went over 186 this morning before making the qualification attempt. "This certainly is a major accomplishment in any racing career," she said. "But no race driver does this alone. I've had help from people too numerous to mention. The car was right and it worked beautifully.

"During the run I was just thinking, 'No mistakes,' and there was an adjective or two in there."

Janet Guthrie started 26th in the 33-car field at the Indy 500 one week later. She fell out with engine trouble after 27 laps. Guthrie returned the following year and finished ninth.

Runners-up
2003: Annika Sorenstam *(see March 16)* became the first woman since Babe Zaharias in 1945 to compete in a PGA Tour event when she teed off in The Colonial at Fort Worth, Tex. Sorenstam shot 71–74 and missed the 36–hole cut.

1963: Mickey Mantle homered off facade atop the third tier at Yankee Stadium against right-hander Bill Fischer of the Kansas City A's. The shot, three feet from becoming the first to leave the Stadium, was almost identical to one

Mantle hit off right-hander Pedro Ramos of the Washington Senators in 1956.

1994: After two successive post-season failures against them, the Knicks finally overcame the Chicago Bulls in the N.B.A. Eastern Conference semifinals, 87–77, in the deciding Game 7 at Madison Square Garden. Chicago, however, was without Michael Jordan, who had retired for the first time in his career. New York lost in the league finals to the Houston Rockets (see June 22).

May 23, 1948
Matchless Feller Meets His Match

By JAMES P. DAWSON

CLEVELAND—Joe DiMaggio drove three successive home runs at Municipal Stadium today before a record gathering of 78,431 fans, to sweep the Yankees to victory over the Indians in the first game of a twin bill. What is believed to be the second largest crowd ever to witness a ball game—it is said only a Yankee–Red Sox record of 81,841 in New York tops today's paid turnout, which displaced the old record of 74,529 here—thrilled to the spectacle of DiMaggio's hitting in the opener. He struck a single his first time up, hit his first homer after Tommy Henrich walked in the fourth, exploded the second when Henrich walked again and Charley Keller singled in the sixth, and capped it all with his third round-tripper, solo, in the eighth.

The matchless Rapid Robert Feller was the victim of DiMaggio's first two for the circuit, a more or less surprising Yankee greeting in the first meeting of the champions with the Iowa strong boy this season. The blow influenced Rapid Robert's rapid withdrawal for a pinch hitter in the seventh and sent Feller crashing to his third defeat. Bob Muncrief felt the pain of DiMaggio's solo homer, the one thrust he yielded as he hurled the final two innings. Once before in his brilliant career DiMaggio hit three homers in one game. That was on June 12, 1937, his second year in the "big time."

Joe DiMaggio hit three home runs in a game more than once. He relaxed between games of a doubleheader after hitting three in the opener against the Washington Senators in September 1950. (Associated Press)

With his three round-trippers and a single, DiMaggio swept across the runs which gave the Yanks the decision in the opener, 6 to 5, with the aid of a dramatic exhibition of relief pitching by the redoubtable Joe Page. Adding to the thrill of DiMaggio's robust slugging in the opener, and the drama of a pitching piece in which Page fanned two Tribe club wielders on six pitches with the bases loaded in a tense ninth inning to preserve for Allie Reynolds his sixth victory, was the fact that the Yanks rallied from a four-run deficit to score this triumph.

Bill Veeck, the young president of the Indians, looked on, distressed, from the press box through the opener. Bill "escaped" from the Cleveland Clinic Hospital because he just couldn't resist the lure of his record crowd, which would have been greater but for the rain that fell today. Veeck is convalescing from a third operation on his right leg.

DiMaggio's homers put the Yanks in front and it was fortunate, for Reynolds wobbled badly in the seventh, eighth and ninth. When Allie had walked Dale Mitchell and pitched two balls to Hal Peck, swinging for Jim Hegan, Manager Harris called Page.

DiMaggio's tempo must have been too fast for the double-feature routine and Wallopin' Joe went hitless in the second game. When he didn't hit, neither did his mates, and the Indians romped to a 5–1 victory.

Runners-up

1958: Wilt Chamberlain, the all-America center from the University of Kansas, announced that he was giving up his senior year of eligibility to turn pro as a member of the Harlem Globetrotters. He barnstormed with the Trotters for one year before joining the N.B.A. with the Philadelphia Warriors.

2002: Sam Snead, owner of the smoothest swing in golf and three-time winner of the Masters and the P.G.A. but never the United States Open, died at his home in Hot Springs, Va., after a series of small strokes. He was 89. "Whenever I needed to remind myself how to swing a golf club," said Tom Watson, the five-time British Open champion, "I'd look at Sam's swing."

1942: Cornelius (Dutch) Warmerdam of Long Beach, Calif., the supreme pole-vaulter of the World War II years and early 1950's, soared 15 feet 7¾ inches at a meet in Modesto, Calif., setting a world vault record that lasted until 1957. Warmerdam, using bamboo poles in the prefiberglass era, cleared 15 feet or more 43 times in 1940–44; no one else made that height until 1951.

May 24, 1935
Hot Dogs for Dinner!

A night game at Crosley Field in Cincinnati in 1935. President Franklin D. Roosevelt flipped the switch for the first one there, and most players found they were able to catch the ball. (Associated Press)

CINCINNATI (AP)—Night baseball came up from the minors for its first big league tryout tonight, and 25,000 fans and the Cincinnati Reds liked the innovation. Some of the affection of the Reds for the nocturnal pastime was because they defeated the faltering Phillies, 2 to 1. The official paid attendance was announced at 20,422, the third largest crowd of the season.

The flood-light inaugural, with President Roosevelt switching on the lights from Washington, was staged before a host of baseball notables, including Ford Frick, president of the National League, and Prexy Will Harridge of the American. The contest was errorless, despite the fact it was the first under lights for practically all

the players. The hurlers, Paul Derringer for the Reds and Joe Bowman for the Phils, performed in great style, the former allowing six hits and the visitor only four.

Manager Jimmy Wilson of the Phils said the lights had nothing to do with the low hit total. "Both pitchers just had all their stuff working, that's all," he said. "You can see that ball coming up to the plate just as well under those lights as you can in daytime." Jimmy, however, let it be known that he "thinks night baseball is all right, if the fans want it, but I'd rather play in the daytime."

Picture plays were prevalent throughout the game. Reds shortstop Billy Myers went far back into left field for Al Todd's fly in the seventh, the Reds' Sammy Byrd crashed into the center-field wall in the

sixth but held on to Dolph Camilli's drive, while Camilli snatched several throws out of the dirt from the Phil infield at first.

Two long flies were dropped by Philadelphia outfielders, but both were scored as hits. They first led to the Red score in the opening frame, Myers pulling up at second as George Watkins let the ball get away when he fell against the left-field wall. Myers came home as Lew Riggs and Ival Goodman grounded out.

Singles by Billy Sullivan and Harlin Pool and Gilly Campbell's infield outproduced the winning Red marker in the fourth. The Phils got their lone tally in the fifth when Todd singled, took third on Mickey Haslin's drive to center, and counted on Bowman's roller to Myers.

Runners-up

1992: Al Unser Jr. won his only Indy 500 as of 2003 in the closest finish in the history of the event, holding off Scott Goodyear of Canada by .043 seconds. That margin broke the record of .160 seconds in 1982, when Gordon Johncock beat the eventual four-time winner Rick Mears.

1980: The Islanders won their first Stanley Cup, defeating the vaunted Philadelphia Flyers, 5–4, in Game 6 of the finals at Nassau Coliseum when Bobby Nystrom tipped a pass from John Tonelli past goalie Pete Peeters at 7:11 of sudden-

death overtime. The triumph started a four-season Cup championship run by the Islanders (see May 17).

1987: Al Unser Sr. won his fourth Indy 500 at age 47, becoming the oldest to win the event. Unser, driving for the team owner Roger Penske, was a late substitute for Danny Ongais, who suffered a concussion when he crashed one of Penske's top cars in practice.

May 25, 1965
The Phantom Punch?

By ROBERT LIPSYTE

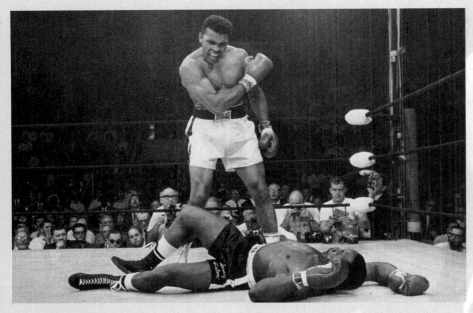

Cassius Clay after dropping Sonny Liston with a short right to the jaw midway through the first round of their heavyweight title rematch in Lewiston, Me. Some in the crowd shouted "Fake! Fake!" (Associated Press)

LEWISTON, Me.—Cassius Clay retained the heavyweight championship tonight when he knocked out Sonny Liston in the first round of their rematch in the schoolboy hockey arena here. Radio and television observers timed the knockout at 1 minute 42 seconds, but Maine boxing officials said it came at one minute. However, the bout, which slipped from the control of Jersey Joe Walcott, the referee, was not declared over until 2 minutes 17 seconds had elapsed. Clay and Liston actually squared off to fight again after it was over.

It will be listed as the fastest knockout on record in a heavyweight title bout, but some of the 4,280 spectators yelled "Fake, fake, fake!" Many were angered by the controversial ending as were those who witnessed the confusing finish of their first bout 15 months ago. The punch—a short right hand—that sent the 215¼-pound Liston to the canvas for the first time in his career did not seem to have knockout power. It all happened something like this:

Clay, weighing 204 pounds, leaped out at the opening bell, skipping forward in his high white shoes, his 8-ounce red gloves far in front of him. He connected immediately with a right to Liston's head, then a left. Liston seemed to shake off the blows, as the crowd, for once, cheered for him. For what seemed longer than the official 48 fighting seconds, Clay danced around Liston counter-clockwise, jabbing him lightly, once more connecting with a solid right. Then he fired the short right and missed with a left hook as Liston sagged to his knees.

Liston collapsed slowly, like a falling building, piece by piece, rolling onto his back, then flat on his stomach, his face pressed against the canvas. Clay danced around him, waving at him, taunting him. Walcott, once the heavyweight champi-

on, tried to wave Clay to a neutral corner. In doing so, he apparently lost the knockdown count being made by Francis McDonough across the ring. As Walcott turned and leaned toward McDonough, Liston began to climb heavily to his feet.

McDonough, a retired Portland printer, continued to count as Liston got back up to his knees, then went down again. McDonough reached the count of 12 before he and Walcott made contact. By then, Liston was up again, squaring off with Clay and ready to fight. Walcott, confused, rushed across the ring and grabbed Clay. He held up Clay's arm, and Clay's entourage poured into the ring. Liston merely dropped his hands to his sides and stood impassively.

Few in the sparse crowd in the cement-block Central Maine Youth Center realized what had happened. The immediate confusion was much like that of the night in Miami Beach when Clay won the title. For six rounds that night Clay outboxed Liston, bobbing out of range of long left hooks. He opened a cut under Liston's left eye, but did not seem to do much real damage to the so-called "ugly bear," who had twice scored one-round knockouts over Floyd Patterson. But Liston never answered the bell for the seventh, remaining on his stool as the Miami crowd leaped, screaming, to its feet. Later, Liston said he had injured his left arm in the first round and was unable to use it. Tonight there was the same kind of consternation. As the crowd surged forward against a cordon of state and city policemen—some yelling "Fix! Fix!"—Clay stood against the blue velvet ropes, telling the fans to "shaddup," telling them his victory was a triumph of the "righteous life."

Runners-up

1935: Playing in one of his final games for the visiting Boston Braves against the Pittsburgh Pirates at Forbes Field, Babe Ruth *(see Feb. 26)* hit three home runs. The third one, the 714th and last of his career, a shot of more than 600 feet off Guy Bush, was the first to clear the right-field grandstand at the park.

1994: Mark Messier made good on a public "guarantee," scoring three goals to lead the Rangers to a come-from-behind 4–2 victory over the Devils in Game 6 of their Eastern Conference playoff series at Byrne Meadowlands Arena. It was

the turning point of the series, which the Rangers won two nights later. Within three weeks, New York won the Stanley Cup *(see June 14).*

1935: In the space of an hour during the Big Ten championships in Ann Arbor, Mich., Jesse Owens of Ohio State University *(see March 9)* became a national celebrity: he broke three world records, in the broad jump, the 220-yard dash and the 220-yard hurdles, and tied another, in the 100-yard dash.

Perfect Wasn't Good Enough

Harvey Haddix of the Pirates during one of his 12 perfect innings against the Braves in Milwaukee. He lost in the 13th on an error and a home run, later changed to a double, by Joe Adcock. (Associated Press)

MILWAUKEE (UPI)—Harvey Haddix of the Pittsburgh Pirates pitched twelve perfect innings tonight but lost in the thirteenth. The first hit he yielded, to Joe Adcock, gave a 2–0 victory to the Milwaukee Braves. Haddix, who retired thirty-six men in a row, became the first major league pitcher to carry a perfect performance past nine innings.

Felix Mantilla was the first man to face the slender, 33-year-old curveball specialist in the thirteenth. He hit a grounder to the Pirates' third baseman, Don Hoak,

who threw it into the dirt at the feet of the first baseman, Rocky Nelson. Mantilla was safe on the throwing error. Haddix' perfect string was snapped but the no-hitter was intact. Ed Mathews, the next man up, sacrificed the fleet Mantilla to second. Hank Aaron, the major's leading batter, received an intentional base on balls.

Then Adcock connected. The hit barely cleared the right-center-field fence and the big first baseman hesitated a moment before starting around the bases. Then two boys crawled under the barricade

and snatched the ball. Adcock at first was credited with a home run, and the final score was announced as 3–0. But then he was declared out for passing Aaron between second and third base and his home run became a double. The jubilant Aaron, who had cut across the diamond without touching third, was sent back by his mates to touch third and then home.

Confusion developed immediately after Adcock's blow cleared the fence. The umpires stopped the action as players swarmed out on the field. Aaron and Mantilla were ordered to retrace their steps and cross the plate. The National League president, Warren Giles, said later in Cincinnati that he believed the final score of the game eventually would be changed by official ruling to 1–0.

Seven major league pitchers have hurled, and won, nine-inning perfect games. Don Larsen of the Yankees did it most recently, in the 1956 World Series against the Dodgers. Until his downfall in the thirteenth Haddix had used a fast ball that was always on target and a curve that cleverly nipped the corners. The closest thing to a base hit during the regulation nine innings was Johnny Logan's line drive in the third that the shortstop, Dick Schofield, speared on a leaping catch. Haddix fanned eight men. Haddix' loss was his third this season and the toughest in baseball history.

The National League ruled that Joe Adcock was out for passing Henry Aaron. He therefore was credited with a double, not a home run, and the official score was 1–0. "It didn't matter to me whether it was 1–0 or 100–0," Harvey Haddix said. "We lost the game, and that's what hurts me most."

Runners-up

1991: Rick Mears, a one time off-road racer from Jupiter, Fla., won his fourth Indy 500, tying the record of A.J. Foyt and Al Unser Sr., when he made a daring wide Turn 1 move past Michael Andretti 12 laps from the finish and held on for a three-second victory. Mears's other victories were in 1979, '84 and '88.

1928: The quadrennial World Cup soccer tournament came into being when Jules Rimet, president of FIFA, soccer's world congress and ruling body, persuaded

it to organize a new competition, open to all member nations, beginning in 1930. The Jules Rimet Trophy is given today to each championship team.

1985: Danny Sullivan, a former New York City taxi driver and bon vivant, recovered from a high-speed 360-degree spin on Lap 120 to win the Indy 500 by 2.4 seconds over the legendary Mario Andretti.

May 27, 1937
Nothing Screwy About This Guy

By JOHN DREBINGER

CINCINNATI—Unexpectedly entering a fray which in the beginning was not at all of his choosing, Carl Hubbell today came up with his twenty-fourth consecutive National League victory in a two-year string as the Giants, riding handsomely on the crest of Melvin Ott's seventh homer of the year, brought down the Reds, 3 to 2.

The famous Hub came into the game in the last half of the eighth with the score deadlocked at 2-all, and with no more effort than one would employ in dusting off a shelf, he retired three Reds on infield grounders. In the upper half of the ninth he sat placidly in the Giant dugout as his no less distinguished roommate, Master Melvin, swung desperately at the slanting shots served up by the left-handed Lee Grissom. Earlier in the day Mel had cracked a triple off the screening in front of the right-field bleachers, and so the odds were slightly against him on this occasion.

But there is a strange bond of comradeship among these older Giants who date back to the days of John J. McGraw, and Mel swung with tremendous fervor. The result was a towering smash that cleared the screening and dropped into the bleachers more than 400 feet from the plate. Presently the Giants' inning ended with no

Carl Hubbell, the New York Giants' "meal ticket." His screwball and remarkable control earned him 253 regular-season victories, including 24 in a row in 1936-37. (Associated Press)

further scoring and Hubbell sedately marched out to the mound. He retired three more Reds, this time on pop flies, and it was over. It was as easy as that.

For the screwball maestro it marked his eighth successive pitching victory of 1937 against not a single setback, and this, added to the sixteen straight with which he concluded the 1936 campaign, gives him the amazing all-time mark. It was also only the second time in this unprecedented string that saw Hubbell receive credit for a game in which he did not start.

Sharing the spotlight with the spectacular team of Hubbell and Ott was Dashing Dick Bartell, whose bat exploded a pair of doubles which drove in the other two Giant tallies, the second one tying the score in the eighth. Dick Coffman held the Reds in check until he vacated for a pinch hitter in the eighth. After that it was just a case of the oldest master stepping up, chalking his cue and continuing his unbroken run.

Carl Hubbell's streak was broken on May 31 when the Brooklyn Dodgers beat him, 10–3, before a Memorial Day crowd of 61,756 at the Polo Grounds. The pitcher who has come closest to Hubbell's record is the sinkerballer Roy Face of the Pittsburgh Pirates, who won 22 consecutive games in 1958–59.

Runners-up

1972: Mark Donohue, the Trans-America and United States road-racing king, scored his greatest victory in the Indianapolis 500, taking the lead 13 laps from the end in Roger Penske's McLaren turbo Offy and finishing at an average speed of 163.465 miles an hour. Donohue was killed in a crash at the Ostreichring in Austria in 1975 *(see Aug. 19)*.

1975: The Philadelphia Flyers defeated the Buffalo Sabres, 2–0, in Game 6 at Buffalo's Memorial Auditorium, winning their second straight Stanley Cup title.

Flyers goalie Bernie Parent was named most valuable player of the post-season for the second time in succession.

1968: The National League voted to expand to 12 teams in 1969, adding the Montreal Expos and the San Diego Padres. Because the American League had already created two new teams for '69, each league formed two divisions that led to a post-season tier of playoff games. To some, these League Championship Series stole some of the World Series' glamour.

May 28, 1957
They Took Our Hearts, Too

By JOSEPH M. SHEEHAN

CHICAGO—The Brooklyn Dodgers and the New York Giants received permission today from the National League to switch their respective bases of operation to Los Angeles and San Francisco. The permission, granted unanimously by the other club owners at the league's mid-season meeting here, was conditional on two items that continued to leave room for conjecture that there might be a shift as soon as next season.

The approval in advance of the transfers was predicated on two points: that the Giants and Dodgers request the shifts before Oct. 1, 1957, and that they make the moves together. If these conditions are met, Warren C. Giles, the president of the National League, is empowered by the action taken today to approve the transfer applications. If one club wants to move and one wants to stay, the league would have to reconsider, Giles said. Walter F. O'Malley, the president of the Dodgers, and Horace C. Stoneham, the president of the Giants, both emphasized that it still was far from definite that they would move their clubs.

"In fairness, all I can say now is that this action opens the door for exploration of further possibilities," said O'Malley. While listening with an attentive ear to the blandishments of Los Angeles, the Dodger president still is on record as hoping that the long-stalled campaign to build a new, downtown Brooklyn stadium for the Dodgers will get off the ground.

"At this time I wouldn't say that we would go," said Stoneham. "This permission merely gives us a further chance to examine the possibilities and probabilities." The Giant owner recently received an attractive offer to move the Giants to San Francisco but, perhaps, is under less

Walter O'Malley, the Dodgers' owner, being greeted by officials in California in October 1957 while exiting his private plane marked "Los Angeles Dodgers." Meanwhile, all Brooklyn mourned. (Associated Press)

immediate pressure than the Dodgers to leave New York.

The third trial balloon of what had reportedly been a prospective three-club switch of locations failed to escape. It had been rumored that to obviate the chance of a National League void being left in New York as a result of the possibly impending departure of the Dodgers and Giants, that the Redlegs would move to New York from Cincinnati, where they operate in an equally obsolete and even smaller ballpark than the Polo Grounds or Ebbets Field. Gabe Paul, vice president and general manager of the Redlegs, had said before the meeting, "We are happy in Cincinnati and have no intention of initiating a proposal of any shift."

One analysis of the action here—as O'Malley and Stoneham are well aware—

is that it should have a catalytic effect on someone, somewhere. Backed against the wall as they are because of declining attendance, which is a result of obsolete facilities and metropolitan New York's saturation with televised baseball, the Dodger and Giant presidents unquestionably are receptive to making a change.

Despite assurances by Walter O'Malley and Horace Stoneham that the National League vote merely allowed them to explore possibilities, the Dodgers and Giants opened the 1958 season on the West Coast. The Dodgers played in the Los Angeles Coliseum for four seasons while their permanent home was being built in Chavez Ravine. The Giants used Seals Stadium in downtown San Francisco until Candlestick Park opened in 1960.

Runners-up

1989: Emerson Fittipaldi and Al Unser Jr. entered Turn 3 of the next to last lap of the Indy 500 in the lead and side by side in as stunning a finish as the race has seen. Fittipaldi, slightly behind and below Unser, appeared to come up and touch Unser's left rear wheel, sending him on a frightening spin into the out side wall and allowing Fittipaldi to cross the finish line the winner.

1956: Dale Long of the Pittsburgh Pirates homered off the Brooklyn Dodgers' Carl Erskine at Forbes Field, becoming the first player to hit a home run in eight

consecutive games. Don Mattingly of the Yankees, in 1987, and Ken Griffey Jr. of the Seattle Mariners, in 1993, later tied the record.

1951: Having gone 0 for 26 since being called up from the Minneapolis Millers of the American Association, Willie Mays of the New York Giants got his first major league hit, a home run off the Boston Braves' Warren Spahn at the Polo Grounds. Mays retired in 1973 with 3,282 other hits, 659 of them home runs.

May 29, 1953
The Highest of Highs

KATMANDU, Nepal (Reuters)—The British expedition has conquered Mount Everest, a radio message flashed from Namche Bazar to the British Embassy here today. The message said Edmond Hillary, a 34-year-old New Zealand beekeeper and mountaineer, and Tensing Norkay, the famous Sherpa guide, had reached the hitherto unscaled summit from Camp Eight. The news of this success had to be rushed by runner from the British expedition's base camp on Khumbu Glacier to the radio post at Namche Bazar.

It is understood here that this was the expedition's third attack on the last slopes leading to the summit, a first double attempt having failed. Experts here said the success was largely due to the fine weather, combined with properly acclimatized climbers and the excellent organization and leadership of Col. H.C.J. Hunt. Full details of the exploit are not expected to reach here for some days.

It is believed here that the news was transmitted specially to London by diplomatic channels so Queen Elizabeth could be told on the eve of her coronation that the British expedition had conquered the mountain. The British climbers had succeeded in their plan to give her a world-shaking coronation present. Mount Everest, the 29,002-foot giant, was the last main outpost of the world unknown to man.

The thirteen members of the expedition formed the eleventh team to try to conquer the mountain in the past thirty years. Many climbers have died in the high ice and snow of the Himalaya giant. The Sherpa guide, Tensing Norkay, is a 42-year-old native veteran of more assaults on Mount Everest than any other man.

With 362 porters, twenty Sherpa guides and 10,000 pounds of baggage the expedition left the Nepalese base of Katmandu on March 10. Thus it took eighty days from start to finish.

The climbers carried three flags—the Union Jack, the United Nations flag and the Nepalese flag—to plant on the summit. They made an approach to the "Goddess Mother of the Snows" from the south, or Nepalese side. It was the route reconnoitered by Sir Eric Shipton, who led a British expedition in 1951, and it was the approach by which the Swiss so nearly succeeded last year. All previous parties had started from the Tibetan side, now closed to explorers since the Chinese Communists have moved in.

Tensing Norkay, a Sherpa guide on the summit of Mount Everest. He and Edmund Hillary, a New Zealand beekeeper and mountaineer, planted three flags there—the Union Jack and those of Nepal and the United Nations. (Associated Press)

Runners-up

1922: Justice Oliver Wendell Holmes wrote on behalf of the United States Supreme Court that organized baseball cannot be subject to antitrust legislation because "it would not be called commerce in the commonly accepted uses of those words." The ruling allowed major league teams to operate as a permanent cartel, with little competition against them.

2001: The Supreme Court decided that Casey Martin, the disabled golfer who had battled the P.G.A. Tour's walking rule for four years, had the right to ride in a cart during tournament play. The Tour had sought to impose the rule, arguing that walking is an inherent part of the game. The case was particularly controversial because it put the high court in the position of weighing the nature of a sport's rules for the first time.

1985: British hooligans rooting for the Liverpool soccer club stormed a section of stands filled with fans of the Juventus team from Turin, Italy, during the European Cup final at Heysel Stadium in Brussels. A concrete retaining wall collapsed and 38 people were crushed or trampled to death, 32 of them Italians, and more than 400 were injured. It was the worst sports riot on record.

May 30, 1969
Four Hands on the Wheel

By DAVE ANDERSON

Mario Andretti after driving Andy Granatelli's STP Hawk-Ford to victory in the Indianapolis 500 despite a harrowing slip in Turn 3. "I love you, kid," Granatelli told him. (Associated Press)

INDIANAPOLIS—Inside his red blazer, perspiration was soaking his maroon-and-white striped shirt and wrinkling his purple-and-black striped tie. Andy Granatelli had been entering racing cars in the 500-mile race here since 1946 without winning, but now his driver, Mario Andretti, was an apparent victor.

"Should we go to our garage or to the Firestone garage?" an aide asked Granatelli.

"I won't talk to you about it," snapped Granatelli. "Don't ask me those questions."

Granatelli's superstition was justified. At about that very moment today, Andretti was guiding his blazing-red car toward the No. 2 turn on the 150th of the 200 laps.

Suddenly, the car skipped toward the wall. "I got caught in Mike Mosley's draft," Andretti disclosed later. "The car went sideways. I almost hit the wall: I fought the wheel and got it straightened out. But I was lucky."

Andretti, a slim 138 pounds on his 5-foot-6-inch frame, guided his Hawk-Ford the remaining laps without incident for his first victory here in his first year as one of Granatelli's drivers. But as he waited in the pit area, the 5–7, 250-pound Granatelli maintained his superstition. "I didn't believe it until I saw Mario 100 feet from the flag," Granatelli said, "and I knew he could coast in."

Granatelli remembered the previous two races here, when his turbine cars,

now outlawed, lost in the closing minutes. But this time, Andretti was driving a piston-engine car. "I could've gone another 500 miles," Andretti said, laughing.

"That's because of the STP," said Granatelli, ever the promoter. Granatelli is president of the STP Corporation, whose initials stand for scientifically treated petroleum, an oil additive for automobiles. Wherever he goes, he slaps STP stickers on just about everything, including the backside of the cocktail waitresses in the nearby Holiday Inn. Prior to the race, Granatelli handed out a $500 bill to the chief mechanic of each of the 22 cars that used STP—an outlay of $11,000, of which Andretti will get half, in addition to the prestige of winning the Indianapolis 500.

"This is the greatest," Andretti said. "I don't know why, but you strive so hard for it, I guess that's it." As a rookie here in 1965, Andretti finished third and later won the United States Auto Club title that year. "I went on the 'Joey Bishop Show,'" he recalled, "and I was introduced as the rookie of the year at Indianapolis, not a word about me winning the driving championship. That's what I mean."

Andretti, who grew up in Trieste, Italy, before his family came to the United States, wrecked a Lotus-Ford here 10 days ago in practice. He competed with the discomfort of the burns he received, now healing, above his upper lip, the lower part of his nose and across both cheeks. "It's itchy now," Mario Andretti conceded, "but I had cream on it during the race."

"I love you, kid," Granatelli said, glancing fondly at his tiny driver.

"But you're a sloppy kisser," Andretti said, referring to the kiss Granatelli gave him on greeting him after the victory.

Runners-up

1955: Bill Vukovich, the Indy 500 winner in 1953 and 1954 and the foremost race car driver in America, was killed on Lap 141 while leading the 500 when he plowed into a four-car tangle of wreckage immediately in front of him on the backstretch. His Hopkins Special burst into flames and he died before members of the track safety patrol could extricate him.

1982: Twenty-one-year-old Cal Ripken Jr. of the Baltimore Orioles began his consecutive-games-played streak, starting at third base against the Toronto Blue Jays at Memorial Stadium in Baltimore. The streak lasted for more than 13 years and 3 months (see Sept. 6) and allowed him to surpass Lou Gehrig of the Yankees as baseball's ultimate iron man.

1936: Louis Meyer, 32, of Huntington Park, Calif., drove his Ring-Free Special to a then-unprecedented third Indy 500 victory, winning in 4 hours 35 minutes and averaging 109.069 miles an hour. Meyer's other victories came in 1928 and '33.

May 31, 1967
Fate Rides Shotgun

By FRANK M. BLUNK

INDIANAPOLIS—A.J. Foyt Jr. of Houston won the 51st running of the 500-mile race today when auto racing's newest and fastest creation, a whispering turbine, went out of action with a broken ball-bearing holder in its gear box with only three laps to go and holding a 45-second lead. Foyt, with previous victories here in 1961 and 1964, became the fourth man in the history of this race to wear the victory garland wreath three times. Louis Meyer, Mauri Rose and Wilbur Shaw were the others. The first two Foyt triumphs were in front-mounted, Offenhauser-powered roadsters. Today he had a Ford engine in the rear end of a Coyote chassis, a racer of his own design.

Parnelli Jones of Torrance, Calif., was in charge of Andy Granatelli's STP Turbine Special. He had given notice yesterday that this car would be difficult to beat. It had caused a furor among other owners and drivers when it appeared on the track early this month. And there were many of the old-timers who said "wait and see." They knew that the turbine machine was having gear box and brake troubles. Before the race was halted after 18 laps yesterday, Jones and the turbine special had thrown a scare into the rest of the field. The turbine's speed was superior to that of any of its piston-engine rivals. It moved into and out of the speedway's corners silently and with ease.

But the transmission of the turbine's smooth flowing power to all four wheels had been a big problem for Granatelli, the

car's builder, since its first running. Numerous gear boxes were tried and finally, just before the first qualifying day on May 13, Granatelli announced that he had hit upon the correct setup. Today, however, when Jones passed by on his 180th lap, with only 20 more laps remaining,

A. J. Foyt holding up three digits moments after winning the Indianapolis 500 and the Borg Warner Trophy for the third time. His ring finger was extended with the others 10 years later. (Associated Press)

Granatelli gave him a signal to "ease up." Jones was then 48 seconds ahead and had Foyt, running second, within view. There had been no warning, Jones said later, of the gear trouble. "It just broke and all of a sudden I dropped from a 150-mile-an-hour leader to a nonfinishing also-ran."

Foyt's three victories at Indianapolis, all achieved within seven years, have come after the leader had run into trouble. But Foyt, 32, doesn't back away from the challenges of auto racing. Instead, he accepts the risks, as nearly as possible, on fate's terms. There is talk that his father, who was a successful builder of race cars in Houston, wants him to retire. The black-haired, brown-eyed Foyt Jr. is one

of the few drivers who have become millionaires. Some friends insist that his wife, Lucy, whom he married in 1955, prays for him to quit.

"Retire? The worst of us wait until we're driven to it, by injury or fear," he once said. "You have to want to drive so damn much, or else you wouldn't do it at all. I love racing. I don't fear death. I don't think about it. I'm young. I'm at my best." It all started for Foyt when he was 8 years old. He was presented with a blood-red miniature racing car. "I thought it was the most beautiful thing that ever was," Foyt said in his soft Texas accent. In his teens, everything with wheels was "beautiful" to A.J.—motorcycles, stock cars, midget racers, Indianapolis-type machines. Spinning from dirt track to asphalt, from backwoods ovals to high-powered competition, Foyt tried them all, any place, for any purse.

The small fortune he picked up today for winning will satisfy him for now. But after his last Indy triumph, in 1964, he flew to Bremen, Ohio, for a sprint-car race and then returned for the victory dinner to receive his $153,650 in prizes. "It all adds up," explains A.J. "You drive the big ones and the little ones. This wasn't meant to be a soft sport."

A.J. Foyt won his fourth and final Indy 500 at age 42 in 1977, driving the Coyote-Foyt that he designed and built to a 28-second victory over Tom Sneva. Two other drivers have won four 500's: Al Unser Sr. (see May 24) and Rick Mears (see May 26).

Runners-up

1991: Pat Riley, who coached the Los Angeles Lakers to four N.B.A. titles in the 1980's, became head coach of the Knicks. He brought them within one game of the league title, in 1994, and reached two Eastern Conference finals during his four years in New York.

1983: The Philadelphia 76ers, coached by Billy Cunningham, defeated the defending champion Los Angeles Lakers, 115–108, in Game 4 at the Spectrum in Philadelphia to win the N.B.A. title. The Sixers' center and team leader, Moses

Malone, had predicted three straight four-game sweeps in the playoffs, saying, "Fo', fo', fo'." He wasn't far off. It took the Sixers not 12 games to seize the title but 13.

1987: After squandering a three-games-to-one lead in the Stanley Cup finals, the Edmonton Oilers defeated the rugged Philadelphia Flyers, 3–1, in what amounted to a sucden-death Game 7 at Northlands Coliseum to win their third N.H.L. title in four years.

JUNE

June 1, 1992
Super Mario Sunshine

By JOE LAPOINTE

CHICAGO—Hockey's longest season, and one of its most troubled ones, ended tonight when the Pittsburgh Penguins defeated the Chicago Blackhawks, 6–5, in a wild finale to clinch the Stanley Cup with a four-game sweep of the final round. It was the second consecutive National Hockey League championship for Pittsburgh, which didn't win any in the first 23 years of the franchise. It was the first sweep in the final series since 1988, when Edmonton beat Boston in a series that lasted five games because one game ended in a tie after a power failure.

Mario Lemieux, the captain of the Penguins, scored one goal and added two assists and won the Conn Smythe trophy for the second consecutive season as the most valuable player in the playoffs. Can his team win three or four consecutive championships like the dynasties of Edmonton, Montreal and the Islanders? "That's a pretty strong word, when you talk about dynasty," Lemieux said. "We'll know next year at this time."

In the postgame celebration, Lemieux was asked about comments made by Mike Keenan, the coach of the Blackhawks, who accused Lemieux of "diving" too much to influence the penalty calls of referees. "I'm just going to go in the dressing room and try to dive in the Cup right now," Lemieux said.

The victory was the Penguins' 11th in a row, tying a league record set earlier this spring by Chicago. Dirk Graham, the captain of the Blackhawks, scored a hat trick in the first period. Jeremy Roenick, his star teammate, scored twice, including the final goal midway through the third period to add drama to the finish. The game was tied at 3–3 after one period and at 4–4 after two before Larry Murphy

Mario Lemieux toting the Stanley Cup after the Penguins swept the Blackhawks for their second straight N.H.L. title. It was a special victory for the Penguins, whose coach, Bob Johnson, died of a brain tumor the previous November. (Associated Press)

and Ron Francis scored for the Penguins to open up a two-goal lead early in the third.

It was a joyous conclusion for the Penguins, who struggled throughout the season with many problems off the ice. Their coach, Bob Johnson, died of a brain tumor and was replaced by Scotty Bowman. The team ownership changed hands. And Lemieux suffered several injuries, including chronic back problems and the fracture of a bone in his left hand when he was hit by the stock of the

Rangers' Adam Graves in the second round of the playoffs.

"I thought of him every game in the playoffs," Murphy said of Johnson. "It's not a situation where you say out loud, 'Let's win one for Bob.' But every guy on this team knows we are at the level we are because of Bob Johnson."

Said Bowman, who won four Cups with the Montreal Canadiens in the 1970's: "I started this job Oct. 1. Now it's June. If I was a lady, it's long enough to have a baby."

Runners-up

1946: Assault, ridden by Warren Mehrtens and trained by Max Hirsch, won the Belmont Stakes to complete the third Triple Crown in six years, following Whirlaway's achievement in 1941 (see June 7) and Count Fleet's in 1943. There were 11 Triple Crown winners through 2003.

1994: In one of the remarkable performances in N.B.A. playoff history, Reggie Miller gave the Indiana Pacers a 93–86 victory over the Knicks in Game 5 of the Eastern Conference finals by scoring 25 of his 39 points in the fourth quarter, singlehandedly wiping out the Knicks' double-digit lead. New York, however,

came back to win the series in seven games.

1986: Pat Bradley of Westport, Mass., sank a 15-foot birdie putt on the last hole of the L.P.G.A. championship at the Jack Nicklaus Sports Center in Kings Island, Ohio, giving her a one-stroke victory over Patty Sheehan. The victory made Bradley the first woman to achieve a career Grand Slam in golf, with victories in all four women's majors—the United States Open, the du Maurier Classic, the Nabisco Championship and the L.P.G.A.

June 2, 1974
How It All Began

ROME (AP)—Chris Evert won her first major international tennis tournament today by defeating Martina Navratilova of Czechoslovakia, 6–3, 6–3, in the women's singles final of the Italian open. Miss Evert, a 19-year-old star from Fort Lauderdale, Fla., also won the women's doubles with Olga Morozova of the Soviet Union when Mrs. Helga Masthoff and Heide Orth of West Germany defaulted.

In her singles final, Miss Evert's great consistency and experience were too much for Miss Navratilova, a 17-year-old Czech appearing for the first time in a big international tournament. Miss Evert played impeccably from the baseline during the 80-minute match, went to the net more often than usual, and ruthlessly exploited her opponent's weaker net play with deadly lobs and passing shots that clipped the sidelines.

The women drew warm applause in the seventh game of the opening set when each conceded the other a point on a dubious line call. There were six service breaks in the first set, four for Miss Evert. She broke in the seventh and ninth games, jumping from a 3–3 tie to a 6–3 victory. In the second set, she took a 4–1 lead and went on to win the match.

The default in the women's doubles final by Mrs. Masthoff, because of a knee injury, caused some controversy. The tournament director protested that Mrs. Masthoff had not reported her injury to the proper authorities.

Chris Evert and Martina Navratilova played in the finals of 22 Grand Slam tournaments. Navratilova won 14 of them, including seven of nine Wimbledon finals and three of four United States Open championship matches. The 15-year rivalry between them elevated women's tennis, partly because they were a study in contrasts: a Czech expatriate who became open about her lesbianism against the American girl next door. But both were remarkably evenly matched. Evert won 157 singles titles in her career; Navratilova claimed 167.

Chris Evert winning the French Open championship against Olga Morozova in 1974. Evert, a 19-year-old "girl next door" from Fort Lauderdale, Fla., captured at least one Grand Slam singles title in each of the next 13 years. (Associated Press)

Runners-up

1941: Lou Gehrig, the great Yankee first-baseman and Hall of Famer who had to end his career in 1939 after playing in a record 2,130 consecutive games (*see May 2*), died at his home in the Bronx at age 37 of amyotrophic lateral sclerosis. His death came almost 16 years to the day after he replaced Wally Pipp in the Yankees' lineup.

1935: Babe Ruth, aged 40 and batting .181, was released from his contract by the Boston Braves (*see Feb. 26*) and announced his retirement in his 22nd major league season. He ended his career with a .342 average and 714 home runs—not to mention a pitching record of 94–46 and a run of 29⅔ scoreless innings in the World Series that stood for 43 years.

1990: Suzy Favor of the University of Wisconsin completed an 800- and 1,500-meter double in the N.C.A.A. Track and Field Championships at Duke University. She won the 1,500 for the fourth straight year and claimed an unprecedented ninth individual N.C.A.A. track title.

June 3, 1932
'The Little Napoleon' Surrenders

[Unsigned, *The New York Times*]

NEW YORK—Pleading ill health, which has prevented him from giving his full time and attention to his team, John J. McGraw, outstanding figure in baseball for twoscore years, today resigned as manager of the New York Giants, a post he had held for thirty years. William H. (Memphis Bill) Terry, star first baseman of the team, was named as his successor by Charles A. Stoneham, president of the club. McGraw, however, will continue his association with the club, for which he won ten pennants, as vice president, stockholder and a general adviser, although making it clear that Terry is to assume full responsibilities in the management of the team and is to receive a free hand in its direction.

The resignation of McGraw removes from active participation in baseball the man whose name is synonymous with the game everywhere, even in Japan, where the sport enjoys a prominence second only to this country. During his tenure at the Polo Grounds McGraw established one mark that still stands unparalleled— the guiding of a team to four pennants in a row. A study of the records indicates the astonishing success of McGraw, who, as the master strategist, became known years ago in baseball parlance as "The Little Napoleon." In his earlier days McGraw was as dominating a figure as ever stepped upon the diamond. His first and last objective was to win and along that line he bought, sold and traded more players than any other manager the game has known.

McGraw's exciting exploits and his turbulent outbursts gave color to the sport. He learned his combativeness as a member of the celebrated Baltimore Orioles and when he came to New York he brought with him that same fiery spirit. It was not long after he assumed the managership of the Giants that his praises were being sung by sports followers throughout the city who enjoyed the spectacle of McGraw popping out on the field, eager to protest an umpire's decision at the slightest provocation.

Associated Press Photo
(Underwood)

John McGraw retired after guiding the Giants to 2,763 victories during his 33 years managing the club. (Associated Press)

June 3, 1932
One Bronx Bomber

By WILLIAM E. BRANDT

Lou Gehrig taking a practice cut at Yankee Stadium three months after hitting four home runs in a single game. Gehrig, forever playing in Babe Ruth's glow, was again overshadowed on his record-setting day when another New York baseball legend, John McGraw, retired. (Associated Press)

PHILADEPHIA—Henry Louis Gehrig's name today took rank in baseball's archives along with Bobby Lowe and Ed Delehanty, the only other sluggers who, in more than half a century of recorded diamond battles, ever hit four home runs in one major league game. Largely because of Gehrig's quartet of tremendous smashes the Yankees outstripped the Athletics in a run-making marathon, winning, 20 to 13, after twice losing the lead because of determined rallies by the American League champions.

Homers by Combs, Lazzeri and Ruth enabled the Yankees to tie the all-time record of seven homers by one club in one game. The Yanks, with their twenty-three hits, also set a new modern club-batting record for total bases, with fifty.

Gehrig in his first four times at bat hammered the ball outside the playing area. In the first and fifth innings he sailed balls into the stands in left center. In the fourth and seventh he fired over the right-field wall. Lou had two chances to hit a fifth homer and thus surpass a brilliant record in baseball's books. He grounded out in the eighth, but in the ninth he pointed a terrific drive which Simmons captured only a few steps from the furthest corner of the park. A little variance to either side of its actual line of flight would have sent the ball over the fence or into the stands.

As it was, Lou's four homers tied the all-time record of Lowe in hitting for the circuit in four successive times at bat in 1894. Only three of Delehanty's were in successive times at bat.

Runners-up

1975: Pelé, the World Cup champion from Brazil and soccer's most famous player (see June 21 and Nov. 19), joined the New York Cosmos, bringing international exposure to the North American Soccer League. He signed for $7 million over three years as the world's richest player in team sports.

1995: Pedro Martínez of the Montreal Expos took a perfect game into the 10th inning at Jack Murphy Stadium in San Diego when Bip Roberts of the Padres doubled to lead off the frame. The Expos had scored a run in the top of the

inning; Martínez got a 1–0 victory but not the perfecto.

1888: The San Francisco Examiner published Ernest Thayer's "Casey at the Bat." Thayer, editor of The Harvard Lampoon in college before going to work for The Examiner's founder, William Randolph Hearst, originally published "Casey" anonymously and as a poem. The piece was an instant hit, and reading it brought joy to generations of Americans, if none to Mudville.

The Final Hurdle

MADRID (AP)—Edwin Moses' 122-race winning streak, the longest in the history of track, ended today when Danny Harris, another American, beat him in the 400-meter hurdles at an international meet here. Moses, the world-record holder with a time of 47.02 seconds, last lost on Aug. 26, 1977, in West Berlin, when he was beaten by Harald Schmid of West Germany. Harris, 21 years old, won in 47.56. Moses finished second in 47.69, followed by Nate Page of the United States in 50.12.

"I ran a good race and the guy that beat me is 10 years younger and ran the race of his life," Moses said tonight. "It's very early in the season for me to be running in Europe. I'm not as sharp as I would be normally. This is one of my best times for so early in the season. I'm not disappointed at all with the race I ran."

Moses led over the first two of the 10 hurdles, but Harris took the lead at the fifth hurdle and stayed in front. Moses had trouble at the last hurdle. "I hit the 10th hurdle and that really cost me the race," Moses said. "I expect to do much better. He was very lucky to win the race. He built up an early lead. There's probably no other person in the world who could run this time."

Moses tried to recover after hitting the hurdle but could not. "He moved out slightly," Moses said of Harris. "I came back toward the end but there was not enough time."

Moses was smiling as he ran a lap of honor after the race. A half-hour later, the crowd of about 11,000 was still chanting his name. After allowing Moses the solitary lap of honor, Harris shook his hand. He then said: "It's been a great day for me. It makes me proud to have beaten an athlete of his caliber."

It was the first meeting between Moses and Harris since the 1984 Olympics in Los Angeles, when they finished first and second. Moses, 31, had won 107 consecutive finals and 15 preliminaries. Moses's streak was the longest for a track event, but not for a field event. Iolanda Balas of Rumania had 180 straight victories in the women's high jump in the 1950's and 1960's.

Edwin Moses stretching his 400-meter hurdles streak to 103 victories while winning a gold medal at the 1984 Los Angeles Olympics in 47.75 seconds. The silver medal went to Danny Harris in 48.13. It was Harris who broke Moses's streak 19 races and three years later. (Associated Press)

Runners-up

1968 Don Drysdale of the Los Angeles Dodgers, who would go 14–12 with a 2.15 earned run average this year and lose the Cy Young Award to the St. Louis Cardinals' Bob Gibson with his 1.12 e.r.a., set a major league record of six consecutive shutouts by defeating the Pittsburgh Pirates at Dodger Stadium, 5–0.

1976: The Boston Celtics defeated the Phoenix Suns, 87–80, in Game 6 of the N.B.A. finals at Memorial Coliseum in Phoenix to win their 13th title in 20 years, four games to two. The Celtics' shooting guard Jo Jo White was named the most valuable player in the finals.

1980: Gordie Howe, the former great right winger for the Detroit Red Wings (see Nov. 27), retired from the Hartford Whalers at age 52 after 32 years in both the N.H.L. and the World Hockey Association. His 26 years and 1,767 games played in the N.H.L. are records that are unlikely to ever be broken.

June 5, 1977
Walton Stands Up to the Man

By DAVE ANDERSON

The Portland Trail Blazers, led by Bill Walton, defeated the Philadelphia 76ers, 109–107, on this date to win the N.B.A. championship by four games to two. Walton scored 20 points, snatched 23 rebounds, blocked 8 shots and made 7 assists as the Blazers, in only their seventh season, swept to the title after losing the first two games. The following column appeared in The Times on June 7.

PORTLAND, Ore.—Early in Bill Walton's second season with the Portland Trail Blazers, he was asked to assess his career that had been hounded by injuries. "When I'm healthy," he said, "I play real good, I think."

"Then," the 6-foot-11-inch center was asked, "nobody has seen the real Bill Walton yet?"

"I don't think so."

But everybody has seen the real Bill Walton now. Healthy virtually throughout his third season and his first playoffs, the real Bill Walton has stood up and the other Trail Blazers have stood up with him as the National Basketball Association champions. No more nasty remarks about his vegetarian diet, please; his teammate, Maurice Lucas, also is a vegetarian.

For the traditionalists, at least Bill Walton sheared his long red beard and ponytail to more conservative lengths. And he wasn't talking about Patty Hearst any

Bill Walton, right, fighting for position against Kareem Abdul-Jabbar of the Lakers in the 1977 N.B.A. semifinals. The Trail Blazers pushed aside Los Angeles and then dispatched the 76ers in the finals. (Associated Press)

more. He didn't have time. He was too busy waving his arms and directing the offense or rebounding on defense during the Trail Blazers' conquest of the Philadelphia 76ers in six games. Bill Walton was everything he used to be at the University of California, Los Angeles, when John Wooden was his coach. Eddie Donovan, the New York Knicks' general manager, has a theory as to why.

"I think Jack Ramsay reached Walton," says Eddie Donovan. "Of all the coaches in our league, Jack Ramsay is the closest to being the John Wooden type—scholarly, available. I think Walton responded to that." Bill Walton surely responded to Jack Ramsay, but so did his teammates. "They're talented," the coach said, "and they're willing to play together."

Being willing to play together is what basketball is all about. "The coach can say what he wants," Jack Ramsay said, "but the players have to respond." Bill Walton led that response— as the captain, as the leader, as the center that an N.B.A. championship team invariably needs. Bill Walton also responded to the aura of the N.B.A. championship series, basketball's showcase event.

"This was better even than at U.C.L.A.," the center said, "because this was against the best players in the world."

Runners-up

1943: Count Fleet, ridden by Johnny Longden, won the sixth Triple Crown—and the fourth in nine years—by defeating Fairy Manhurst by 25 lengths in the Belmont Stakes. Count Fleet's time for the mile and a half was 2:28⅕, the best since the Belmont went to that distance in 1926.

1937: War Admiral, with Charlie Kurtsinger up, won the Triple Crown in the Belmont despite a torn heel apparently injured in the starting gate. The 3-year-old son of Man o' War went on to take Horse of the Year honors but was soon overshadowed by Seabiscuit, the "people's champ" (see Nov. 1).

1993: Julie Krone, 29, became the first woman jockey to ride a winner in a Triple Crown race when she took Colonial Affair to a 2¼-length victory over Kissin Kris in the 125th running of the Belmont.

June 6, 1992
Seles Toughs It Out

By ROBIN FINN

PARIS—Monica Seles provided a guttural soundtrack for this most grand of Grand Slam finales today, and in the end, she didn't lose her voice or her French Open crown. Steffi Graf provided a silent and tireless threat, and after climbing back from a paralyzing first set, valiantly rescued herself from five match points. But because of the killer instincts of Seles, the No. 1 player in the world, the herculean effort by the German to reclaim a title she last held in 1988 was in vain, and she lost, 6–2, 3–6, 10–8.

For nearly three hours, the 18-year-old Seles used her spring-loaded strokes to try to discourage Graf, and she finally gained her third consecutive French Open title, and the sixth Grand

Monica Seles uncoiling one of her signature two-handed forehands at Steffi Graf during the French Open finals. Seles slugged her way to a third consecutive triumph on the red clay at Roland Garros in Paris. (Bettmann/Corbis)

Slam title of her career, when Graf made an habitual move at just the wrong time. On the sixth match point, Graf skirted her backhand in order to attack the ball with her most intimidating shot, a full-blown forehand, but instead of putting Seles into reverse, the shot was smacked into the net and cost its disappointed launcher the match.

"I was trying to be the one who was aggressive," said the 22-year-old Graf, who is ranked No. 2 in the world and would have gained her 11th Grand Slam title with a victory. "I just wish I would have played better on those big points; it definitely was a special match, but it's really difficult to feel great about it 10 minutes after it's

over." The victory by Seles required 2 hours 43 minutes of effort from the participants and, more important, made the exhausted Yugoslav the first woman in 55 years to win three straight French Open titles. The last woman to have such a hold on the event was Hilde Sperling of Germany from 1935–37.

In the final set, which lasted 91 minutes, Seles served three times to end the match and had to struggle to get past Graf's most determined Grand Slam campaign since she defeated Gabriela Sabatini in last year's Wimbledon final. "But she's definitely a tough player, and even if it's close, and even if she's tired, she's always going for it," Graf said about Seles, who

later agreed with that somewhat grudging but clearly accurate evaluation. "I could have stayed out there longer if I had to," Seles said. "I have that kind of personality, that even if it's taking my last breath on the court, I'm going to run for the ball."

Seles now seems invincible whenever her calendar shows a Grand Slam date. The victory today was her fifth straight in the Grand Slams in which she has played, and the fifth she has won in the last six over all. (She didn't play at the 1991 Wimbledon.) The teenager has won all six Grand Slam finals she has been in. "I think it was the most emotional match I've played ever, not just in a Grand Slam, but in any tournament," Seles said.

Runners-up

1999: A suddenly resurgent Andre Agassi of Las Vegas defeated Andre Medvedev of Ukraine in the French Open in four sets, becoming the fifth man to win all four Grand Slam events—the Australian, the French and the United States Opens and Wimbledon. The others who have won all four: Rod Laver of Australia, Fred Perry of Britain, Roy Emerson of Australia and Don Budge of Oakland, Calif.

1946: The Basketball Association of America, forerunner of the N.B.A. (see Aug. 11), was formed with Maurice Podoloff as its president. Of the 11 franchises that

composed the B.A.A. in the 1946–47 season, only three remain—the Boston Celtics, the New York Knickerbockers and the Golden State Warriors (originally Philadelphia Warriors).

1944: Sports officials across the country, including all major league team owners, canceled games and events as the Allied forces began D-Day operations in Normandy. The next time baseball postponed an entire day's schedule was Sept. 11, 2001.

June 7, 1941
True to His Name

By BRYAN FIELD

Whirlaway enjoying a congratulatory pat from Eddie Arcaro as the trainer Ben A. Jones, right, kept him steady in the winner's circle at Belmont Park. Whirlaway became the fifth Triple Crown champion in racing history. (Associated Press)

NEW YORK—Whirlaway today did the expected in his own proud manner when he won the seventy-third Belmont Stakes before 30,801 persons on the final afternoon of a record-breaking Belmont Park meeting. The chestnut colt from the Calumet Farm raced through the stretch so easily that he had his ears pricking, and he also had that mightiest triple crown tilted jauntily on his handsome forelock. When he finished the historic mile and a half run that grossed $52,270 in 2:31 flat over a fast track, the son of Blenheim II and Dustwhirl became the fifth horse in American racing history to capture the Kentucky Derby, Preakness and Belmont Stakes.

Warren Wright, owner of Whirlaway and the Calumet Farm, had to choose between seeing his son or his horse, and of course he chose to go to his boy's graduation in the West. Yet he heard by radio about Calumet's most successful days at any track, since his juvenile colt, Some Chance, captured the $15,640 National Stallion Stakes, which had its twenty-ninth running. Whirlaway was so good that he made ducks and drakes of his opposition. Robert Morris was second, beaten three lengths, and five lengths before Yankee Chance. Itabo trailed. The winner was a standout 1-to-4 favorite and returned only $2.50 and $2.10, there being no show betting.

Perhaps the best way to describe the manner in which Whirlaway dominated the field is to tell what Eddie Arcaro, the winning jockey, did in the race, and what

he said about it. Before a half mile had been run Arcaro startled thousands by suddenly sending Whirlaway dashing to the front, a reversal of riding tactics from all of Whirlaway's previous races. It looked revolutionary from the stands, and indeed it was, for suddenly it was learned that the boy had had racing orders from Trainer Ben Jones.

But this is what happened, as Arcaro tells it: "I was last with Whirlaway going away and I was going to stay last for a while. But at the mile post [a mile to go], there was no pace. It was very slow. So I yelled to those other jocks: 'I'm leaving.'" It was then that the watchers in the stand saw Whirlaway shoot to the front. He dashed far ahead in a twinkling. Through the backstretch Whirlaway opened six or eight lengths. Robert Morris, Itabo and Yankee Chance followed in Indian file.

Would Whirlaway shoot his bolt? Had he got away from Arcaro? Was his headstrong trait coming out in a different way? All of these questions were asked and unanswered as the race went on. The big challenge, and the only one of the race, came from the far turn to the head of the stretch. There Alfred Robertson moved forward with Robert Morris. Robert Morris cut that big lead, but he never made Arcaro go to a drive nor did Eddie ever make use of the whip.

Here's just what that challenge amounted to, in Robertson's words after the finish: "I thought we had a chance when I moved, but it was no use." That "no use" just about describes it. Whirlaway was safely home with the triple crown safely his. Before him only Sir Barton, Gallant Fox, Omaha and War Admiral completed the sweep of Derby, Preakness and Belmont.

Runners-up

1986: Woodford Cefis (Woody) Stephens, 72, one of the most learned trainers in racing history, won an unprecedented fifth straight Belmont Stakes when Danzig Connection, an 8-to-1 shot ridden by Chris McCarron, beat Johns Treasure by 1¼ lengths.

1978: Center Wes Unseld sank the deciding foul shots to lead the Washington Bullets, coached by Dick Motta, to a 105–99 Game 7 victory over the SuperSonics in Seattle and give the Bullets (years later renamed the Wizards)

their only N.B.A. title. "The opera isn't over," Motta said in what became a team rallying cry, "until the fat lady sings."

1996: In a changing of the guard among the lighter weights, Oscar De La Hoya (22–0) scored a savage four-round technical knockout of Julio César Chávez (97–2–1) in a World Boxing Council junior welterweight title bout in Las Vegas. De La Hoya, 23, became heir to Sugar Ray Leonard and Chávez would never be the same fighter again.

June 8, 1986
Master of the Head Fake

By ROY S. JOHNSON

BOSTON—Watching Larry Bird perform must be very much like being on the same court with him, only safer. The unfortunate teammate who looks away or relaxes for just an instant may get smacked in the temple with the basketball. Bird doesn't take it well when one of his passes is fumbled out of bounds. He glares disdainfully at the offender.

The spectator who blinks isn't subjected to that, but he may miss the most intriguing part of Bird's talents—the subtleties that sometimes make it seem as if the game he's playing is his alone: the body language—a twitch of his shoulder, hands or his head. The eye movement, distracting the defender's concentration. The extra dribble that moves his man another inch, creating just enough room for him to thread a pass to a teammate or transform a well-covered shot into an open one. The bit of hesitation that creates chaos for everyone but him.

The Boston Celtics gained their 16th championship this afternoon at Boston Garden largely because Bird reached that plane. He scored 29 points, snatched 11 rebounds, fed his teammates for 12 assists

Larry Bird driving to the basket against the Rockets' Rodney McCray in Game 1 of the 1986 N.B.A. finals. Bird's talent and tenacity lifted the Celtics to three titles during the 80's and elevated the N.B.A. to a new level of popularity. (Associated Press)

and even disrupted the Houston Rockets with three steals. His efforts solidified his selection as the most valuable player of the final series. "He is undoubtedly in my mind at least the best basketball player playing the game today," said his teammate Dennis Johnson.

Despite his team's 55–38 halftime lead today, Bird—with 16 points, eight rebounds and eight assists—wasn't happy at intermission. He felt he wasn't "going at it enough."

"If I get a few more shots," he said, "we could have put it away in the first half."

When Bird wants the ball, he doesn't have to ask. "They know," he says of his teammates. "Just by getting mad and storming around, I got everybody's attention. I didn't want this day to slip away from me."

Bill Fitch, the Rockets' coach, was wary of Bird. "I truly think that when he gets like that, he believes he can do anything he wants," Fitch said. "I love it. There are an awful lot of guys on this team who can learn from that. It's like they say, how do you teach four dumb dogs? Throw one smart one out there and the others'll learn from him. Larry's that smart dog."

Runners-up

1966: The 47-year-old N.F.L. and the seven-year-old American Football League agreed to merge in 1970. The new N.F.L. would have two 13-team conferences: the A.F.C., composed mostly of former A.F.L. teams such as the Oakland Raiders, the Jets and the Boston Patriots, and the N.F.C., with teams such as the Giants, the Chicago Bears and the Green Bay Packers (see May 10).

1985: A newly muscled Chris Evert won the French Open, finally defeating her nemesis Martina Navratilova, 6–3, 6–7, 7–5, to temporarily regain the No. 1 ranking in women's tennis (see June 2). Between 1974 and '86, Evert won the French a record seven times; on three of those occasions, Martina was her victim.

1965: The Kansas City Athletics made the Arizona State University outfielder Rick Monday the No. 1 selection in baseball's first free-agent draft. Monday reached the major leagues in 1966 but played most of his 19-year career with the Chicago Cubs and the Los Angeles Dodgers (see April 25).

A Horse for the Ages

By JOE NICHOLS

Ron Turcotte, atop Secretariat, sizes up the field behind him in the final turn of the Belmont Stakes en route to capturing the Triple Crown. Secretariat won by an astounding 31 lengths and ran the 1½ miles in 2:24, the fastest ever. (Associated Press)

NEW YORK—Secretariat won the Belmont Stakes today with a finality that was incredible. The Meadow Stable star flashed to success in the 1½-mile event by the improbable margin of 31 lengths over Twice a Prince, his runner-up, and, even with the big margin, he set a track record time of 2:24.

The performance was executed under a splendid ride by Ron Turcotte, and was most noteworthy in that it enabled Secretariat to become the ninth winner of the Triple Crown for 3-year-olds. A quarter of a century ago Citation turned the trick, and Secretariat is the first since then to do so. He won the Kentucky Derby at 1¼ miles on May 5, and the Preakness at 1³⁄₁₆ miles on May 19.

A crowd of 69,138, the second-largest turnout to see a Belmont Stakes, attended the 105th running of the race. It had five contestants, and the advance indications were that it would turn out to be a duel between Secretariat, whose payoff at the end was $2.20 for $2 to win, and Sham, who competes in the silks of Sigmund Sommer. Sham was in there for a while, but he found the going too tough as the contest went on, and he wound up in the most unlikely spot—last place.

The race, as regards tight competition, was hardly a tingler, considering the huge margin of victory. But it held continuous excitement because of the superequine achievement of Secretariat. At the start he went to the front with Sham, who was ridden by Laffit Pincay, and for a spell the pair raced together, the others being "nowhere." Approaching the three-quarter pole, Turcotte turned around to spot his pursuer, who was two lengths behind. Assured that his margin was a comfortable one, Turcotte just sped away to the score, which had to be the easiest one of

Secretariat's career, while Sham cracked completely under the fast pace.

It was obvious through the going that Turcotte was out for the record with Secretariat, just as he was in the Kentucky Derby. He corroborated the speculation when he returned to the winner's circle, saying, "When we got to the stretch, and I saw those figures on the tote board, I knew that I was going to a record." Incidentally, the world record for a mile and a half (on turf, and not on the dirt, like the Belmont) is 2:23, set by Fiddle Isle at Santa Anita in 1970. The American record on dirt, which was broken today, was 2:26⅕. Set by Going Abroad at Aqueduct in 1964.

Secretariat is trained by Lucien Lauren and owned by Mrs. John (Penny) Tweedy, who directs the activities of the Meadows interests founded by her late father, Christopher T. Chenery. The horse, a Virginia-bred son of Bold Ruler and Somethingroyal, now has a record of 12 victories in his 15 races. His share of today's purse raised his career earnings to $895,242.

"He's just the complete horse," Turcotte said. "I let him run a bit early to get position in the first turn. Once he got in front of Sham, he wasn't about to give anything away. I kept looking back. The last 70 yards or so I seen on the toteboard teletimer I was breaking the record pretty good, so I let him go on a little. Just a hand ride. I never hit him once."

Secretariat was the ninth and by all estimates the greatest Triple Crown winner of the 20th century. Affirmed (see June 10) was the last three-crown champion to date, in 1978. Ron Turcotte was paralyzed from the waist down during a racing spill at Saratoga, N.Y., in 1978.

Runners-up

1985: The Los Angeles Lakers, coached by Pat Riley, defeated the Boston Celtics, 111–100, at Boston Garden in the decisive Game 6 to win their first N.B.A. championship over the Celtics in nine series against them since 1959. The Lakers' Kareem Abdul-Jabbar, a former New Yorker, likened the long-sought victory to that of the Brooklyn Dodgers over the Yankees in 1955.

1899: James J. Jeffries of Los Angeles, a 206-pounder who once was an aspiring boilermaker, knocked out the defending champion Bob Fitzsimmons of Cornwall, England, who weighed only 167 pounds, in the 11th round of their world heavyweight championship fight at Coney Island in Brooklyn.

1993: The Montreal Canadiens, behind brilliant goaltending by Patrick Roy, defeated Wayne Gretzky and the Los Angeles Kings, 4–1, giving them a four-game sweep in the Stanley Cup finals and their 24th N.H.L. title. The postgame celebration in Montreal turned into a riot, with 168 people injured and an estimated $10 million in property damage.

June 10, 1978
Losing Isn't Everything

By STEVE CADY

NEW YORK—Affirmed fought off Alydar one more time today, and his courage under the fiercest of pressure in the 110th Belmont Stakes brought him a sweep of the triple crown. No horse ever worked harder for it, or deserved it more. For the last half-mile of the mile-and-a-half "test of the champion," Affirmed and Alydar ran head to head. At the finish, with a crowd of 65,417 at Belmont Park and a television audience of millions on the brink of a nervous breakdown, Affirmed's head was still in front.

At the parimutuel windows, that meant $3.20 for $2. To Affirmed's people, it meant the fulfillment of a lifetime dream. Even Steve Cauthen, the Harbor View Farm colt's unflappable 18-year-old jockey, didn't know quite how to explain what his golden 3-year-old had done in those last desperate yards. "I can't believe it," he said, reflecting the unanimous reaction of racing fans to what had to be one of the most dramatic Belmonts in history.

Never has a triple crown sweep been sealed by such a narrow margin. It took a photo-finish camera to determine that Affirmed had won by a head. But young Cauthen knew he had it. He stood up in the saddle a few yards past the finish, and waved his left hand high in the air. Florida-bred Affirmed, now with 14 firsts and two seconds in 16 starts, became the third triple

crown winner in six years and the second in two years, the first time there were consecutive sweeps. Today's Belmont, making Affirmed the 11th triple crown winner, was the kind of close-combat struggle that demonstrated why humans have been so fascinated by thoroughbred racehorses for centuries.

From a slow early pace that helped front-running Affirmed the last half-mile was furious. The final time of 2:26⅘ was the third fastest in Belmont Stakes history, bettered only by Secretariat's 2:24 and Gallant Man's 2:26⅗. No final half-mile in the Belmont was ever run any faster than Affirmed and Alydar ran it. And racing history itself has seldom seen two 3-year-olds as good as Affirmed and Alydar in the same season.

Never in that long history have two horses fought each other so frequently in a rivalry that has produced such close margins. In nine meetings, Affirmed and Kentucky-bred Alydar have raced a total of nine miles. Affirmed has won seven of those battles, but his net margin is still just under three lengths. His total margin in the triple crown series was fewer than two lengths, by far the slimmest of any triple crown winner. He beat Alydar in the Kentucky Derby five weeks ago by a length and a half, and beat him in the Preakness by a neck.

It's a good thing Affirmed is a racehorse, not a sentimentalist. He was just about the only one in his camp with completely dry eyes after today's excruciatingly tense duel in the sun.

Steve Cauthen and Affirmed, on the rail, finishing a nose in front of Alydar and Jorge Velásquez in the Belmont Stakes in the climax of the horses' memorable rivalry. In three Triple Crown races, the two colts were separated by less than two lengths. (Associated Press)

Runners-up

1948: Tony Zale, of Gary, Ind., regained the world middleweight title in a fierce bout, knocking out Rocky Graziano, of New York City, after 1 minute 8 seconds of the third round at Ruppert Stadium in Newark. It was the last of three brawls between the pair. Three months later Zale lost the title to Algerian-born Marcel Cerdan of France and retired.

1977: Thirty-nine-year-old Al Geiberger of Woodenville, Wash., shot 59—the first sub-60 round ever recorded in a P.G.A. Tour event—in the second round of the Memphis Golf Classic at Colonial Country Club. His round included 11 birdies,

an eagle and an 8-foot birdie putt on No. 18. Chip Beck and David Duval (see Jan. 24) have since shot 59's.

2000: The New Jersey Devils (see June 24) defeated the Dallas Stars, 2–1, at 8:20 of the second overtime when Jason Arnott scored the deciding goal in Game 6 in Dallas to win their second Stanley Cup title in five years. The remarkable series featured four one-goal games, a triple-overtime thriller and the double-overtime finale. The Devils' Scott Stevens was named most valuable player.

June 11, 1978
The Rookie Sensation

[Unsigned, *The New York Times*]

MASON, Ohio—Nancy Lopez left all of the other members of the Ladies Professional Golf Association chasing rainbows again today when she picked up her biggest pot of gold so far, winning the 24th L.P.G.A. Championship and the $22,500 first prize in her fourth straight victory. The amazing 24-year-old rookie, never really threatened since she opened the final round five shots ahead of the field, shot a two-under-par 36, 34–70 for a 72-hole total of 275, a tournament record. Mary Mills shot the previous low of 278 to win in 1964.

By shooting 13 under par for four rounds on the 6,312-yard Kings Island course, Miss Lopez finished six strokes in front of Amy Alcott, who had 71 today for 281. Miss Lopez, continuing to be in a class by herself, gained her sixth triumph and first national title since turning professional last summer. Once again she played steady golf, utilizing her ability as the most accurate woman off the tees, the best putter, and one of the half-dozen longest hitters on the tour. She also continued to display a vivacious charm that has made her a big draw in the L.P.G.A.

Ray Volpe, commissioner of the tour, would not say what most persons feel—that Miss Lopez is the best gallery attraction the L.P.G.A. has ever had—

Nancy Lopez sinking a birdie putt during the final round of the Bankers Trust Classic in Rochester, N.Y. Lopez won a record fifth consecutive L.P.G.A. tournament and her popularity seemed to know no bounds. (Associated Press)

but did say, "Nancy is certainly one of the best things that has happened to the L.P.G.A." Miss Alcott, a Californian who is only 11 months older than Miss Lopez, praised the winner. "She's one hell of a competitor and I've never seen anyone who accepts what she does with such humility," the second-place finisher said.

Miss Lopez became the second rookie to win the L.P.G.A. championship (Sandra Post won the title in 1968). Following her triumph, Miss Lopez said, "Now that I have won four in a row I'd like to break the record and win five in a row."

She displayed her calm, concentrated approach to the game right at the start today when she missed the second green with her approach and made an unimpressive chip shot to the pin. She then drained a right-to-left 16-foot putt for par. She saved par on the seventh with a similarly-breaking 10-foot putt after a weak chip, and parred the first nine holes to make it virtually impossible to catch her. When Miss Lopez dropped her final putt, most in the record crowd of over 20,000 cheered her wildly, with many giving the now familiar call of "Nan-Cee." She ran to her father, Domingo, and gave him a big hug.

Domingo Lopez said, "She loves to play for the people."

Runners-up

1950: Ben Hogan *(see June 16),* who survived a near-fatal car crash in February 1949 and returned to tournament competition in January, defeated Lloyd Mangrum and George Fazio in an 18-hole playoff to win his second United States Open title, at Merion Golf Club in Ardmore, Pa.

1982: Larry Holmes knocked out Gerry Cooney, billed in some circles as the "great white hope," in the 13th round of their heavyweight championship fight at Caesars Palace in Las Vegas. Holmes, an underestimated champion who

defended his title 21 times between 1978 and '85, was 53–3 with 37 knockouts when he initially retired in 1991.

1955: At the famous LeMans, France, racing circuit, more than 80 spectators were killed when a Mercedes sports car driven by Pierre Levegh of France hit a pit road barrier at high speed, burst into flames and hurtled parts into a congested grandstand nearby. It was by far the single greatest loss of life in auto-racing history.

June 12, 1991
Jordan Transformed

By CLIFTON BROWN

INGLEWOOD, Calif.—It ended seven years of frustration for Michael Jordan. It ended 25 years of frustration for the Chicago Bulls. And it ended in perfect fashion for the Bulls, because they did it not by relying solely on Jordan, but by relying on each other. The Chicago Bulls are the new National Basketball Association champions, by virtue of their emotional 108–101 victory over the Los Angeles Lakers tonight. By ending the series in five games and winning the final four games of the series, the Bulls turned what was supposed to be a classic confrontation into a personal coronation.

Chicago steamrolled through the playoffs with a 15-2 record, smothering teams with their defense, dazzling them with their offense and surprising them with their confidence. When it was over, Jordan shed tears of joy. He was unanimously voted the most valuable player of the series, after a 30-point, 10-assist performance that led to a moment he will treasure for a lifetime. So too will the city of Chicago treasure the Bulls' winning their first title in their 25-year history.

"No one can ever take this away from me," said Jordan, whose voice cracked on several occasions in the postgame news conference. "This has been a seven-year struggle for me. It should get rid of the stigma of being a one-man team. We have players surrounding myself that make us

Michael Jordan, surrounded by his wife and father, weeps as he holds the Bulls' first championship trophy after carrying the team with no reward for seven seasons. He twice led the Bulls to three straight titles, 1991 to '93 and 1996 to '98. (Getty Images)

an effective basketball team. I don't know if I'll ever have this same feeling again."

Thanks to John Paxson and Scottie Pippen, Jordan will feel good all summer. Pippen capped a sensational playoff series with a stunning all-round game—32 points, 13 rebounds, 7 assists and 5 steals. But it was Paxson (20 points, 9-for-12 shooting) who made the clutch shots in the waning minutes of the game, scoring 10 points in the final 6 minutes. With the score tied at 93, Paxson made two jump shots and a driving layup to give the Bulls a 99–93 lead. Chicago never trailed again, but Paxson wasn't finished. He added another jump shot from the top of the key to give Chicago a 103–96 lead with 1:58 left.

Then after the Lakers closed to within

102–101 with 1:13 left, Paxson struck again. Jordan drove into the lane, and as usual three Lakers surrounded him and left Paxson wide open. Jordan made the pass, Paxson hit the 18-foot jump shot, and the Bulls led, 105–101, with 56 seconds left. In the end, Jordan and the Bulls were too good. No longer will people wonder whether Michael Jordan's game is conducive to winning a championship. "We'll probably celebrate until training camp next year," Pippen said. "But we've been through a lot. We deserve it."

Michael Jordan and the Bulls this season truly learned how to win. He led the team to five more N.B.A. titles in the next seven years, including the famous "three-peat" over the Phoenix Suns in 1993 (see June 14 and 20).

Runners-up

2002: Led by Shaquille O'Neal and Kobe Bryant, the Los Angeles Lakers, coached by Phil Jackson, beat the New Jersey Nets, 113–107, in Game 4 of the N.B.A. finals at the Meadowlands. The Lakers became only the fifth team in league history to win three straight titles—and three of those teams were coached by Jackson.

1948: Calumet Farm's Citation, ridden by Eddie Arcaro and trained by Jimmy Jones, beat Better Self by eight lengths to win the Belmont Stakes and become the fourth horse of the decade, after Whirlaway (1941), Count Fleet ('43) and Assault ('46), to win the Triple Crown.

1930: Max Schmeling of Germany became the only fighter to win the world heavyweight championship on a foul when Jack Sharkey of Boston was disqualified by Referee Jim Crowley for a low blow in the fourth round at Yankee Stadium. Schmeling and Sharkey, whose real name was Joseph Zukauskas, were fighting for the title vacated by Gene Tunney, who had retired.

June 13, 1948
Goodbye to All That

By ARTHUR DALEY

NEW YORK—Nostalgia dripped all over Yankee Stadium today in the wake of weeping skies as an amazing crowd of 49,641 turned out to celebrate the twenty-fifth anniversary of the opening of the House That Ruth Built and to welcome back the heroes of the 1923 team which brought the first world championship to the Bronx Bombers. In impressively sentimental ceremonies Babe Ruth's famed No. 3 was permanently retired and his uniform formally presented to the baseball shrine at Cooperstown as eyes grew moist and fans choked up at the touching scene.

But all was not pathos. The game between the '23 heroes and later day stars, a rugged two-inning affair played before the current day Yankees defeated the Indians, 5–3, was delightfully hilarious despite creaking bones and faltering limbs. It had Abner Doubleday spinning in his grave, the major spin coming when the Old-Timers were generously given four outs in the second frame. They didn't need any of them, either, because they already had won, 2–0. They won because the still lean Bob Meusel, who used to hit line drives in the old days, lofted a simple blooper to right center which bounced off Red Rolfe's glove for a hit. At least that's what the official scorer called it, after succumbing to his most generous and gentlemanly instincts.

The climax, however, came when the two men who made the Yankees what

they are today, Ed Barrow and Babe Ruth, came ambling from opposite dugouts to embrace unashamedly at home plate. That was a thrill which made the fans forget the rain, the lowering skies and the damp discomfort of a raw, unpleasant day. They had to swallow hard, then, engulfed as they were in a wave of emo-

Babe Ruth, using a bat to support his fragile frame, bids adieu to fans and players on the 25th anniversary of Yankee Stadium, the house that he frequently filled. Ruth, 53, died of throat cancer two months later. (Nat Fein/The New York Herald Tribune)

tion. Thrilling, too, was the tender message the band played, "Auld Lang Syne." Should old acquaintance be forgot? Never. Not when they are such stalwarts as these. The twenty pennants which bedecked the Stadium facade eloquently bespoke the dynasty they created.

There was a reverent hush when the Bambino, no longer the hulking, dynamic and domineering figure he once was, strode hesitatingly to the microphone and

spoke in his muted and strangely croaking voice. He told the fans in sincere and simple words how wonderful the occasion was for him and of his pride in having hit the first home run ever struck at the Stadium. It had been a tiring day for the ailing Sultan of Swat. First of all, it was an emotional drain on him to greet his old buddies in the dressing room. To them he was still the king. Obsequiously they approached him for his autograph. That was something to see, these case-hardened old companions getting the signature of their pal and idol. But he was the central figure of the day. Without him it would have been empty.

It was a physical drain on him, too. He sat in the dank, chilling runway behind the dugout for a quarter of an hour, waiting for the drizzle to halt. A topcoat was thrown across his once sweeping shoulders and buttoned around his tender throat. He smiled wanly as the merry Waite Hoyt entertained Bob Meusel, Wally Pipp and some of the other Old-Timers with his reminiscences. "They took a good many years to retire your number, Babe," Hoyt remarked with a chuckle. "They retired mine in 1930—damn quick, too. And without notice, too." The Babe grinned.

Babe Ruth was in the late stages of throat cancer when this first Old-Timers game was held in a major-league park and the first uniform number was retired. He died two months later, on Aug. 16.

Runners-up

1953: Ben Hogan *(see June 16)* won the United States Open for a record-tying fourth time, tying the mark of Willie Anderson and the great Bobby Jones and defeating Sam Snead by six shots with a final-round 71 at the Oakmont Country Club near Pittsburgh. Jack Nicklaus tied the record with his fourth Open title in 1980 *(see June 15)*.

1935: James J. Braddock, 29, a New Jersey longshoreman, won a unanimous 15-round decision over Max Baer of Germany to gain the world heavyweight title at Madison Square Garden in New York. Braddock held the crown for almost two years, until 21-year-old Joe Louis knocked him out in 1937 *(see June 22)*.

1998: Haile Gebrselassie of Ethiopia broke the world 5,000-meter record held by Daniel Komer of Kenya by running 12:39.36 in Helsinki. It was Gebrselassie's 14th world record. Two weeks before, he had broken the 10,000-meter mark held by Paul Tergat of Kenya when he ran 26:22.75 in Hengelo, the Netherlands.

June 14, 1994
Breaking the Jinx

By JOE LAPOINTE

NEW YORK—They hoisted the big silver trophy high, passed it around, shook it over their heads. Sometimes they kissed it. Slowly, they skated a ceremonial victory lap around the crowded, littered ice surface of Madison Square Garden. The Rangers, led by their captain, Mark Messier, were cheered mightily and repeatedly by a capacity crowd of 18,200 fans and watched by an international television audience, including President Clinton, who held the phone long enough to offer them his congratulations when they finally came inside.

The players seemed to be in no hurry to leave the ice after almost nine months of hockey. Some of their fans had waited 54 years for this moment. Why not savor it? No National Hockey League team that existed in 1940 and still plays now had gone so long between hoists of hockey's championship chalice. And now the Rangers had it because they beat the Vancouver Canucks tonight in a spine-tingler of a Game 7 in the finals. When it ended, amid the anxiety and perspiration of a 3–2 victory, fireworks exploded overhead. Tears and champagne flowed. A fan held up a sign that said "Now, I Can Die in Peace." The witnesses chanted "We Won the Cup! We Won the Cup!" and "1940! 1940! 1940!"

Messier, who scored one of the goals, spoke of the pressure of winning the cup in the charged atmosphere of Manhattan, about "the magnitude of the city" and about a conversation he had before the game with Mike Keenan, the coach. "They talk about ghosts and dragons," Messier said. "I said to Mike, 'You can't be afraid to slay the dragon.' We're going to celebrate this like we've never celebrated anything in our lives."

When President Clinton spoke, he congratulated Brian Leetch, the Ranger defenseman who won the Conn Smythe trophy as the most valuable player in the postseason tournament. Leetch had the first goal tonight, Adam Graves the second, and Messier the third. "Congratulations, man," Clinton said to Leetch. "I've been sitting here in the White House watching this, cheering for you, biting my fingernails, screaming and yelling."

He noted that the Rangers are a United States–based team and that Leetch is the first American to win the playoff m.v.p. award. "You didn't choke," Clinton said. "You just kept playing. America is proud of you tonight." When he hung up, Leetch said, jokingly, "Was that Dana Carvey?" referring to the comedian who used to imitate former President George Bush on "Saturday Night Live."

Tonight's victory came in a seven-game series that went the distance after the Rangers had taken a 3-games-to-1 lead. Behind the bench and behind the scenes, it was a personal triumph for Keenan, the coach, and Neil Smith, the general manager. Keenan was coaching his first year in New York after losing in the final round twice with Philadelphia and once with Chicago. For Smith, it was the pinnacle of a five-year term in office, the first major executive position of his career.

Mark Messier celebrating a second-period goal against the Canucks in Game 7 of the Stanley Cup finals at Madison Square Garden. The Rangers won, 3–2, forever ending mock cries of "1940! 1940!"—the last year they had won the title. (Associated Press)

Runners-up

1998: Michael Jordan (see June 12) took over the decisive Game 6 of the N.B.A. finals against the Utah Jazz in the final minute, leading the Chicago Bulls from a 3-point deficit to an 87–86 victory at the Utah Delta Center in Salt Lake City. It was the Bulls' second "three-peat" and sixth championship of the decade, and Jordan was the series most valuable player for the sixth time.

1965: Right-hander Jim Maloney of the Cincinnati Reds struck out 18 Mets and allowed no hits over 10 innings at Shea Stadium in New York, only to lose, 1–0, when Johnny Lewis homered in the 11th inning. In August, Maloney pitched a 10-inning no-hitter against the Chicago Cubs at Wrigley Field—and that one he won.

1949: Eddie Waitkus, the Philadelphia Phillies' first-baseman, was shot in the chest at the Edgewater Beach Hotel in Chicago by 19-year-old Ruth Ann Steinhagen, who had never met Waitkus but had been obsessed with him for years. Waitkus recovered and played for the 1950 pennant-winning Phillies. Steinhagen, charged with attempted murder, was committed to a mental institution for three years.

Lightning Strikes Twice

By ROSCOE MCGOWEN

BROOKLYN (Wednesday)—They turned on the greatest existing battery of baseball lights at Ebbets Field tonight for the inaugural night major league game in the metropolitan area. A record throng for the season there, 40,000, of whom 38,748 paid, came to see the fanfare and show that preceded the contest between the Reds and the Dodgers,. The game, before it was played, was partly incidental; the novelty of night baseball was the major attraction. Larry MacPhail, the Dodger's owner, had two fife and drum corps and a band, and there was a series of sprinting exhibitions by Jesse Owens, the hero of the 1936 Olympics.

But Johnny Vander Meer, a tall, handsome twenty-two-year-old Cincinnati southpaw pitcher, stole the entire show by hurling his second successive no-hit, no-run game, both coming within five days, and making baseball history that probably will never be duplicated. His previous no-hitter was pitched in daylight last Saturday against the Boston Bees, the Reds winning, 3–0. Tonight the score was 6–0. The records reveal only seven pitchers credited with two no-hitters in their careers and none who achieved the feat in one season.

More drama was crowded into the final inning than a baseball crowd has felt in many a moon. Until that frame only one Dodger had got as far as second base, Lavagetto reaching there when Johnny issued passes to Cookie and Dolph Camilli in the seventh. But Vandy pitched out of that easily enough and the vast crowd was pulling for him to come through to the end. Johnny mowed down Woody English, batting for Luke Hamlin; Kiki Cuyler and Johnny Hudson in the eighth, fanning the first and third men, and when Vito Tamulis, fourth Brooklyn hurler, treated the Reds

likewise in the ninth, Vandy came out for the crucial inning.

He started easily, taking Buddy Hassett's bounder and tagging him out. Then his terrific speed got out of control and, while the fans sat forward tense and almost silent, walked Babe Phelps, Lavagetto and Camilli to fill the bases. All nerves were taut as Vandy pitched to Ernie Koy. With the count one and one, Ernie sent a bounder to third baseman Lew Riggs, who was so careful in making the throw to catcher Ernie Lombardi that a double play wasn't possible.

Leo Durocher, so many times a hitter in the pinches, was the last hurdle for Vander Meer, and the crowd groaned as he swung viciously to line a foul high into the right field stands. But a moment later Leo swung again, the ball arched lazily toward short center field and Harry Craft camped under it for the put-out that brought unique distinction to the young hurler. It brought, also, a horde of admiring fans onto the field, with Vandy's teammates ahead of them to hug and slap Johnny on the back and then to protect him from the mob as they strug-

gled toward the Red dugout. The fans couldn't get Johnny, but a few moments later they got his father and mother, who had accompanied a group of 500 citizens from Vandy's home town of Midland Park, N.J. The elder Vander Meers were completely surrounded and it required nearly fifteen minutes before they could escape.

Johnny Vander Meer, who went 15–10 in 1938, pitched for 13 seasons in the major leagues, never completing another no-hitter. His lifetime record was 119–121.

Johnny Vander Meer of the Reds pitching against the Brooklyn Dodgers during his second successive no-hitter. The night game was the first ever played at Ebbets Field. Jesse Owens ran pregame sprints as a sideshow. (The New York Times)

Runners-up

1980: Jack Nicklaus, aged 40, won a record-tying fourth United States. Open title, defeating Isao Aoki of Japan by two strokes with a final-round 68 at Baltusrol Golf Club in Springfield, N.J. It was Nicklaus's 18th major title and his four-round total of 272 was the lowest ever recorded in the Open.

1977: In the most widely deplored trade in Mets history, Chairman M. Donald Grant sent 32-year-old Tom Seaver to the Cincinnati Reds for the journeymen Steve Henderson, Doug Flynn, Pat Zachary and Dan Norman. Seaver went on to

win 122 more games—more than one-third of his career total of 311 victories—as a non-Met.

1984: Tommy Hearns of Detroit knocked out Roberto Duran of Panama at 2 minutes 7 seconds of the second round at Caesars Palace in Las Vegas and unified the world superwelterweight title. Hearns, trained by Emmanuel Steward, won major titles in the welterweight, junior middleweight, middleweight and light heavyweight divisions.

June 16, 1951
Hogan Tames the Monster

By LINCOLN A. WERDEN

BIRMINGHAM, Mich.—Ben Hogan is still the champion. In another great comeback, the little Texan retained the United States Open golf title by closing with a 67 at the enormously difficult Oakland Hills Country Club to finish with a 72-hole aggregate of 287. Trailing the leader, Bobby Locke of South Africa, at the end of the second round yesterday by five strokes and co-leaders Locke and Jimmy Demaret after the third this morning by two, Hogan won in a smashing finale by two strokes.

With a large sector of the record crowd of 17,500 hemming in the eighteenth green to view another phase of his courageous bid to keep the crown, Hogan rolled in a 14-foot putt for a concluding birdie 3. Surrounded by a cordon of police he made his way to the clubhouse amid the cheers of the spectators who had witnessed another stirring chapter in the golfing story of Hogan. Then Hogan, the man who returned to the game after an almost fatal accident in 1949 to triumph in the historic play-off at Merion a year ago in one of the greatest of all sports comebacks, had to wait 1 hour and 45 minutes before he knew his claim on the trophy was secure.

Until Hogan did the trick, no one among the 162 who started play here in the opening round had been able to beat the controversial par 70 of the course. "Under the circumstances," stat-

Ben Hogan after winning his second straight U.S. Open at Oakland Hills in Michigan. A year earlier, at Merion in Pennsylvania, he won in a remarkable comeback from a near-fatal car crash. (Associated Press)

ed Hogan as he sat in the locker room patiently awaiting the latest news of Locke's progress, "it was the greatest round I have played. I didn't think I could do it. My friends said last night that I might win with a pair of 69's. It seemed too much on this course. It is the hardest course I have ever played. I haven't played all the courses in the world, but I don't want to, especially if there are any that are tougher than this one."

He started Thursday with a 75, a bit ruffled by his failure to solve the course. Neither was he satisfied yesterday with a 73, nor this morning with a 71. He blamed himself for overclubbing, for making mistakes. "I guess all of the boys are making more," he confessed.

But the 71 this morning was something in the way of an inspiration for the thrill-hungry crowd. All week they had heard reports of or seen for themselves the narrow fairways with strategically placed traps, the greens of rolling contours and two par-4 holes that many thought should have been rated at 5. And no one was under par! Hogan changed this attitude completely as he played the first nine in 32. Hogan seemed determined to "beat" the course. He looked grim. He was concentrating. In fact, on the final putt for the 67, he stood over the ball at least 30 seconds before stroking. He wanted to do his best and he did.

Runners-up

1978: The Louisiana left-hander Ron Guidry of the Yankees, on his way to a record of 25–3 with a 1.74 earned run average for his Cy Young Award season, struck out a team-record 18 batters in a 4–0 victory over the California Angels in the Bronx.

1998: With a 4–1 victory over the Washington Capitals at the MCI Center in the District of Columbia, the Detroit Red Wings completed back-to-back sweeps of the Stanley Cup finals. Coach Scotty Bowman (*see Dec. 19*), formerly with the Montreal Canadiens and the Pittsburgh Penguins, tied the record of Montreal's Hector (Toe) Blake with eight Cup titles.

1934: Glenn Cunningham of the University of Kansas set a world record in the mile, 4:06.7, beating his Princeton rival Bill Bonthron by 40 yards on a cinder track at Princeton's Palmer Stadium. Cunningham was severely burned as a boy and told he would never walk again yet persevered to become the premier middle-distance runner of his era.

Nicklaus Repels an Army

By LINCOLN A. WERDEN

OAKMONT, Pa.—Jack Nicklaus, a 22-year-old rookie professional, beat Arnold Palmer by three strokes in an 18-hole golf playoff today and won the sixty-second United States Open championship. Nicklaus scored a par 71, Palmer a 74. Although the husky 200-pounder from Columbus, Ohio, learned at the age of 16 how to outscore professional golfers by winning the Ohio open, the triumph this afternoon over the 6,894-yard Oakmont Country Club course was his first since he left the amateur ranks last November.

In beating the favored Palmer, Nicklaus became the first man to take the Open in his initial season as a pro. The extra session proved a surprise to a partisan gallery of 11,000, which called constantly, "Come on, Arnie." But the crowd failed to rattle Nicklaus, who outdrove his illustrious rival and outputted him on the undulating greens of this rugged course. At the end of six holes, Nicklaus had a four-stroke lead. Presently, however, as almost everyone expected, Palmer put on one of his characteristic rallies. This one accounted for birdies on the ninth, eleventh and twelfth holes and reduced Nicklaus's margin to one stroke. Unfortunately for Palmer, who won the 1960 Open at Denver when Nicklaus was second as an amateur, the rally could not be sustained.

Nicklaus and Palmer had ended the regulation seventy-two holes yesterday

Arnold Palmer, left, and Jack Nicklaus going their separate ways on the first tee in the second round of the U.S. Open at Oakmont. Nicklaus, a rookie pro, beat Palmer in an 18-hole playoff for the title. (Associated Press)

tied for first with scores of 283. Today, there were some moments of confusion, but Nicklaus appeared to be calmer and more relaxed in what was a duel that tested emotions as well as golfing skills. Some of the tension was shown at the eighteenth, where Palmer conceded Nicklaus the title before the latter had holed out. Nicklaus had called for a ruling after driving into the rough when he found his ball lodged in a bad spot. He was ordered to continue, and did so after Palmer had knocked his second short of the bunker to the right, below the green.

After a recovery wedge, Nicklaus pitched a No. 9 iron to the green and putted close. Palmer, on with his third, then putted and missed. After he again

knocked his ball toward the cup, Palmer picked up the coin that Nicklaus had used to mark his place on the green and offered congratulations to the new champion. But as Nicklaus was surrounded by well-wishers, he was reminded that he had not holed out. The happy Ohioan complied by going back and tapping in a tiny putt for the 5 that officially made him one of the youngest champions ever to win the game's most cherished honor.

Despite his youth, Nicklaus isn't the youngest to win this title. That honor went to Horace Rawlins, the first winner, who was 19 when he won in 1895 at Newport, R.I. Bobby Jones was 21 when he won the first of his four Opens in 1923.

Runners-up

1993: In Denver, owners voted 26–2 to expand the baseball playoffs for the first time in 25 years. Eight teams would now qualify for the post-season, and a best-of-five-game series would be added to accommodate wild-card play. The post-season, of course, was stretched deep into late October.

1976: The American Basketball Association ended its nine-year run by agreeing to merge four of its six teams—the New York Nets, the Denver Nuggets, the

Indiana Pacers and the San Antonio Spurs—into the dominant N.B.A., which became a 22-club circuit for the 1976–77 season.

1973: In the lowest final round in the history of a major professional tournament, Johnny Miller of Napa, Calif., who started the day six shots off the lead, shot 63 at Oakmont Country Club near Pittsburgh to win the United States Open by one stroke over John Schlee.

June 18, 1960
Nerves of Steel

By LINCOLN A. WERDEN

DENVER—Golf's man of steel won the United States Open championship today. Refusing to concede defeat when he trailed by seven strokes going into the final round, Arnold Palmer scored an incredible closing 65 for the greatest winning finish anyone has made in the game's top tournament. While thousands cheered him at the Cherry Hills Country Club, the 30-year-old Ligonier (Pa.) professional brought his 72-hole total to 280. He won by two strokes.

In a dramatic fourth round, Palmer played the first nine holes in 30. That equaled the Open record set by Jimmy McHale, a Philadelphia amateur, in 1947. It also turned Palmer from an also-ran into a challenger. Palmer started the round with four straight birdie 3's. A tremendous bid by 20-year-old Jack Nicklaus, the National Amateur titleholder from Columbus, Ohio, fell just short. Nicklaus finished with a par 71 for 282 and runner-up laurels. No amateur since Johnny Goodman in 1933 has carried off this title. But the score by Nicklaus, an Ohio State University junior, is the lowest ever by an amateur, including Bob Jones, in this championship.

Nicklaus was caught in the midst of tremendous interest because his playing partner on the last two rounds was Ben Hogan. The 47-year-old Texan made his bid when Mike Souchak, the leader by two strokes entering the final round, started to falter. Hogan reached the brink of a fifth championship, a feat never achieved in this tournament. But the seventy-first and seventy-second holes smashed his fondest hopes. Hogan was 4 under par until then. But he slipped to a 6 on the 17th hole when he had to take off his right shoe and sock and hit out of water near the green. And he scored 7 on the 18th for a round of 73 when he hooked a shot into the lake.

Playing back of Nicklaus and Hogan, Palmer learned what was happening ahead and adhered to pars on the last four holes for the victory. It brought him a first prize of $14,400. Palmer is a determined fellow on a golf course. He is the son of a professional and grew up in a golfing atmosphere. After winning the Masters in April, he said his goal this year would be to win here, the British Open and the Professional Golfers Association championship.

Palmer was confident as he drove the first green and started his string of birdies. He had thirteen birdies in earlier rounds of 72, 71 and 72 and bagged seven more in the final eighteen holes. "I never lost my desire to win here. But you must have the breaks, too," Palmer said after he had won.

The only other closing rush to the title that approached Palmer's was a 66 by Gene Sarazen as he triumphed in 1932 at Fresh Meadow. Palmer, who attended Wake Forest College, won the National Amateur in 1954 and subsequently joined the pro ranks, a life-long ambition. This was his eighth appearance in the Open championship. He tied for fifth in his best previous performance last year at Winged Foot.

Arnold Palmer, having charged back from seven strokes down in the final round, prepares to hurl his visor to the crowd after winning the U.S. Open at Cherry Hills in Denver. He said simply, "I never lost my desire." (Associated Press)

Runners-up

1941: Joe Louis, near defeat late in the fight, knocked out unrelenting Billy Conn of Pittsburgh in the 13th round of their scheduled 15-rounder at the Polo Grounds in New York City. Louis's heavyweight title defense was his 18th since he wrested the crown from James J. Braddock in 1937.

2000: In one of the greatest performances in golf history, Tiger Woods (see Feb. 7) devastated the United States Open field at Pebble Beach in California, scoring four birdies over the back nine to win by a staggering 15 strokes with an Open record-tying 12-under-par 272. Jack Nicklaus had the same total in an epic 1980 round (see June 15).

1897: "Wee" Willie Keeler, the 5-foot-4-inch Baltimore Orioles outfielder whose credo was to "hit 'em where they ain't," batted safely in his 44th consecutive game, setting a major league record that lasted until Joe DiMaggio of the Yankees broke it in 1941. Keeler hit .424 this year.

June 19, 2000
Svengali of the N.B.A.

By HARVEY ARATON

Lakers Coach Phil Jackson giving Shaquille O'Neal the what-for in a regular-season game in 2002. After leaving the Bulls with six N.B.A. titles in 1998, Jackson kept right on winning with the Lakers in 2000. (Associated Press)

The Los Angeles Lakers won their first N.B.A. championship under Phil Jackson on this date, defeating the Indiana Pacers, 116–111, in Game 6 of the finals at the Staples Center. It was the seventh title in nine seasons for Jackson, the former Bulls coach, who folded his arms in serene contentment as the Lakers came from behind to win. The following column appeared in The Times *on June 7, the day the series began.*

LOS ANGELES—Greetings, fans, from sunny Southern California, center of the basketball universe, now that I, Phil Jackson, am on the verge of winning a ring without Michael Jordan. I admit I am not the same earthy fellow I was 15 years ago, when I coached in the basketball bushes and talked about organic experiences and went out for late-night fish 'n' chips at roadside shacks in Pensacola. Am I a sellout just because I wear suspenders under my suit jacket and do online trading spots on television for P.D. Waterhouse? Times change. Garcia's gone. Consider me part new-age psychologist, part 60's guru, some kind of spiritual cross between Tony Robbins and Leonard Nimoy.

Just look at the results and listen to the music. Shaq, the heretofore playoff flop and Gen X cynic, will soon be rappin' from the top of the mountain, and from that lofty perch will clearly see that he's only scratched the surface of his potential. Give me two more years with him—the Daddy will be wearing the world's longest bell bottoms and groovin' to the Strawberry Alarm Clock.

"Meditation, oooh...."

People (read: Pat Riley) may ask, "Who wouldn't win with Shaq and Kobe?" But here are two more questions that are not exactly a koan. Who to this point has won with Shaq and Kobe? And what other coach has had championship success with veterans weaned on 1980's values and the contemporary stars of the hip hop culture? By the time this is over, even ol' Riles will have emerged from his annual brooding season and just admit that I am a genius because, as Artur Schnabel said, "The pauses between the notes—ah, that is where the art resides."

Take it from me, he wasn't talking about Shaq at the free-throw line. Or Glen Rice trying to beat his man off the dribble, Ron Harper shooting the 3-pointer or A.C. Green shooting anything but a dunk. Let's face it, other than the two marquee attractions, I haven't exactly been working here with the cast of the "Sopranos." Basketball, however, can be such a simple game when you are not one of those impossible control freaks, when you can sit back, cross your legs, caress your whiskers and apply the ancient Zen teachings.

I believe that the Pacers are dead fish. Five or six games, and it's a wrap.

June 20, 1960
Reclaiming the Crown

By JOSEPH C. NICHOLS

Referee Arthur Mercante directing Floyd Patterson to a neutral corner before beginning the count over an unconscious Ingemar Johansson in the fifth round of their world heavyweight title fight. (Associated Press)

NEW YORK—Floyd Patterson tonight became the first man in the history of boxing to regain the heavyweight championship of the world. The 25-year-old fighter from Rockville Centre, L.I., knocked out the defending titleholder, Ingemar Johansson of Goteborg, Sweden, with a left hook in 1:51 of the fifth round of their scheduled fifteen-round fight at the Polo Grounds. Patterson was clearly the master of the man who sent him to a humiliating defeat and deprived him of his title last June 26. He out-boxed the Swede at almost every turn, withstood Johansson's famed right hand, then showed power sufficient to bring him the triumph with two quick, sharp strokes.

The surprisingly large crowd of 31,892 fans thrilled to Patterson's conquest. Johansson, 27, who weighed 194¾ pounds to Patterson's 190, had been the 8-to-5 choice to retain his crown. A year ago Patterson had been the favorite at 5 to 1.

In bringing about Johansson's downfall, Patterson used a "picture-punch" left hook. He ripped the blow across to the chin early in the fifth and Johansson went down heavily. But it was plain he was not senseless. He was certain to get up, and he did at the count of 9. Patterson was unhurried now in the approach to his task. He stalked Johansson eagerly and even recklessly, as if aware that Johansson couldn't hurt him. Johansson kept his eyes wide open, almost unnaturally so, as Patterson came at him. But he didn't have enough vision to pick off Patterson's next wallop.

This punch, like the earlier one, traveled in the perfect arc that makes the left hook the deadly blow it is. It hit the mark perfectly, right on the Johansson jaw, and down went the Swede. Referee Arthur Mercante went through the motions of the full count, but Patterson knew his foe was out as soon as Johansson hit the canvas. The new champion leaped for joy even as Mercante was tolling off 10. When the count was completed, Patterson was mobbed by his handlers and the many fanatics climbing into the ring. Johansson was completely out, and he remained out for several minutes after his handlers had helped him to his corner. He was still in a daze as he was escorted down the ring stairs.

Johansson's setback was the first in his professional career of twenty-three fights. Fourteen of his twenty-two triumphs had been knockouts. Patterson's record before tonight showed thirty-five victories in thirty-seven starts, with twenty-six knockouts. The only one to beat him besides Johansson was Joey Maxim, who outpointed Floyd before the latter became the heavyweight king.

There was tension throughout the fight, most of it generated by the belief that Johansson's mighty right-hand punch—last year likened to the Hammer of Thor—could end matters whenever it hit the target. Patterson was most careful in not presenting a target, but Johansson succeeded, at least once, in crashing his right to the jaw. When it landed, Patterson surprised the excited crowd, and the eager Johansson, by remaining on his feet. This was in the second round, the only one of the four complete rounds that Johansson won.

Floyd Patterson lost the heavyweight title for a second time to Sonny Liston in 1962 (see Sept. 25). Patterson failed in three attempts to win it back yet again—against Liston in 1963, Muhammad Ali in '65 and Jimmy Ellis in '68.

Runners-up

1964: Ken Venturi overcame heat exhaustion and 100-degree temperatures to win the United States Open by four strokes over Tommy Jacobs at the Congressional Country Club in Bethesda, Md. Venturi shot 66 in the morning round and 70 in the afternoon; he staggered on the 16th tee during the morning round and thought he might have to withdraw, but was attended by a physician and recovered in time for the final round.

1982: Facing a brutal lie in the rough off the 17th green at Pebble Beach in California, Tom Watson chipped the ball 16 feet into the cup for birdie with a sand wedge, winning his first United States Open title and denying Jack Nicklaus, who finished two strokes back, an unprecedented fifth Open crown.

1993: Michael Jordan led the Chicago Bulls to their third straight N.B.A. championship, defeating the Phoenix Suns, 99–98, in Game 6 at Phoenix's America West Arena. It was the third "three-peat" in league history. Only the Minneapolis Lakers (1952–54) and the Boston Celtics (1959–66) had won as many as three straight titles.

June 21, 1970
The Pearl of Brazil

By JUAN de ONIS

MEXICO CITY—Brazil, with a crushing 4–1 victory over Italy, won the ninth World Cup soccer championship today and gained permanent possession of the Jules Rimet Trophy, symbol of world supremacy in the sport. Edison Arantes, better known as Pelé, scored Brazil's only goal in the first half, which ended in a 1–1 tie and setup Brazil's three second-half goals. The 29-year-old Brazilian forward showed why he is called the King of Soccer, but Brazil's defense, until now the weak spot in a young team, shared the glory with Pelé.

Led by the team captain, Carlos Alberto Torres, the best left full-back in the tournament, the Brazilian defense smothered Italy's counter attacking offense, except for one moment of confusion. Italy's alert forward, Roberto Boninsegna, stole the ball from the Brazilian defender, Wilson Piazza, at 37 minutes of the first half and with Brazil's goalie, Feliz Mielli, out of his nets, shot home a goal that temporarily tied the game.

The scoring had been opened by Pelé at 18 minutes on a pass from Roberto Rivelino that crossed the Italian defense zone. Pelé, who is only 5 feet 7 inches tall but outjumps most defensemen, headed the ball into the nets past a desperate lunge by the goalkeeper, Enrico Albertossi. At the 65-minute mark (each half is 45 minutes), Gerson Olivera Nuñez, Brazil's great playmaker, took a pass from Pelé on the run at the

edge of the penalty area. He drove a left-footed shot deep into the nets past a helpless Albertossi and the game was decided.

Six minutes later, Pelé headed a long pass from Gerson toward Jair Ventura, who beat out Albertossi from three feet out. It was Jair's seventh goal, which placed him second to Gerhard Muller of West Germany, who scored 10 goals before his team was eliminated in the semifinals, in the race for high scorer. The final goal came at 87 minutes. Pelé, with three Italian players converging on him, rolled a perfect pass to Carlos Alberto, who boomed home a 30-foot shot from the right side of the penalty area.

The victory was greeted with delirious joy by the 10,000 Brazilian fans who came here to Aztec Stadium for the tournament and by the majority of the Mexican crowd. Pelé and the other Brazilian stars were mobbed on the field for 10 minutes after the game. This was Brazil's third world championship, following earlier triumphs in Sweden in 1958, when Pelé first appeared as a 17-year-old, and in Chile in 1962.

Brazil is the first country to win three times in the competition, instituted in 1930, which is held every four years. Brazil got to the final undefeated in five games during the elimination round in which 16 national teams participated. Brazil's victories were over Czechoslovakia, England, Rumania, Peru and Uruguay.

Pelé lifting the Jules Rimet Trophy, emblematic of soccer supremacy, after Brazil's defeat of Italy in the World Cup. It was the Brazilians' third Cup title — all with their legendary player on the loose. (Reuters)

Runners-up

1988: The Los Angeles Lakers became the first N.B.A. team since the 1969 Boston Celtics to win successive titles, defeating the Detroit Pistons, 108–105, in Game 7 of the finals at the Forum in Inglewood, Calif. Coach Pat Riley had publicly "guaranteed" a repeat, but it took Los Angeles 24 post-season games, the most in league history, to do it.

1963: Bob Hayes, a 20-year-old freshman from Florida A&M University with a distinctive running style—elbows out, knees high—earned the title "world's fastest human" by shattering the 100-yard-dash record in 9.10 seconds at the Amateur Athletic Union championships in St. Louis.

1964: Jim Bunning of the Philadelphia Phillies, later a Hall of Famer and a United States senator from Kentucky, pitched a perfect game against the Mets in a Father's Day doubleheader at Shea Stadium, striking out pinch-hitter Johnny Stephenson for the final out. It was the first regular-season perfect game since 1922 and the first in the National League since 1880.

June 22, 1938
Fight, Might and Whata Right!

By JAMES P. DAWSON

Joe Louis sizing up Max Schmeling after the first of three opening-round knockdowns. Schmeling's trainer literally threw in the towel after the third knockdown. (Associated Press)

NEW YORK—The exploding fists of Joe Louis crushed Max Schmeling tonight in the ring at Yankee Stadium and kept sacred that time-worn legend of boxing that no former heavyweight champion has ever regained the title. The Brown Bomber from Detroit, with the most furious early assault he has ever exhibited here, knocked out Schmeling in the first round of what was to have been a fifteen-round battle to retain the title he won last year from James. J. Braddock. He has now defended it successfully four times.

In exactly 2 minutes and 4 seconds of fighting Louis polished off the Black Uhlan from the Rhine, but, though the battle was short, it was furious and savage while it lasted, packed with thrills that held three knockdowns of the ambitious ex-champion, every moment tense for a crowd of about 80,000. This gathering,

truly representative and comparing favorably with the largest crowds in boxing's history, paid receipts estimated at between $900,000 and $1,000,000 to see whether Schmeling could repeat the knockout he administered to Louis just two years ago here and be the first ex–heavyweight champion to come back into the title, or whether the Bomber could avenge this defeat as he promised.

As far as the length of the battle was concerned, the investment in seats, which ran to $30 each, was a poor one. But for drama, those who came from near and far felt themselves well repaid because they saw a fight that, though it was one of the shortest heavyweight championships on record, was surpassed by few for thrills. With the right hand that Schmeling held in contempt Louis knocked out his foe. Three times under its impact the German fighter hit the ring floor. The first time Schmeling regained his feet laboriously at the count of three. From the second knockdown Schmeling, dazed but game, bounced up instinctively before the count had gone beyond one.

On the third knockdown Schmeling's trainer and closest friend, Max Machon, hurled a towel into the ring, European fashion, admitting defeat for his man. The towel sailed through the air when the count on the prostrate Max had reached three. The signal is ignored in American boxing, has been for years, and Referee Arthur Donovan, before he had a chance to pick up the count in unison with knockdown timekeeper Eddie Josephs, who was outside the ring, gathered the emblem in a ball and hurled it through the ropes.

Returning to Schmeling's crumpled figure, Donovan took one look and signaled an end of the battle. The count at that time

was five on the third knockdown. Further counting was useless. Donovan could have counted off a century and Max could not have regained his feet. The German was thoroughly "out." It was as if he had been poleaxed. His brain was awhirl. His body, his head, his jaws ached and pained, his senses were numbed from that furious, paralyzing punching he had taken even in the short space of time the battle consumed.

Following the bout, Schmeling said he was fouled. He said that he was hit a kidney punch, a devastating right, which so shocked his nervous system that he was dazed and his vision was blurred. To observers at the ringside, however, with all due respect to Schmeling's thoughts on the subject, the punches which dazed him were thundering blows to the head, jaw and body in bewildering succession, blows of the old Alabama Assassin incarnate tonight for a special occasion. Louis wanted to erase the memory of that 1936 knockout he suffered in twelve rounds. It was the one blot on his brilliant record. He aimed to square the account and he did.

"Now I feel like a champion," Louis said on his arrival in his dressing room. "I've been waiting a long time for this night and I sure do feel pretty glad about everything. I was a little bit sore at some of the things Max said. Maybe he didn't say them, maybe they put those words in his mouth, but he didn't deny them, and that's what made me mad." What Louis referred to probably was the statement attributed to Schmeling a month ago, to the effect that the Negro would always be afraid of him. Something must have rankled Joe, for the savagery with which he battered down the German was never displayed in his other bouts here.

Runners-up

1986: Diego Armando Maradona's "hand of God" goal in the World Cup quarterfinals at Mexico City helped Argentina defeat England, 2–1. Most believe the ball was punched into the net, not headed—an act missed by the referee. But it helped cast Maradona's reputation as the greatest soccer player of his era (see June 29).

1937: Joe Louis, 23, knocked out James J. Braddock in the eighth round of their world heavyweight title fight at Comiskey Park in Chicago to become the first

black champion since Jack Johnson lost to Jess Willard in 1915 (see April 5). Louis went on to hold the title through 25 defenses until he retired as champion in 1949 (see March 1).

1994: John Starks of the Knicks shot 2 for 18 from the field, including 0 for 11 from 3-point range, as New York lost Game 7 of the N.B.A. finals to the Houston Rockets at The Summit, 90–84. It was the closest the Knicks have come to the league championship since their 1973 title behind Willis Reed.

June 23, 1967
The All-American Miler

By WILLIAM N. WALLACE

Jim Ryun, aged 20, at the University of Kansas. Ryun, an early bloomer, still held four of the top five high-school times in the mile and four of the six best times in the 1,500 meters as of 2003. (Associated Press)

BAKERSFIELD, Calif.—Jim Ryun, the precocious 20-year-old sophomore from the University of Kansas, set a world record for the one-mile run tonight at the Amateur Athletic Union's national track and field championships here. Ryun, winning by some 40 yards, ran the classic distance in 3 minutes 51.1 seconds. That was two-tenths of a second faster than Ryun's recognized world mark of 3:51.3, set a year ago at Berkeley, Calif.

It was a tremendous race that saw the first seven finishers run the distance in under four minutes. The seventh-place finisher, 17-year-old Martin Liquori of Essex Catholic High School in Cedar Grove, N.J., posted a time of 3:59.8. Jim Grelle, a seasoned miler from Portland, Ore., had a time of 3:56.1 for second place, then came Dave Willborn, University of Oregon, 3:56.2; Tom von Ruden, Oklahoma State, 3:56.9; Roscoe Divine, Oregon, 3:57.2; Sam Bair, Kent State, 3:58.6, and Liquori.

Paul Wilson, a 19-year-old sophomore at the University of Southern California, also set a world's record. Wilson cleared 17 feet 8 inches in the pole vault event to eclipse the former mark of 17-7 set by his teammate, Bob Seagren, last June 10.

Ryun's quarter times were 59.2 seconds, 59.8, 58.6, and then a blasting 53.5 as he went for the world mark. He next took a leisurely jog around Bakersfield College's Memorial Stadium as the crowd of 10,000 cheered him mightily. Ryun had taken the lead just after the start, a lead that grew longer and longer. As the collective quarter times were announced over the public address system, the crowd sensed a record was at hand and urged on the slight, tall, dark-haired Ryun. Said Ryun afterwards, "I felt well and I wanted to run a fast race." That was succinct and simple.

On June 5, 1964, at Compton, Calif., eight men ran a mile race in under four minutes. Ryun, then a 17-year-old junior at Wichita (Kan.) East High School, placed eighth. His time was 3:59. Tonight's effort was Ryun's 12th mile run since then under four minutes and Grelle's 19th in his longer career.

Jim Ryun is a United States congressman from Kansas, now serving his fourth term.

Runners-up

1972: Title IX, the revolutionary federal law that opened wide the doors to women in high school and collegiate sports as well as in academics in general, was signed by President Richard M. Nixon. The statute, which barred sex discrimination at schools receiving federal funds, effectively forced colleges to create sports programs for women if they wanted to keep their revenue-producing sports programs for men.

1922: Foreshadowing the popularity of golf in America, Walter Hagen of Rochester, N.Y., scored a one-stroke victory over Jim Barnes and George Duncan at Royal St. George's Golf Club in Sandwich, England, becoming the first United States–born player to win the British Open. Jock Hutchison of Pittsburgh won the title the previous year *(see June 26)*, but he was born in Scotland.

1917: The Red Sox' Ernie Shore pitched the third "perfect game" of the 1900's, though he didn't start it. Babe Ruth did but was ejected for arguing a ball-four call to the Senators' leadoff batter. Shore entered, the runner was caught stealing and Shore got the next 26 outs. A 1991 rule change deprived him of the honor because he didn't pitch a full nine innings.

June 24, 1995
The Devils Get Their Due

By DAVE ANDERSON

EAST RUTHERFORD, N.J.—In the years when the Soviets first discovered hockey, a conductor on the Trans-Siberian Express confronted an American passenger. "Tell me about your hockey teams," the conductor said. "Basta Broons. Chcaga Blikhaks. Tronta Miplelifs. Mintrl Cinidins." That conductor never mentioned the New Jersey Devils, the franchise that had not yet been organized. But wherever that conductor is now, he is asking about the Nijrze Divls, who tonight skated with the Stanley Cup in celebrating their sweep of the Detroit Red Wings.

Even if the franchise is moved to Nashville, the Devils have put New Jersey on the world sports map. Never before has a "New Jersey" team won what is considered a world championship. And don't say the Giants. Yes, the Giants won two Super Bowls, but in the National Football League standing they have always been a "New York" team with New York roots. The Cosmos won the North American Soccer League's Soccer Bowl three times, once in Giants Stadium, but that victory hardly qualified as a world title. And even if it had, the Cosmos were never known as the New Jersey Cosmos, just as the Cosmos.

The Devils, in contrast, are as New Jersey as the Turnpike, as New Jersey as the Shore.

Through the years, several New Jersey athletes have been considered the world's best. Jersey Joe Walcott and Jim Braddock were heavyweight champions. Carl Lewis has sprinted and long-jumped to eight Olympic gold medals. Milt Campbell won the Olympic decathlon. And some New Jersey teams have been the best in their realms. Seton Hall's 1953

Claude Lemieux reveling with the Stanley Cup after the Devils swept the Red Wings for their first N.H.L. title. Never before had a team with "New Jersey" as part of its name succeeded so mightily. (Associated Press)

basketball team won the National Invitation Tournament. The 1937 Newark Bears, with several future Yankees, dominated the International League and won baseball's Little World Series.

Until now, New Jersey has mostly been linked to sports history as a site: the first baseball game in 1846 (in Hoboken) and the first college football game in 1869 (Princeton–Rutgers in New Brunswick). But until the Devils' ascent, the world had never associated New Jersey with a cham-

pionship sports team, the world had never focused on the players representing a team across the Hudson from the Big Apple.

Two of those players, Claude Lemieux and Stephane Richer, already have their names on the Stanley Cup from their days with the Canadiens, a couple of Quebeçois who each list West Orange, N.J., as their residence now. Just a couple of Jersey guys representing those Nijrze Divls that a conductor on the Trans-Siberian Express is asking about.

Runners-up

1952: Eddie Arcaro of Cincinnati, aged 36, became the first American-born jockey to win 3,000 races when he rode a horse named Ascent to a victory at Arlington Park, near Chicago. By the time Arcaro retired in 1962, after 31 years of racing, he had won 4,779 times. Johnny Longden and Gordon Richards, who won 4,000 races in the United States, were natives of England.

1922: The N.F.L. was born when the American Professional Football Association, organized in 1920, changed its name to the National Football League. Earl

(Curly) Lambeau paid $250 for the franchise rights to the Green Bay Packers, originally of the A.P.F.A. and founded by his employer, the Indian Packing Company.

1962: The Yankees defeated the Detroit Tigers, 9–7, in a 22-inning, seven-hour marathon at Tiger Stadium that ended when Jack Reed, a little-used outfielder, hit a two-run homer into the left-field upper deck. Jim Bouton pitched the last of the 22nd for the victory.

June 25, 1998
Hitting the Mother Lode

By IRA BERKOW

Sammy Sosa of the Cubs taking his trademark hop after hitting his 60th homer of the season in 2001. Sosa hit 60 or more homers in three separate seasons – 66 in 1998, 63 in '99 and 64 in 2001. (Reuters)

Sammy Sosa of the Chicago Cubs broke the record for home runs in a month on this date when he hit his 19th in June in an interleague game against the Detroit Tigers, breaking the 61-year-old record set by the Tigers' Rudy York. Sosa went on to hook up with Mark McGwire of the St. Louis Cardinals in a historic home run race that lasted until the season's end, McGwire finishing with 70 and Sosa 66. The following article appeared in The Times *on June 30.*

CHICAGO—Once upon a time, Sammy Sosa was the kind of mad-hatter batter who swung so violently and so indiscriminately that, it was said, he would attack even a white paper cup if it came floating toward home plate. "I remember pitching against him when I was with the Mets," said Mark Clark, now a teammate of Sosa's on the Cubs, "and you could bounce a ball in front of the plate, and he'd swing at it. He'd go for a high, bad slider. You knew he could hurt you, but you felt you could handle him in tight situations. Not anymore. He's been incredible."

Incredible may be an understatement, in a sports world of galloping hyperbole.

This evening at leafy Wrigley Field, Sosa concluded the most remarkable home run-hitting month in the history of baseball by hitting a home run. After striking out twice and flying to right field in the Cubs' 5–4 loss to Arizona, Sosa came to bat in the eighth inning. On a 3–2 pitch, he clubbed the ball with such ferocity off Alan Embree that it reached the left-field bleachers nearly before Sosa had finished his follow-through. Two fans ran onto the field, reaching Sosa as he rounded second base, before security guards escorted them off.

This was his 20th home run in a record-breaking month, topping by two the record held by Rudy York, who hit 18 in August 1937 for the Tigers. If Sosa belted homers as he did in June for each month of the season, he would wind up with 120. Turns out that not even the compactly, powerfully built, easygoing right fielder for the Cubs is on that pace. More modestly, he is on track to break the one-season home run record of 61 set by Roger Maris in 1961. About the halfway point of the season, Sosa has stroked 33 homers, which put him even with Seattle's Ken Griffey Jr. and four behind the St. Louis masher, Mark McGwire.

"I'm no Mark McGwire," Sosa said today. "He's the man. If anybody's going to break Roger Maris's record, it's going to be him. Me, I'm just another kid on the block having a pretty good season." He has been more than just another kid on the block for several years now, although he has not been as appreciated or as generally applauded as he is this season. He has not only slugged homers like crazy, but is also hitting for average—his .327 is 70 points higher than his 10-year major league average—and has knocked in 79 runs.

"He has matured as a ballplayer,"said Jim Riggleman, the Cubs' manager. "He has become more patient, waiting for the pitcher to get the ball in the strike zone."

Sosa is 29 years old, and didn't begin playing organized baseball until he was 14, in San Pedro de Macoris, the town in the Dominican Republic that has sent an extraordinary number of players to the majors. "It's amazing how far he's come when you consider where he came from," said Omar Minaya, the Mets' assistant general manager, who was a scout for the Texas Rangers in 1985 when he signed Sosa for $3,500. "I remember him coming from a poverty-stricken background, where he lived in a two-room house with his widowed mother and four brothers and two sisters."

Sosa remembers selling oranges for 10 cents apiece and shining shoes for 25 cents. Last year, he signed a four-year contract with the Cubs for $42 million. "I think about when I had very little," he said. "That's changed."

Runners Up

1948: Losing on two of the three judges' cards after 10 rounds, 32-year-old Joe Louis (*see June 22*), who had announced beforehand that this would be his last fight, knocked out Jersey Joe Walcott in the 11th round to retain his world heavyweight title at Yankee Stadium. It was his second defeat of Walcott in seven months.

1965: At an expansion meeting in New York, N.H.L governors, an elite group of the owners of the six original league teams, gave themselves the power to grant six new franchises for the 1967–68 season—for an admission of $2 million each. The new teams were the Los Angeles Kings, Oakland Seals, Minnesota North Stars, St. Louis Blues, Philadelphia Flyers and Pittsburgh Penguins. United States teams henceforth dominated the league.

1969: Regaining his faded brilliance, Pancho Gonzalez, 41, defeated Charlie Pasarell in the longest Wimbledon match on record. The early-round match took 112 games to complete and lasted 5 hours and 12 minutes. Play was called because of darkness on June 24 was completed the following day. Gonzalez later lost to his protégé, Arthur Ashe.

June 26, 1921
Stealing St. Andrews

[Unsigned, *The New York Times*]

NEW YORK—A lofty ambition, long cherished but never before achieved, was realized today when Jock Hutchison, the good-natured, always-smiling, happy-go-lucky Scot, professional at the Glen View Golf Club, Chicago, and a member of the American professional golf team, won the British Open championship at St. Andrews, Scotland, in the playoff with Roger Wethered, the young Oxford student, who was tied with him for the honors when the regular 72-hole destination was reached.

For years, as individuals, members of the American professional fraternity have gone to the other side in quest of the honor, but until this year the British home guard has always been able to turn them back with disappointing regularity. This year, however, through the efforts of Golf Illustrated, the style of attack was changed somewhat.

Instead of a hit-and-miss, go-as-you-please, each-man-for-himself plan, it was decided to send a representative team. After currying the country for the best talent available and for funds, the project was finally put through and twelve men named for the team to represent this country. Only eleven made the journey, Wilfred Reid finding it impossible to get away when the time came. The result is now pleasing history.

One of the members of that team was successful in capturing the greatest honors that can come to a golfer, for this year's tournament was something more than a British Open championship. It was an international event, with the stars of Great Britain, Australia, Spain, France and America competing. In winning from a field that sparkled with brilliancy, Hutchison earned his honors.

Jock Hutchison, 87, left, and Fred McLeod, 89, after teeing off as honorary starters at the Masters in 1972. A half-century earlier, Hutchison had become the first American pro to win a major tournament across the pond. (Associated Press)

Three other members of the team—two from the metropolitan area—finished well up in the list, far ahead of golfers whose rule had been accepted as supreme for years. One of these was Tommy Kerrigan of the Siwanoy Club, an American home-bred, who won third place, two strokes behind the leaders, and another was Jim Barnes of the new Pelham Country Club who, with Walter Hagen, former national open champion, tied with five others for sixth place.

But for a putting weakness that developed in the course of his second round, Kerrigan might today be wearing the crown, while Barnes, after three consistent rounds of 74—perfect golf—lost out only in the final eighteen holes of the play.

Barnes's showing, in the face of the handicap he has been under, was remarkable. He was not well when he left for the tournament and he received another setback after he landed, necessitating his forsaking golf and going to his old home in Cornwall to rest for the big event. He tied for the honors at the end of the third round but lack of condition caused him to tire and destroyed his chances of victory.

Hutchison's victory, coming on the heels of America's previous setbacks at Hoylake and Turnberry, comes with an especial sweetness and it comes to a player who is universally liked. Happy-go-lucky Hutch will wear his honors with becoming modesty and defend them with a true champion's ability.

Runners-up

1959: Ingemar Johansson of Sweden knocked down world heavyweight champion Floyd Patterson seven times in the third round before a crowd of 30,000 at Yankee Stadium to win the title on a technical knockout. One year later Patterson became the first heavyweight to regain the title *(see June 20)*.

1911: John McDermott of Atlantic City, N.J., became the first American-born golfer to win the United States Open, which for 16 years had been owned by Britons. He won with an 80 in a three-way playoff round, trumping an 82 by Mike Brady of Boston and an 85 by George Simpson, a former amateur champion of Scotland, at the Chicago Golf Club.

1944: More than 50,000 fans packed the Polo Grounds in New York for a unique exhibition game between the city's three major league teams to raise war bonds for World War II. The teams rotated, with one team sitting out an inning. The final score was Brooklyn Dodgers 5, New York Yankees 1, New York Giants 0.

June 27, 1999
The Pied Piper of Skateboarding

By DAVID FISCHER

Tony Hawk, the Babe Ruth of skateboarding, performing the first 900 at the sixth X Games in San Francisco. The risky two-and-a-half-revolution off a halfpipe took him years and a few teeth to accomplish. (Rob McConaughy)

SAN FRANCISCO—He had tried the trick for several years, never landing it, and in the process had suffered cracked ribs, several concussions, a back injury and the loss of a handful of teeth. His attempts to become the first skateboarder to complete a 900, a dangerous two-and-a-half revolution spin off a vertical ramp called a halfpipe, had all ended in painful failure. "Some tricks you think you will never get," the world's most famous skateboarder is fond of saying about his work ethic. "All you can do is keep at it."

Tonight, in the sixth X Games at Pier 30 overlooking San Francisco Bay, Tony Hawk of San Diego became the first skateboarder ever to land the 900, his sport's equivalent of the four-minute mile.

He was locked in a friendly battle with four of his toughest competitors—Andy Macdonald, Bob Burnquist, Bucky Lasek

and Neal Hendrix—all daredevil ballet dancers on urethane wheels hoping to capture the X Games' coveted best trick medal. On his first try at the 900, Hawk came up short on his revolutions. He failed again on his second, third, fourth and fifth attempts. Twice he landed on his board, only to have it slide out from under him. For Hawk, whose credo is never say "last try," the near misses only fueled his desire to reach his personal Holy Grail.

By this point, his four chief rivals had stopped competing, choosing to watch Hawk get into "the zone." In skateboarding's premier event of vert jumping, Hawk is the only man to watch. And the four were banging their boards on the ramp in thunderous applause as he kept climbing up the stairs after each of the failed attempts, which by now had reached 10. "I saw him when he did the kick-flip 540 for

the first time," Hendrix told ESPN. "I thought that was great. But this just blows that moment away."

Hawk, 27, has been wowing crowds for more than 15 years with his skateboarding magic. He was dubbed a prodigy by Sports Illustrated at 18 during the sport's Dark Ages, and has since won skateboarding competitions worldwide—by best reckoning, 73 of 103 pro contests. He gave an underground sport a face for a nation of scabby-kneed kids, while inventing nearly 80 aerial tricks, including the Madonna (because it takes your breath away). Though he was the first boarder to turn the 720 in competition, the 900 was a different story—two 360's and a 180.

Tonight at Pier 30 on his 11th try, he seemed to defy gravity, launching himself high above the halfpipe. Spiraling with gymnastic skill, a twirling mass somersaulting two and a half rotations, he landed nearly perfectly on his waiting skateboard, his feet seemingly glued to it. He lightly touched the ground with his right hand, then rose up, riding the trick out clean. There was a wild ovation from the capacity crowd of 8,000 on the pier. The other skaters jumped to the bottom of the halfpipe and lifted Hawk until he seemed to soar above them.

"This is the best day of my life, I swear to God!" Hawk said through the public address system. "I couldn't have done it without you [fans]."

Tony Hawk retired from competition after these X Games, when sales of Hawk-branded items had already grossed more than $250 million annually. The "Tony Hawk's Pro Skater" video game series has generated about $450 million in sales since its introduction in the fall of 1999.

Runners-up

1988: Mike Tyson (see Nov. 22), having stated that his only purpose in the ring was to inflict pain, beat Michael Spinks, looking like a deer in the headlights, into submission in 1 minute 31 seconds of the first round of their bout for the unified world heavyweight title in Atlantic City. The knockout was the fourth quickest in heavyweight championship history.

1972: Left-winger Bobby Hull of the Chicago Blackhawks (see March 12) became the first superstar to leave the N.H.L. for the upstart World Hockey Association,

joining the Winnipeg Jets as a player-coach. The 33-year-old Hull got a 10-year contract worth at least $2.5 million—far from a princely sum a decade later.

1992: Dan O'Brien, the world decathlon champion from Idaho and the focus of a $25 million Reebok ad campaign aimed at the Barcelona Games, failed to clear the 15-foot-9-inch minimum height in the pole vault in three attempts at the Olympic Trials in New Orleans. Amazingly—and alarmingly for Reebok—he did not make the Olympic team.

June 28, 1976
Everybody's Favorite

By THOMAS ROGERS

DETROIT — The Yankees got their first look at Mark Steven Fidrych, the 21-year-old right-handed rookie sensation, tonight. And the hard-hitting Yankees had to be impressed. The fidgety, 6-foot-3-inch bundle of nerves fed the Yankees a diet of on-target fastballs that enabled the Detroit Tigers to top the Yankees, 5–1, in the opener of a three-game series before a jubilant crowd of 47,855 at Tiger Stadium and a national television audience.

Fidrych, called "The Bird" by Detroit fans for his habit of flopping around the mound and his constant chattering to himself, allowed seven hits and only one was damaging. It was Elrod Hendricks's third homer of the season, a shot into the lower right-field stands. As well as winning for the eighth time in nine decisions and pitching his eighth complete game, he also stopped the 20-game hitting streak of Mickey Rivers. The Yankee center fielder grounded out four times.

Ken Holtzman, who allowed the Tigers five runs on six hits, also pitched strongly until the eighth inning. He was tagged for two runs in the first on a walk to Ron LeFlore and Rusty Staub's fourth homer of the season. And he threw a home-run pitch to Aurelio Rodriguez in the seventh, which the third baseman lined into the right-field seats. But in between he was as

Mark Fidrych of the Tigers signing autographs before a game at Yankee Stadium. Chattering on the mound, mugging with fans, winning — "I didn't have any idea this was going to happen," he said. (Bettmann/Corbis)

tough as Fidrych, retiring 17 of the 19 batters.

Referring to the Tigers' rookie star, Staub, the ex-Met, said: "There's an electricity that he brings out in everyone, the players and the fans. He's different. He's a 21-year-old kid with a great enthusiasm that everyone loves. He has an inner youth, an exuberance."

"I just throw as hard as I can and as fast as I can," said Fidrych. "I'm kind of surprised at my success in the majors. I didn't have any idea this was going to happen. I'm just trying to take each game one at a time and hope to win as many as I can."

Mark Fidrych, the American League Rookie of the Year in 1976, finished with a 19-9 record for the fifth-place Tigers. But soon the fireworks were over, as arm injuries limited him to just 10 more victories.

Runners-up

1997: Former heavyweight champion Mike Tyson was disqualified from his bout against W.B.A. titleholder Evander Holyfield in Las Vegas for biting and bloodying both of Holyfield's ears in the third round. The bites left Holyfield howling in pain and resulted in Tyson's disqualification and permanent banishment from fighting in Nevada.

1957: Baseball Commissioner Ford Frick removed three Cincinnati Redlegs from the starting lineup of the July 9 All-Star Game at St. Louis after Cincinnati fans stuffed the ballot box. First baseman George Crowe and outfielders Gus Bell

and Wally Post were removed and replaced by Stan Musial of the Cardinals, Willie Mays of the New York Giants and Henry Aaron of the Milwaukee Braves.

1958: Mickey Wright, 23, became the first player to win the top two prizes in women's golf in the same season, defeating Louise Suggs in the United States Open at Pontiac, Mich., after beating Fay Crocker in the L.P.G.A. championship at Penn Hills, Pa., three weeks before. Meg Mallon of the United States (1991) and Se Ri Pak of South Korea (1998) also won both titles in one year.

With an Assist From God

By ALEX YANNIS

MEXICO CITY—In a game that was billed as a battle of continents, Argentina edged West Germany, 3–2, to win the World Cup today and set off a wild celebration among South American and Mexican soccer fans at Aztec Stadium. Argentina took a 2–0 lead, getting goals by Jose Luis Brown in the 22d minute and by Jorge Alberto Valdano in the 56th. But the West Germans rallied and tied the game on goals by Karl-Heinz Rummenigge in the 74th minute and by Rudi Voeller in the 81st before Jorge Luis Burruchaga gave Argentina the victory in the 84th minute.

It was the second World Cup for Argentina, which captured the coveted trophy when it was host of the tournament in 1978. For West Germany, winner of the tournament in 1954 and 1974, the loss was its second consecutive failure in the final. It also kept alive the tradition that American teams win in the Americas, and Europeans in Europe.

"I was convinced this was our year," said Diego Armando Maradona, the Argentine star who, although scoreless, was involved in all three goals. "The people of Argentina wanted this. I'm happy the World Cup belongs to South America again." Although the Germans were able to prevent the 25-year-old Maradona from scoring, it often meant that he was double-teamed, with Lothar Matthaeus getting help from a teammate. Maradona, arguably the

Diego Maradona exulting with a teammate during a World Cup victory over South Korea. Maradona scored five goals in all and led Argentina to its second Cup title against West Germany in the final. (David Cannon/Getty Images)

best player in the world, required the extra attention after having scored five goals earlier in the tournament, including three remarkable ones within the previous week. One brilliant goal helped eliminate Belgium in the semifinals. Earlier, a handball that Maradona proudly described as a goal assisted by the "hand of God," eliminated England.

Today, Maradona was a threat who gave purpose to his entire team, especially after the West Germans staged their comeback. "Our downfall was our happiness after we got the second goal," said Rummenigge, playing his 95th international game. "I think maybe we figured the game was ours."

It certainly looked that way because the Argentines acted as if they had been hit by a bolt of lightning while the West Germans had the momentum. But Maradona overcame the shock, displaying his vision and quickness only three minutes later when he led Burruchaga with a pass down the right side. Despite pressure from Hans-Peter Briegel, Burruchaga kept the ball and his wits about him as he entered the penalty area and then fired it past Harald (Toni) Schumacher, who had not allowed a goal in his previous three games.

"Fate was not in our favor," said West Germany Coach Franz Beckenbauer. "My players deserve credit for performing in such unfavorable conditions. The altitude was bad and the crowd was encouraging for Argentina."

Runners-up

1950: In perhaps the most surprising upset in soccer history, the United States team, composed mostly of amateurs with jobs such as mailmen or carpenters, defeated Great Britain, 1–0, in a first-round World Cup match in Brazil. Some British newspapers assumed wire service score lines had to be an error and reported the result as a 10–1 British victory.

1958: With a 17-year-old phenomenon named Pelé scoring two goals and stealing the show, Brazil defeated Sweden, 5–2, in the World Cup final at Stockholm. Pelé scored six goals in all in the tournament, which was the first to receive

international television coverage that increased the game's—and Pelé's—worldwide popularity.

1941: Singling against knuckleballer Dutch Leonard and Walt Masterson of the Washington Senators in either end of a doubleheader, Joe DiMaggio of the Yankees hit safely in his 41st and 42nd consecutive games, breaking the American League record set by George Sisler of the St. Louis Browns in 1922. Next up for DiMaggio was "Wee" Willie Keeler (see June 18).

The Score Didn't Matter

[Unsigned, *The New York Times*]

NEW YORK—Did you hear about what Denton T. (Cy) Young did up at the American League Park today? He didn't exactly beggar description, but he came mighty nigh it. He beggared the Elberfeld aggregation so far as runs were concerned, and he made hitless Yankees out of the whole outfit, and he smashed out singles thisaway and thataway, and he scored people that he liked, and he scored people that we don't know whether he cares much about or not, and he was the jolly old plot of the piece, and there wasn't an inning that you could lose track of him.

The score, which is an entirely immaterial consideration, was 8. That's all, just 8.

Young's performance in shutting out the Yankees without a hit stamps him as the most remarkable pitcher in the history of major league baseball. Not only is he the oldest pitcher in National or American League ranks, but he is the only player in the history of the National pastime who has shut out an opposing team without a hit on three different occasions. In addition, he shares with John M. Ward the unique distinction of pitching a no-hit game with no player reaching first base. Ward performed the feat for Providence against Buffalo in 1880, while Young established his record on May 15, 1904, against the Philadelphia Athletics while pitching for Boston. Today only one New York player reached first base—Niles, on a base on balls.

"Cy" Young pitched his first no-hit game for Cleveland against Cincinnati in 1897. This was in the National League. His next shut-out game was against the Philadelphia Athletics in 1904, and his third today. In addition to his remarkable record for no-hit games, Young holds the record for effective pitching in the major league, pitching fifty-four innings without a run in 1904.

Young was born at Gilmore, Ohio, March 29, 1876, stands 6 feet in height, and weighs 210 pounds. Canton, Ohio, was where "Cy" made his first appearance, and the Cleveland Club took him in charge that year, 1890. He remained with Cleveland until that club was transferred to St. Louis, where he remained one year, and then went to Boston the first year of the American League.

Young is the most remarkable ball player the game has yet produced when good work for a long period is considered.

Cy Young with the Cleveland Indians in an undated photo, probably from 1909 or '10. Easily the greatest turn-of-the-century pitcher, he holds the major league record for victories with 511. (Associated Press)

Runners-up

1929: Bobby Jones of Atlanta won the United States Open at Winged Foot Golf Course in Mamaroneck, N.Y., by 23 strokes over the runner-up, Al Espinosa of Chicago, in a 36-hole playoff. It was the third of Jones's four Open titles from 1923 to '30. Jones crushed Espinosa in the playoff, 141 strokes to 164.

1962: Sandy Koufax of the Los Angeles Dodgers pitched the first of his four career no-hitters, striking out 13 as he defeated the Mets, 5–0. Koufax threw a no-hitter every year, including one perfect game, between 1962 and '65.

1970: Riverfront Stadium opened in Cincinnati as home of the Reds and the football Bengals for a game between the Reds and the Atlanta Braves. Riverfront, which preceded the opening of Three Rivers Stadium in Pittsburgh by two weeks and that of Veterans Stadium in Philadelphia by nine months, was typical of the sterile, cookie-cutter, multipurpose stadiums with artificial turf then being built. All are now gone.

JULY

July 1, 1961

Miss Wright Rules Supreme

By LINCOLN A. WERDEN

SPRINGFIELD, N.J.—Mary Kathryn (Mickey) Wright, a slim, blonde player from San Diego, Calif., became the Women's United States Open golf champion today. She left no doubt about the stature of her game as she played the lower course of the Baltusrol Golf Club this morning in 69. To cap her third victory in this championship she finished with a par-equaling fourth round of 72. That gave her a 72-hole aggregate of 293. Betsy Rawls, the defender, finished second at 299 with a last round of 76.

"It's just great," said Miss Rawls as she greeted Miss Wright. Miss Rawls holds the record of winning four championships.

"I feel wonderful but exhausted," said Miss Wright as she left the final green. The Californian, who can pound the ball farther than any of her colleagues, seemed decidedly cool as she accepted the plaudits of a gallery of 4,000.

The winner of the crown in 1958 and 1959, Miss Wright suffered a case of the jitters yesterday. That almost proved disastrous for it resulted in a second-round 80. But she was calm and relaxed as she started the fourth round with a birdie 4. She went over par only twice in this crucial round, on the third and thirteenth, where

Mickey Wright hitting a fairway wood on the L.P.G.A. tour in 1960. Three years later, when television began broadcasting women's golf, she won a record 13 tournaments. It remains a feat unlikely to be matched. (Associated Press)

she was trapped. So consistently did she play that she had thirty-six putts for her last round and hit sixteen greens in regulation figures.

With her $1,800 winner's share, Miss Wright now leads the pro women's brigade with earnings of $11,247. Louise Suggs, who finished fourth here with 301 after a one-over-par 73 on her fourth round, had occupied first place until the Open. She has $10,334.

Miss Wright's 72, 80, 69, 72 was five over par for the championship course. Her 69 was one of the best scores in the history of the tourney, considering the length of the course, and one of the best competitive performances ever credited to a woman golfer in the United States. She acknowledged this triumph as "the greatest of them all."

The blue-eyed champion, who is nearsighted and wears glasses while playing golf, is 5 feet 9 inches tall and weighs 150 pounds. She was born on St. Valentine's Day, Feb. 14, 1935. She started playing golf in 1947 and five years later was the national junior champion. The winner of the Ladies Professional Golfers Association crown in 1960, Miss Wright automatically rules supreme now in women's golfing ranks.

Runners-up

1951: Bob Feller of the Cleveland Indians, who had to talk his pitching coach into letting him stay in the game, became the first pitcher of modern times to pitch three no-hitters in his career, defeating the Detroit Tigers, 2–1, in the first game of a doubleheader at Cleveland's Municipal Stadium.

1977: With Elizabeth II watching from the Royal Box at Wimbledon, Virginia Wade of Britain completed a stirring come-from-behind victory in the finals over Bette Stove of the Netherlands, 4–6, 6–3, 6–1. Wade is the last Briton of either sex to win the national title; the Englishman Fred Perry won in 1936.

1980: Steve Ovett of Britain broke the world record in the mile in 3 minutes 48.8 seconds at Bislett Stadium in Oslo, breaking his countryman Sebastian Coe's mark by two-tenths of a second (see Aug. 28). Coe, who was watching, had just broken the world 1,000-meter record in 2:13.4, surpassing the standard set by Rick Wohlhuter of the United States six years before.

The Million-Dollar Gate

By ELMER DAVIS

JERSEY CITY—Jack Dempsey is still heavyweight champion of the world—it might almost be said that for the first time he is really the champion. Georges Carpentier, in many respects the most serious opponent Dempsey has ever faced, stood up against him this afternoon in Tex Rickard's stadium here and could not last through the fourth round. And at that, Carpentier fought better than most American critics believed possible.

His end came at a few seconds after 3:30 o'clock, when the fourth round had been going on one minute and sixteen seconds. Dempsey found the Frenchman's face with his left and followed it up with a hard right just in front of the ear. Carpentier went down, but on the count of nine leaped to his feet and seemed in shape to give the champion more trouble. But he never had the chance. Dempsey led a light left to the face and then, as Carpentier swayed aside from the blow, Dempsey drove a tremendous smash with his right hand into Carpentier's ribs below the heart. This was quickly followed by a smashing right to the jaw.

The blow to the body was a hard enough blow in itself, because that spot had already been hammered and weakened by a score of fierce short-arm jolts in the desperate infighting of the previous rounds, but at the blow to the jaw Carpentier dropped again—dropped on his right side and lay there while Referee Harry Ertle swung his arm above him and counted. At the count of eight Carpentier stirred and made a desperate effort to rise; but he could not move. Nine, ten—and Dempsey's championship was secure. So ended the "battle of the century," fought before 90,000 people—a fight

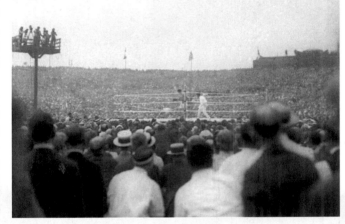

A crowd of 90,000 watch as heavyweight champion Jack Dempsey stands in a neutral corner after flooring Georges Carpentier, at rear of ring, in Jersey City, N.J. Tex Rickard took in the then-staggering sum of $1.6 million at the gate. (Associated Press)

which had aroused more interest, in all probability, than any other in all history.

The fight was held in a huge, hastily constructed wooden arena in Boyle's Thirty Acres: There was a novelty not only in the size of the crowd, but in the composition of it. The throng included thousands of women and a considerable number of public officials such as rarely have been seen in this country at a professional boxing bout. The crowd was the largest ever to see a sporting event in the United States. In another way, Mr. Rickard, promoter of the fight, achieved a new record. The gate receipts, estimated at $1,600,000 by Mr. Rickard, were far above all previous records. All day long the crowd had been gathering for the

championship battle. From 9 o'clock in the morning, when the gates were opened, until a few minutes before three in the afternoon, when the event of the day was scheduled to begin, a steady stream of people marched steadily across the muddy fields leading to the saucer-shaped arena.

Late this afternoon, Carpentier returned to his training camp in Manhasset, N.Y., and informed a representative of The New York Times that he knows no man in the world who is in the same class as Dempsey. He said he put forth every ounce of his strength in the fight. On Carpentier's behalf, however, his old friend Thierry Mallet, acting as spokesman, said an injury to Carpentier's thumb eight days ago, which led to the breaking of the thumb in the second round today, was a contributing cause toward his defeat. Mallet did not attribute the defeat of the Frenchman to this cause, however. Carpentier's external injuries appeared to be a slight cut under the eye, a slightly swollen nose and a badly swollen right hand, due to the fracture of a bone in the thumb. The injury to the thumb, it was said, was the most serious injury he sustained.

Dempsey's first thought as he came victorious from the ring was of his mother. He took a pencil and wrote her the following telegram:

"Mrs. C. Dempsey, 8572 South State St., Salt Lake City, Utah:

"Dear Mother: Won in the fourth round. Received your wire. Will be home soon as possible. Love and kisses. Jack."

Runners-up

1938: In an all-American women's final, Helen Wills Moody won a record eighth Wimbledon singles title by defeating her California rival Helen Jacobs, 6–4, 6–0. The mark stood until the Czechoslovakian expatriate Martina Navratilova won her ninth Wimbledon crown by dispatching Zina Garrison of Houston, 6–4, 6–1, in 1990.

1977: Bjorn Borg of Sweden outlasted Jimmy Connors of the United States in one of the most dramatic Wimbledon finals in history. Down by 0–4 in the deciding fifth set, Connors staged a remarkable comeback to tie at 4–4, but he double-faulted in the ninth game and the crowd cheered. Responding with an obscene gesture, he dropped three straight points, and Borg served out the match, 3–6, 6–2, 6–1, 5–7, 6–4.

1988: An era ended at Wimbledon when Martina Navratilova's six-year winning streak was snapped in the finals by 19-year-old Steffi Graf of West Germany, 5–7, 6–2, 6–1. The baton of supremacy having been passed, Graf went on to win the Grand Slam with a victory over Gabriela Sabatini of Buenos Aires in the United States Open (see Sept 10).

July 3, 1954
Answered Prayers

By LINCOLN A. WERDEN

Babe Didrikson Zaharias hoisting the women's U.S. Open golf trophy for the third and final time. It was a sublime moment for Zaharias, who was battling cancer. Having sunk the final putt, she declared: "My prayers have been answered." (Associated Press)

PEABODY, Mass.—Mrs. Mildred (Babe) Didrikson Zaharias completed her comeback bid by winning the United States women's open golf championship today. Over the Salem Country Club course the famed woman all-around athlete, who underwent an operation for cancer in the spring of 1953, regained the title she held in 1948 and 1950 with a seventy-two-hole score of 291.

Visibly tiring on the last six of the 36 holes that she played today, Mrs. Zaharias admitted that this triumph was one of the highlights of a long athletic career. A member of the Olympic track team and winner of two events in the 1932 games, Mrs. Zaharias has competed in many sports and was declared the "greatest woman athlete of the half century" in an Associated Press poll several years ago.

After receiving a thunderous ovation upon holing the final putt of her fourth round for a 75, following a 73 this morning, Mrs. Zaharias declared that "my prayers have been answered. When I was in the hospital I prayed that I could play again. Now I'm happy because I can tell people not to be afraid of cancer. I've had over 15,000 letters from people and this victory today is an answer to them—it will show a lot of people that they need not be afraid of an operation and can go on and live a normal life."

Those who followed Mrs. Zaharias on the concluding day of the championship were anxious to see how the physical strain might affect her in this arduous tourney. She proved equal to it all. "I really wanted to win this one," the Babe explained, "and I'm glad I could hold my concentration."

Betty Hicks of Durham, N.C., with 75 and 77 for her closing rounds, finished second at 303. Mrs. Zaharias's 12-stroke advantage was one of the widest victory margins in history. The record is the 14-stroke edge enjoyed by Louise Suggs in 1949. At the seventy-second hole, she pushed her drive into the trees. She didn't elect to play safe, but boldly pitched through an opening to the fairway. From below the hill, she pitched her third shot to the green and was down in two putts for a 5. The Babe doffed her straw hat in response to the applause of the crowd. The first United States woman golfer to win the British championship, a title she captured in 1947, Mrs. Zaharias has now won four of twelve tournaments since she underwent her operation at Beaumont, Tex., in 1953.

Babe Didrikson Zaharias died of cancer at age 42 in September 1956.

Runners-up

1912: Left-hander Rube Marquard of the New York Giants defeated the Dodgers, 2–1, at Washington Park in Brooklyn to win his 19th consecutive game, a major league record for a single season that still stands. Carl Hubbell of the Giants set the mark for most straight victories over all in 1937 (*see May 27*).

1990: Larry Tudor of Santa Ana, Calif., set a certified world "open distance" paragliding record of 303 miles. Finding some two dozen hot, light air masses called thermals, he soared as high as 13,500 feet and floated from an airpark in Hobbs, N.M., to a fast-food restaurant in Elkhart, Kan. The 300-mile barrier had never before been broken.

1983: Two world 100-meter records were set within 15 minutes of each other at the National Sports Festival at the Air Force Academy in Colorado Springs. Evelyn Ashford of Roseville, Calif., set the women's record of 10.79 seconds and Calvin Smith, a University of Alabama senior, set the men's mark of 9.93.

July 4, 1939
Hail and Farewell

By JOHN DREBINGER

An emotional Lou Gehrig delivering his valedictory before a full house at Yankee Stadium. He called his incurable disease a "bad break," but described himself "the luckiest man alive." (UPI)

NEW YORK—In perhaps as colorful and dramatic a pageant as ever was enacted on a baseball field, 61,808 fans thundered a hail and farewell to Henry Lou Gehrig at the Yankee Stadium today.

To be sure, it was a holiday and there would have been a big crowd and plenty of roaring in any event. For the Yankees, after getting nosed out, 3 to 2, in the opening game of the double-header, despite a ninth-inning home run by George Selkirk, came right back in typical fashion to crush the Senators, 11 to 1, in the night-

cap. Twinkletoes Selkirk embellished this contest with another home run. But it was the spectacle staged between the games which doubtless never will be forgotten by those who saw it. For more than forty minutes there paraded in review two mighty championship hosts—the Yankees of 1927 and the current edition of the Yanks who definitely are winging their way to a fourth straight pennant and a chance for another world title.

From far and wide the 1927 stalwarts came to reassemble for Lou Gehrig Appreciation Day and to pay their own tribute to their former comrade-in-arms who had carried on beyond all of them only to have his own brilliant career come to a tragic close when it was revealed that he had fallen victim of a form of infantile paralysis. In conclusion, the vast gathering, sitting in absolute silence for a longer period than perhaps any baseball crowd in history, heard Gehrig himself deliver as amazing a valedictory as ever came from a ball player.

So shaken with emotion that at first it appeared he would not be able to talk at all, the mighty Iron Horse, with a rare display of that indomitable will power that had carried him through 2,130 consecutive games, moved to the microphone at home plate to express his own apprecia-

tion. He spoke slowly and evenly, and stressed the appreciation that he felt for all that was being done for him. He spoke of the men with whom he has been associated in his long career with the Yankees—the late Colonel Jacob Ruppert; the late Miller Huggins, his first manager, who gave him his start in New York; Edward G. Barrow, the present head of baseball's most powerful organization; the Yanks of old who now stood silently in front of him, as well as the players of today.

"What young man wouldn't give anything to mingle with such men for a single day as I have for all these years?" he asked. "You've been reading about my bad break for weeks now. But today I think I'm the luckiest man alive. I now feel more than ever that I have much to live for."

When Gehrig returned to the Yankee dressing rooms he was so close to a complete collapse it was feared that the strain upon him had been too great and Dr. Robert E. Walsh, the Yankees' attending physician, hurried to his assistance. But after some refreshment, he recovered quickly and faithful to his one remaining task, that of being the inactive captain of his team, he stuck to his post in the dugout throughout the second game.

Long after the tumult and shouting had died and the last of the crowd had filed out, Lou trudged across the field for his familiar hike to his favorite exit gate. With him walked his bosom pal and team-mate, Bill Dickey, with whom he always rooms when the Yanks are on the road. Lou walks with a slight hitch in his gait now, but there was supreme confidence in his voice as he said to his friend: "Bill, I'm going to remember this day for a long time."

Runners-up

1910: Jack Johnson, aged 28, stopped former champion James J. Jeffries in a 15th-round technical knockout in their world heavyweight championship fight in Reno, Nev. Jeffries, aged 35, had come out of retirement in an attempt to dethrone Johnson.

1975: Billie Jean King (see Sept. 20) won the women's singles at Wimbledon for the sixth time, defeating Evonne Goolagong-Cawley of Australia, 6–0, 6–1, in 39 minutes. King won 20 Wimbledon titles over all. Martina Navratilova, whose career overlapped King's by several years, won 19.

1983: Dave Righetti pitched the first no-hitter for the Yankees since Don Larsen's perfect game in the 1956 World Series (see Oct. 8), defeating the Boston Red Sox, 4–0, at Yankee Stadium. Righetti struck out Wade Boggs, who would retire with 3,010 lifetime hits, for the final out.

July 5, 1980
The Unforgettable Match

By NEIL AMDUR

WIMBLEDON, England—Bjorn Borg posted a five-set victory over John McEnroe today that not only gave the Swede his fifth consecutive Wimbledon singles title but also gave tennis followers something to cherish long after both players have left the sport. Like well-conditioned fighters, they traded shots for 3 hours 53 minutes on the center court of the All-England Lawn Tennis and Croquet Club. The top-seeded Borg won, 1–6, 7–5, 6–3, 6–7, 8–6, only after the determined second-seeded McEnroe had saved 7 match points in the fourth set, including 5 in a dramatic 34-point tiebreaker that will stand by itself as a patch of excellence in the game's history.

"Electrifying," said Fred Stolle, a former Australian great, of the tiebreaker that the 21-year-old McEnroe finally won, 18 points to 16, to deadlock the match, after Borg had earlier lost 2 match points on serve at 5–4, 40–15. If this marathon was not the greatest major championship final ever played—and tennis historians treasure the past with reverence—it ranked as one of the most exciting. Lance Tingay of The London Daily Telegraph, who was watching his 43d final here, put it at the top of his Wimbledon list.

"For sure, it is the best match I have ever played at Wimbledon," said the 24-year-old Borg, who now has won a record 35 singles matches in a row here, including five-set finals from Jimmy Connors in 1977 and Roscoe Tanner last year. Connors and Tanner, like McEnroe, are left-handers. This one was more of a struggle of indomitable wills that would not buckle, even under the normally strenuous circumstances of a championship final. Heightening the drama were the contrasting playing styles and personalities of the participants—Borg, the stolid, silent man of movement, and McEnroe, the brash, aggressive serve-and-volleyer, dubbed by one Fleet Street tabloid as "Mr. Volcano" for his outbursts during yesterday's stormy four-set triumph over Connors in the semifinals.

McEnroe spoke only with his racquet and spirit today, flooring Borg with his kicking serve and deep first volleys for almost two sets and then defying the Swede's attempt to close out the match in the fourth set. That Borg lost the fourth set and then played one of the best sets of his career, losing only 3 points in seven service games, reaffirmed the notion that he must be ranked alongside Rod Laver and Bill Tilden among the sport's greatest champions.

The match wound up, perhaps almost fittingly, with Borg and McEnroe throwing their favorite punches. Attacking off his second serve at 15–40, McEnroe punched a forehand volley into the corner. Borg countered with the backhand cross-court winner. "He's gone through every kind of testing," Roger Taylor, a British player during Laver's reign, said of Borg. "If you were going to find any chinks, this would have been it today."

Bjorn Borg after defeating John McEnroe in their epic five-set struggle at Wimbledon. The fourth set, simply the best ever played in a major championship match, went to McEnroe after a 34-point tiebreaker. But Borg prevailed for his fifth straight All-England title. (Associated Press)

Runners-up

1947: Larry Doby of the Cleveland Indians became the first black player in the American League, three months after Jackie Robinson broke the color line with the Brooklyn Dodgers. Doby, 22, who became a seven-time All-Star and Hall of Famer and twice led the league in home runs, pinch-hit and struck out in the seventh inning against the Chicago White Sox at Comiskey Park.

1975: Arthur Ashe defeated Jimmy Connors in four sets in an all-American final at Wimbledon, becoming the first African-American to win there. The match was played amid charged feelings because Connors had said in a lawsuit the month before that Ashe had slandered him for refusing to join the United States Davis Cup team.

1982: In perhaps the greatest performance of his storied career, striker Paolo Rossi scored all of Italy's goals to eliminate Brazil, 3–2, in a World Cup second-round match at Barcelona, Spain. Italy went on to win its third World Cup (see July 11) as Rossi scored six tournament goals.

Grass Court Queen for a Day

By FRED TUPPER

WIMBLEDON, England—Althea Gibson fulfilled her destiny at Wimbledon today and became the first member of her race to rule the world of tennis. Reaching a high note at the start, the New York Negro routed Darlene Hard, the Montebello (Calif.) waitress, 6–3, 6–2, for the all-England crown.

The ladies took the stage amid a sea of waving programs as the temperature touched 96 in the shade. Miss Gibson was in rare form. She had beaten Darlene three times running in the past year and was off in high. Her big service was kicking to Miss Hard's backhand with such speed that Darlene could only lob it back. Behind her serves and her severe ground shots, Althea moved tigerishly to the net to cut away her volleys. Quickly she had four games running against one of the finest net players in the game. Darlene, white-faced in the heat, kept shaking her head at her failure to find an offensive shot. The set was gone in 25 minutes at 6–3.

At the beginning of the second set, Althea was unhurried. Her control was good and she calmly passed Miss Hard every time she tried to storm up to the barrier. The game grew faster as Miss Gibson's service jumped so alarmingly off the fast grass that Darlene nodded miserably as her errors mounted. It was all over in 50 minutes. "At last! At last!" Althea said, grinning widely as the Queen congratulated her and presented the trophy.

Later Miss Gibson paired with Miss Hard to swamp Mary Hawton and Thelma Long of Australia, 6–2, 6–1, in the doubles for her second championship.

But the match of the day and the sensation of the year saw Gardnar Mulloy gain the honor of being the oldest man in Wimbledon history to win a title. The 42-year-old Denver executive teamed with 33-year-old Budge Patty, the Californian who lives in Paris, to upset the top-seeded Neale Fraser and Lew Hoad, 8–10, 6–4, 6–4, 6–4, and break an Australian domination in the men's doubles that went back seven years.

Althea Gibson, aged 30 at the time she won at Wimbledon, became the first African-American of either sex to win a United States Open title two months later. She repeated her victories at both tournaments the following year and played on the L.P.G.A. golf tour from 1964 to '71. She has rarely appeared in public in recent decades.

Althea Gibson returning a shot to Darlene Hard in their Wimbledon final. She not only became the first black player to win a major tournament but also won the J.S. Open in 1957 and both tournaments again in '58. (Associated Press)

Runners-up

1933: The first All-Star Game was held at Comiskey Park as part of World's Fair activities in Chicago, with the American League defeating the National, 4–2. Babe Ruth homered in the third inning. Founded through the enterprise of the Chicago Tribune writer Arch Ward, the exhibition was the precursor of all-star games in all major United States sports.

1975: In a heralded 1¼-mile match against the Kentucky Derby winner Foolish Pleasure at Belmont Park in New York, Ruffian, the popular 3-year-old filly, broke down about three-eighths of a mile into the race and had to be destroyed. The veterinarian for the New York Racing Association described the severe fracture above the horse's right ankle as "just like breaking a stick."

1994: Leroy Burrell of Lansdowne, Pa., broke Carl Lewis's 100-meter world record of 9.86 seconds by running 9.85 in an annual meet at Lausanne, Switzerland. Burrell's mark stood until Donovan Bailey of Canada ran 9.84 seconds at the 1996 Olympic Games in Atlanta.

July 7, 1912
'World's Greatest Athlete'

By Marconi Transatlantic Wireless Telegraph to *The New York Times*

STOCKHOLM—For the second time in the history of the Olympic Games the Stars and Stripes floated today from all three flag poles on which are hoisted the national emblems of the countries obtaining first, second and third places in final events. The previous occasion was at Athens in 1896, when American athletes won all the points in the standing broad jump. The event today in which the Americans made a clean sweep was the final of the 100-meter flat race. Barely a yard separated the first and fifth men at the finish, and a mighty shout arose from the 20,000 present when the numbers were posted, showing that Ralph Craig of Detroit was first, Meyer, the New Yorker, second, and Lippincott of Philadelphia third.

Besides these successes on the cinder path, James Thorpe of the Carlisle Indian School won the pentathlon, with J.J. Donoghue of California third. This event is designed to show the all-around ability of athletes, and consists of the running broad jump, throwing the javelin, 200 meters run, throwing the discus, and 1,500 meters run. Thorpe won first place in all except the javelin throw, in which he was third.

Commenting on Thorpe's success, Commissioner Sullivan of the United States said to The Times correspondent: "His all-around work was certainly sensational. It is a complete answer to the charge that is often made, that Americans specialize in athletics. In fact, the pentathlon was added to the games especially for the benefit of foreigners, but we have shown that we can produce all-around men, too. It also answers the allegation that most of our runners are of foreign parentage, for Thorpe is a real American, if there ever was one."

Thorpe made six points in the pentathlon, compared with 15 points for P.R. Bie of Norway, who was second, and 26 points for Donoghue, who was third. Thorpe's marks were: running broad jump, 7 meters 7 centimeters; javelin, 52 meters; 200 meters flat, 23 seconds; discus, 35 meters 37 centimeters; 1,500 meters flat, 4:44.

Altogether today the American athletes made sure of eleven more points in the contest for the Olympic championship. Matt Halpin of New York, a member of the Olympic Committee, told The Times correspondent tonight that he was much delighted over the day's successes. He said: "Although we expected that Thorpe would win the pentathlon, his great performance exceeded our hopes. Donoghue will show up much better in the decathlon."

Jim Thorpe, a 24-year-old Native American whose Carlisle Indian School football exploits were soon to become well known (see Nov. 9), won a second gold medal in the decathlon eight days later. The greatest athlete of his day, he played major-league baseball from 1913 to '19 and pro football from 1915 to '28. Because he had played semipro baseball before the Stockholm Games, his medals were stripped from him by the International Olympic Committee in 1913. They were returned to his descendants in 1983 (see Jan. 18), 30 years after his death in poverty in Los Angeles.

Jim Thorpe watching a shot put attempt during the decathlon competition at the Stockholm Olympics. He won gold medals in the pentathlon and the decathlon, leading King Gustav of Sweden to call him "the world's greatest athlete." Thorpe is said to have replied, "Thanks, King." (UPI)

Runners-up

1937: Dizzy Dean of the St. Louis Cardinals suffered a broken toe when hit by a drive by the Cleveland Indians' Earl Averill in the All-Star Game at Griffith Stadium in Washington. Returning to action two weeks later, Dean favored the toe and injured his arm. He was never the same pitcher again.

1986: Jackie Joyner-Kersee of the United States broke the world heptathlon record at the first Goodwill Games in Moscow, finishing the two-day, seven-event competition with 7,148 points, 202 more than the previous international mark set by Sabine Paetz of East Germany.

1985: Unseeded Boris Becker, 17, of West Germany, became the youngest Wimbledon champion ever and the first unseeded player to win, firing 21 aces in the final to defeat Kevin Curren, 27, of South Africa, 6–3, 6–7, 7–6, 6–4. Becker won three All-England championships as well as two other major tournaments before retiring in 1999.

July 8, 1889
The First 'Title' Fight

[Unsigned, *The New York Times*]

NEW ORLEANS—Never, during even a Presidential election, has there been so much excitement as there is here now, even when the brutal exhibition is over and it is known that John L. Sullivan was successful and that seventy-five rounds were necessary to "knock out" Jake Kilrain. All the streets and vacant spaces around the Northeastern Railroad Station were crowded until the last train got away, at 2:25 this morning, and before daylight the streets in front of the newspaper offices were crowded by people waiting for the bulletins that never came.

Before the last excursion train left the city it ceased any longer to be a secret that the fight would take place at Richburg, Miss., a small station on the New Orleans and Northeastern Railroad, 104 miles from New Orleans. The ring was erected by pine torchlight during the night on the highest of hills in the rear of Richburg. In the fourth and fifth rounds Kilrain made Sullivan run around the ring after him, falling when he got too near him. After running about the ring for a while in the tenth round, Kilrain fell to avoid being hit. He pursued the same tactics in the next one, until Sullivan cried out: "Stand up and fight like a man; I'm no sprinter! I'm a fighter!"

This sort of procedure went on for a long time, Kilrain running and dodging and Sullivan calling on him continually to "fight like a man." But Kilrain insisted on fighting or, rather, running as "Charlie" Mitchell, his trainer, directed. In the thirty-ninth round Sullivan asked the referee to make his opponent "stand and fight," and made a claim of a foul, which the referee refused.

In the forty-fourth Sullivan became sick, but even then Kilrain was afraid to

John L. Sullivan outlasting Jake Kilrain, center of ring, in their secretive, bare-knuckled 75-round heavyweight title fight in Richburg, Miss. All subsequent heavyweight championship bouts were fought openly—and with gloves. (The Ring)

venture near him. He asked him to make the fight a draw, but Sullivan refused, and emphasized the refusal by knocking Kilrain down. He was angry now, and in the next round he not only knocked Kilrain down but he stamped upon him, which prompted a claim of foul from Kilrain's friends. This was not allowed, and it was repeated in the next round, after Sullivan had thrown Kilrain and fallen upon him. The crowd was now satisfied that only chance would enable Kilrain to win, and it jeered him for his Fabian tactics.

In the sixty-seventh, sixty-eighth, sixty-ninth and seventy-first rounds Sullivan managed to catch his fleeing antagonist and each time knocked him down. Each of the next four rounds ended by Kilrain falling to avoid being knocked down. At the end of the seventy-fifth the referee cautioned Kilrain not to repeat his tactics, but it was seen that Kilrain was in no condition to continue. Kilrain was frightfully bruised and bled profusely. Sullivan was but little marked. The official time of the unofficial fight was 2 hours 16 minutes and 25 seconds.

Runners-up

1967: University of Kansas sophomore Jim Ryun *(see June 23)* ran 3 minutes 33.1 seconds in the 1,500 meters at the British Commonwealth meet at the Los Angeles Coliseum, defeating Kip Keino of Kenya and breaking the 1960 world record of 3:35.6 by Herb Elliott of Australia. Ryun's record fell to Filbert Bayi of Tanzania in 1974.

1941: Ted Williams of the Boston Red Sox walloped a three-run homer off Claude Passeau of the Chicago Cubs with two out in the bottom of the ninth inning in the All-Star Game at Briggs Stadium in Detroit, giving the American League a stunning 7–5 victory.

2000: Roger Clemens of the Yankees beaned Mike Piazza of the Mets on the front of the helmet with a fastball in an interleague night game at Yankee Stadium. Piazza suffered a concussion and did not play in the All-Star Game. The incident served as a subplot in the World Series that fall when Clemens threw Piazza's shattered bat back at him from the mound in Game 2 *(see Oct. 22).*

The Duel at Turnberry

By JOHN S. RADOSTA

TURNBERRY, Scotland— In an epic head-to-head match even more gripping than yesterday's tie at 65, Tom Watson came from three strokes behind today to beat Jack Nicklaus by one shot for the British Open golf championship. Watson shot 65 on seven birdies and two bogeys while Nicklaus carded 66 on four birdies and no bogeys. This wasn't just golf, it was theater. Watson pulled up even at the 15th with a monster 60-foot putt, and the outcome appeared to be settled on the par-5 17th, where Nicklaus took two putts from four feet for a par while Watson went ahead with an easy birdie.

On the 18th, Nicklaus pushed his drive to what looked like a hopeless position beside a stand of gorse. Watson, on the fairway and away, confidently lofted a soft No. 8-iron shot to two feet from the flagstick. Nicklaus blasted from the rough to the green, 32 feet short. Now it looked like a two-shot loss. But not yet: Still unbeaten, Nicklaus gallantly and incredibly rolled in that 32-foot putt for a birdie 3. But it was futile. Watson admitted he was nervous over his 2-foot putt, but he knocked it in for a matching birdie—and his second British Open in three years and second major title this season.

Nicklaus put his hands on Watson's shoulders and said

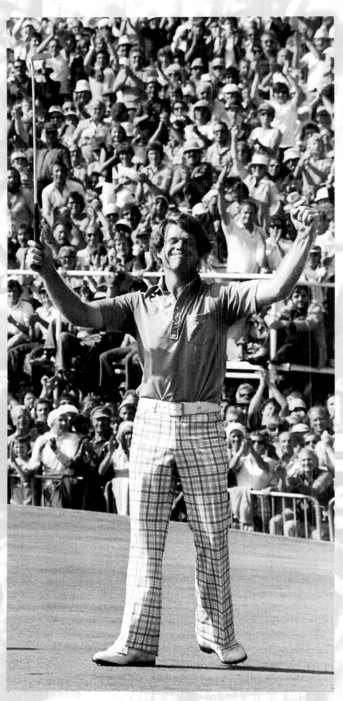

Tom Watson after sinking a 2-foot putt to win the British Open by one stroke over Jack Nicklaus at Turnberry in Scotland. The mano-a-mano battle is widely considered the most dramatic in the history of major tournament golf. (Associated Press)

something like, "You know, I'm tired of giving it my best shot and finding it's not enough." The same thing had happened in April, when Watson beat Nicklaus for the Masters, his first major victory of the season. Nicklaus, 37, who won the British Open in 1966 and 1970, has now finished second six times, a record. There are many who consider him the greatest golfer of all time. Certainly for the last decade, since he deposed Arnold Palmer, he has been the king of the game.

Now there is no question that Watson, 27, has the best chance to succeed Nicklaus. He meets him with respect but no fear, and he relishes the battle. Nicklaus has always said of this young man that his strength lies in his temperament and iron will. Nicklaus had to yield to it in the final round of this year's Masters, and yielded again today.

Despite his history of choking in final rounds, Watson has developed cool nerves and confidence in himself. With the help of Byron Nelson, he also has honed a swing that he says will stand up under pressure. Watson's 72-hole aggregate was 268, eight strokes below the record 276 set by Arnold Palmer in 1962 and matched by Tom Weiskopf in 1973. Nicklaus scored 269 after precisely matching Watson the first three days on 68, 70 and 65.

Runners-up

2000: Pete Sampras of Florida passed Roy Emerson of Australia as the all-time leader in Grand Slam victories, winning his 13th such title with a four-set victory over Patrick Rafter at Wimbledon. It was Sampras's 53rd victory in 54 matches at the All-England Club. Sampras won his 14th Slam title at the United States Open in 2002.

1969: The great Tom Seaver of the Mets, aged 24, lost a bid for a perfect game against the Chicago Cubs when Jimmy Qualls, a light-hitting rookie outfielder who batted .250 with only 31 hits this year, singled with one out in the ninth at Shea Stadium.

1994: In the World Cup's most dramatic game, Brazil defeated the Netherlands, 3–2, in the quarterfinals at the Cotton Bowl in Dallas. All five goals came within 30 minutes in the second half, with a free kick by Branco in the 81st minute deciding the game. Brazil beat Sweden in the semifinals and Italy in the championship game.

Women of the World

By JERE LONGMAN

PASADENA, Calif.—They played to near collapse, through 120 minutes of soccer, 90 minutes of regulation melting into 30 minutes of overtime under a brutal sun, and still no one had put the ball into the net in the final of the Women's World Cup. And so the United States won soccer's world championship over China by the sport's most tense and capricious arbiter—penalty kicks.

Five players from each team set the ball up 12 yards from goal in the penalty-kick phase, leaving the shooters and goalkeepers alone, one on one, to decide the match as much by chance as by skill. All a goalie can do is guess, act on instinct. If she guesses correctly, she is a hero. If not, there is no resistance to be offered, only a futile leap or a dive one way, while the ball flies unimpeded in the opposite direction.

When this breathless game was over, the Americans had put five penalty kicks into the net, while China could manage only four. After curling her decisive, left-footed kick inside the right post, the defender Brandi Chastain whipped off her jersey, twirling it like a lariat over her head as 90,185 fans erupted in celebration and confetti cannons dusted the field at the Rose Bowl.

It was the largest crowd to watch a women's sporting event in the United States—in the world, organizers believe. Chastain's kick consummated three weeks of unprecedented interest in a sport that filled huge arenas with soccer moms and dads and their daughters, who painted their faces red, white and blue in star-spangled admiration of the American players. Grownups finally began recognizing the sporting heroes their kids had discovered long ago. Even President Clinton was in attendance today, having been drawn into the swirl of popularity surrounding the United States team.

Perhaps gone forever is the myth that women's sports cannot attract crowds and that the games that women play are somehow lesser than the games men play. The Women's World Cup will undoubtedly be remembered as an epochal moment in women's sports, along with the Billie Jean King–Bobby Riggs tennis match in 1973, and the passage of Title IX in 1972, which essentially forbid discrimination on the basis of gender.

Although many find penalty kicks an unsatisfying way to decide a match—the 1994 men's World Cup was decided here the same way— the victorious American women still made a forceful case for a professional league of their own that would start after the 2000 Summer Olympics in Sydney, Australia. This was the second world championship for the United States, which won the inaugural Women's World Cup in 1991, before taking a bronze in 1995. The Americans also won the 1996 Summer Olympics, but they had lost twice to China this year. And until Chastain's rescuing penalty kick, today's result was in doubt.

America's most confident and accurate taker of penalty kicks, midfielder Michelle

Carla Overbeck as netting the first shootout goal as the U.S. defeated China in the Women's World Cup at the Rose Bowl. The high drama began when 120 minutes of play ended in a scoreless tie. (Getty Images)

Akers, left woozily at the end of regulation and spent the rest of the game in the American locker room with heat exhaustion. Despite a career threatened by chronic fatigue syndrome, Akers dominated today's game in defensive midfield, sliding ferociously, sledgehammering teammates and opponents in her path and using her head to catapult away one Chinese kick after another. She was the first great star of this team, and Coach Tony DiCicco calls her the greatest woman ever to play the game.

Runners-up

1934: In the second annual All-Star Game, at the Polo Grounds in New York, Carl Hubbell of the Giants struck out five future Hall of Famers in a row: Babe Ruth, Lou Gehrig, Jimmie Foxx, Al Simmons and Joe Cronin. Despite the legendary feat, the American League won, 9–7.

1989: The Chicago Bulls named the former Knicks forward and Bulls assistant Phil Jackson as head coach to replace Doug Collins. He led them to six N.B.A. titles in nine seasons (with more than a little help from Michael Jordan). After a one-year retirement, Jackson joined the Los Angeles Lakers in 2000 and coached them to three league titles through 2003 *(see June 19)*.

1971: Former Boston Red Sox slugger Tony Conigliaro, victim of one of baseball's worst beanings, announced his retirement at 25. An emerging home run champion, Conigliaro was hit in the head by California Angels fastballer Jack Hamilton in August 1967. The pitch broke Conigliaro's cheekbone and damaged his sight. Although he briefly tried a comeback in 1975, he was never the same.

July 11, 1989
'The Sky's the Limit With Bo'

By MICHAEL MARTINEZ

Bo Jackson of the Royals watching his nearly 450-foot home run in the first inning of the 60th All-Star Game in Anaheim, Calif. Jackson, also a brilliant running back for the N.F.L. Raiders, became a Pro Bowl selection late in the 1990 season. (Associated Press)

ANAHEIM, Calif.—In his life and times as a big league baseball player, Bo Jackson has done the kinds of things expected of legends. He has made the spectacular diving catch, hit the electric home run, thrown out the runner sliding across the plate. He has done them often enough to be admired for his wondrous talent. But they are still merely glimpses.

Tonight, on one of the game's grandest stages, Jackson took his rising star to another height. In the 60th All-Star Game, in front of 64,036 at Anaheim Stadium, the Kansas City Royals left fielder turned the

night into something special. He hit a first-inning homer nearly 450 feet, drove in two runs and stole a base, then was named the game's most valuable player in the American League's 5–3 victory over the National League.

"He's a very dynamic player," said Wade Boggs, who followed Jackson with a home run of his own in the first. "He can do a lot of things: run, throw, hit, hit for power. He can do it all." The victory was the A.L.'s second in the last two years, the first time it has won consecutive midsummer games since 1957–58.

In only his third full season in the

league, Jackson is already considered an impact player. He earned the most votes among the fans in voting to determine the game's A.L. starters, and he brought 21 home runs into the All-Star break. But there are still some who say he cannot continue to play both baseball and football—he works down the freeway for the Los Angeles Raiders during the fall and winter—on a professional level. "A couple of years ago, people said I couldn't do both," Jackson said when the night was over. "But that's not fair to me, to say what a man can or can't do."

Only 26 years old, Jackson has made the most of his chance. The Royals regard him as a most valuable entity; the Raiders see him as one of their most important offensive players. To baseball, he is perhaps a legend in the making. One other player in All-Star Game history has hit a home run and stolen a base in one game: Willie Mays, who did it in 1960.

In December 1990 Bo Jackson became the only athlete in history to be named to both the All-Star and the Pro Bowl games. A month later he suffered a hip injury in an N.F.L. playoff game, which ended his football career. In April 1993, after a year-and-a-half layoff from baseball for hip replacement surgery, he homered in his first at-bat for the Chicago White Sox. He retired two seasons later.

Runners-up

1982: Italy (see July 5) won its third World Cup, and first in 44 years, beating West Germany, 3–1, in the final at Madrid and tying Brazil at the time for the most Cup titles. Paolo Rossi capped his return from a two-year suspension for reported involvement in illegal gambling by scoring the Italians' first goal and setting up the second with a beautiful display of ball control.

1973: Dwight Stones, a 19-year-old from Los Angeles who had leapt into stardom the year before at the Munich Olympics, set a world high-jump record of 7 feet

6½ inches in a meet between the United States and West Germany in Munich.

1924: Eric Liddell, a 22-year-old divinity student from Scotland, set an Olympic record in winning the 400-meter sprint in 47.6 seconds at the Olympic Games in Paris. Liddell, whose specialty was the 100 meters, passed up that event because the final was held on Sunday, his Sabbath. His story was portrayed decades later in the Academy Award–winning "Chariots of Fire."

July 12, 1924
Nurmi, the Flying Finn

By EDWIN L. JAMES

COLOMBES, France—It was Paavo Nurmi's moment again in the Olympic Stadium. As fresh as if he had just come from a country walk, he finished two minutes ahead of his countryman, Willie Ritola, today in the most grueling cross-country race ever run in Olympic history. Thirty-nine men, all hard and fit athletes, started in the 10,000-meter cross-country race, but only fifteen finished. The finish of some of those fifteen was most pitiful.

Behind Nurmi and Ritola, both from Finland, there came into the stadium a big American boy, R. Earl Johnson of Pittsburgh. Entering about a minute behind Ritola, he slowly but steadily edged his way round the half circle of the stadium toward the tape. He was still running, but his run was fast becoming an amble. Ten yards behind Johnson came an Englishman, Harper, who struggled even more painfully. His legs moved as if each had a ten-pound weight attached to it. For a moment it

seemed doubtful if he could reach the tape. He did, but he stood groping blindly with his hands, seeking support, and was caught fainting in the arms of his countrymen.

Scarcely had he fallen when through the Marathon gate came other figures, even more pitiful. Two Frenchmen were running together. At the bend one of them staggered, and as dazed as a man who had been struck by a hammer tottered off the track onto the field. The cheers of the crowd roused him. Back he came and, swaying now right and left, he staggered forward. Twice he nearly fell. If the Frenchman could keep going he would take fifth place behind his countryman, Lauvaux, who had reached home. But tottering backward and forward, he fell at last, twenty yards from the tape, rolled over like a man shot.

From the far side of the stadium, just by the gate, came shouts for help. The Spaniard, Andia Aguilar, running dazed and stupefied, turned to the left instead of right, then fell, splitting his scalp and knocking all the remaining consciousness out of his head. These were scenes inside the stadium. Outside there were worse. One after another in a heap six men fell not a quarter of a mile from home, broken by the pace and the pitiless sun which was blazing down.

It was partly the pace set by Nurmi that caused the disaster, but more the terrific heat of the sun. However, Nurmi and Ritola, were amazing. Since the week began the latter has raced thirty-nine kilometers and in every case has been first or second. Today he suffered more than Nurmi did but reached the tape still alert enough to trot off the course behind his fellow countryman. Nurmi's time was 32:54⅘ minutes.

The indefatigable Paavo Nurmi of Finland cruising to victory in a 5,000-meter race in Berlin in September 1930. Nurmi won nine gold medals in Olympic middle- and long-distance races from 1920 to '28. (Associated Press)

Runners-up

1930: Bobby Jones became the first golfer to break par for the four rounds of the United States Open, shooting 5-under-par 287 at Interlachen Country Club in Hopkins, Minn. It was Jones's fourth Open title and the third leg of his unparalleled Grand Slam (*See Sept. 27*).

1998: In the most improbable World Cup final upset since Uruguay defeated Brazil in 1950, France, playing at home in Saint-Denis, defeated Brazil, 3–0. Zinedine Zidane, France's exquisite playmaker, headed in a pair of corner kicks.

1979: Chicago White Sox owner Bill Veeck's "Disco Demolition Night" promotion at Comiskey Park went awry when fans set fire to disco records on the field as planned between games of a doubleheader against the Detroit Tigers but then refused to return to their seats. The second game had to be forfeited.

July 13, 1966
Jim Brown Quits Football for the Movies

LONDON (AP)—Jim Brown of the Cleveland Browns, of the National Football League, the leading ground-gainer in pro football history, will announce his retirement today. The 30-year-old fullback will make the announcement at a news conference here, where he is making a motion picture. Although Brown still has one year to go on a two-year contract at a salary reported to be $60,000-plus a year, he has decided to step out at the top of his career.

The 228-pounder, who was the league's most valuable player in 1965, has gained almost seven miles in his N.F.L. career. In nine years of pro ball, he won the rushing championship eight times. Art Modell, the owner of the Browns, had told Brown he expected him to be in camp at Hiram, Ohio, when the experienced players report to Coach Blanton Collier. However, the movie in which Brown is working will not be completed until late September. The Browns, the defending Eastern Conference champions, will open their regular season on Sept. 11 at Washington and will have played three games before the end of September.

In his pro career, the former all-America fullback from Syracuse carried the ball 2,359 times and gained 12,312 yards for an average of 5.2 yards a carry. He scored 126 touchdowns. In 1965,

Jim Brown turning the corner against the Packers in his last game, for the N.F.L. championship in January 1966. Green Bay beat Cleveland, 23-12, and suddenly the movies beckoned. (Associated Press)

Brown won the ground-gaining title with 1,544 yards, averaging 5.3 yards a carry. He scored 21 touchdowns. The loss of Brown will be a blow to Cleveland, which has won the Eastern title the last two years. Behind Brown, Cleveland has Charlie Scales, a 5-foot-11-inch 215-pounder, who carried the ball only 19 times for 72 yards last year, and Jamie Caleb, who spent most of last season on the reserve squad.

Although Brown had hinted that he might not play this season and had said

positively he would not continue in 1967, the news of his decision to quit came as a surprise. In mid-June, Modell had warned Brown that his pay would be suspended if he failed to report to camp. Modell said it would be unfair to coaches, fans and other clubs not to clarify Brown's position.

Brown won the rushing title as a rookie in 1957 and retained the crown five straight years, through 1961. He finished behind Jim Taylor of Green Bay in 1962 and led again in 1963, 1964 and 1965.

Runners-up

1996: Cigar (see March 27) swept to his 16th straight victory, winning the Citation Challenge at Arlington Park outside Chicago and matching the record modern-era winning streak set by Citation from 1946 to '48. Cigar's streak was halted in August by the 39-to-1 long shot Dare and Go in the Pacific Classic, and he was retired in November.

1985: Breaking his own world record, 22-year-old Sergei Bubka of the Soviet Union (see Aug. 5) became the first pole-vaulter to clear 6 meters, or 19 feet 8¼

inches, long considered unattainable, when he soared past that height in the Paris International Track and Field Meet.

1934: Babe Ruth of the Yankees became the first player to hit 700 home runs when he connected against right-hander Tommy Bridges of the Detroit Tigers at Navin Field in Detroit. Only Ruth and Henry Aaron of the Milwaukee and Atlanta Braves have reached the 700 mark.

July 14, 1946
Williams Beats the Williams Shift

BOSTON (AP)—On the strength of Ted Williams' thumping bat, the not-to-be denied Red Sox outscored the Indians, 11–10, in the first game of a twin bill today and then went on to take the second by a more moderate score, 6–4. The double triumph stretched Boston's American League lead to 11 games over the second-place Yankees. All Theodore Samuel Williams did in the first game was clout three homers and a single, drive in eight runs and score four times. Ted the Kid thus joined a large group of sluggers who have belted three homers in a single contest.

Lou Boudreau, Cleveland pilot who in the nightcap set up the most unusual defense against Williams ever seen in Fenway Park, also had himself a time in the opener. Boudreau hit a homer and four successive doubles in that first game during which the two teams sprayed hits all over and out of the field.

When Williams went to bat in the second game, during which he received his ninety-fifth and ninety-sixth bases on balls, Shortstop Boudreau concentrated six men in right field. The Cleveland manager played back on the grass midway between first and second. Jimmy Wasdell, the first sacker, posted himself on the grass near the foul line. The third baseman was on the grass on the right side of second base and the right and center fielders patrolled as deep as possible in that sector. The set-up was successful once when Boudreau snagged a hot grounder and threw Thumpin' Theodore out at first. The first time Williams batted in the second contest he lined a double down the right field foul line. The smash was just too high for Wasdell, who leaped with his gloved hand outstretched.

Williams' first four-sacker, on a one-and-nothing pitch off Steve Gromek, was a tremendously high smash which bounded off the top of the wall between the bull pen and the right field bleachers, more than 400 feet from the plate. His second was a line drive on the first ball thrown by Don Black in the fifth inning. That landed in the runway between the bleachers and grandstand in right field and bounced high into the stands. Williams' third four-ply poke was another liner which screamed into the stands where they curve in deep right. The first homer came with the bases filled and the third was belted while two mates were aboard.

Ted Williams may well have been the greatest hitter in the history of baseball. That an opposing team would concentrate six men on the right side of the field, conceding him a hit to left, hints at the respect in which he was held.

Williams remains the last of the .400 hitters, having batted .406 in 1941, his third big-league season. He hit .388 at age 39 in 1958, was an All-Star 17 of the 18 full seasons he played, had a lifetime average of .344 and, as a career codicil, hit a home run in his last at-bat at age 42 (see Sept. 28). Williams lost three full seasons in his prime during World War II and most of two others during the Korean War yet still came within 300-odd hits of 3,000. Ever opinionated, frequently contrary, he died at age 83 in 2002.

The Cardinals' infield shifts sharply to the right with Ted Williams at bat in the 1946 World Series in St. Louis. Indians manager Lou Boudreau unveiled a stop-Williams defense similar to this one during the regular season. (Associated Press)

Runners-up

1970: Pete Rose of the Cincinnati Reds bowled over catcher Ray Fosse of the Cleveland Indians with two out in the last of the 12th inning at Rose's home park, Riverfront Stadium, to score from second on a single and give the National League a 5–4 victory in the All-Star Game. It was the league's eighth straight victory in the classic.

1985: The Baltimore Stars of the summertime United States Football League, coached by Jim Mora, won their second straight U.S.F.L. title over the Oakland Invaders, 28–24, at Giants Stadium in New Jersey as Kelvin Bryant ran for three touchdowns. One year later, the league folded, having gained the grand total of $1 in its federal court challenge to the N.F.L.

1991: Meg Mallon of Ramona, Calif., who had not won on the L.P.G.A. tour for four seasons, shot a final round of 67 to win the United States Women's Open at Colonial Country Club in Fort Worth by two strokes over Pat Bradley of Westford, Mass. The victory came two weeks after Mallon outdueled Bradley to win the L.P.G.A. championship.

July 15, 1923
Bobby Jones Wins His First Major

By WILLIAM D. RICHARDSON

INWOOD, L.I.—Robert Tyre Jones Jr. of Atlanta, Ga., twenty-one years old on March 17 last, is tonight America's national open golf champion. Tied yesterday by Robert A. Cruickshank, former Scottish amateur star, who came to America and turned pro three years ago, with a score of 296 at the conclusion of the regulation 72-hole test at the Inwood Country Club, Jones was the winner in the play-off today by two strokes. It was not until the last hole was played that the question of who is to wear this year's crown was decided in favor of the youthful amateur.

When the Southern youngster, competing in his fourth national open tournament, tapped his putt into the cup for a par 4 on the last hole, it made his total for today's eighteen holes 76, but the issue was decided two strokes previous to that. It was decided when Jones played his second shot coming to the home hole—a truly miraculous shot out of the rough that sped almost 200 yards and ended less than two yards away from the flapping flag on the eighteenth green. It was a shot that, in addition to proving Jones one of the most courageous fighters in the world, will take its place among the epochal strokes that are a part of golf's lengthy history.

Made in the stress of battle,

Bobby Jones, 21, in the U.S. Amateur at Flossmoor, Ill., in 1923, while he was student manager of the Harvard golf team. Two weeks later he won the U.S. Open. He captured 12 other major championships by age 28 and retired in 1930. (Associated Press)

it sealed the fate of the little Scottish gamecock, just as it opened up the portals of fame to the man who brought it off. It was a superb shot made by a superb golfer in a superb manner. Without a moment's hesitation, Jones drew his No. 1 iron out of the bag, took a momentary look at the lie, glanced at the flag and swung. The ball flew off the face of his club, rose in the air and carried squarely on the green, 190 yards away. A tremendous shout went up as the ball struck on the green, bit its way into the turf, and brought up its journey about two club lengths away from the hole for a possible birdie three. Jones twice tapped his ball. When it dropped into the cup on the second tap it signalized his first great victory.

Then one of the greatest scenes of all was enacted. The crowd rushed out on the green. Two of Bobby's fellow townsmen from Atlanta hoisted him on their shoulders and he was borne triumphantly toward the clubhouse. A kiltie, blowing away on the bagpipes, furnished musical accompaniment. His youthful face wreathed in smiles, Jones was kept busy several minutes accepting the congratulations and plaudits of the golf-mad spectators who had witnessed one of the greatest of all play-offs.

Runners-up

1972: Lee Trevino of Horizon City, Tex., sank a 30-foot chip shot with a 9-iron to save par on the 17th hole at Muirfield in Scotland to beat Jack Nicklaus by a stroke and win his second straight British Open title. Trevino won six major tournaments, including two United States Opens (1968 and '71).

1994: One month after leading the New York Rangers to the Stanley Cup, Mike Keenan announced that he was stepping down as their coach because a delayed bonus payment in his view voided his contract. The move struck some

Rangers fans as outright desertion. Two days later he became coach and general manager of the St. Louis Blues for $2 million a year.

1901: Twenty-two-year-old Christy Mathewson of the New York Giants, the dominant pitcher of the first decade of the modern era, pitched a no-hitter as they defeated the St. Louis Cardinals, 5–0, at the Polo Grounds. Mathewson won 373 games and was among the initial five players inducted into the Hall of Fame in 1936 (see Feb. 2).

July 16, 1988
Flo-Jo's Form Overtakes Her Fashion

By FRANK LITSKY

Florence Griffith Joyner set a women's world record in the 100 meters on this date at the United States Olympic track and field trials. The following article appeared in The Times *on Monday, July 18.*

INDIANAPOLIS—As good a runner as she is, Florence Griffith Joyner has been better known through the years for her sense of fashion. Start with the fingernails. At the Los Angeles Olympics in 1984, when they were 4 inches long, she painted three of them red, white and blue. She painted a fourth gold, for the color of the medal she hoped to win in the 200 meters. Instead, she finished second and won a silver medal.

In 1986, when the nails reached 6½ inches, they prevented her from styling her hair, so she trimmed them. The nails are again almost 4 inches long and painted bright red, the color of the United States Olympic uniforms. In the United States Olympic track and field trials here, most of the women in the 100-meter dash wore conventional running shorts. In three of Griffith Joyner's four races, she wore body suits with the left leg cut off; in the other, she wore a black body suit with both legs. "One-leg-

Florence Griffith Joyner winning the 200 meters at the U.S. Olympic trials six days after breaking the world 100-meter mark. Her fashion statement this time: a two-legged body suit, muscles defined. (Associated Press)

gers," she called her cut-down outfits. "I designed them myself."

For all her style, Florence Griffith Joyner will be better remembered for running the three fastest 100 meters ever in 24 hours: Saturday's world record of 10.49 seconds and Sunday's 10.70 and 10.61. For the first time in a long career, she had reached the top.

She is 28 years old, slim but strong at 5 feet 8 inches and 130 pounds. She trains with weights four times a week and can squat with 320 pounds. She ran for California State–Northridge and later for U.C.L.A. In 1980, she finished fourth in the 200 meters in the United States Olympic trials, just failing to make the team. "I had four years to make the next team," Griffith Joyner said, "and possibly to become a medalist. I became determined to do that."

She succeeded, and she won the silver medal behind Valerie Brisco in the 1984 Olympics. Here, she ran unlike any other woman in history.

At the 1988 Seoul Olympics, Florence Griffith Joyner won gold medals in the 100 and 200 meters (see Sept. 29) and the 4×100-meter relay. She died of a heart seizure at her home in Mission Viejo, Calif., at age 38 in 1998.

Runners-up

2001: Jacques Rogge of Belgium succeeded Juan Antonio Samaranch of Spain, who had served for 21 years as president of the International Olympic Committee. Rogge's election was seen as an I.O.C. move toward greater openness and less attention to lavish perks.

1950: Some 174,000 people, probably the most ever to attend a sporting event, gathered at the new Maracaña Stadium in Rio de Janeiro to watch Uruguay, in only its second World Cup appearance, upset Brazil, 2–1, in the final. It was the first Cup action in 12 years because of World War II.

1947: Rocky Graziano of New York City knocked out world middleweight champion Tony Zale of Gary, Ind., in the sixth round of their title fight at Chicago Stadium. Zale, however, had knocked out Graziano the year before for the title and kept the upper hand in their famous rivalry by doing it again in 1948.

July 17, 1941
The Streak Still Stands

By JOHN DREBINGER

CLEVELAND—In a brilliant setting of lights and before 67,468 fans, the largest crowd ever to see a game of night baseball in the major leagues, the Yankees tonight vanquished the Indians, 4 to 3, but the famous hitting streak of Joe DiMaggio finally came to an end. Officially it will go into the records as fifty-six consecutive games, the total he reached yesterday. Tonight in Cleveland's municipal stadium the great DiMag was held hitless for the first time in more than two months.

Al Smith, veteran Cleveland left-hander and a Giant cast-off, and Jim Bagby, a young right-hander, collaborated in bringing the DiMaggio string to a close. Jolting Joe faced Smith three times. Twice he smashed the ball down the third-base line, but each time Ken Keltner, Tribe third sacker, collared the ball and hurled it across the diamond for a put-out at first. In between these two tries, DiMaggio drew a pass from Smith.

Then, in the eighth, amid a deafening uproar, the streak dramatically ended, though the Yanks routed Smith with a flurry of four hits and two runs that eventually won the game. With the bases full and only one out Bagby faced DiMaggio and, with the count at one ball and one strike, induced the renowned slugger to crash into a double play. It was a grounder to the shortstop, and as the ball flitted from Lou Boudreau to Ray Mack to Oscar Grimes, who played first base for the Tribe, the crowd knew the streak was over.

However, there were still a few thrills to come, for in the ninth, with the Yankees leading, 4 to 1, the Indians suddenly broke loose with an attack that for a few moments threatened to send the game

Joe DiMaggio extending his hit streak to 56 consecutive games with a first-inning single against Al Milnar of the Indians at Cleveland on July 16, 1941. He was stopped in a night game the following day. (Associated Press)

into extra innings and thus give DiMaggio another chance. Gerald Walker and Grimes singled, and, though Johnny Murphy here replaced Lefty Gomez, Larry Rosenthal tripled to score his two colleagues. But with the tying run on third and nobody out the Cleveland attack bogged down in a mess of bad base-running and the Yanks' remaining one-run lead held, though it meant the end of the streak for DiMaggio, who might have come up fourth had there been a tenth inning.

"I can't say that I'm glad it's over," DiMaggio said after the game. "Of course, I wanted it to go on as long as it could. Now that the streak is over, I just want to get out there and keep helping to win ball games." It was on May 15 against the White Sox at the Yankee Stadium that DiMaggio began his string, which in time was to gain nationwide attention. As the great DiMag kept clicking in game after game, going into the twenties, then the thirties, he became the central figure of the baseball world.

On June 29, in a doubleheader with the Senators in Washington, he tied, then surpassed the American League and modern record of forty-one games set by George Sisler of the St. Louis Browns in 1922. The next target was the all-time major league high of forty-four contests set by Willie Keeler, the famous Oriole star, forty-four years ago under conditions much easier then for a batsman than they are today. Then there was no foul-strike rule hampering the batter. But nothing hampered DiMaggio as he kept getting his daily hits, and on July 1 he tied the Keeler mark. The following day he soared past it for No. 45, and he kept on soaring until tonight. In seeking his fifty-seventh game, he finally was brought to a halt.

Joe DiMaggio's consecutive-game hitting streak has been among the most enduring records in sports. Pete Rose of the Cincinnati Reds has come the closest to matching it, hitting in 44 consecutive National League games in 1978.

Runners-up

1961: Commissioner Ford C. Frick ruled that Roger Maris of the Yankees had to break Babe Ruth's record of 60 home runs in 154 games, or separate marks would appear in the record books. Maris broke Ruth's record in 163 games (see Oct. 1).

1994: In the first World Cup final ever decided by penalty kicks, Brazil defeated Italy, 3–2, after 120 minutes of scoreless play before a crowd of 94,194 at the Rose Bowl. Roberto Baggio of Italy missed a free shot into the net from 12 yards to decide the game after Dunga had made what ultimately became the winning kick. Both teams had been vying to win their fourth Cup title.

1983: Tom Watson sank a 20-foot birdie putt on the 16th hole to break a three-way tie in the British Open at Royal Birkdale in Southport, England, in one of the tightest championships ever held across the pond. Watson parred the last two holes for a total of 275, one stroke ahead of Hale Irwin and Andy Bean, for his fifth British title and second in a row.

July 18, 1999
A Faultless Day for Everyone

By MURRAY CHASS

David Cone being carried off the field at Yankee Stadium after pitching a perfect game against the Montreal Expos. Joe Girardi, his catcher, and Manger Joe Torre, wearing a wristwatch, served as escorts. (Barton Silverman/The New York Times)

NEW YORK—In an improbable setting, David Cone performed an improbable feat today. He pitched the Yankees' second perfect game in little more than a year, and he did it playing in front of Don Larsen, who pitched a perfect World Series game for the Yankees in 1956 (see Oct. 8). Larsen was at Yankee Stadium to help celebrate Yogi Berra Day, and after Larsen threw the ceremonial first pitch to Berra, Cone took command of the mound and retired all 27 Montreal batters he faced as the Yankees clubbed the Expos, 6–0. It was only the 16th perfect game in major league history.

Following David Wells's perfect game against Minnesota by one year, two months and one day, Cone made the Yankees the first team to pitch perfect games in successive seasons and the first to have three perfect games to their credit. "I probably have a better chance of winning the lottery than this happening today," an exuberant Cone said. "What an honor. All the Yankee legends here. Don Larsen in the park. Yogi Berra Day. It makes you stop and think about the Yankee magic and the mystique of this ball park."

When the foul pop-up lofted by Orlando Cabrera, the ninth batter in the Expos' lineup, on Cone's 88th pitch of the day descended softly into third baseman Scott Brosius's glove for the 27th out, Cone dropped to his knees and grabbed his head, "in disbelief," he said. Joe Girardi, the catcher, was the first to reach him. "I just put a bearhug on him and took him down," Cone said. "I didn't want to let go. Somebody dragged me off him. I wasn't going to let go. That's how good I felt about Joe Girardi and what he means to me not only professionally but personally."

Working in 98-degree heat, Cone threw only 20 called balls and increased the velocity of his fastball as the game progressed. He had the Expos lunging at sliders the entire game. Unable to hit his sliders or his fastballs with authority, they struck out 10 times and hit 13 balls into the air.

With 26 outs from 26 batters, Cone looked around the stadium, soaking in the scene as he prepared to face No. 27, Cabrera. Cabrera, a 24-year-old Colombian, had already done some quick figuring. "If he throws a perfect game," he told some teammates, "I'm going to be the last out." Cabrera swung and missed, took the second pitch for a ball, then hit yet another ball into the air. "I was glad it went up and not down," Brosius said. "I was glad to see a pop-up and not some kind of weird ground ball."

"It's getting to be a habit, huh?" Larsen said as he rode the elevator to get to the clubhouse, where he threw his arms around Cone.

Runners-up

1987: Don Mattingly of the Yankees homered in his eighth consecutive game, tying the major-league record set by Dale Long of the Pittsburgh Pirates in 1956. Mattingly's shot came off José Guzmán of the Texas Rangers in Arlington, Tex. Ken Griffey Jr. of the Seattle Mariners also tied the mark in 1993.

1927: Ty Cobb of the Philadelphia A's collected his 4,000th hit, doubling against Sam Gibson of the Tigers in Detroit. Only Pete Rose, with 4,256 hits, and Cobb, who retired with 4,189, have reached the 4,000 plateau.

1951: Jersey Joe Walcott of Camden, N.J., 37, became the oldest heavyweight champion in history when he knocked out Ezzard Charles of Cincinnati in the seventh round of their fight at Forbes Field in Pittsburgh. Walcott reigned for 14 months. George Foreman was eight years older than Walcott when he became the champion by knocking out Michael Moorer in 1994 (see Nov. 5).

July 19, 1996
The Flame Still Burns

By GEORGE VECSEY

ATLANTA—Muhammad Ali floats above the Summer Games, no longer an elusive butterfly but a great glowing icon as large as a spaceship. He casts his light on every athlete, every spectator, every volunteer, all the people who walk these humid streets with just a little more zip in their step, now that they have seen Ali.

The whole world gasped in shock tonight when Ali suddenly materialized on that platform at the far end of Olympic Stadium, the perfect choice to light the cauldron. Who would have thought of Ali? Who would have predicted he could stand in front of the world, his body slowed by Parkinson's syndrome, and hold a flaming torch and transfer searing fire to a contraption that would raise the fire to the cauldron?

The people from the Atlanta organizing committee can be flagellated for the clogged traffic and the rampant greed and tackiness of these Games, but Billy Payne and his colleagues must be praised for their innate understanding that Muhammad Ali, the former Cassius Clay, was the perfect symbol for the ceremony. Everybody knew the theme of these Games was "look how far we've come," to justify this event being given to Atlanta. The ceremony's creators paid careful, artistic attention to the safe black poets and singers and athletes and martyrs of the South. And reviving the Rev. Martin Luther King's "I Have a Dream" speech was as predictable as it was proper.

Ali was the shocker, the wild card.

But Ali has always been full of surprises. He could float like a butterfly and sting like a bee, could charm the world as a beautiful youth when he won the gold at the Summer Games of 1960, he could

Muhammad Ali, aged 54, his movements slowed by Parkinson's syndrome, lights the Olympic flame in the opening ceremony of the Atlanta Games. The U.S. swimmer Janet Evans is at rear. (Associated Press)

spout doggerel and he could beat bad Sonny Liston, could be cruel to opponents, could defy the draft board, could come back and regain his heavyweight championship. Somewhere along the line, even to most of white America, Ali stopped being a frightening symbol of a "foreign" religion and a menacing black man and a threat to the welfare of his homeland, and he became a fragile legend, damaged by the punches of his brutal sport, unable to rouse the wit and flash of his youth.

Putting him on that platform was a stroke of genius that transformed a very nice ceremony into a celebration, a block party. I was sitting in the stadium with a black male colleague and a white female colleague, and when we saw Ali shining on that platform, we exchanged high-fives at the audacious perfection of it. Ali was at the Games. Ali was on the hill. Raise the flame. Float like a butterfly, sting like a bee, all of us.

Runners-up

1976: Nadia Comaneci, a 4-foot-11-inch, 80-pound 14-year-old from Romania, became the first gymnast in Olympic history to score a perfect 10; the scoreboard, unprepared for four digits, read: "1.00." She earned the mark with an exquisite uneven parallel bars routine in the Montreal Games and received six other 10's and three gold medals *(see July 21).*

1910: At age 43, Cy Young of the Cleveland Naps (later renamed the Indians), won his 500th game, defeating the Washington Senators, 5–4, at League Park in

the District of Columbia. Young retired in 1911 with 511 victories. Only Walter Johnson of the Senators, with 417, has won 400 or more games.

1947: Babe Didrikson Zaharias *(see July 3),* the greatest female athlete of the half-century, extended her unprecedented string of pro golf victories to 17 by defeating Dot Kielty, 9 and 8, in the final round of the Broadmoor Women's Invitational at Colorado Springs. At the awards ceremony, Didrikson told her rival, "All you have to do is hitch up your girdle and swing."

July 20, 1979
The Swashbuckler

By JOHN S. RADOSTA

ST. ANNE'S, England—Severiano Ballesteros, a 22-year-old Spaniard with the face of an altar boy and the style of a blade-swinging corsair, came from two strokes behind today to win the 108th British Open by three shots. After he had sunk a par putt of three feet on the 18th green, two of his brothers, Vicente and Baldomero, rushed out and surrounded him in an emotional embrace. Their eyes were filled with tears. Indeed, the man nicknamed Sevvy was already welling up with tears as he strode up the 18th fairway, enveloped by the cheers of thousands of admirers.

For an agonizingly long time this afternoon, the tournament was wide open and within anyone's grasp. A tie looked inevitable when as many as five players were clustered within a bracket of one-under to one-over par. One by one the other contenders gave up shots while Ballesteros parred his way through the daunting final nine of the Royal Lytham and St. Anne's Golf Club. He shot 70, one under for this links course on the coast of the Irish Sea, for a one-under, 72-hole total of 283. A wild driver who has to make his pars and even birdies from sand traps, roughs and occasionally parking lots, he was the only player to beat par for 72 holes. His previous rounds were 73, 65, 75.

Ballesteros was one of many players who posted big numbers in yesterday's wind, rain and cold. He said if he could get off to a good start today, he had a chance. He came out charging with a birdie 2 on the first hole, where he sank a 15-foot putt.

Ballesteros does not know the meaning of caution. His game reminds one of the young Arnold Palmer. He almost always has been an erratic driver—very long but quite wild, left or right. In the last two days he has hit the fairway only once while using his driver. Yesterday, he missed the golf course by driving out of bounds on the second hole. As a result, Ballesteros has become one of Europe's best players from the rough and bunkers. Fifteen times this week he was in green-side bunkers and 14 times he got down with one putt. Today he saved four pars with his miracle shots.

After making the turn at 34, one under par, he bogeyed the 10th, where his second shot flew to an adjoining tee. Then he birdied the 339-yard 13th without hitting fairway or green. He bogeyed the 14th on a rare three-putt when he tied for the lead with Ben Crenshaw. But he immediately compensated with a birdie on 16—from a parking lot. Reviewing that hole later, Ballesteros said it had presented no problem. He was on the favorable side for his approach and there was a left-to-right wind to steer his sand iron shot to the green, 15 feet from the flag. Then he sank the putt for a birdie.

Crenshaw, who came out of the field to lead for a while, shot 71–286 for a second-place tie with Jack Nicklaus, the three-time winner and defending champion, who carded 72. Crenshaw dashed his chances with a double-bogey 6 on the 17th hole.

Seve Ballesteros, who knew the weeds as well as the fairways, acknowledging the cheers on the 18th green at Royal Lytham and St. Anne's in Lancashire, England, after winning the British Open. (Associated Press)

Runners-up

1937: Don Budge of Oakland, Calif., staged one of the most remarkable comebacks in tennis history, defeating Baron Gottfried von Cramm of Germany, 8–6, in the final set of the Davis Cup semifinals at Wimbledon and enabling the United States to beat England the next week in the finals. Budge was down two sets to love and 4–1 before winning in the final set on the sixth match point.

1858: All-Star baseball teams from Brooklyn and Manhattan played the first in a series of three games at the Fashion Park Race Course on Long Island. According to the encyclopedia Total Baseball, it was the first time admission (50 cents) was ever charged at a game. It was 11 more years before the first players, the Cincinnati Red Stockings, were paid.

1924: Johnny Weissmuller of Chicago (see Aug. 10) won the gold medal in the 100-meter freestyle at the Paris Olympics in 59.0 seconds, setting a new Olympic record but falling well short of his world mark of 57.4 earlier that year. It was a United States medal sweep, as Duke Kahanamoku and his brother Sammy of Hawaii took the silver and bronze.

July 21, 1976
Nadia Comaneci: The Perfect 10

By DAVE ANDERSON

MONTREAL—On the uneven bars, she whirls as easily as a sparrow fluttering from limb to limb on a tree. On the balance beam, she clings to it as surely as a squirrel would. On the vault, she lands as softly as a sea gull on a beach. In her floor exercises, she is part go-go dancer, part ballerina, part cheerleader. And today Nadia Comaneci, her dark pigtails tied with red and white yarn, won her first Olympic gold medal as the all-round champion in women's gymnastics. But at 14 years old, she is not a woman. An athlete, yes; an artist, yes. But with her 80-pound rubber body, she's hardly much more than a child. That, of course, is the essence of her charm.

The Rumanians knew that Nadia was technically superior to any of the Soviet gymnasts. They also knew that Olga Korbut had used her charm to upstage her teammate, Ludmilla Tourischeva, the brooding beauty who won the all-round gold medal at Munich four years ago. Gymnastics has been one of the purest forms of sport for 150 years, but now, ever since television recorded Olga Korbut's tears and triumphs at Munich, gymnastics also is show biz, especially Olympic women's gymnastics. And so the Rumanians reminded Nadia to smile and wave. Not boastfully. Softly and naturally was enough, both for her and for the television people.

At 14, as a Barbie doll with bangs, Nadia Comaneci was perfect as Olga Korbut's television successor. She also was perfect as a gymnast. Five times (all three on the uneven bars, twice on the beam) she has been awarded a perfect 10 score. It registers as "1.00" on the electronic scoreboard because 9.99 is the

Nadia Comaneci of Romania dismounting from the uneven bars at the Montreal Olympics. Her repeated 10's came out as "1.00's" on the scoreboard, which wasn't ready for anything beyond 9.99. (Associated Press)

board's limit. The perfect 10 score was considered unattainable in the Olympics until Nadia attained it once Sunday, twice Monday and twice today. Not that she considered it unattainable. "I've done it," she said, "20 times now."

One a scale of 1 to 10, she has made the scoring scale outmoded. On a scale of 1 to 10, she really deserves an 11 for what she has accomplished in relation to the scores of other gymnasts. Because of the restrictions of the scoring scale, many gymnastic observers thought that her dominance over the other competitors was not as wide as it should have been. Her aptitude for gymnastics was discovered in kindergarten. It was confirmed in a recent aptitude test that some of the European nations give their gymnasts.

"The numbers from 1 to 100 are mixed up on a piece of paper," says Art Maddox, the pianist for the United States Olympics women's gymnasts. "You get four minutes to go from one number to another. It might sound easy, but it's not. I'm told that Nadia had the highest score anybody ever got—72, as I remember." Aptitude is one thing. Performance is another. And today, in winning the all-around gold medal Nadia performed virtually impeccably at the Forum, the Montreal Canadiens' hockey shrine.

In today's competition, she opened with a respectable 9.85 on the vault, added her third consecutive 10 on the uneven bars, another perfect 10 on the beam and concluded with a 9.9 in her floor exercises. By that time, all the other competitors were watching her except the Soviet athletes, who never seem to look at her as she performs. That assured Nadia Comaneci's coronation as the queen of the Olympics, the successor to Ludmilla Tourischeva in skill and to Olga Korbut in show biz.

Runners-up

1973: Henry Aaron of the Atlanta Braves (see April 8) became the second player in history, behind Babe Ruth in 1934, to hit 700 home runs when he launched a two-run shot off left-hander Ken Brett of Philadelphia in an 8–4 loss to the Phillies at Atlanta–Fulton County Stadium.

1952: Parry O'Brien, a University of Southern California student, won the shot-put gold medal at the Helsinki Olympics in Finland. O'Brien, who also won gold at the '56 Melbourne Games in Australia and was the first to exceed 60 feet, revolutionized shot-putting by starting with his back to the circle and then unwinding into the throw with all the momentum he could gather.

2002: Ferrari's Michael Schumacher of Germany won the French Grand Prix at Magny-Cours. He clinched his third consecutive Formula One drivers title and fifth championship in nine years, tying the record set by Juan Manuel Fangio of Argentina in the 1950's.

July 22, 1996
'Pocket Hercules'

By GEORGE VECSEY

Naim Suleymanoglu of Turkey at the Atlanta Games. A shade under 5 feet tall yet able to lift almost three times his bodyweight of 141 pounds, he won gold medals in three straight Olympics. (Associated Press)

ATLANTA—Naim Suleymanoglu of Turkey became the first weight lifter in history to win three gold medals, and he also set a world record, in the 141-pound competition today at the Summer Games. Suleymanoglu, known to the world as Pocket Hercules, won in one of the most dramatic confrontations possible as he and his closest rival, Valerios Leonidis of Greece, traded three straight world-record lifts. Not quite 5 feet tall, Suleymanoglu snatched 324½ pounds and then raised 413¾ in the clean-and-jerk for a total of 738¼. Leonidis failed in his final attempt for the gold medal, but did set his own world record in the clean-and-jerk in his next-to-last lift.

When Suleymanoglu was in New York three months ago, he was asked who his biggest competition would be. He said, in two of the few words he used in English, "the Greek." He was right about that. Leonidis matched him right up to the final attempt today in a competition that had the joint rocking. The championship was held in the cavernous basement of the Georgia World Congress Center, an exhibition hall hard by the Georgia Dome. The two Greek weight lifters had a large cheering section, and they played to the crowd, particularly Yorgos Tzelilis, who alternately pounded his chest and waved his palms toward the heavens, asking for more cheers.

The first half of the competition was the snatch, in which the bar is raised from the floor to the overhead position in one motion. The lower-rated lifters risked hernias and falling bars first, and then the favorites took over. Leonidis went first and lifted 308 pounds. At 4:45 P.M., Suleymanoglu strode to the floor and lift-ed 319 pounds. At 4:50 P.M., Leonidis came back and lifted 319. At 4:56 P.M., Suleymanoglu came back and tried 324½ pounds but never got it above his waist and dropped it, almost daintily. At 4:59 P.M., Leonidis could not raise 324½ pounds but he was still ahead of Suleymanoglu because of his lower body weight, nearly a pound and a half less. At 5 P.M., Suleymanoglu raised 324½ pounds, held it and then dropped the bar before raising his two fists nearly shoulder high, an extravagant gesture for him. He had the lead halfway through.

The second half was the clean-and-jerk, which involves two motions, one to the shoulders and then overhead. Again, the bottom half of the draw went first. At 5:45 P.M., Suleymanoglu, with little emotion or extra motion, lifted 396 pounds. At 5:48 P.M., Leonidis equaled him. Then two announcements were made: Juan Antonio Samaranch, the president of the International Olympic Committee, was present, and Suleymanoglu would try to raise 407 pounds, which would be a world record. Suleymanoglu came out and promptly set the world record, then pointed to himself.

This is the third time the world has turned on the television and discovered Naim Suleymanoglu. He was born into the huge Turkish community in Bulgaria and came up through the Bulgarian youth programs. Turkey paid $1 million to Bulgaria to facilitate his changing citizenship in 1988 in time for him to be eligible for the Summer Games. Now he has accumulated 46 world records and 232 gold medals, including three Olympic championships. Asked if he was the greatest lifter in history, he said people would have to make that judgment for themselves.

Runners-up

1990: Greg LeMond of Medina, Minn (*see July 23*), who in 1989 had overcome a gunshot wound to return to competitive cycling, came back from a serious viral infection in April and a 105th-place finish in the Giro d'Italia in June to win his third Tour de France in five years and second in succession. He finished 2 minutes 16 seconds ahead of Claudio Chiappucci of Italy.

1976: Kornelia Ender, 18, of East Germany, equaled her own world record in the 100-meter butterfly and broke the world mark in the 200 butterfly within the space of 27 minutes at the Montreal Olympics. She won four gold medals in the Games. Enders's feats were tarnished in 1991 when former East German coaches confessed that their swimmers had trained with anabolic steroids (*see Nov. 24*).

1991: Kari Castle, a 31-year-old hang glider, took off near Lone Pine, Calif., in the Sierra Nevada, caught repeated gusts of hot, light air and, dangling in a harness from the tiny craft's underside, landed 210 miles away near Austin, Nev. 8 hours 20 minutes later. She became the first woman to glide more than 200 miles, reaching a height of some 16,000 feet.

July 23, 1989
Greg LeMond's Tightest Race

By SAMUEL ABT

Greg LeMond on the 15th stage of the Tour de France, amid rugged hills between Gap and Orcières-Merlette. He won his second title by 8 seconds – the narrowest margin in the race's history. (Getty Images)

PARIS—By racing from Versailles into Paris in a stunning 26 minutes 57 seconds today, Greg LeMond of the United States won the Tour de France for the second time. His margin of victory over Laurent Fignon of France, 8 seconds, was the smallest ever in the world's greatest bicycle race.

The Tour had already covered 2,000 miles in three weeks when LeMond set off on the last stage today 50 seconds behind the overall leader, Fignon. The final stage was a 15-minute time trial, in which a rider's time, not his position relative to other riders, is what matters. Few besides the 28-year-old LeMond, who has made a remarkable comeback from injury, believed he had a chance to make up the

50 seconds on Fignon. "It's still possible," LeMond said yesterday, but most people doubted him. As half a million people watching the finish on the Champs Elysées burst into cheers, LeMond proved all the doubters wrong.

"I just went all out," said LeMond, who also won in 1986. "I thought I could win, but I knew I needed something special." LeMond won the time trial easily, finishing 33 seconds faster than Thierry Marie, a Frenchman, who was timed in 27.30. LeMond needed all his speed and power as Fignon placed third, 58 seconds slower than LeMond. The American's time translated into a speed of 34 miles per hour, the fastest ever for a time trial in the Tour de France by about 3 miles per hour.

The margin of victory was the smallest by 30 seconds in the history of the Tour de France, which began in 1903 and has been interrupted only by both world wars. LeMond waited in the finish area for the arrival of Fignon, who set off two minutes after him. As the seconds went by, LeMond said later, "All I could think was how terrible it would be to lose by one second." As it became clear that Fignon was not going to win, LeMond broke into a huge grin and punched one uppercut after another into the air.

In finishing one-two, LeMond and Fignon made remarkable comebacks this year. LeMond was accidentally shot while hunting turkey in California in April 1987, nine months after he became the only American to win the Tour de France. Fignon, who will be 29 next month, won the Tour de France in 1984 and 1985 but then developed tendinitis in his left heel. After surgery in 1985, he had only occasional success until he won the recent Italian tour.

Runners-up

1996: Performing on a badly sprained ankle in the Atlanta Olympics, Kerri Strug of Tucson, Ariz., painfully landed her second vault and fell into the arms of Coach Bela Karolyi, having scored 9.712 points in the routine. It was enough to win a team gold medal for the United States women gymnasts.

1995: Miguel Indurain of Spain became the first cyclist to win the Tour de France five consecutive times, defeating Alex Zulle of Switzerland by 4 minutes 35 seconds. Four others—Jacques Anquetil of France, Eddie Merckx of Belgium,

Bernard Hinault of France and Lance Armstrong of the United States (see July 25) have also won five times.

1960: Betsy Rawls, 32, of Spartenburg, S.C., won the United States Women's Open for a record fourth time at Worcester (Mass.) Country Club. She overcame a seven-stroke deficit in the third round with a 68 and took the title with a final-round 75 to win by one shot over Joyce Ziske. Mickey Wright of San Diego (see July 1) also won four United States Women's Opens.

The Pine Tar Home Run

By MURRAY CHASS

NEW YORK—Baseball games often end with home runs, but until today the team that hit the home run always won. At Yankee Stadium today, the team that hit the home run lost. If that unusual development produced a sticky situation, blame it on pine tar. With two out in the ninth inning, George Brett of the Kansas City Royals hit a two-run home run against Rich Gossage that for several minutes gave the Royals a 5–4 lead over the Yankees. But Brett was called out by the umpires for using an illegal bat—one with an excessive amount of pine tar. The ruling, after a protest by Billy Martin, the Yankees' manager, enabled the Yankees to wind up with a 4–3 victory.

"I can sympathize with George," Gossage remarked after the game, "but not that much." The outcome, which the Royals immediately protested, is certain to be talked about for years to come, because it was one of the more bizarre finishes any game has ever had. "I couldn't believe it," Brett said, infinitely more calm than when he charged at the umpires after their controversial call. "It knocks you to your knees," added Dick Howser, the Kansas City manager. "I'm sick about it. I don't like it. I don't like it at all. I don't expect my players to accept it."

What the Royals refused to believe or accept was that the umpires ruled the home run did not count because Brett's bat had too much pine tar on it. Pine tar is a sticky brown substance batters apply to their bats to give them a better grip. Baseball rule 1.10 (b) says a bat may not be covered by such a substance more than

18 inches from the tip of the handle. Joe Brinkman, the chief of the crew that umpired the game, said Brett's bat had "heavy pine tar" 19 to 20 inches from the tip of the handle and lighter pine tar for another three or four inches.

The umpire did not use a ruler to measure the pine tar on Brett's 34½-inch bat; they didn't have one. So they placed it across home plate, which measures 17 inches across. When they did, they saw

George Brett after umpires ruled that his potential game-winning ninth-inning homer didn't count because there was too much pine tar on his bat. Yankees Manager Billy Martin had brought up the matter. (Associated Press)

that the pine tar exceeded the legal limit. The four umpires conferred again, and then Tim McClelland, the home plate umpire, thrust his right arm in the air, signaling that Brett was out. His call prompted two reactions:

Brett, enraged, raced out of the dugout and looked as if he would run over McClelland. Brinkman, however, intercepted him, grabbing him around the neck. "In that situation," Brinkman said later, "you know something's going to happen. It was quite traumatic. He was

upset." Meanwhile, Gaylord Perry of the Royals, who has long been accused of doing illegal things with a baseball, tried to swipe the evidence, according to Brinkman. "Gaylord got the bat and passed it back and tried to get it to the clubhouse," Brinkman said. "The security people went after it, but I got in there and got it. Steve Renko, another Kansas City pitcher, had it. He was the last in line. He didn't have anyone to hand it to."

Why the stadium security men went after the bat was not clear. "I didn't know what was going on," Howser said. "I saw guys in sport coats and ties trying to intercept the bat. It was like a Brink's robbery. Who's got the gold? Our players had it, the umpires had it. I don't know who has it—the C.I.A., a think tank at the Pentagon." The umpires declined to show the bat, which they said was on its way to the American League office. Presumably, Lee MacPhail, the league president, will study the bat and measure the pine tar tomorrow, then rule on the Royals' protest.

Four days later, Lee MacPhail upheld the Royals' protest, overruled the umpires and put the Royals back in front, 5–4. On Aug. 18, the two teams met at Yankee Stadium to finish the game from the point of the home run and the Royals won by the same 5–4 score. Players still use pine tar on their bats and continue to apply it liberally well above the handle. There have been uproars over bats doctored with cork implants since 1983 but none dealing with the sticky stuff, perhaps because of tighter enforcement by the umpires.

Runners-up

1996: Michael Irvin, the Dallas Cowboys' Pro Bowl receiver, was suspended for the first five games of the season by Commissioner Paul Tagliabue after pleading no contest to a charge of cocaine possession. The suspension effectively marked the end of Dallas's N.F.L. dominance in the 90's.

1987: Nineteen-year-old Boris Becker of West Germany defeated a gassed John McEnroe, 28, of Douglaston, N.Y., in an epic Davis Cup elimination match at Hartford, Conn. Believed to be the longest Davis Cup match ever played, it

lasted 6 hours 38 minutes; the second set alone went 2 hours 35 minutes. Final score: 4–6, 15–13, 8–10, 6–2, 6–2.

1976: John Naber, a 20-year-old student at the University of Southern California, won his fourth and final gold medal of the Montreal Olympics when he became the first swimmer to break the two-minute barrier in the 200-meter backstroke. His time was 1 minute 59.19 seconds.

July 25, 1999
The Ultimate Overachiever

By FRANK LITSKY

NEW YORK—Even before October 1996, when he was found to have advanced testicular cancer, Lance Armstrong had much to prove. He had always been bright and charming, but he had also been brash, almost angry for having to show that he could overcome life's stacked deck. His victory in the Tour de France in Paris today made him only the second American to win the world's most prestigious bicycle race (Greg LeMond won it three times). It was the ultimate payoff for someone who had an unsettled childhood, achieved remarkable success on a bike, almost died and then found rejection from the cycling community he had enriched.

There was even rejection of sorts the last two weeks. French newspapers insinuated that he had taken illegal performance-enhancing drugs. It turned out that with permission of cycling authorities, he had used a skin cream to treat a rash caused by saddle sores. The cream had minimal amounts of a banned substance that did not affect performance. Armstrong said he had taken no drugs since his chemotherapy two and a half years ago, "I've been on my deathbed," he said, "and I'm not stupid."

In 1993, his first full season as a professional, Armstrong had been experiencing groin pain, but dismissed it as the price of riding hard saddle five or six hours a day. The findings were devastating. He had an especially lethal variety of testicular cancer that had spread to his lungs and abdomen (which had 12 tumors, some as large as golf balls) and his brain (two lesions). After two operations the cancer disappeared—"a miracle," he said.

In this ultimate team sport, Armstrong has always been a team player. In the 1995

Lance Armstrong, center, wearing the yellow jersey of the overall leader, riding past a field of sunflowers between Le Bourg d'Oisans and Saint-Étienne during the 11th stage of the Tour de France. (Agence France-Presse)

Tour de France, a Motorola teammate, Fabio Casartelli of Italy, crashed and died during a high-speed mountain descent. Armstrong vowed to win a one-day stage of the Tour for Casartelli, and three days later he did. In the final meters, Armstrong raised his eyes and index fingers, pointing to the heavens. "There's no doubt there were four feet pushing those pedals that day," Armstrong said.

Lance Edward Armstrong was born Sept. 18, 1971, in Dallas. He does not talk about his early family life, although his mother, Linda, has said she dropped out of high school when she was 17 to give birth to Lance and then found a job to support

him. At 19, she married Terry Armstrong, who adopted Lance, but the marriage dissolved. He has always been protective of his mother. In 1993, after he had won the world road-racing championship in Oslo, he was invited to meet the Norwegian King, Harald V. His mother was not invited. He told the officials: No mom, no Lance. Mom got to meet the King.

Lance Armstrong won the Tour de France five consecutive times through July 2003. He passed several random drug tests, but after the 1998 race had been tainted by a drug scandal reporters hounded him with questions for much of the '99 Tour.

Runners-up

1976: In his first international competition, Edwin Moses (see June 4), a 20-year-old senior at Morehouse College in Atlanta, set a world record of 47.64 seconds in the 400-meter hurdles as he won the gold medal at the Montreal Olympics. The former record holder, John Akii-Bua of Uganda, was a no-show because African countries boycotted the Games over apartheid in South Africa.

1970: The U.S. Tennis Association announced a revolutionary scoring change for the Open: a nine-point tiebreaker (at 4–4 the next point wins) would be used in all future matches. In 1974 the U.S.T.A. switched to the 12-point breaker (the win-

ner must have at least 7 points with a margin of 2).

1976: Jim Mortgomery of Madison, Wis., became the first swimmer in history to crack the 50-second barrier in the 100-meter freestyle as he won the gold medal at the Montreal Olympics in 49.99 seconds. The record lasted all of three weeks. As of 2003, Pieter van den Hoogenband of the Netherlands held the mark, now 47.84 seconds.

Mathias Leads a Decathlon Sweep

By ALLISON DANZIG

HELSINKI, Finland—Bob Mathias paced an American sweep of the grueling Olympic decathlon event tonight, shattering his own world record and raising to thirteen the number of gold medals taken by the United States in these games. A bandage covering his painful leg injury, the Tulare, Calif., giant retained the title he won in 1948 as darkness was enveloping the huge arena after twelve hours of competition.

Mathias ran the 1,500 meters in the final ordeal of the two-day grind of ten events in 4 minutes 50.8 seconds, to raise his total to 7,887 points. Milton Campbell, 18-year-old athlete from Plainfield, N.J., finished second with 6,975 and Floyd Simmons of Charlotte, N.C., was third with 6,788. In the Olympic trials in his hometown early this month, Mathias had set a new decathlon record of 7,825. He excelled that performance today by 62 points under the pressure of competition from the world's best and despite the fact that he had suffered a muscle twinge in broad jumping yesterday.

Shifting from foot to foot, still weary from his grueling last effort in the 1,500, Mathias said he had felt before starting the event today that he could better his own record. "After the high hurdles yesterday, I didn't think I could do it. But I did it and now I'm finished," Mathias told United Press International, as newsmen, team members, well-wishers and the Finnish version of pushing, clawing bobby sockers crushed in about him. "This will be my last decathlon," said the 21-year-old wizard of strength and endurance. "You can't keep this up forever."

For a while this afternoon it seemed that Mathias might not break his record. His performance in the 100 meters, broad jump, hurdles and discus had not been up

Bob Mathias, the defending Olympic decathlon champion, throwing the discus at the Helsinki Games. He won a second gold despite having tweaked a leg muscle in the broad jump the day before. (Associated Press)

to his efforts at Tulare and though he excelled in the shot-put and 400 meters and equaled his high jump mark, he was 99 points behind his record as he came up to the pole vault. But this youngster from the Far West has the heart of a lion. Despite his fatigue, he vaulted 13 feet 1½ inches on his second try to beat his Tulare effort by 9⅜ inches.

"I heard some great man in the stands figuring my point totals," Mathias told UPI. "I don't even know what his name was. But after the pole vault I went over and he said if I could keep up my usual distances in the javelin and run the 1,500 under 4.54 minutes I could beat the record. I thought for

sure I could do that." And with his performance in the 1,500, Mathias was in. In almost complete darkness, with the track lighted only by the illumination from the electric scoreboard, he traveled the distance in 4:50.5 and the thousands acclaimed a great champion who had far excelled his amazing achievement as a 17-year-old schoolboy at London four years ago.

Bob Mathias, 6 feet 3 inches and 204 pounds, played for Stanford in the Rose Bowl and competed in the Olympics in the same year. He served four terms in the United States House of Representatives from 1967 to '74.

Runners-up

1980: It was a great day for Britain at the Moscow Olympics as Daley Thompson won the decathlon while Steve Ovett and Sebastian Coe *(see Aug. 28)* ran one-two in the 800 meters. Thompson won another gold medal in the decathlon at the 1984 Los Angeles Games, equaling the world record of 8,798 points by Jürgen Higsen of West Germany.

1981: Pat Bradley of Westport, Mass., defeated Beth Daniel of Charleston, S.C., in a dramatic United States Women's Open at La Grange Country Club in Illinois by dropping a 70-foot birdie putt on the 15th hole and shooting a final-round

66 to win by one stroke. Bradley's 279 total remained an Open record for seven years; Juli Inkster held the mark as of 2003 with a 272 total at the 1999 Open.

1997: Giants owner Wellington Mara, whose father invested $500 to buy the team in 1925, and Don Shula, who coached the Miami Dolphins to a perfect season in 1972 and won a record 328 regular-season N.F.L. games with the Baltimore Colts and Miami, were inducted into the Pro Football Hall of Fame.

July 27, 1952
Going the Distance

By ALLISON DANZIG

HELSINKI, Finland—Emil Zatopek stood as the wonder runner of the ages today as the track and field competition of the Olympic Games came to a close with the United States supreme by an overwhelming margin after eight days of record-breaking performances such as the world has never beheld before. The once-peerless Paavo Nurmi, Finland's own, had to yield his pedestal as the greatest distance runner in history when the 30-year-old Czechoslovak Army major killed off the field to win the classic marathon by a half-mile in 2 hours 23 minutes 3.2 seconds for his third gold medal of the games.

Three days after he had captured the 5,000-meter run in record time and a week after he had shattered the mark by 42.6 seconds in repeating his 10,000-meter victory of the 1948 games at London, this little phenomenon of almost super-human endurance and with the most agonizing running style within memory sped 26 miles, 385 yards 6 minutes and 16 seconds faster than an Olympic marathon had ever been traversed before.

When Zatopek came through the tunnel into the stadium, two and a half minutes before his nearest rival, 70,000 people, among whom was the Duke of Edinburgh, cheered his every step around the track. As he dashed across the finish line, fresh enough apparently to have been able to go on for another ten miles, despite his facial contortions and wabbing head, the multitude stood and broke into a frenzied roar of adulation. Rejecting the blanket that was thrown around his shoulders and swiftly changing his shirt, he received his gold medal in the victory ceremony and then circled the track to a continuous ovation surpassing all others of the games.

That Zatopek should run the marathon after the 10,000 and 5,000-meter races was a most remarkable undertaking. He had failed to score a double at London when he came in a close second to Gaston Reiff of Belgium in the 5,000 and here he was going far beyond that and attempting the most punishing grind of all over Helsinki's paved roads after only two days of rest. On top of that he had never before run the full marathon distance.

After his victory today no one who saw his powerful finish, as compared with the pitiful physical state of some of his rivals who had confined their efforts to this one race, will believe that there is any limit to the wonders Zatopek can perform in a track uniform. Some one shouted to the Americans in the press box, "Lucky for you fellows that Zatopek didn't run in the 100 and 200 sprints."

Emil Zatopek, a Czechoslovak Army major, beating Alain Mimoun of France in the 5,000 meters at the Helsinki Olympics. Four days earlier he had won the 10,000, and three days later he captured the marathon. (Agence France-Presse)

Runners-up

2003: Lance Armstrong of the U.S. (see July 25) became the fifth cyclist in history to win the Tour de France five times and the second to win it five times in succession. Miguel Indurain fo Spain (1991-95) is the only other consecutive five-time winner.

1996: A pipe bomb spiked with nails and screws exploded at the Atlanta Olympics' Centennial Park, killing a 44-year-old Georgia woman and wounding at least 111. A Turkish television cameraman died of a heart attack while running to cover the blast. A suspect was charged in the case in 2003. Another suspect, Richard Jewell, was exonerated earlier as the F.B.I. was criticized for its investigative tactics in the case and the news media were upbraided for all but trying him in print and on the air.

1985: Steve Cram of Britain broke his countryman Sebastian Coe's 1981 world record in the mile (see Aug. 28) when he was timed in 3 minutes 46.3 seconds, nearly a second faster, at the Grand Prix meet at Bislett Stadium in Oslo, Norway. Cram's mark was broken when Noureddine Morceli of Algeria ran 3:44.1 in 1993.

July 28, 1999
Sanders Puts It in Writing. He's Gone

By THOMAS GEORGE

NEW YORK—As quietly and as unassumingly as he entered the National Football League, Barry Sanders has left it, simply issuing a statement today that he is retiring after 10 seasons as a Detroit Lions running back.

His statement, in part, read: "Today I officially declare my departure from the N.F.L. I leave on good terms with everyone in the organization. The reason I am retiring is simple: my desire to exit the game is greater than my desire to remain in it. I have searched my heart through and through and feel comfortable with this decision. I wish my teammates, coaches and the entire Lions organization all the best." Little fanfare. No glitzy news conference. Just a written statement and then, like one of his shimmering runs, poof! He was gone.

Sanders was spotted today at Gatwick Airport near London after having arrived from Detroit. "I'm going into retirement and I don't see my plans changing," he told reporters. He said he would spend two days in London before visiting Amsterdam and Paris. Asked why he happened to be in London, Sanders answered: "I don't know the right way to retire. This is just my way of doing it."

His father hinted last May that it could happen this way. Few took him seriously then, but many do now. This is what William Sanders said in the spring: "He can do just like Jim Brown did in '65— walk away from the game and never let it faze him." He said that someday Barry Sanders may simply not show up. That day has come.

Several N.F.L. owners agreed with Commissioner Paul Tagliabue's view when asked about relaxing the league's salary cap within the collective bargaining agreement so that Sanders could be traded. Tagliabue's response was simply no. "Obviously we're very disappointed because we lose a great player," Bobby Ross, the Lions' head coach, said. "From what I know about Barry, when he makes up his mind, he makes up his mind."

It is a puzzling situation. Sanders, 31, is still in the prime of his career despite having played a decade, and he is only 1,457 yards shy of breaking Walter Payton's career rushing record of 16,726 yards. He shows no hint of slowing or of his sparkling skills waning. He is the premier running back in the N.F.L. and one of its brightest stars. He stands only 5 feet 9 inches but packs a solid 203 pounds. Spinning, twisting, dashing, cutting and electrifying is his running style. He grew up in Wichita, Kan., and won the 1988 Heisman Trophy at Oklahoma State.

That year he set or tied 34 collegiate records. He arrived in Detroit as the No. 3 overall draft pick in 1989 (behind Troy Aikman in Dallas and Tony Mandarich in Green Bay). That year he rushed for 1,470 yards, won rookie of the year honors and proceeded to become an N.F.L. staple. He has been a league

The great Barry Sanders eyeing the end zone on a 1996 touchdown run against the Bears. "When he makes up his mind, he makes up his mind," Lions Coach Bobby Ross said of Sanders's abrupt retirement. (Associated Press)

most valuable player (1997) and a fixture on league Pro Bowl and All-Pro teams. He has been a quiet but shining star.

Never one to dance in the end zone after scoring a touchdown. Seldom one to complain about anything. Actually, seldom one to speak about anything.

Runners-up

1984: President Ronald Reagan opened the Summer Olympics at Los Angeles Coliseum, with Gina Hemphill, granddaughter of Jesse Owens, circling the track with the torch and Rafer Johnson, the 1960 decathlon champion, lighting the flame.

1993: Ken Griffey Jr. of the Seattle Mariners tied the major league record for home runs in eight consecutive games, matching Dale Long of the Pittsburgh Pirates (1956) and Don Mattingly of the Yankees (1987). Griffey, 23, tied the mark with a 404-foot shot off Willie Banks of the Minnesota Twins in the Kingdome.

1994: Left-hander Kenny Rogers of the Texas Rangers pitched a perfect game, the 11th regular-season one in history, defeating the California Angels, 4–0, at the Ballpark in Arlington. Center-fielder Rusty Greer saved the masterpiece with a diving catch with none out in the top of the ninth inning.

July 29, 1976
A Cuban Runner Smokes the Field

By FRANK LITSKY

MONTREAL [Thursday]—Alberto Juantorena, a Cuban who looks more like a football player than a runner, made Olympic history today. He became the first man to win the 400-meter and 800-meter titles in one Olympic Games. Last Sunday, Juantorena won the 800-meter gold medal in world-record time, and today he attempted to complete the 400–800 double that had eluded Mel Sheppard in 1908, Ted Meredith in 1912, Arthur Wint in 1948 and Mal Whitfield in 1948 and 1952. All won one final, but not the other.

Many of the 65,000 spectators in Olympic Stadium were cheering for the three American finalists and fearing Juantorena. The fears were fulfilled. Fred Newhouse of Baton Rouge, La., as usual, led for 200 meters. Then they rounded the last turn, and Juantorena started rolling. As they straightened out for home, he was close to Newhouse. With 50 meters left he caught him, and the power from his 6-foot-2-inch, 185-pound body carried him home first by a yard. Herman Frazier of Philadelphia finished five yards behind Newhouse. Juantorena's time was 44.26 seconds, the third fastest in history and the fastest at sea level. The only faster times were 43.81 by Lee Evans and 43.97 by Larry James behind Evans in the 1968 Olympics at Mexico City, in thinner air, 1½ miles above sea level.

"I caught Newhouse in the last 50 meters," said the 24-year-old Juantorena, "because I had power and muscles I keep for the last part of the race."

"I'm not pleased I got a silver medal," said the 27-year-old Newhouse. "I gave it all I had. I thought I won the race. I didn't think anyone could beat me. Twenty yards from the tape, that's when I realized he was with me. Even then, I thought I could still win. He was tiring."

How good is Juantorena? "He ain't God," said Newhouse, "but he's a good runner."

"I'm no superman," said Juantorena, closing the subject.

Alberto Juantorena of Cuba, right, winning the 800 meters at the Montreal Games. Four days later he won the 400 meters, completing a 400-800 double that had escaped all Olympians before him. (Associated Press)

Runners-up

1996: On his third attempt in the long jump at the Atlanta Games, Carl Lewis, 35, leapt 27 feet 10¾ inches to win his fourth Olympic long jump, tying him with former discus champion Al Oerter of the United States as the only athletes to win four gold medals in the same event. Oerter *(see Oct. 15)* won his medals in the 1956, '60, '64 and '68 Olympics.

1989: Javier Sotomayor of Cuba became the first high jumper to break the 8-foot barrier when he cleared that height, breaking his own world record of 7 feet 11½ inches, at the Caribbean Championships in San Juan, Puerto Rico. Sotomayor set the current high jump mark of 8 feet ½ inch in 1993.

1989: Texas Rangers owner George W. Bush made one of the worst trades in baseball history, obtaining outfielder Harold Baines and a utilityman from the Chicago White Sox for shortstop Scott Fletcher and two prospects, one of whom was Sammy Sosa *(see June 25).* It was the "biggest mistake of my adulthood," the future president said in 2000.

July 30, 1966
All England Hails 'Wembley Goal'

By W. GRANGER BLAIR

LONDON—England, deprived of a victory by a German goal in the last 15 seconds of regular play, broke through in overtime today and won the World Cup, emblematic of international soccer supremacy, by beating West Germany, 4–2. England's first World Cup victory was witnessed by a crowd of 100,000 in Wembley Stadium. It was a match marked by the kind of hard, clean play that had been noticeably absent from a number of the earlier games in the tournament. When it was over and the spectators were shouting "England, England," Bobby Moore, the captain of the English eleven, led his team to the royal box to receive the solid gold cup from Queen Elizabeth.

A lesser team than England might have been demoralized by that game-tying goal in the last 15 seconds of the regulation 90 minutes, when England was leading, 2–1. In a skirmish in front of the English goal, Wolfgang Weber, a German halfback, kicked the ball into the net for the equalizer. That the Germans were in a position to score stemmed largely from England's refusal to adopt stalling tactics to keep the ball. Only once did the English team stall—about three minutes before the end of regulation play. The crowd began booing and the home eleven quickly swung back to the offensive, thereby giving the Germans their golden opportunity.

Eleven minutes after the 30-minute overtime period began, Geoff Hurst scored for England on a 10-yard shot. He booted in another goal on a breakaway dash in the final seconds. He had scored on a header in the opening minutes of the match. Hurst's first goal in overtime seemed doubtful for a moment. The linesman first indicated that the ball had hit the top bar, but had not gone in. But he and the referee

conferred and England was awarded the goal as the crowd cheered. Whatever doubts German fans might have had about the legitimacy of the English lead were dispelled when, with virtually the entire German team pressing on the English cage in a desperate attempt to score, Hurst broke away with the ball, drove downfield and easily beat the German goalie.

The scoring began when Helmut Haller, an outstanding German forward, fired a low, powerful shot into the English goal 10 minutes after the opening whistle. Hurst tied it for England nine minutes later, when he headed in a nicely lofted free kick by Moore, who was chosen by soccer writers as the most valuable player of the tournament. Offensive rushes marked the rest of the first half. Throughout the cup series England had displayed a solid defense, and it was no less so today. Ten minutes before regulation play was to end, Martin Peters, an English forward, found an opening in a melee in front of the German goal and blasted the ball past the sprawling German goalie, Hans Tilkowski. Then came the Weber goal that sent the game into overtime.

Geoff Hurst's decisive first goal for England in overtime came to be known as

England captain Bobby Moore kissing the World Cup trophy after his team beat West Germany at Wembley Stadium for the title. Geoff Hurst's deciding goal in overtime is still debated. (Associated Press)

the "Wembley goal" and is probably the most hotly disputed in the history of soccer. The question was whether the ball crossed the goal line after bouncing off the top bar. The Soviet linesman, Tofik Bakhramov, ruled at first that it did not. He and the Swiss referee, Gottfried Dienst, conferred, however, and the call was overturned. Video technology has since been used in an attempt to answer the question, but the debate still rages.

Runners-up

1976: Bruce Jenner, a 26-year-old from San Jose, Calif., with matinee idol looks, won the gold medal in the decathlon at the Montreal Olympics with 8,618 points, breaking the world record of 8,454 points set by Nikolai Avilov of the Soviet Union in the 1972 Munich Games.

1933: Dizzy Dean of the St. Louis Cardinals struck out a major-league record 17 batters as the Gashouse Gang beat the Chicago Cubs, 8–2, at Sportsman's Park. The performance made Dean, from Lucas, Ark., a national celebrity (see Sept. 21). Afterward he said, "Heck, if anybody told me I was setting a record, I'd have got me some more strikeouts."

1990: George Steinbrenner was barred from further involvement in the management of the Yankees by Commissioner Fay Vincent because of his association with and $40,000 payment to Howard Spira, whom Vincent called "a known gambler." Steinbrenner was reinstated in 1992 and resumed control of the team the following spring.

U.S. Boxers Haul Gold

By STEVE CADY

Sugar Ray Leonard, who wore pictures of his girlfriend and son on his socks, against Ulrich Beyer of East Germany in the Montreal Olympics. Leonard won the gold metal against Andrès Aldama of Cuba. (Associated Press)

MONTREAL—Digging and blasting like prospectors who know exactly what they're doing, American boxers shook loose an avalanche of gold tonight in the Olympic finals at the Forum. When the last stick of dynamite had been detonated by Leon Spinks in the light heavyweight class, the young team many experts thought would be outslugged by East Europeans and Cubans had walked off with five gold medals. They could have used a pack-mule to lug the gold, because no other United States boxing team has ever won any more of it than they did

tonight before an appreciative standing-room crowd of 20,000.

"This is the greatest night in the history of amateur boxing for America," said Rollie Schwartz, manager of the team. The United States won five golds once before, in the 1952 Olympics, but it got no silvers or bronzes that year. This time, a silver and a bronze increased the medal total to seven.

In order, the American winners on the 11-bout program were Leo Randolph, an 18-year-old bantamweight from Tacoma, Wash.; Howard Davis of Glen Cove, L.I., in

the lightweight class; Sugar Ray Leonard, a light-welterweight from Palmer Park, Md.; Mike Spinks of St. Louis, Leon's younger brother, in the middleweights, and Leon, whose overhand right stretched Sixto Soria of Cuba flat on his face in the third round of their slugfest.

Spinks, a 23-year-old Marine Corps corporal from St. Louis, mixed it with Soria right from the beginning, knocking him down with a vicious right five seconds from the end of the opening round. Leon Spinks's 20-year-old brother, Mike, also was a walking hand-grenade in his bout with Rufat Riskiev of the Soviet Union. The younger half of American boxing's first Olympic brother team decked his opponent with a long right in the second round, staggered him for a mandatory standing 8-count in the third and then doubled him up with a shot to the stomach.

While the granite-jawed Spinks brothers provided the heaviest hitting of a star-spangled night, it was by no means the only dynamite set off by the American team. Davis and Leonard both put on dazzling displays of boxing and punching, Davis in a 5–0 decision over tank-like Simion Cutov of Rumania and Leonard against hard-punching Andrès Aldama of Cuba. Leonard discarded his usual fancy tactics and hammered Aldama with left hooks and long rights. In the second and third rounds, he staggered the Cuban for two mandatory standing 8-counts and then sent him reeling into the ropes in the closing seconds.

"This is my last fight," Leonard said later. "My journey has ended. My dream is fulfilled." The 20-year-old collegian plans to major in business administration at the University of Maryland.

Runners-up

1891: Amos Rusie of the New York Giants pitched a no-hitter, defeating the Brooklyn Bridegrooms (later the Dodgers), 6–0, for one of his 33 victories that year. His dominance, comparable to that of Cy Young of the Cleveland Spiders of the National League, led to an 1893 rule change that stretched the distance from the pitcher's rubber to home plate from 50 feet to 60 feet 6 inches.

1954: Joe Adcock of the Milwaukee Braves set a major league record of 18 total bases in five at-bats by hitting four home runs and a double as they defeated the Brooklyn Dodgers, 15–7, at Ebbets Field. Shawn Green of the Los Angeles

Dodgers had 19 total bases (four homers, a double and a single) against the Milwaukee Brewers in 2002.

1932: Babe Didrikson (see July 3) of Beaumont, Tex., arguably the greatest woman athlete of the 20th century, won the gold medal in the javelin in 143 feet 4 inches at the Los Angeles Olympics. She also won gold in the 80-meter hurdles and the high jump, but that medal was later reduced to silver because she used a then-illegal "western roll" across the bar.

AUGUST

August 1, 1996
Michael Johnson Stands Alone

By JERE LONGMAN

ATLANTA [Thursday]—He crossed the finish line, saw the stunning world record at 200 meters and let out a scream. Later, Michael Johnson slumped to the track on all fours. He had the same reaction to his time of 19.32 seconds as did the other 82,884 spectators at Olympic Stadium. Disbelief. The bronze medalist in the race was so startled that he thought it was insufficient to shake Johnson's hand. So he bowed. In one of the greatest performances in the history of track and field, Johnson became the first man to win the 200-meter and 400-meter sprints at the same Olympics. Monday night, he won the 400 meters in 43.49 seconds, an Olympic record. Never before has a sprinter possessed such blistering speed for the 200 and the muscular endurance for the 400.

His winning time in tonight's 200 whittled more than three-tenths of a second off the previous record of 19.66 seconds that Johnson set on this same track on June 23 at the Olympic trials. No one has ever lowered the 200-meter record by such a hefty margin. Immediately, Johnson was being compared to Bob Beamon, whose phenomenal long jump at the 1968 Summer Games surpassed the existing record by more than two feet.

As remarkable as his victory was, Johnson was not the only person to accomplish the 200-400-meter sprint dou-

ble tonight. Marie-Jose Pérec of France became the second woman to win both events at the Olympics, winning her 200-meter race in 22.12 seconds. If the full house at Olympic Stadium warmly

Michael Johnson reacting to his stunning world-record time of 19.32 seconds in the 200 meters at the Atlanta Games. He is the only man in history to have won both the 200- and 400-meter sprints in a single Olympics. (Barton Silverman/The New York Times)

applauded Pérec's victory, it launched into frenzied celebration of Johnson's shattering performance. He ran the first 100 meters in 10.12 seconds, then shifted into hammering overdrive to run the second 100 meters in 9.20 seconds. The world record for 100 meters from a stationary start is 9.84 seconds.

Frankie Fredericks of Namibia finished second tonight in 19.68 seconds, only two-hundredths of a second off Johnson's previous record, but he was still four yards behind at the finish. Ato Boldon of Trinidad won the bronze in 19.80 seconds, which would have won or tied for first at every previous Olympics but one; tonight

he was a distant third. The race was so fast that the 1992 champion, Mike Marsh of the United States, finished last with a time of 20.48. "I said before, the person who won the 100 meters was the fastest man alive," said Boldon, who also finished third in the 100 meters. "I think the fastest man alive is sitting to my left."

That man, of course, was Johnson. On Monday night, his victory in the 400 meters had been overshadowed when Carl Lewis won his ninth gold medal with another victory in the long jump. Tonight, Johnson had center stage. Even he had trouble comprehending what he had just accomplished. Until just over a month ago, the 200 meters had been the most stubborn and resistant record in track and field. Pietro Mennea of Italy ran 19.72 seconds in 1979, and the record stood for more than 16 years. Now, in little more than a month, Johnson has chopped it down by four-tenths of a second. In a race decided by hundredths of a second, four-tenths may as well be four minutes.

"I can't describe what it feels like to break the world record by that much," Johnson said. "I thought 19.5 was possible, but 19.3 is unbelievable."

As of 2003, no one has even approached the 19.66 seconds Michael Johnson ran in the Olympic trials before the 1996 Games, much less his world record of 19.32.

Runners-up

1978: Pete Rose's National League–record 44-consecutive-game hitting streak, which he shares with Willie Keeler *(see June 18),* ended when Larry McWilliams and Gene Garber of the Atlanta Braves blanked him in five plate appearances at Fulton County Stadium as the Braves routed the Cincinnati Reds, 16–4.

1975: Volatile Billy Martin, fired as skipper of the Texas Rangers, was named manager of the Yankees, replacing Bill Virdon. It was the first of Martin's five

stints as manager in a love-hate relationship with George Steinbrenner that lasted four full seasons and parts of four others until 1988. Martin won two pennants and one World Series.

1945 Mel Ott of the New York Giants became the first National Leaguer to hit 500 home runs with a shot off Johnny Hutchings of the Boston Braves at the Polo Grounds. Ott retired early in the 1947 season with 511 homers.

August 2, 1992
The Seventh Wonder of the Games

By MICHAEL JANOFSKY

Jackie Joyner-Kersee about to throw the javelin in the Olympic heptathlon in Barcelona, Spain. Born into poverty in 1962, she was named after Jacqueline Kennedy. Her grandmother said, "Someday this girl will be the First Lady of something." (Associated Press)

BARCELONA, Spain—For all the wondrous performances of her career, the medals, the records, the inspiration she has been for others, what Jackie Joyner-Kersee accomplished in the last two days might overshadow it all. She is 30 years old, well into her 11th year of competing in the heptathlon, and tonight she won an Olympic gold medal, her second in the seven-event grind, something no woman had ever done. And if it weren't for a hamstring injury eight years ago in Los Angeles, which left her in second place by 5 points, this would have been her third celebration. No matter.

"God willing, if I'm around in 1996 to meet the challenge, to finish my career on American soil would be a dream come true," Joyner-Kersee said, referring to Atlanta, where the Summer Games will be that year.

But this latest victory, in which she led after every event, signifies more than an Olympic championship and the sixth-best finish of her career with 7,044 points, a margin of 199 over Irina Belova of the Unified Team and 395 over the bronze medalist, Sabine Braun of Germany. Rather, this was a triumph over adverse psychological, physical and meteorological conditions. As such, it could easily be regarded as her best heptathlon ever, never mind that her standing world record, from the last Olympics, 7,291, is likely to remain unmatched by any contemporary heptathlon athlete or even her.

"For me, it's the challenge," Joyner-Kersee said. "The challenge to try to beat myself or do better than I did in the past. I try to keep in mind not what I have accomplished but what I have to try to accomplish in the future. After 1988, even though I won the gold, I wanted to come back in 1992. But I had to put that behind me. I knew I had to do better. I know other people see me as invincible, but I can't let what I have accomplished control what I'm trying to do."

Still on the track after the 800, amid the chaos of her victory lap with an American flag in her hand, Joyner-Kersee found herself talking to Bruce Jenner, the 1976 Olympic decathlon champion. That was just a little coincidental, because her husband had helped inspire her through the heptathlon by reminding her of Bob Mathias, the only decathlete to win back-to-back Olympic titles in non-boycott years, 1948 and 1952. Now here she was with Jenner, a latter-day and worthy successor. And this was a moment.

"You're the greatest athlete in the world," he told her. "Man or woman, the greatest athlete in the world."

Runners-up

1979: Yankee catcher Thurman Munson, 32, a leader on three pennant winners and two World Series championship teams and the first Yankee captain since Lou Gehrig four decades before, died when the jet plane he was piloting crashed near the Canton, Ohio, airport. He was headed to his nearby home for a visit with his wife and children.

1980: Teofilo Stevenson of Cuba became the first boxer to win the heavyweight gold medal at three consecutive Olympics, outpointing Pyotr Zaev of the Soviet Union in three rounds at the Moscow Games. Stevenson would have been a force in United States pro boxing had his government not deprived him of the opportunity.

1948: Fanny Blankers-Koen of the Netherlands, 30 years old and the mother of two, became an international women's pioneer by winning the 100 meters at the London Olympics in 11.9 seconds. It was the first of her four gold medals in the Games—100 meters, 80-meter hurdles, 200-meter dash, 4x100-meter relay.

August 3, 1984
'I Was Thinking, Stick, Stick'

By DAVE ANDERSON

LOS ANGELES [Friday]—Behind the lavender fence, Mary Lou Retton's coach, Bela Karolyi, was waiting to encourage her. But even before he could give her any advice about the vault on which she needed a perfect 10 to win the Olympic gold medal, Mary Lou Retton looked up at him with those big cocker-spaniel eyes. She wasn't waiting for her coach to say something. Instead, she had something to tell him.

"I'm going to stick it," she said.

Name a candy bar after her. Or at least a stick-pin. Mention to Michael Jackson that he should rewrite the lyrics to one of his hits and title it "Stick It" in her honor. Mary Lou Retton is not merely the Olympic gold medalist in all-around gymnastics. Mary Lou Retton is an American folk heroine now, an Olympian for the ages. With what Don Peters, the United States gymnastics coach, described as a "backward somersault in a laid-out position with a full twist, 360 degrees, a Tshukahaka," she stuck herself into Olympic history Tonight as the first American gymnast, man or woman, to win a gold medal.

Mary Lou Retton might stick herself into history again Monday night with two more gold medals in the vault and the floor exercises in the women's individual events. And she's doing all this on a right knee that jeopardized her appearance here before arthroscopic surgery removed torn cartilage two months ago. "She was declared out of the Olympics," says Bela Karolyi, "declared out of any hard landing." But on her hard landings here at Pauley Pavilion all week, Mary Lou Retton has had no pain. Only glory.

In gymnastics, "stick it" is not an impolite expression. In gymnastics, "stick it" means landing after a flip as if you had a foot-long spike on the sole of each foot. It means landing so solidly that you stick to the mat without a wobble. And it's now the new phrase in the American vocabulary, just as Mary Lou Retton is the new name. "I was thinking, 'Stick, stick,'" she said later. "I like the added pressure, it makes me fight harder."

The 16-year-old daughter of Ron Retton, who played basketball with Jerry West at West Virginia and later was a shortstop in the Yankees' farm system, remembered stretching out on the floor of the family room in her Fairmont, W. Va., home in 1976 and watching Nadia Comaneci of Rumania win the all-around gold medal at Montreal. "I was just a beginner then, I never thought about the gold medal," she recalled. "I just thought Nadia was great."

All over America tonight, little girls were stretched out on the floor watching Mary Lou Retton. "What she did will be a great thing for American gymnastics," Bela Karolyi says. "You will see little girls joining gymnastics clubs now instead of sitting around the cafeteria." But there will never be another quite like her. Mary Lou Retton will always be an American original.

Mary Lou Retton after a perfect 10 in the vault, giving her the Olympic gold medal in the all-around in Los Angeles. Thousands of American girls joined gymnastic clubs after watching her perform on television. (Associated Press)

Runners-up

1921: Baseball's new commissioner, Judge Kenesaw Mountain Landis (see Nov. 12,, imposed a lifetime ban on eight members of the 1919 Chicago White Sox for their roles in throwing that season's World Series to the Cincinnati Reds (see Sept. 28). "Regardless of the verdict of juries," Landis said, "no player that...undertakes or promises to throw a ballgame...will ever play professional baseball."

1936: At the Olympic Games in Berlin, Jesse Owens, an African-American, won the gold medal in the 100 meters after German Chancellor Adolf Hitler had espoused Aryan racial superiority. It was the first of four gold medals for Owens; one of them, over the German Lutz Long in the broad jump, came while Hitler, from his stadium box, and 110,000 others watched. (see Aug. 4).

1960: In an unprecedented trade of managers, mostly for publicity purposes, the Cleveland Indians sent Joe Gordon to the Detroit Tigers for Jimmy Dykes. Neither man helped his new second-division club: Detroit's Bill DeWitt fired Gordon when the season ended and Cleveland's Frank Lane dismissed Dykes after 1961.

August 4, 1936
Owens Steals the Führer's Show

By ARTHUR J. DALEY

BERLIN—The United States stole away what to date had been a distinctly German show by winning four of the five championships contested this bleak afternoon, as the greatest Olympic Games of them all swung through their third day. Once again a huge crowd of 90,000 gathered for the morning preliminaries, and once again another capacity throng of 110,000 later packed the Reich Sports Field Stadium. They came to cheer for more German victories, but remained instead to turn their hosannas in the direction of the Americans.

The invincible Jesse Owens won the broad jump at the Olympic record distance of 8.06 meters (26 feet 5²¹⁄₆₄ inches).

Miss Helen Stephens walked off with the women's 100-meter final in world record time. Glenn Hardin slammed to victory in the 400-meter hurdles, and John Woodruff, University of Pittsburgh Negro freshman, gave America its first 800-meter triumph in twenty-four years. And topping off the achievement of the Star-Spangled brigade, Owens twice broke the 200-meter mark around a turn, as well as the Olympic standard, hitting the identical figures of 21.1 seconds in both trials.

The only championship to evade the eager Americans' grasp was the women's discus crown. And that went to Germany as Miss Gisela Mauermeyer broke the Olympic record with a toss of 47.63

meters amid the exuberant shouts of her compatriots. But Germany's share in the harvest was a relatively minor one. The United States closed so far ahead in the race for the men's track and field team championship that every one else already is lapped at least a full circuit behind. The American total is 83 points to 38¾ for the Reich and 30¼ for Finland.

The German threat is apparently at an end. Smooth lies the path of the United States toward a goal it has always achieved—the Olympic team title. Yet these Germans have been performing in such astounding fashion all along that counting them out of the running is done reluctantly, even though the ammunition the Teutons have left is of the powder cap variety. The broad jump had been the one event of his three in these eleventh Olympics that Owens had been most certain of winning. Lutz Long, so unheralded in German sporting circles that he is neither a policeman nor a soldier, tied Owens at 7.87 meters with two leaps remaining and forced this human bullet to catapult out near his own new world record of 26 feet 8¼ inches in order to emerge victorious at all.

So delighted was Chancellor Hitler by the gallant fight that Long had made that he congratulated him privately just before he himself left the stadium. In fact, his eagerness to receive the youthful German was so great that the Führer condescended to wait until his emissaries had pried Long loose from Owens, with whom he was affectionately walking along the track arm in arm. All the Negro received was his second gold medal, which probably satisfied him well enough at that.

Jesse Owens setting an Olympic long-jump record in Berlin. It was one of four gold medals he won in the Games. Adolf Hitler, hoping that Lutz Long of Germany might win the event and propagate the myth of Aryan superiority, was watching from his box. (Associated Press)

Runners-up

1985: Tom Seaver, pitching for the Chicago White Sox, won the 300th game of his career by beating the Yankees, 4-1, at Yankee Stadium. At roughly the same time, at Anaheim County Stadium in California, Rod Carew of the Angels collected his 3,000th hit with a single off Frank Viola of the Minnesota Twins.

1945: Byron Nelson of Fort Worth, Tex., coming as close to perfect golf as anyone ever has, completed a record 11-tournament victory streak on the P.G.A. Tour by beating Ed Furgol by four strokes in the Canadian Open at Thornhill Country Club in Toronto. Nelson's average during the course of his epic run was 67.86

strokes. He bought a Texas ranch with his winnings and retired to it the following year at 34.

1957: In one of the most stirring racing comebacks ever, Juan Manuel Fangio of Argentina came from about a minute off the lead in his Maserati to win the German Grand Prix at Nurburgring over Mike Hawthorn of Britain, who was driving a Ferrari. The victory, in the last race of Fangio's career, gave him his fifth Formula One title, still a record.

August 5, 1991
Bubka! Bubka! Bubka!

By MICHAEL JANOFSKY

NEW YORK [Monday]—It has reached the point in his remarkable career as a pole vaulter that Sergei Bubka of the Soviet Union seems only to be toying with his event, breaking world records so often as to render the next crowning moment barely more special than the last. His evening's work in Malmo, Sweden, tonight produced the latest in a string of 28 such accomplishments, as he became the first vaulter to clear 20 feet outdoors with a winning height of 20 feet ¼ inch in the Dag Galan Grand Prix meet.

Bubka's stunning résumé now includes 13 world records outdoors and 15 indoors since 1984, as well as victories at the first two world championships, in 1983 and 1987, and at the 1988 Olympics. Only Paavo Nurmi, the legendary distance runner from Finland, had more world records to his credit, 29, stretched across a decade through 1931, but at a variety of distances, from the mile through 20,000 meters.

Bubka's has been a singular pursuit, through an arcane skill that requires an urgent need of speed, strength and courage to transform horizontal energy into vertical, then supreme body control to leave the bar high upon the uprights. For this record, it took three attempts, the last of the competition. He had almost decided to forgo the effort after his first attempt. He had complained of fatigue before the meet, having had only one rest day since competing

Sergei Bubka of Ukraine during the 1994 Goodwill Games in St. Petersburg, Russia. The only pole-vaulter ever to clear 20 feet, he was the Olympic gold medalist in 1988 and won five world titles between 1983 and '95. (Getty Images)

in Monaco on Saturday.

But so often when Bubka vaults, his spirit and the crowd's become one. After clearing two earlier heights, 18-8¼ and 19-2¼, which won the competition, he decided he would try the record height just once. But a crowd in excess of 20,000 wanted more. As so many others have before, they began chanting: "Bubka! Bubka! Bubka!"

No doubt, such a record height might have elicited even stronger reactions of amazement if Bubka had not swooped over similar heights earlier this year during the indoor season. In an eight-day period through March 23, he set world indoor records three times, becoming the first to vault 20 feet anywhere with an effort of 20-¼ in San Sebastián, Spain. He followed that with efforts of 20-½ in his hometown of Donetsk in the Ukraine four days later and one of 20-1 in Grenoble, France, four days after that. His outdoor season began with another record, 19-11, in Shuzouka, Japan, on May 6, followed by incremental improvements to 19-11¼ in Moscow on June 9 and 19-11¾ in Formia, Italy, on July 8.

Sergei Bubka's great strength and the fact that he gripped the pole higher than others contributed to his prowess. His records have endured. Not only was he the only vaulter as of 2003 to have exceeded 20 feet, but he also still held the world record, 20 feet 1¾ inches, at Sestriere, Italy, in 1994.

Runners-up

1984: Joan Benoit of Freeport, Me., who had undergone arthroscopic knee surgery only four months before, won the first women's Olympic marathon, finishing in 2 hours 24 minutes 52 seconds, about a third of a mile ahead of the favorite, Grete Waitz *(see Nov. 2)* of Norway.

1986: The longtime Philadelphia Phillie Steve Carlton *(see Sept. 15)*, now of the San Francisco Giants, became the second pitcher in history to amass 4,000 strikeouts when he fanned Eric Davis of the Cincinnati Reds in an 11–6 loss by the Giants at Candlestick Park. Carlton retired in 1988 with 4,136 K's, the most by any left-hander.

1921: The first major-league baseball game was broadcast by radio station KDKA in Pittsburgh. Harold Arlin was the announcer as the Pirates defeated the Philadelphia Phillies, 8–5, at Forbes Field. The following year, the entire World Series was broadcast by station WJZ in Newark, N.J., with the sportswriter Grantland Rice calling the plays.

August 6, 1926
Gertrude Ederle Swims the Channel

By T.R. YBARRA

DOVER, England—Gertrude Ederle, the plucky little New York girl, swam across the English Channel today in 14 hours 31 minutes, thus winning not only the honor of being the first woman to accomplish this feat but breaking by a goodly margin the best record made by a male cross-Channel swimmer. The speediest cross-Channel swim made before today was that of the Italian swimmer Sebastian Tirabocchi, who swam from France to England in 1923 in 16 hours 23 minutes.

Gertrude Ederle's successful swim came fifty-one years after the Channel was first conquered by an English swimmer, Captain Matthew Webb. In 1911 the Channel was crossed by another Englishman, T.W. Burgess, who now has achieved the added glory of having trained the young American girl and of having guided her today from start to finish of her magnificent swim.

Miss Ederle, 19, plunged into the water this morning at 7:09 o'clock at Cape Gris-Nez, France. She landed at Kingsdown, near Deal, England, at 9:40 o'clock this evening. For three desperate hours she fought the ebb and flow of the tide, with the British shores looming temptingly before her yet apparently hopelessly out of reach. But she gritted her teeth and stuck to it, putting every ounce of strength and will power into her strokes. She knew that if she could only stick it out a favorable turn in the tide might let her reach the coveted shore. Instead of making for Shakespeare Cliff or

St. Margaret's Bay, as swimmers usually do, Gertrude made toward Deal. And at last the favorable current for which she was praying swept her toward the cliffs of England.

Nineteen-year-old Gertrude Ederle of New York City, a three-time medalist at the 1924 Paris Olympics, becoming the first woman to swim across the English Channel. "I just knew if it could be done, it had to be done, and I did it,' she said. (Associated Press)

Alec Rutherford, a British expert on Channel swimming, was aboard the tugboat that accompanied Ederle and reported the following for The Times.

I watched this pretty, tiny atom of humanity in her red bathing dress and skull cap, with goggles like a motorist's, battle for 14 hours. She was accompanied by the tug Alsace, carrying the Stars and Stripes and a wireless apparatus for flashing to America messages during each mile of progress. Among those on the tug were the father and sister of

the swimmer and Burgess, her trainer. Chalked on the less side of the tug in front of Miss Ederle's eyes were the words: "This Way, Ole Kid!" with an arrow pointing forward. Burgess said that twice during the swim he wanted Miss Ederle to come out of the water—the first time at noon and the second time at 6 o'clock. It was her father and sister who would not let her come out, he said.

It was when Miss Ederle had passed south of Goodwin Lightship that the party for the first time decided that victory seemed possible. The crowds on shore began to gather in thousands all along the beach and automobiles by the hundreds all sounded their horns. Tugs in the Channel hooted their sirens and scores of flares were lit on the beach to guide her in. As she approached the shallow water, hundreds of people, regardless of their clothes, waded in the water and surrounded her. Miss Ederle walked ashore unaided, quickly followed by her father who clasped her in his arms and wrapped her in a dressing gown. Waiting on the tug in Dover Harbor after the Channel triumph, she said: "I just knew if it could be done, it had to be done, and I did it."

Gertrude Ederle returned home to New York City to a tickertape parade attended by some two million people. By 1933 she became deaf, the loss of hearing having been attributed to the Channel swim. She later spent many years teaching swimming to deaf children.

Runners-up

1981: Ending a strike that had wiped out seven weeks of the schedule, baseball owners and players divided the campaign into a split-season format, with the first-half winners (Yankees, A's, Phillies and Dodgers) facing those from the second half in an extra round of divisional playoffs. The arrangement was somehow unjust: the Cincinnati Reds had the best overall record, 66–42, but never made the playoffs.

1948: Bob Mathias, a 17-year-old California high school senior, became the youngest

men's gold medalist in the history of Olympic track and field by winning the decathlon at the London Games. He won again at the Helsinki Games in 1952 (*see July 25*).

1952: At age 46 (or 47 or 52), Satchel Paige (*see Feb. 9*) of the St. Louis Browns became the oldest player ever to pitch a complete-game shutout in the major leagues, striking out nine and defeating Virgil Trucks and the Detroit Tigers, 1–0, on seven hits in 12 innings at Sportsman's Park in St. Louis.

August 7, 1999
'L.T! L.T! L.T!' They Chanted

By THOMAS GEORGE

CANTON, Ohio—Lawrence Taylor stood near the steps of the Pro Football Hall of Fame today and talked about being knocked down and about getting up, about honor, class, friendship and family. He talked about football. Giants football. His son, Lawrence Jr., had presented him as a member of the Class of '99—Taylor said those moments almost made him cry—and they stood together onstage in a long embrace, whispering into each other's ears an exchange meant only for father and son. A memory for both that will last a lifetime.

So it went for Taylor and for each of the inductees, an overflow of emotion and memories that will last forever, and bronze busts in their likeness placed in the Hall to last as long. Taylor, Eric Dickerson, Tom Mack, Ozzie Newsome and Billy Shaw pushed the number in the Hall of Fame to 199.

More than 300 Giants fans were here today, including team owner Wellington Mara, who was inducted into the Hall last year. Giants fans filled an entire section in the upper tier of the crowd and were loud and bold in their blue and white. "L.T.! L.T.! L.T.!" they chanted, all day long. Taylor noticed. "I was a little nervous before I came out," he said, "but then I saw all the Giants stuff through the glass door and I knew I was in Giants territory. I think back; how did I get here?"

Others wondered, too. There was no denying his impact on pro football, a fearless linebacker who rushed the passer and pursued ballcarriers with venom and power and then delivered punishing tackles. Taylor was the key cog in two Giants Super Bowl championships, in 1987 and 1991. But his selection to the Hall was controversial to some because

Lawrence Taylor of the Giants regaining his breath on the sideline in 1989. Blending speed, power, aggression and more than a touch of intimidation, he changed the way the linebacker position was played in the 80's. (Getty Images)

of his off-field problems since he retired from the Giants in 1993, including drug arrests and his admission of cocaine addiction.

"I do understand the game and how this is an honor," Taylor said. He was humble. He was reflective. He talked about one of his teammates, a peer at linebacker, Harry Carson, who was in the crowd. Carson had been critical of Taylor's post-football behavior. The two "had some words" and "hadn't talked for a while," Taylor said, but there was Carson in attendance supporting him.

"Harry Carson," Taylor said, pointing at him. "What you have done here today is the classiest thing I have ever seen. Thank you. I love you." Carson kissed his fingers and pointed back at Taylor, then touched his chest.

Lawrence Taylor, who played for the Giants from 1981 to '93 and revolutionized the way linebacking was played, was perhaps the greatest at his position to ever play the game. Some argue that Dick Butkus, whose career with the Chicago Bears lasted from 1965 to '73, was at least Taylor's equal. By 2003 only Butkus's uniform number, 51, had been retired by his team.

Runners-up

1954: In a race billed as the "Mile of the Century," pitting against each other the only two men who had broken the four-minute mile barrier, Roger Bannister of Britain (*see May 6*) defeated John Landy of Australia in 3 minutes 58.8 seconds at the British Empire Games at Vancouver, British Columbia.

1999: Wade Boggs, formerly of the Boston Red Sox and the Yankees but now with the Tampa Bay Devil Rays, became the 23rd player to reach 3,000 hits but the only one to do so with a home run. He connected against the left-hander Chris Haney of the Cleveland Indians at Tropicana Field in Florida.

1932 Babe Didrikson and her United States teammate Jean Shiley both cleared the world-record height of 5 feet 5¼ inches in a jump-off at the Los Angeles Olympics, but the judges ruled that Didrikson had "dived" across the bar head first, torso second. She was given the silver medal while Shiley got the gold. The uproar soon caused the rules to be changed, but too late for the Babe.

Medalists Go Commercial

By HARVEY ARATON

BARCELONA, Spain—On the gold-medal stand tonight, in their corporate-sponsored suits with logos purposefully hidden, the multimillionaire professionals from the National Basketball Association were flanked by teams from tiny breakaway republics that could barely scrape together the funds necessary to attend. To their right was the Croatian team it had just defeated for the gold medal, 117–85, in their bland, identification-less uniforms straight out of the 1950's. To their left were the Lithuanians, jubilant bronze medalists after their 82–78 victory over the Unified Team, in their tie-dyed shirts and shorts that were paid for by a rock band, the Grateful Dead.

The beat had gone on for the United States Olympic basketball team right until the finish, but that didn't mean its participation in the 1992 Summer Olympics, and its successful mission to bring back the gold, was the greatest concern there ever was. "Actually, the greatest basketball I've ever been involved in was in Monte Carlo," said Magic Johnson. He was referring to the Dream Team's intra-squad scrimmages.

The Dream Team might have conquered the world, but ambiguity ruled the final night, from the Toni Kukoc–led Croatian team's ability to prevent a total drubbing to the sight of Jordan draping the American flag over his right shoulder to block out the logo of a company that is a rival to the one he is associated with. "Everyone agreed that we would not deface the logo," said Jordan, referring to the dispute between the Dreamers and the United States Olympic Committee. "The flag can't deface anything."

Its raising was not without memorable touches, as Johnson's smile and teary eyes lit up the arena, as John Stockton sang the words to the anthem and Larry Bird held his hand over his heart. But Bird, while saying he appreciated the opportunity to have joined what is the greatest assemblage of team talent in the history of the sport, also understood what was lacking, through no fault of its own, from its success. "I've cried at home when I've seen Americans win close races," said Bird. "I think you would've seen a lot more emotion up there if we hadn't won every game by 50 points."

Commercialism in the Olympics hardly began with members of the 1992 United States basketball team covering up the logos on their corporate-sponsored suits. In the 1968 Winter Games, Jean-Claude Killy of France had countless logos on his ski equipment. And I.O.C. president Avery Brundage banned the Austrian ski star Karl Schranz from the 1972 Olympics because of his sponsorship deals.

By the 1984 Los Angeles Games, the pendulum had swing the other way when a program of corpor-ate sponsorships was initiated by Peter Ueberroth, president of the Los Angeles Olympic Organizing Committee. The Games had grown so large that ticket sales and huge television rights payments alone were no longer sufficient to keep local Olympic organizing committees in the black.

Magic Johnson after the U.S. Dream Team won the basketball title. Never before was a group of Olympians so cocky. In an editorial titled "America's Nightmare Team," The Times labeled them "a boorish pack of prima donnas." (Associated Press)

Runners-up

1928: Ulise (Pete) DesJardins of Miami Beach, Fla., won the springboard gold medal at the Amsterdam Olympics. Three days later DesJardins, called the Little Bronze Statue because of his 5-foot-3-inch stature and perpetual tan, won the platform competition, too—a double unmatched until Greg Louganis of the United States (*see Aug. 12*) achieved it at Los Angeles in 1984.

1988: After 74 years as the site of baseball games played only in the daylight, Wrigley Field (*see April 20*) opened for its first night game, rained out in the fourth inning, between the Philadelphia Phillies and the Chicago Cubs. "Maybe," a woman said, "the Cubs will play better in the dark."

1920: Howard Ehmke of the Detroit Tigers allowed three hits and shut out the Yankees, 1–0, at Navin Field in the fastest game in American League history—1 hour 13 minutes. Because of television timeouts, more hitting, indiscriminate use of relief pitchers and other factors, the average length of a World Series game in 2002 had reached 3 hours 37 minutes.

Say It Ain't So, Wayne

By GEORGE VECSEY

NEW YORK—In Edmonton, it is still summertime. People still flock to the world's largest indoor mall. The Oilers are still printing up their schedules for the next hockey season. But life has changed forever in Edmonton. Wayne Gretzky is gone. Nothing terrible happened. He did not total his car trying to break a different kind of record out on the highways of Alberta. He did not succumb to alcohol or drugs or any of the other perils. He was not caught pulling stock deals or writing bad checks. He was merely traded to the Los Angeles Kings today, with his acquiescence, and things will never be the same.

Babe Ruth was sold. Wilt Chamberlain was traded. Tom Seaver was traded. Kareem Abdul-Jabbar was traded. Other franchise players have been traded near the peaks of their careers. But it could be argued that no other team athlete has ever been traded while he was the most dominant player of his time and perhaps ever of his game. Edmonton was already on the map—that spot way up there on the North American continent—but Gretzky taught people where to look for it. Little boys on the Alberta wheat farms, waiting for their ponds to freeze over, may not understand it. Eskimos near the Arctic Circle, waiting for Hockey Night in Canada to start again in October, may not understand it. Yuppies of Edmonton, with their season tickets for 40 Oiler games in the Northlands Coliseum, may not understand it. Gretzky is gone.

The oil bust having lasted so long in Edmonton, Peter Pocklington, the owner of the Oilers, may very well need the millions of dollars he receives in the Gretzky deal. It was Peter Puck and his hockey man, Glen Sather, who snookered the Ontario teen-ager away from a fellow World Hockey Association speculator, Nelson Skalbania, after Gretzky's eight-game career as a part-time high school student in Indianapolis. Now Gretzky is leaving Edmonton for Los Angeles, perhaps to further the career of his new wife, Janet Jones, perhaps to see how he might do in front of the cameras, perhaps just to stay warm in the winters without having to snuggle into the fur coats he can well afford.

Perhaps having done just about everything a hockey player can do, he now wants the creative challenge of seeing whether he can revive a franchise as lukewarm as the Forum ice. He never said he would stay forever. He just scored 583 goals for the Oilers and, in the last five seasons, helped win four Stanley Cups.

The Great Gretzky. Even in steamy towns along the Gulf of Mexico, where hockey rarely materializes, they have heard of this Wayne Gretzky. Skinny dude from Canada. Long blond hair. Gentle face and gracious manner. Scores all those goals. In Canada there are children who eat their cereal and drink their juice and buy a certain brand of sports wear because Wayne Gretzky says so. But he is more than the sum of his endorsements.

Wayne Gretzky surveying his new surroundings two months after being dealt from Edmonton to Los Angeles. No other athlete has ever been traded while being far and away the most dominant player of his sport. (Associated Press)

Runners-up

1936: Jesse Owens (*see Aug. 4*) won his fourth gold medal of the Berlin Olympics when he ran the opening leg on the United States 4x100-meter relay team, which set a world record in 39.8 seconds. Owens and Ralph Metcalfe were replacements for Marty Glickman and Sam Stoller, the only Jews on the team, who were withdrawn by United States Olympic officials at the last minute.

1963: Roger Craig's 18-game losing streak with the Mets came to an end when Jim Hickman hit a grand slam in the ninth inning for a 7–3 victory over the Chicago Cubs at the Polo Grounds. Craig went 5–22 this year, though he was considered an ace on the Mets' 51–111 team. The Mets' Anthony Young lost 27 games in a row in 1992–93.

1900: In the first annual Davis Cup tennis competition, Malcolm Whitman, Dwight Davis (for whom the Cup was named) and Holcombe Ward of the United States defeated a British team, 3–0, at the Longwood Cricket Club near Boston. Davis Cup play dominated the international tennis schedule until the 1970's.

August 10, 1928
Tarzan Sets Olympic Record

Johnny Weissmuller competing in Tokyo in 1928. Defending his Olympic 100-meter title in Amsterdam three months earlier, he inadvertently gulped a mouthful of water, quickly swallowed it and won the fourth of his five gold medals. (Associated Press)

AMSTERDAM, Holland (AP)—In the final round of trials and eliminations today in the Olympic water sports carnival, Johnny Weissmuller, Chicago speedster and defending champion in the 100-meter free-style, set a new Olympic record in the semi-finals of that event. Weissmuller, ace of the American swimming forces, flashed over his favorite distance with huge, space-devouring strokes in 58⅗ seconds. István Bárány, Hungarian, who finished second, gave the American speed king a fight through every inch of the first fifty meters, making the turn with him on even terms. Weissmuller forged ahead with a tremendous burst of speed in the final thirty meters, flailing the water with mighty strokes.

With Weissmuller in the final tomorrow will be George Kojac, the New York schoolboy, and Walter Laufer of Chicago. Victory in the men's 100-meter dash already is conceded Weissmuller, with Laufer and Kojac likely to complete the first three names on the board. Alberto Zorilla, the Argentinian, who won the 400-meter championship in spectacular style yesterday; Katsuo Takaishi, the Japanese, and Bárány of Hungary, other finalists, appear only as dangerous contenders to Laufer and Kojac. They hold little threat to Weissmuller's supremacy.

Arne Borg, Swedish champion, who came to grief yesterday, losing to Zorilla and Charlton of Australia in the 400-meter finals, was scratched from the second heat of the 100-meters in which he was scheduled to start. The official reason given was that he was stale. Swimming pool devotees and others said that Borg was none too eager to try conclusions with Weissmuller and risk a second defeat. In Swedish circles there has been much comment of Weissmuller's being scratched in the 400 meters, and hints were broadly expressed that the American feared Borg. Weissmuller was being quoted as having promised to give "Mr. Borg a little medicine in the 100 meters."

Weissmuller, who shattered the one-minute barrier at the Olympic Games at Paris in 1924 in 59 seconds even, swam with such apparent carefreeness in his heat that some spectators interpreted his attitude as contemptuous. After permitting Spence, who was swimming in the adjacent lane, to remain head to head with him for seventy-five meters, the American put on a little spurt at the finish and won by about a yard.

Johnny Weissmuller won the gold medal in the 100-meter freestyle the following day, equaling his Olympic record as he edged Istvan Bárány for the fourth of five career gold medals. Weissmuller won his fifth later in the Games in the 4×200-meter freestyle. While training for the 1932 Los Angeles Games, he was spotted by a Hollywood producer and cast in the starring role of Tarzan, the ape man. Weissmuller would make 12 Tarzan movies.

Runners-up

1984: Mary Decker of the United States fell to the track in the 3,000 meters at the Los Angeles Olympics when her right foot became entangled with the bare left foot of 18-year-old Zola Budd of South Africa, who was running for Britain. Both were favorites in one of the most celebrated matchups of the Games; neither won, as the gold medal went to Maricica Puica of Romania.

1929: Grover Cleveland Alexander of the St. Louis Cardinals *(see Oct. 10)* won the 373rd and final game of his career by defeating the Philadelphia Phillies, 11–9, at Shibe Park in Philadelphia and passing Christy Mathewson of the New York Giants for most career victories in the National League. Years later Mathewson, who retired in 1916, was awarded his 373rd after a study of records; the two have shared the career lead since.

1932: Clarence (Buster) Crabbe, of Oakland, Calif., won the 400-meter freestyle gold medal at the Los Angeles Games in 4 minutes 48.4 seconds, an Olympic record. He soon graduated from athletics to Hollywood, playing Buck Rogers, Flash Gordon and Tarzan in the 1930's and 40's.

August 11, 1984
'The Time of My Life'

By FRANK LITSKY

LOS ANGELES [Saturday]—The Carl Lewis Show ended tonight in triumph and a world record. The 23-year-old Lewis, from Willingboro, N.J., won his fourth gold medal in track and field in the Games of the XXIII Olympiad. In the men's 400-meter relay, the United States team of Sam Graddy of Atlanta, Ron Brown of Phoenix, Calvin Smith of Bolton, Miss., and Lewis won by 7 meters in 37.83 seconds for the only track and field world record of these Olympics. A United States team that included Smith and Lewis set the previous record of 37.86 in last year's world championships.

Lewis's previous gold medals came in the 100-meter dash last Saturday night, the long jump Monday night and the 200-meter dash Wednesday night. His four gold medals came in the same events in which the late Jesse Owens won his four in the 1936 Berlin Olympics. "Jesse Owens is still the same man to me he was before," said Lewis. "He is a legend. I'm just a person. I still feel like the same Carl Lewis I was six years ago, except I'm a little older and a lot more people come to my press conferences."

At the medal ceremony, Lewis wore brand new jogging shoes. The shoes were white and trimmed in, yes, gold. After the ceremonies, Lewis's relay teammates carried him off the field. That surprised many people because teammates have often criticized Lewis for demanding privileges not available to others.

"I think Carl has handled himself very well," said Smith. "He's a great person to have as a teammate."

"Carl is a good friend," said Brown. "He set some goals and he achieved them. People should respect that. A lot of people think he is a showboat, but I don't think so."

Carl Lewis as the star of stars in the Los Angeles Olympics after winning the 100-meter gold medal. He collected three more golds, in the 200 meters, the long jump and the 400 relay, duplicating event for event Jesse Owens's feat in 1936. (Associated Press)

Lewis has heard the criticism. He said he was misunderstood. "Too many people built me up before the Games," he said. "All I am is Carl Lewis. I came to these Games with the intention of winning four gold medals. I did it. I've enjoyed the Olympic Games. This has been the time of my life." Lewis said he would give the gold medal he won in the long jump to Ruth Owens, Jesse's widow. That was Owens's favorite event, and he said he picked that one for Mrs. Owens "because it means the most to me."

After the four gold medals comes rest. "I have no plans after today," said Lewis. "I'm very, very exhausted. I have to go to Europe next week, but as of right now I have no other plans." Well, he said, he had one plan. "Tonight," he said, "I plan to go jump in my pool fully dressed."

Runners-up

1994: Major league players called a strike for the eighth time in 23 seasons. The dispute, centering on the owners' demand to control costs by putting a limit on player payrolls, meant the cancellation of the World Series for the first time in the game's history (see Sept. 14). Tony Gwynn of the San Diego Padres lost a reasonable chance to hit .400.

1949: The struggling six-team National Basketball League and the Basketball Association of America merged, forming a 17-team N.B.A. One of the N.B.L. teams to join the N.B.A. was the Syracuse Nationals (now the Philadelphia 76ers), made famous by the dominant center Dolph Schayes.

1991: John Daly, 25, completed a story of Rocky-like proportions by winning the P.G.A. Championship at Crooked Stick Golf Club in Carmel, Ind., as a last-minute replacement for Nick Price. Daly, who became an overnight golf sensation, had to drive all night from Memphis to make his first-round tee time. He also won the British Open in 1995.

August 12, 1984
A Portrait of Power and Grace

By LAWRIE MIFFLIN

Greg Louganis in the springboard preliminaries at the Los Angeles Games. He won on both the springboard and platform, and when he repeated those victories at the 1988 Seoul Olympics, some called him the Baryshnikov of diving. (Associated Press)

LOS ANGELES [Sunday]—With a display of power and grace that astounded even those who are used to his dazzling performances, Greg Louganis won his second gold medal of these Olympic Games today, taking the men's 10-meter platform competition with a world-record score of 710.91 points. He became the first platform diver to break the 700-point plateau, eclipsing the 688.05 he accumulated in preliminaries yesterday. That score broke a year-old record of 687.90 that was his.

"You want your best performance to come in the Olympic Games," said the 24-year-old Californian. Louganis's gold medal today also was the 81st for the United States in these Games, breaking the record of 80 achieved by the United States in 1904 and by the Soviet Union in 1980.

Repeatedly asked to compare the achievements of Louganis to those of Carl Lewis, the runner and long jumper who won four gold medals here, Ron O'Brien, who coached the United States diving team, said, "Greg's two golds are equal to Carl Lewis's four, maybe even better. You have to put it in perspective and look how dominant he is." Louganis, who also won the 3-meter springboard gold medal Wednesday, is so superior to everyone else in his sport that he not only makes every dive look beautiful, but he makes the most frightening dives look almost effortless.

His final dive, a reverse three-and-a-half somersault, is the same maneuver that killed the Russian Sergei Shalibashvili last summer at the World University Games, when he flung his head back to execute the first somersault and hit it on the platform. Louganis seems to stretch his talents to the fullest when the pressure is greatest—pressure he puts on himself when his competitors aren't close enough to push him. Before his 10th and final dive, he said he was very nervous, even though he had virtually clinched the gold medal.

"You want to hit 10 good dives, you can't let up at any time, you can't play safe," he said. "I was scared going into the last dive. But I stood there and told myself that no matter what I do here, my mother will still love me. That thought gives you a lot of strength."

He also said that he sings to himself on the platform in the waiting moments just before each dive. "It's usually 'Believe in Yourself' from 'The Wiz' that I sing," said Louganis, who has studied dance since he was less than 2 years old, and earned his undergraduate degree in drama from the University of California at Irvine. "You're up there 33 feet above the water, with not a whole lot on, and seven people judging you, and it's a very vulnerable position. You've got to have a lot of confidence in yourself."

Runners-up

1974: Nolan Ryan of the California Angels, who came within two outs of a no-hitter in his previous start, struck out 19 Boston Red Sox in a game at Anaheim Stadium, equaling the mark held by Tom Seaver with the Mets and Steve Carlton with the St. Louis Cardinals (see Sept. 15). The record is now held by Roger Clemens, who struck out 20 with the Red Sox in 1986 (see April 29).

1978: New England Patriots receiver Darryl Stingley was paralyzed from the chest down in a preseason game after being hit by the fierce Oakland Raiders safety Jack Tatum on a crossing pattern over the middle. Mike Utley, a Detroit Lions guard, and Dennis Byrd, a Jets defensive end, were partially paralyzed in regular-season games in 1991 and '92, respectively.

1975: John Walker of New Zealand broke the 3 minutes 50 seconds barrier in the mile when he was clocked in a world-record 3:49.4 in Göteborg, Sweden, breaking the mark of 3:51.0 by Filbert Bayi of Tanzania earlier in the year. Walker got stronger as he progressed; his split times were 56.3, 59.2, 58.0 and 55.9.

August 13, 1919
A Horse Named Upset Beats Man o' War

By FRED VAN NESS

SARATOGA, N.Y.—The Glen Riddle Farm's great two-year-old, Man o' War, met with his first defeat here today in the running of the Sanford Memorial. He was forced to bow to Harry Payne Whitney's Upset in a neck-and-neck finish in this six-furlong dash. Though defeated, Man o' War was not discredited. On the contrary, the manner in which he ran this race stamped him, in the opinion of horsemen, as the best of his division without question. Though failing to get his nose in front, he stood out as the best horse in the race by a large margin, for he had all the worst of the racing luck.

Beginning with a very bad start, he came on to give battle to a horse which had a start of three to four lengths on him. There was scarcely a witness of this race who did not believe after it was all over that Man o' War would have walked home, with anything like a fair chance. For those who had hoped for a pretty race without anything to mar it, it was unfortunate that the acting starter, C.H. Pettingill, one of the placing judges, spent several minutes trying to get the horses lined up and then sent them away with only those near the rail ready for the start. The start was responsible for the defeat of Man o' War, it turned out.

Off almost last, Man o' War gained his speed in a few strides and then started to pass horses all along the back stretch. Steadily Man o' War drew up on Upset. On the last part of the turn into the stretch, Man o' War took third position, about two lengths back of Upset. A few strides down the stretch Golden Broom suddenly gave up, and Upset ran past him. In another instant Man o' War had dashed by his chestnut rival and it became a question whether Upset could last to win. Steadily Man o' War drew up on Upset. A hundred feet from the wire he was three-fourths of a length away. At the wire he was a scant neck out of the first position and in another twenty feet he would have passed the Whitney horse.

What made the race of Man o' War so impressive was the fact that he came from so far behind and that also he conceded fifteen pounds to Upset. On the very performance of the two today the Whitney horse would not appear to have a chance to win under an even break. The Sanford Memorial, for which John Sanford donated a cup on this occasion because of the presence of Man o' War and the widely heralded Golden Broom, who finished third, was by far the most interesting event that has been held during the Saratoga meeting. One of the largest crowds of the meeting, about 20,000 persons, saw the running of the race.

Man o' War, who beat Upset in their six previous meetings, never lost another race. He was retired to stud in 1920 and foaled 64 stakes winners, including the 1937 Triple Crown winner, War Admiral.

The appropriately named Upset (4), ridden by Willie Knapp, holds off Man o' War, with Johnny Loftus up, to win the Sanford Memorial in Saratoga, N.Y. It was the only defeat in 21 races for Man o' War, who quickly became a legend. (Associated Press)

Runners-up

1999: Steffi Graf of Germany retired from tennis at age 30, saying she had lost her unflagging will to excel. She left with 22 Grand Slam tournament titles, including the French Open championship over Martina Hingis two months before. Only Margaret Court of Australia has more Slam titles, 24.

1989: Payne Stewart of Orlando, Fla., won the P.G.A. Championship at Kemper Lake Golf Course in Hawthorne Woods, Ill., by shooting 31 on the last nine holes and overtaking 10 other players with a final-round 67. It was the first of three major championships for the man who was the last golfer to wear knickers.

1906: Jack Taylor of the Chicago Cubs lasted three innings against the Brooklyn Dodgers at Washington Park in Brooklyn, ending his consecutive complete-games streak, which had begun in 1901, at 187. It was a different era then, with "closers" not part of anyone's vocabulary. In 10 years Taylor failed to finish 8 of 286 starts.

August 14, 1903
Jeffries Was No Gentleman

[Unsigned, *The New York Times*]

SAN FRANCISCO—James Jeffries, holder of the title of heavyweight champion of the world, made secure his claim to first place in the pugilistic world by defeating James J. Corbett, the former champion, after ten rounds of fast and fierce fighting in the Mechanics' Pavilion here to-night. Ten thousand men seated about the arena saw the fight, the crowd representing an expenditure for seats aggregating $34,000. This was the largest crowd ever assembled at a ringside in this country, and the third largest sum in dollars and cents ever contested for. The two that exceeded it in receipts were the Corbett–Jeffries fight at Coney Island, $66,000, and the Corbett–McCoy fight at Madison Square Garden, New York, $63,000. The fight by the final four rounds:

Round 7. Corbett used his feet to good advantage at this stage. He tried to use his once lightning left, but it was a lame excuse. He came in quickly and sent his right to the heart, but Jeffries came back with a left on the body. Corbett was holding on saying: "He can't knock me out. He can't knock me out. Go on, Jim, see if you can knock me out." Corbett took a left on the head, and an uppercut to the chin. Corbett was fighting faster on his feet, using his fancy boxing tactics, but they were of no use against his burly opponent.

Round 8. Corbett staggered Jeffries with a left to the nose and half a dozen lefts and rights on Jeffries's face, which he accepted pleasantly. Corbett endeavored to stab Jeffries in the eyes, but thus far his blows had not raised a bump. Corbett fought cleverly, sending in half a dozen lefts and rights on the jaw. He seemed to improve 100 per cent, and the great crowd was in a state of wild excitement. They cheered him to the echo. This was

Corbett's round. He had changed his style and was using some of his old-time cleverness in ducking and blocking.

Round 9. Jeffries came at Corbett with a rush. Corbett's left cheek showed a lump from one of Jeffries's close-arm blows.

Round 10. Jeffries stood straight up and came after his man without hesitation Corbett seemed to be making a waiting fight. They exchanged lefts to the face and Jeffries made a vicious effort. Jeffries sent a left hook to the stomach and Corbett went down for nine seconds. He got up

and received a left in the stomach and a right on the jaw. He went down, and after the count of seven Tommy Ryan threw up the sponge. Corbett was suffering pain and a chair was brought for him. After a minute's rest he recovered and got up and shook hands with Jeffries.

James Jeffries held the heavyweight championship from 1899 to '05, successfully defending it seven times. He retired as champion but came back at age 35 as the "Great White Hope" against Jack Johnson in 1910 (see July 4).

James Jeffries, left, and James J. Corbett before their heavyweight title fight in San Francisco. Jeffries retained his title and retired the following year, but was coaxed back to face Jack Johnson in 1910. Corbett, who had dethroned John L. Sullivan in 1892, never fought again. (The Ring)

Runners-up

1959: The American Football League was formed with six franchises to be awarded to Dallas, Houston, Minneapolis–St. Paul, Denver, New York and Los Angeles. The Minnesota team never materialized, and Boston, Buffalo and Oakland were added. The eight teams began play in 1960 and were called, in order, the Texans (now Kansas City Chiefs), Oilers (Tennessee Titans), Broncos, Titans (now Jets), Chargers (now San Diego), Patriots (New England), Bills and Raiders.

1977: In the first major tournament played under a new sudden-death rule, Lanny Wadkins sank a six-foot putt for par on the third playoff hole at Pebble Beach in California to defeat Gene Littler and win the P.G.A. Championship. By 2000,

the P.G.A. had reverted to a three-hole playoff (see Aug. 20).

1936: The United States won the first Olympic basketball tournament at the Berlin Games, defeating Canada, 19–8. The game was played on a tennis court of clay and sand under intolerable conditions—a driving rainstorm that turned the footing to a sea of mud. "College Joe" Fortenberry and three others from McPherson, Kan., accounted for all but 1 of the points for the United States, which won 63 straight Olympic games until beaten by the Soviet Union in 1972 (see Sept. 10).

August 15, 1993
Norman's Putts That Missed

By JAIME DIAZ

TOLEDO, Ohio—Perhaps it is simply not meant to be for Greg Norman at the Inverness Club. Or perhaps it was just Paul Azinger's time. Either way, nothing but fate can describe the dramatic end of the 75th PGA Championship today. After the two players tied over 72 holes, Norman watched two putts in sudden death roll hard against the left edge of the hole only to spin out to the left. The first miss, from 20 feet, cost him an outright victory and his second consecutive major championship. The second, from 5 feet, which came after Azinger lipped out a 6-footer of his own, gave the 33-year-old Floridian his first major championship.

Azinger fired a closing three-under-par 68 over a drier, stingier Inverness Club that included birdies on four of the final seven holes, the last one coming from 6 feet on the 71st hole. Like Norman, he narrowly missed a birdie putt on the first extra hole. Norman, who began the day with a one-stroke edge over a tightly bunched leaderboard, closed with a battling 69, tying Azinger at 12-under-par 272. With his lipouts, he lost a chance both to make history and, in a sense, rewrite it.

Had he won, it would have been the first time a player had won the British Open and the PGA Championship since Walter Hagen did it in 1924. As it was, Norman became, with his performance in the British Open and here, the first player ever to play eight consecutive rounds in the 60's in major championships. Perhaps more significantly, a victory would have expiated the pain of his defeat in the same championship on the same course in 1986, when Bob Tway holed a sand shot for a birdie on the 72d hole to defeat him. Instead, he has now lost a playoff in each of the four major championships.

In the sudden-death playoff, which began on the 18th hole, Norman hit a wedge approach to almost exactly the same spot as he had in regulation. This time, he hit his putt a shade more to the right. A foot from the cup, it looked to be in, but instead it dipped along the left edge of the hole and spun out at a 90-degree angle. After Azinger followed with a narrow miss for a winning birdie from 18 feet, the players went to the second playoff hole, the 361-yard 10th. There, Norman hit a pitching wedge from light rough some 25 feet past the hole. Azinger followed from the fairway with a wedge to 6 feet pin-high to the right. Putting first, Norman misjudged the speed of his birdie putt and left it 4½ feet short of the hole, in almost the identical place from where he had missed a birdie putt in regulation.

Azinger hit his putt to win a shade too hard and watched it lip out of the right edge of the cup. After Azinger tapped in for par, Norman tried to finesse his sharp breaking right to left downhiller, but watched it break too much and spin out of

Greg Norman flips his putter after missing a birdie putt to win the P.G.A. in regulation at the Inverness Club in Ohio. He lost to Paul Azinger on the first hole of a sudden-death playoff after another potential winning putt lipped out. (Associated Press)

the left side of the hole. "I think I feel more down because of the first putt I had in the playoff," said Norman. "I hit as perfect a putt as I could have hit to win. But I can handle adversity pretty well. I lost to a great player. I'm happy for him, but I wish it was me."

Runners-up

1948: Babe Didrikson Zaharias, Olympic gold medalist, baseball player and pro golfer, won the third United States Women's Open title, shooting a final-round 78 to defeat Betty Hicks of Long Beach, Calif., by eight strokes at the Atlantic City Country Club in Northfield, N.J. Didrikson (see July 3) won three Opens in all. Her prize money in this one: $1,200.

1993: Damon Hill of England, son of the 1960's racing star Graham Hill, who died in a 1975 plane crash, became the first second-generation winner of a Formula One race when he drove his Williams-Renault to victory in the Hungarian Grand Prix at Budapest. Racing families are not as common in Formula One as in Nascar or Indy competition.

1975: Baltimore's bantam Earl Weaver, who managed the Orioles to four pennants and one world championship but forever antagonized umpires, was ejected from both games of a doubleheader by Ron Luciano. Weaver, ejected 90 times in his career, was thrown out before the second game even started during a heated lineup card exchange.

August 16, 1998
A Record for Gordon Is Only Miles Away

By TARIK EL-BASHIR

Jeff Gordon winning the Pepsi 400 at Michigan Speedway at the apex of the greatest run any Nascar driver has had in 30 years. He won 10 races a season from 1996 through '98. (Associated Press)

On this date Jeff Gordon became the seventh driver in modern Nascar history to win four straight races, coming from deep in the field to take the Pepsi 400 at Michigan Speedway, southwest of Ann Arbor. The following article, by Mr. el-Bashir, appeared in The Times *on Aug. 20.*

NEW YORK [Thursday]—Having already established himself as the driver to beat this season, Jeff Gordon has a chance to preserve his place in Nascar history this weekend with a fifth straight victory. A triumph by Gordon at Bristol, Tenn., on Saturday would set a record for consecutive victories in modern Nascar Winston Cup racing. Six other drivers—Mark Martin, Bill Elliott, Harry Gant, Dale Earnhardt, Darrell Waltrip and Cale Yarborough—share with Gordon the record of four straight victories.

"It's not easy to dominate in Nascar," Earnhardt said. "But Gordon and his team are certainly doing that. We did the same thing in 1987 when everything went our way and we won 11 races. You can't explain it; the cards just fall your way. Right now, the No. 24 bunch is head and shoulders above the rest."

If Gordon wins for the fifth straight time this weekend it will be his ninth victory of the season. The string of victories began last month at Pocono, where the efficient work of his pit crew late in the race put him out front for good. The streak continued in Indianapolis six days later. After Dale Jarrett ran out of gas, Gordon drove away from the field to become the first two-time winner of the Brickyard 400. He collected a prize pack-

age, including a bonus from Winston of more than $1.6 million, the largest in American motorsports history. The week after that, Gordon ran down Mike Skinner at Watkins Glen, N.Y., taking the lead with only five laps remaining as Skinner was forced to slow and conserve fuel. That third straight victory was also Gordon's third won from the pole position.

The streak, however, appeared in jeopardy at Brooklyn, Mich. Gordon was in position to finish high, but had not led a lap all day. Then, once again, he benefited from the wizardry of his pit crew. He came into the pit in third place late in the race, left in second place, and drove by Martin a few laps later to take his fourth straight checkered flag. "The records are great because when your career is over you can look back and say that was cool you did that," Gordon said.

During his streak, Gordon has started from the pole once, the outside of the front row once and from inside of the second row twice. He has led by as few as nine laps (Michigan) and as many as 154 of 200 (Pocono). Over all, Gordon has run up front for 325 of the 650 laps in the four races.

Jeff Gordon failed in his bid for a record fifth successive victory as Mark Martin won the Bristol 500 in Tennessee the following week. Gordon won 10 races in 1996, '97 and '98—a three-year run unmatched in Nascar history.

Runners-up

1948: Babe Ruth, whose home runs changed the way baseball was played, popularized sports in America and made the Yankees the most famous sports franchise of the 20th century, died of throat cancer in New York City at age 53. Six thousand mourners packed St. Patrick's Cathedral for his funeral three days later as another 75,000 gathered outside in the rain.

1930: Jim Dandy, a 100-to-1 shot from California, defeated the Triple Crown winner Gallant Fox by six lengths to win the Travers Stakes at Saratoga Racetrack in New York. Seeking an explanation for the upset, The Times wrote: "Many go back to the old maxim: 'Anything can happen in the mud.'"

1954: Sports Illustrated, which helped popularize sports in the United States, debuted with the first cover featuring Eddie Mathews of the Milwaukee Braves batting under the lights at County Stadium. Time's founder, Henry Luce, underwrote the magazine throughout its first decade, which would never have happened today.

Beaned by a Pitch, Ray Chapman Dies

[Unsigned, *The New York Times*]

NEW YORK—The body of Ray Chapman, the Cleveland shortstop, who died early today in St. Lawrence Hospital after being hit in the head by a pitched ball thrown by Carl Mays at the Polo Grounds yesterday afternoon, was taken to his home in Cleveland tonight. A group of baseball fans stood with bared heads at the Grand Central Terminal as the body was taken through the gates to the train. The ball player's widow, who went with the body, was accompanied by her brother and a friend, Indians Manager Tris Speaker, and Joe Wood, one of the players.

Chapman's death has cast a tragic spell over the baseball fans of the city, and everywhere the accident was the topic of conversation. Chapman was a true sportsman, a skillful player, and one of the most popular men in the major leagues. And this was to have been his last season in professional baseball. Carl Mays, the Yankees pitcher who threw the ball which felled Chapman, voluntarily went before Assistant District Attorney Joyce and was exonerated of all blame. The game which was to have been played between Cleveland and New York was put over until Thursday and the players of both clubs joined in mourning.

Although there is some bitterness against Mays among some of the Cleveland players, Manager Speaker, in a telephone conversation with Colonel T. L. Huston, part owner of the New York club, said he and his clubmates would do everything in their power to suppress this feeling. "It is the duty of all of us," said Speaker, "of all the players, not only for the good of the game, but also out of respect to the poor fellow who was killed, to suppress all bitter feeling."

Chapman died at 4:40 o'clock this morning, following an operation performed by Dr. T. M. Merrigan, surgical director of the institution. Chapman was unconscious after he arrived at the hospital. The operation began at 12:29 o'clock and was completed at 1:44. The blow had caused a depressed fracture in Chapman's head three and a half inches long. Dr. Merrigan removed a piece of skull about an inch and a half square and found the brain had been so severely jarred that blood clots had formed. The shock of the blow had lacerated the brain not only on the left side of the head where the ball struck but also on the right side where the shock of the blow had forced the brain against the skull, Dr. Merrigan said.

Mays is greatly shocked over the accident. He said he threw a high fast ball at a time when Chapman was crouched over the plate. He thought the ball hit the handle of Chapman's bat, for he fielded the ball and tossed it to first base. It wasn't until after that, when he saw Umpire Connelly calling to the stands for a physician, that he realized he had hit Chapman in the head. Manager Miller Huggins of the Yankees believes Chapman's left foot may have caught in the ground in some manner which prevented him from stepping out of the ball's way. Manager Huggins explained that batsmen usually had one foot loose and free at just such moments and Chapman had got out of the way of the same kind of pitched balls before.

Although there have been several serious beanings in the major leagues, some of which led to the curtailment of careers, Ray Chapman remains the only player to have been killed by a pitch. Batting helmets, invented in the 50's, may well have helped to prevent deaths.

Ray Chapman of the Indians in an undated photo. The Yankees' Carl Mays, who hit him, was a known headhunter, but Chapman's spikes may have caught in the dirt, keeping him from dodging the pitch. (Bettmann/Corbis)

Runners-up

1938: Henry Armstrong won the world lightweight title in a bloody 15-round split decision over Lou Ambers at Madison Square Garden in New York, becoming the first boxer to hold titles in three different weight classes simultaneously. He also held the welterweight and featherweight crowns. Armstrong retired in 1945 with a record of 145-20-9 with 98 knockouts.

1988: Butch Reynolds of Akron, Ohio, ran the 400 meters in 43.29 seconds at the International Grand Prix Sportfest in Zurich, breaking the 20-year-old world record of 43.86 set by Lee Evans of the United States at the Mexico City Olympics. Reynolds's mark stood for 11 years until it was shattered by Michael Johnson at the World Track and Field Championships in Seville, Spain (*see Aug. 26*).

1968: JoAnn Carner of Seekonk, Mass., beat Anne Welts of Seattle at Birmingham (Mich.) Country Club for her fifth United States Women's Amateur title, one short of Glenna Collett Vare's record of six in the 1920's and 30's. As a pro the hugely popular Carner, 'Big Mamma" to her tour mates, won five Vare Trophies for lowest scoring average and three L.P.G.A. Player of the Year titles.

George Brett Is Now a Happening

By DAVE ANDERSON

George Brett of the Royals singling in the first inning off Ed Figueroa of the Rangers in Texas. Chasing the 1941 shadows of Ted Williams and his .406 average, Brett had four hits, raising his mark to .401. (Associated Press)

NEW YORK—George Brett has blown his cover. For about a week his batting average had been slithering along around .390, like a water moccasin in a swamp. But with four hits today he suddenly moved above the surface to .401, and now he can't hide anymore. Now he's a media event. Now the constant inquisitions might be more difficult for the Kansas City Royals' third baseman to cope with than the constant confrontations with opposing pitchers.

Not since 1941 when Ted Williams hit .406 for the Boston Red Sox has anybody batted over .400 in the major leagues. But suddenly George Brett has a chance. All he has to do is average two hits in every five at bats for the rest of the season. The way he's hitting, that's the easy part. The hard part will be dealing with the writers, radio men, television announcers and photographers who now will swarm around him as never before.

Rod Carew could tell George Brett about that. Three seasons ago Rod Carew, then with the Minnesota Twins, was batting over .400 in early July when the swarm began. In addition to the increased attention from the daily media, Time magazine, Sports Illustrated and Sport magazine did cover stories on him. Newsweek and People magazine had pieces on him. ABC News had TV cameramen following him around. Perhaps the swarm of newsmen prevented Rod Carew from hitting .400, perhaps not. Shortly after the swarm began, Carew dropped under .400 and he skidded to .374 on Aug. 26 before spurting to finish at .388 for the sixth of his seven American League batting titles. He had 239 hits that year. Seven more and he would have batted .401.

Because he missed 35 games with thumb and ankle injuries, George Brett will need about 200 hits this season. From now on, every one will be documented. Back in 1941 there were no television cameras and no sports magazines covering Ted Williams over the last two months of the season. And back in 1941 a .400 hitter was not that unusual. Bill Terry had hit .401 for the New York Giants in 1930, Rogers Hornsby had hit .424, .403 and .401 for the St. Louis Cardinals during the 1920's.

Now it has been nearly 40 years since baseball has had a .400 hitter; now George Brett has a chance to accomplish something special. "I've never been this hot this long," the 27-year-old left-handed hitter said. "I'm just going to try to keep telling myself that I'm hot. The thing I don't want to do is put pressure on myself. But it's hard not to think about what I'm hitting. My batting average is in the papers every day and every time I go up to hit in Royals Stadium, it's up there out in center field on the scoreboard that's as high as a six-story building."

George Brett finished with a .390 average in 1980. By 2003, the closest anyone had come to batting .400 since then was .394 by Tony Gwynn of the San Diego Padres in the strike-shortened 1994 season.

Runners-up
1989: Dallas Green was fired as Yankee manager by George Steinbrenner, marking the 17th time the majority owner of the team changed skippers since he took control in 1973 (*see Jan. 3*). Steinbrenner went through three more managers before finding comfort and talent with Joe Torre in 1996.

1992: Larry Bird of the Boston Celtics (*see June 8*), "a hick from French Lick" in Indiana, as he once put it, but one of greatest players in the history of basketball, announced his retirement because of back trouble at age 35. He led the Celtics to three N.B.A. titles and won three most valuable player awards in his 13 seasons.

1993: Walter Ray Williams Jr. of Ocala, Fla., the most dominant Professional Bowlers Association star since Mark Roth in 1978 and a five-time world horseshoe champion as well, rolled four perfect games in the Greater Harrisburg (Pa.) Open, tying the mark of seven in a year by Amleto Monacelli in 1989.

Where's the Strike Zone?

By ARTHUR DALEY

NEW YORK—There was one rather disturbing occurrence today, one that should not be permitted to pass without comment. The zany Bill Veeck pulled the craziest stunt of his attention-getting career when he signed a 3-foot-7-inch midget to a contract and arranged for him to go to bat in a major league game as a pinch-hitter. He was walked, of course, because the midget strike zone was too small to find.

Veeck's madcap antics have never before violated good taste. But this one is positively indecent, an ignoble burlesque of a noble sport. Eddie Gaedel's name has appeared in a major league box score and he now is an official part of baseball history along with Ty Cobb, Honus Wagner and Babe Ruth. That is outrageous even though it was perfectly legal, as the chagrined umpires were dismayed to find.

Perhaps Veeck got the idea from James Thurber's hilarious short story, "You Could Look It Up," the best sports fiction this reporter ever read. It was wonderful as fiction. As fact it's on the revolting side. Thurber's midget hero, you might remember, performed yeoman service as a walking pinch-hitter until one smart pitcher tossed him an easy, irresistible sucker pitch in the key moment of the key game. So the midget hit the ball for an easy out.

Eddie Gaedel, a 3-foot-7-inch stuntman, batting against the Tigers at Sportsman's Park. Inserted as a pinch-hitter by St. Louis Browns owner Bill Veeck and wearing uniform No. 1/8, he walked on four pitches and bowed twice before reaching first base. (Associated Press)

Veeck is a great idea man. His promotional schemes even have reached a point where he can attract 18,396 fans into Sportsman's Park to see the Browns, a minor miracle at the very least. But in hiring a midget as a legally signed player of the Brownies, Wild-William overreached himself. As far as major league stature is concerned the Brownies are midgets and they don't need a pint-sized player to make it more obvious.

The Eddie Gaedel stunt followed a birthday party celebrating the American League's 50th anniversary between games of a doubleheader. During the festivities, he popped out of a papier-mâché cake. Bill Veeck, however much given to excess, was about 30 years ahead of the curve of promotions and commercialism in baseball. The bobblehead doll nights and other give-aways, team mascots moving in the stands, fireworks exploding from scoreboards—all pay homage to Veeck, who owned the Cleveland Indians, the Browns and the Chicago White Sox at one time or another and died in 1986.

Runners-up

1921: Ty Cobb of the Detroit Tigers *(see May 18)* singled against Elmer Myers of the Boston Red Sox in a game at Navin Field for his 3,000th hit, following Cap Anson, Honus Wagner and Nap Lajoie at that level. Aged 34 at the time, Cobb remains the youngest ever to reach that mark.

1981: Renaldo Nehemiah, formerly of the University of Maryland, broke the 13-second barrier in the 110-meter hurdles when he was clocked in a world-record 12.93 seconds at a meet in Zurich, Switzerland. So remarkable was the record that it has been lowered by only 0.02 seconds in more than 20 years.

1975: Mark Donohue, the great road-racing champion and former Indianapolis 500 winner *(see May 27)*, died from brain injuries he suffered when his car blew a tire and crashed spectacularly during a practice run before the Austrian Grand Prix on the Ostreichring track.

August 20, 2000
Tiger Makes It Three Straight Majors

By CLIFTON BROWN

Tiger Woods in the P.G.A. Championship at Valhalla Golf Club in Louisville, Ky. He beat Bob May in a three-hole playoff, winning his third straight major tournament and second consecutive P.G.A. (Getty Images)

LOUISVILLE, Ky.—Facing a courageous challenger who refused to give in, the world's best golfer showed the world just how good he is. Winning his third consecutive major championship today, and winning his second consecutive P.G.A. Championship, Tiger Woods prevailed by one stroke in a three-hole playoff against Bob May, ending a day overflowing with spectacular golf. Woods became only the second player to win three majors in one year, joining Ben Hogan, who won the Masters, the United States Open and the British Open in 1953. Woods also became the first back-to-back

winner at the P.G.A. Championship since Denny Shute won the P.G.A. title in 1936 and 1937.

But Woods's year has been even more dominant than Hogan's year in 1953. Woods won this year's United States Open by a record-setting 15 strokes, he won the British Open by eight strokes, and today, Woods and May set the P.G.A. Championship scoring record (18-under-par 270), breaking the previous mark of 17 under par set by Steve Elkington and Colin Montgomerie in 1995. Incredibly, Woods holds the scoring record at all four major championships—the Masters (18

under par), the United States Open (15 under par), the British Open (19 under par) and the P.G.A. Championship (18 under par). At 24, he has won five career majors faster than anyone, and he is the first player in history to win four of five majors, dating to last year's P.G.A. Championship.

Yet, hardly anyone expected what happened today at Valhalla Golf Club—Woods being pushed to the brink of defeat by a 31-year-old, relatively obscure player, who had never won a PGA Tour event, let alone a major championship. But when May made him play his best, Woods was brilliant. Woods forced the playoff by making a pressure-packed 5-foot birdie putt at No. 18, then he closed the three-hole playoff by making a wonderful up and down from the greenside bunker at No. 18 to protect his one-shot lead.

That bunker shot came after his tee shot hit a tree and dropped nearly straight down onto a cart path. The ball bounced so high it hit the tree again. It landed on the cart path and sped down a hill onto trampled grass. His second shot landed in the rough, with his third shot going into the bunker. An extraordinary effort by May was not enough to defeat the game's most extraordinary player. Woods could not remember being tested more severely.

"This was probably one of the greatest duels I've ever had in my life," Woods said. "It was a very special day, to have two guys playing at a level that you don't see unless you have the concentration heightened to where it was at. We never backed off from one another. Birdie for birdie, shot for shot, we were going right at each other. That's as good as it gets."

Runners-up

1964: Phil Linz of the Yankees and Manager Yogi Berra went at each other in a heated row in Chicago when Linz played a harmonica on the team bus after a fourth straight loss put New York 4½ games behind in the pennant race. The music turned out to be sweet, however, when the Yankees beat the White Sox for the pennant.

1955: Arnold Palmer, winner of the United States Amateur in 1954, won his first professional tournament, the Canadian Open, at the Weston Club in Toronto. He won 59 other pro titles, including eight majors (see April 6 and June 18),

and with his skill, shirttail-out manner and telegenic appeal popularized golf perhaps more than any other player.

1973: Two days after winning the All-American Soap Box Derby in Akron, Ohio, Jim Gronen, 14, of Boulder, Colo., was stripped of the championship when it was found that an illegal electromagnet had been secreted inside his race car so that the metal baffle plate at the start line would pull the car forward, giving it a competitive advantage. It was the biggest scandal in the 37-year history of the festival.

August 21, 1914
Young Walter Hagen Wins the Open

[Unsigned, *The New York Times*]

CHICAGO—Walter C. Hagen, 22 years old, native professional of Rochester, N.Y., today displaced Francis Ouimet as open golf champion of America, by winning the tournament at Midlothian with a medal score of 290 for the seventy-two holes. Ouimet fell off in his play, taking 298 for his total, and it fell to the lot of Charles Evans, Jr., Western amateur champion, hampered by a wrenched right ankle, to furnish Hagen's chief opposition. Outplaying the whole field in a spectacular finish that electrified the long gallery, Evans made two rounds of 71 and 70 and finished with 291, just one stroke behind Hagen.

Evans's score of 141 for today was the best double round of the tournament, and was accomplished despite several missed putts. His ankle seemed to bother his putting more than his long work and iron shots. His tee shots spanned some 300 yards of the fairway, nearly every time. His irons were nearly all perfect, but, in the last nine holes, he missed three short putts and had no luck with long ones. He finally drove the edge of the eighteenth green, 277 yards, and had left one putt for a half with Hagen. The spectators stood on tiptoe while the Chicagoan tried the thirty-foot putt. He missed by twelve inches and the championship went to Hagen.

Ouimet lost the title with graceful equanimity. He had no fault to find, he said, having fallen off his game, as others had done before. He won the title last year at Brookline, tying with Harry Vardon and Edward Ray, British professionals, at 304. In the playoff Ouimet made 72 to Vardon's 77 and Ray's 78.

Hagan's victory was accomplished by steady playing. Yesterday he made a record of 68 for the course by good work

Walter Hagen in an undated photo from the 1920s. Colorful and gregarious, he especially dominated the P.G.A., winning 40 career tournaments and four straight titles under match-play format from 1924 to '27. (Pacific & Atlantic Photos)

aided by spectacular putting. He took 74 in the afternoon, leading the field at the end of the first day with 142. Today, he fell off a trifle, taking 75 for the first round and 73 for the second. The best of his game came on the last nine holes, where, holing putt after putt, he made 35, two under par. The new champion was born in Rochester, learned golf there and had not made any record outside his native city until the present tournament. He is slight in build, but follows Vardon's system of shooting straight for the flag all the time.

Walter Hagen won 10 other major titles and ranks behind only Jack Nicklaus, with 20, and Bobby Jones, with 13. Hagen was golf's first true pro player. A crowd favorite because of his frequent exchanges with the gallery, he was a master shotmaker and something of a hustler who wasn't above using a little psychology on his opponents. The columnist Arthur Daley of The Times *said of Hagen, "He was the first golfer to earn a million from the sport and the first to spend it, too."*

Runners-up

1947: The Maynard (Pa.) Midgets won the first National Little League Tournament (later the Little League World Series), beating Lock Haven, Pa., 16–7, in Williamsport, Pa. Founded in 1939 by Carl Stotz, a Pennsylvanian, Little League baseball grew into a national, then international movement, enriching the lives of countless children and families.

1982: Rollie Fingers of the Milwaukee Brewers became the first reliever in history to record 300 saves when he pitched the final two innings of a 3–2 victory over

the Seattle Mariners at the Kingdome. The premier closer for the Oakland A's team that won five division titles and three World Series (*see Oct. 17*), he retired in 1935 with 341 saves.

1864: The Travers, the oldest major stakes race for 3-year-olds, was run for the first time at the year-old Saratoga Race Course in upstate New York. The race was named after the state's racing association president, William Travers, and the inaugural winner was Kentucky, owned by none other than Travers himself.

August 22, 1965
Marichal Clubs Roseboro With a Bat

By LEONARD KOPPETT

SAN FRANCISCO—In a burst of uncontrollable temper under circumstances still unclear, Juan Marichal of the San Francisco Giants attacked John Roseboro of the Los Angeles Dodgers today with a baseball bat. Marichal's bat hit Roseboro on the top of the head at least twice and opened a two-inch cut that bled profusely. The injury was apparently no more serious than that, but as Roseboro accompanied his teammates on a flight to New York this evening, he was being observed for symptoms of brain concussion.

It happened before 42,807 spectators, the largest Candlestick Park crowd of the year, and many television viewers in the Los Angeles area. It occurred in the third inning of the fourth and final game of a series in which the Dodgers and Giants have been battling for the National League lead. The Giants went on to win, 4–3, but the eventual effect of the incident on the pennant race could be profound. Marichal was ejected from the game and a lengthy suspension is a distinct possibility once the league president, Warren Giles, gets his report from the chief umpire, Shag Crawford.

The flare-up precipitated free-for-all scuffling that interrupted the game for 15 minutes. Both teams were left emotionally shaken. Fights that erupt under pennant pressure are not unusual, but they are always fist fights. Players, coaches and managers of both teams here could not recall ever seeing an attack with a bat. Fights usually break out after an exchange of "bean balls," pitches thrown close to batters' heads to "keep them loose." There had been such an exchange in this game—but everyone concerned seemed to agree it was not the thing that angered Marichal.

Juan Marichal (27) of the Giants attacks the Dodgers' John Roseboro with his bat at Candlestick Park while Sandy Koufax (32) approaches. The blows bloodied Roseboro, but he was not seriously injured. (Associated Press)

The two directly concerned, Roseboro and Marichal, left the park long before the game ended. Their accounts could not be obtained anyway, since a dozen policemen had barred the dressing rooms to reporters until the end of the game. As pieced together, the story seemed to be that Marichal believed that Roseboro, in throwing the ball back to the pitcher, tried to hit Marichal in the back of the head. Marichal turned and went after Roseboro with his bat. Not a word was spoken, according to Crawford, who was the umpire at home plate and was two feet from the action.

The next three men to arrive on the scene were Sandy Koufax, the Dodger pitcher who had just taken the return throw from Roseboro; Charlie Fox, the Giants' coach at third base, and Tito Fuentes, rookie Giants' shortstop who had been in the on-deck circle. Fuentes also was brandishing a bat, but he did not appear to be using it as a weapon. In the melee that followed within a few seconds, peacemaking seemed desperately urgent, and there didn't seem to be the usual taking of sides. Everyone seemed horrified by the nature of the attack and by the sight of blood streaming down Roseboro's face.

Juan Marichal was suspended for nine days and fined $1,750. Years later Marichal failed to gain entry to the Hall of Fame in his first two years of eligibility. He was elected only after John Roseboro, by then a friend, publicly campaigned for him.

Runners-up

1998: In the midst of his pursuit of Roger Maris's record of 61 home runs—he finished with 70 *(see Sept. 8)*—Mark McGwire of the St. Louis Cardinals acknowledged that for more than a year he had been using androstenedione, a testosterone-producing supplement that is banned by the N.F.L., the N.C.A.A. and the I.O.C. because it is thought to provide an unfair advantage.

1851: The schooner *America* defeated 14 British boats in a race around the Isle of Wight. *America's* owners were awarded the Hundred Guinea Cup, which they presented to the New York Yacht Club on condition that it be put up for grabs in international sailing competition. In 1870 it was renamed the America's Cup. It remained in United States hands until 1983, when *Australia II* captured it *(see Sept. 26)*.

1999: Was it the pool? Ian Thorpe of Australia knocked more than two seconds off the 400-meter world freestyle record with a clocking of 3 minutes 41.83 seconds at the Pan Pacific Championships in Sydney. Eleven other records were set in eight days there.

August 23, 1926
Mrs. Mallory and Her Stirring Comeback

By ALLISON DANZIG

NEW YORK—The sceptre in American women's tennis returned to Mrs. Molla Mallory today. Time turned back at Forest Hills as the New York woman, holder for six years of the title, fought her way to a stunning victory over Miss Elizabeth Ryan of California to regain the crown which she lost to Miss Helen Wills in 1923 and to tie the record for all time of the number of championships won by a single player, either man or woman. In all the thirty-nine years of the women's national championship there has probably never been a more sensational victory scored in a final round than Mrs. Mallory's today.

Trailing at 0–4 in the final set, in which she was within a single stroke of defeat in the fourteenth game, the New York woman threw the 3,000 spectators in the Stadium into a frenzy of delight as she fought her way through four games in a row with a savageness of stroking that crushed all opposition. Miss Ryan, clearly the favorite from the start up to this point, wilted before the devastating attack, which completely broke up her volleying game. She fought desperately through seven more games to hold off Mrs. Mallory's penetrating forcing shots, and then, amid screams of joy from the whole gallery, Mrs. Mallory brought the play to a climax by breaking through service and winning her own game for the match. The score was 4–6, 6–4, 9–7.

It is not often that a tennis gathering runs the gamut of emotions that those 3,000 spectators experienced today. There were moments when the suspense was so terrific that it set hearts to pounding wildly as the match hung in the balance on a single stroke. Because Mrs. Mallory's cause was almost unanimously regarded as hopeless, the onlookers broke into applause at her every winning shot, cheered her on excitedly as she fought her way to victory in the second set, and then the safety valve was blown off as she staged her rally in the final chapter. The stadium fairly rocked as Mrs. Mallory won the last point, and of all those 3,000 people none was so unrestrainedly exuberant as the champion.

Mrs. Mallory danced with joy, throwing her racquet in the air, waving to the cheering stands and unrestrainedly giving vent to her glee. One would have thought, as she received the championship cup from Jones W. Mersereau, President of the United States Lawn Tennis Association, that Mrs. Mallory was experiencing a new thrill. Certainly she showed greater happiness than she did over any of her victories in the past. And well she might. Looked upon as having passed the prime of her career and given little consideration as a championship contender, the New York woman showed that the same courageous fighting spirit and iron will to win that kept her at the top for seven years and that enabled her to triumph over Mlle. Lenglen at Forest Hills in 1921 are still as strong as ever within her.

Molla Mallory returning a backhand volley, circa 1925. A fierce ground-stroker, she spurned long points and tenaciously went for winners. She and her colossal rival Helen Wills each won the U.S. championship seven times. (Corbis)

Runners-up

1936: Bob Feller, 17, making his first major-league start for the Cleveland Indians, struck out 15 batters in a 4–1 victory over the St. Louis Browns in Municipal Stadium. Feller, from Van Meter, Iowa, came one short of the American League record set by the Philadelphia Athletics' Rube Waddell in 1908. On Sept. 13 Feller tied Dizzy Dean's major-league record of 17 strikeouts.

1931: Lefty Grove's American League record-tying 16-game winning streak was snapped when Philadelphia A's outfielder Jim Moore misjudged a fly ball, giving the St. Louis Browns a 1–0 victory at Sportsman's Park in St. Louis. Grove, eventually a 300-game winner, shared the streak record with Walter Johnson and Joe Wood.

1999: Jenny Thompson, a former Stanford University star, broke the world 100-meter butterfly record of 57.93 seconds set by her countrywoman Mary T. Meagher in 1981. Thompson's time in the Pan Pacific Championships in Sydney, Australia, was 57.88 seconds.

August 24, 1989
A Hero's Exile

By MURRAY CHASS

NEW YORK—Saying he believed that Pete Rose had bet on baseball games, including those of the team he managed, Commissioner A. Bartlett Giamatti announced an agreement today that bans Mr. Rose permanently from baseball.

The five-page agreement, reached after four months of sporadic negotiations, encompasses virtually everything the commissioner wanted to achieve, including reaffirmation of the authority of his office, and grants Mr. Rose only the ability to continue denying that he bet on baseball games. The carefully worded legal document stipulates that Mr. Rose can apply for reinstatement after a year under Major League Rule 15 (c). The rule, which applies to anyone ruled ineligible, states that "no application for reinstatement from the ineligible list may be made until after the lapse of one year..."

The agreement, signed by Mr. Rose and Mr. Giamatti, does not specify that the Cincinnati Reds' manager was suspended for betting on baseball games and does not say that he bet on games. It says, in fact, that "nothing in this agreement shall be deemed either an admission or a denial" by Mr. Rose of the charges that he bet on games. Nevertheless, at a news conference announcing Mr. Rose's "banishment for life," Mr. Giamatti, in reply to a question, said, "In the absence of a hearing and therefore in the absence of any evidence to the contrary, I am confronted by the factual record of the Dowd report, and on

the basis of that, yes, I have concluded that he bet on baseball." And on the Reds? "Yes."

Mr. Rose, at his own news conference at Riverfront Stadium in Cincinnati, said, "Regardless of what the commissioner said today, I did not bet on baseball."

The Dowd report, a 225-page document supported by seven volumes of exhibits compiled by John M. Dowd, the special counsel hired by the commissioner, contained voluminous testimony chronicling Mr. Rose's gambling activities. At one point in the negotiations with Mr. Rose's attorneys, Francis T. Vincent Jr., the deputy commissioner, proposed that Mr. Rose be made to wait for seven years before applying for reinstatement, according to a lawyer familiar with the talks. Mr. Vincent, the lawyer said, eventually lowered the period to five years and then to three years before the two sides agreed on

Reds Manager Pete Rose during spring training in 1989, five months before he was banished from baseball by Commissioner A. Bartlett Giamatti. Giamati concluded that Rose had bet on games, including ones involving the Reds. (Associated Press)

using Rule 15 (c).

Both Mr. Giamatti and Reuven Katz, Mr. Rose's lawyer, said they had made no deal about reinstatement. It is not automatic, the commissioner said; nor is it guaranteed. "The burden to show a redirected, reconfigured, rehabilitated life is entirely Pete Rose's," Mr. Giamatti said at the news conference at the New York Hilton. Mr. Rose said today that he would "never bet on any kind of sports again—team sports."

Mr. Rose, whose 4,256 hits are the most any player has ever had, is easily the most prominent person to be banned from baseball since 1921 when Shoeless Joe Jackson and seven other members of the Chicago White Sox were banished by the first commissioner, Kenesaw Mountain Landis, for conspiring to fix the 1919 World Series (see Sept. 28). Mr. Rose said he would apply for reinstatement as soon as he is permitted to do so. An ineligible person may apply as often as he wants, but of the 14 who have been banned, none has been reinstated.

As of late 2003, Pete Rose had been denied election to the Baseball Hall of Fame, which remained a divisive issue among fans. Although Commissioner Giamatti said he concluded that Rose had bet on baseball games, including those of the Reds, Rose continued to deny those findings. In August 1990 he entered a federal work camp in Marion, Ill., where he served a five-month sentence for tax evasion on income from his betting winnings and collectible shows.

Runners-up

1875: Matthew Webb of England became the first swimmer to cross the English Channel, a feat tried by men for more than a century. Webb set out from Dover and swam the 21-mile divide in 21 hours 45 minutes, arriving in France the day after he left.

1963: John Pennel, a senior at Northeast Louisiana State College, became the first outdoor pole-vaulter to clear 17 feet, with a mark of 17 feet ¾ inches at the Florida Gold Coast A.A.U. meet in Miami. He chose to use a fiberglass pole at

a time when most vaulters were using wooden ones. Only a year before, the 16-foot barrier had been breached by John Uelses (see Feb. 2).

2000: Michelle Akers of Shorecrest, Wash., the heart and soul of the Women's World Cup championship teams of 1991 and '99 (see July 10) and the United States Olympic gold medal team of '96, announced her retirement from the squad because of injuries. The 34-year-old Akers was the second United States women's all-time scorer behind Mia Hamm.

August 25, 1991
The Fastest Race in History

By MICHAEL JANOFSKY

TOKYO—For all the amazing races and remarkable long jumps, the gold medals, records, titles and honors that have defined Carl Lewis's life in track and field, little of the past could have foretold his stunning performance tonight in the 100-meter final of the world championships. And certainly there was nothing in the past to match it. Enduring growing doubts about his ability to run faster and questions about his age, now that he is seven weeks past his 30th birthday, Lewis won the fastest race in history, setting a world record of 9.86 seconds.

He led an American sweep as six of the eight runners finished in under 10 seconds. Only twice before—in the final of the 1988 Seoul Olympics and in one of the semifinals tonight—had as many as three sprinters broken 10 seconds. In a race for the ages, it seemed only appropriate that one of the aged should win, with a time that sliced 4-hundredths of a second off the world record set by his friend and 24-year-old teammate, Leroy Burrell, just 10 weeks ago at the national championships in New York. In the race tonight, Burrell broke the previous record as well, finishing second in 9.88 seconds. Dennis Mitchell of the United States was third at 9.91, followed by Linford Christie of Britain in 9.92, Frank Fredericks of Namibia and Brigham Young University in 9.95 and Ray Stewart of Jamaica in 9.96. Only Robson Da Silva of Brazil and Bruny Surin of Canada failed at the 10-second barrier, with times that could have won a thousand other races, 10.12 and 10.14, respectively.

While the times give the race its place in history, they do only partial justice in illustrating the significance of the moment for Lewis. Even he had trouble putting things into perspective for a roomful of reporters at a post-race news conference. He laughed about scolding from his coach, Tom Tellez, before the race about his not doing his best in finals of major competitions. And he cried through a poignant remembrance of his father, William, who died in 1987.

"This is a special time," Lewis said haltingly. "He can't be here with me, but I know he's with me. When there's a clear sky, he's able to see through the clouds. Tonight, he was able to see through the dark, and I was happy I was able to do what I could do."

Carl Lewis later called this the greatest performance of his career. The record was broken by Leroy Burrell, who ran 9.85 seconds at a meet in Switzerland in 1994 (see July 6).

Carl Lewis nearing the finish line in record time in the 4x100-meter relay at the world track championships in Tokyo. One week earlier he set an eye-opening world mark of 9.86 seconds at age 30 in the 100 meters. (Associated Press)

Runners-up

1985: Dwight Gooden, aged 20, of the Mets *(see Sept. 12)*, won his 14th consecutive game and became the youngest pitcher in history to win as many as 20 games when he beat the San Diego Padres, 9–3, at Shea Stadium. He finished the season 24–4 with 268 strikeouts, a 1.53 earned run average and the Cy Young Award.

1996: Tiger Woods, aged 20, won an unprecedented third straight United States Amateur title, rallying from two strokes back with three holes to play to defeat Steve Scott of the University of Florida at Pumpkin Ridge Golf Club in Cornelius, Ore. Two days later Woods turned pro. In '94 he had become the youngest amateur champion and the first African-American ever to win the title.

1952: Virgil Trucks of the Detroit Tigers threw his second no-hitter of the season, defeating the Yankees, 1–0, in the Bronx. He had no-hit the Washington Senators, 1–0, at Detroit's Briggs Stadium in May. It was everything or nothing for Trucks—his season record for the eighth-place Tigers was 5–19.

August 26, 1939
First Day for the Small Screen

By ROSCOE McGOWEN

NEW YORK—The pennant fever hit Flatbush today when 33,535 of the most hopeful fans in any major league city swarmed into Ebbets Field to see the double-header with the league-leading Reds. Their temperature dropped a bit when Bill McKechnie's men took the opener, 5–2, but rose again with a 6–1 Dodger triumph in the nightcap. The double-header marked major league baseball's television debut before two prying "eyes" of station W2XBS in the Empire State Building. One "eye" or camera was placed near the visiting players' dugout, or behind the right-hand batters' position. The other was in a second-tier box back of the catcher's box and commanded an extensive view of the field when outfield plays were made.

Red Barber interviewing Brooklyn Dodgers manager Leo Durocher at Ebbets Field before the first major league game ever televised. Nearby are Reds manager Bill McKechnie (1), Dixie Walker, behind Barber, and Dolph Camilli, right. (Associated Press)

Over the video-sound channels of the station, television-set owners as far away as fifty miles viewed the action and heard the roar of the crowd, according to the National Broadcasting Company. It was not the first time baseball was televised by the NBC. Last May at Baker Field a game between Columbia and Princeton was caught by the cameras. However, to those who, over the television receivers, saw last May's contest as well as those of today, it was apparent that considerable progress has been made in the technical requirements and apparatus for this sort of outdoor pick-up, where the action is fast. At times it was possible to catch a fleeting glimpse of the ball as it sped from the pitcher's hand toward home plate.

Bucky Walters, Dodger nemesis, allowed only two hits in the opener in annexing his 21st victory and his sixth straight over Brooklyn. Luke (Hot Potato) Hamlin, trying for No. 16, blew a 2–0 lead over Walters in the eighth and was knocked out, charged with his 10th loss. In the nightcap Hugh Casey breezed through to his ninth triumph, aided by Dolph Camilli's twenty-second homer of the year off Johnny Niggeling with Cookie Lavagetto aboard in the second frame.

Dolf also contributed a scorching double in the third that knocked the veteran knuckleball hurler out. The Dodgers scored four times in that frame, Lavagetto's double driving in one run, Camilli's another and Ernie Koy's single off Whitey Moore bringing the other pair home.

Forty-six years later, the coverage of baseball was so refined that fans at home knew instantly from a videotape replay that an umpire's call was wrong. The mistake led to the St. Louis Cardinals' losing a World Series game and ultimately the Series itself (see Oct. 26).

Runners-up

1933: Helen Wills Moody of Carmel, Calif., endured her first tournament loss since she was upended by Suzanne Lenglen of France at Cannes in 1926 *(see Feb. 16)*—after a stretch of 158 victories. The defeat came by default in the third set against Wills's rival Helen Jacobs in the United States nationals at Forest Hills, N.Y.

1960: John Devitt of Australia was judged the winner over Lance Larson, a University of Southern California student, in the 100-meter freestyle final at the Rome Olympics, although experimental electronic timers showed Larson with a time of 55.1 seconds to Devitt's 55.2. The German chief judge ordered Larson's time increased to Devitt's to agree with his visual estimate; a United States protest of the decision was denied.

1999: Michael Johnson of Dallas shattered Butch Reynolds's 11-year-old world record in the 400 meters in a remarkable 43.18 seconds at the World Track and Field Championships in Seville, Spain. Three years earlier at the Atlanta Olympics, Johnson had broken the 200-meter world mark in another extraordinary performance *(see Aug. 1).*

'No Exceptions,' and No Renee Richards

By ROBIN HERMAN

Renee Richards was denied admission to the United States Open tennis tournament in Forest Hills, N.Y., on this date when she refused to take a chromosome test established for all women entrants. "There will be no exceptions," the tournament's director, Mike Blanchard, said. "I guess we have Dr. Renee Richards to thank for instituting this." The following article appeared in The Times *on August 31.*

NEW YORK—Before she underwent a sex-change operation last November, Dr. Renee Richards was known as Dr. Richard Raskind, an amateur tennis player who in 1974 ranked third in the East and 13th nationally in the men's 35-and-over division. Last week, before curious crowds buzzing with debate, the 42-year-old ophthalmologist reached the semifinal round of a women's tournament in South Orange, N.J.

When Dr. Richards was accepted into the Tennis Week open by the tournament director, a longtime friend, 25 women players withdrew in protest. They argued that Dr. Richards's presence was unfair, that despite her operation and resulting feminine appearance, she still retained the muscular advantages of a male and genetically remained a male. Dr. Richards questions the validity of sex identification through genes, and insists that bodily, psychologically and socially she is female. "I do not feel that I have an unfair advantage over other women in athletic competi-

tion," said Dr. Richards, who is 6 feet 2 inches tall. Under her new name and sex, she has been given new official papers, such as a passport, certificate to practice medicine and other licenses. "In the eyes of the law," she says, "I am female."

Dr. Richards had planned to enter the United States Open, which begins tomor-

The transsexual player Renee Richards in a 6-1, 6-4 loss to Virginia Wade at the U.S. Open in 1977. She obtained a court order allowing her to play after being barred for refusing to take a chromosome test the year before. (Associated Press)

row. But she was thwarted by the United States Tennis Association, which for the first time instituted a chromosome test as a prerequisite for women entries. Dr. Richards has refused to take the test and is considering legal action against the U.S.T.A.

Should Dr. Richards, an admitted transsexual, be permitted to compete against women who have been females from birth? By instituting the sex test, the U.S.T.A. is belatedly following the lead of

the International Olympic Committee. At the 1968 Olympics in Mexico, the I.O.C. made the chromosome test mandatory for competitors in women's events. In most cases a male will show an XY pattern of chromosomes, a female XX. The only athlete known to have failed a femininity test was Ewa Klobukowska, a Polish sprinter. She was ruled ineligible for the European Cup women's track and field competition in 1967. A year later the I.A.A.F. took away the gold and bronze medals she had won in the 1964 Olympics.

Although Dr. Richards had a sex-change operation just last year, she emphasizes that she does not belong to the imposters against whom sex tests were first meant to guard. Dr. Richards entered and won her first women's tournament last month in La Jolla, Calif. At that time she did not make it known that she was a transsexual. Reporters investigating her background subsequently discovered her former identity. "I'm not a full-time major league tennis player," she said at South Orange. "I'm here to make a point. It's a human rights issue. I want to show that someone who has a different lifestyle or medical condition, has a right to stand up for what they are."

Challenging the imposition of the chromosome test, Renee Richards obtained a court order admitting her into the 1977 United States Open. She lost in the first round to the No. 3 seed and Wimbledon champion Virginia Wade (see July 1).

Runners-up

1982: Twenty-three-year-old Rickey Henderson of the Oakland A's stole his 119th base of the season in the third inning of a 5–4 loss to the host Milwaukee Brewers, breaking Lou Brock's major-league record set with the St. Louis Cardinals in 1974. Henderson finished the year with 130 stolen bases, still the single-season record, and broke Brock's career record of 938 steals in 1991 (*see May 1*).

1978: Second baseman Joe Morgan of the Cincinnati Reds, one of the greatest packages of speed and power in baseball history, became the first major

leaguer to hit 200 home runs and steal 500 bases when he homered off Mike Krukow in a game against the Chicago Cubs at Riverfront Stadium.

1973: The N.H.L. voted to expand from 16 teams, adding the Washington Capitals and Kansas City Scouts (now the New Jersey Devils) for the 1974–75 season. The league was up to 21 teams with the absorption of World Hockey Association franchises by 1979–80, unleashing supply-and-demand forces that are plaguing the league today.

August 28, 1981
Coe Over Ovett. Ovett Over Coe

By NEIL AMDUR

NEW YORK—Sebastian Coe of Britain ran the mile in 3 minutes 47.33 seconds at an international track and field meet in Brussels tonight, marking the third time in 10 days that the world record for the distance had been broken. Coe, 24 years old, regained the record from a countryman, Steve Ovett, who had run the mile in 3:48.40 two days before in Koblenz, West Germany. Ovett had originally entered tonight's race but withdrew several weeks ago, saying that when he races Coe for the first time in the mile, he wants to do so on British soil.

That Coe and Ovett, both Englishmen, have never met in a mile, instead maintaining their intense rivalry through separate world-record races, remains an irony in an event that has seen a surge of record-breaking. Until this summer,

Ovett's 3:48.53 in Oslo last year had been the record. On Aug. 19, in Zurich, Coe ran 3:48.53. On Wednesday, one week later, Ovett reclaimed the record with his 3:48.40.

"It was fast," Coe said of tonight's performance, which took place before a cheering crowd of nearly 50,000 at Heysel Stadium. "But I think there is still a little bit more to come out of it." In cutting 1.07 seconds from the previous record, Coe brought about the biggest reduction in the time for the mile since 1975, when John Walker of New Zealand ran 3:49.4, eclipsing the 3:51.0 clocked earlier that year by Filbert Bayi of Tanzania.

Tom Byers of the United States paced the field tonight through a first lap of 54.92 seconds, a time that Coe had said would set him up for a chance at the

record. The half-mile time, 1:52.67, with Coe stalking Byers, was almost a second faster than the pace in Ovett's race two days earlier. A temperature of 71 degrees and an enthusiastic crowd provided Coe perfect finishing conditions in a field that included Mike Boit of Kenya, who finished second in 3:49.45, and Steve Scott, the Californian and holder of the American record (3:49.68), who was third in 3:51.48.

The mile has long been track and field's most popular event. One reason is its familiarity as a standard measure of distance in the United States and Britain. A second was the old competitive barrier of four minutes, an easily identifiable standard that withstood repeated challenges until Roger Bannister's historic 3:59.4 in 1954 *(see May 6)*.

"Bannister used to send a commemorative tie to each runner who broke four minutes," Craig Masback, an American sub-four-minute miler, wrote in The New York Times last month in assessing the mile's mystique. "Though he would have to open an outlet of Tie City to fill the current need, the aura surrounding four-minute miles endures. In spite of the record's having fallen below 3:50, four minutes remains to the casual sports fan an easily remembered benchmark separating a good performance from an average one. And for the philosopher of life, it is still a symbol of individual human achievement."

The ever versatile Sebastian Coe held world records in the mile, 800 meters and 1,000 meters. His mile mark fell to Britain's Steve Cram, who ran 3:46.32 in 1985. The current mile record, 3:43.13, is held by Hicham El Guerrouj of Morocco.

Sebastian Coe of Britain winning the 1,500 meters at the 1980 Moscow Olympics with his countryman and rival, Steve Ovett (279), finishing third. Coe and Ovett traded world records in the mile in 1981. (Associated Press)

Runners-up

1977: The great Pelé played in his final game as the New York Cosmos defeated the Seattle Sounders, 2–1, for the North American Soccer League championship before a crowd of 35,548 in Portland, Ore. Pelé retired to Brazil and eventually became the nation's minister of sports.

1954: Arnold Palmer, 24, of whom a lot more would be heard in the years just to come *(see June 18)*, won the United States Amateur championship at the Country Club of Detroit in Grosse Pointe Farms, Mich. He wiped out a two-hole

morning deficit with a final-round 70, good for a 1-up victory over the 43-year-old veteran Robert Sweeny.

1978: Donald Vesco of Loma Linda, Calif., raced his special 21-foot-long Kawasaki motorcycle named Lightning Bolt to a cycling land speed record of 318.598 miles an hour at the Bonneville Salt Flats in Utah. The mark was broken by Dave Campos of New Mexico on a Harley-Davidson called Easy Rider in 1990.

August 29, 1974
One Day a Schoolboy, Next Day a Pro

By GERALD ESKENAZI

NEW YORK—Moses Malone became the highest salaried teen-age athlete in the United States today by choosing a seven-year professional basketball deal, with a potential value of $3 million, instead of playing for the University of Maryland. The 19-year-old from Petersburg, Va., 6 feet 11 inches tall, was acclaimed as the country's top high school basketball star last season. Although he posted only a C average throughout high school, more than 300 colleges offered him scholarships—about a quarter of all the colleges in the United States that field basketball teams.

In becoming the first player to go directly from high school to pro basketball, Malone was also offered a $120,000 scholarship fund by the Utah Stars of the American Basketball Association. He will get $30,000 as a bonus for every year of college he completes if he decides to attend any college of his choice in the off season.

Young Malone's mother works as a $100-a-week packer in a supermarket. She said, "I put the price on the meat." The price of basketball talent was the main theme today during the Malone news conference, held at the Royal Box of the Americana Hotel. His mother, Mary, sat quietly next to her 210-pound only child. All questions of money were dismissed as "personal" by his lawyer, Lee Fentress of Washington, and by Jim Collier, the Stars' president. They had been with Malone day and night for the previous four days, interrupted occasionally by Coach Lefty Driesell, who left the Maryland campus to try to persuade Malone to keep his commitment to the school. Malone had agreed to go to Maryland, where classes began this week. Driesell is considered one of the country's most persuasive recruiters.

Moses Malone of the Utah Stars making sure a tap-in had fallen against the New York Nets in October 1974. Two months earlier he had become the first basketball player to jump straight from high school to the pros. (Associated Press)

However, the Stars drafted Malone last spring, which meant they had the rights to negotiate with him. Many observers believed they had selected him as a publicity stunt, since no player ever had been asked to make the move directly to the pro ranks. Collier, the club owner, conceded he might face situations a pro club never had to contend with before because of Malone's age. "We've got a teen-ager on our hands," he said. "We'll have to place him with the right people on the club."

An increasing number of players, including current stars such as Kobe Bryant of the Los Angeles Lakers and Kevin Garnett of the Minnesota Timberwolves, have followed Moses Malone's precedent of going straight to the pros from high school. In 1987, nine collegiate underclassmen or high schoolers declared for the N.B.A. draft. In 2002, 45 did.

Runners-up

1977: Lou Brock of the St. Louis Cardinals stole two bases against the San Diego Padres at Jack Murphy Stadium, bringing his career total to 893 and breaking the mark that Ty Cobb set 49 years before. Brock retired in 1979 with 938 stolen bases and is second all-time to Rickey Henderson (see May 1).

1920: John Kelly of the United States won a gold medal in the single sculls at the Antwerp Olympics in Belgium, narrowly beating the great British rower Jack Beresford. Kelly, the father of Grace Kelly, the actress and later princess of

Monaco, won gold in the double sculls with Paul Costello 30 minutes later.

1965: Casey Stengel, 75, who led the Yankees to 10 pennants and seven World Series titles between 1949 and 1960, retired as manager of the Mets for health reasons after a 56-year career in baseball. He was an outfielder for the Brooklyn Dodgers and New York Giants, among other teams, early in the century.

August 30, 1991
Shattering the 'Unbreakable' Record

By MICHAEL JANOFSKY

TOKYO—For more than two decades, it was considered the one record that would stand for the ages: Bob Beamon's extraordinary long jump in the 1968 Mexico City Olympics. If the record would ever be broken it would have to come in the thin air of high altitude, and if anyone was going to break it, it would be Carl Lewis, the outstanding Olympian who has chased Beamon for a decade. But all those suppositions were swept aside at the world track and field championships tonight as Mike Powell of Alta Loma, Calif., made a stunning leap of 29 feet 4¼ inches, 2 inches beyond Beamon's mark, the oldest record in track and field.

At the same time, Powell also passed Lewis, who had finally fulfilled the quest of a lifetime not 15 minutes before when he bettered Beamon's 29-foot-2½-inch record by a quarter of an inch. Even though the leap would not have counted as a world record because the tail wind was too strong, the mark was still a milestone for Lewis, who had never before cleared 29 feet. The competition ended not long after that as Lewis reached 29 feet twice more but failed to improve on his best mark. At the moment his final effort fell short, the actions of both jumpers revealed instantly what a momentous event had just occurred.

Powell leaped into the air and came down dancing, then charged toward a nearby official, hugged him and danced away. "I was so

Mike Powell of the U.S. in the long jump at the world track and field championships in Tokyo. He broke the record that seemingly couldn't be broken—Bob Beamon's mark of 29 feet 2½ inches in the 1968 Olympics. (Getty Images)

happy," Powell said later, the mood still evident. "I just wanted to share it with somebody and he happened to be in the way." At the same time, Lewis looked dazed, almost as if he had been shot and didn't know it.

They were entirely justified in their reactions. In the years since Oct. 18, 1968, when Beamon soared through the rarified air more than 7,000 feet above sea level in Mexico City, one record has replaced another in every other of the sport's many disciplines. But not in the long jump, where Beamon's mark loomed as gargantuan now as it did then, when he stretched the existing record by almost two feet. In the process of chasing Beamon's record down, Lewis built a staggering record in the long jump— victories in 65 consecutive meets over 10 years, 56 jumps of 28 feet or better and a personal best of 28-10¼, which he accomplished twice. At no time was he ever not favored to win, and as the victories mounted, surpassing Beamon became an obsession, if not with the 30-year-old Lewis, then certainly with the public.

Powell, meanwhile, had spent part of the last eight years as one of Lewis's many foils. Fifteen times they competed against each other, and Lewis's advantage was 15–0. Still, Powell's confidence never flagged, and this week it was brimming. "I was so psyched up, so motivated, I was almost hyperventilating," he said.

Runners-up

1979: In a classic, tumultuous United States Open match, notorious Ilie Nastase lost to infamous John McEnroe in four sets after Nastase had been held in default by the umpire only to be reinstated by the referee. Both players hurled invectives at each other in the televised night match and play was delayed some 20 minutes while fans erupted, tossing beer cans and other trash on the court.

1904: Thomas Hicks of Cambridge, Mass., won the third modern Olympic marathon in St. Louis in 3 hours 28 minutes 53 seconds, collapsing at the finish line amid 90-degree heat and 90 percent humidity. Another of the 32 starters, Fred Lorz of the Mohawk Athletic Club of New York, finished 15 minutes ahead of Hicks but was disqualified when it was learned he rode in a car for 11 of the 26-plus miles.

1978: Sadaharu Oh of the Yomiuri Giants of Japan's Central League, the 38-year-old Hank Aaron of the Far East, hit his 800th home run, by far the most in the history of Japanese baseball. The historic ball landed in the shoe of a fan who had removed it to feel more comfortable.

August 31, 1972
84 Lbs. of Vinegar

MUNICH, West Germany (UPI)— Everything about Olga Korbut of the Soviet Union is tiny except her talent as a gymnast, and that was big enough to win her two gold medals and one silver in individual competition at the 20th Olympics tonight. Miss Korbut so dominated the evening performances that East Germany's accomplished Karin Janz, who also won two gold medals and one bronze, was only mildly acknowledged.

Miss Korbut, 17 years old, 4-feet 11-inches tall and weighing only 84 pounds, was adopted by the fans from her first appearance in the preliminary exercises earlier this week. She then proceeded to show them she had the ability to match her charm. She won the individual gold medal for the balance beam exercises with 19,400 points and the floor exercises with 19,575. In each case, she just squeaked by a compatriot. Tamara Lazakovitch won the silver medal with 19,375 points in the first event and, in the second, the silver went to Liudmila Turistschewa with 19,550.

The bronze medals in those disciplines went to Miss Janz with 18,975 points, and Miss Lazakovitch, with 19,450. Miss Janz won her gold in the long horse and the uneven parallel bars. In the first event, she garnered

19,675 points and in the second 19,525. Miss Korbut and the East Germany glamor girl, Erika Zuchold, tied for second place in the uneven bars with 19,450 points. In the long horse, Miss Zuchold got another silver with 19,275. Miss Turistschewa of the U.S.S.R. was third with 19,250.

Olga Korbut's performance at the Munich Games, caught by ABC's television cameras and transmitted around the world, turned her into an international celebrity virtually overnight and made gymnastics a premier attraction of the Olympics. Its popularity continued to soar with the perfect 10's scored by Nadia Comaneci of Romania at the Montreal Games in 1976 (see July 21).

Eighty-four-pound Olga Korbut, 17, of the Soviet Union, earning a gold medal on the balance beam in the Munich Olympics. She turned women's gymnastics into one of the Games' marquee events virtually overnight. (UPI/Bettman)

Runners-up

1959: Sandy Koufax, aged 23, of the Los Angeles Dodgers, just emerging as the most overpowering pitcher of his era *(see Sept. 9),* tied Bob Feller's major league single-game strikeout record of 18 in a 5–2 victory over the San Francisco Giants before a crowd of 82,974 at Los Angeles Memorial Coliseum. Koufax struck out 15 of the last 17 Giants to face him.

1934: The first College Football All-Star Game, pitting a star team of college seniors against the N.F.L. championship team of the previous season, was played to a scoreless tie before a crowd of 79,432 at Soldier Field in Chicago. The

charity game, invented by the Chicago Tribune sports editor Arch Ward, became a highlight of the national sports calendar for 42 years.

1980: Giorgio Chinaglia scored seven goals, a North American Soccer League single-game record, in leading the Cosmos over the Tulsa Roughnecks, 8–1, in the N.A.S.L. playoff quarterfinals before a crowd of 40,285 at Giants Stadium in New Jersey. The Cosmos won the N.A.S.L. championship, their third in four years.

SEPTEMBER

September 1, 1985
The Hottest, Richest Foot

By STEVE POTTER

DARLINGTON, S.C. (AP)—Bill Elliott, driving a conservative race, watched three of his top competitors go up in smoke on his way to winning both the Southern 500 Grand National stock car race today and a $1 million bonus. Elliott, who earned his 10th victory in 20 starts this season, made it three out of four in the Grand National "Big Four" and picked up the Winston Million, the biggest single payoff in the history of auto racing, as he outran Cale Yarborough, the five-time Southern 500 winner, to the finish line by six-hundredths of a second. "It all turned out, but I knew if I made one mistake, Cale would be right there to take advantage of it," Elliott said.

Eight days before Bill Elliott won the Southern 500 and the $1 million prize, the following article, by Mr. Potter, appeared in The Times.

NEW YORK—It has been 13 years since anyone has dominated stock-car racing as Bill Elliott has this season. The 29-year-old driver from Dawsonville, Ga., has won 9 of 18 races run so far this year. Driving a Ford Thunderbird prepared by his father and brothers, Elliott has won more than $750,000 in 1985. He not only leads the Winston Cup point standing, but on Labor Day he has an opportunity to add $1 million to his prize money total.

At the Nascar banquet last November in New York, Gerald Long, the president of R.J. Reynolds Tobacco Co., announced that Reynolds would pay that sum to any driver who won three of the four most prestigious stock car races on the 1985 calendar. Elliott breezed to victory in the Daytona 500 in February, nursed his car

back from a two-lap deficit to capture the Winston 500 at Talladega, Ala., in May, but then lost the World 600 at Charlotte, N.C., on Memorial Day when his brakes failed. Elliott's final opportunity to claim the bonus comes in the oldest race on the stock car circuit, the Southern 500 at Darlington, S.C., a week from tomorrow.

Close competition among many drivers and cars has helped boost stock-car racing's popularity in the last decade, and Nascar has helped keep the competition close through judicious and frequent rule changes. And although "stock cars" are far from stock, under their sheet metal exterior, most of them are more or less similar. If any one car model seems to be gaining a significant advantage over the rest of the field, Nascar's rule makers take out their pencils and start revising the rule book. So far this season they have acted twice to slow Ford models, although some insiders point out that all of the Fords have not been going fast, just the Elliotts. The rules changes have angered Ernie Elliott, who builds the team's engines. "I feel like Nascar has aimed these rules changes specifically at us," he said to a television interviewer after the sanctioning body announced new carbure-

tor rules in June. Later he added, "We've still got some things up our sleeves though."

Bill Elliott won 11 races in 1985, second only to Richard Petty's 27 in '67, but lost his season-long points lead in the last event of the season. Darrell Waltrip, who won just three races, took the Winston Cup championship instead.

Bill Elliott receiving the 1985 Daytona 500 trophy with his wife at his side and his daughter, wearing his helmet, behind him. He soon hit the jackpot by winning the Winston 500 at Talladega and the Southern 500 at Darlington. (Associated Press)

Runners-up

1989: Eight days after announcing an agreement that banned Pete Rose from baseball for life, Commissioner A. Bartlett Giamatti *(see Aug. 24)*, a Renaissance scholar, English professor and former president of Yale University, died after a heart attack on Martha's Vineyard, Mass. He was 51.

1972: In a race long considered the United States' by eminent domain, Valery Borzov of the Soviet Union won the 100-meter gold medal at the Munich Olympics, defeating Robert Taylor of the United States in 10.14 seconds. The American Eddie Hart, Borzov's greatest threat in the event, was disqualified the day

before in the quarterfinals for arriving late for the start.

1946: The golfer Patty Berg *(see April 26)* won the first United States Women's Open at Spokane (Wash.) Country Club, defeating Betty Jameson, 5 and 4, in the 36-hole final. The Open soon became a showcase for women's golf. Berg, whose role in women's golf as both a player and a leader cannot be overestimated, became one of the founders of the Ladies Professional Golf Association in 1949.

Night Stalker of the Open

By HARVEY ARATON

NEW YORK—He was not going to lose, not now, not this far into his birthday, having so appropriately fallen on the day America's workers had the chance to sit home and watch the all-time champion of blue collar tennis. High above the Stadium Court, Arthur Ashe, who as much as anyone must have known this, began talking about 1978, a United States Open final between Jimmy Connors and Bjorn Borg. "Were you here for that one?" Ashe asked, during a changeover late in the fifth set. "He was unbelievable that day. He was flying. He just took Borg apart." Ashe knew the scores, 6–4, 6–2, 6–2. "If you're talking about Connors's performances here, to me, that was first."

He paused for a moment, running through a mental file to make sure he was not forgetting any others. Then he nodded confidently. "This," he said, "is second."

Ashe, himself a champion here in 1968, looked through the glass of the press box, at a crowd seized with delirium, and at Connors parading around his half of the court after another mad rush to the net had put him into a fifth-set tie breaker against a 24-year-old, Aaron Krickstein. The match was well into its fifth hour and the court was all shadow now, so it was easy to see that Connors, the Night Stalker of the Open, was exactly where he wanted to be. "This is what I live for, to win a match 7–6 in the fifth," he would say before going off to find a doctor to examine his battered bones and a trainer to administer the mother of all rubdowns.

And that is how we come to this place, to 39-year-old Jimmy Connors in the quarterfinals of an Open he has simply taken over. Of all the explanations and the analyses that were heard tonight,

Connors's was the simplest and indisputably the best. He lives for those fifth-set tie-breaker moments, and who else would make that claim? The kids play this game for the rankings, the money, the endorsements. They play the match to get it over with, so the computer can record the victory and the bank can accept the deposit. They play with the burden of millions on their backs, and they do it for the most part without passion, joy or understanding of their work.

John McEnroe, to cite a player closer to Connors's age, chases his own legend around the world, doomed to run a distant second. But Connors has few of the kids' concerns and none of McEnroe's historical angst. He said, "This is still my job," but it is one he holds not out of necessity but of choice. Here is that rare athlete who had the champion's run, experienced mortality and somehow has been granted a second, less-pressured life he can live with. "I'm in a beautiful position, finally, after 22 years," he said tonight at a news conference during which he wouldn't sit down for fear of making a "sudden move in the

wrong direction." In other words, everything hurt. "I can play against all of these kids the way they played against me all those years." He meant without fear of losing, none whatsoever.

Jimmy Connors, the 39-year-old people's choice of Flushing Meadows, exulting after his fourth-round U.S. Open victory over Aaron Krickstein, 24. The triumph took five sets, 4 hours 42 minutes, and an uncommon spirit of resolution. (Associated Press)

Runners-up

1960: Wilma Rudolph of Tennessee State University, hobbled as a child by polio that required leg braces, became the world's fastest woman by winning the 100-meter dash at the Rome Olympics (her semifinal heat of 11.3 seconds had tied the world record). She also won gold medals in the 200 meters and the 4x100 relay.

1972: Dave Wottle of Canton, Ohio, distinctive for always running with a cap, unleashed a furious kick in the 800 meters at the Munich Olympics, passing Kenyan Mike Boit and leaning across the finish line to nip Yevgeny Arzhanov of

the Soviet Union. Wottle, an R.O.T.C. member in college, forgot to remove his cap during the national anthem at the medal ceremony and later issued an apology.

2001: Mike Mussina came within one strike of throwing the fourth perfect game in Yankee history when Carl Everett of the Boston Red Sox singled to left on a 1–2 count with two outs in the ninth inning at Fenway Park. "I'm going to think about it until I retire," Mussina said.

September 3, 1972
Down But Not Out

By ARTHUR DALEY

MUNICH, West Germany—With a fancier flourish than ever was used by Paavo Nurmi and Finland's other great Olympic distance-running champions of yesteryear, the 23-year-old Lasse Viren rebounded from the brink of disaster to win the classic 10,000-meter title today. Knocked down in a traffic tangle somewhere near the midway mark, the handsome young man with the tightly cropped beard climbed off the deck and set out in pursuit of the leaders 60 yards ahead. After he caught them, he not only went on to score a smashing victory but also set a world record of 27 minutes 38.3 seconds.

That had to be the most amazing part of the high drama of today's track and field phase of an international carnival that continues to draw packed houses of 80,000 customers for both morning and matinee sessions. They bathed in bright sunshine and in the reflected glory of the greatest day West Germany ever produced in Olympic competition, three gold medals. But the show stealer had to be Viren, who may be leading a renaissance to Finland's past glories in distance running. From 1912 to 1936 the Finns took 24 Olympic championships and dominated that phase of the competition. But the Russian invasion of Finland in 1939 and the ensuing war seemed to bring a long pause to Finnish distance running. This may signal the return.

It hardly could have been more dramatic. For most of the early going Dave Bedford of Britain, a colorful character who talks a better race than he runs, was out in front. It was an almost unchanging procession: Bedford, Merus Yifter of Ethiopia, Emiel Puttemans of Belgium, Mariano Haro of Spain, Viren and eventu-

Lasse Viren (228) of Finland in the Olympic 10,000 meters in Munich. He was knocked down in traffic earlier, got up, closed a 60-yard gap, passed David Bedford (274) of England for the lead and still won in world-record time. (Associated Press)

ally Frank Shorter of the United States. When Viren tumbled in the backstretch along with Mohamed Gammoudi of Tunisia, the 5,000-meter champion of 1968, both seemed finished. The Tunisian actually dropped out. But the indomitable Finn hadn't started to run. In less than half a lap he had rejoined the leaders and was definitely back in contention.

With 9½ laps to go, Viren whipped past Bedford and sent the Britisher into permanent decline. With two laps Haro, the surprising Spaniard, took brief command. Viren reclaimed the lead, fought Puttemans around the last turn and beat

him by eight yards. Yifter was third and Haro fourth. In fifth place was Shorter and his time of 27:51.4 represents an American record. After the race Viren waved his way for an extra circuit of the track. He was joined by four long-haired and trousered Finns and his newfound friends joyously waved a Finnish flag. It was a lovely touch for the embellishment of a noble victory.

On Sept. 10, Lasse Viren won his second gold medal of the Munich Games, winning the 5,000 meters in an Olympic-record 13:26.4. He also became a double gold medalist in the 5,000 and 10,000 at the 1976 Games at Montreal.

Runners-up

1911: William Larned of Summit, N.J., won his fifth straight United States national tennis championship at Forest Hills, N.Y., defeating Maurice McLoughlin of San Francisco in straight sets at age 38. Larned, the premier male player of the early century, won seven United States titles between 1901 and '11.

1935: Sir Malcolm Campbell of Kent, England, became the first person to drive over 300 miles an hour when he pushed his 28-foot, 12,000-pound, 2,500-horse-power *Blue Bird* to a land speed record of 301.203 m.p.h. at the Bonneville

Salt Flats in Utah (see Nov. 15). Campbell soon turned his attention to setting world water speed records.

1895: John Brallier, a quarterback from Indiana College in Pennsylvania, accepted $10 and "cakes" (expenses) to play for Latrobe, Pa., in a game against neighboring Jeannette—and for decades was considered the first pro football player. The Pro Football Hall of Fame uncovered evidence in 1963 that William (Pudge) Heffelfinger was the first (see Nov. 12).

September 4, 1972
Of Gold and Drugs

By NEIL AMDUR

MUNICH, West Germany—To nobody's surprise, Mark Spitz won his seventh gold medal of the Olympics tonight with a seventh world-record swimming performance. But the luster of Spitz's final race and subsequent world-record victories by Mike Burton, Melissa Belote and Karen Moe were tarnished by the stunning disqualification of an asthmatic American swimming gold medalist on drugging charges.

The 22-year-old Spitz, in what may have been his final race before he retires to pursue a career in dentistry, swam the butterfly leg in the 400-meter medley relay. The Californian turned a tight team duel with East Germany into a two body-length lead for Jerry Heidenreich on the anchor free-style leg, as the Americans clocked 3 minutes 48.16 seconds. The victory in the concluding race of the swimming competition gave Spitz four individual golds [100 and 200-free-style and 100 and 200 butterfly] and three relay titles— an achievement unequaled by a single athlete in one Olympics.

But even as Spitz and his teammates received a standing ovation from the capacity crowd of 10,000, some members of the American team were in tears over the disqualification of Rick DeMont, a 16-year-old high school senior from San Rafael, Calif. DeMont, who won the 400-meter free-style earlier in the competition, was dropped from the finals of the 1,500 minutes before the race tonight because his doping test had turned up positive following the 400.

Kenneth Treadway, manager of the

men's team, said that DeMont regularly takes a prescription known as Malax, which contains an ephedrine. DeMont listed the special medication on his Olympic forms during final processing in the

Mark Spitz displaying the five swimming gold medals he had by Aug. 31 at the Munich Games. Within the next five days he won a sixth and a seventh— the most ever, regardless of sport, in a single Olympics. (Associated Press)

United States, but American team doctors apparently did not clear the prescription with the medical committee of the International Olympic Committee. "He's been taking that medication since he was a little boy," said Mrs. Betty DeMont, who tried to comfort her tearful son when he was informed of the disqualification at poolside.

According to the drug control manual of the I.O.C. medical committee, ephedrine is included among a group of

drugs or related amphetamines that can affect an athlete's performance. "They have a particular point of attack in the vegetative nervous system, in addition to their central stimulating effect and the resulting elimination of fatigue," the manual, printed earlier this summer, states on the reason for the ban. "These drugs, as well as some of different pharmaceutical nature, which act similarly such as ephedrine . . . increase the fonicity of the sympathetic nerves which must be active in any great exertion."

The decision to disqualify DeMont was made after a recheck of his urinalysis today, and a second meeting of the I.O.C. Medical Committee. His first urinalysis after the 400 had proved positive. The committee granted DeMont an opportunity to explain the situation earlier today, but ruled that he was to be disqualified from the 1,500. "The question of whether he will have to return his medal will be submitted to the I.O.C. Executive Committee," Prince Alexandre de Merode, chairman of the Medical Committee, said. The tests proved positive 12 parts in a million—a trace one doctor here described as an "infinitesmal amount."

Mark Spitz retired from swimming after the Games, becoming a poster boy and making commercials for Schick and Speedo. He later had a successful career in real estate. Rick DeMont had to return his gold medal. Later the assistant head swim coach at the University of Arizona, he has continually asked for it back, only to be denied.

Runners-up

1951: Maureen (Little Mo) Connolly, 16, of San Diego, became an American tennis sensation by winning the United States women's nationals at Forest Hills, N.Y., in three sets over Shirley Fry of Akron, Ohio. Connolly won three straight U.S. titles *(see Sept. 7)* and, in 1953, the first Grand Slam by a woman, but her career was cut short by a horse-riding accident.

1993: Jim Abbott of the Yankees, the former University of Michigan star and United States baseball Olympian who was born without a right hand, pitched a 4–0

no-hitter against the visiting Cleveland Indians. He got Carlos Baerga to ground out to shortstop Randy Velarde for the final out.

1976: Billy Haughton, driving the 3-year-old trotter Steve Lobell, won the Hambletonian Classic, trotting's crown jewel, in an exhausting fourth-heat race-off in scorching weather at the Du Quoin State Fairgrounds in Illinois. The horse collapsed in his stable after going into shock but was later revived. The Hambletonian now has a three-heat limit.

September 5, 1972
The Munich Massacre

By DAVID BINDER

MUNICH, West Germany—Eleven members of Israel's Olympic team and four Arab terrorists were killed today in a 23-hour drama that began with an invasion of the Olympic Village by Arabs. It ended in a shootout at a military airport some 15 miles away as the Arabs were preparing to fly to Cairo with their Israeli hostages.

The first two Israelis were killed early this morning when Arab commandos, armed with automatic rifles, broke into the quarters of the Israeli team and seized nine others as hostages. The hostages were killed in the airport shootout between the Arabs and German policeman and soldiers. In addition to the slain Israelis and Arabs, a German policeman was killed and a helicopter pilot was critically wounded. Three Arabs were wounded. The bloodshed brought the suspension of the Olympic Games and there was doubt if they would be resumed. Willi Daume, president of the West German Organizing Committee, announced that he would ask the International Olympic Committee to meet tomorrow to decide whether they should continue.

The bloodbath at the airport, which ended around midnight, came after long hours of negotiation between Germans and Arabs at the Israeli quarters in the Olympic Village where the Arabs demanded the release of 200 Arab commandos imprisoned in Israel. Finally the West German armed forces supplied three helicopters to transport the Arabs and their Israeli hostages to the airport at Fürstenfeldbruck. From there all were to be flown to Cairo. A Boeing 707 provided by the Lufthansa German Airlines was waiting.

Two of the terrorists, carrying their automatic rifles, walked about 170 yards from the helicopters to the plane. And then they started back to pick up the other Arabs and the hostages. As the Arabs were returning, German sharpshooters reportedly opened fire from the darkness beyond the pools of light at the airport. The

Arabs returned fire. How the hostages were killed was still in doubt. One theory was that an Arab threw a grenade into a helicopter in which some or all of the hostages were bound hand and foot.

Partial explanation of how the Arabs knew so much about the Israeli compound in the Olympic Village came from Dr. Bruno Merk, the Interior Minister of Bavaria. He said that at least one of the terrorists was an official employee in the village and that there was reason to believe some of his confederates had also obtained accreditation. The idea of trying to liberate the hostages at the Olympic Village was rejected, Dr. Merk said, because it could have "involved athletes from other nations" living nearby.

After the terrorists killed two Israelis and took control of the Olympic Village, a number of events continued until activities were suspended late in the day. Despite the carnage at the airport, Avery Brundage, chairman of the International Olympic Committee, famously said, "The Games must go on," and 34 hours later competition resumed.

The coffin of David Berger, one of 11 Israeli team members killed at the Munich Games. Above right, a Palestinian terrorist within the Olympic Village. "They're all gone," the ABC-TV announcer Jim McKay intoned when confirmation came in. (Associated Press)

Runners-up

1994: Wide receiver Jerry Rice of the San Francisco 49ers *(see Dec. 14)* scored three touchdowns in a 44–14 victory over the Los Angeles Raiders at Candlestick Park. The last touchdown, on a reception from Steve Young late in the fourth quarter, was the 127th of Rice's career, breaking Jim Browr's N.F.L. record. Rice had 192 regular-season touchdowns through 2002.

1960: Cassius Clay of Louisville, Ky., won a unanimous decision over the three-time European champion Zbigniew Pietrzytkowski of Poland to win the gold medal in the light-heavyweight division at the Rome Olympics. The 18-year-old Clay had his first pro bout as a heavyweight seven weeks later against Tunney Hunsaker, the police chief of Fayetteville, W. Va.

1918: The national anthem was sung for the first time at a sporting event in the middle of the seventh inning of Game 1 of the World Series between the Boston Red Sox and the Chicago Cubs at Comiskey Park. The Series, the last won by the Red Sox, was held at the White Sox' park for more seating and four weeks early because the government ordered the regular season ended early because of World War I.

Ripken Steps Into the History Books

By MURRAY CHASS

BALTIMORE—In the brightest, most dramatic development of a season damaged by an unresolved labor dispute, Cal Ripken defied the odds of probability and baseball reality tonight, playing in his 2,131st consecutive game. That was one more game than Lou Gehrig achieved in his legendary streak that stood untouched—and was believed to be untouchable—for 56 years.

Gehrig's record, which Ripken broke on the Baltimore Orioles' home field at Camden Yards, was not as glamorous as many others in baseball lore—Babe Ruth's 60 home runs in a season and 714 in his career, for example—but Ripken's ability to break it was perhaps an even more remarkable feat. Playing every game for 13½ seasons certainly was thought to be beyond the grasp of the modern-day player.

"Tonight, I stand here, overwhelmed, as my name is linked with the great and courageous Lou Gehrig," Ripken said at the conclusion of an hourlong post-game ceremony. "I'm truly humbled to have our names spoken in the same breath. Some may think our strongest connection is because we played many consecutive games. Yet I believe in my heart that our true link is a common motivation—a love of the game of baseball, a passion for our team and a desire to compete on the very highest level."

The record-setting game against the California Angels was sufficiently scintillating to attract President Clinton, Vice President Al Gore, Joe DiMaggio and other notables. They joined a crowd of 46,272 in saluting the 35-year-old Ripken at every opportunity—when Rex Barney, the former pitcher and public address announcer, announced his name in the starting lineup; when he ran on the field for the start of the game, and when he batted for the first time, at the start of the second inning.

On Ripken's second time at bat, in the fourth inning, he lined a 3–0 pitch from Shawn Boskie into the left-field seats for his 15th home run of the season and a 3–1 Oriole lead en route to a 4–2 victory. The blow continued Ripken's sizzling recent hitting. Throughout the streak, some have criticized Ripken for not resting once in a while, saying his daily presence on the field tired him and weakened his hitting. But the home run was the third he had hit in the last three games, and his two hits in four at-bats raised his batting average to .390 in the last 10 games.

Fans saved their longest and loudest ovation for the moment at the end of the California half of the fifth inning, when the game became official and the number 1 was unfolded to replace the number 0 on the warehouse wall behind the right-field stands, making the 10-foot numbers read 2 1 3 1. For 20 thunderous, spine-tingling minutes, the Camden Yards populace roared for Ripken, forcing him out of the first-base dugout time and time again. At the 10-minute mark, Rafael Palmeiro, the Orioles' first baseman, and Bobby Bonilla pushed Ripken into a lap around the field.

"They said we'll never get this game going if you don't run around the field," Ripken said at a news conference after the post-game ceremony. "I said I didn't have the energy to make it. They said, 'Then walk.'"

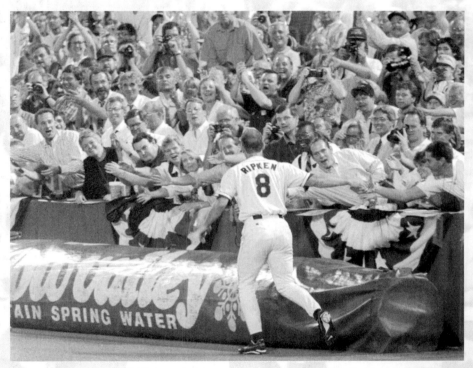

The eyes of Baltimore are on Cal Ripken as he takes a victory lap around Camden Yards after playing in 2,131 consecutive games, one more than Lou Gehrig. It took Ripken 13 seasons to break the record but only 20 minutes to celebrate it. (Associated Press)

Runners-up

1920: Establishing himself as the finest tennis player in the world (see Sept. 19), 27-year-old Bill Tilden of Philadelphia defeated Bill Johnston of San Francisco in five arduous sets to win his first United States tennis championship. Tilden had defeated Gerald Patterson of Australia at Wimbledon in July.

1960: In an epic duel against his U.C.L.A. teammate C.K. Yang of Taiwan, Rafer Johnson won the gold medal in the decathlon by 58 points at the Rome Olympics. Johnson lost 7 of the 10 events, but his superiority in the shot-put, the discus and the javelin and his ability to stay close in the final 1,500 meters was the difference.

1976: Chris Evert won her second straight United States Open tennis title, defeating Evonne Goolagong of Australia, 6–3, 6–0, and capping her three-year run as the top women's player in the world. Only 21 years old, Evert had already won two Wimbledon titles, two French Opens and two United States Open championships.

September 7, 1953
'Little Mo,' the Grand Slammer

By ALLISON DANZIG

Maureen Connolly digging out a backhand half-volley return against Angela Mortimer at Wimbledon in 1952. Connolly was never beaten in a singles match there, winning three straight titles from 1952 to '54. (Associated Press)

NEW YORK—Maureen Connolly, the little, blonde Californian from San Diego, who will shortly attain the age of 19, carried off the women's amateur championship of the United States today at Forest Hills for the third successive year. In doing so she completed the first grand slam of the world's four major tournaments scored by a woman. She repeated her victory of last year's final over Doris Hart of Coral Gables, Fla., whom she also defeated in a magnificent final at Wimbledon in July.

In forty-three minutes, Miss Connolly, with her devastating speed and length off the ground and showing vast improvement since last year, took the match before some 12,000 on the stadium of the West Side Tennis Club, 6–2, 6–4. Miss Hart, a finalist five times and a strong hitter in her own right, resorted to every device, including changes of spin, length and pace, in an effort to slow down her opponent. But Miss Connolly went implacably on to victory in one of her finest performances. She was irresistible except for a momentary wavering when she stood within a stroke of ending matters at 6–2 in the final set and

yielded two more games to Miss Hart.

Following the triumph of Miss Connolly, Tony Trabert, an ex-sailor less than three months out of the Navy, won the men's championship in as stunning a final-round reversal as Forest Hills has seen in many years. With the onslaught of the level fire power of 16-inch rifles, Trabert, of Cincinnati, silenced the guns of the favored champion of Wimbledon, Victor Seixas of Philadelphia, and in exactly one hour won the match, to the acclaim of the crowd. The score was 6–3, 6–2, 6–3. Like Miss Connolly, the 23-year-old six-footer became one of the few to go through a championship without losing a set.

Maureen Connolly lost only one set in completing her Grand Slam, which came 15 years after Don Budge (see Sept. 24) secured the first. She won three successive Wimbledon championships (1952–54) and three United States championships (1951–53) as a teenager.

In July 1954 she was riding her horse Colonel Merryboy when she was struck by a cement truck, receiving a severely broken leg. Unable to play again professionally, she became an instructor. She died of cancer at age 34 in 1969. Bud Collins, the tennis historian and commentator, wrote: "It was the shortest of great careers, but few got more done in many more years."

Runners-up

1892: Using a short, straight punch called a jab, which had never been seen in the ring, the challenger James (Gentleman Jim) Corbett of California knocked out John L. Sullivan of Boston, the first recognized heavyweight champion, in the 21st round of their title fight at the Olympic Club in New Orleans. Sullivan created socially acceptable "modern" boxing with padded gloves, if not fewer rounds.

1997: Martina Hingis, 16, of Switzerland, won her third Grand Slam tennis title of the year, defeating unseeded Venus Williams, 17, of California, in straight sets to win the United States Open women's singles championship. Hingis ended the year as the reigning No. 1 women's player with a record of 75–5.

1993: Mark Whiten, a journeyman outfielder for the St. Louis Cardinals, hit four home runs and drove in 12 runners in the second game of a doubleheader against the Cincinnati Reds at Riverfront Stadium for the best single-game batting performance in major league history. The 12 runs batted in tied the 70-year old major league record by the Cardinals' Sunny Jim Bottomley.

September 8, 1969
Twice Is Nice

By NEIL AMDUR

NEW YORK—Rod Laver achieved the second grand slam of his tennis career today. With all the competitive trademarks of the true champion, the 31-year-old king of the court overcame Tony Roche, his 24-year-old Australian countryman, 7–9, 6–1, 6–2, 6–2, in the final of the United States Open championship at the West Side Tennis Club in Forest Hills, Queens.

Laver entered the record books as the only player to have achieved two sweeps of the Australian, French, British and American championships, the international events that make up the grand slam. Don Budge registered the first slam in 1938. Laver completed his initial sweep in 1962, but as an amateur and with such established pros as Richard (Pancho) Gonzales, Ken Rosewall, Lew Hoad and Tony Trabert ineligible for the competition. That situation has been changed with the approval of open tournaments.

"Tenniswise, winning this tournament was a lot tougher because of all the good players," the modest, freckle-faced redhead said. "Pressurewise, I don't think it was any tougher. There's always pressure when you're playing for something over nine months."

The fine line that separates Laver from Roche, Arthur Ashe, Roy Emerson and others is his ability to concentrate on the big serve or decisive volley at 15–30 or 30–40. Laver trailed, 30–40, in the opening game of the second set. A service break at this point could have carried Roche to a two-set lead. But three strong first serves saved the game. Laver won the last three service games of the set at love.

The crucial moment in the match, when it seemed to turn dramatically, came in the second game of the third set, after play had been suspended by rain. Roche had won his serve at love for a 1–0 lead. When the players returned 30 minutes later, the pressure was on Laver. Roche pushed Laver to deuce twice in that second game. But two more big

Rod Laver of Australia with the U.S. Open trophy at Forest Hills, N.Y., after becoming the only player in tennis to win two Grand Slams. He lost just two sets in the finals of the four major tournaments. (Associated Press)

serves, hopping deep to Roche's backhand, gave Laver the impetus to hold service and then break Roche in the next game, in which he was helped by Tony's netted forehand approach volley and long overhead at deuce. "Tony didn't seem to be digging in as much," Laver said of the player who had beaten him in

five of their seven previous meetings. "I felt his concentration was off."

Rod Laver remains the only player in history to complete two tennis Grand Slams. Don Budge (1938), Maureen Connolly (1953), Margaret Court (1970) and Steffi Graf (1988) had one each.

September 8, 1998
A Mighty Swing, a Grand Record

By MURRAY CHASS

ST. LOUIS—Mark McGwire, the St. Louis Cardinals' Paul Bunyan with a bat, made the most out of the least tonight, setting Major League Baseball's home run record by hitting his 62d and shortest home run of the season. Swinging at the first pitch from Steve Trachsel of the Chicago Cubs with two out in the fourth inning, McGwire lined a low-flying shot that just cleared Busch Stadium's left-field fence not far from where the fence meets the foul line. The drive was estimated, in baseball's method of measuring home runs, at 341 feet, 6 feet shorter than his previous shortest this season.

McGwire, a 34-year-old right-handed hitter, has hit five home runs that soared more than 500 feet, the longest estimated at 545 feet at Busch last May 16 that was his 16th. The blow that made McGwire the greatest single-season home run hitter of all major league time was atypical of his patented high-flying projectiles that soar majestically into the air and descend into some distant seat in the stands. This one nevertheless broke the tie that the red-headed McGwire had forged only the day before. In 1961, Maris hit his 61st home run in the Yankees' 163d and last game. In 1927, Babe Ruth hit his 60th home run in the Yankees' 154th and last game. This was the Cardinals' 145th game, which they won, 6–3.

McGwire thus beat Sammy Sosa of the Cubs to the record. The talented and likable players have been engaged in a spirited race to the record that has captivated the nation and returned to the sport many fans who had become disenchanted by the labor dispute in 1994–95. McGwire leads Sosa, 62 homers to 58, but the man who will enter the record book will be the one who has the most home runs at the end of the season on Sept. 27. For now, as Sosa said he told McGwire after the historic home run: "You're the man. You did it."

Before hitting this one, before the game, McGwire was handed the bat with which Maris hit the home run that broke Ruth's legendary record. He swung it, then touched his heart with it and said, "Roger, you're with me."

Mark McGwire finished his record season with a flourish, clouting two home runs off Mike Thurman and Carl Pavano of the Montreal Expos to raise his total to 70.

Mark McGwire of the Cardinals had no trouble focusing on Roger Maris's home-run record amid the popping flashbulbs of Busch Stadium. He hit No. 62 in his next at-bat off the Cubs' Steve Trachsel. (Associated Press)

Runners-up

1984: Martina Navratilova *(see Dec. 6)* won her sixth consecutive Grand Slam tournament by defeating Chris Evert in the United States Open in three tight sets. In 1983 Navratilova won Wimbledon, the United States Open and the Australian (then held in December). In '84 she won the French Open, Wimbledon and the United States Open—a "Straight Slam"—the four majors in sequence, though not within a calendar year.

1906: Dan Patch, the greatest pacer of all time, set a world record by turning a mile in 1 minute 55 seconds at the Minnesota State Fair Grounds in Hamline. Patch was retired in 1909 having lost only two heats and not a single race. His 1:55.0 mark stood for 54 years until Adios Butler broke it in 1:54.3.

1914: Boston's "Miracle" Braves, who had been in the National League cellar on July 15, 11½ games behind the New York Giants, took over the league lead with an 8–3 victory over the Giants at Fenway Park. They beat the Philadelphia A's in the World Series in the greatest single-season comeback (60–16 in the season's second half) in baseball history.

September 9, 1965
His Fourth No-Hitter Is Perfect

LOS ANGELES (AP)—Sandy Koufax of the Los Angeles Dodgers pitched a perfect game tonight in a 1–0 victory over the Chicago Cubs and became the first pitcher in baseball history to pitch four no-hitters in his career. Outpitching Bob Hendley in a brilliant duel between lefthanders, Koufax hurled his fourth no-hitter in four years and surpassed the record for multiple no-hitters held by Bob Feller, Cy Young and Larry Corcoran.

Hendley, who allowed only one hit, yielded a run in the fifth inning when the Dodgers scored without a hit. Lou Johnson walked to open the inning, was sacrificed to second, stole third and raced home when Chris Krug, the catcher, threw wild. That was enough for the Dodgers, who remained half a game behind San Francisco in the National League pennant race. The only hit off Hendley—and the only hit of the game—was Johnson's bloop double to right field with two out in the seventh inning.

Koufax, 29 years old, whose career was in jeopardy three years ago because of a circulatory ailment in his pitching hand, retired 27 Cubs in order. Koufax struck out 14, lifting his major-league-leading total to 332, as he posted the first perfect game in his 11-year career, the eighth in modern baseball history and only the third in National League annals. Jim Bunning of Philadelphia accomplished the feat last year.

Koufax, bringing his won-lost record to 22–7, was overpowering with his assortment of fast balls and breaking stuff. He struck out the last six batters he faced and seven of the last nine. In the eighth, he faced two of the Cubs' hardest-hitting players, Ron Santo and Ernie Banks. He struck out both, then ended the inning by fanning Byron Browne, a rookie left fielder.

In the ninth as the tension mounted in the crowd of 29,139, Koufax fired a third strike past the young Cubs' catcher, Krug. A pinch-hitter, Joey Amalfitano, also went down swinging—on three pitches. Then it was up to another pinch-hitter, Harvey Kuenn, the former American League batting champion. Kuenn also went down swinging—and Koufax had his first perfect game. He also closed in on another of baseball's most spectacular achievements, Feller's strikeout record of 348 in one season. Koufax now is 16 shy of matching that feat.

Koufax, who won the Cy Young award as the best pitcher in the majors in 1963 when he posted a 25–5 record, pitched his first no-hitter against the New York Mets, June 30, 1962, winning 5–0. His second came May 11, 1963, against San Francisco, with the Dodgers winning 8–0. Koufax made it three no-hitters last year, June 4, against Philadelphia, winning 3–0.

Sandy Koufax pitching on a field of dreams late in his perfect game against the Cubs at Dodger Stadium in Los Angeles. He struck out the last six batters he faced, including Chris Krug, here, leading off the ninth. (Associated Press)

Runners-up

1968: The first United States Open of tennis's new era was held, pitting professionals against amateurs. The men's title went to the amateur Arthur Ashe of Richmond, Va. (see Feb 6), who defeated Tom Okker of the Netherlands, a professional, in five sets. Ashe received $15 a day in expense money; Okker pocketed the $14,000 winner's check even though he lost.

1974: In what amounted to a changing of the guard in tennis, 22-year-old Jimmy Connors of Belleville, Ill. (see Sept. 2), needed only 78 minutes to defeat 39-year-old Ken Rosewall of Australia, 6–1, 6–0, 6–1, in the United States Open.

Billie Jean King of Long Beach, Calif., won her fourth and final Open singles title, defeating Evonne Goolagong of Australia, 3–6, 6–3, 7–5.

1993: Baseball owners realigned the two leagues into three divisions each for 1994 and added a new best-of-five-game playoff round for each, featuring two wild-card teams in all. The expanded playoffs began in '95 after the '94 post season was canceled. The first double wild-card World Series was in 2002, when the California Angels beat the San Francisco Giants in seven games.

September 10, 1972
Basketball or Chaos?

By NEIL AMDUR

MUNICH, West Germany [Sunday]—In a chaotic finish unparalleled for the sport of basketball, the Soviet Union snapped the 63-game winning streak of the United States, 51–50, early this morning and won the Olympic gold medal. The official result of the game, however, was delayed pending a protest made by Hank Iba, the American coach, and a hastily arranged meeting of a five-member jury of the International Amateur Basketball Federation (F.I.B.A.).

Ken Davis, a player representative for the American team, said the players would not accept a silver medal if the appeal was turned down. Davis said the vote had been unanimous. A short while later, the F.I.B.A. jury said that it would announce its decision at 8 A.M. Sunday, New York time.

Iba's protest concerned the almost unbelievable events that occurred during the final few seconds of the game, after the United States took the lead for the first time on two foul shots by Doug Collins with three seconds left. The Soviet Union took possession after the shots and put the ball in play from under its basket. The inbounds pass was deflected, however, and when time ran out, the American players began jumping up and down excitedly on the court believing they had won the game and the gold medal.

Their joy was short-lived. A ruling was issued at courtside by Robert Jones, secretary-general of F.I.B.A. The exact details of the ruling remain in conflict

over whether Jones had decided that the Soviet Union had called time before putting the ball in play or whether the official clock was in error and showed only one second when the Soviet team took possession. Either way, Jones informed the officials and the two coaches that the clock would be reset with three seconds left and the Soviet team again would have one last play.

U.S. basketball players celebrating their supposed championship at the Munich Olympics. The joy vanished quickly. Officials reset the clock with 3 seconds left and the Soviets scored off a full-court pass to win. (Associated Press)

The 68-year-old Iba, who had coached American gold medal teams in 1964 and 1968, angrily stalked after the referees and the F.I.B.A. officials and had to be restrained by his players. After order was restored at courtside, a Soviet player tried a desperation baseball pass that traveled the length of the court to Aleksander

Belov, a muscular 6-foot-8-inch forward, who was being guarded under the American basket by Kevin Joyce and James Forbes. All three players went up for the ball, but Joyce and Forbes were knocked to the floor in the battle for position. Belov grabbed the ball at the full extension of his jump, brought it down and then went back up again for the layup that sealed the Soviet victory before a stunned and confused crowd.

Chaos ensued. Iba again rushed to the scorer's table, Forbes wept unabashedly, and photographers, newsmen and irate fans flooded onto the floor. "I don't think it's possible to have made that play in three seconds," Iba shouted. "There's no damn way he can get that shot off in time." Under international rules, the clock does not start on inbounds plays until the ball is touched. "I've never seen anything like this in all my years of basketball," Iba said later. Both referees, a Bulgarian and Brazilian, signed the score-sheets after the game. Iba, however, refused and issued the formal protest that prompted the meeting of the F.I.B.A. jury.

The five-member jury voted 3–2 along East–West lines to support the decision of F.I.B.A.'s Robert Jones, which meant the Soviet Union remained the winner, 51–50. Judges from Hungary, Poland and Cuba ruled in favor of the Soviet team while those from Italy and Puerto Rico sided with the United States. The silver medals of the United States team members remain unclaimed.

Runners-up

1960: Abebe Bikila of Ethiopia won the marathon at the 1960 Rome Olympics while running barefoot over the cobblestones of the Appian Way. Bikila, 28, a member of the Ethiopian Imperial Bodyguard, repeated as the winner in the 1964 Tokyo Games, though with white shoes and socks. His time was a record 2 hours 12 minutes 11.2 seconds, and he was the first ever to win two Olympic marathons.

1988: Nineteen-year-old Steffi Graf of West Germany won the United States Open, defeating Gabriela Sabatini of Argentina in three sets and joining Don Budge,

Maureen Conrolly, Rod Laver and Margaret Court as the only players to have won a Grand Slam. Between the 1987 and '90 French Opens, Graf appeared in 13 straight Grand Slam tournament finals, winning 9 *(see June 6)*.

1989: In perhaps his signature moment as a two-sport star, Deion Sanders returned a punt 68 yards for a touchdown in his N.F.L. debut with the Atlanta Falcons five days after hitting a home run in a game for the Yankees. Sanders is the only athlete to play in a World Series (Atlanta Braves, 1992) and a Super Bowl (San Francisco 49ers, 1995; Dallas Cowboys, '96).

September 11, 1985
The All-Time Hit King

By IRA BERKOW

CINCINNATI—Ten miles from the sandlots where he began playing baseball as a boy, Pete Rose, now 44 years old and in his 23rd season in the major leagues, stepped to the plate tonight in the first inning at Riverfront Stadium. He came to bat on this warm, gentle evening with the chance to make baseball history. The Reds' player-manager, the man who still plays with the joy of a boy, had a chance to break Ty Cobb's major-league career hit record, 4,191, which had stood since Cobb retired in 1928.

The sell-out crowd of 47,237 that packed the stadium hoping to see Rose do it now stood and cheered under a twilight blue sky beribboned with orange clouds. Now he eased into his distinctive crouch from the left side of the plate, wrapping his white-gloved hands around the handle of his black bat. His red batting helmet gleamed in the lights. Everyone in the ball park was standing. The chant "Pete! Pete!" went higher and higher. Flashbulbs popped.

On the mound was the right-handed Eric Show of the San Diego Padres. Rose took the first pitch for a ball, fouled off the next pitch, took another ball. Show wound up and Rose swung and hit a line drive to left-center. The ball dropped in and the ball park exploded. Fireworks being set off was one reason; the appreciative cries of the fans was another. Streamers and confetti floated onto the field. Rose stood on first base and was

Pete Rose a moment after supplanting Ty Cobb as No. 1 on the all-time hit list. After waves of cheers and tenderness from fans and old friends, Rose put his head on first-base coach Tommy Helms's shoulder and wept. (Associated Press)

quickly mobbed by everyone on the Reds' bench. The first base coach, Tommy Helms, one of Rose's oldest friends on the team, hugged him first. Tony Perez, Rose's longtime teammate, then lifted him. Marge Schott, the owner of the Reds, came out and hugged Rose, and kissed him on the cheek. A red Corvette was driven from behind the outfield fence, a present from Mrs. Schott to her record-holder.

Rose had removed his batting helmet and waved with his gloves to the crowd. Then he stepped back on first, seemed to take a breath and turned to Helms, threw an arm around him and threw his head on his shoulder, crying. The tough old ball player, his face as lined and rugged as a longshoreman's, was moved, perhaps even slightly embarrassed, by the tenderness shown him in the ball park. Then from the dugout came a uniformed young man. This one was wearing the same number as Rose, 14, and had the same name on the back of his white jersey. Petey Rose, a 15-year-old redhead and sometime bat boy for as long as he can remember, fell into his pop's arms at first base, and the pair of Roses embraced. There were tears in their eyes.

Pete Rose later told Sports Illustrated *about another thought he had while standing on first base after his record hit: "Clear in the sky I see my dad, Harry Francis Rose, and Ty Cobb. Ty Cobb was in the second row. Dad was in the first."*

Runners-up

1983: Jimmy Connors, 31, the people's choice at Flushing Meadows *(see Sept. 2),* won his fifth and final United States Open tennis title, defeating the Czech expatriate Ivan Lendl in four sets. Connors won eight Grand Slam tournaments on all three playing surfaces—grass, clay and hard court—and reached the finals of seven others.

1918: After a regular season shortened by a month because of World War I, the Boston Red Sox defeated the Chicago Cubs, 2–1, in Game 6 at Fenway Park to win the World Series. Red Sox left-hander Babe Ruth won two games and extended his consecutive scoreless streak to 29⅔ innings. It was Boston's fifth world title in five tries but, as of 2002, their last.

1994: Unseeded Andre Agassi of Las Vegas resurrected his tennis career, ripping through all five seeds ahead of him, including Michael Stich of Germany in a three-set final, to win his first United States Open. Although Agassi soon married the actress Brooke Shields, his image-is-everything days (his consort Barbra Streisand once gushed about his playing "like a Zen master") were over.

September 12, 1984
The Quintessential Gooden

By JOSEPH DURSO

NEW YORK [Wednesday]—In a dazzling display of virtuoso pitching by a 19-year-old rookie, Dwight Gooden fired the Mets to a 2–0 victory over the Pittsburgh Pirates tonight, struck out 16 batters and hurtled past strikeout records set by Tom Seaver, Nolan Ryan and Herb Score.

The tall and taciturn right-hander from Tampa, Fla., overpowered the Pirates on five hits, gave no walks and pitched his second straight shutout and seventh straight victory and ended the evening with more strikeouts than any other rookie in history. He passed that milestone in the sixth inning when he struck out Marvell Wynne. It was his 11th strikeout of the night and the 246th of his brief career in the big leagues, and it broke the record set by Score for the Cleveland Indians 29 years ago.

But there was more. By the time he had finished, Gooden had a total of 251 strikeouts in 202 innings in 29 games. He also had broken Ryan's club record of 14 strikeouts by a rookie in a game, set in 1969, and Seaver's one-season record of 13 games with 10 or more strikeouts, set in 1971. Gooden, who pitched a one-hitter against the Cubs last Friday night, now has won 16 games in his first season past the Carolina League, where he struck out 300 batters in 191 innings last year. And he stopped the Pirates last night on 120 pitches, only 28 of them called balls.

"He's great," said Chuck Tanner, the Pirate manager. "He's a smoothie, and we'll see him doing it years from now. Our guys weren't saying anything at all in the dugout. They didn't have time. They were striking out so fast, they had to run back on the field."

"Sometimes you think about it," Gooden said later of his success, in a rare touch of personal reaction. "You think about it going home, or lying in bed before falling asleep. You think, 'Am I dreaming?'"

Dwight Gooden won the Rookie of the Year title in 1984, went 24–4 with 268 strikeouts in winning the Cy Young Award in '85 and helped lead the Mets to the World Series championship in '86. But his was a story of paradise lost: he was admitted to a drug rehab center in 1987 and was never again as dominant. He did have a last hurrah for the Yankees in '96—a 2–0 no-hitter against Seattle at Yankee Stadium (see May 14).

The Mets' Dwight Gooden, aged 19, unleashing his overpowering fastball against the Pittsburgh Pirates at Shea Stadium in June 1984. His potential seemed infinite. "Sometimes you think about it," he said of his success. "You think, 'Am I dreaming?' " (Associated Press)

Runners-up

1992: Monica Seles of Yugoslavia, by now almost totally dominating women's tennis, won her sixth Grand Slam tournament in three years by breezing through the United States Open without dropping a set. She played the entire tourney in little more than seven hours, defeating Arantxa Sánchez Vicario of Spain, 6–3, 6–3, in the final.

1979: Carl Yastrzemski of the Boston Red Sox collected his 3,000th major league hit with a single off Jim Beattie in a 9–2 victory over the Yankees at Fenway Park. Yastrzemski retired in 1983 and as of 2002 remained baseball's last Triple Crown winner, in '67 having topped everyone in the American League in batting average, home runs and runs batted in.

1951: With a fearsome gash over his left eye that was threatening to stop the fight, Sugar Ray Robinson unleashed a savage 10th-round attack against Randy Turpin of Britain to score a technical knockout and regain the world middleweight championship at the Polo Grounds in New York. Robinson had lost the title to Turpin two months before at Yankee Stadium.

Aussies on Top

By NEIL AMDUR

NEW YORK—Mrs. Margaret Court swept everything, including her grand slam in singles, and little Ken Rosewall collected his biggest payday as a professional on the final day of the $160,000 United States Open tennis championships today.

"I felt the pressure quite a bit at times," Mrs. Court said after her final. "I played very tentative, but I sort of made myself concentrate. I'm tired. I guess I haven't realized that it's all over." Mrs. Court, an Australian who at 5 feet 9 inches is two inches taller than Rosewall, overshadowed the women's field. She achieved the last leg of her singles grand slam with a 6–2, 2–6, 6–1 triumph over Rosemary Casals, a victory worth $7,500. The only other woman player to win the grand slam was the late Maureen Connolly as an amateur in 1953. Mrs. Court had won three of the four amateur events three times in the past.

The 21-year-old Miss Casals became the first player in two years here to take a set against Mrs. Court when she won the second. Both women appeared nervous and admitted afterward that the play had been "tentative and spotty" because of the stakes. "I had a lot of trouble with my serve," said Miss Casals, a Californian. "And Margaret has such long arms that they seemed to go all around the court."

Mrs. Court broke Miss Casals in the second and sixth games of the third set, concentrating her attack on her rival's

backhand volley and driving deeply off the ground. "There was a lot of tension," she said. "I was praying on that last serve that Rosie hit into the net." Mrs. Court's husband, Barry, was one of the first to congratulate her after the match. "What was the first thing she said to you afterward?" a friend asked Barry. "She said she couldn't believe it," he answered.

The 35-year-old Rosewall, who received a gold ball and a handshake for winning the National Amateur event 14 years ago, drove out of the West Side Tennis Club in Forest Hills, Queens, with a new Ford Pinto and a check for $20,000 after his 2–6, 6–4, 7–6, 6–3 victory over Tony Roche. It was the biggest payoff for a tournament since the Open era began in tennis three years ago. Roche, the Australian left-hander beaten by Rosewall in the semifinals at Wimbledon and seeded fourth here, received $10,000 as the runner-up for the second straight year.

Margaret Court of Perth, Australia, won more major singles titles, 24, than anyone else in the history of tennis. In this year of her Grand Slam, her record in matches was 104–6. Tall and strong, formidable on both serve and volley, she made women's tennis far more athletic.

Margaret Court, above, closing out the second Grand Slam in women's tennis in the U.S. Open at Forest Hills, N.Y. At top right, Ken Rosewall, 35, winning his second U.S. title 14 years after his first. (Michael Evans/The New York Times)

Runners-up

1970: Seventy-three years after the Boston Marathon's debut, the New York City Marathon, organized by the New York Road Runners Club, kicked off with 175 participants who had paid the $1 entry fee. Only 55 runners finished the four circuits of Central Park. Gary Muhrcke of Freeport, N.Y., was the first winner, in 2 hours 31 minutes 38 seconds.

1998: Locked in a record-setting derby with Mark McGwire even though McGwire had broken Roger Maris's home run record five days before (see Sept. 8), Sammy Sosa of the Chicago Cubs hit Nos. 61 and 62 off the Milwaukee Brewers' Bronswell Patrick and Eric Plunk, respectively, at Wrigley Field. Sosa (see June 25) finished with 66 homers to McGwire's 70.

1992: In a note that spoke volumes about how offenses had come to dominate the N.F.L., punters Chris Mohr of Buffalo and Joe Prokop of San Francisco did not appear in the Bills' 34–31 victory over the 49ers at Candlestick Park. The game featured 1,086 yards of offense and, for the first time in league history, not a single punt.

September 14, 1994
The Day the Owners Killed the Series

By MURRAY CHASS

NEW YORK—With a four-paragraph resolution providing the final out instead of a ball nestling into a glove or soaring over a fence, major league baseball owners called off the rest of the season today, sweeping away 89 years of the World Series and sending the game staggering into the great unknown. Led by Bug Selig, the acting commissioner, the owners voted, 26–2, to cancel the remainder of the regular-season schedule, two rounds of the playoffs and the World Series. They blamed the players' 34-day strike and what they charged was the union's unwillingness "to respond in any meaningful way" to the clubs' demand for cost containment.

But Donald Fehr, the players' labor leader, countered by saying: "When people think back to what the final image of the 1994 season will be, it may be Bud Selig at a press conference in Milwaukee protesting the pain and gnash-

Fans at Yankee Stadium, above, as players prepared to strike in August 1994. Gates at all major league parks, like Jacobs Field in Cleveland, below, were closed in September, canceling the World Series for the first time in 90 years. (Associated Press)

ing of teeth but nevertheless going ahead and dashing the hopes and dreams of many people. It was their decision to make. They decided their circumstances were more important."

The inability of the players and the owners to settle their bitter dispute over the clubs' proposal to limit payrolls short-circuited a season that had been one of the most scintillating in years. Washed away are the chances of the Yankees to appear in the playoffs for the first time since 1981 and Don Mattingly for the first time ever; the assault on Roger Maris's home run record by Matt Williams, Ken Griffey Jr. and others, and the pursuit of a .400 batting average by Tony Gwynn.

For the first time since 1904, the World Series, which had survived world wars and an earthquake since its inception in 1903, will not be played. That cancellation occurred when the National League champion New York Giants refused to play Boston's American League champions chiefly because of a feud between the Giants' owner and the president of the new league.

The baseball strike, the eighth work stoppage in 23 seasons, became the longest shutdown in the game's history, surpassing the 50-day strike in 1981 when it extended 18 games into the '95 season. It was settled in March 1995 when a federal judge forced the owners to return to the rules of the old labor pact.

Runners-up

1968: Denny McLain of the Detroit Tigers became the first major leaguer to win 30 games in a season since Dizzy Dean of the St. Louis Cardinals in 1934 when he defeated the Oakland A's, 5–4, at Tiger Stadium. He finished the season 31–6 with 280 strikeouts and a 1.96 earned run average. No one has come closer than 27 victories since.

2002: Tim Montgomery of Gaffney, S.C., set a world record of 9.78 seconds in the 100 meters during the International Amateur Athletic Federation Grand Prix final in Paris. He broke the three-year-old mark set by Maurice Greene of Kansas City, Kan., by a hundredth of a second.

2002: Oscar De La Hoya of East Los Angeles, Calif., the most popular welterweight since Sugar Ray Leonard in the 1980's, scored an 11th-round technical knockout over Fernardo Vargas of Oxnard, Calif., for the world junior middleweight title in Las Vegas. The bout, which grossed $50 million, raised De La Hoya's record to 35-2-0 with 28 knockouts.

A Record Game Is a Record Loss

By JOSEPH DURSO

ST. LOUIS—Steve Carlton of the St. Louis Cardinals set a major league record tonight by striking out 19 New York Mets. But the Mets still won the game, 4–3, on a pair of two-run home runs by Ron Swoboda and extended their lead to 4½ games with 15 to play. Carlton, a 24-year-old lefthander, struck out the side in four of the nine innings as he surpassed the record of 18 strike-outs set by Sandy Koufax, Bob Feller and Don Wilson. He even fanned Swoboda twice—on his first and third times at bat. But on his second and fourth trips to the plate, the Maryland muscleman drove home runs into the left-field seats—both times with a man on base, both times with the Mets trailing by one run.

As a result, the Mets swung even higher on their high-flying trapeze with two and a half weeks to play. They put 4½ games between themselves and the Chicago Cubs, who lost to the Montreal Expos and continued one of the stunning tailspins of the baseball season. The Mets' victory—despite Carlton's virtuoso performance—was No. 27 in their last 34 games. They trailed Chicago by 9½ games on Aug. 13, but since then have soared to the top of the Eastern Division of the National League, and tonight marked the 20th straight game in which their pitchers did not allow an enemy home run.

Carlton, though, suffered a bittersweet even-ing precisely because he threw the home-run pitch twice to the right-handed Swoboda. The 6-foot-4-inch 200-pounder from Miami pitched his way into the baseball record books by striking out half of the 38 batters he faced. He got 27 outs—19 on third strikes—but allowed nine hits and two walks, and took his 10th defeat against 16 victories.

Going into the ninth inning tonight, Carlton had 16 strikeouts, meaning he had to fan the side to establish the record. He had already struck out three Mets in the first, second and fourth innings. He had struck out Amos Otis three times and four other Mets twice apiece. Then in the final inning, he struck out Tug McGraw, who had relieved Gary Gentry in the seventh inning of a game that had been delayed twice by rain for a total of 81 minutes. That was No. 17. Next came Bud Harrelson, and he looked at strike three for No. 18. And finally, Otis—just recalled from the minor leagues—swung and missed a third strike for No. 19 and the record.

"It was the best stuff I ever had," said Carlton, like a sculptor who has just created a masterpiece and then accidentally chipped it. "When I had nine strike-outs, I decided to go all the way. But it cost me the game because I started to challenge every batter."

Steve Carlton was traded to the Philadelphia Phillies in 1972 for Rick Wise in one of the worst deals in baseball history. Carlton pitched as well that season as any pitcher ever has, winning 27 games for an inept team that won just 59 with 310 strikeouts and an earned run average of 1.97. In all, he won 241 games and four Cy Young awards with the Phillies.

Steve Carlton at Busch Stadium after striking out a major-league record 19 Mets – yet still losing the game on a pair of Ron Swoboda home runs. "It's irritating, it's frustrating," Carlton said. "It's part of baseball." (Associated Press)

Runners-up

1978: Muhammad Ali, 36, became the first boxer in history to win the world heavy weight title three times when he scored a unanimous 15-round decision over 25-year-old Leon Spinks in the Superdome at New Orleans. Ali had lost the title for the second time in his first bout against Spinks the previous February.

1990: Underscoring baseball's movement toward late-inning "closers," a relatively new term in the game's lexicon, Bobby Thigpen of the Chicago White Sox became the first pitcher to chalk up 50 saves in a season in a 7–4 victory over the Boston Red Sox at Comiskey Park. Thigpen finished with 57 saves, the record through 2002.

1963: Quarterback George Izo of the Washington Redskins threw a 99-yard touch down pass to Bobby Mitchell in a game against the Cleveland Browns. Five years later to the day, the Redskins' Sonny Jurgensen threw one to Gerry Allen against the Chicago Bears. There have been seven other such passes in N.F.L. history.

September 16, 1950
Hello, Browns, Not So Nice to Know You

By LOUIS EFFRAT

PHILADELPHIA—
Until at least Dec. 3, when they clash again, the Cleveland Browns, who played their first game in the National Football League tonight, will merit a solid claim of superiority over the Philadelphia Eagles. With a convincing 35–10 rout of the two-time champions of the N.F.L. before 71,237 fans at Municipal Stadium, Paul Brown's resourceful athletes produced the answer to the most repeated question in professional gridiron history: "Can the Browns beat the Eagles?"

It took four years and cost some $8,000,000 before a contest between the N.F.L. and the All-America Conference kings could be arranged. Made possible by the A.A.C. capitulation last winter, the long-awaited game finally was staged, only because the Browns, along with the San Francisco Forty-Niners and the Baltimore Colts, joined the N.F.L. And now that it has come to pass, it could be that some N.F.L. folks are sorry. Judged by tonight's performance, the Browns, who were the only champions the now-defunct A.A.C. ever knew, may, for a number of years, anyway, dominate the league as it did the Conference.

Certainly, the beautifully coached Browns, with Otto Graham, as great as he ever was at Northwestern and since he became a professional, leading the attack, Greasy Neale's Eagles were made to look

The great Marion Motley about to be tackled by the Giants' Jim Duncan, foreground, at the Polo Grounds in October 1950. It was just the sixth N.F.L. game for the Browns, who went on to win the league title. (Associated Press)

bad. The Eagles' defense against Graham's passes was woefully weak, even if they managed to minimize the Cleveland trap plays, featuring Marion Motley. Graham went overhead thirty-eight times and completed twenty-one, good for 346 yards and three touchdowns. His was a magnificent display of aerial artistry and his was a job so well done that the difference between the elevens was greater even than the actual margin.

On his first touchdown pass, Graham fired to Dub Jones, completely fooling the Philadelphia defense. Jones caught the ball on the 25 and continued unmolested

for the touchdown. Graham threw to Dante Lavelli for twenty-six yards and a touchdown in the second and to Mac Speedie for thirteen yards and six points in the third. With Steve Van Buren in uniform but not called upon because of the toe he fractured during training, with Bosh Pritchard out with a bad knee and with Clyde (Smackover) Scott, a dynamic runner until he was injured in the second period, lost for the last thirty-five minutes, the Eagles perhaps were outmanned by the Browns. However, none could dispute that the Clevelanders were the better, stronger, smarter club tonight.

Runners-up

1973: O.J. Simpson of the Buffalo Bills became the first player in pro football history to rush for 250 yards in one game in a 31–13 victory over the New England Patriots at Foxboro, Mass. He ran for 2,003 yards that season (see Dec. 16), an N.F.L. record at the time.

1981: Trailing on the judges' scorecards and with his trainer, Angelo Dundee, saying, "You're blowing it, son," Sugar Ray Leonard staged a furious rally against Thomas Hearns in the 13th and 14th rounds that gave Leonard the world

welterweight title by technical knockout in Las Vegas. It was Leonard's 31st victory in 32 pro bouts and Hearns's first loss in 33.

1960: Amos Alonzo Stagg, a father of American football, stepped down as coach of Stockton Junior College in California at age 98 after a 71-career on the sideline, including 40 years at the University of Chicago. Stagg watched football evolve from an amalgam of soccer and rugby and invented the end-around play, shifting offenses, the man in motion and the huddle. He died at 102.

September 17, 1954
Marciano Runs His Record to 47-0

By JOSEPH C. NICHOLS

NEW YORK—Rocky Marciano retained the world heavyweight championship at the Yankee Stadium tonight. The undefeated boxer from Brockton, Mass., knocked out the former titleholder, Ezzard Charles, in the eighth round of a scheduled fifteen-round contest. A left hook and a right cross to the jaw put Charles down for the full count after he had been floored earlier in the session for the count of four with a long right to the head. On the second knockdown in the concluding round, Charles just managed to reach his feet a split second after Referee Al Beri had counted ten but Ez made no move to continue the hostilities.

The victory was Marciano's No. 47 in as many professional fights, a record unique in the history of the heavyweight division. And his knockout was the forty-first such conquest in his professional career. It was the second fight between the pair and the result was just about what most fans expected. Marciano was the favorite, at odds of 9 to 2, to dispose of the skillful Negro from Cincinnati, with a knockout ending being generally predicted.

In their first fight, last June 17, Rocky was expected to dispose of Ez by a knockout, but the latter surprised the boxing world by waging a willing, game fight that went the limit before Rocky got the unanimous decision. In contrast to their other clash, tonight's contest was one-sided, with Marciano winning every round except the first one on this observer's scorecard. Besides registering the two knockdowns in the eighth round, Rocky also felled his opponent in the second session. He dropped him in the second with a right to the jaw, followed by a two-fisted attack to the body.

After he was dropped in the second, Ezzard seemed to have the steam taken out of him. In all the fifteen rounds of their previous fight, Ezzard stood up under Rocky's vaunted punch without going down once. When he did find out that the Brockton Rock really could punch, Charles became cautious, and his leads were infrequent.

A turn of fortune appeared to come Charles' way in the sixth when Marciano, emerging from a clinch, showed a nasty cut straight up the tip of his nose. Ezzard made this wound a target, and also punched for a cut that opened beside Rocky's left eye in the eighth, but the

champion showed that he had enough to stand up against this sort of punishment. Despite the fact that his victory was a decisive one and virtually foreordained, Marciano lost the sympathy of a good many in the crowd by his inclination to skirt the rules. Twice he was guilty of hitting after the bell, and once he was warned for heeling Ezzard in a close-quarters exchange.

This was Rocky Marciano's last fight. He retired in 1956 to spend more time with his wife and family (see April 27) and was killed in a plane crash in 1969. He remains the only undefeated heavyweight champion.

Rocky Marciano landing the eighth-round punch that decked Ezzard Charles for the first time in Marciano's final fight. When Charles got back up, a left hook to the jaw and a right cross put him down for good. (Bettmann/Corbis)

Runners-up

1920: The American Professional Football Association, organized by George Halas, was formed in a Canton, Ohio, auto showroom. The original teams, which each paid a $100 admission fee, included the Decatur Staleys, the Canton Bulldogs and the Dayton Triangles. Two years later the A.P.F.A., then comprising 14 teams, changed its name to the National Football League.

1994: Julio César Chávez of Mexico, who had sustained the first loss of his 90-fight career earlier in the year, scored an eighth-round technical knockout over

Meldrick Taylor to retain his W.B.C. superlightweight belt in Las Vegas. A Mexican Independence Day crowd celebrated his return to form.

1984: Reggie Jackson (see Oct. 18) of the California Angels, who hit his first home run for the Kansas City A's 17 years earlier to the day, slugged the 500th of his career off Bud Black of the Kansas City Royals at Anaheim Stadium. The 13th player to reach 500 homers, Jackson retired from the Oakland A's with 563 in 1987 and stood eighth on the all-time list as of 2003.

September 18, 1977
A Brash Captain Keeps the Cup

By STEVE CADY

NEWPORT, R.I.—"If I only had a little humility," Ted Turner once confessed in his high-speed Georgia drawl, "I would be perfect." That appraisal might be disputed by Commissioner Bowie Kuhn and others with whom Turner, the suspended owner of the Atlanta Braves baseball club, has feuded. But tonight, as he basked in the glow of a successful America's Cup defense some of his critics had hoped he would not be chosen to make, the so-called Mouth of the South was probably as close to perfection as he would want to come. Courageous completed a four-race sweep over the yacht Australia this afternoon, good for a 23d successful defense. Courageous's time margin today was 2 minutes 25 seconds, and her yachtsmen either were pushed or went voluntarily into the waters of Newport Harbor within seconds after she docked.

All summer long, except for an occasional lapse, the 38-year-old skipper of Courageous had behaved with what for him was monklike humility as he fought his way past two newer 12-Meter yachts for the role of cup defender. With a cigar in his mouth, a railroad engineer's cap on his head and a wise-crack, an insult or a compliment ready for any occasion, the 6-foot-3-inch, mustachioed Captain Courageous suggests a variety of heroes from Mark Twain and Horatio Alger to Errol Flynn. What adjectives fit? Take your pick.

Flamboyant, volatile, charming, witty, handsome, outrageous, disrespectful, uncouth, irreverent, jaunty, courteous, rude. Whatever the choice, depending on which side of the fence the jurors occu-

Ted Turner, captain of the Courageous, salutes a crowd that gathered to greet him in Atlanta the day after he swept the yacht Australia in the America's Cup series. Turner, 38 and irreverent, was an outsider in the genteel Cup establishment. (Associated Press)

pied, it did not matter much tonight. The skipper who came here in 1974 with a slow boat named Mariner was the man of the hour in Newport and the rest of the yachting world.

The Ted Turner who emerged in the America's Cup defense has always tended to be camouflaged by the more highly publicized images: a rebel, a maverick, a gadfly, a runaround, a tyrant, a flake and so forth. But Turner played it straight this time, in the genteel, blue-blazer world of the New York Yacht Club, and the sacred cup was never more secure. All he had to do was win some boat races, something he has been doing with increasing success since he began at the age of 11, after his family had moved from Cincinnati, his birthplace, to Savannah, Ga.

He was a winning dinghy sailor at Brown University, a winner in one-design classes and an almost monotonous winner in the ocean-racing circuit. And now he has become the biggest winner of all. "Exposure to defeat," Turner said after the Mariner debacle in the 1974 trials, "is a very important thing." For the now-respectable Mouth of the South, the battle with Bowie Kuhn may not be over. But the America's Cup war has been won. As Turner himself would say, "Anybody got a cigar?"

Bowie Kuhn issued a one-year suspension against Ted Turner in January 1977 for tampering in a successful attempt to sign the San Francisco Giants outfielder Gary Matthews. Besides founding the first television superstation, WTBS, Turner founded CNN, TNT and the quadrennial Olympic-style Goodwill Games, which were held from 1986 through 2000.

Runners-up

1984: The Detroit Tigers clinched the American League East Division title with a 3–0 victory over the Milwaukee Brewers, becoming the fourth team in baseball to inhabit first place for a season wire to wire. The Tigers and the others—the 1923 New York Giants, the '27 Yankees and the '55 Brooklyn Dodgers (see Oct. 4)—all won world championships.

1999: One year after his and Mark McGwire's remarkable assault on the record books, Sammy Sosa (see June 25) of the Chicago Cubs hit his 60th home run of the season. Eight days later McGwire, of the St. Louis Cardinals, hit his 60th

as the pair, aided no doubt by pitching made thinner by expansion and other changes in the game, became the first ever to hit 60 home runs twice.

1963: The last game was played at the historic Polo Grounds in New York, site of Fred Merkle's boner (see Sept. 23) and Bobby Thomson's home run (see Oct. 3) and home of the Giants from 1890 to 1957, the Yankees in the early 20's and the Mets in '62–63. A crowd of 1,752 saw the Philadelphia Phillies score a 5–1 victory over the Mets, who moved into Shea Stadium in 1964.

The Dominator

By ALLISON DANZIG

NEW YORK—A new mark in modern American tennis was set today when William T. Tilden 2d won the national championship for the sixth successive year and captured his second challenge trophy outright. Playing before a gallery of 14,000 wild and enthusiastic spectators who filled the stadium at the West Side Tennis Club to capacity, the Philadelphian defeated William Johnston in a thrilling five-set match that required two hours and ten minutes to play. The score was 4–6, 11–9, 6–3, 4–6, 6–3.

Not since 1922 has Johnston made such a great fight against the champion as he did today, nor has any match of the six in which they have met in the final of the championship aroused a gallery to more thunderous applause than reverberated through the concrete enclosure almost continuously during this struggle. Johnston's well-wishers were there in thousands and Tilden's were too, and between them they made the welkin ring as it has not rung all season at Forest Hills.

Forgetting those two crushing defeats at the hands of Tilden in 1923 and last year, Johnston went out on the courts and fought with all the blistering pace and deadliness that characterized his game in 1915 when he conquered Maurice McLaughlin and Dick Williams to win the title for the first time. Volleying flawlessly with punching strokes and whipping his mighty forehand across the net at a low altitude, the Californian carried the attack to his opponent with such impetuousness that for the first and second sets Tilden had to call upon all his brilliancy as a shot-maker to stay on even terms with him. Taking the first set by breaking through in the tenth game, Johnston never faltered in the second chapter until in the eighteenth

game he stood at set point.

At this stage the gallery was in a state of such excitement that it could hardly control itself. Every shot was followed with breathless interest, every winning stroke of Johnston's threw the spectators almost into a state of frenzy. It was the same keyed-up gallery, ready to break into pandemonium at any moment, that saw Johnston take the first two sets from Tilden in the 1922 final.

Three times Johnston stood within a single stroke of taking this set, but nervousness and the inability to control his shots in the critical moments cost him the game, one of the longest in the match, and Tilden took the next two games for the set. This failure to rise to the occasion in a moment of great opportunity characterized Johnston's play for the rest of the match. He wasted a lead of 3–1 in the third set and after breaking through Tilden's service to lead at 2–1 in the final set he allowed a lead of 40–15 to slip away in the fourth game, and instead of going ahead at 3–1 the score became 2-all. These lapses on the Californian's part caused a great deal of anguish to his thousands of admirers. An indication of how close the match was is furnished in the point score. Only two points separated them in the totals, Tilden

having 191 to 189 for Johnston. Johnston made 147 errors to Tilden's 140, while the Californian scored five more earned points than did the other, 49 to 44.

From 1920 to '26, Bill Tilden dominated tennis as no one before or since. Part of sport's golden age with Babe Ruth, Jack Dempsey and Red Grange, Tilden not only was invincible in the United States nationals but also won Wimbledon both times he played there and led the United States to seven straight Davis Cup victories.

Bill Tilden in a tournament in Florida in 1933. Tall, rangy and powerful, he was a colossal figure in tennis at a time when the balls and the uniforms, not to mention the opponents, all were white. (Associated Press)

Runners-up

1959: Jack Nicklaus, a 19-year-old junior at Ohio State University, sank a birdie putt on the final hole to defeat the defending champion Charlie Coe of Oklahoma for a 1-up victory in the United States Amateur championship at the Broadmoor Golf Club in Colorado Springs. Nicklaus turned pro after again winning the Amateur in 1961 at Pebble Beach in California.

1988: Greg Louganis of the United States (*see Aug. 12*) narrowly escaped serious injury when he hit his head while performing on the springboard at the Seoul Games. Five stitches and eight days later, in possibly the most dramatic

moment in diving history, he defeated the 14-year-old Xiong Ni of China and won both the springboard and 10-meter platform gold medals for the second straight Olympics.

1949: Ralph Kiner of the Pittsburgh Pirates homered in a 6–4 loss to the New York Giants at Forbes Field, becoming the first National Leaguer to hit 50 or more home runs twice. The Mark McGwire or Sammy Sosa of his era, in which homers were harder to come by, Kiner hit 51 in 1947 and 54 this year. He led the league in homers each year from 1946 to '52.

September 20, 1973
Take That, Gents!

By NEIL AMDUR

HOUSTON—Mrs. Billie Jean King struck a proud blow for herself and women around the world with a crushing 6–4, 6–3, 6–3 rout of Bobby Riggs tonight in their $100,000 winner-take-all tennis match at the Astrodome. In an atmosphere more suited for a circus than a sports event, the 29-year-old Mrs. King ended the bizarre saga of the 55-year-old hustler, who had bolted to national prominence with his blunt putdowns of women's tennis and the role of today's female. Mrs. King, a five-time Wimbledon champion and the most familiar face in the women's athletic movement, needed only 2 hours 4 minutes to reaffirm her status as one of the gifted and tenacious competitors in sport, male or female.

A crowd of 30,492, some paying as much as $100 a seat, watched the best three-of-five-set struggle, the largest single attendance ever for a tennis match. Millions more viewed the event on national television. The match also was seen in 36 foreign countries via satellite. Mrs. King squashed Riggs with tools synonymous with men's tennis, the serve and volley. She beat Bobby to the ball, dominated the net and ran him around the baseline to the point of near exhaustion in the third set, when he suffered hand cramps and trailed, 2–4. Most important, perhaps for women everywhere, she convinced skeptics that a female athlete can survive pressure-filled situations and that men are as susceptible to nerves as women.

It was Riggs, for example, who only yesterday had claimed "I have no nerves," who double-faulted at 4–5, 30–40 to decide the first set. And it was another Riggs double-fault, at deuce in the ninth game of the final set, that gave Mrs. King her third match point. An uproar of cheers followed

when Riggs drove a high backhand volley into the net. Later, away from the tumult and the shouting, Mrs. King admitted that she, too, had suffered cramps in her leg in the sixth game of the final set. "It was a combination of nerves and just all that running," she said. "When I felt the first twinge, I said, 'Oh God, not now— not this close.' I was really worried."

Riggs praised Mrs. King. "She was too good," said the 1939 Wimbledon singles champion. "She played too well. She was playing well within herself, and I couldn't get the most out of my game. It was over too quickly."

Instead of the traditional walk onto the court, the players entered the stadium with the flourish of something out of a Cecil B. DeMille movie. Mrs. King came first on a Cleopatra-style gold litter that was held aloft by four muscular track-and-field athletes from nearby Rice University and an Astrodome employee. One of the toga-clad carriers was Dave Roberts, one of the world's finest pole-vaulters. Riggs was transported into the stadium in a gold-wheeled rickshaw pulled by six professional models in tight red and gold outfits who had been dubbed "Bobby's Bosom Buddies" during his stay here. It was apparent why.

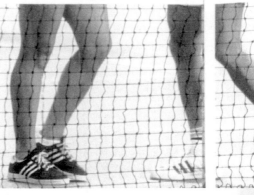

Bobby Riggs congratulating Billie Jean King after she dismissed him in their nationally televised winner-take-all match. For all his supposed chauvinism, he was surprisingly cordial in defeat. (Bettmann/UPI)

Riggs did not leave the match empty-handed. Like Mrs. King, he was guaranteed a minimum of $75,000 for ancillary rights to the promotion. His other endorsements and contracts should swell his take to over $300,000. Mrs. King, the biggest money-winner in the history of women's athletics and the foremost spokesman for equality in sport, is certain to reap even greater financial returns from tonight's victory. But as she said yesterday, "pride matters a lot more than money."

Runners-up

1998: Cal Ripken Jr. *(see Sept. 6)* removed himself from the Baltimore Orioles' line-up in the final game of the season at Camden Yards against the Yankees, ending his record streak of consecutive games at 2,632. It was the 38-year-old Ripken's first game off in 16 years. He retired after the 2001 season.

1913: Francis Ouimet, a 20-year-old amateur from Brookline, Mass., defeated Harry Vardon and Ted Ray of Britain in a playoff to win the United States Open golf championship. The victory by Ouimet, who had entered the tournament only

because it was held in his hometown, sparked a wave of American interest in the British sport.

1982: The N.F.L. players' union announced the first in-season strike in the 63-year history of the league for a share of the league's new $2.1 billion five-year television deal. The work stoppage lasted 57 days and reduced the season from 16 games to 9. One thing the union won was the right to obtain copies of all player contracts; previously, salary figures had been anybody's guess.

September 21, 1934
Oh, Those Dizzy and Daffy Dean Boys

By ROSCOE McGOWEN

Dizzy Dean, winning pitcher Paul Dean, Manager Frank Frisch and catcher Bill DeLancey, from left, after Game 6 of the 1934 World Series in Detroit. Dizzy shut out the Tigers the following day for the championship. (Associated Press)

NEW YORK—Those highly publicized Dean brothers lived up to every advance notice as they hurled the Cardinals to a double victory over the Dodgers at Ebbets Field today. The elder brother, Dizzy, allowed three safeties, the first coming in the eighth inning, as the Cards took the opener, 13 to 0. But good as Dizzy was, he went into eclipse behind the extraordinary feat of his youthful brother, who gave 18,000 fans the thrill that comes once in a baseball lifetime by hurling a no-hit game. The Cards made seven safe blows off Ray Benge to win, 3 to 0.

Paul's work was just one point short of perfection. He issued one pass, drawn by Len Koenecke in the first inning after two were out, but thereafter the Stengel athletes just marched to the plate and right back again with monotonous regularity.

The tension among the players on the Cardinal bench and among the fans could almost be felt as Paul went to the mound in the ninth. Thousands of fans rose to their feet and leaned forward to watch every move on the field, while two or three Cardinals in the dug-out could be seen holding their fingers crossed. With two out in the ninth, only Ralph Boyle stood between Paul and his goal, and Buzz came closest to spoiling everything. He drove a slashing liner toward short that sizzled into Durocher's glove on the short hop and Leo couldn't hold it. But he pounced on the ball like a cat and by a lightning throw just beat Boyle to first to end the game.

Paul fanned six men, three of them in the last two innings, and thirteen other Dodgers were retired on balls not hit out

of the infield. It was the greatest day the Dean brothers ever experienced, a day in which one all-time record was smashed and two amazing predictions by Dizzy were fulfilled.

In winning his twenty-seventh game Dizzy broke a mark established by Cy Young in 1899 as a Cardinal hurler to win the most games in a season. Cy won 26 and lost 15 that season. Dizzy has lost only seven. When Paul won the nightcap it marked his eighteenth victory, and thus made good Dizzy's boast in the Spring that "Paul and I will win forty-five games for the Cardinals this year." The dizziest prophecy of all which was made good was voiced in the Cardinals' hotel this morning, when the elder Dean told a St. Louis writer that "Zachary and Benge will be pitching against one-hit Dean and no-hit Dean today." Dizzy fell down only on his own assignment by allowing three hits instead of one.

Dizzy Dean and Paul (Daffy) Dean won seven games in 10 days to give the Cardinals the pennant on the final day of the season. "Me and Paul'll win two games apiece" in the World Series against the Detroit Tigers, Dizzy predicted. Indeed, Dizzy won Games 1 and 7, while Daffy took Games 3 and 6. Dizzy was struck on the forehead by a thrown ball as a pinch-runner in Game 4 and was taken to a hospital. Later he quipped, "The doctors X-rayed my head and found nothing."

Runners-up

1970: In the first of the Monday Night Football broadcasts, soon to become a prime-time television institution, the Cleveland Browns defeated the Jets, 31–21. Keith Jackson, Howard Cosell *(see April 25)* and Don Meredith—the "Danderco" to Cosell—reported the action. The broadcasts were the idea of Roone Arledge of ABC and Pete Rozelle, the N.F.L. commissioner.

1968: Texas Coach Darrell Royal unveiled a new backfield formation called the wishbone in a 20–20 tie against the University of Houston at Memorial Stadium in Austin. Halfbacks lined up farther from the line of scrimmage than the fullback,

creating the appearance of a wishbone. Texas won two national titles with it in 1969 and '70, and the formation permanently changed college football.

1964: The Philadelphia Phillies lost to the Cincinnati Reds, 1–0, on Chico Ruiz's steal of home at Connie Mack Stadium in Philadelphia. It was the first of 10 straight defeats for the Phils, who lost a six-and-a-half-game lead and the pennant in one of the game's most abject collapses. Manager Gene Mauch contributed to it by overusing the starters Jim Bunning and Chris Short to clinch the pennant early.

September 22, 1927
The 'Long Count'

By JAMES B. DAWSON

RINGSIDE, SOLDIER FIELD, CHICAGO—His refusal to observe the boxing rules of the Illinois State Athletic Commission, or his ignorance of the rules, or both, cost Jack Dempsey the chance to regain the world's heavyweight championship here tonight in the ring at Soldier Field. By the same token this disregard of rules of ring warfare, or this surprising ignorance, saved the title for Gene Tunney, the fighting ex-marine, who has been king of the ring for just a year.

The bout ended with Tunney getting the decision, and the vast majority in the staggering assemblage of 150,000 people, who paid, it is estimated, $2,800,000 to see this great sport spectacle, approved the verdict. The decision was given by referee Dave Barry and Judges George Lytton, wealthy department store owner, and Commodore Sheldon Clark of the Sinclair Oil Company. It was announced as a unanimous decision. Tunney won seven of the ten rounds, losing only the third, sixth and seventh, in the last of which Dempsey made his great mistake.

In that seventh round Dempsey was being peppered and buffeted about on the end of Tunney's left jabs and hooks and sharp though light right crosses, as he had been in every preceding round, with the exception of the third. In a masterful exhibition of boxing, Tunney was evading the attack of his heavier rival and was countering cleanly, superbly, for half of the round or so. Then Dempsey, plunging in recklessly, charging bull-like, suddenly lashed a long, wicked left to the jaw with the power of old. This he followed with a right to the jaw and quickly drove another left hook to the jaw, under which Tunney toppled like a falling tree, hitting the canvas with a solid thud near

Dempsey's corner, his hand reaching blindly for a helping rope which somehow or other refused to be within clutching distance.

Then Dempsey made his mistake, an error which, I believe, cost him the title. The knockdown brought the knockdown timekeeper, Paul Beeler, to his feet automatically, watch in hand, eyes glued to the ticking seconds, and he bawled "one" before he looked upon the scene in the ring. There he saw Dempsey in his own corner, directly above the prostrate, brain-numbed Tunney, his hand resting on the middle ring strand. Beeler's count stopped. Referee Barry never started one.

It is the referee's duty to see to it that a boxer scoring a knockdown goes to the corner farthest from his fallen foe and it is the duty of the knockdown timekeeper to delay the count from the watch until this rule is obeyed. The challenging ex-champion stood there, arms akimbo on the top ropes of the ring in his own corner, his expression saying more plainly than words: "Get up and I'll knock you down for keeps, this time for keeps." Finally, Dempsey took cognizance of the referee's frantic motions. He was galvanized into action and sped hurriedly across the ring to a neutral corner.

But three or four, or possibly five precious seconds had elapsed before Dempsey realized at all what he should do. In that fleeting time of the watch Tunney got the advantage. No count was proceeding over him, and quickly his senses were returning. When Referee Barry started counting with Timekeeper Beeler, Tunney was in a state of mental revival where he could keep count with the tolling seconds and did, as his moving lips revealed. Slowly the count proceed-

ed. It seemed an eternity between the downward sweep of the arm of Referee Barry and the steady pounding of the fist of Timekeeper Beeler. Tunney's senses came back to him. He got to his feet with the assistance of the ring ropes and with visible effort at the count of "nine." He was groggy, stunned, shaken.

But Dempsey was wild in this crisis, as Tunney, back pedaling for dear life, took to full flight, beating an orderly, steady retreat with only light counter moves in the face of Dempsey, aroused now for the kill. Soon Dempsey tired of his own exertions. The former champion stopped dead in his tracks in mid-ring and with a smile spreading over his scowling face motioned disgustedly, daringly, for Tunney to come on and fight.

But Tunney was playing his own game, and it was a winning game. He did not want to expose himself to that deadly Dempsey punch again, and he would not. Leo P. Flynn, Dempsey's manager, made no effort after the fight to disguise or conceal his feelings or those of Dempsey. "The watch in our corner showed fifteen seconds from the time Tunney hit the floor until he got up at the count of nine," Flynn said. "The legal count over a fallen boxer is ten seconds, not fifteen. Dempsey was jobbed."

Dempsey, however, was hoisted on his own petard. The rule compelling a boxer to go to the corner furthest removed from a fallen foe is traceable to Dempsey himself. Its adoption followed the Manassa Mauler's battle in 1923 with the giant Firpo when Dempsey stood directly above the fallen Firpo, striking the South American just as soon as his knees left the floor without waiting for Firpo to come erect from a knockdown.

Runners-up

1911: Cy Young (*see June 30*) of the Boston Braves, won his 511th and final game, a 1–0 victory over the Pirates at Forbes Field in Pittsburgh. Young's career bridged the periods when the pitching rubber was 50 feet and 60 feet 6 inches from home plate. Remarkably durable (he also had 316 losses), he pitched until he was a portly 44, when he was bunted into retirement.

1969: Willie Mays (*see Sept. 29*) of the San Francisco Giants hit his 600th home run off Mike Corkins of the Padres in a game at Jack Murphy Stadium in San

Diego. He became the second to reach that level, after Babe Ruth. Mays finished with 660 home runs and stood third on the all-time list through 2002.

1987: N.F.L. players, making an average of $230,000 a year but insistent on free agency, staged their second strike in five years. This one led to the owners' decision to use unknown replacement players for three weeks of the season, with all games counting in the standings; the regular players came back without a new contract after 24 days.

September 23, 1908
A Boner Buries the Giants

[Unsigned, *The New York Times*]

NEW YORK—Censurable stupidity on the part of player Merkle in today's game at the Polo Grounds between the Giants and Chicagos placed the New York team's chances of winning the pennant in jeopardy. His unusual conduct in the final inning of a great game perhaps deprived New York of a victory that would have been unquestionable had he not committed a breach in base-ball play that resulted in Umpire O'Day declaring the game a tie.

With the score tied in the ninth inning at 1 to 1 and the New Yorks having a runner, McCormick, on third base waiting for an opportunity to score and Merkle on first base, Bridwell hit into center field. It was a fair hit ball and would have been sufficient to win the game had Merkle gone on his way down the base path while McCormick was scoring the winning run. But instead of Merkle going to second base to make sure that McCormick had reached home with the run necessary to a victory, Merkle ran toward the club-house, evidently thinking that his share in the game was ended when Bridwell hit the ball into safe territory.

Manager Chance of the Chicago Club quickly grasped the situation and directed that the ball be thrown to second base, which would force out Merkle, who had not reached that corner. Chance, who plays first base for the Chicago club, ran

to second base and the ball was thrown there, but immediately Pitcher McGinnity interfered in the play and a scramble of players ensued, in which, it is said,

Fred Merkle in 1908, the year his base-running gaffe cost the New York Giants the pennant. Instead of advancing from first to second on a ninth-inning hit to make sure that a game-winning run from third would count, he headed to the clubhouse. (Corbis)

McGinnity obtained the ball and threw it into the crowd before Manager Chance could complete a force play on Merkle, who was far away from the baseline. Merkle said that he had touched second base, and the Chicago players were equally positive that he had not done so.

Manager Chance then appealed to

Umpire O'Day, who was head umpire of the game, for a decision in the matter. The crowd, thinking that the Giants had won the game, swarmed upon the playing field in such confusion that none of the "fans" seemed able to grasp the situation, but finally their attitude toward Umpire O'Day became so offensive that the police ran into the crowd and protected the umpire, while arguments were being hurled pro and con on the point in question by Manager Chance and McGraw and the umpire.

Umpire O'Day finally decided that the run did not count, and that inasmuch as the spectators had gained such large numbers on the field that the game could not be resumed. O'Day declared the game a tie, but the management of the Giants has recorded it as a 2 to 1 victory.

Fred Merkle's blunder indeed cost the Giants the National League pennant and effectively ruined his reputation as a player. The umpire's decision was appealed to the league's president, Harry C. Pulliam, who finally ruled the game a tie. The Giants and Cubs finished the season dead-locked for first, so the tied game was finally replayed and the Cubs won it to capture their third and last pennant. Pulliam, whose indecision about sched-uling a makeup game led to his being pilloried in the New York press, shot himself to death at the New York Athletic Club the following July.

Runners-up

1952: Rocky Marciano, 28, of Brockton, Mass., *(see Sept. 17)* knocked out Jersey Joe Walcott, 38, of Camden, N.J., in the 13th round to win the world heavy weight championship at Municipal Stadium in Philadelphia. Walcott had reigned for 14 months since winning the title from Ezzard Charles of Cincinnati.

1962: Maury Wills of the Los Angeles Dodgers, who restored to baseball the all but lost art of base stealing, thus changing the way the game was played, broke Ty Cobb's 47-year-old record by swiping his 96th and 97th bases of the

season at Sportsman's Park in St. Louis. He set a record of 104, broken by Lou Brock of the St. Louis Cardinals in 1974.

1988: The "40-40 Club" came into vogue in baseball when Jose Canseco of the Oakland A's stole his 39th and 40th bases of the year and hit his 41st home run in a game against the Milwaukee Brewers. Barry Bonds (San Francisco Giants, 1996) and Alex Rodriguez (Seattle Mariners, '98) are the other charter members.

September 24, 1938
Success, Success, Success

By ALLISON DANZIG

NEW YORK—The book was closed today on the greatest record of success ever compiled by a lawn tennis player in one season of national and international tennis competition. J. Donald Budge of Oakland, Calif., stood as the first player in history to win all four of the world's major tennis titles in the same year when he defeated Gene Mako of Los Angeles in the Forest Hills Stadium in the final round of the national championship. The score was 6–3, 6–8, 6–2, 6–1.

The triumph of the 23-year-old red-headed giant completed a campaign of unparalleled achievement on three continents. No one before him has held at one and the same time the American, British, French and Australian crowns, all of which have fallen in 1938 to the rapacity of Budge's 15-ounce racquet for a grand slam that invites comparison with the accomplishment of Bobby Jones in golf. In this respect, at least, Budge takes precedence over William Tilden, the Frenchmen, Henri Cochét and Rene Lacosté; Ellsworth Vines, Wilmer Allison, Fred Perry, the Briton, and all the other great modern champions. Jack Crawford of Australia came closest to winning four major crowns when, in 1933, he won three of the titles and led Perry, three sets to one, in the American final.

A gallery of 12,000 looked

on under a stinging sun as Budge made history. That the stadium was not filled to capacity was probably attributable to the conviction that the outcome of his meet-

Donald Budge, aged 20, in 1935. Three years later the tall redhead from California became the first player in tennis to win all four major tournaments—the Australian, French, British and U.S. titles—in a single year. (Associated Press)

ing with his doubles partner was foreordained. Despite the amazingly fine tennis Mako had produced to concoct the defeat of John Bromwich in the semi-finals, few, if any, conceded the stalwart, blond Los Angeles youth the slightest chance of staying the all-conquering march of the Oakland terror.

If Mako had the satisfaction of being the only player in the tournament to wrest a set from the champion, it was not because Budge willed it that way. It was salvaged from a 2–5 deficit after Mako had slumped badly in the face of Budge's pitilessly raking bombardment. It would be considerably less than justice not to accord Mako that full measure of praise he deserves for the brilliant tennis he put forth in winning six of the next seven games. His flat forehand was striking like lightning. His backhand slice stood up unwaveringly from any angle. He used the lob and drop shot with his usual aplomb. It was a worried-looking Budge who stared at Mako's beautiful back-hand drive that went passing by him for the final point of the set.

With the start of the third set, however, command of the match reverted to the champion. Budge turned loose a tornado of controlled speed such as had been visited upon no other opponent in the tournament, with his service making the chalk fly on the lines.

September 25, 1986
What a Way to Win!

By ROY S. JOHNSON

HOUSTON—The Houston Astros wrapped up an improbable season with an improbable ending today as Mike Scott pitched a no-hitter that clinched their first division championship in six years. The Astros, who have been in first place since July 19 after being picked by many to finish at the bottom of the division, had maintained all along that they wanted to earn the title by winning the clinching game, rather than depending on the misfortunes of their closest competitors. But no one envisioned that they would complete their quest in such an emotional and dramatic fashion.

Scott, who was traded to the Astros by the Mets for Danny Heep four seasons ago, struck out 13 batters and allowed only three base-runners in a masterly 2–0 triumph over the San Francisco Giants. Scott, the league leader in strikeouts (298) and earned run average (2.25), won his 18th game of the season against 10 losses as Houston reached the League Championship Series for the first time since 1980 and only the second time in the 25-year history of the franchise.

The Astros began the day knowing that a victory by the Atlanta Braves over the Cincinnati Reds earlier this afternoon was all they needed to clinch the title. But after they learned during batting practice that the Reds had gained a 6–4 victory, the Astros knew they could clinch by themselves. Well into the game, however, their quest for the title seemed secondary to Scott's performance. Going into the ninth inning, he said he was "more pumped up than nervous" as the crowd of 32,808 gave him a standing ovation. "I just wanted to keep us in the game," Scott said. "We would have been real disappointed if we didn't win and had to go to Atlanta and do it in front of 5,000 people."

Scott, a 6-foot-3-inch right-hander who is 31 years old, had never pitched a no-hitter at any level, and after the first pitch of the game it didn't seem as if this would be his first one. His elusive split-fingered fastball hit Dan Gladden, the Giants' leadoff hitter, squarely in the back. "For the first two innings, he had what I would call mediocre stuff," said Alan Ashby, the Astros' catcher. "But after that, it was Katy, bar the door." More than two hours after that first errant pitch, Scott entered the ninth by striking out Gladden and Rob Thompson and gaining the final out on a ground ball by Will Clark to Glenn Davis, the first baseman, who fielded the ball cleanly and completed the play unassisted.

"I told him to take it himself because I didn't want to bobble it," said Scott, who was running toward first in a not-so-wholehearted effort to cover the bag. The Astros mobbed their pitcher. In contrast to the destructive scene that marred the Mets' division-clinching victory last week, not one fan came onto the Astrodome field. Fourteen mounted policemen seemed to be enough of a deterrent.

In the best-of-seven-game league

Mike Scott and the Astros hail his no-hitter over the Giants, which clinched the N.L. East title. Scott's gift to baseball in 1986 was the split-fingered fastball, which he used to strike out 306 and win the Cy Young Award. (Associated Press)

championship series, Mike Scott won both games he started against the Mets, allowing one earned run in 18 innings. The Mets won the pennant, however, by 7–6 in Game 6 as Jesse Orosco struck out Kevin Bass with the tying run on third base in the last of the 16th inning.

Runners-up

1988: Matt Biondi of Palo Alto, Calif., won his fifth gold medal at the Seoul Olympics, falling two short of Mark Spitz's seven in 1972 *(see Sept. 4)*, when he swam the butterfly leg on the United States 4x100-meter medley relay. A powerful 6 feet 6 inches and 200 pounds, Biondi won eight gold medals over all in three Olympics (Los Angeles 1984, Seoul '88, Barcelona '92).

1962: Sonny Liston of St. Louis knocked out the two-time champion Floyd Patterson at 2 minutes 6 seconds of the first round with two lefts and a devastating right to win the world heavyweight championship at Comiskey Park in Chicago. The glowering Liston got into boxing while serving time for robbery at the Missouri State Penitentiary.

1989: Wade Boggs of the Boston Red Sox collected 200 hits for a major league-record seventh straight season when he went four for five in a 7–4 victory over the Yankees at Fenway Park. He won five batting titles during those seasons, with a high of .368 in 1985.

September 26, 1999
A Charge From Beyond the Fringe

By DAVE ANDERSON

BROOKLINE, Mass.—Justin Leonard's putt crawled up, up and across the ledge on the 17th green and dived into the hole like a field mouse. As Leonard struggled during the week, Ben Crenshaw, the American captain, kept promising that "Justin's going to make a putt." And he already had, a 30-footer on the 15th green today that squared his match with José Maria Olazabal after having been 4 down. But now the little Texan had made a 45-footer for a birdie 3 that will be remembered as the most theatrical putt in Ryder Cup history.

In their elation, several American players and their wives rushed to celebrate with Leonard, but soon remembered that Olazabal still had to putt for what might be a tying birdie. So did Crenshaw, now crouched behind the green, saying, "All right." Next to him, Bruce Edwards, Tom Watson's long-time caddie, who was here as an assistant to Crenshaw, turned to the captain. "If he misses, you win," Edwards said. "Oh, my God," Crenshaw said quietly. "You're five seconds away," Edwards said, "from the greatest comeback in the history of the Ryder Cup."

But it would be more like five minutes. Olazabal, the Spaniard who had played so well for the European team in other cup matches, knew he had to make his 25-footer. He studied the uphill line, walked around and peered at the contours near the cup, finally took his stance over the ball, then stepped back, studied the line again, took his stance again and putted. "Please miss," Edwards whispered what all the Americans were wishing. "Please miss."

Olazabal's ball moved up the slope and across the ledge, but when it stayed left of the hole, the American players rushed Leonard. But Crenshaw, who seemed to have been holding his breath all that time, moved forward, knelt and kissed the green, then joined the celebration as Olazabal shook hands with the American captain. With Leonard 1 up going to the 18th hole, the United States Ryder Cup team was assured of the half-point it needed for an unprecedented 4-point comeback in the 12 singles matches for a 14½-13½ triumph at The Country Club that had both proper and improper Bostonians roaring as if the Red Sox had won a World Series.

And for Ben Crenshaw, his crusade had been a success. It hadn't been easy. In the August controversy over some American golfers' request for money they could donate to their individual charities, he had questioned the commitment of Tiger Woods, David Duval, Phil Mickelson and Mark O'Meara. Critics had second-guessed his two wild-card choices, Tom Lehman and Steve Pate, as well as some of his final pairings. "I don't know how these things happen," he said. "I do know how it happened, though. By these fellows and the way they can play golf."

Justin Leonard exults over sinking a 45-foot putt on the 17th green against José Maria Olazabal of Spain that gave the U.S. Ryder Cup team a 14-13 comeback victory over Europe. It was the greatest final-day recovery in Cup history. (Agence France-Presse)

Runners-up

1961: Roger Maris of the Yankees *(see Oct. 1)* tied Babe Ruth's 1927 home run record by hitting his 60th of the season into the right-field seats at Yankee Stadium in a 3–2 victory over the Baltimore Orioles. The shot, which came off right-hander Jack Fisher, came in Maris's 159th game, which became an issue because Ruth hit his in 154 games.

1988: Ben Johnson of Canada left the Seoul Olympics in disgrace after being stripped of his 100-meter gold medal when he tested positive for steroids. His three-day-old world record of 9.79 seconds was erased and the gold medal was awarded to Carl Lewis of the United States.

1983: Australia II, skippered by John Bertrand, became the first foreign boat in nearly a century to win the prestigious America's Cup, defeating Dennis Conner's Liberty, 4-3, and wresting the trophy from the New York Yacht Club, which had held it for 132 years *(see Aug. 22)*. Australia II won in large measure because of its innovative keel design. Conner returned the Cup to the United States in 1987 *(see Feb. 4)*.

September 27, 1930
The Golf Grand Slam

By WILLIAM D. RICHARDSON

ARDMORE, Pa.—When Gene Homans's ball grazed the side of the cup on the twenty-ninth hole at the Merion Cricket Club today, Bobby Jones not only became the national amateur champion for 1930 but the holder of a record that probably will survive through the ages. At 28, this rarely-gifted golfer from Atlanta, who defeated Homans 8 up and 7 to play in today's final and who has come closer to mastering the intricacies of the game than any one else, has performed a feat that no one hitherto had considered possible.

Within the short span of five months, Bobby has played in the four major golf events—the British amateur and open championships and the American open and amateur—and won them all, outscoring the professionals at their own game in the two open tournaments and out-stripping all his fellow amateurs in the others. Moreover he is the first man in the history of American golf to win the National amateur five times, he and Jerry Travers, who was in the gallery that followed the marvelous Atlantan today, having been tied at four victories each until this afternoon.

No one in the great throng of fully 18,000 spectators, who made a great human fringe around the green and a solid mass packed in the fairway that Jones had just played from, could help but feel that here was golf history being made. It was an epochal moment, and the demonstration that came after it was one that will never be forgotten. Playing the hole, a two-shotter with two level fairways and an island green tucked away back in the woods, Jones was a dormie 8. But a moment before he had missed a chance to close out the match on the previous hole by misjudging a little pitch shot out of the rough and putting his ball into a bunker alongside Homans's.

Both sides of the fairway were lined

Bobby Jones, left, receiving the U.S. amateur trophy from Findlay Douglas, president of the U.S. Golf Association. Jones had just completed the Grand Slam at Merion by defeating Gene Homans, right, 8 and 7. (Associated Press)

with persons ten and twelve rows deep as he and Homans drove off. It was Gene's honor, Bobby having conceded him a birdie 2 on the No. 9 hole. The ex–Princeton star, realizing by now, of course, that it was all over, drove to the left. Having nothing to lose, Bobby lit into his drive and sent his ball flying down the fairway. It was a long drive, almost reaching the edge of the little stream that runs across the fairway near the 300-yard mark. Homans had to play first and sent a beautiful mashie shot onto the green, a trifle beyond the hole. A moment later Bobby's ball came sailing on, stopping short of the pin.

Despite the fact that all those thousands were standing as close as they could get, the dropping of a pin in the grass would have been heard as Bobby, looking a little haggard and drawn, walked over to his ball after his caddie had handed him his pet putter, known the world over as Calamity Jane. One of those quizzical glances that he gives the hole, the familiar cocking of the Jones head, a slight movement of the wrists as they brought the club back and then forward.

The ball started on its journey up to the hole over the closely cropped grass. He didn't quite have the line, but it stopped so close to the side of the hole that Homans would have had to sink his in order to prevent the match from ending there and then. Knowing full well that it was all over Gene took comparatively little time over his own putt, hit the ball and, almost before it passed by the side of the hole, he was over wringing Bobby's hand. Immediately a great shout was sent up, then the tumult that reverberated for miles. It lasted for several minutes. There was a wild rush toward Jones who, had it not been for the presence of a squad of marines, would have been crushed.

Runners-up

1998: Mark McGwire of the St. Louis Cardinals, who broke Roger Maris's record of 61 home runs early in the month *(see Sept. 8),* finished his record season with a flourish, clouting two home runs off Mike Thurman and Carl Pavano of the Montreal Expos at Busch Stadium to raise his total to 70.

1973: Nolan Ryan of the California Angels fanned 16 Minnesota Twins in an 11-inning 5–4 victory at Anaheim Stadium, setting the single-season record of 383 strikeouts. Rich Reese became victim no. 383, enabling Ryan to surpass Sandy Koufax of the Los Angeles Dodgers, who struck out 382 in 1965.

2000: Rulon Gardner, 29, of Afton, Wyo., the 298-pound United States heavyweight in Greco-Roman wrestling, pulled off one of the major upsets of the Sydney Olympics in Australia, defeating Aleksandr Karelin of Russia, 1–0, when Karelin, 290 pounds, made the mistake of breaking a hold. Karelin, 33, had been undefeated in 14 years of international competition.

'There's Nothing More I Can Do'

By ARTHUR DALEY

Ted Williams of the Red Sox being greeted by Jim Pagliaroni after connecting for a home run in his final major league at-bat, at Fenway Park. "That's the end," he said, retiring in the most dramatic fashion possible. (Associated Press)

BOSTON (UPI)—Ted Williams ended his playing career today by hitting a home run against the Baltimore Orioles in his last time at bat. The 42-year-old Boston Red Sox star had planned to play in the team's last three games at New York this week-end. But he disclosed after the Red Sox had beaten the Orioles, 5–4, that he was calling it quits immediately.

The club had announced that Williams would retire at the end of the season. The slugging outfielder gave no reason for his sudden decision to retire four days early. Williams's farewell home run was the 521st of his career. It was a 420-foot drive off Jack Fisher with the bases empty in the eighth inning. The crowd of 10,454 had given Williams a standing ovation as the big left fielder strode to the plate for his final appearance, swinging two bats. Williams lashed at a 1–1 pitch and the ball was gone.

Besides the 521 home runs, Ted Williams retired with a .344 average. He won six batting titles and led the American League in homers and runs batted in four times. The following column, by Mr. Daley, appeared in The Times *two days later.*

NEW YORK—In retrospect the special trip must be regarded as ridiculously premature. But in the late spring of 1952 a certain long-time admirer of Theodore Samuel Williams went many miles out of his way to attend a Boston Red Sox exhibition game in Florida. "Ted will be on his way to Korea any day now," he said, almost as if he required an excuse. "This may be my last chance to see him swing a bat."

For all that anyone knew at that time the summary recall of the great slugger for a second service stint as a Marine aviator might have finished him as a ballplayer. So monumental are his talents, though, that it didn't. He returned and picked up a couple more batting championships, his fifth and sixth.

A similar pilgrimage had been planned for this week-end at the Stadium when Williams was scheduled to play the last three games of his career and then rack up his bat for the last time, a glorious career at an end. But Ted unexpectedly jumped the gun. He struck his own resounding farewell note in his final time at bat amid the thunderous ovation of fans at Fenway Park. He hit a titanic homer over the Red Sox bullpen.

"That's the end," said Ted sadly, canceling himself out of the Yankee Stadium series. "There's nothing more I can do." None can blame him. He quit in the most dramatic fashion possible. "All I want out of life," he said when he first joined the Red Sox in 1939, "is that when I walk down the street folks will say: 'There goes the greatest hitter who ever lived.'" That matchless swing has been seen for the last time and baseball will be the poorer by Ted's departure.

September 28, 1920
The Black Sox Scandal

[unsigned, *The New York Times*]

CHICAGO—Seven star players for the Chicago White Sox and one former player were indicted late this afternoon, charged with complicity in a conspiracy with gamblers to "fix" the 1919 world's series. The indictments were based on evidence obtained for the Cook County Grand Jury by Charles A. Comiskey, owner of the White Sox, and after confessions by two of the players told how the world's championship was thrown to Cincinnati and how they had received money or were "double-crossed" by the gamblers.

The eight players indicted are:

EDDIE CICOTTE, star pitcher.

"SHOELESS JOE" JACKSON, left fielder and heavy hitter.

OSCAR "HAP" FELSCH, centre fielder.

CHARLES "SWEDE" RISBERG, shortstop.

GEORGE "BUCK" WEAVER, third baseman.

ARNOLD GANDIL, former first baseman.

CLAUDE WILLIAMS, pitcher.

FRED McMULLEN, utility player.

The specific charge against the eight players is "conspiracy to commit an illegal act," which is punishable by five years' imprisonment or a fine up to $10,000, but this charge may be changed when the full indictments are drawn by the Grand Jury. No sooner had the news of the indictments become public than Comiskey suspended the seven players, wrecking the team he had given years to build up and almost certainly forfeiting his chances to beat out Cleveland for the American League pennant. His letter notifying the players of their suspension follows:

Shoeless Joe Jackson in an undated photo. Jackson and seven other members of the 1919 White Sox were indicted by a Chicago grand jury for throwing the World Series to the Reds. "Say it ain't so, Joe," a reporter quoted a boy as saying. (Associated Press)

"Chicago, Sept. 26.

"To Charles Risberg, Fred McMullen, Joe Jackson, Oscar Felsch, George Weaver, C.P. Williams and Eddie Cicotte:

"You and each of you are hereby notified of your indefinite suspension as a member of the Chicago American Baseball Club. Your suspension is brought about by information which has just come to me directly involving you and each of you in the baseball scandal resulting from the world's series of 1919.

"If you are innocent of any wrongdoing you and each of you will be reinstated; if you are guilty you will be retired from organized baseball for the rest of your lives

if I can accomplish it. Until there is a finality to this investigation it is due to the public that I take this action, even though it costs Chicago the pennant.

"CHICAGO AMERICAN BASEBALL CLUB

"By CHARLES A. COMISKEY"

Officials of the Grand Jury lifted the curtain on the proceedings and declared that Cicotte and Jackson made open confessions, Cicotte admitting receiving $10,000 and throwing two games, and Jackson admitting receiving $5,000 of $20,000 promised him by the gamblers and telling of his efforts to defeat his own team.

Cicotte's confession came after he and Alfred S. Austrian, counsel for the White Sox management, had conferred with Judge Charles A. McDonald in the latter's chambers. Toward the end of this conference they were joined by Assistant State Attorney Hartley Replogle. A few moments later he and Cicotte proceeded to the grand jury room. There the great baseball pitcher broke down and wept. "My God! Think of my children," he cried.

The eight White Sox players, tried in June 1921, were acquitted in 2 hours 47 minutes. The confessions of Joe Jackson, Eddie Cicotte and Claude (Lefty) Williams were reported missing and were never heard by the jurors. Kenesaw Mountain Landis, appointed commissioner the previous year (see Nov. 12), banned all eight from the game immediately after the verdict. Jackson, Cicotte and Risberg continued to play baseball for some years in outlaw leagues or on semi-pro teams. Jackson later owned and operated a liquor store. He died in Greenville, S.C., at age 62 in 1951.

Runners-up

1941: Ted Williams of the Boston Red Sox became the last player to hit .400 for a season, getting six hits in eight at-bats against the Philadelphia Athletics in a doubleheader at Shibe Park. He finished at .406 (.4057), deciding to play in both games although he effectively started the day at .400 (.39955).

1938: Catcher and manager Gabby Hartnett hit the "homer in the gloamin'" at Wrigley Field, helping the Chicago Cubs beat the Pittsburgh Pirates for the National League pennant. Hartnett's game-ending, dusk-descending shot, off

Mace Brown, gave the Cubs a one-game lead with one to play. Chicago clinched the title the following day but was swept in the World Series.

1988: Orel Hershiser of the Los Angeles Dodgers pitched 10 shutout innings against the San Diego Padres in his last regular-season start, giving him 59 consecutive scoreless innings and breaking Don Drysdale's record of 58⅔ innings set while a member of the Dodgers two decades before (see June 4).

September 29, 1954
On the Wings of the Wind

By JOHN DREBINGER and LOUIS EFFRAT

NEW YORK—At precisely 4:12 o'clock by the huge clock atop the center-field clubhouse at the Polo Grounds this afternoon, Leo Durocher peered intently at his hand and decided it was time to play his trump card. It was the last half of the tenth inning in the opening game of the 1954 world series. The tense and dramatic struggle had a gathering of 52,751, a record series crowd for the arena, hanging breathlessly on every pitch.

The score was deadlocked at 2-all. Two Giants were on the base paths and on the mound was Bob Lemon, twenty-three-game winner of the American League, who had gone all the way and was making a heroic bid to continue the struggle a little further. Then Leo made his move. He called on his pinch-hitter extraordinary, James (Dusty) Rhodes from Rock Hill, S.C., to bat for Monte Irvin. Lemon served one pitch. Rhodes, a left-handed batsman, swung and a lazy pop fly sailed down the right-field line. The ball had just enough carry to clear the wall barely 270 feet away. But it was enough to produce an electrifying three-run homer that enabled the Giants to bring down Al Lopez' Indians, 5 to 2.

It was a breath-taking finish to as nerve-tingling a struggle as any world series had ever seen. The game had started as a stirring mound duel between 37-year-old Sal Maglie and the Tribe's brilliant Lemon. It saw Vic Wertz, sturdy first sacker, rake Giant pitching for four of the Indians' eight hits. His first one was a triple that drove in two first-inning runs off Maglie. In the third the Polo Grounders wrenched those two tallies back from Lemon. Then, in the eighth, with the score 2–2, Maglie faltered. He walked Larry Doby, and Al Rosen, hitless to this point,

banged a scorching single off shortstop Al Dark's bare hand. That brought in Don Liddle, a mite of a southpaw, who almost lost the game on the spot. With the runners leading off their bases, Wertz connected for another tremendous drive that went down the center of the field 450 feet, only to have Willie Mays make one of his most amazing catches.

Traveling on the wings of the wind, Willie caught the ball directly in front of the green boarding facing the right-center bleachers and with his back still to the diamond. Mays, his usual happy self, said

later that "I don't know whether I made a greater catch at any time. I just try to get a good jump on the ball and go get it. I thought I had that one all the way." Unanimously, the Indians agreed that the catch by Mays was the turning point in the encounter. Willie's incredible snare with none out took the Tribe out of a most promising inning. "It was one of the greatest catches I ever have seen," Lopez averred. Doby, a center-fielder, echoed his manager's praise of Mays. And Wertz said, "I never hit a ball so hard in my career as the one Willie caught."

Willie Mays, back to the plate, catching Vic Wertz's 450-foot drive to center field in Game 1 of the 1954 World Series. The most famous catch in baseball history, it helped the New York Giants sweep the Indians. (Associated Press)

Runners-up

1988: Four days after setting a world record of 10.49 seconds in the 100 meters at the Seoul Olympics, Florence Griffith Joyner (*see July 16*) of the United States set a world mark of 21.34 seconds in the 200. The first mark broke the 1984 record of 10.76 seconds by Evelyn Ashford of the United States; the second shattered the joint standard of 21.71 by Marita Koch and Heike Drechsler of East Germany in the 70's and 80's.

1991: The United States regained the Ryder Cup with a 14½–13½ victory over Europe on the Ocean Course at Kiawah Island, S.C. Bernhard Langer of

Germany missed a six-foot putt on the 18th hole in the deciding match, giving Hale Irwin a tie and the half-point the United States needed for the victory.

1996: Jeff Gordon (*see Aug. 16*) raced to his 10th Nascar victory of the year in the farewell Winston Cup race at North Wilkesboro Speedway in North Carolina, giving him a seemingly insurmountable 111-point lead over his teammate Terry Labonte for the season's title. But consistent finishes pay: Labonte, despite just two victories, had just enough of them to win the driver's title.

The Record That Stood for 34 Years

[Unsigned, *The New York Times*]

NEW YORK—Babe Ruth scaled the hitherto unattainable heights today. Home run 60, a terrific smash off the southpaw pitching of Zachary, nestled in the Babe's favorite spot in the right-field bleachers, and before the roar had ceased it was found that this drive not only had made home run record history but also was the winning margin in a 4 to 2 victory over the Senators. This also was the Yanks' 100th triumph of the season. Their last league game of the season will be played tomorrow.

When the Babe stepped to the plate in that momentous eighth inning the score was deadlocked. Koenig was on third

base, the result of a triple, one man was out and all was tense. It was the Babe's fourth trip to the plate during the afternoon, a base on balls and two singles resulting on his other visits plateward. The first Zachary offering was a fast one, which sailed over for a called strike. The next was high. The Babe took a vicious swing at the third pitched ball and the bat connected with a crash that was audible in all parts of the stand. The boys in the bleachers indicated the route of the record homer. It dropped about half way to the top, a fitting wallop to break the Babe's record of 59 in 1921.

While the crowd cheered and the

Yankee players roared their greetings the Babe made his triumphant, almost regal tour of the paths. He jogged around slowly, touched each bag firmly and carefully, and when he imbedded his spikes in the rubber disk to record officially Homer 60 hats were tossed into the air, papers were torn up and tossed liberally and the spirit of celebration permeated the place. The Babe's stroll out to his position was the signal for a handkerchief salute in which all the bleacherites, to the last man, participated. Jovial Babe entered into the carnival spirit and punctuated his kingly strides with a succession of snappy military salutes.

The only unhappy individual in the Stadium was Zachary, one of the most interested spectators of the home run flight. He tossed his glove to the ground, muttered to himself, turned to his mates for consolation and got everything but that.

The ball that the Babe drove, according to word from official sources, was a pitch that was fast, low and on the inside. The Babe pulled away from the plate, then stepped into the ball, and wham. According to Umpire Bill Dinneen at the plate and Catcher Muddy Ruel, the ball traveled on a line and landed a foot inside fair territory about half way to the top of the bleachers. But when the ball reached the bleacher barrier it was about ten feet fair and curving rapidly to the right. The ball was caught by Joe Forner of 1937 First Avenue, Manhattan. He is about 40 years old and has been following baseball for about thirty-five, according to his own admission. He was far from modest and as soon as the game was over rushed to the dressing room to let the Babe know who had the ball.

Babe Ruth hitting his famous 60th home run against the Washington Senators at Yankee Stadium. When he went to right field in the top of the ninth, fans waved handkerchiefs and the Babe responded with military salutes. (Reuters)

Runners-up

1945: Having returned from World War II three months before, Tigers slugger Hank Greenberg clinched the American League pennant for Detroit with a ninth-inning grand slam off Nelson Potter that beat the St. Louis Browns, 6–3, at Sportsman's Park in St. Louis. The Tigers beat the Chicago Cubs, four games to three.

1962: The Mets, tagged in their first year with Manager Casey Stengel's immortal line "Can't anybody here play this game?" lost a major league-record 120th game in the season's finale, 5–1, to the Chicago Cubs at Wrigley Field. As if

to offer a fitting close, the Mets' Joe Pignatano lined into a triple play in his last major league at-bat.

1967: The three greatest thoroughbreds of the day—Buckpasser, Damascus and Dr. Fager—were brought together for a historic meeting in the Woodward Stakes at Belmont Park in New York. Damascus, ridden by Bill Shoemaker and trained by Frank Whiteley Jr., won by 10 lengths over Buckpasser, who struggled to finish a half-length ahead of a weary Dr. Fager.

OCTOBER

October 1, 1961
Roger Maris Surpasses the Babe (*)

By JOHN DREBINGER

NEW YORK—Roger Maris today became the first major league player in history to hit more than sixty home runs in a season. The 27-year-old Yankee outfielder hit his sixty-first at the Stadium before a roaring crowd of 23,154 in the Bombers' final game of the regular campaign. That surpassed by one the sixty that Babe Ruth hit in 1927. Ruth's mark has stood in the record book for thirty-four years. Artistically enough, Maris's homer also produced the only run of the game as Ralph Houk's 1961 American League champions defeated the Red Sox, 1 to 0, in their final tune-up for the world series, which opens at the Stadium in two days.

Maris hit his fourth-inning homer in his second time at bat. The victim of the blow was Tracy Stallard, a 24-year-old Boston rookie right-hander. Stallard's name, perhaps, will in time gain as much renown as that of Tom Zachary, who delivered the pitch that Ruth slammed into the Stadium's right-field bleachers for No. 60 on the next to the last day of the 1927 season. Along with Stallard still another name was bandied about at the Stadium after Maris's drive. Sal Durante, a 19-year-old truck driver from Coney Island, was the fellow who caught the ball as it dropped into the lower right-field stand, some 10 rows back and about 10 feet to the right of the Yankee bull pen.

Maris was fooled by Stallard on an outside pitch that he stroked to left field for an out in the first inning. He let two pitches go by when he came to bat in the fourth with one out and the bases empty. The first one was high and outside. The second one was low and appeared to be inside. Stallard's next pitch was a fast ball that appeared to be about waist high and right down the middle. In a flash, Roger's rhythmic swing, long the envy of left-handed pull hitters, connected with the ball.

Almost at once, the crowd sensed that

Roger Maris watching the flight of his 61st home run off Tracy Stallard of the Red Sox at Yankee Stadium. The shot broke Babe Ruth's record and ignited a controversy since Maris had 163 games for his mark while Ruth had 154. (Associated Press)

this was it. An ear-splitting roar went up as Maris, standing spellbound for just an instant at the plate, started his triumphant jog around the bases. As he came down the third-base line, he shook hands joyously with a young fan who had rushed onto the field to congratulate him. Crossing the plate and arriving at the Yankee dugout, he was met by a solid phalanx of team-mates. This time they made certain the modest country lad from Raytown, Mo., acknowledged the crowd's plaudits. He had been reluctant to do so when he hit No. 60, but this time the

Yankee players wouldn't let Roger come down the dugout steps. Smiling broadly, the usually unemotional player lifted his cap from his blond close-cropped thatch and waved it to the cheering fans. Not until he had taken four bows did his colleagues allow him to retire to the bench.

Ruth's record, of course, will not be erased. On July 17, Commissioner Ford C. Frick ruled that Ruth's record would stand unless bettered within a 54-game limit, since that was the schedule in 1927. Maris hit fifty-nine homers in the Yanks' first 154 games to a decision. He hit his sixtieth four games later. However, Maris will go into the record book as having hit the sixty-first in a 162-game schedule. Maris finished the season with 590 official times at bat. Ruth, in 1927, had 540 official times at bat. Their total appearances at the plate, however, were nearly identical—698 for Maris and 692 for Ruth.

No asterisk in the baseball record book noting that Roger Maris set his record in 163 games while Babe Ruth reached his in 154 ever really existed—the records were simply listed separately. But the twin listing itself was controversial, implying to some that Maris's record was somehow inferior. In 1991 a major-league baseball committee on statistical accuracy voted to remove the distinction, giving the record fully to Maris. He did not live to see the change, having died of cancer in Houston at age 51 in 1985.

Runners-up

1932: Babe Ruth hit his "called shot" home run into the Wrigley Field bleachers in the fifth inning of Game 3 of the World Series. Some historians say Ruth was not pointing to the center-field stands before Charlie Root's two-strike pitch but rather was notifying the Chicago Cubs' bench jockeys that he still had one more pitch to hit. The point is, he hit it, breaking a 4–4 tie and helping the Yankees to a four-game sweep.

1975: Muhammad Ali retained his world heavyweight championship when Joe Frazier was unable to answer the bell for the 15th round of their unforgettably fierce

and punishing bout that came to be known as the Thrilla in Manila. Ali later said of the bout, "Closest thing to dyin' I know of."

1967: The Boston Red Sox, concluding their "impossible dream" season, clinched their first pennant since 1946 with a 5–3 victory over the Minnesota Twins at Fenway Park. Carl Yastrzemski, superb in the clutch, went 4 for 4 and had 10 hits in his last 13 at-bats to grab the pennant and become the last player as of 2002 to win the triple crown.

October 2, 1978
Bucky Dent's Improbable Clout

By JAMES TUITE

BOSTON—Somehow, it all defied logic. After more than 300 hours of baseball in 162 games spanning half a year, the season was distilled into 172 minutes on a sunny October afternoon. Yet, here was the reductio ad absurdum: the New York Yankees, torn by bitterness and 14 games out of first place a month ago, sat atop the American League East today, headed for a pennant confrontation with the Kansas City Royals. "I've been dreaming of this," said Bucky Dent, of the seventh-inning homer he hit over the leftfield wall. "You know you dream about things like that when you're a kid. Well, my dream came true."

Dent was talking about a looping drive that cleared the formidable rampart by at least five feet and sent Chris Chambliss and Roy White scurrying home ahead of him. That sent the Yankees ahead of the Boston Red Sox, 3–2, and proved to be the mightiest blow of their 5–4 victory. A double by Thurman Munson that scored Mickey Rivers provided another Yankee run in the seventh, this one off of Bob Stanley. He had replaced Mike Torrez after the Yankees put a Dent in their former teammate. A Reggie Jackson homer in the eighth put the game away.

The record books will probably find it difficult to explain that Rivers and a bat-boy deserve asterisks for Dent's home run. After Dent painfully fouled a ball off his ankle, Rivers handed a bat to Tony Sarandrea, the 18-year-old batboy. "Give this to Bucky," said Rivers. "Tell him there are lots of hits in it. He'll get a home run." Dent switched to the new bat and gave lie to Hemingway's observation that "a man can be destroyed but not beaten." That may apply to old fishermen but not to the Yanks: they defeated the Red Sox without destroying them.

For the Bostons, still on a natural high after winning 12 of their last 14 games and eight of them in a row, gallantly fought back. Their partisans among the 32,925 noisy viewers here saw them make a game effort with two more runs in the eighth but only after the Yanks had collected a decisive one on a looping homer to centerfield by Jackson. "It was a fast ball right over the plate," said Jackson, who detoured on his way back to the dugout to shake the hand of his part-time adversary and Yankee president, George Steinbrenner. That sealed the tasty conquest for Ron Guidry, who needed help from Rich Gossage in the seventh. Said Gossage, who achieved his 27th rescue of the season: "I wasn't worried out there. If I got beaten I was going to lose on my own effort."

"We've come back from bigger deficits," said Graig Nettles. "It was nothing to worry about. The best part was that we did it against Torrez. He's been bad-mouthing us all season, ever since he left the Yanks." Torrez, whose erratic pitching has not endeared him to the Boston fans in recent weeks, was rolling comfortably along with the two-run cushion provided by Carl Yastrzemski's homer in the second and a Jim Rice single that scored Rick Burleson in the sixth.

The Yankee players all had praise for Bob Lemon, who took over the club from Billy Martin during his tumultuous early months. "Lemon knew us all the way," said Nettles. "He was perfect for bringing us together. It wouldn't have worked if they had brought someone else in as manager." Lemon got an extra chuckle out of today's victory, for he had played on the Cleveland team that beat Boston the last time the Red Sox were forced into a one-game playoff. The year was 1948. As for Dent, he was not worried about his injured foot. "A little ice and champagne will fix that," he said smiling.

The Yankees went on to defeat the Kansas City Royals, three games to one, in the league championship series. They won the World Series in six games over the Los Angeles Dodgers after being down, two games to none.

Bucky Dent connecting for a three-run, seventh-inning home run off the Red Sox' Mike Torrez that all but clinched a division title for the Yankees in a one-game regular-season playoff at Fenway Park. Dent had only four other homers all year. (Associated Press)

Runners-up

1968: Bob Gibson struck out a World Series record 17 batters in pitching the St. Louis Cardinals over the Detroit Tigers, 4–0, in Game 1 at Busch Stadium. Gibson, who had 13 shutouts and a 1.12 earned run average in the regular season, bested the 31-game winner Denny McLain. The "Year of the Pitcher" led to off-season changes such as the lowering of the mound and creation of a tighter strike zone.

1980: Larry Holmes, aged 30, defended his World Boxing Council heavyweight championship with an 11th-round technical knockout of Muhammad Ali, 38, in Las Vegas. Ali, who had been retired for two years, was trying to win the heavyweight title for an unprecedented fourth time *(see Dec. 11)*.

1994: Don Shula, 64, and the Miami Dolphins defeated David Shula, 32, and the Cincinnati Bengals, 23–7, at Riverfront Stadium in Cincinnati. It was the first time in pro sports that a father and son faced each other as head coaches. Don Shula became the winningest coach in N.F.L. history (347–173–6 in the regular season and the playoffs). David (19–52) was fired after four seasons.

October 3, 1951
'The Shot Heard Round the World'

By JOHN DREBINGER

NEW YORK—In an electrifying finish to what long will be remembered as the most thrilling pennant campaign in history, Leo Durocher and his astounding never-say-die Giants wrenched victory from the jaws of defeat at the Polo Grounds today, vanquishing the Dodgers, 5 to 4, with a four-run splurge in the last half of the ninth. A three-run homer by Bobby Thomson that accounted for the final three tallies blasted the Dodgers right out of the World Series picture, and tomorrow afternoon at the Stadium it will be the Giants against Casey Stengel's American League champion Yankees in the opening clash of the world series.

Seemingly hopelessly beaten, 4 to 1, as the third and deciding game of the epic National League play-off moved into the last inning, the Giants lashed back with a fury that would not be denied. They routed big Don Newcombe, while scoring one run. Then, with Ralph Branca on the mound and two runners aboard the bases, came the blow of blows. Thomson crashed the ball into the left-field stand. Forgotten on the instant was the cluster of three with which the Brooks had crushed Sal Maglie in the eighth.

For a moment the crowd of 34,320, as well as all the Dodgers, appeared too stunned to realize what had happened. But as the long and lean Scot from Staten Island loped around the bases behind his two team-mates a deafening roar went up, followed by some of the wildest scenes ever witnessed in the historic arena under Coogan's Bluff. The Giants, lined up at home plate, fairly mobbed the Hawk as he completed the last few strides to the plate. Jubilant Giant fans, fairly beside themselves, eluded guards and swarmed on the field to join the melee. When the players finally completed their dash to the center-field clubhouse, the fans, thousands deep on the field, yelled themselves purple as Thomson repeatedly appeared in the clubhouse windows in answer to the most frenzied "curtain calls" ever accorded a ballplayer.

The pennant, which the Giants so dramatically won in the second play-off series in National League history and the first to go the full three games, brought to a climax one of the most astonishing uphill struggles ever waged in the annals of the sport. Off to an atrocious start in the spring when they blew eleven in a row, the Giants plugged away firmly for weeks to make up the lost ground. But as late as Aug. 11 they were still thirteen and a half games behind the high-flying Brooks who, hailed by experts as the "wonder team" of the modern age, threatened to win by anywhere from fifteen to twenty lengths.

Then, on Aug. 12 began the great surge. Sixteen games were won in a row and from there the Polo Grounders rolled on to finish in a deadlock with the Dodgers at the close of the regular schedule. Majestically they swept ahead on Monday in the opener of the three-game play-off series in Brooklyn. Then disaster engulfed them as they came to the Polo Grounds Tuesday to be buried under a 10–0 score. And they were still struggling to get out from under as late as the ninth inning today when Thomson, whose two-run homer had won on Monday, exploded his No. 32 of the year that ended it all. It sailed into the lower left-field stand a little beyond the 315 foot mark. The ball, well tagged, had just enough lift to clear the high wall. And with that Leo Durocher almost leaped out of his shoes as he shrieked and danced on the coaching line.

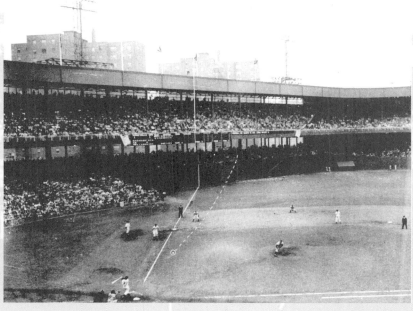

"And the Giants win the pennant! ..." The most famous home run in baseball history leaves the bat of the New York Giants' Bobby Thomson at the Polo Grounds. Ralph Branca of the Brooklyn Dodgers is on the mound. (Associated Press)

Runners-up

1974: Frank Robinson, 39, was named by the Cleveland Indians as major league baseball's first black manager. Robinson, who replaced Ken Aspromonte as player-manager, homered in his first at-bat in 1975 as a designated hitter. President Gerald Ford described Robinson's appointment as "welcome news for baseball fans across the nation."

1989: Art Shell, a member of the Pro Football Hall of Fame, was named by the Los Angeles Raiders as the first black N.F.L. head coach since the league gained national recognition in the 1920's. Fritz Pollard, a black running back, served as player-coach for the Hammond (Ind.) Pros from 1923 to 1925, in the infancy of the N.F.L.

1947: Pinch-hitter Cookie Lavagetto of the Brooklyn Dodgers broke up what would have been the first no-hitter in World Series history when he sliced a game-winning double off the right-field screen at Ebbets Field with two outs in the ninth against Bill Bevens of the Yankees in Game 4. The hit evened the Series, won by the Yankees, at two games to two.

October 4, 1955
For Brooklyn, This *Is* Next Year

By JOHN DREBINGER

NEW YORK—[Tuesday]—Brooklyn's long cherished dream finally has come true. The Dodgers have won their first World Series championship. The end of the trail came at the Stadium today. Smokey Alston's Brooks, with Johnny Podres tossing a brilliant shutout, turned back Casey Stengel's Yankees, 2 to 0, in the seventh and deciding game of the 1955 baseball classic. This gave the National League champions the series, 4 games to 3. As the jubilant victors almost smothered their 23-year-old left-handed pitcher from Witherbee, N.Y., a roaring crowd of 62,465 joined in sounding off a thunderous ovation.

Seven times in the past had the Dodgers been thwarted in their efforts to capture baseball's most sought prize—the last five times by these same Bombers. This was the first time a team had won a seven-game world series after losing the first two games. And Podres, who had vanquished the Yankees in the third game as the series moved to Ebbets Field last Friday, became the first Brooklyn pitcher to win two games in one series. Tommy Byrne, a seasoned campaigner, carried the Bombers' hopes in this dramatic struggle in which victory would have given them their seventeenth series title. But Byrne, whose southpaw slants had turned back the Dodgers in the second encounter, could not quite cope with the youngster pitted against him.

In the fourth inning a two-bagger by Roy Campanella and a single by Gil Hodges gave the Brooks their first run. In the sixth a costly Yankee error helped fill the bases. It forced the withdrawal of Byrne, though in all he had given only three hits. Stengel called on his right-handed relief hurler, Bob Grim, who did well

enough. But Bob couldn't prevent Hodges from lifting a long sacrifice fly to center that drove in Pee Wee Reese with the Brooks' second run of the day.

The Yankees' biggest threat against Podres came in the last of the sixth when Billy Martin walked and Gil McDougald outgalloped a bunt for a hit to put two on with nobody out. Yogi Berra then stroked an outside pitch, the ball sailing down the left-field foul line. It appeared to be a certain hit, but Sandy Amoros, racing at top speed, stuck out his glove and caught the ball in front of the stand. Martin, meanwhile, had played it fairly safe and was only a few feet up from second. But McDougald had gone well down from first, with the result that when Sandy fired the ball to Reese, the shortstop, who in turn relayed it to Hodges at first, McDougald was doubled off the bag by inches. It was a killing play for the Yanks.

Fittingly, the final out of the game was a grounder by Elston Howard to Reese, the 38-year-old captain of the Flock. Ever since 1941 had the Little Colonel from Kentucky been fighting these Yankees. Five times had he been forced to accept the loser's share. Many a heart in the vast arena doubtless skipped a beat as Pee Wee scooped up the ball and fired it to

first. It was a bit low and wide. But Hodges reached out and grabbed it inches off the ground. Gil would have stretched halfway across the Bronx for that one.

The 1955 World Series title was the only one the Brooklyn Dodgers ever won. They lost to the Yankees in seven games in 1956, and in 1957, seeking a new park with plenty of parking in a better neighborhood, the team's owner, Walter O'Malley, announced that he was moving to Los Angeles for the 1958 season (see May 28).

Brooklyn's Sandy Amoros snaring Yogi Berra's drive down the left-field line in Game 7 of the World Series at Yankee Stadium. The catch, which the Dodgers turned into a double play, allowed Brooklyn to win its only Series. (Associated Press)

Runners-up

1987: N.F.L. owners used unknown "replacement" players for the first time in league history when the regular players struck for the right to gain free agency. Average attendance dropped from 59,824 the week before to 16,947, but the strike and the replacements lasted for more than three weeks.

1963: Behind the brilliant pitching of Sandy Koufax, who beat Whitey Ford in Games 1 and 4, tied a World Series record with 14 strikeouts in one of them and allowed just three runs in 18 innings over all, the Los Angeles Dodgers swept

the Yankees for the Series championship. Koufax had gone 25–5 in the regular season; Ford, 24–7.

1991: The Rangers traded their goal-scoring center Bernie Nicholls and two prospects to the Edmonton Oilers for the all-star center Mark Messier. He was the first and most important ingredient in the Rangers' winning the Stanley Cup behind Coach Mike Keenan in 1994 *(see June 14).*

October 5, 2001
Bonds Breaks Record, and Then Some

By SELENA ROBERTS

SAN FRANCISCO—The instant Barry Bonds unleashed his spring-loaded swing tonight, the moment his black maple bat made sweet contact on a pitch, the 1–0 fastball delivered by Dodgers starter Chan Ho Park shot into the night sky. There was no mistaking its destination, or its place in baseball history. As Bonds's record-breaking 71st home run arched over the brick wall at Pacific Bell Park, it looked like a piece of confetti falling from a distance. As it landed in the right-center-field seats, the home run triggered a celebration that accompanied the Giants' sculptured left fielder on his home run trot.

Suddenly, the most glorified baseball record was his, and his alone, with Bonds separating himself from St. Louis's Mark McGwire. In 1998, McGwire did the unthinkable when he soared past Roger Maris's 37-year-old record of 61 home runs by finishing with 70 (*see Sept. 8*). Twenty-four hours after matching McGwire with No. 70 in Houston, Bonds created his own unfathomable scenario at home. After hitting No. 71 in the first inning, he came back with No. 72 in the third inning on a 1–1 pitch by Park.

This is the totality of Bonds's incredible power at age 37. And it is why few pitchers have wanted to challenge him over the last two weeks. But with his team out of the pennant race, Dodgers Manager Jim Tracy allowed Park to dare Bonds. Park did not have a chance against a man motivated by the Giants' playoff race, moved by the recent death of a friend and hungry for baseball history. That was made in the first inning on a 442-foot home run. In the batter's box, Bonds took a moment to savor the ball's flight, but quickly rounded the bases to find his

Barry Bonds of the Giants, center, hugging his son, Nikolai, after hitting his 70th home run, tying Mark McGwire's record, in Houston. The following night, in San Francisco, he clouted his 71st and 72nd off the Dodgers' Chan Ho Park. (Associated Press)

teammates, along with his son, Nikolai, at home plate to greet him.

As banners announcing Bonds's 71st home run unfurled on the light posts above center field, fireworks went off over the boats gathered in McCovey Cove. Beneath the roar from those in the stands, while the sound of horns emanated from the cove beyond right field, Bonds lifted Nikolai and kept pointing to the heavens. A minute later, Bonds made his way into the seats behind home plate to kiss his

wife and mother. Then his cellphone rang. It was his father, the former baseball All-Star Bobby Bonds, calling from Bridgeport, Conn., the site of his charity golf tournament.

After a four-minute stoppage, the game resumed and the buzz continued. As if piling on the record books, Bonds hit No. 72.

Barry Bonds (see Nov.11) *hit his 73rd and final home run of the season off Dennis Springer of the Dodgers at Pacific Bell Park two nights later.*

Runners-up

1953: The Yankees won their fifth consecutive World Series—no other team besides the 1936–39 Yankees has won more than four straight—by defeating the Brooklyn Dodgers, 4–3, in Game 6 in the Bronx. Billy Martin singled in the winning run against Clem Labine in the bottom of the ninth inning with his 12th hit of the Series.

1941: Mickey Owen's passed ball on a third strike to Tommy Henrich in Game 4 at Ebbets Field became one of the classic muffs in World Series history. The Brooklyn Dodgers held the lead, 4–3, with two outs in the top of the ninth

inning and thought they had evened the Series when the ball got by Owens. The Yankees then rallied with four runs for a three-to-one Series lead and won the title the following day.

1985: Coach Eddie Robinson of Grambling State University in Louisiana won his 324th game, breaking the college football record set three years earlier by Paul (Bear) Bryant of Alabama (*see Nov. 28*), as the Tigers defeated Prairie View A&M, 27–7, at the Cotton Bowl in Dallas. Robinson became the first college coach to reach 400 victories in 1995.

October 6, 1928
The Genius of Polo (Before Ralph Lauren)

By ROBERT F. KELLEY

WESTBURY, L.I.—United States polo is still the greatest in the world. From the rim of defeat and with a patched-up line-up put together in a desperate last-minute attempt to stand off the strongest rush that polo had faced in this country in a quarter of a century, Tommy Hitchcock today led a new United States team to the greatest triumph it has ever scored. In the third game with Argentina for the championship of the Americas, the United States came through, and came through with plenty to spare, 13 to 7. After the third period there was never any question of the ultimate winner.

The biggest crowd ever to witness a polo game in this country fought for admission. One hour before the whistle of Captain Wesley White started play the seats in both the west and east stands had been sold and hundreds of persons stood outside the gates trying to find a way in. The officials then opened up the ends of historic International Field at Meadow Brook and the spectators stood four deep. More than 40,000 were grouped around the playing area.

Winston Guest, Earle A.S. Hopping and Hitchcock kept a constant rain of drives pouring into Argentine territory. Out in front the black-haired, pale-faced W. Averill Harriman was riding the finest polo ponies in the world, and when the ball came out to him he carried on. Six times

Harriman carried on to a point for this country, and throughout he played the same type of hard-riding, brilliant No. 1 which had caused so much trouble during the first game and finally carried through

Tommy Hitchcock, arguably the greatest polo player ever, in an undated photo. He was a fearless rider and accurate long hitter, and his style meshed nicely with that of the U.S., which relied on long passing to advance the ball. (The Museum of Polo and Hall of Fame)

the winning goal in that game to give his country the chance to go on to a third match.

Hitchcock found himself playing in the No. 3 position for the first time in his career. The genius of United States polo at least played as fine a game as any ever

turned in at that position. He was superb on defense, driving through the narrowest sort of openings to come through with the ball and carry on to an attack, and on other occasions dropping from nowhere all alone to break up the South American combination play. Hitchcock rode through to four goals this afternoon, and his game was far and away better than anything he had displayed in this series. Hitchcock had at last come out of his slump and the United States team rode along the crest with him.

From the beginning it was apparent that this was a different United States team. Hitchcock came out for the start wearing the strange (for him) No. 3 on his back. He was soon in the thick of play and helped with the opening rush of the game. This went wide but it was not much later that the first United States score came. It was on a free hit from the 30-yard line, which is like handing a balloon to Hitchcock and asking him to break it.

The blond-headed Tommy Hitchcock's fame soon was eclipsed by that of his teammate W. Averill Harriman. Harriman became United States ambassador to the Soviet Union and Britain under President Harry S. Truman and was a two-term governor of New York. Polo lost much of its popularity as a spectator sport after it was removed from the Olympics in 1936.

Runners-up

1926: In one of his outsized World Series performances, Babe Ruth hit three home runs in Game 4 at Sportsman's Park as the Yankees beat the St. Louis Cardinals, 10–5; the Cardinals won the Series, however, four games to three. Two years later Ruth duplicated the feat in Game 4 on the same field as the Yankees beat the Cardinals, 7–3, completing a four-game sweep.

1993: Michael Jordan (see June 12) announced his retirement after three straight N.B.A. championships with the Chicago Bulls and seven league scoring titles. After playing pro baseball—and batting .202—with the Class AA Birmingham

Barons in 127 games the following year, he "unretired" and returned to the Bulls.

1955: The 3-year-old trotter Scott Frost, with Joe O'Brien in the sulky, won the Kentucky Futurity at Lexington's Red Mile, becoming the first Triple Crown winner in harness racing. In August, Scott Frost had won the sport's two other most prestigious races, the Yonkers Trot in New York and the Hambletonian in Goshen, N.Y.

Quarterback Call: 'Toss 28 Weak'

By MICHAEL JANOFSKY

CHICAGO—The moment finally came on the second play from scrimmage in the third quarter today. Jim McMahon, the Chicago Bears' quarterback, called "Toss 28 Weak," a pitchout for Walter Payton and a play the Bears have run countless times before. Only this time there was something special about it. This time Payton ran the pitchout to his left behind the fullback Matt Suhey and the left guard Mark Bortz for a 6-yard gain and a place in history. The yards moved him past Jim Brown to become the National Football League's career leading rusher.

Brown, who gained 12,312 yards from 1957 through 1965 with the Cleveland Browns, had led Payton by 66 before today. Payton's run lifted him past Brown by 5 yards, and he finished the game, a 20–7 victory over the New Orleans Saints, with 154, for a career total of 12,400 and 775 this season, the best of his career. Payton's performance set another record. He ran for 100 yards or more for the 59th time; until today, he and Brown had shared the record at 58.

Because of the inconsistent nature of the Bears' recent play and the fact that they were leading the Saints by only 13–7, Payton wanted to minimize the disruption when the historic moment came. Although in recent weeks he had discussed with Bears' officials what sort of ceremony might be held the moment after he broke the record, very little was done when it actually happened. The game was stopped so that the officials could give Payton the ball. He was immediately engulfed by his teammates and many of the Saints, offering congratulations. Then he walked over and shaked the hand of Bum Phillips, the Saints coach. Finally, he walked the ball off the field to the Bears' sideline before play resumed.

"We didn't have enough points to stop the game for longer," said Payton, who had scored on a 1-yard run with three seconds remaining in the first half. "I wanted to get everybody off the field so we could score some more." Payton said he felt "relieved" that the chase was finally over. After speaking by telephone for several minutes to President Reagan, who offered his congratulations from aboard Air Force One, Payton described how the chase had begun to bother him.

"For the past three weeks, I have tried to conceal it, but there has been a lot of pressure," he said. "It's been really hard to deal with; I'm glad I don't have to do this every week. There was a lot of pressure, and if you don't know how to deal with it, you can go astray."

Walter Payton retired after the 1987 season with 16,726 yards. He died of bile duct cancer at age 45 in November 1999. Emmitt Smith of the Dallas Cowboys broke Payton's record in October 2002.

The sun sets on Walter Payton in his last regular-season home game for the Bears, at Soldier Field in December 1987. Aggressive, tough, fast and elusive, he retired as pro football's all-time leading rusher. (Associated Press)

Runners-up

1952: Billy Martin made a shoetop catch of a bases-loaded pop-up by Jackie Robinson of the Brooklyn Dodgers in the seventh inning of Game 7 of the World Series at Ebbets Field, saving a 4–2 Yankees lead and allowing them to win their fourth straight world championship. The record run equaled that of the 1936–39 Yankees.

1995: Mark Allen of Boulder, Colo., won his sixth Ironman Triathlon (see Feb. 18) title in seven years in Kailua-Kona, Hawaii, overtaking the leader, Thomas Hellriegel of Germany, at the 24-mile mark of the marathon. It was the 37-year-old Allen's closest finish since his first Ironman victory, by 58 seconds over Dave Scott in 1989.

1945: The Green Bay Packers scored 41 points in the second quarter—an N.F.L. one-quarter record equaled by the Los Angeles Rams in 1950—as they routed the Detroit Lions, 57–21, at State Fair Park in Milwaukee. The peerless receiver Don Hutson (see Nov. 30) caught four touchdown passes and kicked five extra points, setting an all-time single-quarter mark of 29 points.

October 8, 1956
Larson's Well-Timed Masterpiece

By JOHN DREBINGER

NEW YORK—Don Larsen is a footloose fellow of whom Casey Stengel once said, "He can be one of baseball's great pitchers any time he puts his mind to it." Larsen had his mind on his work today. He pitched the first no-hit game in world series history. Not only that, but he also fired the first perfect game—no batter reaching first base—to be posted in the major leagues in thirty-four years. This nerve-tingling performance, embellished with a Mickey Mantle home run, gained a 2–0 triumph for the Yankees over the Dodgers and Sal Maglie at the Stadium. It enabled Casey Stengel's Yankees to post their third straight victory for a 3–2 lead in the series.

With every fan in a gathering of 61,519 hanging breathlessly on every pitch, Larsen, a 27-year-old right-hander, slipped over a third strike on Dale Mitchell to end the game. Dale, a pinch-hitter, was the twenty-seventh batter to face Larsen. As he went down for the final out, the gathering set up a deafening roar, while jubilant Yankees fairly mobbed the big pitcher as he struggled to make his way to the dugout.

The unpredictable Larsen had triumphed at a time when the Bombers needed it most, with one of the most spectacular achievements in diamond history. Last spring the tall handsome Larsen had caused considerable to-do in the Yankees' St. Petersburg training camp. In an early dawn escapade, he wrapped his automobile around a telephone pole. He later explained he had fallen asleep at the

wheel. Today big Don remained wide awake through every moment of the nine innings, turning in a performance in which only four batted balls had a chance of being rated hits. One was a foul by inches. Three drives were converted into outs by

Don Larsen making the final pitch of the only perfect World Series game ever thrown. Brooklyn Dodgers pinch-hitter Dale Mitchell struck out to end Game 5 at Yankee Stadium. Second baseman Billy Martin and a string of zeros looked on. (Bettmann/Corbis)

miraculous Yankee fielding plays.

In the second inning Jackie Robinson banged a vicious grounder off Andy Carey's glove at third base for what momentarily appeared a certain hit. But Gil McDougald, the alert Yankee shortstop, recovered the ball in time to fire it for the putout on Jackie at first base. In the fifth, minutes after Mantle had put the Yanks ahead, 1–0, with his blast into the right field stand, Gil Hodges tagged a ball that streaked into deep left center, seemingly headed for extra bases. But Mantle, whose fielding in the series has at times been a trifle spotty, more than made amends. He tore across the turf to make a reaching backhanded catch.

On the next play, Sandy Amoros leaned

into a pitch and rocketed a towering drive toward the right field stand. This drive promised to tie the score, but at the last moment the ball curved foul. And then, in the eighth, Hodges once again was victimized. Gil drove a tricky, low liner to the left of Carey. The Yankee third sacker lunged for the ball and caught it inches off the ground.

In the ninth, only Mitchell, batting for Maglie, remained between Larsen and everlasting diamond fame. The former American League outfielder and sure-fire pinch hitter with the Cleveland Indians ran the count to one ball and two strikes. Mitchell fouled off the next pitch and as the following one zoomed over the plate Umpire Babe Pinelli called it strike three. Mitchell whirled around to protest the call and later he said it was a fast ball that was outside the strike zone. But Dale was in no spot to gain any listener. The Yanks were pummeling Larsen and the umpires were hustling off the field.

Doubtless for Pinelli, this, too, could have provided his greatest thrill in his long career as an arbiter. For after this series, Babe, as dean of the National League staff of umpires, is to retire.

Despite his magical afternoon, Don Larsen was an itinerant pitcher. Traded from the Yankees three years later, he finished with an 81–91 record for eight teams in 14 seasons. His masterpiece still stands as the only no-hitter, much less perfect game, in World Series history.

Runners-up

1927: The Yankees' "Murderers' Row" outfit, considered perhaps the greatest baseball team of all time with Babe Ruth *(see Sept. 30),* Lou Gehrig, Bob Meusel and Tony Lazzeri in the heart of the lineup, swept the Pittsburgh Pirates in the World Series with a 4–3 victory at Yankee Stadium. Earle Combs scored the winning run in the ninth on a wild pitch by Pirates reliever Johnny Miljus.

1973: Pete Rose's hard slide into Bud Harrelson to break up a double play in Game 3 of the playoffs at Shea Stadium brought the Cincinnati Reds and the Mets onto the field and precipitated a near riot. Fans pelted Rose with debris in left

field until Mets players calmed them down to alleviate the risk of forfeit. New York won, 9–2, and took the playoffs in five games.

1961: Left-hander Whitey Ford *(see Jan. 16)* set a World Series record of 33 consecutive scoreless innings, breaking Babe Ruth's 1916 and '18 record of 29⅔ innings with the Boston Red Sox *(see Oct. 9),* when he went five shutout innings against the Cincinnati Reds in Game 4 at Crosley Field. The Yankees won, 7–0, and took the Series in five games.

October 9, 1997
A Lovefest for Dean Smith

By MALCOLM MORAN

CHAPEL HILL, N.C.—Dean Smith, the coach whose basketball lineage traces from James Naismith and the first peach basket, formally ended an era today. His retirement after 36 years as coach at the University of North Carolina, and 879 victories that surpassed the total of every other college coach, inspired all manner of responses. They came from President Clinton, who telephoned him. From Michael Jordan, whose jump shot as a freshman led Smith's Tar Heels to the first of his two national championships, who called him his second father. And from students who wedged themselves against windows outside the athletic building that bears his name and where the announcement was made.

Smith, who played at the University of Kansas for the Hall of Fame coach Phog Allen, who had played for Naismith, has forever changed the game of basketball through the players and coaches he has taught. Last winter, Jordan joined the former Smith recruits James Worthy and Billy Cunningham among those selected as the 50 leading players in the history of the National Basketball Association. Thirty of Smith's players have reached all-America status. Eight of the last nine United States Olympic teams have included at least one of his Tar Heels. Last season, no fewer than 15 of his former players appeared on N.B.A. rosters.

As Smith announced his decision to retire this afternoon, Larry Brown, one of his former players who now coaches the Detroit Pistons, stood quietly in a corner of the room. But Smith's role as an instructor for the game's brightest minds does not stop with Brown. George Karl has taken the Seattle SuperSonics to the N.B.A. finals. Roy Williams of Kansas and Eddie

Fogler of South Carolina, longtime Smith assistants, have risen to the top of their profession. Their mentor lifted a program troubled by National Collegiate Athletic Association rules violations in the early 1960's and transformed it into a national model of athletic and academic efficiency. The Tar Heels have won at least 20 games for 27 consecutive seasons. They have built winning percentages of .728 in Atlantic Coast Conference regular-season play and .716 in the intense conference tournament. Perhaps more important, 97.3 percent of the players to receive a letter under Smith have earned their degrees.

As the campus responded today to the shock of Smith's decision, the depths of his relationships became as clear as the coach's lasting contributions: his support of desegregation efforts, his recruitment of African-American athletes, his strategic innovations that included the four-corners offense and the foul-line huddle. "He's like a second father to me," Jordan said at the Chicago Bulls training center in Deerfield, Ill.

Smith introduced his successor, 60-year-old Bill Guthridge, an assistant for the past 30 years who had wanted to end his career with Smith rather than take his place. Although Smith's contract ran through 2001, the task of extending his

Dean Smith, the North Carolina basketball coach, after the Tar Heels defeated Stanford for his 500th victory in 1983. He was only 14 years and 379 games away from home. (Associated Press)

career was becoming impossible. From a year ago to mid-May, Smith remembered, he had one free weekend to see his grandchildren.

Last Thursday, he informed Dick Baddour, the athletic director, that he was 80 percent certain he would resign. Wednesday evening, after the players completed the mile run that is a required prelude to practice, they were called into an unscheduled meeting. Smith informed them of his decision, and broke down. "It was like, just wake me up, this can't be happening," said Antawn Jamison, a junior who had chosen not to apply to the N.B.A. draft.

Runners-up

1934: Joe Medwick's spikes-up slide into Detroit Tigers third baseman Marv Owen with the Cardinals leading, 11–0, in Game 7 of the World Series precipitated a riot by fans at Detroit's Navin Field. Medwick was showered with debris when he retook his position, and Commissioner Kenesaw Mountain Landis *(see Nov. 12)* removed him to quell the disturbance.

1916: Babe Ruth of the Red Sox, a king of pitchers before he became the Sultan of Swat, allowed a first-inning run and tossed 13 scoreless innings in a Game 2

World Series victory over the Brooklyn Robins (later the Dodgers) at Braves Field in Boston. In his second full season, Ruth, 21, had won 23 games and led the American League with a 1.75 earned run average.

2000: Center Brett Hull of the Dallas Stars passed his father, Bobby *(see March 12),* of the Chicago Blackhawks, for seventh place on the all-time N.H.L. goal list with his 611th score as Dallas defeated the Toronto Maple Leafs, 3–1, at Maple Leaf Gardens.

October 10, 1926
Alexander the Great Fans Lazzeri

By JAMES R. HARRISON

In the seventh inning of Game 7 of the World Series between the Yankees and the Cardinals at Yankee Stadium, St. Louis was leading by 3–2 with two outs, but New York had the bases loaded. It was the last great Yankees rally of the Series. The Cardinals' second baseman and manager, Rogers Hornsby, summoned a famous pitcher, well past his prime at 39, to relieve Jesse Haines and face the dangerous 22-year-old rookie Tony Lazzeri.

NEW YORK—Forty thousand pairs of eyes peered anxiously through the gray mist toward the bullpen out in deep left. There was a breathless pause, and then around the corner of the stand came a tall figure in a Cardinal sweater. His cap rode rakishly on the corner of his head. He walked like a man who was going nowhere in particular and was in no hurry to get there. He was a trifle knock-kneed and his gait was not a model of grace and rhythm.

Any baseball fan would have known him a mile away. It was Grover Cleveland Alexander. Alexander the Great was coming in to pull the Cardinal machine out of the mudhole. The ancient twirler, who had gone nine full innings the day before, was shuffling in where younger men feared to tread.

On any other day he would have been sitting contentedly on the bench, chewing his quid and ruminating on life. This time he was plucked out from the bullpen and

Grover Cleveland Alexander with the Cardinals at age 39 in 1926. History remembers him for his World Series shootout at the O.K. Corral, but he won 373 games and dominated all hitters for years. (Associated Press)

thrust into the limelight as the last hope of the Cardinals. He warmed up in that leisurely, methodical way of his, and as he faced Tony Lazzeri, fresh young slugger from the Coast, he was outwardly as unconcerned as if it were a spring exhibition game. Throughout the park there came a silence. The fans slid forward to the edge of their seats. Hardly a mother's son of them seemed to be moving a muscle, but old Alex was undisturbed.

He had been through all that before. Apparently there wasn't a nerve in his body. Ball one to Lazzeri was low and the crowd stirred, but Alex calmly carved the outside corner with a strike, like a butcher slicing ham. Another one outside and Lazzeri fouled it into the stand. The Yankee was now in the hole. "This lad is in a tighter fix than I am," thought Alex, and so he essayed a low curve that one of the Singer midgets couldn't have hit. Lazzeri swung and missed. The deed was done. Alex took off his glove and shuffled again to the bench. The Cardinals, young and impetuous, pounded his back and hugged him madly, but old Alex took it with placid good humor—not the shadow of a smile on his face.

Only once did he turn his head and send a half-smile toward the stand and we suspect that that was his only gesture of triumph.

Runners-up

1920: With runners on first and second off with the crack of the bat, Cleveland Indians second baseman Bill Wambsganss caught a line drive, stepped on second and tagged the runner coming from first for the only triple play—an unassisted one at that—in World Series history. The Indians defeated the visiting Brooklyn Robins (later the Dodgers), 8–1, in Game 5 and won the title in seven games.

1924: Earl McNeely's grounder apparently hit a pebble and bounced over third baseman Freddie Lindstrom's head in the last of the 12th inning of Game 7 at Griffith Stadium, giving the Washington Senators a 4–3 victory over the New York Giants and their only World Series championship. The great Walter Johnson, aged 36, got the victory in relief.

1964: Mickey Mantle hit his 16th World Series home run, moving past Babe Ruth on the all-time list. The dramatic shot, off Barney Schultz of the St. Louis Cardinals on the first pitch in the bottom of the ninth inning in Game 3 at Yankee Stadium, gave New York a 2–1 victory. Mantle hit two more homers in the Series for a final total of 18, but the Yankees lost in seven games.

October 11, 1890
The Old Detroit's Sleek New Model

[Unsigned, *The New York Times*]

WASHINGTON—Now is the time for the Manhattan Athletic Club of New York to crow, and her representatives are taking advantage of their turn to whoop things up. Several hundred men wearing the pretty "cherry diamond" of the club are having a jollification here to-night over the result of the National Amateur Athletic Union's championship of the United States, contested on the grounds of the Columbia Athletic Club. The Manhattans are now the undisputed champions of the country, and while many thought before the games began that this club would defeat the New York Athletic Club in the race for the Bailey, Banks & Biddle plaque, representing the championship of clubs, no one believed the margin between them to-night would be as large as it is.

The New York Athletic Club won the plaque two years in succession, but the past year was the first time the Manhattans competed for it. Three world's amateur records were surpassed in the contests. The most notable feat was the running of John Owen, Jr., Detroit Athletic Club, in the 100-yard dash, who covered the distance in 9⅘ seconds. The record heretofore both in this country and in England was 10 seconds, this time having been made by a number of runners. Owen's performance equals the professional record, and was the most wonderful exhibition of sprinting ever seen in amateur contests. L.H. Cary of the Manhattan Athletic Club was second to Owen by about 18 inches, while Fred Westing, Manhattan Athletic Club, was third by 26 inches. All three finished close together and all were within even time, 10 seconds. Owen won the championship last year, and had a ten-second record before.

John Owen Jr., right, and Michael C. Murphy, his notoriously strict coach and trainer at the Detroit Athletic Club, at a photo studio start line. Owen became the first amateur to break 10 seconds in the 100-yard dash. (Detroit Athletic Club and the Burton Historical Collection, Detroit Public Library)

The track was in the best possible condition for the contest, and went far toward establishing this new record. There is a claim made that the ground was not level, but if there is any incline it is very slight, and a member of the Record Committee of the Amateur Athletic Union said tonight that he thinks the record will be allowed.

The timing in each event was excellent. It was done by C.C. Hughes, Manhattan Athletic Club; C.A. Reed, Boston Athletic Association, and M.B. Bishop, Staten Island Athletic Club. In the heat where Owen made his 100-yard record, Mr. Hughes's watch failed to stop, but the other two agreed.

John Owen's record of 9.8 seconds in the 100-yard dash stood for 31 years until it was broken by Charles Paddock of the Los Angeles Athletic Club in 9.6. The 100-yard dash gave way to the 100-meter competition in most major athletic meets during the 1930's.

Runners-up

1972: In the signature moment of his career, Johnny Bench of the Cincinnati Reds, generally acknowledged as the greatest catcher in history, led off the last of the ninth inning in decisive Game 5 of the playoffs with a home run off the Pittsburgh Pirates' Dave Giusti at Riverfront Stadium to tie the score at 3–3. The pennant-winning run soon scored on a wild pitch by Pirates reliever Bob Moose.

1999: In one of the most remarkable performances of his career, Pedro Martínez, who did not start because of an ailing back, nevertheless came in to pitch six no-hit innings of relief as the Boston Red Sox defeated the Indians, 12–8, in the deciding game of their division series at Jacobs Field in Cleveland. The Sox lost to the Yankees in the League Championship Series.

1959: Bert Bell, commissioner of the N.F.L. since 1946, died of a heart attack at Philadelphia's Franklin Field during an Eagles game. As owner of the Eagles in '35, Bell proposed the first college draft; as commissioner, he oversaw the merger with the All-America Football Conference and the N.F.L.'s television popularity. He was succeeded by Pete Rozelle (see Jan. 26).

October 12, 1963
Unstoppable Force, Immovable Object

By GORDON S. WHITE Jr.

Texas' Tommy Ford (24) blowing through the Oklahoma line in the Cotton Bowl as the Longhorns supplanted the Sooners as the nation's No. 1 team. Coach Darrell Royal bested his one-time mentor, the great Bud Wilkinson. (University of Texas)

DALLAS—Texas laid claim to the No. 1 ranking among the nation's college football teams today by toppling Oklahoma, king of the hill the last two weeks, with a decisive 28–7 victory in the Cotton Bowl. Texas was in the No. 2 spot behind the Sooners prior to the game. The Sooners had moved from third to first by whipping Southern California, then the front-runner.

The annual classic, which sends Longhorn and Sooner fans into a New Year's Eve spirit, was played before a capacity crowd of 75,504. The sellout was the 18th in a row in the rivalry. The ground power of Coach Darrell Royal's Texans nearly drove Oklahoma off the field at the start. Texas showed no mercy in rolling up 102 yards on the ground in the first period. With Duke Carlisle, Tommy Ford, Phil Harris, Tony King and others carrying the ball, Texas totaled 239 yards over land in the game.

Oklahoma, which dominated the top spot in the early 1950's, bowed to the Longhorns for the sixth straight time. Royal, once an assistant to Coach Bud Wilkinson of Oklahoma, has lost only once to his former boss since taking over at Texas. That occurred during his first season at Texas, in 1957.

Royal's forces were unstoppable today. Taking the opening kickoff, Texas moved to a score before Oklahoma even got its hands on the ball. The hero of that strong move was Carlisle, a powerful running quarterback, who disdained the pass for a fake in which he either kept the ball or pitched back. Five times on the opening drive of 68 yards in 13 plays, Carlisle kept and chose to run through big holes in the Oklahoma line. Twice he picked up 14 yards. He went 2 yards for the first touchdown on a fourth-and-goal situa-

tion. Tony Crosby kicked the first of his four conversions, and Texas was off and running.

The Longhorns held a 21–0 lead late in the third period before the Sooners scored. Texas, a slight underdog, pushed around a defense that was supposed to have been hard to move. Carlisle picked up 83 yards and Ford 78 to lead the ground-gainers. Oklahoma's big fullback, Jim Grisham, ran for 73.

"I didn't feel safe until we led, 21–7, and had the ball on our last touchdown drive," Royal said later.

Darrell Royal's Longhorns finished 11–0 by defeating Navy and Heisman Trophy winner Roger Staubach in the Cotton Bowl, 28–6. It was the first of Texas's three national titles under his direction. Royal developed the wishbone offensive formation, still widely used in college football, in 1968 (see Sept. 21).

Runners-up

1986: One strike away from reaching the first World Series in their 26 years, the California Angels were cruelly denied when Dave Henderson of the Boston Red Sox hit a game-tying two-run homer off Donnie Moore in Game 5 of their play-off series at Anaheim. The Sox won in 11 innings, then swept the stunned Angels in the next two games to steal the pennant.

1929: Leading by 8–0 in the seventh inning of Game 4 at Shibe Park and set to even the World Series at two games apiece, the visiting Chicago Cubs collapsed as the Philadelphia Athletics erupted for 10 runs and a three-games-to-one lead.

The Cubs' Hack Wilson lost a ball in the sun for an inside-the-park three-run homer. Permanently shellshocked, the Cubs lost in five.

1920: Man o' War (see Aug. 13), the 3-year-old speed king known to his devotees as "Big Red," defeated Sir Barton, the previous year's Triple Crown winner, by seven lengths in a match race at Kenilworth Park in Ontario. In a financial move that became common decades later, Man o' War then was then retired to stud by his owner, Samuel Riddle of Philadelphia, with a record of 20–1.

October 13, 1960
Mazeroski's Historic Whack

By JOHN DREBINGER

PITTSBURGH—The Pirates today brought Pittsburgh its first world series baseball championship in thirty-five years when Bill Mazeroski slammed a ninth-inning home run high over the left-field wall of historic Forbes Field. With that shot, Danny Murtaugh's astounding Bucs brought down Casey Stengel's Yankees, 10 to 9, in a titanic struggle that gave the National League champions the series, four games to three.

Minutes later a crowd of 36,683 touched off a celebration that tonight is sweeping through the city like a vast conflagration. For with this stunning victory, which also had required a five-run Pirate eighth, the dauntless Bucs avenged the four-straight rout inflicted by another Yankee team in 1927.

As for the 70-year-old Stengel, if this is to be his exit—his retirement has been repeatedly rumored—the Ol' Professor scarcely could have desired a more fitting setting short of a victory. Headed into the last of the eighth inning, Stengel had a 7–4 lead and appeared to have the series title wrapped up. But then the Corsairs suddenly erupted for five runs, the final three scampering across on an electrifying home run by Hal Smith.

The rally was set up by what doubtless was the crucial play of the entire series. With a runner on first base, Bill Virdon hit a vicious grounder to short that looked like a double play until the ball took a freak hop and struck Tony Kubek in the larynx.

Kubek had to leave the game and was rushed to the Eye and Ear Hospital here. The play opened the gates to two runs. And after a lapse by Yankee reliever Jim Coates, who failed to cover first base on a routine grounder, more followed as Smith

belted the ball high over the left-field wall, putting the Bucs in front, 9–7.

But still the battle raged. In the ninth the Yanks counted twice, once again putting two runners on base against reliever Bob Friend. Mickey Mantle singled to right, scoring Bobby Richardson and sending Dale Long to third. Gil McDougald, in as a pinch-runner for Long, scored on a grounder to first when the Pirates' Rocky Nelson could not complete a double play.

In the last of the ninth, it was the clout by Mazeroski, first up, that ended it. Ralph Terry, the fifth Yankee hurler, was the victim. With a count of one ball and no strikes Mazeroski whacked the ball over the left-field brick wall directly over the 402-foot mark. He said later that his homer was hit off a high fast ball. Verification was sought from Terry in the Yankee dressing room.

"I don't know what the pitch was. All I know is it was the wrong one," Terry said.

Gleeful Pittsburgh fans and a coach, Frank Oceak, greeting the Pirates' light-hitting Bill Mazeroski as he rounds third base after swatting a walk-off home run against Ralph Terry in the ninth to dispatch the Yankees in Game 7 of the World Series. (Associated Press)

Runners-up

1903: Bill Dinneen pitched a four-hit, 3–0 shutout over the visiting Pittsburgh Pirates in Game 8 to lead the Boston Pilgrims (later the Red Sox) to the championship of the first "world" series ever played. The then-best-of-nine-game classic was the product of a challenge by the Pirates' owner, Barney Dreyfuss, to the champions of the two-year-old American League.

1971: For television purposes the first World Series game was played at night. Commissioner Bowie Kuhn pointedly declined to wear a topcoat to ward off the cold. The great Roberto Clemente (see March 20) got three hits and Bruce

Kison threw six innings of shutout relief as the Pittsburgh Pirates defeated the Baltimore Orioles, 4–3, in Game 4 at Three Rivers Stadium.

1998: The N.B.A. canceled the first two weeks of the season when collective bargaining talks between owners and players broke down. Other weeks were lost as the 191-day lockout continued; the regular season did not open until Feb. 5, 1999, and lasted just 50 of the usual 82 games. This was the longest work stoppage in league history.

An Orphan With a Nation as Family

TOKYO (AP)—Billy Mills took up running to get in shape as a boxer while attending an Indian school for orphans and went on to score one of America's greatest track triumphs. "I'm flabbergasted, I can hardly believe it," the Marine lieutenant beamed today after beating 37 of the world's top endurance racers for the Olympic gold medal in the 10,000 meters.

A complete dark horse who barely sneaked onto the United States squad in the last race of the qualifying trials at Chicago, he was about a 1,000-to-1 shot. "Still, I always felt I had an outside chance because I had been training well," he said. "I have been running 100 miles a week until the last two weeks. Then I settled down to long, easy running. I felt the spark and spring coming back to my legs."

The winner, who had run the 10,000 only five times previously and never beaten the leading United States hope, Gerry Lindgren, said he knew he had a good chance with five laps to go. Mills said he believed he could outkick Mohamed Gammoudi of Tunisia, the second-place finisher.

The surprise 10,000-meter champion is 26 years old, 5 feet 11 inches tall and weighs 155 pounds. He was born in Pine Ridge, S.D., a town with a population of 2,000. He was in the eighth grade when he started running, just to condition himself for the boxing ring. After losing his first two bouts—winding up with a pair of big black eyes—he decided to stick to running exclusively. His mother died when he was a baby and his father passed away when he was 12.

Mills, who is part Sioux Indian, was placed in the Haskell Institute at Lawrence, Kan., as an orphan and stayed

there until he entered the University of Kansas. He was a two-mile and cross-country champion at Kansas. As a distance runner bidding for an Olympic berth, he attracted little notice. In five 10,000-meter races, he won only one—and that was an interservice event against negligible competition. His best previous time for the distance was 29:10.

"I thought I would cry," he said when he saw the United States flag hoisted on the flagpole at the medal ceremonies. "And I did." Mills's wife, Patricia, mother of their 6-month-old baby, also wept.

Billy Mills's victory was among the most stunning in Olympic history. Sprinting from the top of the home-stretch before a crowd of 75,000, he overtook both Mohamed Gammoudi and Ron Clarke of Australia, the favorite, by three yards in 28 minutes 24.4 seconds. The leaders had lapped several runners in the field, and the finish was congested. According to the Olympic historian David Wallechinsky, Clarke, the 10,000 world record-holder, said, "It was like a dash for a train in a peak-hour crowd."

Because of the congestion, Mills was unable to take a victory lap. On a rainy day in 1984 he returned to a silent National Stadium in Tokyo along with his wife, Pat, the Olympic filmmaker Bud Greenspan and a film crew and took that lap. "Toward the end of my lap," he told the writers Lewis Carlson and John

Billy Mills, a Native-American Marine lieutenant from Kansas who was given no chance in one of the best 10,000-meter fields ever assembled, wins the gold medal at the Tokyo Olympics. "I thought I would cry," he said, "and I did." (Associated Press)

Fogarty, "I heard one person clapping. It was Pat, clapping for me. I started to cry. I needed that victory lap so badly. I started crying, and rather than let the group see me cry, I lifted my face up to the rain, walked up the track a way to get my composure, then finished the lap."

Mills and his wife live in Sacramento, Calif. He owns and operates a speakers bureau and is the national spokesman of Running Strong for American Indian Youth, a nonprofit organization that helps communities with self-sufficiency programs, youth activities and cultural identity projects.

Runners-up

1905: Christy Mathewson shut out the Philadelphia Athletics for the third time in six days in the World Series, winning decisive Game 5 by 2–0 at the Polo Grounds and delivering the championship to the New York Giants. The 25-year-old Mathewson (see Feb. 2), who won 31 games in the regular season, did not allow a runner past second base in his 27 remarkable innings.

1976: Chris Chambliss hit Mark Littell's first pitch in the last of the ninth for a home run at Yankee Stadium, giving New York a 7–6 victory over the Kansas City Royals in decisive Game 5 of the League Championship Series. It was the

Yankees' 30th pennant, easily a major league record, but their first in 12 years.

1916: Jim Barnes of England sank a four-foot putt on the 36th hole of the final day of play and defeated Jock Hutchison of Pittsburgh, 1-up, in the first P.G.A. Championship ever played. The tournament was held at Siwanoy Country Club in Bronxville, N.Y. The P.G.A. switched from match to medal play (total strokes not holes won) in 1958 when Dow Finsterwald won the first four-day, 72-hole tournament.

October 15, 1989
The Greatest Gretzky

EDMONTON, Alberta (AP)—He was called the Great Gretzky even before he played his first game in the National Hockey League. Tonight, in just his 11th season and before the adoring fans of his former team, he became the greatest scorer in N.H.L. history. Wayne Gretzky, at age 28, broke Gordie Howe's record of 1,850 points with a goal late in the third period of the Los Angeles Kings' game against the Edmonton Oilers. He also scored an overtime goal that gave the Kings a 5–4 victory.

The record-setting point came when Gretzky backhanded the puck past the Oilers' goaltender, Bill Ranford, with 53 seconds remaining in regulation time, tying the score at 4–4. After watching the puck enter the net, Gretzky leaped into the air and was surrounded by his Kings teammates. The fans in the sellout crowd at Northlands Coliseum, many of whom had passed by a statue of Gretzky on their way into the building, gave him an ovation that lasted more than two minutes.

The game was stopped as Howe, along with John Ziegler, the N.H.L. president, and Mark Messier, who succeeded Gretzky as captain of the Oilers, presented him with gifts marking the occasion. Messier presented Gretzky, his longtime teammate before a blockbuster trade on Aug. 9, 1988, with a diamond bracelet containing 1.851 carats, spelling out "1,851." Howe, Gretzky's boyhood idol, then said: "In all honesty, I've been looking forward to today. It's really nice for me to be a part of this." Howe scored an N.H.L.-record 801 goals and added 1,049 assists in 26 seasons. His record for goals is one of the few significant marks that Gretzky does not yet own. The two goals tonight gave Gretzky 642.

After Howe spoke, Gretzky addressed the crowd. "I've really been excited in the last week," he said. "An award such as this takes a lot of help. Both teams that are here today are a big part of these 1,800 points. I'd like to thank the Edmonton fans for their support, and I'd like to thank the Edmonton organization for their support." Gretzky also thanked his parents and wife and saluted Howe. "Gordie still is the greatest, in my mind, and the greatest in everyone else's mind," he said.

The goal that broke the record was classic Gretzky. He had been on the ice for almost three uninterrupted minutes and was hanging behind the net, waiting. Dave Taylor, stationed on the far right side, threw a pass in front. Gretzky skated in front of the net and backhanded the puck between Ranford and the post. The crowd roared as Gretzky and the Kings celebrated. The game was stopped for 10 minutes while Gretzky was honored. Gretzky entered the game 1 point shy of Howe's mark. He needed less than five minutes to get it, earning an assist on the game's first goal.

"It's been like a movie script," the Kings' owner, Bruce McNall—the man who brought Gretzky to Los Angeles—said after the game. "Nobody would buy it. It's so unbeliev-

able." Gretzky was revered by Edmonton fans while leading the Oilers to four Stanley Cups and he left the city in tears when he was sent to Los Angeles. He had predicted before the season that he would break Howe's mark on his first visit of the season to the Northlands Coliseum. Gretzky's specialness, Howe had said, made the loss of the record easier to take. "If it was, pardon the expression, some clown breaking it, it would have bothered me," Howe said earlier. "But not Wayne."

Wayne Gretzky of The Kings with Gordie Howe, his hero, after breaking Howe's points record. Gretzky had predicted he would become the N.H.L's greatest scorer on this very day before his old fans in Edmonton. (Associated Press)

Runners-up

1988: In a scene straight from the movie "The Natural," Kirk Gibson of the Los Angeles Dodgers hobbled from the dugout in the ninth inning of Game 1 of the World Series at Dodger Stadium and pinch-hit a come-from-behind game-winning two-run homer off Dennis Eckersley of the Oakland A's. The Dodgers went on to win the Series in five games.

1968: Al Oerter of West Babylon, N.Y., became the first track and field athlete to win four gold medals in the same event when he won the discus throw in 216 feet 6 inches at the Mexico City Games. His streak started at the 1956 Melbourne

Games in Australia. Carl Lewis of the United States won four straight gold medals in the long jump between 1984 and '96.

1970: Brooks Robinson, the greatest-fielding third baseman in baseball history, was magical with his glove and reactions on play after play as the Baltimore Orioles upended the Cincinnati Reds in the World Series in five games. Robinson was named the Series most valuable player after also hitting .429 with two home runs and nine runs batted in.

October 16, 1968
Olympics Ouster

By JOSEPH M. SHEEHAN

Tommie Smith and John Carlos of the United States raised gloved hands with fists clenched in a black power salute and bowed their heads on the victory stand during the playing of the national anthem on this date after they had finished first and third in the 200 meters at the Mexico City Olympics. The following article appeared in The Times *two days later.*

MEXICO CITY [Friday]—The United States Olympic Committee suspended Tommie Smith and John Carlos today for having used last Wednesday's victory ceremony for the 200-meter dash at the Olympic Games as the vehicle for a black power demonstration. The two Negro sprinters were told by Douglas F. Roby, the president of the committee, that they must leave the Olympic Village. Their credentials were also taken away, which made it mandatory for them to leave Mexico within 48 hours.

The decision to dismiss the athletes was made early this morning after the committee had been summoned into a conference by the executive committee of the International Olympic Committee. Members of the United States committee, who were divided on the question of whether action should be taken, emphasized that the dismissals were by edict of the international unit. The I.O.C. indicated, it was said, that it might bar the entire United States team from further participation if the athletes were not disciplined.

In a statement issued early this morning, the United States committee expressed its "profound regrets" to the International Olympic Committee, the Mexican Organizing Committee and the people of Mexico for the "discourtesy displayed" by Smith and Carlos. "The untypical exhibitionism of these athletes violates the basic standards of good manners and sportsmanship, which are so highly valued in the United States," the statement said. "Such immature behavior is an isolated incident" and "a repetition of such incidents by other members of the

Tommie Smith, center, and John Carlos of the U.S. extend black-gloved fists and stare downward on the victory stand in the Mexico City Games. They were suspended under pressure from the International Olympic Committee. (Associated Press)

United States team can only be considered a willful disregard of Olympic principles."

At Wednesday's 200-meter victory ceremony, Smith, the winner, and Carlos, who finished third, wore black scarves around their necks and black gloves (Smith on his right hand and Carlos on his left). After receiving their medals from the Marquis of Exeter, the president of the International Amateur Athletic Federation, Smith and Carlos raised their gloved hands with fists clenched and kept their heads deeply bowed during the playing of the national anthem and raising of the United States flag in their honor.

This demonstration produced a mixed

reaction among United States officials and members of the United States squad, black and white. Some hailed it as a gesture of independence and a move in support of a worthy cause. Many others said they were offended and embarrassed. A few were vehemently indignant.

The 24-year-old Smith, a rangy, long-legged athlete who stands 6 feet 3 inches, is from Lemoore, Calif., and is a student at San Jose State University, where Harry Edwards, who initiated the black power manifestations in athletics, was a teacher last year. Carlos, 23, who is 6 feet 4 inches tall, was born and raised in New York, but now lives in San Jose and also attends San Jose State.

October 16, 1969
The Amazin' Mets. For Once It's True

By JOSEPH DURSO and WILLIAM BORDERS

Catcher Jerry Grote, right, embraces winning pitcher Jerry Koosman while third baseman Ed Charles, left, cavorts as the Mets defeated the Orioles in Game 5 of the World Series. It was a day on which even the skyscrapers leapt. (Associated Press)

NEW YORK—The Mets entered the promised land today after seven years of wandering through the wilderness of baseball. In a tumultuous game before a record crowd of 57,397 in Shea Stadium, they defeated the Baltimore Orioles, 5–3, for their fourth straight victory of the 66th World Series and in five games captured the championship of a sport that had long ranked them as comical losers.

They did it with a full and final dose of the magic that had spiced their unthinkable climb from ninth place in the National League—100-to-1 shots who scraped and scrounged their way to the pinnacle as the waifs of the major leagues. At 3:17 o'clock on a cool and often sunny afternoon, their impossible dream came true when Cleon Jones caught a fly ball hit by Dave Johnson to left field. And they immediately touched off one of the great, riotous scenes in sports history, as thousands of persons swarmed from their seats and tore up the patch of ground where the Mets had made history.

It was 10 days after they had won the National League pennant in a three-game sweep of the Atlanta Braves. It was 22 days after they had won the Eastern title of the league over the Chicago Cubs. It was eight years after they had started business under Casey Stengel as the lovable losers of all sports. They reached the top, moreover, in the best and most far-fetched manner of Met baseball. They spotted the Orioles three runs in the third inning when Dave McNally and Frank Robinson hit home runs off Jerry Koosman. But then they stormed back with two runs in the sixth inning on a home run by Donn Clendenon, another in the seventh by Al Weis and two more in the eighth on two doubles and two errors.

The deciding run was batted home by Ron Swoboda, who joined the Met mystique in 1965 when the team was losing 112 games and was finishing last for the fourth straight time. But, like most of the Mets' victories in their year to remember, the decision was a collective achievement by the youngest team in baseball, under Manager Gil Hodges—who had suffered a heart attack a year ago after the Mets "surged" into ninth place.

With the kind of jubilation it reserves for its special heroes, New York went pleasantly mad when the Mets won. From the sleek skyscrapers of Wall Street, where a spontaneous tickertape blizzard greeted the victory, to the undistinguished bars of a hundred neighborhoods, where the toasts were in draft beer, the shouted cry was: "We're No. 1!" Teachers suspended classes because their transistor-equipped students were not paying attention anyway; bosses closed offices early for the same reason, and even policemen shrugged happily as they despaired of keeping order in the streets.

"We did it!" Swoboda shouted in the Mets' locker room. "This is the summit," cried third baseman Ed Charles, 36 years old and until a couple of months ago beyond hope for this particular thrill. "We're No. 1 in the world and you just can't get any bigger than this."

"Some people still might not believe in us," said Jones, "but then, some people still think the world is flat."

Runners-up

1912: Fred Snodgrass of the New York Giants dropped an easy fly to right-center field in the 10th inning of decisive Game 8 (Game 2 finished in a tie when called because of darkness) of the World Series at Fenway Park. The error opened the way to a two-run rally against Christy Mathewson that gave the Boston Red Sox a 3–2 victory and the championship and forever tarnished Snodgrass's name.

1962: Bobby Richardson snared Willie McCovey's scorched line drive with two outs in the last of the ninth inning at Candlestick Park with the tying and winning runs in scoring position to give Ralph Terry and the Yankees a 1–0 victory over the San Francisco Giants in Game 7 for New York's record 20th World Series championship.

1964: Don Schollander, 18, of Lake Oswego, Ore., became the first swimmer to win four gold medals in an Olympics when he won the 100-meter and 400-meter freestyles (the latter in a world record of 4 minutes 12.2 seconds) and anchored the 4x100-meter and 4x200-meter relays at the Tokyo Games. Schollander was also the first American to win four gold medals since Jesse Owens at the 1936 Berlin Olympics.

Three Straight for the Rowdy A's

By JOSEPH DURSO

Rollie Fingers, a poster-boy for the mustachioed A's, working on a new pair of shoes during spring training in 1974. He was voted M.V.P. of the World Series, winning one game and saving two against the Dodgers. (Associated Press)

OAKLAND, Calif.—The Oakland A's, fussing and feuding to the end, swept to their third straight baseball championship tonight when they defeated the Los Angeles Dodgers, 3–2, and won the 71st World Series. Only one team in baseball history has won more World Series in consecutive years than the controversial and frequently rowdy American League champions—the New York Yankees. The Yankees won four straight starting in 1936 and five straight starting in 1949, but tonight the A's moved right behind them into the record book.

"Their record speaks for itself," conceded Manager Walter Alston of the Dodgers, whose team won 102 games this summer with the best performance in the major leagues. "They play the game the way it should be played. They don't make

any mistakes." They didn't make any tonight before 49,347 fans in the Oakland–Alameda County Stadium as they stopped the Dodgers for the third night in a row and took the Series four games to one. At least, they didn't make any mistakes that could not be salvaged by late theatrics, and the theatrics were supplied chiefly by Joe Rudi in the seventh inning when he broke a 2–2 tie with a resounding home run off Mike Marshall, who was pitching in his 113th game of the year.

Rudi settled the issue just after the fans in the left-field seats had littered the grass with debris and at least one whisky bottle. The game was delayed briefly while the Dodgers considered taking shelter, but the outcome was not long delayed after the game was resumed and Rudi swung against Marshall. In an era of workhorse

relief pitching, Marshall was working for the fifth time in a five-game match. But Oakland produced an iron man of its own: Rollie Fingers, the man with the Svengali mustache who appeared 76 times during the six-month regular season and four times in the Series. The 29-year-old Ohioan worked the final two innings tonight, protected the lead provided by Rudi and then was voted the most valuable player on the scene.

So for the third October in a row, champagne flowed in the often tumultuous clubhouse of Charles O. Finley's ball team, including some that Reggie Jackson poured over the head of the commissioner of baseball, Bowie Kuhn, on national television. But some of the best men on the Oakland team were still demanding to be traded from Finley's heavy-handed grip. The best pitcher, Jim (Catfish) Hunter, was still pursuing a grievance claim for half his $100,000 salary and his outright release. And there were reminders of the customary bickering in a season that was enlivened by a fistfight or two and by the best record in recent times: four Western Division titles in a row, three American League pennants in a row and three world championships.

Jim (Catfish) Hunter, the 1974 Cy Young Award winner, won his grievance after the season and signed a free-agent contract with the Yankees (see Dec. 15). By 1977 Reggie Jackson was with them, too, and the Oakland dynasty was over.

Runners-up

1989: Shortly before the start of Game 3 of the World Series at San Francisco, a devastating earthquake rippled through Candlestick Park. More than 200 people were killed in the Bay Area, though none at the stadium, which sustained minor structural damage. The Series, an afterthought when the Oakland A's swept the Giants, was interrupted for 10 days.

1964: Fred Hansen of Cuero, Tex., won the gold medal in the pole vault at the Tokyo Olympics, defeating Wolfgang Reinhardt of Germany with an Olympic record of 16 feet 8¾ inches. Hansen used one of the new slingshot fiberglass Sky

Poles that had recently transformed vaulting. Within the previous two years, John Uelses (see Feb. 2) and John Pennel (see Aug. 24), both of the United States had broken the forbidding 16- and 17-foot barriers with fiberglass.

1994: Joe Montana (see Jan. 10), the great San Francisco 49ers quarterback now with the Kansas City Chiefs, staged a theatrical last hurrah in his final season, marching 75 yards in 81 seconds to defeat John Elway and the Denver Broncos, 31–28, at Mile High Stadium in a memorable Monday night game. Montana retired the following April.

October 18, 1924
Red Grange, the Galloping Ghost

URBANA, Ill., (AP)—A flashing, red-haired youngster, running and dodging with the speed of a deer, gave 67,000 jammed into the new $1,700,000 Illinois Memorial Stadium the thrill of their lives today, when Illinois vanquished Michigan, 39 to 14, in what probably will be the outstanding game of the 1924 gridiron season in the West. Harold (Red) Grange, Illinois phenomenon, All-America halfback, who attained gridiron honors of the nation last season, was the dynamo that furnished the thrills. Grange doubled and redoubled his football glory in the most remarkable exhibition of running, dodging and passing seen on any gridiron in years—an exhibition that set the dumbfounded spectators screaming with excitement.

Individually, Grange scored five of Illinois' six touchdowns in a manner that left no doubt as to his ability to break through the most perfect defense. He furnished one thrill after another. On the very first kickoff Grange scooped up the ball on the Illinois five-yard line and raced 95 yards through the Michigan eleven for a touchdown in less than ten seconds after the starting whistle blew. Before the Michigan team could recover from its shock, Grange had scored three more touchdowns in rapid succession, running 66, 55 and 40 yards, respectively, for his next three scores. Coach Bob Zuppke took him out of the line-up before the first quarter ended. He returned later to heave several successful passes and score a fifth touchdown in the last half.

Michigan, bewildered by the catastrophe, unleashed a rain of forward passes in an attempt to recoup, but 9 of its 13 heaves were grounded and 1 intercepted. The 3 successful passes were good for a total of 37 yards. Illinois completed 5 passes for a total of 70 yards, 2 others grounding. Meanwhile, Grange surpassed all of his former exploits in every department. He handled the ball 21 times, gained 402 yards and scored 5 touchdowns. Unbiased experts agree that his

Harold (Red) Grange posing at the University of Illinois in an undated photo. In the first quarter against Michigan in 1924 he returned a kickoff 95 yards for a touchdown and rushed 66, 55 and 40 yards for three other scores. (Bettmann/Corbis)

performance was among the greatest ever seen on an American gridiron.

On the second kickoff, Grange received the ball and raced 10 yards. Illinois lost the ball on downs but recovered by the same method on its 33-yard line. Then Grange tore off 66 yards for a second touchdown around right end. A moment later, on the same play, he ran 55 yards for a touchdown and shortly after scored his fourth of the quarter from Michigan's 40-yard line. In each instance he started behind perfect interference and side-stepped Michigan's safety men in the final sprint. He has a way of dodging, almost coming to a dead stop before whirling in another direction, that leaves his tacklers flat-footed and amazed.

The game was won and lost in the first thrill-packed moments when Grange, extricating himself repeatedly from

seemingly hopeless tangles of tacklers, crossed the goal line and permanently shook the Michigan morale. The shock which his four touchdowns produced on the highly keyed Wolverines dazed the Michigan crowd and team, and when the game was over many were still attempting to explain the defeat.

Harold (Red) Grange's performance made him the most storied college football player of the 20th century. He was the first collegiate star to turn pro, signing with the Chicago Bears in 1925 in the N.F.L.'s infancy and quickly popularizing it, playing 19 games in 17 cities in 66 days. Damon Runyon wrote: "He is three or four men rolled into one. He is Jack Dempsey, Babe Ruth, Al Jolson, Paavo Nurmi and Man o' War." Grange suffered a knee injury in his second season and retired in 1934.

The Long Jump That Defied Belief

By NEIL AMDUR

Bob Beamon of the United States digging into the sand pit while landing a record 29-foot-2½-inch long jump at altitude in the Mexico City Olympics. No one had ever jumped beyond 27 feet 4 inches before. (Associated Press)

MEXICO CITY—Two astonishing track and field achievements—a 29-foot-2½-inch long jump and a 43.8-second sprint in the 400-meter run—dramatically reaffirmed today the tenacity and competitive spirit of United States athletes. Faced with mounting mental and social pressures that could have cost them coveted places on the Olympic awards platform, Bob Beamon and Lee Evans responded with gold-medal performances that rivaled the first 4-minute mile and the first 17-foot pole vault for breath-taking spontaneity.

Beamon, 22, from Jamaica, Queens, startled the crowd of 45,000 in Olympic Stadium with an unbelievable opening attempt in the long jump. The world record for the event was 27-4¾, but Beamon, with his speed, height off the board and thinner air at the 7,350-foot altitude here, flew by 27 feet, 28 feet and 29 feet with a mark that may stand for years. Ralph Boston, Beamon's teammate, who shared the listed world record with Igor Ter-Ovanesyan of the Soviet Union, was third. "I figured the pressure was on me and Ralph, so I knew I had to go 100 per cent," the 6-foot-3-inch Beamon said afterward. Beamon's best jump before today had been a wind-aided 27-6½.

Beamon got tremendous height on his opening jump. His arms flapped like a bird and he seemed to take off like one. When the numbers 8.90 [meters] were placed on the scoreboard in front of the long-jump area, the metric figures corresponding to 29-2½, the crowd let out an unbelieving roar and Beamon jumped up and down in front of the stands. The 21-year-old Evans scored a driving, determined triumph in the 400-meter run with his 0:43.8, which was an amazing seven-tenths of a second under the recognized world record and two-tenths better than Evans's pending performance at South Lake Tahoe, Calif., last month.

That Beamon and Evans performed so marvelously was a tribute to their instinctive will to win. American athletes—black and white—had been under enormous pressure in the last 24 hours as a result of a United States Olympic Committee ruling that stripped Tommie Smith and John Carlos, the two Negro sprinters, of their Olympic credentials. Evans is a close friend of the pair and was one of the early leaders in the protest plans for an Olympic boycott by Negro athletes. Evans wore a pair of black socks as a silent sign of protest today.

Reggie Jackson, Mr. October

By JOSEPH DURSO

NEW YORK—With Reggie Jackson hitting three home runs in three straight times at bat, the Yankees swept all those family feuds under the rug tonight and overpowered the Los Angeles Dodgers, 8–4, to win their first World Series in 15 years. They won it in the sixth game of a match that had enlivened both coasts for the last week, and that rocked Yankee Stadium tonight as hundreds of fans poured through a reinforced army of 350 security guards and stormed onto the field after the final out.

For a team that already had made financial history by spending millions for players on the open market, the victory in the 74th World Series also brought new baseball history to the Yankees: It was the 21st time that they had won the title, but the first time since they defeated the San Francisco Giants in 1962 toward the end of their long postwar reign. And it marked a dramatic comeback from the four-game sweep they suffered last October at the hands of the Cincinnati Reds.

But for Jackson, the $3 million free agent who led the team in power hitting and power rhetoric, this was a game that perhaps had no equal since the World Series was inaugurated in 1903. He hit his three home runs on the first pitches off three pitchers, and he became the only man in history to hit three in a Series game since Babe Ruth did it for the Yankees twice, in 1926 and again in 1928. But nobody had ever before hit five in a World Series—let alone five in his last nine official times at bat—a feat that the 31-year-old Pennsylvanian accomplished during the last three games in California and New York.

Tonight his home runs on successive swings came off Burt Hooton in the fourth inning, Elias Sosa in the fifth and Charlie Hough in the eighth. In the tumult on the field after the final out, Jackson ran breathless into the clubhouse from right field with such speed that the Dodger pitcher Don Sutton later said, "That was one of the best broken-field runs I've ever seen."

"Perhaps for one night," Jackson reflected later inside the Yankees' tumultuous locker room, "I reached back and achieved that level of the overrated superstar. Babe Ruth was great. I'm just lucky."

Reggie Jackson said, "I'm the straw that stirs the drink." Indeed he was for the six Oakland A's or Yankee World Series teams he played for within 11 years during the 70's and early 80's. He hit 563 home runs in his 21-year career and retired the all-time leader in Series slugging with a .755 average.

Reggie Jackson admiring his record third consecutive home run in the sixth and final game of the World Series at Yankee Stadium. The pitcher was the Dodgers' knuckleballer, Charlie Hough. (Associated Press)

Runners-up

1924: Notre Dame's backfield gained a total of 310 yards in defeating Army, 13–7, at the Polo Grounds in New York. On the following day The New York Herald Tribune's Grantland Rice famously wrote: "Outlined against a blue-gray October sky, the Four Horsemen rode again. In dramatic lore, they are known as Famine, Pestilence, Destruction and Death. These are only aliases. Their real names are Stuhldreher, Miller, Crowley and Layden."

1960: Five days after losing the World Series to the Pittsburgh Pirates *(see Oct. 13),* Casey Stengel was fired as manager of the Yankees and replaced by Ralph Houk, a coach. Stengel won 10 pennants and 7 world championships in his 12 years with the team. Realizing that his age was a factor in his dismissal, he said, "I'll never make the mistake of being 70 again."

1950: Connie Mack, 87, stepped down as manager of the Philadelphia Athletics after 50 years at the helm and was succeeded by Jimmie Dykes. Born Cornelius McGillicuddy, Mack was a catcher for 11 years in the 1800's before being chosen by Ban Johnson, founder of the American League, to manage the new Philadelphia team. Mack always wore a business suit in the dugout.

English Teacher Wins Decathlon

By NEIL AMDUR

MEXICO CITY—Bill Toomey, a 29-year-old teacher of English, won the grueling decathlon with an Olympic record of 8,193 points tonight and gained the 11th track and field gold medal for the United States in these Games. Helped by a pressure performance in the pole vault and strong showings in the running aspects of the 10-event competition, Toomey beat three Germans—Kurt Bendlin, Hans-Joachim Walde and Manfred Tiedtke—for the most prestigious title in sports: a crown worn by such prominent American athletes as Jim Thorpe, Bob Mathias, Milt Campbell and Rafer Johnson.

Toomey, born in Philadelphia but a resident of Laguna Beach, Calif., needed a solid time in the final event, the 1,500-meter run,

Bill Toomey in a quadruple-exposure photo taken before he won the Olympic gold medal as best all-around athlete at Mexico City. He is shown throwing the javelin, putting the shot, running and hurdling. (Associated Press)

to assure himself of what some observers believe is the determinant of the "world's greatest athlete." Toomey led Bendlin, a West German and the world record holder, by 56 points, 7,764 to 7,708, and needed a time of 4 minutes 35.1 seconds in his heat of the 1,500 meters to set a world record. But he settled for a victorious 4:57.1. As Toomey entered the final stretch ahead by eight meters, a big smile swept across his handsome face and he pointed his fingers up as a sign of victory. His Olympic record beat the mark of 8,001 points set in the 1960 Games by Johnson.

The decathlon is determined on a point

scale rather than individual competition and athletes receive a specified number of points for each performance in the 10 events. The better the performance, the more points an athlete can receive. Thus, when Toomey missed his first two jumps at the opening height in the pole vault, he faced the possibility of receiving no points in the event if he failed on his third attempt. He succeeded and reached 13 feet 9½ inches. Toomey's best showings came in the 100-meter dash, 400-meter run, high jump and 110-meter high hurdles where he either led his 30 rivals or was close to the top.

Toomey was a long jumper and quarter-

miler at the University of Colorado when he decided to switch to the decathlon five years ago. Track observers told him to think twice. After all, they said, wasn't that rather late in life to begin such a physically and mentally demanding assignment? Mathias was 18 when he won an Olympic gold medal in 1948 and Campbell and Johnson also were considerably younger. But Toomey's speed and versatility were his strongest assets. He probably would have established a world record except that he lost precious seconds in the 1,500-meter run, the final event, because of the high altitude here of 7,350 feet above sea level.

Runners-up

1999: The Atlanta Braves advanced to their fifth World Series of the decade when the Mets' Kenny Rogers walked Andruw Jones to force in the winning run for a 10–9 Braves victory in the bottom of the 11th inning of Game 6 of the League Championship Series at Turner Field.

1957: Maurice (Rocket) Richard (see March 17) of the Canadiens, the highest-scoring player in N.H.L. history at the time, became the first to break the 500 barrier for career goals when he slapped a 20-foot shot past Glenn Hall of the

Chicago Blackhawks at the Montreal Forum. He retired in 1960 with 544 goals. Fourteen players now have more than 600.

1936: The Associated Press released its first ranking of college football teams, choosing Minnesota, coached by Bernie Bierman and led by tackle Ed Widseth, as the best in the country. The poll kicked off a national debate about "Who's No. 1?" that exists to this day in both football and basketball at the collegiate level.

October 20, 1968
Fearless Fosbury Flops to Glory

By JOSEPH DURSO

NEW YORK—Fearless Fosbury is a 21-year-old senior at Oregon State University with a major in civil engineering, two bad feet, a worn-out body, an unbelievable style of high-jumping head first on his back, a habit of talking to himself in midair—and a gold medal and an Olympic record. He started jumping over bars in the fifth grade with the orthodox scissor-kick, and cleared 3 feet 10 inches. In high school, despite the dire warnings of every coach who watched him, he invented the "Fosbury Flop" and reached 6–7. And today in Mexico City he amazed 80,000 persons by clearing 7 feet 4¼ inches for an Olympic record.

Before he springs from the pad like some great rocket lifting off, Dick Fosbury meditates, worries, psyches himself. Once he pondered four and a half minutes before approaching the bar. On the way over, he goads himself with a pep talk. When he lands, it's usually on his shoulder blades but sometimes on his neck. "I have a bad back," Fosbury said after his victory, "and I lost a big patch of skin on the back of my left heel. Then I tripped on some stone steps the other day and strained a ligament in my right foot. I guess I use positive thinking. Every time I approach the bar I keep telling myself, 'I can do it, I can do it.'"

When he did it tonight, Fosbury gave the world a spectacular display of his "thing," which he describes as follows: "I take off on my right, or outside, foot rather than my left foot. Then I turn my back to the bar, arch my back over the bar and then kick my legs out to clear the bar." The people at Oregon State are studying hundreds of films of their flying civil engineer in action, but so far nobody has figured out a way to duplicate his style. It is totally unlike the scissor-kick, the Western roll, the Eastern cutoff and other techniques. Even Fearless Fosbury is amazed. "Sometimes I see movies," he says, "and I really wonder how I do it."

However, Fosbury foresees the day when boys all over America will be soaring over bars upside-down. "I think quite a few kids will begin trying it my way now," he said. "I don't guarantee results, and I don't recommend my style to anyone. All I say is if a kid can't straddle, he can try it my way."

Dick Fosbury had discovered as a schoolboy that by lowering his center of gravity by stretching out on his back he could actually jump higher. Within a decade of his gold medal, the scissors kick had been rendered old-fashioned and the great majority of Olympic high jumpers were using Fosbury's technique.

Dick Fosbury using the "Fosbury Flop," a then-unorthodox head-first, back-to-the-bar method of high jumping, at the Mexico City Games. He cleared 7 feet 4¼ inches for a gold medal and a world record. (Associated Press)

Runners-up

1988: Untouchable Orel Hershiser, who had ended the regular season with a scoreless streak of 59 consecutive innings, pitched visiting Los Angeles to a 5–2 victory over the Oakland Athletics as the Dodgers won the World Series in five games. Hershiser had a 1.00 earned run average for his two complete-game victories, was named the Series' most valuable player and later won the Cy Young Award unanimously.

1991: Ayrton Senna of Brazil clinched his third Formula One world racing championship when he drove his McLaren-Honda to a second-place finish at the Japanese Grand Prix in Suzuka. He outpointed Nigel Mansell of Britain for the overall title. Senna, who ranked third on the all-time victory list, was killed in 1994 in a crash at the San Marino Grand Prix in Imola, Italy.

1968: In one of the grand showdowns of Olympic history, Kip Keino of Kenya defeated the world record-holder Jim Ryun (*see June 23*) of the U.S. in the 1,500 meters at the Mexico City Games. Running at altitude, where he was comfortable, Keino blazed to an Olympic mark of 3:34.9, almost two seconds behind Ryun's record, but finished 20 meters ahead of him.

October 21, 1975
Fisk Begs 'Stay Fair! Stay Fair!'

By JOSEPH DURSO

Carlton Fisk providing the body English that kept his 12th-inning, game-winning shot barely fair at Fenway Park in Game 6 of the World Series against Cincinnati. Reds pitcher Pat Darcy looks on. (Associated Press)

BOSTON—The Boston Red Sox rose to dramatic heights tonight when they defeated the Cincinnati Reds, 7–6, on a 12th-inning home run by Carlton Fisk just barely inside the left field foul pole and stretched the World Series into a seventh and deciding game. It was a tingling four-hour marathon that ended at 12:33 after the Red Sox had raised all sorts of rumpus before a roaring crowd of 35,205 in Fenway Park and a national television audience. They took a 3–0 lead the first time they batted, they lost it five innings later, they fell behind by 6–3 in the eighth

and then four outs from losing the final honors of the baseball season, they struck back with theatrical flourishes.

Their first flourish was a three-run pinch-hit homer in the bottom of the eighth by Bernie Carbo, who had pinch-hit a home run a week ago in Cincinnati. Then, while a record total of 12 pitchers tried to establish some sort of order on both sides, the Red Sox failed to score with the bases loaded and nobody out in the ninth; they survived a Cincinnati threat in the 11th on a circus catch by Dwight Evans in right field, and they won

it on the second pitch to Fisk in the 12th. As a result, the champions of the American League tied the champions of the National League at three games apiece in one of the most colorful matches in the 72-year history of the World Series.

"The way I hurt all over," said Sparky Anderson, manager of the Reds, after they had missed a great chance for their first championship in 35 years, "it was probably as good a ball game as I've ever seen. A great game in a great series. And that catch by Evans in the 11th was as good a catch as you'll see."

"It was a fantastic game," agreed Fisk, a 27-year-old catcher from Vermont, who ended it against Pat Darcy in the 12th. "You're not exactly on top of the world when you're trailing a club like the Cincinnati Reds, 6–3, with four outs to go. Pete Rose came up to me in the 10th and said, 'This is some kind of game, isn't it?' And I said, 'Some kind of game.'"

The Carlton Fisk Game, as it came to be called, was among the handful of most dramatic games in history and gave baseball a needed boost during a time of lagging popularity. Cincinnati won the first of two straight World Series titles the next day, 4–3, on Joe Morgan's ninth-inning single to center off Jim Burton. For all but Reds fans, however, the game was anticlimactic after the night before.

Runners-up

1998: The Yankees, who won 125 games in the regular and post-season to rank as one of the greatest teams ever, completed a World Series sweep of the San Diego Padres with a 3–0 victory at Jack Murphy Stadium. New York's Scott Brosius, who batted .471 and hit two home runs in Game 3, was named the Series' most valuable player.

1976: Johnny Bench slugged a two-run homer and a three-run shot in Game 4 at Yankee Stadium as the Cincinnati Reds won, 7–2, to sweep New York in the

World Series. Bench batted .533 in the classic. It was the Big Red Machine's second straight world title under Manager Sparky Anderson.

1980: The Philadelphia Phillies won their first and only World Series to date behind their most valuable player, Mike Schmidt, defeating the Kansas City Royals in decisive Game 6 by 4–1 at Veterans Stadium. In a sign of the times, police officers on horseback ringed the field in the ninth inning to prevent fans from pillaging the field or endangering the players and umpires.

October 22, 2000
Throwing a Bat and Piercing the Mets

By BUSTER OLNEY

NEW YORK—Roger Clemens threw fastballs that reached 99 miles an hour, but drew even more attention for firing a broken bat in the direction of the Mets' Mike Piazza tonight, pitching eight shutout innings and heightening the emotions of the Subway Series that is being controlled by the Yankees.

Facing Piazza for the first time since hitting the Mets catcher in the head with a fastball in July, Clemens sparked an astonishing bench-clearing incident in the first inning by hurling the broken bat. But Clemens retreated to a private room in the clubhouse, refocused and continued his recent postseason domination, allowing only two hits and striking out nine in a 6–5 victory over the Mets in Game 2 of the World Series at Yankee Stadium. Now the Yankees lead the Series two victories to none.

Clemens and his manager, Joe Torre, became animated when questioned after the game about Clemens's intent when he threw the bat at Piazza. "There was no intent there," Clemens said repeatedly. Torre said: "It was just emotional. Should he have done it? No."

Clemens's beaning of Piazza three and a half months ago has hovered over this Series, and although Torre has accused the news media of reopening the wound in the last week, the Mets' hostility toward Clemens has never really dissipated. Everything Clemens did tonight would be seen by the Mets through the prism of that incident in July. And some of the Yankees had been concerned about his mood after a week in which the news media had revisited the beaning time and again. Clemens wore linebacker's eyes to the mound. He wears a mouthpiece when he pitches, and his lower jaw was locked, his chin pushed

forward, except when he cursed, either at himself or the batter, and at no one in particular.

After Clemens had disposed of Timo Perez and Edgardo Alfonzo, Piazza was announced as the next hitter and the crowd of 56,069 roared. Clemens pumped two fastballs for strikes. Then, after throwing a ball out of the strike zone, he fired inside, shattering Piazza's bat into at least three pieces. The ball went foul and the barrel of the bat bounced toward Clemens, who fielded it as he would a grounder, then turned and fired the fragment sidearm toward Piazza, the bat head skimming and skittering along the ground just in front of Piazza.

Piazza was stunned, and he turned and stared at Clemens, moving toward the pitcher, turning the bat handle in his hand, stepping across the base line. The Mets' coaching staff and players immediately

rushed from their dugout. Clemens held his hand up, as if to ask the umpire for a new ball, but then came face to face with Piazza, appearing to tell him that he thought the barrel was the ball. Piazza shouted at Clemens, asking him what his problem was. Then the Mets' bench coach, John Stearns—who had tried to confront Clemens the day after the beaning—bulled his way toward the pitcher, screaming. Torre grabbed Stearns, who used to play for him, and tried to calm him down, and gradually, as Clemens and Piazza were separated, the situation came under control without punches.

Four nights later, the Yankees won the first Subway Series in 44 years, finishing off the Mets in Game 5 at Shea Stadium. Luis Sojo grounded the winning hit up the middle off Al Leiter in the ninth inning, leading to a 4–2 victory.

Roger Clemens of the Yankees throwing the barrel of Mike Piazza's shattered bat back in his direction in Game 2 of the World Series against the Mets. The incident became a cause célebre in light of Clemens's beaning of Piazza in July. (Barton Silverman/The New York Times)

Runners-up

1989: Alain Prost of France won the Formula One world championship in the Japan Grand Prix at Suzuka when his McLaren teammate and rival for the title, Ayrton Senna of Brazil (see Oct. 20), was disqualified for getting an illegal push-start after running into Prost's car and taking him out of the race. Senna crossed the finish line first, but to the disabled went the spoils.

1972: Gene Tenace, the World Series' most valuable player after hitting .348 with four home runs, drove in all of the Oakland A's runs and Rollie Fingers got the

save as the Athletics defeated the Cincinnati Reds, 3–2, in Game 7 at Riverfront Stadium for their first of three successive world championships (See Oct. 17).

2000: Corey Dillon, a one-man-gang running back for the Cincinnati Bengals, rushed for 278 yards in a 32–21 victory over the Denver Broncos at Paul Brown Stadium in Cincinnati, breaking the single-game mark of 275 set by Walter Payton of the Chicago Bears in 1977 (see Nov. 20).

October 23, 1994
Solo Sailor, Instant Heroine

By BARBARA LLOYD

NEW YORK—It was a bright, clear night in Cape Town when the French solo sailor, Isabelle Autissier, sailed across the finish line in her record-setting first stage of the BOC round-the-world yacht race early today. The next closest competitor was still 1,200 miles away, reason enough for Autissier to become France's newest sports heroine. "Barring a gear failure, she has such a commanding lead now that it seems impossible for anyone to catch her in the remaining 16,000 miles of the race," said Mark Schrader, the BOC race director, from Cape Town.

The 38-year-old Autissier, alone on her 60-foot sailboat, Ecureuil PoitouCharentes 2, bucked 40-knot winds as she sailed past Cape Town's Table Mountain today. She arrived at about 3:30 A.M., having completed her 6,800-mile voyage from Charleston, S.C., in 35 days, 8 hours, 52 minutes. The passage was two days faster than the BOC record set in 1990 by another French sailor, Alain Gautier. Still at sea are 17 men. "It's incredible," Autissier said, clinging to the bow of her boat as hundreds of well-wishers chanted: "Vive la France!" "I'm astonished, even now I don't realize what I've accomplished," she said.

Autissier, who is the only woman competing in the 1994–95 BOC Challenge race, is also the only woman to have completed a 27,000-mile BOC competition. Sailing in the 1990–91 BOC race, she finished seventh, having been dismasted along the way. She vowed at that time to come back and win. "She was the most determined person and the most focused on what she would do in the next four years," said Schrader.

Autissier used her New York–to–San

Isabelle Autissier of France popping a magnum of champagne after winning the first leg of the BOC round-the-world yacht race. She sailed a 60-foot boat alone from Charleston, S.C., to Cape Town in 36 days. (Reuters)

Francisco run last spring as a 14,000-mile shakedown for the BOC. That voyage left her extraordinary abilities written on the wind. The trip, which Autissier did with a crew of three men, shaved 14 days off the 76-day San Francisco record. Her run to Cape Town has established another new standard.

But how did she do it? "Obviously, 1,200 miles is just an incomprehensible lead in a 7,000-mile leg," said Schrader. "If it was just one factor—the person, the boat, or the tactics—her margin of winning would be very small. But it was all of that."

Her boat, built with an innovative swing keel, is undeniably fast. And she is an astute student of weather, having been trained in meteorology in France for a year before the race. But beyond that, she exudes confidence, and has proved that she is willing to trust her own judgment. "There was a point in time where she risked it all," said Schrader, referring to Autissier's bold decision about 2,500 miles from Cape Town to head into an area where there are usually calms. "She saw something there that no one else saw," he said. "She was going to win, and win big, or lose it all."

Runners-up

1993: Joe Carter of the Toronto Blue Jays lined a pitch from Mitch Williams of the Philadelphia Phillies over the left-field fence at the Skydome for a three-run ninth-inning homer that catapulted the Jays to a dramatic 8–6 victory in Game 6 of the World Series. It gave Toronto a second straight world title.

1945: Brooklyn Dodgers president Branch Rickey announced that the former U.C.L.A. football star and Negro league player Jackie Robinson (*see April 10*) had signed to play with the team's Montreal farm club in 1946. Robinson, a former Army lieutenant, had been handpicked and advised by Rickey on how to handle the racism he might face from some white players.

1994: Dale Earnhardt won his seventh Winston Cup season championship, taking the AC Delco 500 at Rockingham, N.C., and beating Mark Martin by 444 points for the driving title. It was the Intimidator's seventh crown and tied him with Richard Petty (*see Feb. 18*)—King Richard, as they called him within the sport—on the all-time Nascar list.

Wilt the Stilt, Big at the Garden

By HOWARD M. TUCKNER

NEW YORK—At Madison Square Garden tonight the Knickerbockers ran smack into the biggest thing to hit basketball since the abolishment of the center jump. The big thing was Wilt (the Stilt) Chamberlain, the Philadelphia Warriors' 7-foot-2-inch rookie center. The show he put on for 15,527 fans was both beautiful and frightening. Chamberlain, performing as gracefully as a backcourt man, scored 43 points in his league debut and the Warriors triumphed, 118–109.

It was the opening National Basketball Association contest for both teams, but the Knick players and the crowd probably will remember Wilt's performance long after the end of the seventy-five-game campaign. Chamberlain, the affluent giant who quit Kansas State in his junior year and joined the Harlem Globetrotters at $60,000 a season, played a near-perfect game tonight.

His rebounding was magnificent. Time and again he fought off elbows, hips and, on several occasions, fists to capture the ball off the backboard. He pulled down twenty-eight rebounds, one-quarter of the entire Philadelphia total. When he gained possession of the ball, he would whip it down court to start Philadelphia's fast break. More often than not, he was down court quickly enough to receive a return pass and stuff the ball in on turn shots inside the keyhole or on hard drives into the basket.

On set plays, the Knicks, who had held Chamberlain to a 25-point average in three pre-season games, played him man-to-man with either Charlie Tyra or Johnny Green assigned to fluster him. The New Yorkers' strategy was to keep Chamberlain outside the foul line and to allow Wilt to try his hand at hooks or long push shots. To keep him away from the basket, Tyra used all legal means (rushing and hand-waving) and a few other tricks, such as grabbing Wilt's shirt or slipping a quick elbow into the small of his back.

But Wilt would have none of this. Despite his proportions, he is one of the fastest men in pro basketball and he had Tyra chasing him all over the court. Finally Wilt would spot an opening and dash under the basket with Tyra in pursuit. The entire Knick defense would collapse on him. Guy Rodgers, Philadelphia's deft ball handler, then would flip a high pass in Wilt's vicinity and an arm—an arm two and a half feet long—would reach out for it from the maze of other arms. It belonged to Chamberlain. Then he would fake, spin and two more points could be chalked up for the Warriors.

Wilt hit on seventeen of twenty-seven field goal attempts and nine of fifteen foul shots during the game. Rodgers and Paul Arizin provided fine assistance for Chamberlain, scoring 19 points each.

Wilt Chamberlain (see March 2) combined size, strength and grace to dominate N.B.A. games the way no one had before. He led the league in scoring his first seven seasons, a feat matched only by Michael Jordan. In Chamberlain's third season (1961–62) he averaged 50.4 points a game and finished with 4,029; no one else has come near him.

Wilt Chamberlain of the Philadelphia Warriors trying to put back a rebound against the Knicks at the old Madison Square Garden. He was overwhelming the N.B.A. in his first season after a year with the Harlem Globetrotters. (Corbis)

Runners-up

1992: A Canadian team won a World Series for the first time as 41-year-old Dave Winfield's two-run double off the Atlanta Braves' Charlie Leibrandt with two out in the top of the 11th inning of Game 6 at Fulton County Stadium gave the Toronto Blue Jays a 4–3 victory.

1999: Ricky Williams of the University of Texas became the leading scorer in Division I-A history when his two touchdowns in the last 2 minutes 3 seconds of a 30–20 victory over Baylor gave him 428 career points. He broke the record of 416 points by Roman Anderson of Houston in 1989.

1857: The world's first soccer team, the Sheffield Football Club, was formed by two army officers, Col. Nathaniel Cresswick and Maj. William Priest, in England. They simultaneously drew up rules, drawing on the best features of rudimentary winter games at schools such as Charterhouse, Rugby and Eton, and created the constitution of the Sheffield club.

Mookie Wilson's Grounder. Bill Buckner's Legs

By DAVE ANDERSON

Because of its unpredictable turns, strategic moves and staggering finish, Game 6 of the 1986 World Series between the Mets and the Boston Red Sox is widely considered one of the greatest baseball games ever played.

NEW YORK—In the uproar after the Mets somehow won, 6–5, with three runs in the 10th inning tonight, Chub Feeney, the retiring president of the National League, put both the World Series and the wonderful world of baseball in their proper perspective. "Impossible," he shouted, hurrying out of Shea Stadium. Not since Bobby Thomson hit his pennant-winning home run for the New York Giants off Ralph Branca in the ninth inning of their decisive 1951 playoff game with the Brooklyn Dodgers had a New York team won such an important game in such an improbable, if not impossible, manner. Two outs, nobody on, two runs behind. But somehow the Mets won.

Just when these Red Sox thought they had won the franchise's first World Series championship since 1918, the Mets somehow patched and pasted together three runs on singles by Gary Carter, Kevin Mitchell and Ray Knight, a wild pitch by Bob Stanley and Mookie Wilson's grounder that Bill Buckner, the Red Sox first baseman, let slip through his aching legs. And tomorrow night Ron Darling has an opportunity to measure the Mets for their World Series rings in the decisive seventh game.

"I'm not an emotional guy, I never run on the field," said Davey Johnson, the Mets' manager. "But when I saw the ball get by Buckner, I was out on the field." Davey Johnson also was out of his own doghouse. With one out in the bottom of

Bill Buckner of the Red Sox heads to the clubhouse after misplaying Mookie Wilson's grounder, allowing the Mets to even the World Series at three games apiece. The Sox were within one out of their first Series title since 1918. (Associated Press)

the 10th inning, Johnson sat down in the Mets' dugout, his hands stuffed in the slash pockets of his blue Mets' jacket, his mind still on the ninth inning when Howard Johnson had struck out as a pinch-hitter with runners on first and second in a 3–3 game. Moments later the Mets might've won that game on Lee Mazzilli's fly ball to left field if Johnson had bunted the runners over. But he had struck out instead.

"I had two choices. I could let a rookie bunt," Davey Johnson said, alluding to Kevin Elster, "but if I do that I'd have had to use a pinch-runner for Ray Knight at second base, and I didn't want to do that. I never play conservative, but I sent a good hitter up to bunt. I didn't like the way he swung on the bunt, so then I let him hit and he struck out." Elster joined the Mets from their Jackson, Miss., farm late in the season. Johnson also might have second-

guessed himself for taking Darryl Strawberry out of the game at the start of the ninth inning. "There's a case when I'm running out of pitchers," the Mets' manager said. "I don't want my pitcher hitting fourth in the next inning."

The Mets' manager put Mazzilli, who had singled and scored the tying run in the eighth, in right field. In a double switch, Johnson brought in Rick Aguilera to pitch and put him in Strawberry's fifth slot in the batting order. But lo and behold, in the 10th inning, Mitchell was up there instead of Strawberry, who had been hitting .200 in the Series with only four hits. In tonight's game, Strawberry walked twice before grounding out and hitting a high fly ball.

Maybe if Johnson had kept Strawberry in the game, Strawberry would have made the final out in the 10th inning as the Red Sox won the World Series for the first time since 1918. Or maybe Strawberry would have hit a two-run homer to tie the game. No one will ever know what would have happened if Strawberry had stayed in the game. But now everybody, especially the Red Sox, knows that Mitchell's single kept the Mets' rally alive. Not that Johnson was taking any credit for what happened in the Mets' 10th inning.

"In that 10th inning," the manager was asked, "did you make any little moves that helped?"

"No," he said, "I was sitting there praying that we'd get something going, if you know what I mean."

Two nights after the impossible Game 6, the Mets came back from a 3–0 deficit against Bruce Hurst in the final innings of Game 7 to win by 8–5 and take their second world championship. As of 2003, the Red Sox were still waiting for their first title since 1918.

Runners-up

1999: Months after capturing his second United States Open with the longest winning putt in the tournament's history, Payne Stewart was killed with five others when his Learjet crashed in South Dakota. All aboard apparently lost consciousness or died during flight, most likely from lack of oxygen. Shadowed by Air Force jets, the plane crashed after running out of fuel.

1947: Columbia University, coached by Lou Little, defeated mighty Army, guided by Earl (Red) Blaik, 21–20, at Baker Field in New York as Bill Swiacki caught nine passes, including a dramatic one with one arm that set up the winning score.

Columbia, then a waning Eastern powerhouse, broke the Cadets' 32-game unbeaten streak, which dated from World War II (*see Dec. 1*).

1990: Evander Holyfield, a 208-pound former cruiserweight, won the undisputed world heavyweight title by knocking out James (Buster) Douglas, the bloated 246-pound title-holder, in the third round of a bout in Las Vegas. The loss ended a brief championship reign for Douglas, who had dethroned Mike Tyson in a stunning 10-round knockout eight months before (*see Feb. 11*).

October 26, 1980
The Toast of the Town

By NEIL AMDUR

NEW YORK—Alberto Salazar, a 22-year-old senior at the University of Oregon, survived chilly, blustery weather and 14,011 challengers from 44 countries to win the New York City Marathon today. Salazar, who was born in Cuba and who now lives in Wayland, Mass., dispelled a marathon myth and won his first 2-mile-385-yard race in an astonishing 2 hours 9 minutes 41 seconds, a course record. It was the fastest first marathon in history, eighth on the world list and the second fastest by an American. As many as 2 million New Yorkers may have lined the course from Fourth Avenue in Brooklyn to the finish line at Tavern on the Green in Central Park, despite the 40-degree temperatures.

Only one day before the race, when asked to assess his chances, the 6-foot, 140-pound Salazar had stunned veteran road racers by saying, "I feel confident I can go the whole distance...if somebody runs 2:10 tomorrow, I'll run 2:10." Rodolfo Gomez of Mexico, who was even with Salazar until he stopped for a drink at 21.4 miles, was second in 2:10:14.

Despite his size and dark, handsome features, Salazar is hardly a picturesque runner. He has no high-knee lift that is associated with speed, his long legs have a duck-like wobble, and he lands far back on his heels instead of his toes. But what Salazar lacks in style, he more than compensates for with a confidence and mental determination that has become famous among his peers. During a race in Falmouth, Mass., several years ago, he was administered last rites and put into an ice bath when his body temperature reached 103 degrees and he passed out after having finished second to Bill Rodgers, who won this race the last four

Alberto Salazar, left, winning his third consecutive New York City Marathon in 1982. His 1980 time of 2 hours 9 minutes 41 seconds – he expected to run 2:10 – was the fastest ever for a debut in the race. (Barton Silverman/The New York Times)

years and finished fifth today.

On his original marathon entry blank that asked for a projected time here, Salazar wrote "2:10." Today, sensing that Gomez had slowed for fluids, Salazar accelerated, seemingly oblivious to the so-called "wall" that is supposed to confront marathoners after 20 miles. Within a few city blocks along Fifth Avenue, he extended his lead from 5 to 30 yards. "I had always heard about the magical 20-mile mark," said Salazar, who began training

for his first marathon only because he had no collegiate cross-country eligibility this fall. "The most I hurt was the last 300 yards."

Alberto Salazar's victory in New York was the fastest marathon debut in history. The following year he broke the 12-year-old world marathon record at New York in 2:08.13. His third straight victory in 1982 was the last time an American won the New York City Marathon.

Runners-up

1996: The Yankees won their 23rd World Series—and first in 18 years, their longest drought—with a 3–2 victory over the Atlanta Braves at the Stadium. John Wetteland, the Series' most valuable player with four saves, got Mark Lemke for the final out in the decisive Game 6. Wade Boggs rode a Police Department "victory horse" around the outfield.

1985: The Kansas City Royals were three outs away from elimination when Umpire Don Denkinger's bad call on a play at first—Jorge Orta was called safe on a ground ball—led to a two-run Game 6 rally that evened the World Series

against the St. Louis Cardinals at Royals Stadium. The Royals won their only world title on a Bret Saberhagen shutout the following night.

1929: Yale Coach Mal Stevens inserted 5-foot-6-inch, 144-pound quarterback Albie Booth while losing to Army, 13–0, at the Yale Bowl in Connecticut. He became an overnight sensation by scoring every point in a 21–13 upset by running for two touchdowns, making a 65-yard punt return for another and kicking all three extra points.

OOO OOO OOO O: Couldn't Be Touched

By IRA BERKOW

Jack Morris of the Twins against the Angels in August 1991. Fast, cunning and experienced, he bested John Smoltz and defeated the Braves in a 10-inning Game 7 duel two months later in the World Series. (Getty Images)

Minneapolis—Nothing was happing, nothing, nothing, nothing, nothing but increasing tension. The zeros on the scoreboard tonight in the Metrodome were dropping inning after inning after inning, as if a row of hens were working overtime. It appeared that the best and concluding moments of this baseball season—maybe the best of any baseball season—might last forever.

This was the seventh game of the World Series, and after three, four, five, six, seven innings, nobody could score. People tried: The Minnesota Twins got a runner to third in the third inning; the Atlanta Braves did likewise in the the fifth. But nothing happened. The pitchers, Jack Morris of the Twins and John Smoltz

of the Braves, were matching sets of excellence, bookends of bravado.

It was preposterous. It couldn't get more dramatic. It did. In the eighth, both teams loaded the bases with one out, but the Twins turned a double play to end the Braves' threat. In the bottom of the inning, the Braves did precisely the same thing to the Twins, behind Mike Stanton, who had replaced Smoltz.

It went into the ninth inning, 0–0. That is, 16 zeros. Nothing had happened, and it just kept on happening. And into the 10th: zero, of course, to zero. The longest Game 7 with no score in the history of the World Series.

And there it ended. Dan Gladden hit a broken-bat double, and there was a sacri-

fice bunt and two intentional walks, and then with the bases loaded and a pulled-in outfield, Gene Larkin, a seldom-used infielder, stepped up to pinch-hit. He was facing Alejandro Peña, now on the mound for the Braves. The noisy home crowd of 55,000 was on its feet and creating a snowstorm by waving its white homer hankies. And Larkin responded. He looped a fly ball over the outstretched glove of left fielder Brian Hunter, for a single to score the lone run of the game.

Suddenly it was over. Suddenly the Twins had won. But the Braves did not lose. They just didn't win the World Series, is all. Four of the first six games between the Braves and the Twins had been decided by one run, and three had been determined only in the home half of the final inning, to break up a tie game—one concluding in the ninth inning and one in the 12th, with plays at the plate, and, last night, in the 11th, with Kirby Puckett's game-ending home run for the Twins.

But we needed this game, Game 7, and that's the simple truth. It was only fitting and proper. It was all so unlikely, all so upside-down, but this seems to restore the cosmic balance: Two teams that finished last in their divisions the year before win the pennants. Each team knowing in its heart it cannot lose, that the fates have ordained that this is their season.

Runners-up

1999: The Yankees won their third world championship in four years and 25th over all when Roger Clemens and Mariano Rivera, the Series' most valuable player, shut down the Atlanta Braves, 4–1, at the Stadium for a four-game sweep. It was New York's second straight Series sweep and gave them 12 consecutive Series victories dating to 1996.

2002: Emmitt Smith of the Dallas Cowboys broke the 15-year-old N.F.L. career rushing record held by Walter Payton of the Chicago Bears (see Oct. 7) when he reached 16,728 yards with an 11-yard surge in the fourth quarter in a loss

to the Seattle Seahawks. The mother and brother of Payton, who died in 1999, watched from a box at Texas Stadium.

1962: Dawn Fraser, a 25-year-old Australian who was a gold medalist in the 1960 Olympic Games, became the first woman to break the one-minute barrier in the 100-meter freestyle at an Empire Games trial in Melbourne. Women swimmers long considered the 60-second mark the way male runners had looked upon the 4-minute mile.

October 28, 1962
The Old Giants' Winning Arm

By ROBERT L. TEAGUE

NEW YORK—As if the league-leading Washington Redskins weren't even there, Y.A. Tittle of the Giants played catch with fleet-footed friends this afternoon at Yankee Stadium. The results were a record-equaling seven touchdown passes for Tittle and a 49–34 triumph for New York. Only twice before had any National Football League quarterback wreaked so much havoc with his throwing arm in a single joust. Eons ago, Sid Luckman of the Bears established a league high of seven scoring passes in one game. Later that was matched by Adrian Burk of the Eagles.

Today, a vociferous throng of 62,844 saw the Giants abruptly halt Washington's unbeaten streak at six, and re-establish New York's ranking as the club most likely to succeed in the Eastern Conference. Joe Walton crossed the goal line three times with Tittle's passes. Joe Morrison scored with two and Frank Gifford and Del Shofner sprinted into the end zone with one apiece for the 1961 conference champions.

All told, the 35-year-old Tittle made connections on 27 of 39 passes—and 12 of the completions came in succession. He thus accounted for 505 yards, more than any of his predecessors on the Giants ever had. As the final score suggests, Tittle was virtually compelled to reach the apogee of his 15-year career as a pro. Norm Snead turned in his greatest performance to date as Washington's second-year quarterback. He made four touchdown throws. Two of these went to Bobby Mitchell on plays covering 80 and 44 yards.

Shofner was Tittle's primary target, although it was Gifford who was in on the longest Giant pass of the day—63 yards. The lanky Shofner gained 269 yards on 11 catches, which equaled Gifford's club record for receptions in one game. Shofner also eclipsed the Giants one-day mark of 212 yards gained by a pass catcher set by Gene Roberts in 1949.

At times, Tittle and Shofner seemed oblivious of the Redskins, as if warming up for a big game at some later date. Again and again, Del embarrassed Claude Crabb, Washington's rookie defensive back, in the secondary. What made the Tittle-Shofner combination so effective, of course, was the stubbornness of New York's forward blockers—Ray Wietecha, Darrell Dess, Roosevelt Brown, Jack Stroud and Reed Bohovich. They gave Tittle plenty of time and room to study the field, and gave the receivers time to bamboozle or outrun their shadowers.

On the other hand, Snead was hard pressed more often than not, and frequently was flattened by the Giants before he could get a pass off. The tacklers in most of these instances were Jim Katcavage, Rosey Grier, Andy Robustelli and Dick Modzelewski.

Playing in an era when passing did not dominate the game to the extent it does today, Y.A. Tittle threw 33 touchdown passes in 1962. The 12-2 Giants faced Vince Lombardi's Green Bay Packers in the N.F.L. championship game, losing by 16–7 in 35-mile-an-hour winds at Yankee Stadium. Tittle retired in 1964.

Y.A. Tittle of the Giants getting off a pass in a game against the Redskins. He threw for a record-tying seven touchdowns – three to Joe Walton, two to Joe Morrison, and one each to Frank Gifford and Del Shofner. (The New York Times)

Runners-up

1995: The Braves became the first team to win a World Series in three cities (Boston, 1914; Milwaukee, '57; Atlanta '95) as they defeated the Cleveland Indians, 1–0, behind Tommy Glavine at Fulton County Stadium. From 1991 to 2002, though, the Braves were National League East champions 11 times with only one world title to show for it.

1981: After losses to the Yankees in 1977 and '78, the Los Angeles Dodgers finally won the World Series, coming back from a two-games-to-none deficit and winning their fourth straight, 9–2, at Yankee Stadium. Three days before, a frustrated George Steinbrenner had emerged from an elevator in the Yankees' hotel with a fat lip and a broken hand—the result of a scuffle, he said, with two fans.

1973: Secretariat, the greatest horse who ever raced (see June 9), concluded his career with a victory in the Canadian International Championship Stakes at Woodbine Racecourse in Toronto. He was retired to stud with 16 victories in 21 races. In 1989, suffering from laminitis, an inflammation of the hoof, he was put down at age 19 at Claiborne Farm in Paris, Ky.

David Skunks Goliath at Harvard

[Unsigned, *The New York Times*]

Centre College of Kentucky upsetting supposedly invincible Harvard, 6-0, before a crowd of 45,000 at Cambridge, Mass. There was no stopping the Praying Colonels' quarterback, Bo McMillin. (Centre College)

In arguably the upset of the century in college football, tiny Centre College of Danville, Ky., with a student enrollment of slightly more than 200, defeated Harvard on this date, 6–0, in Cambridge, Mass. The Crimson had a 25-game unbeaten streak, dating to 1916. The teams had met the year before at Harvard, with Centre gaining a surprising tie at intermission before losing in the second half.

CAMBRIDGE, Mass.—Charley Moran's Centre College eleven defeated Harvard, 6 to 0, in the stadium today, emulating Chicago, which beat the Princeton Tigers a week ago. Before 45,000 fans, the Danville team first played Harvard to a standstill and then delivered the winning punch, a swiftly delivered blow which carried the Southern team across the goal line before the third period was two minutes old. The reverse came like a shock to Harvard.

The real story of the game is that of the opening seconds of the second half. Centre had driven to Harvard's 32-yard mark in the first period, but had been stopped dead, and Glass, a substitute halfback, had missed a long shot at field goal. This time, however, there was no stopping. Centre, on its first play after it had the Harvard goal line in sight, won the game.

Last year the Praying Colonels' second touchdown and the one Harvard had to match to set a 14–14 score in the first half was made by the famous quarterback Bo McMillin. Today McMillin turned the trick again. He dashed through the line to his right, with Roberts interfering for him. Once through the line, he half reversed, saw an opening and dashed off to his left and straight for the side line. Up to this time he had not even been slapped by a Harvard tackler, and there were only two men between him and the Harvard goal line. These were Gherke and Johnson. They were at McMillin's right and not very far ahead of him. Neither had a chance to make a head-on tackle, and so they chased him to the side line.

McMillin kept on going, faster and faster. At the side line both Gherke and Johnson threw themselves at him, but with the cleverness of a Mahan, McMillin stopped short, took only a brushing blow from the Harvard men, and then was off like the wind for the goal line, now only 10 yards away. He was overtaken from behind because of the delay, but not until he had crossed the last yard of ground.

Here were 6 points, but when Bartless missed the try for goal, Harvard breathed more freely. The Crimson had not shown anything in the first half, but the second was still young and a touchdown and goal would win after all. Harvard bent itself to the task of pulling the game out of the fire. The attempt was a gallant one, but it was not attended by success. How nearly the Crimson drive did succeed is another story in itself, for Harvard will never come nearer winning another game, when driven to the final trench, than it did against Centre College this afternoon.

Centre College, a Presbyterian men's school in 1921, today has 1,070 students, equally divided between men and women. Still playing football in the Southern Collegiate Athletic Conference (Division III), it has won seven conference titles in the last 18 years.

Runners-up

1979: Commissioner Bowie Kuhn barred Willie Mays from his part-time coaching position with the Mets and from any other association with baseball when he began working as a greeter at Bally's casino in Atlantic City, N.J. Kuhn also blacklisted Mickey Mantle when he worked for Claridge's in 1983. Peter Ueberroth, Kuhn's successor, reinstated them in 1985.

1950: Marion Motley, the great fullback for the Cleveland Browns in the pre–Jim Brown era (see Sept. 16), had perhaps his greatest day as a pro, rushing for 188 yards in 17 carries—or 11.5 yards a pop—in a 45–7 victory over the Pittsburgh Steelers at Cleveland's Municipal Stadium. Motley became the first black Pro Football Hall of Fame member in 1968.

1908: Ulrich Salchow of Sweden won the first Olympic gold medal in figure skating at the London Summer Games (the Winter Olympics were not established until 1924). Salchow, the Brian Boitano of his day, invented the jump named after him: a takeoff from one skate, a 360-degree turn and a landing on the other skate.

October 30, 1974
How a Bee Stung a Bear

By DAVÉ ANDERSON

KINSHASA, Zaire—Muhammad Ali became today the second man in boxing history to regain the world heavyweight championship, with an eighth-round knockout of George Foreman. Under an African moon a few hours before dawn, the 32-year-old Ali sent his 25-year-old rival crashing to the floor with a left and a chopping right. It was a bee harassing a bear, stinging incessantly until his arm-weary adversary succumbed to sheer persistence.

Inspired by the chant of "Ali, bomaye," meaning "Ali, kill him" from the cheering assembly of nearly 60,000 in the Stade du 20 Mai, boxing's most controversial champion created the most bizarre chapter in his bizarre career in a bizarre bout in which each fighter earned $5 million in Africa's first heavyweight title bout. Ali at times was content to lay on the top rope and permit Foreman to pummel him almost at will. But every so often, the old bee would sting the young bear with jabs that snapped back Foreman's head. Instead of sitting on his stool after the third round, Ali strolled over to make a face into the closed-circuit TV cameras at ringside.

Despite a violent siege, Ali, disdaining his usual butterfly tactics, took Foreman's most powerful punches without flinching and without wobbling except for a brief moment in the second round. Suddenly, with Foreman stumbling on weary legs near the end of the eighth, Ali exploded a left-right combination. Spinning backward, Foreman flopped onto the canvas. Ali had predicted that "after the 10th round, Foreman will fall on his face from exhaustion." As it developed, in the eighth Foreman toppled onto his rump from exhaustion. Groping to his feet, he was counted out by Zack Clayton, the referee, at 2 minutes 58 seconds of the round.

"Foreman was humiliated," Ali said later. "I did it. I told you he was nothing but did you listen? I told you I was going to jab him in the corners, I told you I was

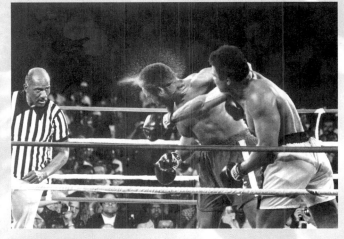

Perspiration flies from the head of the champion George Foreman as he takes a right from Muhammad Ali during their title fight in Zaire. Foreman was knocked out in the eighth round. He said years later that as he lay on his training table, he thought he was dying. (Associated Press)

going to take all his shots. I told you he had no skill. I told you he didn't like to be punched."

Ali's reaction was similar to his attitude in 1964 after he won the heavyweight title when Sonny Liston declined to come out for the seventh round of their Miami Beach bout. Ali, then known as Cassius Clay, was a 7–1 betting underdog that time. He was a 4–1 underdog to Foreman, unbeaten in 40 previous bouts. Ali has now won 45 of 47 bouts, with 32 knockouts. His only losses were to Joe Frazier and to Ken Norton.

In his three title bouts, Foreman had needed only 11 minutes 35 seconds in dethroning Frazier and successfully defending his crown against Joe (King) Roman and Norton, but in the ring under a canopy in the Zaire capital's soccer stadium, he was unable to pound Ali into submission with the same punches that had demolished the other three. "I lost the fight," Foreman commented, "but I was not beaten. He's now the champion. He has to be respected."

In the fourth, Ali opened with a quick flurry of jabs that jarred Foreman's head. But still Ali was content to lay on the ropes again. Foreman's legs appeared weary as he walked after Ali and often lunged ineffectively. When the fifth began, Ali maintained his strange tactics. Other boxers had been toppled quickly by Foreman's sledge-hammer punches but Ali obviously had prepared himself well for this task. Surely his body will be sore tomorrow, but somehow, despite the punches to his face, there was no obvious sign of the punishment.

Stumbling along, Foreman chased Ali throughout the seventh, but his face had puffed, especially around the right eye that had been cut in training, causing a six-week postponement. Foreman was hoping to measure Ali for the big punch that had finished 24 consecutive opponents but his arms were powerless. Suddenly, with the left-right combination, Ali produced the knockout. Moments later, perhaps overcome with emotion, he sat down in the ring for several moments as his idolators swarmed onto the canvas to surround him.

Runners-up

1954: The N.B.A. played its first game with the 24-second clock, adopted at the urging of Danny Biasone, owner of the Syracuse Nationals *(see April 22)*, to bring more scoring to the game. The rule's revolutionary effect was immediately apparent as the Rochester Royals beat the Boston Celtics, 98–95.

1966: Johnny Unitas, the Baltimore Colts' man with the golden arm *(see Dec. 28)* and arguably the greatest passing quarterback in N.F.L. history, threw for 252 yards to break Y.A. Tittle's record with the Giants as the all-time passing leader. In 1973, Unitas, then with the San Diego Chargers, became the first player to top 40,000 yards in the air.

1971: Ed Marinaro of Cornell University ran for 272 yards in a victory over Columbia at Schoellkopf Field in Ithaca, N.Y., surpassing 4,000 yards for his three years of eligibility and breaking the career rushing record compiled by Steve Owens of Oklahoma in 1967–69. Marinaro rushed for an average of 174.6 yards a game, still the Division I record.

October 31, 1964
Kelso Is a Horse for the Ages

By JOE NICHOLS

NEW YORK—Kelso broke two world records at Aqueduct in winning the Jockey Club Gold Cup today. He became the greatest money-earner in the history of thoroughbred racing by adding the first money of $70,590 to his previous gains. And he ran the two miles in 3:19⅕, faster than any other covered the distance on a dirt track. The famous 7-year-old gelding owned by Mrs. Richard C. du Pont had an easy time taking the same race that he had won the previous four years, beating his nearest rival by 5½ lengths. That rival was Louis Wolfson's 3-year-old Roman Brother, who had the margin of six lengths over the other 3-year-old in the race, Paul Mellon's Quadrangle. The others in the weight-for-age race were Polizonte, Cedar Key and Monade.

Kelso's bankroll now totals $1,803,362, enabling him to go ahead of Round Table, who retired with $1,749,869. Kelso's next engagement will be in the Washington, D.C. International, on the turf at Laurel on Veterans Day. If he wins that race, there is a strong chance that, in the word of his trainer, Carl Hanford, it will be his "swan song" to racing. Thus what could have been Kelso's last New York appearance was witnessed by 51,122 cheering fans.

The time record that Kelso broke was one of his very own making. When he won the Jockey Club Gold Cup in 1960, he was clocked in 3:19⅖, under 119 pounds. His burden, which included Ismael Valenzuela, in today's race, was 124, and his winning price was $2.90 for $2. Research has failed to bring up a faster dirt race at the 2-mile distance than the one that Kelso turned in today. However, a horse called Polazel did 2 miles on the turf course at Salisbury, England, in 3:15, on July 8, 1924.

Valenzuela kept Kelso in a comfortable spot through the running, back of the early pace-setter, Cedar Key, and Quadrangle. When the field passed the stands the first time Kelso was third and running smoothly. There was a change in the order when Cedar Key wilted and dropped back, at which time Kelso moved into the lead. This was on the backstretch the second time. Approaching the turn, Roman Brother made a bid at the pace-setter but Kelso only sprang away to go on and win without any threat or trouble. The fractions for the race were 0:48⅘, 1:38, 2:04 and 2:53⅗. Kelso's winning time could have been faster for, as Valenzuela said, "he was running easy at the finish."

The mighty Kelso, with Eddie Arcaro in the saddle, winning the Metropolitan Handicap under 130 pounds in a sensational stretch drive at Belmont Park in Elmhurst, N.Y., in May 1961. (Bettmann/Corbis)

"I had plenty of horse and let him run along easy until we passed the board the first time and I saw that 0:48⅘ for the half on the teletimer," he said. "Then I realized I had plenty of horse and when we got into the backstretch, I picked him up and yelled at him. He just took off. I don't know whether I hit him or not coming to the stretch. Maybe once. But I was waving the stick at him. I looked around and they were not closing on us. He was running real easy at the finish."

In his racing career, Kelso has been in 55 contests and has won 35, 28 of which were stakes. He was named the horse of the year the last four seasons. He started slowly this year, though, and the Jockey Club Gold Cup was only his second "big" success of the year, the other being the Aqueduct on Labor Day. A Kentucky home-bred, he was ordered de-sexed by a veterinarian when he was a yearling because he was of scrawny proportions, with no indication of filling out. Mr. du Pont accepted the victory trophy from Ogden Phipps, the president of the Jockey Club, after the race. Also honored with gifts were Hanford and Valenzuela.

Kelso's victory in the Jockey Club Gold Cup clinched his fifth consecutive Horse of the Year award. Kelso, who was retired in March 1966, finished in the money in 53 of his 63 races, earning nearly $2 million. Cigar, who ran from 1993 to '96, in an age of much higher purses, is racing's all-time money winner with almost $10 million.

Runners-up

1925: Red Grange *(see Oct. 18)* almost single-handedly defeated mighty Pennsylvania in his first game in the East, as the University of Illinois beat the Quakers, 24–2, before 65,000 at Franklin Field in Philadelphia. The redheaded senior ran for 363 yards and three touchdowns, twice ripping off broken-field runs of 60 yards.

1986: Julius (Dr. J.) Erving, the Philadelphia 76ers forward who raised basketball to another level by his widely copied soaring moves toward the basket *(see May 13)*, announced that he would retire at the end of the season. In 16 seasons he led the Sixers to one N.B.A. title (1983) and the New York Nets of the old American Association to two championships (1974 and '76).

1950: Earl Lloyd, a forward drafted out of West Virginia State University, became the first black player to appear in an N.B.A. game when he made his debut with the old Washington Capitols. The Capitols folded nine weeks later and Lloyd spent the rest of his nine-year career with the Syracuse Nationals (later the Philadelphia 76ers).

NOVEMBER

November 1, 1913
Inventing the Forward Pass

By HARRY CROSS

WEST POINT, N.Y.—The Notre Dame eleven swept the Army off its feet on the Plains this afternoon and buried the soldiers under a 35-to-13 score. The Westerners flashed the most sensational football that has been seen in the East this year, baffling the Cadets with a style of open play and a perfectly developed forward pass which carried the victors down the field 30 yards at a clip. Football men marveled at this startling display of open football. Bill Roper, former head coach at Princeton, who was one of the officials of the game, said that he had always believed that such playing was possible under the new rules but that he had never seen the forward pass developed to such a state of perfection.

The Eastern gridiron has not seen such a master of the forward pass as Charley Dorais, the Notre Dame quarterback. A frail youth of 145 pounds, as agile as a cat and as restless as a jumping-jack, Dorais shot forward passes with accuracy into the outstretched arms of his ends, Captain Knute Rockne, and Gus Hurst, as they stood poised for the ball, often as far as 35 yards away.

The yellow leather egg was in the air half the time, with the Notre Dame team spread out in all directions over the field waiting for it. The Army players were hopelessly confused and chagrined before Notre Dame's great playing, and their style of old-fashioned, close line-smashing play was no match for the spectacular and highly perfected attack of the Indiana collegians. All five of Notre Dame's touchdowns were the result of forward passes. They sprang the play on the Army seventeen times, and missed only four. In all they gained 243 yards with the forward pass alone.

The completion of one of the startling "Dorais to Rockne" passes which beat the Army in 1913 and modified the entire game of football. Here's Knute making a touchdown.

Notre Dame's Knute Rockne, right, scoring on a reception against Army at West Point. Passing was a novelty then, and receivers planted themselves downfield, waiting behind the defense for the roundish ball to arrive. (Notre Dame University)

This was the first time Notre Dame has ever been on the Army schedule, and 5,000 came to the reservation to witness the game. Report had the Indiana team strong, but no one imagined that it knew so much football. Dorais ran the team at top speed all the time. The Westerners were on the jump from the start and handled the ball with few muffs. The little quarterback displayed great judgment at all times and was never at a loss to take the Cadets by surprise. He got around as if on springs and was as cool as a cucumber on ice when shooting the forward pass. Half a dozen Army tacklers bearing down on him in full charge didn't disconcert the quarterback one bit. He got his passes away accurately, every one before the Cadets could reach him. He tossed the football on a straight line for 30 yards time and again.

Eddie Cochem, the St. Louis University coach, was the first to use the forward pass in 1906. Jesse Harper, who coached at Notre Dame in 1913, showed how it could be used by a smaller team to beat a bigger one. Once it was used against a major school on a national stage in this game, the forward pass rapidly gained popularity.

Grete Waitz Runs Alone

By WILLIAM C. RHODEN

NEW YORK—Ever since 1978, when she entered and won her first New York City Marathon, Grete Waitz has so thoroughly dominated the competition that it often seems as if she is running against herself. Mrs. Waitz was running her own private race again today as she achieved her eighth New York victory and her fifth in a row. She finished the 26-mile-385-yard course in 2 hours 28 minutes 6 seconds, running most of it amid the male runners, seemingly oblivious to her female competition.

"I don't know what happened," said the 33-year-old from Norway, who finished more than a mile ahead of Lisa Martin and Laura Fogli. "All of a sudden there were so many men around, and after a while I realized I was all alone." Mrs. Waitz's time was nearly three minutes off the marathon record set in 1981 by Allison Roe, the only woman who has beaten her in New York. "I really had to concentrate," Mrs. Waitz said. "Today's race required a lot more concentration because of the humidity. It wasn't an ideal condition for running."

Mrs. Martin, an Australian who had been a favorite to challenge and possibly defeat Mrs. Waitz today, finished at 2:29.12. The 26-year-old started out quickly in an effort to keep up with Mrs. Waitz and Miss Fogli of Italy. But the pace proved too grueling for her, and as the threesome approached the Pulaski Bridge, Mrs. Martin faded. In fact it was Miss Fogli, the Italian national-record holder, who managed to stay closer to Mrs. Waitz longer than any previous challenger. But she fell back after they crossed the Queensboro Bridge, and paid for her daring move in the final three miles of the race when her legs began to hurt. Of course, Mrs. Waitz had crossed the finish line by then. Later she

said that she was aware of the efforts of her closest competitors to stay on her shoulder. But she said she was more surprised than affected by them.

"I just concentrate on running my race, not on dictating what other runners do," she said. Afterward, Mrs. Waitz, who did not appear fatigued, said that she wasn't sure whether she would run in New York

next year. "The way I feel right now I would say this is the last year," she said, "but you never know. I said that last year, too. I felt pretty good the whole way except for the last three or four miles. I don't think age is a real factor. Age doesn't matter if you enjoy what you're doing."

Grete Waitz won a record ninth New York City Marathon in 1988.

Grete Waitz winning her fifth New York City Marathon in 1983. "Age doesn't matter if you enjoy what you're doing," she said. As if to prove it, she scored her ninth New York victory at age 38 five years later. (Sara Krulwich/The New York Times)

Runners-up

1972: Steve Carlton (*see Sept. 15*), whose 27 victories accounted for almost half of the last-place Philadelphia Phillies' total of 59, was elected the winner of the National League Cy Young Award in his first year with the team after being traded from the St. Louis Cardinals. Carlton won three more such awards, in 1977, '80 and '82.

1995: Joe Torre, a former journeyman manager for the Mets, the Atlanta Braves and the St. Louis Cardinals, was named manager of the Yankees. He led them to

five American League titles and four World Series championships in the next seven seasons.

2002: Relying on a spinner bait for his catches, Rick Clunn of Ava, Mo., weighed in with a three-day bass total of 43 pounds 6 ounces to win the Bassmaster Central Open on Sam Rayburn Reservoir in Jasper, Tex. It was Clunn's 14th national bass championship, tying him with Larry Nixon of Bee Branch, Ark., for second on the all-time list.

November 3, 1899
Last of the Old-Time Sluggers

[Unsigned, *The New York Times*]

James Jeffries, circa 1910. Jeffries retired in 1905 after making his seventh title defense, but was lured back at age 35 five years later to face the black fighter Jack Johnson as the first Great White Hope. (The Ring)

NEW YORK—James J. Jeffries of Los Angeles, Cal., who wrested the heavyweight championship of the world from "Bob" Fitzsimmons of Australia at the Coney Island Athletic Club on June 9, successfully defended his title tonight in a twenty-five-round bout for the championship of the world with "Tom" Sharkey of Ireland. The battle was probably the fiercest that the American fight-going public ever witnessed, for it was between men both of whom are of gigantic physique, both game to the core and masters at the game of boxing.

The battle was a notable one, for the reason that for the first time since John L. Sullivan reigned supreme the title was contested by two old-time fighters, whose stock in trade is brawn and muscle. Not that tonight's battle was devoid of the element that boxing instructors define as the science of self-defense, but it was essentially a "slugging match," in which each of the principals made strenuous efforts to put his opponent out of the fight.

That it went to the limit of twenty-five rounds was evidence of the wonderful condition and vitality of both men, for during the hour and forty minutes, blows hard enough to have felled an ox were given frequently. Both men were badly punished—Sharkey, showing a cut ear and a badly cut eye, while Jeffries was pounded on the neck with Sharkey's vicious left hand until the flesh there was as raw as a piece of beef. When the cheers that greeted the announcement that Jeffries had earned the decision of Referee Siler subsided, three enthusiastic cheers were added for the sturdy ex-sailor, who had taken manfully such a terrible beating from an opponent who had height, reach, and weight on his side.

Sharkey did most of the leading during the early part of the contest, but the Californian had the sailor almost out at the finish. In the last round, after the men had been fighting about two minutes, Jeffries's glove became entangled in the sailor's arm and was pulled off. Sharkey kept away for about twenty seconds and then sailed into his antagonist while the referee was making frantic endeavors to readjust the glove. Jeffries parried his blows, and closed with him, in which position they remained until the gong sounded.

They entered the ring at 19:15 o'clock, and for more than two hours they banged and battered each other in a fashion that was highly approved by the 19,000 spectators who witnessed the bout. It was a battle of giants, and two more magnificent specimens of physical manhood it would be difficult to find. Tom Sharkey was the first of the principal pair to enter the ring. He was attired in green trunks, with the Stars and Stripes as a belt, the whole hidden from view for a moment by a shabby brown bath robe. Jeffries looked determined as he advanced to the centre of the ring to shake hands with the sailor. He towered far above his opponent, despite his crouching position. Marquis of Queensberry rules governed the contest.

Judges, New York State assemblymen, city politicians, actors and businessmen all attended the Jeffries–Sharkey bout, attesting to the acceptance the sport had received since its unsavory reputation a decade before (see July 8). Prizefighting, however, was not made legal across the United States—and did not become hugely popular—until Congress passed the Walker Law, expressly allowing it, in 1920.

Runners-up

1989: Sarunas Marciulionis of the Golden State Warriors and Aleksandr Volkov of the Atlanta Hawks, teammates on the gold-medal Seoul Olympics team in 1988, became the first players from the Soviet Union to play in a regular-season N.B.A. game. Marciulionis, of Lithuania, scored 19 points against the Phoenix Suns, and Volkov, of Russia, was held scoreless against the Indiana Pacers.

1990: In the wildest passing show in college football history, David Klingler and the University of Houston defeated Matt Vogler and Texas Christian, 56–35, in the Astrodome. Klingler, guiding the Cougars' run-and-shoot offense, passed for seven touchdowns and 563 yards, Vogler for five scores and 690 yards. None of the scoring drives took more than 1 minute 40 seconds.

1961: The Boston Patriots of the old American Football League beat the Dallas Texans, 28–21, at Braves Field when a fan who had sneaked onto the field batted away Dallas quarterback Cotton Davidson's pass into the end zone as time ran out. The fan got away and the officials chose not to intervene, bringing the upstart league some much-needed publicity.

End of an Era?

By BUSTER OLNEY

The Diamondbacks mob Luis Gonzalez after his last-of-the-ninth Game 7 single off Mariano Rivera of the Yankees won Arizona's first World Series. Derek Jeter (2) walks off into the night. (Chang W. Lee/The New York Times)

PHOENIX—The Yankees' dynasty was about to be passed down intact, and all that was needed was three outs from Mariano Rivera, who had not failed in the postseason in 1,479 days. They had a 2–1 lead tonight in the bottom of the ninth inning of Game 7 of the World Series, Alfonso Soriano, the youngest Yankee, had hammered an eighth-inning homer off Arizona's Curt Schilling, and Paul O'Neill and other Yankees had gathered at the dugout railing, preparing to rush the field, to charge Rivera and hug him and congratulate each other on a fourth consecutive world championship, their fifth in sixth years.

The prospect of failure was nothing any of them considered; this was Mariano Rivera.

An excited mob formed on the infield minutes later, between first and second base, but the player in the midst of the maelstrom was Arizona's Luis Gonzalez. Rivera walked off, head down, after allowing a game-tying double to Tony Womack and a game-winning single to Gonzalez with the bases loaded and one out. Arizona won Game 7 with a stunning 3–2 victory, ending a World Series filled with stunners. The Yankees had won Games 4 and 5 after hitting game-tying home runs with two outs in the ninth, and they lost the decisive game after coming within two outs of becoming the first team in almost 50 years to win four consecutive championships.

"You saw the light at the end of the tunnel," reliever Mike Stanton said, "and it was taken away."

Randy Johnson—who started and won Game 6 and relieved, won Game 7 and earned three victories in the Series—shared the most valuable player award with Schilling. They were part of the mob in the infield. Derek Jeter sat in the dugout for a minute or so after Gonzalez's hit, staring onto the field, and Manager Joe Torre remained at the railing, watching the Diamondbacks celebrate, before he turned slowly and retreated to the Yankees' clubhouse.

Rivera answered questions quietly, politely, without regret; he had broken bats on all three hits he allowed in the bottom of the ninth.

"I did everything I could," he said.

A half-hour before the Yankees' pregame meeting today, Torre did not know what he would say, or if he really had anything to say, at the end of a long and emotional season that began in February in Tampa, Fla. Torre deferred to others in the clubhouse, who, by and large, view this World Series as an end of an era. The Yankees may continue to win in the years to come, but next year, only four prominent players from the 1996 championship will be with the team.

The trainer Gene Monahan, who joined the Yankees before George Steinbrenner bought the team in 1973, spoke tearfully about how these last six years have been the best of his years with the Yankees and how great it would be to win one more championship. Rivera surprised teammates by saying aloud: "We're going to win. But no matter what happens, it's in God's hands."

Runners-up

1959: Ernie Banks of the Chicago Cubs, the greatest home-run-hitting shortstop of his era and one of the Negro league stars who helped integrate modern baseball, was voted the National League's most valuable player. He hit .304 with 45 home runs and 143 runs batted in, all the while saying, "Let's play two."

1971: Two weeks into his 14th N.B.A. season, Elgin Baylor of the Los Angeles Lakers (see Nov. 15) announced his retirement because of knee problems. A 6-foot-5-inch forward who could play like a guard and foreshadowed Julius Erving and Michael Jordan, Baylor was an 11-time All-Star who averaged 27.4 points a game, third best in league history.

1996: Yankees shortstop Derek Jeter won the American League Rookie of the Year award, receiving all 28 first-place votes awarded. The eighth Yankee to win the award, though the first since Dave Righetti in 1981, Jeter hit .314 and emerged as a team leader with maturity far beyond his 22 years.

Hagen Hangs Tough

By WILLIAM D. RICHARDSON

DALLAS, Tex.—Walter Hagen made new golf history here this afternoon when he defeated Joe Turnesa, young Elmsford Country Club professional, 1 up, in the final round of the 1927 Professional Golfers Association championship. Today's was the fourth straight victory that Hagen has won in this event, which holds an equal place with the open championship. Never before in the history of the game of golf has any one succeeded in doing anything equal to what Hagen has done in this yearly grind at medal and match play.

Great credit is due Turnesa for the grand fight he put up against the old master. It was a fight that would have rewarded him against almost any one else. The young Westchester County professional holed the Cedar Crest Country Club course in 71 in the morning round and had Hagen 3 down at noon. After Turnesa won the first hole in the afternoon to make him 3 up, indications pointed strongly toward the crowning of a new champion. Hagen, however, fought like a tiger from then on. He began to play his old game, which is that of waiting for the breaks to come and seizing them. He got back two holes by winning the second and the third to be only 1 down, lost the fourth when his drive hit a spectator and went into the rough, making him 2 down again, but holed a fine putt to win No. 7 and then squared the match by holing out for a birdie 3 on No. 11.

The turning point came on No. 14. Turnesa, who had halved the previous hole by taking three putts when he had a chance to win, hit a poor drive that left him a long journey away from the green. He was so far, in fact, that when he came to play the shot he missed the green

entirely and had to play his next off hard ground. He recovered strong and had to putt his fourth before Hagen, well on the green in two, putted his third. The result was a 4 for Hagen and a 6 for Turnesa.

Hagen was now 1 up and from there on Walter hung on to that lead for dear life, his faultless play keeping Turnesa in his place. Hagen was always trying for everything, making the breaks when he could and taking full advantage of every opportunity that his opponent gave him. It was a great final, certainly the outstanding final since the playoff in which Hagen lost to Gene Sarazen at the Pelham Country Club in 1923. Incidentally that was the last time that Hagen has been beaten in a P.G.A. event. He has now won four years running and has set up a record that has not only made history but may never be equaled again. The Hagens in golf come few and far between.

Walter Hagen and Bobby Jones, an amateur, were the premier golfers of the Roaring Twenties. In a special 72-hole match in 1926, Hagen defeated Jones, 11 and 10, received a purse of $7,600—then the largest in golf history—and bought his vanquished foe an $800 set of diamond cuff links.

Walter Hagen in the Los Angeles Open at Riviera in 1929. His signature feat was that he won four straight P.G.A. championships (1924–27) under match play, when he could have been eliminated at the end of any one round. (Associated Press)

Runners-up

1994: Trailing on all scorecards, 45-year-old, 250-pound George Foreman knocked out previously undefeated Michael Moorer in the 10th round of their heavyweight title fight in Las Vegas. With one punch Foreman regained the title he had lost 20 years before to Muhammad Ali in Zaire *(see Oct. 30)*.

2002: Randy Johnson of the Arizona Diamondbacks was unanimously voted the National League's Cy Young Award winner by the Baseball Writers Association of America after compiling a 24-5 record for the season with 334 strikeouts.

It was the fourth straight award and fifth over all for the "Big Unit"—one short of Roger Clemens's record.

1982: The New Jersey Nets defeated the Cleveland Cavaliers, 99–91, sending them to an N.B.A.-record 24th consecutive loss over two seasons. The Cavs, hideously outfitted in wine-and-gold uniforms, ended the previous season at 15–67 in a 19-game nosedive and lost their first five of 1982–83 under Coach Tom Nissalke.

November 6, 1991
A New South Africa Goes to the Olympics

By CHRISTOPHER S. WREN

JOHANNESBURG—South Africa will send a racially integrated team of athletes to the Olympic Games in Barcelona, Spain, next July, ending an absence of 32 years, sports officials announced here tonight. But disputes remain over the flag, anthem and emblem to be used by the South African athletes. South Africa last competed in the Olympics in 1960 before being expelled for its apartheid policies, which included sending whites, but not blacks, to represent the country at sporting events abroad.

"This is the first time we can say that South Africa is taking part in the Olympic Games," said Sam Ramsamy, the head of the new National Olympic Committee of South Africa, in announcing the decision to go tonight. "South Africa has never taken part in the Olympic Games before, although a section of South Africa had," Ramsamy said, referring to the country's white minority. "And we are very pleased that we can get a South African team representing South Africa which will have the support of all South Africa at Barcelona."

On July 9, the International Olympic Committee decided at a meeting in Lausanne, Switzerland, to readmit South Africa. But a formal invitation to the 1992 Games hinged on further progress toward the unification of South Africa's racially disparate sports bodies. The process has not been completed, but Olympic officials accept that unification is well on its way. South Africa was expelled from Olympic competition by the I.O.C. in 1970 because of the country's policies of racial discrimination. But its Olympic exile has lasted longer. South Africa last competed in the 1960 Summer Games in Rome with an all-white team, but stayed home in 1964 and 1968 because of threats of boycotts by African nations and countries in the Soviet bloc.

In 1977, the United Nations and the British Commonwealth imposed their own bans on sporting relationships with South Africa. As a result, South African athletes have been unwelcome in virtually all international competition, including the sports that are most popular with South Africans: soccer, rugby and cricket. Some South African athletes, however, were able to compete in the Olympics after gaining citizenship in other countries, including Zola Budd Pieterse (for Britain) and Sydney Maree (for the United States) in 1984.

At a news conference today, Ramsamy displayed a flag with cascading red, blue and green bands set against a mountain. It would replace South Africa's orange, white and blue flag, which is identified with white minority rule. And he said the team's anthem would be the "Ode to Joy" from Beethoven's Ninth Symphony, which is also the Olympic hymn.

Ten months after her country decided to re-enter the Olympics, Elana Meyer, left, of South Africa leads Derartu Tulu of Ethiopia in the 10,000 meters at Barcelona. Tulu won, but a certain victory went to Meyer simply by having competed. (Getty Images)

Runners-up

1869: Rutgers defeated Princeton, 6–4, at New Brunswick, N.J., in the first college football game. It looked more like soccer than modern football: 25 players per team, 1 point for a goal, no throwing or running with the ball, but kicking or batting with hands, feet or head permitted.

1974: In a vote that mirrored baseball's evolving strategy when it came to pitching, Mike Marshall of the Los Angeles Dodgers became the first reliever to win the Cy Young Award. He appeared in a record 106 games, winning 15 and saving 21, as more and more managers resorted to relievers as late-inning "closers."

1929: The Providence Steam Roller played host to the Chicago Cardinals in the first N.F.L. night game. Rain had made the Steam Roller's field unplayable, so the game was rescheduled under the huge floodlights at Kinsley Park Stadium. Providence lost, 16–0, before 6,000 fans. A local newspaper said the football, painted white for the game, "had the appearance of a large egg."

Magic Johnson's Legacy

By IRA BERKOW

Magic Johnson of the Lakers during the N.B.A. Western Conference finals in May 1991. Five months later, with another smile, though this time wan, he announced he had become infected with the AIDS virus. (Associated Press)

NEW YORK—Maybe there's not just one moment you remember about Magic Johnson, the basketball player and the man. Maybe it's a great and wonderful collection of moments, seen in the mind's eye like a film, of Magic's no-look passes, of that quirky, high dribble and then sliding to the hoop for a finger-roll layup. Coming through in each of the frames of the mental film, though, is the smile of Magic Johnson, who played basketball with so much joy. Even when things were low for him in the game, even, for example, after the Lakers fell behind in the last N.B.A. final in a terrific series with the Bulls, he said, "This has been beautiful basketball." His smile was somewhat wan, but he smiled.

Today, in a nationally televised news conference, he again smiled, though again wanly, and told the world that he has learned he has been infected with the AIDS virus. He stood at the microphone, ducking nothing, just as, after losing games, he never ducked the press and explained what had to be explained.

He said that he was feeling fine, but that he would have to retire from basketball. He reminded us that anyone may be susceptible to life's cruelties. "You think it can never happen to you," he said, "that it happens only to other people." He said he was going to be a spokesman on H.I.V., the virus that causes AIDS, and tell people that "if it can happen to Magic Johnson, it can happen to anybody." The message was: Everybody should be more careful, practice safe sex, and smile. He said that he was against the wall, but that he would be swinging.

Though Magic Johnson led the Lakers to five N.B.A. championships and has been the most valuable player in the league three times, Magic Johnson hasn't always succeeded on the basketball court. Yet the smile of Magic Johnson, more than anything else, appeared to typify the man. Anything else, including the inevitable questions that will arise about his sexual preferences, has nothing to do with this man. His infection may change for some how they perceive Magic Johnson. It should not. Magic Johnson is no less the special man than he ever was.

Magic Johnson, the second major sports figure to contract H.I.V., after Arthur Ashe, talked about a comeback with the Lakers in the fall of 1993. Johnson dropped the idea when some players, notably Karl Malone of the Utah Jazz, voiced concern about the dangers of playing with someone who has the AIDS virus. After a layoff of more than three years, Johnson did return for 44 games in 1996.

Runners-up

1975: In one of hockey's biggest trades, the Boston Bruins dealt center Phil Esposito, the two-time most valuable player and long the N.H.L.'s premier goal scorer, to the Rangers for defenseman Brad Park, center Jean Ratelle and two others. Esposito, who later helped bring hockey to Florida in Tampa Bay, never succeeded in New York the way he did in Boston.

1970: Carlos Monzon of Argentina won the world middleweight championship by knocking out Nino Benvenuti of Italy in the 12th round of their fight in Rome. Monzon, who had the longest reign (six years, nine months) of any middleweight, won 82 consecutive bouts from 1964 to '77. He retired with a record of 89-3-9, including 61 knockouts.

1962: Chicago Blackhawks goalie Glenn Hall's N.H.L. consecutive-games record ended at 502 when he could not play because of a back injury. Hall, who played without a mask, never missed a game for seven seasons—two with the Detroit Red Wings and five with the Blackhawks. The mark may stand forever now that teams have more than one goalie.

Adrenaline and a 63-Yard Field Goal

By GERALD ESKENAZI

Tom Dempsey, a New Orleans Saints kicker who was born with half a right foot and without a right hand, kicked a 63-yard field goal against the Detroit Lions at Tulane Stadium on this date. The kick, 7 yards farther than the previous longest field goal in pro history, Bert Rechichar's 56-yarder for Baltimore in 1953, now shares the record as the longest in N.F.L. history. The following article appeared in The Times *two days after the kick.*

Tom Dempsey of the Saints, born with half a foot, booting an historic 63-yard field goal as the Lions' Alex Karras (far left) tries for a block. "I learned from my father as a kid that there was no such word as 'can't,'" Dempsey said. (Associated Press)

NEW YORK—A dozen reasons flashed through Tom Dempsey's mind yesterday as he tried to put into perspective the magnitude of his record 63-yard field goal on Sunday that made him the focus of pro football's millions of fans. "The adrenalin was working," he said by telephone from New Orleans. "The snap was perfect, the ball was placed perfectly—and I had the strength. I'm still stunned today thinking about it. Tomorrow, I'll have to get my mind on the next game. But this is my day."

It was no ordinary day as football Sundays go, and Dempsey is no ordinary player. "I learned as a kid from my father that there was no such word as 'can't,'" he related. "He'd make me try everything, and I wouldn't be satisfied until I was good at everything I tried. And in high school my coach wouldn't let me feel different. I had a tendency to feel sorry for myself. But the coach would say, 'Stop feeling sorry for yourself. Come on, keep working.'"

Dempsey, who was born in Milwaukee on Jan. 27, 1947, moved to California as a youngster and played high school football at Encinitas. He remembered going onto the field as a tackle, wearing a shoe that had been sawed in half and sewn, and that

sometimes he'd hear an opponent say, "Aw, this guy can't do nothing."

"I'd go out there and knock the hell out of them," said Dempsey.

Dempsey does only kicking now, and he wears a custom-made shoe that costs $200. He started kicking the ball when he was in his second and final year at Palomar Junior College. He still wore the sawed-off shoe, but he placed tape across the front of the foot stub. Last year he joined the New Orleans Saints. He entered Sunday's game with a mediocre record for the season of five field goals in 15 attempts. The Detroit Lions, favored by 10 points, were leading, 17–16, with two seconds left. The 66,910 fans in Tulane Stadium grew quiet as it was apparent the Saints were going to try a field goal from

their own 37.

"I usually don't tell the fellows anything before I try a field goal," said Dempsey. "But I went into the huddle and said, 'Fellows, this is going to be a pretty long one—so give me an extra second of blocking.'" When the ball sailed through the uprights—so far away that Dempsey couldn't tell whether it was good—he had broken the mark by 7 yards and lifted the Saints to a 19–17 triumph.

Tom Dempsey's 63-yard field goal was equaled in October 1998 by Jason Elam of the Denver Broncos in a victory over the Jacksonville Jaguars at Mile High Stadium. Kicks generally carry farther in the rarefied Denver air if all other conditions are equal, but a 63-yard field goal is remarkable at any altitude.

Runners-up

1966: Frank Robinson was voted the American League's most valuable player after his triple-crown season (.316 average, 49 home runs, 122 runs batted in) for the world champion Baltimore Orioles. He is the only player to have won M.V.P. awards in both leagues, having received the first one with the Cincinnati Reds in 1961.

1952: Maurice (Rocket) Richard, the brilliant winger for the Montreal Canadiens, scored his 325th career goal against the Chicago Blackhawks at the Montreal

Forum, breaking the 1940 record set by Nels Stewart. Richard retired in 1960 with 544 goals. He stood 19th on the all-time list as of the 2003–4 season.

1998: Jeff Gordon *(see Aug. 16)* came from back in the pack with 25 laps to go to win the NAPA 500 at Atlanta Motor Speedway, tying Richard Petty's 1975 modern-era Nascar record of 13 victories in a season. The victory gave Gordon his third driving championship in four years.

Jim Thorpe Beats the Army

[Unsigned, *The New York Times*]

WEST POINT, N.Y.—Jim Thorpe and his redoubtable band of Carlisle Indian gridiron stars invaded the plains this afternoon to match their prowess against the moleskin gladiators of Uncle Sam's Military Academy, and when the two teams crossed the parade ground in the semi-darkness of late afternoon the Cadets had been shown up as no other West Point team has been in many years. They were buried under the overwhelming score of 27 to 6, figures that no other team has been able to reach against the Cadets since West Point loomed up among the big football teams, and to make the defeat all the more humiliating every Cadet knew deep in his heart that this big score still did not show the relative strength of the two teams, based on today's performances.

It was a game such as the old reservation has seldom, if ever, staged. In a way, it carried a distinct shock to the 3,000 spectators who had firmly believed that the big Army team had passed the stage where such a thing might happen. But the unexpected did happen, with an exhibition of football by the wards of the Nation that distinctly places the Carlisle team among the great elevens of the year. The Indians simply outclassed the Cadets as they might be expected to outclass a prep school. They played football that won by its steadiness rather than novel formations. Speed and accuracy marked every move of the redskins, and they showed that football can still be spectacular while the so-called old style methods are employed most of the time.

Standing out resplendent in a galaxy of Indian stars was Jim Thorpe, recently crowned the athletic marvel of the age. The big Indian captain added more lustre to his already brilliant record, and at times the game itself was almost forgotten while the spectators gazed on Thorpe, the individual, to wonder at his prowess. To recount his notable performances in the

Jim Thorpe of the Carlisle Indian School in a pregame practice in 1912. He was the most celebrated player on the field against Army, but one Cadet halfback that day later eclipsed him in clashes far from home: Dwight D. Eisenhower. (Associated Press)

complete overthrow of the Cadets would leave little space for other notable points of the conflict. He simply ran wild, while the Cadets tried in vain to stop his progress. It was like trying to clutch a shadow. He did not make any of the four touchdowns credited to his team, simply because the brilliant Arcasa, Thorpe's backfield mate, was chosen to carry the ball on three of the four occasions when a plunge meant a score, and Bergie the other time.

Thorpe went through the West Point line as if it was an open door; his defensive play was on a par with his attack and his every move was that of a past master. Thorpe tore off runs of ten yards or more so often that they became common. His zigzagging and ability to hurl himself free of tacklers made his running highly spectacular. In the third period he made a run which, while it failed to bring about anything in points, because of a penalty, will go down in the Army gridiron annals as one of the greatest ever seen on the plains.

After Army punted from behind its own goal line, the ball went directly to Thorpe on West Point's 45-yard line. It was a high kick, and the Cadets were already gathering around the big Indian when he clutched the falling pigskin in his arms. His catch and his start were but one motion. In and out, zigzagging first to one side and then to the other, while a flying Cadet went hurling through space, Thorpe wormed his way through the entire Army team. Every Cadet in the game had his chance, and every one of them failed. It was not the usual spectacle of the man with the ball outdistancing his opponents by circling them. It was a dodging game in which Thorpe matched himself against an entire team and proved the master.

Jim Thorpe, who four months before won Olympic gold medals in the pentathlon and the decathlon at the Stockholm Games (see July 7), *finished the season with 25 touchdowns and 198 points—unthinkable totals for the day. In this game the promising career of an Army halfback ended with a broken knee. His name was Dwight D. Eisenhower, later general of the Army in World War II and 34th president of the United States.*

Runners-up

1946: Army, the defending national champion, undefeated in 25 games, and second-ranked Notre Dame, without a loss this season, played to a historic 0–0 tie before 74,000 at Yankee Stadium. The Irish's Johnny Lujack made a brilliant tackle of the Cadets' Doc Blanchard to keep the game scoreless, and Notre Dame finished No. 1 in the Associated Press poll.

1996: Evander Holyfield, a 5½–1 underdog, battered Mike Tyson into an 11th-round technical knockout in their World Boxing Association heavyweight title fight in Las Vegas. Holyfield sent Tyson to the canvas in the sixth round and staggered him in the 10th. It was the beginning of the end for Tyson, who had lost to Buster Douglas in 1990 before serving three years in prison for rape.

1953: The United States Supreme Court upheld baseball's antitrust exemption for a second time, reaffirming in a 7–2 vote its 1922 position (see May 29) that the game is a local affair and not subject to interstate commerce laws. Among other protections, the ruling effectively kept the reserve clause in force—and players indentured to their teams—for another 22 years (see Dec. 23).

November 10, 1928
Notre Dame Wins One for the Gipper

By RICHARDS VIDMER

Faced with a scoreless tie at halftime, Notre Dame Coach Knute Rockne urged his players to win the game in memory of George Gipp, an Irish player who had died of pneumonia eight years before. Hollywood captured the supposed moment in the 1940 Ronald Reagan movie "Knute Rockne, All American."

Notre Dame's players were not immediately inspired, falling behind by 6–0 at the start of the second half. Not until Rockne summoned Johnny O'Brien in the final quarter did their fortunes dramatically change.

NEW YORK—The referee's whistle blew taps for the Army today. Under the pent-up power of Knute Rockne's nomads from Notre Dame the unbeaten eleven from West Point was buried in its first defeat of the season when the thrill of the whistle sounded the end of the game at the Yankee Stadium.

Through the gathering dusk, into which 85,000 pairs of eyes were peering, the end came with Army on the Notre Dame 1-yard line and Notre Dame a touchdown to the good, gained in the last quarter on a 32-yard pass from Johnny Niemiec to Johnny O'Brien. The score was 12 to 6. Johnny O'Brien made only one play during the game, but that one meant triumph for the South Bend cyclone and the shattered record of an Army eleven that fought desperately, determinedly, but in vain, until the final whistle sounded taps over their beaten bodies.

For three periods, Johnny O'Brien sat on the sidelines, huddled under his blanket with a hope in his heart that he might be called on to do something for Notre Dame. And if he was called on, he would make good. Johnny O'Brien was still on

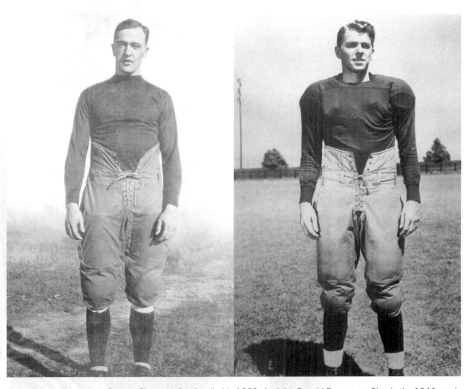

Notre Dame all-American George Gipp, at left, who died in 1920. At right, Ronald Reagan as Gipp in the 1940 movie "Knute Rockne, All-American." Rockne used Gipp's memory as a locker-room rallying charge in 1928. (Associated Press)

the bench through most of the final quarter. The score was 6–6, minutes were ticking away and he hadn't been called on. Notre Dame was marching down the field with steady strides. Notre Dame was apparently headed for another touchdown. Then two things happened. First a bad pass from the centre cost Notre Dame sixteen yards and there was a sudden command from Knute Rockne.

Obeying that command, Johnny O'Brien flung his blanket aside and dashed on to the field, reporting to the referee. O'Brien barked a string of numbers and as the ball was snapped back to Niemiec he winged his way down the field. The goal line was 32 yards away when he started in full flight, but on he went until it was with-

in stepping distance. Then he turned. Timing O'Brien's speed exactly, Niemiec took his time in handling the ball and then he flung it through the air. When Johnny O'Brien turned his head he saw the ball floating down from above. He reached his arms upward and grasped it and then he fell. But he fell over the goal line.

That one play was all that Johnny O'Brien made. He didn't even wait for Niemiec to attempt the extra point, which failed to gain. Johnny was through. He dashed for the side lines, his work done, and done well. He had scored the touchdown that brought victory to Notre Dame, defeat to the Army and another upset to a football season that is getting more topsy-turvy every day.

Runners-up

1963: Gordie Howe of the Detroit Red Wings *(see Nov. 27)* scored his 545th career goal in a 3–0 victory over the Montreal Canadiens at Detroit, breaking the record set by Maurice (Rocket) Richard of the Canadiens. Howe retired in 1980 with 801 N.H.L. goals, a mark that was broken by Wayne Gretzky, then with the Los Angeles Kings, in 1989.

1984: Frank Reich of the University of Maryland staged one of the record comebacks in college football, throwing six touchdown passes in the second half and over-

coming a 31–0 deficit to beat Miami, 42–40, at the Orange Bowl. Reich also orchestrated the biggest comeback in N.F.L. history *(see Jan. 3)*.

1984: The first afternoon-long Breeders' Cup series was held at Hollywood Park in Inglewood, Calif., with Wild Again, a 31–1 long shot, holding off Slew O' Gold and Gate Dancer before a crowd of 64,254 to win the $3 million Cup Classic. The Breeders' Cup immediately became a highlight of the thoroughbred season.

November 11, 2002
The Unbelievable Barry Bonds

By JACK CURRY

NEW YORK—With every swing and nonswing—every titanic shot and 90-foot trot in games from April until October—Barry Bonds was routinely the focus and continually cemented the notion that he was the most valuable player in the National League. The official announcement came today when he was a unanimous choice in winning his record fifth M.V.P. award.

It was no surprise that Bonds, the 38-year-old outfielder for the San Francisco Giants won again. It was a slight surprise that Bonds stumbled out of bed in Japan and spoke about the award in a conference call about an hour later. Bonds is on the major league all-star tour of Japan and he had to wake up early to travel anyway, but this wake-up call came earlier than normal. Obviously, Bonds did not mind feeling groggy after learning that he was picked first on 32 ballots, representing the choices by two writers from each league city. Albert Pujols of the St. Louis Cardinals was a distant second and Lance Berkman of the Houston Astros finished third.

"I'm trying to figure out why a 38-year-old player is still playing like this," Bonds said. "Forget the historical part. I don't know what to say. I'm overjoyed. I'm very happy." Bonds batted .370, becoming the oldest player to ever win an N.L.

Barry Bonds of the Giants gazing at one of his home runs in 2002, the year after his record season (see Oct. 5). So fearful of his power were opposing managers that they often walked him with a runner or two on base. (Barton Silverman/The New York Times)

batting title, ripped 46 homers, drove in 110 runs and set major league records with 198 walks, 68 intentional walks and a .528 on-base percentage. He broke his own year-old record for walks (177), eclipsed Willie McCovey's 33-year-old record for intentional walks (45) and passed Ted Williams's 61-year-old mark of a .551 on-base percentage. These achievements came the year after Bonds set a home run record with 73 in a season.

With every magnificent season, Bonds pushes himself to another stratosphere. Because Bonds is the only baseball player to win five M.V.P. awards, it is logical to compare him to icons in other sports. Kareem Abdul-Jabbar won six M.V.P. awards, and Bill Russell and Michael Jordan secured five each in pro basketball. Wayne Gretzky won nine in hockey and Gordie Howe captured six. When Bonds was asked to compare himself to some of these players, the player who can be surly sounded like a cheerleader who never made the varsity.

"I probably wish I was liked as much as them," Bonds said. "That would be nice. I wish I had the same form of respect that they have. They're all very admired. People really admire their achievements and accomplishments. Everyone has had their ups and downs through the media. I wish my career could be respected as much as theirs. Unfortunately, that's never going to happen."

Although Bonds continues to collect M.V.P. awards the way Tiger Woods collects majors, he still finished the 17th year of his glorious career without a World Series ring. The Giants squandered a five-run lead against the Anaheim Angels in Game 6 and then dropped the decisive game.

Runners-up

1944: "Mr. Inside" and "Mr. Outside," Doc Blanchard and Glenn Davis (see Dec.1), led undefeated Army over Notre Dame, 59–0, at Yankee Stadium, cementing its position as a national powerhouse. It was the worst loss in Irish history, and afterward Notre Dame Coach Ed McKeever sent a telegram: "Have just seen Superman in the flesh. He wears No. 35 on his Army jersey. His name is Felix 'Doc' Blanchard."

1868: The first indoor track and field meet in the United States was held at Empire State Skating Rink in Manhattan. Races began with the sound of a bass drum,

not that of a starting gun, and the track was square and made of clay. William Curtis, who later helped found the New York Athletic Club, won the 75-yard dash in 9.0 seconds. He wore shoes with spikes—common in England but a novelty in the United States.

1990: Derrick Thomas of the Kansas City Chiefs set an N.F.L. record with seven sacks in a 17–16 loss to the Seattle Seahawks at Arrowhead Stadium. Thomas, a nine-time Pro Bowler, died at age 33 in February 2000 a month after being paralyzed in a car crash.

November 12, 1920
The Man Who Rescued Baseball

[unsigned, *The New York Times*]

Kenesaw Mountain Landis on opening day in Washington in 1937. His Hall of Fame plaque reads: "His integrity and leadership established baseball in the respect, esteem and affection of the American people." (Associated Press)

Kenesaw Mountain Landis's appointment as the first commissioner of baseball was a direct result of the Black Sox scandal of 1919, in which eight members of the Chicago White Sox threw the World Series to the Cincinnati Reds (see Sept. 28). The "difficulties" to which the following article refers were the integrity and very existence of the major leagues. Landis, 53 on his hiring, served until his death in November 1944. Bud Selig, the current commissioner, is the game's ninth.

CHICAGO—With Judge Kenesaw Mountain Landis of the United States District Court as arbitrator, a one-man court of last resort, peace will obtain in professional baseball for at least seven years, while the eminent jurist will also continue to strike terror into the hearts of criminals by retaining his position as a Federal Judge.

Sixteen club owners of the National and American Leagues reached this happy solution of their difficulties after a three-hour conference at the Congress Hotel today. They then adjourned, to wait upon Judge Landis in a body and present their proposition to him. After a lonely few minutes' talk with the major league magnates, the Judge accepted the highest responsibility that can be conferred by the promoters of the national sport, and in his acceptance speech made it plain that he was undertaking the task as a public trust, having in mind the millions of fans of all ages who are interested in baseball. By this action, the former three-man National Commission was permanently discarded, and the supreme authority over baseball was centralized in the hands of one man.

In their conference with Judge Landis the major leaguers quickly sensed the fact that he was unwilling to leave his position on the bench despite his great interest in the game which he had characterized several years ago as a national institution. The club owners had made their financial argument so strong that they thought it would be unanswerable, but Judge Landis made it plain that his hesitancy was due solely to his great reluctance to quit the bench. They then suggested the plan which was accepted whereby the jurist could continue to interpret the criminal laws of the land and at the same time keep crooks out of baseball.

When this point was reached Judge Landis proposed that the salary offered him by the baseball magnates be reduced by the amount of his salary as District Court Justice, so that instead of receiving $50,000 a year as the Supreme Court of baseball, he would get $42,500.

This climax to a month of 'crucial' days is believed to mark the beginning of a new era in professional baseball. For the first time in the history of the sport, its promoters have sought and obtained a supreme ruler who has not had, and never expects to have, any interest in the pastime other than that which is born in every red-blooded American. They have selected in Judge Landis a man in whom the men of all branches of sport, as well as business, have such great confidence that if one of his important decisions were ever questioned by a club owner, player or fan, the questioner would be in bad favor with the public and the burden of proof would rest with him. Hitherto, when a club owner has emitted a yell about a verdict of the National Commission, he has been sure of the sympathy of at least the fans of his own town. Now he will not get even that.

After the meeting at his office with the magnates, it was learned that Judge Landis took Clark Griffith, a personal friend and the owner of the Washington team of the American League, over to a window.

"Grif," he said, "I'm going to tell you why I took this job. See those kids down there on the street? See that airplane propeller on the wall? Well, that explains my acceptance. You see that propeller was on the plane in which my son, Major Reed Landis, flew while overseas. Reed and I went to one of the world's series games at Brooklyn. Outside the gate was a bunch of little kids playing around. Reed turned to me and said: 'Dad, wouldn't it be a shame to have the game of these little kids broken up? Wouldn't it be awful to take baseball away from them?'

"Well, while you gentlemen were talking to me, I looked up at this propeller and thought of Reed. Then I thought of his remark in Brooklyn. Grif, we've got to keep baseball on a high standard for the sake of the youngsters."

Runners-up

1892: William (Pudge) Heffelfinger, a three-time all-America guard from Yale, became the first professional football player when he was paid $500 by the Allegheny Athletic Association to play for its team against the rival Pittsburgh Athletic Club. He scored the game-winning touchdown on a fumble recovery.

1979: In a temporary (and chilling) sign of the times, the Philadelphia Eagles' barefoot place-kicker, Tony Franklin, kicked a 59-yard field goal in a Monday night victory over the Dallas Cowboys at Texas Stadium. The kick was four yards off the N.F.L. record held by Tom Dempsey of the New Orleans Saints (see Nov. 8).

1995: Dan Marino (see March 13) of the Miami Dolphins threw for 333 yards in a 34–17 loss to the New England Patriots at Joe Robbie Stadium in Florida, breaking the N.F.L. passing record of 47,003 yards set by Fran Tarkenton of the Minnesota Vikings in 1978. Two weeks later, in Indianapolis, Marino broke Tarkenton's mark for career touchdown passes with 346.

November 13, 1995
The Master of Control

By CLAIRE SMITH

NEW YORK—From 1963 to 1966, Sandy Koufax compiled such incredible numbers as a pitcher that it won the former Los Angeles Dodger endorsements as the greatest left-hander ever. Greg Maddux of the Atlanta Braves has finally provided the right-handed bookend for such accolades: four straight incredible seasons, each deemed worthy of the National League's Cy Young Award.

Maddux extended his string today when members of the Baseball Writers Association of America voted unanimously to honor him again with the award, making Maddux and Steve Carlton the only four-time winners. No pitcher other than Maddux, however, ever won the award even three times in a row.

Maddux, who was 19–2 with a 1.63 earned run average this strike-shortened season, greeted the news with his typical team-first, last and always attitude. His Braves won the World Series, he reminded listeners during today's conference call, and "if there's any way to compare this one to the other three, this one has to be the most special because of that." The award also underlines the obvious: that Maddux is special, at age 29, leaving indelible marks on a game in an era when pitching like his is not only at a premium but is rare.

The 28-member voting panel—two

The Braves' Greg Maddux pitching in 2001. Only three pitchers have won the Cy Young Award unanimously for two years running—Maddux, Sandy Koufax and Pedro Martínez. (Barton Silverman, The New York Times)

writers from each of the league's cities casting votes before the post-season—acknowledged his brilliance by making Maddux the first-place choice on all their ballots for a second straight year. That

matches a feat accomplished only by Koufax, who was selected unanimously in 1965 and 1966. That Koufax and Maddux are the only pitchers to duplicate the feat in an election process that has seen only 13 unanimous selections in its 40-year history strengthens the argument that the two are the most dominant pitchers to toe the rubber from opposite sides.

In his magnificent four-year run in the 1960's, Koufax was 97–27 for a winning percentage of .782. His four-year earned run average was an incredible 1.86. Maddux, a Cy Young winner with the Chicago Cubs in 1992 before signing with the Braves as a free agent, has a 75–29 record over a four-year span in which two seasons were shortened by strikes. His winning percentage for the period is .721; his e.r.a. a pristine 1.98.

The extent of Greg Maddux's dominance in 1995 is apparent in his ratio of strikeouts to walks and his earned run average. He struck out 181 and walked 23—then the best ratio (7.8 to 1) of any starter in history. His 1.63 earned run average was two and a half times better than the National League average of 4.21. Randy Johnson of the Arizona Diamondbacks joined Maddux with four consecutive awards in 2002 (see Nov. 5).

Runners-up

1979: Darryl Dawkins, the mammoth center of the Philadelphia 76ers, completed a monster dunk over Bill Robinzine, shattering the fiberglass backboard against the Kings at Municipal Auditorium in Kansas City. Three weeks later Dawkins shattered another backboard in Philadelphia, and the glass-breaking dunks became video highlights fodder for years to come.

1964: Bob Pettit of the St. Louis Hawks became the first N.B.A. player to score 20,000 career points when he poured in 29 in a road game against the

Cincinnati Royals. Pettit, the league's most valuable player in 1956 and '59, retired with 20,880 points in 1964. He currently ranks 23rd on the all-time list.

1993: In college football's game of the year, second-ranked Notre Dame, coached by Lou Holtz, defeated Coach Bobby Bowden's No. 1 Florida State team, 31–24, at South Bend, Ind. Both teams had 16-game winning streaks coming in. The Irish's Shawn Wooden knocked down a touchdown pass attempt by Charlie Ward as time expired.

November 14, 1943
Luckman Beats His Home-Town Giants

By WILLIAM D. RICHARDSON

NEW YORK—Just prior to the kick-off in today's game between the Bears and the Giants at the Polo Grounds, Sid Luckman, former pupil of Lou Little at Columbia, received two $1,000 war bonds, one a gift of his home-borough admirers in Brooklyn; the other from his own football associates. Right then was when the Giants and Giant fans made their mistake by not matching or out-donating the other donors. Sid seemed to take it as a personal affront, for here is what he did:

Practically single-handed, he administered a 56-to-7 defeat to the Giants, the worst drubbing that club ever has received in National Football League competition. The former black mark was a 49-to-14 rout at the hands of the Redskins in 1937.

He either established or assisted in establishing six new league records. With seven scoring aerials, he broke the mark of six touchdown passes in one game, set by Sammy Baugh of the Redskins against Brooklyn two weeks ago, and added 120 yards to the individual passing total of 333 established by Cecil Isbell of Green Bay. Sid's throws today gained 453 yards. Thanks to Luckman's good right arm, the Bears now hold also the record for yards gained in a single game, 702. The former high-water mark was 613, made by the Bears in 1941. Altogether Luckman completed 23 passes in the thirty times he cocked his arm, and his seven touchdown heaves gave him a total of 23 this season, one from the record, set by Isbell last year.

As a Columbia undergraduate and since he joined the Bears to make them what they seem today—one of the greatest if not the greatest aggregation in football history—Sid has had many a field day, but none to compare with today. If they had added a broad jump or pole vault to

the program, he probably would have broken those marks also.

His was passing artistry of a kind probably never before witnessed on any gridiron, and although his wizardy sent the Giants down to depths they never had explored, the fans gave the black-haired star a tremendous ovation when he trotted from the field after chucking his final toss to Hampton Pool a trifle more than five minutes before the game ended.

Sid Luckman's seven touchdown passes in one game—an achievement equaled but never surpassed—came in a day when rushing, not passing, was predominant in pro football. One month later, Luckman led the Monsters of the Midway to their third league championship in four years in a 41–21 victory over the Washington Redskins.

Sid Luckman looking for a receiver. Bears Coach George Halas hand-picked him to run his new T-formation offense, which required snap decisions. "He never called a wrong play in his life," Halas said. (Associated Press)

Runners-up

1993: Don Shula of the Miami Dolphins (*see Jan. 14*) won his 325th N.F.L. game, surpassing George Halas of the Chicago Bears as the winningest coach in pro football history, as Miami defeated the Philadelphia Eagles, 19–14, at Veterans Stadium. It was Shula's 31st season as a coach; he retired with 347 victories in 1995.

1970: Seventy-five people, including 37 members of the Marshall University football team and the entire coaching staff, were killed when their plane crashed near

Kenova, W. Va., while returning from a game in Kinston, N.C. It was the worst disaster ever to strike a professional or college team.

1943: Sammy Baugh, the Washington Redskins' great quarterback, punter and defensive back, set a record unlikely to be broken with the advent of two-platoon football: in a 42–20 victory over the Detroit Lions at Griffith Stadium, he became the only player in N.F.L. history to pass for four touchdowns and intercept four passes in one game.

November 15, 1965
Craig Breedlove at 600.601 M.P.H.

Craig Breedlove driving his jet-powered Spirit of America across the Bonneville Salt Flats in Utah to a world land speed record of 468.719 miles an hour in October 1964. Thirteen months later he hit 600.601. (Associated Press)

BONNEVILLE SALT FLATS, Utah (UPI)—Craig Breedlove surpassed 600 miles an hour today in regaining the world land speed record in two runs on the Utah salt flats. The 28-year-old Californian drove his jet-powered, four-wheeled Spirit of America at an average speed of 600.601 miles an hour with clockings of 593.178 miles an hour and 608.201 miles an hour over a measured mile.

His official speed was calculated on the basis of the elapsed time for the combined runs, as required by the Federation Internationale de L'Automobile, which certifies international racing events and world records. It was the fifth time since August, 1963, that he had laid claim to the title of fastest man on wheels. He had been the first to crack 400 and 500 miles an hour.

He regained the record from Art Arfons of Akron, Ohio, who drove at a speed of 576.553 miles an hour here on Nov. 7. "That 600 is about a thousand times better than 599," said the new record-holder. "Boy, it's a great feeling. I'm sure we've got

it for the year. Now let's see if ex-king Arthur comes back."

Arfons, his chief competitor in high-speed racing, damaged his racer in his dash to the Nov. 7 record and took it back to Akron. Arfons said tonight in Ohio he would not return to the salt flats this year, but might make a bid early next summer to recapture the record. He said it would be next month before repairs were completed on his racer.

Breedlove's $250,000 racer is powered by a J-79 engine, a surplus Air Force jet plane engine. His sponsor is the Goodyear Tire and Rubber Company. The record runs were so smooth and effortless that Breedlove slowed down at the south end of the course, made a big sweeping turn and parked the streamlined vehicle next to a moving van that served as his mobile repair shop. When timers and pit-crew members saw the car going off the course they sensed trouble and rushed to the scene, where they found Breedlove grinning broadly. He said the car handled "beautifully." He said he used a minimum

stage afterburner on both runs and that the parachutes worked perfectly in bringing the car to a stop.

In the two-year duel between Breedlove and Arfons, Breedlove twice had brushes with death. His original three-wheeled Spirit of America, powered by a J-47 engine, plunged into a salt brine canal during a wild ride across the salt last year, and early this season the new four-wheel model went out of control after the front wheels became airborne. Breedlove modified the car with stabilizing fins to keep the front wheels on the salt. He also reinforced the side panels and nose cowling to prevent buckling of the outer skin by the tremendous air pressure encountered at high speed.

Craig Breedlove's record was broken by Gary Gabelich of Long Beach, Calif., in October 1970. The current mark, set in 1977, is 766.609 miles an hour by Andy Green of Britain. Breedlove tried to break the 800 m.p.h. barrier at age 59 in 1997 but was thwarted when a stray bolt got sucked into Spirit of America's engine.

Runners-up

1960: Elgin Baylor of the Los Angeles Lakers set an N.B.A. record by scoring 71 points in a 123–108 victory over the Knicks in New York, breaking the mark of 64 points he set the previous October. Baylor's record was broken by Wilt Chamberlain of the Philadelphia Warriors in 1961 (*see Dec. 8*).

2001: Roger Clemens of the Yankees (*see April 29 and Oct. 22*) won a record sixth Cy Young Award, one more than Randy Johnson of the Arizona Diamondbacks through 2002. The vote capped a season in which Clemens won 20 of his first

21 decisions and set the American League record for career strikeouts with 3,717.

1992: Richard Petty's 35-year reign as stock-car racing's king (*see Feb. 18*) ended in a fiery crash when his famous No. 43 got caught in a wreck in the Hooters 500 at Atlanta. Unhurt, he salvaged his car for a final lap, retiring with seven Nascar championships and seven Daytona 500 victories, both records.

November 16, 1957
Irish Spoil the Sooners' Party

NORMAN, Okla. (AP)—Oklahoma's record streak of forty-seven football victories was ended today by a Notre Dame team that marched 80 yards in the closing minutes for a touchdown and a 7–0 triumph. Oklahoma, ranked No. 2 in the nation and an 18-point favorite, couldn't move against the rock-wall Notre Dame line and the Sooners saw another of its streaks shattered—scoring in 123 consecutive games.

The defeat was only the ninth for the Oklahoma coach, Bud Wilkinson, since he became head coach at Oklahoma in 1947. It virtually ended any chance for the Sooners of getting a third straight national championship. Although the partisan, sellout crowd of 62,000 came out for a Roman holiday, they were stunned into silence as the Sooners were unable to pull their usual last-quarter winning touchdowns—a Wilkinson team trademark. As the game ended when Oklahoma's desperation passing drive was cut off by an intercepted aerial, the crowd rose as one and suddenly gave the Notre Dame team a rousing cheer.

The smashing, rocking Notre Dame line didn't permit the Sooners to get started either on the ground or in the air. The Sooners were able to make only 98 yards on the ground and in the air just 47. Notre Dame, paced by its brilliant, 210-pound fullback Nick Pietrosante, rolled up 169. In the air, the Irish gained

79 yards by hitting nine of twenty passes. Bob Williams did most of the passing for Notre Dame.

Notre Dame's touchdown drive, biting off short but consistent yardage against the Sooners' alternate team, carried from the 20 after an Oklahoma punt went into the end zone. Time after time, Pietrosante picked up the necessary yard he needed as the Irish smashed through the Oklahoma line. Notre Dame moved to the 8 and the Sooner first team came in to try to make the third Sooner goal-line stand of the day. Pietrosante smashed four yards through center and Dick Lynch was stopped for no

gain. On third down, Williams went a yard through center. Then Lynch crossed up the Sooners and rolled around his right end to score standing up. Monty Stickles converted to give Notre Dame the upset and end collegiate football's longest winning streak.

Notre Dame was the last team to beat Oklahoma, at the start of the 1953 season on the same field that it smothered the Sooners today. Then coach Frank Leahy's Irish beat Oklahoma, 28–21. The next game, Oklahoma and Pittsburgh tied at 7–7. Then the Sooners set sail through forty-seven games until Terry Brennan's Irish stopped the string today.

Dick Lynch rolling around right end for a touchdown from 3 yards out as Notre Dame defeated Bud Wilkinson's Oklahoma team, 7-0, at Norman, Okla. The Sooners' victory streak had lasted since the second week of the 1953 season. (University of Notre Dame)

Runners-up

1999: Pedro Martínez of the Boston Red Sox won the American League Cy Young Award unanimously after establishing himself as the game's dominant pitcher with a 23-4 record and a 2.07 earned run average. He had a shot at the first 30-victory season in 31 years before being sidelined with shoulder trouble in July (see Oct. 11).

1991: Bobby Bowden's Florida State team, ranked No. 1, lost at least a share of the national title to No. 2 Miami, coached by Jimmy Johnson, 17–16, when the Seminoles' Gerry Thomas missed a 34-yard field goal wide right with seconds

remaining. Snakebitten, Florida State again lost to Miami in 1992 when Dan Mowrey pushed a game-tying kick wide right.

1961: Stripped of his college scholarship and barred from the N.B.A. for befriending a fixer of games in high school, Connie Hawkins, a playground legend from New York, played his first pro game with Pittsburgh of the short-lived American Basketball League. Hawkins finally was accepted by the N.B.A., played for the Phoenix Suns and made the Basketball Hall of Fame.

November 17, 1956
Jim Brown's Farewell: 6 Touchdowns

By LINCOLN A. WERDEN

Jim Brown in the 1957 Cotton Bowl. He scored 21 of Syracuse's points on three touchdowns and three extra-point kicks in a 28-27 loss to Texas Christian, heightening his reputation as the greatest college player of the 50's. (Syracuse University)

SYRACUSE—As far as the Colgate football team was concerned, there was just too much Jimmy Brown in the game today. The crushing Syracuse left-halfback from Manhasset, L.I., in an individual performance of all-America proportions, led his team to a 61–7 triumph before a sellout crowd of 39,701.

In his final game for the Orange, Brown accounted for 43 points, scoring six touchdowns and kicking 7 extra-point placements. No other team in this fifty-seven-year-old series had tallied as many points as the Syracuse aggregation did in Archbold Stadium this cold gray afternoon. The highest total credited to any previous Syracuse squad came in 1944. That was 43 points, the total that Brown amassed by the time he made his final exit early in the fourth period. In 1898,

Colgate defeated Syracuse, 58 to 0, and that was the scoring mark shattered by Brown and this alert, fast-moving squad that rolled on to accumulate 511 yards by rushing.

Brown's share of this figure was 197 yards on twenty-two carries. As a result, the senior left-half sent his season's ground-gaining yardage to 986 yards. This erased the previous best by any Syracuse player, which was the 805 yards compiled by George Davis in 1949.

With Governor Harriman among the spectators, the Syracuse fans enjoyed this concluding game of one of the Orange's successful football seasons. There are rumors on the campus that their team may be selected for a post-season bowl game. Colgate, victor over Yale earlier in the season, had been beaten thrice before this contest. Syracuse was the pre-game favorite, having lost only once, by 14–7, to Pitt. But no one anticipated the stunning show Brown was about to put on.

This victory put Syracuse's string at six over the Red Raiders, a record. At halftime, the press box announcer jocularly said: "The score is now Brown 27, Colgate 7." Brown was responsible for scoring all of his team's points in the first half. His longest score of the day was on a pitch-out from quarterback Chuck Zimmerman midway in the first period with Syracuse ahead by 14–0. Brown raced down his right sideline 50 yards for the touchdown. It was 20–7 and Brown's try for the extra point was wide.

Jim Brown's 43 points stood as the National Collegiate Athletic Association's single-game record until Howard Griffith scored 48 points on eight touchdowns for the University of Illinois in 1990.

Runners-up

1968: The notorious Heidi game was played between the Oakland Raiders and the Jets at Oakland–Alameda County Stadium. With New York seemingly safely ahead, 32–29, with 1:05 to play, NBC-TV left the game to broadcast the movie "Heidi." Oakland scored twice in the final 42 seconds to win, 43–32, and armchair viewers were outraged.

1930: Bobby Jones, winner of the Grand Slam two months before *(see Sept. 27)*, announced his retirement from competitive golf at age 28, citing his need to leave golf "in its proper place, as a means of obtaining recreation and

enjoyment." Two years later he and Dr. Alistair MacKenzie designed Augusta National Golf Course in Georgia on the site of a former fruit nursery.

1894: The Daily Racing Form was published for the first time in Chicago, giving bettors reliable information on projected odds for all horse races in the country. The broadsheet was the brainchild of Frank Brunnell, who revolutionized horseplaying in 1905 by theorizing that past record is a determining factor in predicting a horse's likely performance.

Finally, Brilliance Succumbs to Pain

LOS ANGELES (AP)—Sandy Koufax of the Los Angeles Dodgers retired from baseball today at the peak of his career because he feared he might permanently injure his arthritic left arm if he continued to pitch. The man generally recognized as the best pitcher in the major leagues told a news conference that the pain in his left elbow had grown progressively worse since it began three seasons ago. A few minutes before, he said, he had sent a letter to the Dodgers asking them to put him on the voluntary retired list.

Koufax, whose salary of $125,000 this year made him the highest-paid pitcher in history, has set numerous records and won many awards, even after hurting his arm in 1964. "I feel I am doing the right thing and I don't regret one minute of the past 12 years. The only regret is leaving baseball," the 30-year-old pitcher said.

Koufax, whose lightning-fast ball and sweeping curves had befuddled National League batsmen for years, said he had told General Manager E.J. Bavasi just before the season ended that it likely was his last year. He said he informed Bavasi last night he felt he could wait no longer to make the announcement, even though Bavasi wanted him to wait until the Dodger owner, Walter O'Malley, returned within a few days from a tour of Japan with the team. "I felt that I was being too devious when my friends kept asking me what I was going to do," Koufax said. "I didn't want to lie and I didn't want to keep on being devious. I had several calls at home last night. That's when I finally decided to make the announcement."

He said his condition had progressed to the point that he had to have the left sleeves of his coats shortened. The shortening was not much, he said, but it indicated what was happening. He has been taking pills, shots and therapeutic treatments. He said that in the past year he took more and more shots and medication than ever before and this worried him. He said that he had been dropping things with his left hand and learning to do some things with his right. "This is going to get worse as I get older," he said. "But I hope to live longer out of baseball."

Might O'Malley persuade him to change his mind? Sandy laughed. "No, my mind was made up," he said. What will the Dodgers, the National League pennant-winners and World Series losers to the Baltimore Orioles, do without him next year? "Other ballplayers have retired and the team has managed to get by," he replied. "Maybe the Dodgers will need a fourth starting pitcher, but if they can come up with another kid like Don Sutton they'll be all right."

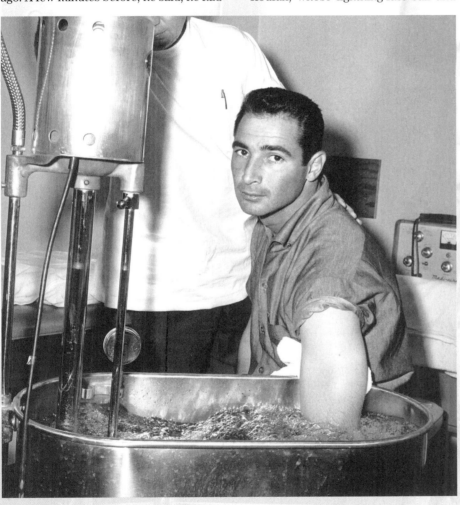

Sandy Koufax, the brilliant Dodgers left-hander, soaking his arm in a whirlpool after a game in April 1964. Before his retirement after the '66 season, his arthritis progressed to the point where he had to shorten the left sleeves of his coats. (Associated Press)

Runners-up

1967: Third-ranked Southern California upset No. 1 U.C.L.A., 21–20, at the Los Angeles Coliseum en route to its first national title since 1962. The game featured the future Heisman Trophy winners O.J. Simpson of the Trojans and Gary Beban of the Bruins. Simpson won the battle, scoring on a 64-yard touchdown run in the fourth quarter on a sore right foot.

1985: Quarterback Joe Theismann, 35, who led the Washington Redskins to the 1983 Super Bowl title, suffered a career-ending compound fracture of his lower right leg when he was sacked by Lawrence Taylor of the Giants in a nationally televised Monday night game at R.F.K. Stadium.

1940: In an act of sportsmanship that has stood tall for decades, Cornell gave back a football victory to Dartmouth after learning that the referee had inadvertently given it an extra down on which it scored the winning touchdown in the final seconds. Cornell agreed that such a victory would not be honorable, and the record has since shown Dartmouth the victor, 3–0.

November 19, 1966
Essence of Soccer

By JOSEPH NOVITSKI

RIO DE JANEIRO—A rich young Brazilian industrialist named Edson Arantes do Nascimento changed clothes in an underground dressing room here tonight and emerged onto the grass of the world's largest stadium as Pelé, the world's best soccer player. This is the stuff of heroic legend anywhere in the world. In Brazil, where soccer is the national sport, the national pastime and the national pride, the homegrown legend nicknamed Pelé scored the thousandth goal of his 13-year professional career. The feat was more than the soccer equivalent of Babe Ruth's 714 home runs.

It was a moment of hoarse, happy release for Brazilians, some of whose political energies, frustrated under a stern military regime, have been poured into soccer. "This is more important than anything that's going on on the moon," shouted one of the tens of thousands of fans pouring out of Maracanã Stadium after Pelé, an inside left, had scored his goal in an otherwise unimportant game.

No modern player of professional soccer, which attracts more spectators than any other sport in the world, has come near the mark set by the short, muscular black Brazilian. The Brazilians shouting and laughing in the stadium, and the millions more listening to radio broadcasts, were proudly certain that their Pelé was the best in the world.

The certainty about Pelé, who has become rich by investing his soccer earnings, seemed only a part of the joy the goal caused for the thousands of fans dancing and cheering on the tiers of concrete seats in the sticky heat of the huge, oval stadium. Professional and amateur sociologists have asserted that cheering at a soccer game is a release for poor,

hungry Brazilians and for their middle-class compatriots. "I turned and hugged a Negro next to me who had a grin that never quit," said a young white secretary. "It seems that you forget any conception of class at Maracanã. I mean nowhere else would I ever hug a man I'd never seen before."

In the last two years, girls and young women have flocked for the first time into the bleachers of Maracanã Stadium. Sociologists have told women's magazines that the phenomenon is evidence of Brazil's change from a traditional society to a modern industrial society, at least in the cities. "They really go to swear out loud and let it all out," said a photographer who often works at the stadium. "You know, when things get rough, and with the political situation, it helps."

The banners, samba bands and firecrackers that used to be part of soccer and political campaigns have been restricted to the outpourings at soccer matches since 1965, when the military government abolished traditional political parties and severely limited elections by popular vote. "The Government ought to contract Pelé as a cabinet minister," said a political reporter who flew from São Paulo to watch the thousandth goal. "He knows how to get people enthusiastic."

After leading Brazil to three World Cup titles, drawing huge crowds in the United States and playing for the New York Cosmos of the North American Soccer League from 1975 to 1977, Pelé returned to Brazil as a sporting ambassador. He now serves as the nation's sports minister.

Edson Arantes do Nascimento of Brazil, known worldwide as Pelé, performing a scissors kick in a September 1968 match. It wasn't so much his scoring that made him a hero, but his sense of timing and creativity. (Associated Press)

Runners-up

1966: No. 1-rated Notre Dame and second-ranked Michigan State played to a 10–10 tie before an overflow crowd of 80,011 at East Lansing, Mich. The game, which transfixed much of the nation, featured Irish quarterback Terry Hanratty and Spartan defensive end Bubba Smith. Notre Dame Coach Ara Parseghian was criticized for preserving the tie and not gambling for the victory in the final two minutes.

1989: The United States, with Tony Meola in goal, clinched its first berth in the World Cup tournament since 1950 with a 1–0 victory over Trinidad and Tobago at Port of Spain. The triumph may yet be recognized as a watershed; Team USA played host to the World Cup only five years later, and the United States men's team gained the quarterfinals against Germany in 2002.

1978: Joe Pisarcik of the Giants needed only to put his knee to the ground to secure a 17–12 victory over the Philadelphia Eagles with 20 seconds left in a game at the Meadowlands, but he tried a handoff and fumbled. Herman Edwards, years later the coach of the Jets, scooped up the ball and raced 26 yards for a touchdown in the most embarrassing loss in Giants history.

November 20, 1982
And at Stanford, the Band Played On

By GORDON S. WHITE Jr. and GEORGE VECSEY

Cal's Kevin Moen leaping in the end zone after weaving past members of the Stanford band for a 25-20 victory as time ran out. The five-lateral kickoff return stunned saxophonists and drummers alike, who figured Stanford had won. (Associated Press)

NEW YORK—Some of the best made plans between bowl committees and universities went astray on the football fields of the West today. Notre Dame was knocked out of bowl consideration at Air Force, Washington was denied a third consecutive trip to the Rose Bowl in a major upset at Washington State, and Stanford was the victim of one of the most bizarre finishes in a college game when California won on a five-lateral kickoff return on the last play.

Stanford was confident it was going to the Hall of Fame Bowl when Mark Harmon's 35-yard field goal with four sec-

onds left gave the Cardinals a 20-19 lead. But on the ensuing short kickoff, California ran one of the most spectacular and confusing kickoff returns for a touchdown ever seen to win, 25–20. Kevin Moen, who started the 55-yard return and ended it by going into the end zone after the fifth lateral, had to run through the Stanford band for the last 10 yards many seconds after the final gun sounded.

Moen picked the ball up at the California 45, lateraled to Richard Rodgers, who ran about 10 yards and flipped to Dwight Garner. After going about 20 yards, Garner tossed back to

Rodgers, who turned and lateraled to Marriet Ford. Ford then tossed the ball to Moen, who had to weave his way through members of the Stanford band. They had stormed onto the field between the back of the end zone and the 10-yard line in preparation of striking up a victory march they never played.

Andrew Geiger, Stanford's athletic director, said he had no plans to protest the runback. "There is nothing to protest," Geiger said. "When a football game ends, it ends. But there were some things involved in that play that I would like to call to the attention of our conference. Crowd control for one. Also that last lateral was a bit questionable. It might have been a forward toss. But, again, that's a judgment call."

Stanford and California are members of the Pacific 10 Conference. "I will possibly make a report," Geiger said. "People were storming onto the field although only the band members—our band members—got near the players. If we can learn something to prevent this happening, it will be helpful.

"We just had a brilliant year," said John Howard, the student manager of the band. "We tried to concentrate on being a good band, and at the last possible moment we pull a play that will make us famous for all eternity."

"Most members of the band are still in shock. They're hitting themselves. They wish they could do what Superman did in the movie, after the earthquake in California—turn back the clock, reverse time, as if it never happened."

Stanford, with a 5-6 record, is not bowl-bound. Thus John Elway, its senior quarterback, cannot add to his long list of thrilling plays.

Runners-up

1960: Chuck Bednarik of the Philadelphia Eagles, last of the great two-way N.F.L. players (see Dec. 26) and one of the hardest tacklers ever, made a ferocious blindside hit against the Giants' Frank Gifford that clinched the Eastern Conference title for the Eagles at Yankee Stadium. The historic hit, though legal, forced Gifford to miss the 1961 season.

1977: When Walter Payton of the Chicago Bears (see Oct. 7) ran for 275 yards in a 10–7 victory over the Minnesota Vikings at Soldier Field he broke the N.F.L. single-game rushing record held by O.J. Simpson. Then with the Buffalo Bills,

Simpson totaled 273 yards in a 1976 game. Payton's mark was broken in 2000 (see Oct. 22).

1991: Seven-time winner Michael Andretti was named Indy Car Driver of the Year, following in the footsteps of his father, Mario, who won the award in 1969 (see May 30). Earlier in the year, Jeff Andretti, Michael's brother, won Rookie of the Year honors at Indianapolis. The Andrettis and Unsers (Bobby, A and Al Jr.) were headliners in Indy racing for almost 40 years.

November 21, 1900
'Play Ball!' Says American League

By WILLIAM TAAFFE

NEW YORK—Ban Johnson, president of the new American League, announced his intention today to expand to Eastern cities and take on the established National League next season. He proclaimed his newly renamed and reconstituted eight-team circuit a major league and said it would stretch from Milwaukee in the West to such cities as Boston, Philadelphia, Baltimore and Washington in the East.

The renamed league, which until last season was called the Western Association, is to begin play with eight teams: the Baltimore Orioles, Boston Pilgrims, Chicago White Stockings, Cleveland Spiders, Detroit Tigers, Milwaukee Brewers, Philadelphia Athletics and Washington Senators.

Only three franchises that were part of the old Western Association will be included in the new American League. These are Chicago, situated in St. Paul through the end of last year; Detroit and Milwaukee. The other clubs that played in the old Western Association, namely Kansas City, Toledo, Minneapolis, Grand Rapids and Indianapolis, will be disbanded.

Johnson has persuaded Connie Mack, manager of Milwaukee last season, to take command of the new Philadelphia club, having promised him a one-quarter ownership in the franchise. When Orioles manager John McGraw said a team in Philadelphia would be "a white elephant," meaning a money loser, Mack replied by making the white elephant the team's symbol. Johnson intends to staff the Washington franchise with the manager and several players from the Kansas City club.

The American League proved stable. In fact, all eight franchises are alive today, despite moves and expansion contortions. *Milwaukee became the St. Louis Browns in 1902, and the Browns became the Baltimore Orioles in 1954. The original Orioles became the New York Highlanders (later the Yankees) in 1903. And the Philadelphia A's moved to Kansas City in 1955.*

The following account about the origins of the league, by Arthur Daley, appeared in The Times *in November 1960. The league at the time was considering the creation of expansion franchises in Los Angeles and Washington, the latter to replace the old Senators, who had moved to Minnesota for the 1961 season.*

NEW YORK—Raw winds knifed in from Lake Michigan and blunted themselves against the ornate coping and windows of the Grand Palace Hotel in Chicago on Nov. 21, 1900. In a third-floor room sports history was being made. In a clear and flowing hand the secretary of the group wrote out baseball's Declaration of Independence. He began it this way:

"We the undersigned, desiring to reorganize The American League of Professional Base Ball Clubs..."

Thus did the American League spring into being as a challenger to the National League. It was the culmination of nine years of thorough and careful planning by a reformed Cincinnati sports writer named Byron Bancroft Johnson. A dominating, domineering figure, Ban Johnson drove the Americans to a position of pre-eminence during his twenty-seven years as president.

Ban Johnson, president and founder of the American League, during grand jury proceedings in the Black Sox scandal in 1920. Johnson formed his circuit to compete with the National League and so created the current major league structure. (Bettmann/Corbis)

Sixty years—less four days—later, the American League will gather in another momentous meeting tomorrow. Once again reorganization will be a topic, but if any raw winds knife against the conclave headquarters at the Savoy Hilton they'll be from the lake in Central Park, not from Lake Michigan. And the preparatory work has not encompassed nine years but twenty-two days.

Runners-up

1981: Jim McMahon, soon to be the No. 1 draft choice of the Chicago Bears (see Jan. 26), capped his record-setting career at Brigham Young by passing for 565 yards and four touchdowns in a 56–28 victory over the University of Utah in Provo. McMahon set 70 N.C.A.A. passing marks at B.Y.U., paving the way for Steve Young, a notable successor.

1987: Ferdinand (see May 3) nosed out Alysheba and won the $3 million Breeders' Cup Classic at Hollywood Park in Inglewood, Calif., in a photo finish. It was the first duel between Kentucky Derby winners since Affirmed beat Spectacular

Bid in a 1979 race. Ferdinand's victory was sentimentally popular because he was ridden by Bill Shoemaker, 57, and trained by Charlie Whittingham, 74, both California favorites.

1931: Notre Dame, undefeated for three years, was upset on a final-minute field goal by Southern California's Johnny Baker, 16–14, before a crowd of 52,000 at South Bend, Ind. It was the first loss for the Irish, then nicknamed the Ramblers, in their new stadium, dedicated the year before to the late Knute Rockne.

November 22, 1986
Cus D'Amato's 20-Year-Old Champion

By DAVE ANDERSON

Mike Tyson, right, pounding Trevor Berbick in the second round while winning the World Boxing Council heavyweight title in Las Vegas. Lethal and relentless, Tyson became the youngest fighter ever to win the championship. (Associated Press)

LAS VEGAS, Nev.—After only 20 years 4 months and 22 days, Mike Tyson needed only 5 minutes 35 seconds tonight to justify what his late mentor, Cus D'Amato, told him several years ago. "If you stay with me," D'Amato said, "you'll be the youngest heavyweight boxing champion in boxing history."

D'Amato died a year ago at age 77 of pneumonia. But after Tyson won the World Boxing Council title tonight by battering Trevor Berbick in a second-round knockout, the 221¼-pound champion smiled through the gap in his teeth. "Cus is up there talking to all the great fighters," Tyson said, "and saying, 'This boy did it.'"

Until tonight, Floyd Patterson, who was D'Amato's first famous protégé, had been the youngest heavyweight champion. Thirty years ago almost to the day, Patterson was five weeks short of his 22d birthday when he knocked out 42-year-old Archie Moore in the fifth round at the Chicago Stadium. But now Tyson has his crown. "I'm the youngest heavyweight champion in the world," Tyson told his co-manager, Jimmy Jacobs, in the ring, "and I'm going to be the oldest."

At that moment, Berbick was trying to regain his equilibrium after Mills Lane, the referee, had wrapped his arms around the 33-year-old Jamaican at 2:35 of the second round. Berbick had been knocked down early in the round with a left hook and

bounced up instantly. But when slammed on the right temple by a left hook, Berbick froze momentarily. In a delayed reaction, he toppled to the middle of the blue canvas. When he tried to get up, his legs wouldn't work. He sprawled into the ropes near his corner. Trying to get up again, he flopped into the middle of the ring. Still wobbling, he finally regained his feet, but the referee moved in to stop the fight. "Berbick was up," Lane said later, "but to allow somebody to get hit in that condition, that's criminal."

Berbick must have felt he was back home in his native Jamaica, trying to find shelter from a hurricane. From the opening bell, Tyson had assaulted him, mostly with the left hook that has now crumpled 26 opponents in his 28–0 record. "But the first time I thought I hurt him," Tyson said later, "was with a left jab early in the first round."

Berbick's mistake was his bravado. Instead of trying to box Tyson, as his trainer Angelo Dundee had suggested, Berbick stood in front of the reform-school graduate, well within punching range. "I was trying to prove to myself that I could take his best shot," Berbick said later. "He punches pretty hard."

The young Mike Tyson was unquestionably one of the greatest heavyweight champions, allowing his opponents no quarter in the ring. But after his loss to James (Buster) Douglas in his 10th title defense in 1990 (see Feb. 11), Tyson's career and personal life unraveled. He was convicted of rape in 1992 and served three years in prison. In his fifth bout after his 1995 return, he was disqualified in a title fight for biting both ears of the champion, Evander Holyfield (see June 28).

Runners-up

1917: Owners of three National Hockey Association teams—the Ottawa Senators, Montreal Canadiens and Montreal Wanderers—met in a Montreal hotel room and joined with a fourth club, the Toronto Arenas, to form the N.H.L. The league expanded within several years to include teams in Quebec, Boston, Chicago, Detroit, Pittsburgh and New York.

1950: The Fort Wayne Pistons beat the Minneapolis Lakers, 19–18, in the lowest-scoring game in N.B.A. history. The Pistons held the ball to keep it away from the 6-foot-10-inch center George Mikan (see April 23), the league's first intim-

idating big man, who scored 15 points. Four years later, the 24-second shot clock was adopted (see April 22).

1981: Kellen Winslow, the prototypical tight end and future Hall of Famer who could block, run and catch with equal brilliance, caught five touchdown passes for the San Diego Chargers in a 55–21 victory over the Oakland Raiders. The touchdown receptions tied the N.F.L. record set by Bob Shaw of the Chicago Cardinals in 1950.

November 23, 1984
Doug Flutie's 'Hail Mary' Pass

By GERALD ESKENAZI

MIAMI—Doug Flutie enhanced his legend today with a last-play touchdown pass that soared 64 yards, just out of reach of three defenders at the goal-line and into the hands of Gerard Phelan to give Boston College a 47–45 victory over Miami. The pass, credited as a 48-yard play, found its way to Phelan, Flutie's roommate. Phelan somehow extracted it out of the evening mist—just as he had countless times in fantasy when the two talked about such a play in their dormitory room.

It was the last spectacular play of a spectacular game, contested on a wet day before a crowd of 30,235 in the Orange Bowl and a national television audience. The matchup was made special by the confrontation between two of college football's most glamorous and appealing quarterbacks—Bernie Kosar, the Miami sophomore, and Flutie, the daring senior scrambler who today became the first collegian to pass for more than 10,000 yards in a career.

Despite his years of heroics, which will wind up with a Cotton Bowl appearance New Year's Day, today's final challenge appeared to be asking a bit much of Flutie. Only 28 seconds remained when Boston College took over on its 20-yard line with Miami holding a 45–41 lead, fashioned on Melvin Bratton's fourth touchdown. Only 6 seconds remained when Flutie took the final snap on the Miami 48.

In the huddle, Flutie called the "Flood Tip" play. In theory, there would be two other wide receivers besides Phelan in the end zone. Phelan's job was to tip the ball to them. Flutie scrambled back, all the way to his 37, and then, under pressure, went to his right. Twice this season he had

passed for touchdowns with no time left, but that was at halftime. This was for the game and a victory against the defending national champion.

Phelan, one of several receivers lined up right of center, was 1 yard past the goal line when the ball arrived. In front of him, three defenders tumbled over one another, attempting to get to the ball. But the other receivers were not nearby. So Phelan caught the ball himself. "He threw it a long, long way," Phelan said. "I didn't think he could throw the ball that far."

"He and I are roommates," said Flutie, the leading candidate for this season's Heisman Trophy, "and we talk all the time about plays like this. I honestly believe when we ran that play we had a legitimate chance. I'm not saying that I anticipated it happening, but I'm saying we had a chance and that's all I ask for." It has seemed to be all he has ever needed.

Doug Flutie (22) rejoicing in the arms of his brother Darren after his desperation 64-yard pass as time ran out somehow found its way into Gerard Phelan's arms in an end zone scrum, giving Boston College a 47-45 victory over Miami. (Associated Press)

Runners-up

1981: The United States District Court in Brooklyn, N.Y., found five former Boston College basketball players guilty of racketeering and bribery charges for shaving points to fix games during the 1978–79 season. Rick Kuhn, a star forward for the Eagles, spent 28 months in prison.

1968: Undefeated Yale was comfortably ahead of unbeaten Harvard, 29–13, with 42 seconds left at Cambridge, Mass., when the Crimson scored two touchdowns and made two 2-point conversions as time ran out in the greatest finale of the

long-storied rivalry. Both teams shared the Ivy League title. The headline in the Harvard student newspaper the next day: "Harvard Wins, 29–29."

1947: Slingin' Sammy Baugh (see Nov. 14), playing in an era when rushing and not passing was king, threw six touchdown passes on "Sammy Baugh Day" at Griffith Stadium as the Washington Redskins beat the Chicago Cardinals, 45–21. Baugh also had six touchdown passes against the N.F.L.'s Brooklyn Dodgers in 1943

Drug Testing on the Front Burner

By MICHAEL JANOFSKY

MOSCOW—Sports ministers and other officials from more than 100 countries approved by acclamation today an anti-drug charter that establishes guidelines for governments to combat trafficking in and use of performance-enhancing drugs. They also recommended that the International Olympic Committee create a panel of experts to test athletes in any country at any time on short notice.

The action, taken during a conference sponsored by the United Nations Educational, Scientific and Cultural Organization, was merely a statement of support for the I.O.C.'s efforts to fight drug use by athletes. The charter has no means of insuring enforcement. But the ministers' approval indicated a willingness to lobby their respective governments for legislative action that would support the charter and make it easier for the drug-testing panel to carry out its objectives.

"This is a big day for the I.O.C.," said Alain Coupat, a senior I.O.C. official. "It means that Unesco recognizes that the fight against doping must be constructed on a global basis, not by state, and that the I.O.C. is the best organization to direct the fight."

The idea of an itinerant panel of drug testers was an extension of the charter's recommendation that athletes from all countries be subject to testing during training. The panel would become a permanent adjunct to the I.O.C. Medical Commission. A team of experts would travel from country to country, testing athletes with little or no notice. Some countries test athletes during training and on short notice, but the United States and many others do not. American and Soviet

Ben Johnson of Canada, center, after winning the 100 meters in world-record time at the Seoul Olympics. Carl Lewis, left, and Linford Christie, right, finished second and third. Johnson lost his gold medal and record after testing positive for steroids. (Getty Images)

athletes are now tested only during the Olympics and other major championships.

The shame of Ben Johnson of Canada being stripped of his 100-meter gold medal and world record at the 1988 Seoul Olympics after testing positive for steroids two months earlier (see Sept. 26) prompted approval of this anti-drug charter and led the I.O.C. to further toughen drug-testing procedures. It later was learned that swimmer Kristin Otto of East Germany, who won six gold medals at Seoul, had been taking steroids

and testosterone under a state-operated program.

Dozens of Olympic athletes have been disqualified for drug usage since testing was initiated in 1968. The first athlete to have a world record nullified by the International Association of Athletic Federations because of a positive drug test was an American discus thrower, Ben Plucknett, in 1981. The I.A.A.F. said he had used an anabolic steroid banned partly because of its dangerous side effects.

Runners-up

1963: Two days after President John F. Kennedy was assassinated in Dallas, and with the nation still in mourning, N.B.A., N.H.L. and American Football League games all were canceled. But the N.F.L.'s Pete Rozelle, saying that "football was Mr. Kennedy's game," played a complete schedule. He later called it his worst decision as commissioner.

1957: The rookie Jim Brown (see Nov. 17) rushed for 237 yards and scored four touchdowns as the Cleveland Browns defeated the Los Angeles Rams, 45–31, at Municipal Stadium overlooking Lake Erie. The yardage total set an N.F.L.

record for a single game, breaking the mark of 223 yards set by Tom Wilson of the Rams in 1956.

1953: Walter Alston, an obscure minor-league manager who had only one at-bat in the major leagues, signed a one-year contract to manage the Brooklyn Dodgers. He signed 22 more such agreements on owner Walter O'Malley's short leash, leading the team to seven pennants and five world championships in Brooklyn and Los Angeles.

November 25, 1980
The Champ Throws in the Towel

By RED SMITH

NEW ORLEANS—Nothing much was happening in the eighth round when Roberto Duran turned away from Sugar Ray Leonard and waved a glove at the referee in a signal to cease and desist. Leonard, aware only that the welterweight champion of the World Boxing Council was not defending himself, hit him a shot to the belly, but Duran did not respond.

"No mas, no mas," Roberto told the referee. "No more box." He walked to his corner, and when Leonard realized that Duran had surrendered the title to him he sprang up like a squirrel on the top rope in a neutral corner. It was 2 minutes 44 seconds into the round, and suddenly the ring was utter confusion. One of Leonard's seconds charged Duran and took a swing at him. Swirling bodies eddied and elbowed. A report flew around that Duran had not quit but had merely misunderstood the referee about something, nobody knew what. There was another that Duran had told his corner he had cramps all over his body.

"Roberto told me," José Sulaiman, president of the W.B.C., said a few minutes later, "that when he threw a right hand in that round, something happened to his shoulder."

Still later, Duran said: "I don't want to fight any more. I've been fighting for a long time." In fact, it has been almost 14 years. He said that in the fifth round he began to feel cramps in his stomach and that the pain spread and grew progressively worse.

This was the first time a champion had voluntarily surrendered his title since Sonny Liston quit to Muhammad Ali, then Cassius Clay, in 1964, claiming a shoulder injury. He ratified the action a year later by taking a dive for Ali in Lewiston, Me. A much more similar denouncement, however, took place in 1949 in Detroit when Marcel Cerdan, middleweight champion, tore the supraspinatus muscle in his right shoulder defending his title against Jake LaMotta. Cerdan, though, fought on left-handed until his seconds persuaded him to retire.

None of those was so startling as this, for Duran was known as the most dedicated, intense warrior in the ring. He had held the lightweight championship for years and had lost only one decision in 72 bouts before taking the 147-pound title from Leonard last June 20 in Montreal. It was said that he could not conceive of losing, and his idolators in his native Panama believed he never would.

When the match ended, officially a knockout in the eighth, Leonard was ahead on the cards of all three judges. Acting as his own judge, Leonard obviously felt that he had it all the way. In the third round when Duran lunged at him and fell far short, Leonard laughed and stuck out his tongue. In the seventh he thrust his face out toward Duran and taunted him with a grimacing, shoulder-shrugging boogaloo. He was not a spectacularly gracious winner.

Sugar Ray Leonard, right, trying to get to Roberto Duran during their welterweight championship bout in the Superdome. In Round 8, with Leonard clearly ahead, Duran suddenly told the referee: "No mas, no mas. No more box." (Associated Press)

Runners-up

1971: Top-ranked Nebraska's running back Jeff Kinney scored his fourth touchdown of the day in the final 98 seconds to outlast No. 2 Oklahoma, 35–31, at Norman, Okla., in a Thanksgiving classic. It was the Cornhuskers' 30th consecutive game without a loss and boosted them toward their second straight national title under Coach Bob Devaney.

1981: Rollie Fingers of the Milwaukee Brewers was elected his league's most valuable player, becoming the first reliever so named. He also won the American League's Cy Young Award this year. Two other relievers, Willie Hernandez of the Detroit Tigers (1984) and Dennis Eckersley of the Oakland A's (1992), have achieved this rare double.

1937: The all-America Byron (Whizzer) White of the University of Colorado rushed for two touchdowns and scored a third on an interception as the Buffaloes defeated the University of Denver, 37–7, at Boulder. White served as a justice on the United States Supreme Court from 1962 to '93.

Parson Bob Vaults to a Second Gold

By ROBERT ALDEN

MELBOURNE, Australia—With one leg held rigidly in the air and both his fists clenched, the Rev. Bob Richards lay in the pole vault sawdust pit gazing up at the crossbar. The bar had tipped as if to fall after he brushed it on his vault. But it did not fall and Parson Bob from Laverne, Calif., won his second Olympic gold medal today. He had triumphed at Helsinki in 1952 and finished third at London in 1948.

Bob's winning vault of 14 feet 11½ inches today broke his own Olympic record. Although it was a gusty and a cold day—the kind of day pole vaulters dread—Richards was in wonderful form. Under the strain of the most intense competition, Richards remained unperturbed. He didn't miss a jump until the bar had reached the 14 feet 11½ inches.

By that time, all the competitors in the Olympic competition except his team-mate Bob Gutowski had been eliminated. While all the other competitors had been undergoing the tortures of jumps narrowly missed and the mental strain of knowing that one more bad effort would mean their elimination, Richards had been clearing the bar with business-like precision.

The battle for the gold medal was, as usual, intense and dramatic. At the start, there were fourteen competitors. Some

Bob Richards at the Melbourne Olympics after repeating his 1952 victory in the pole vault at the Helsinki Games. He defeated his teammate Bob Gutowski, rear, in a duel that nearly reached 15 feet. (Associated Press)

were in trouble almost from the first because of the unfavorable weather conditions. Richards, stocky and muscular, was all business. He wasted little time when it came his turn to jump. He rushed to the starting point with a frown on his face and waited only an instant before he was off on his approach run.

With competitors falling out with each succeeding height from the initial 14 feet 3¼ inches, the bar was finally raised to 14 feet 11½ inches. Gutowski made his first approach, but he went under the bar. Richards made his leap. For the first time during the day, the Parson knocked the bar over. Gutowski tried again. Once more he passed under the bar. Gutowski appeared to be favoring a sore leg.

Richards, still frowning, then made what turned out to be his winning leap. He emerged from the pit smiling for the first time during the day. His hands were pointed to heaven in an attitude of prayer. He said afterward the wind prevented the bar from falling.

Besides becoming the only two-time gold medalist in the pole vault, Bob Richards competed in the decathlon at the 1956 Melbourne Games. The original Wheaties pitchman, he appeared on cereal boxes from 1958 to '69. He was elected to the United States Olympic Hall of Fame in 1983.

Runners-up

1975: Center-fielder Fred Lynn of the Boston Red Sox capped his remarkable first season by winning the American League's rookie of the year and most valuable player awards. Ichiro Suzuki of the Seattle Mariners in 2001 is the only other player to have won both honors in the same year.

1925: The University of Illinois phenomenon Red Grange *(see Oct. 18)* made his pro football debut—forever moving the sport from the back pages to the front— as a Chicago Bear against the crosstown Cardinals at Wrigley Field. He was

held to 36 yards in a scoreless tie yet proved well worth the reported $100,000 given him by his manager, C.C. Pyle.

1976: Tony Dorsett of the University of Pittsburgh ended his regular-season collegiate career as the N.C.A.A.'s all-time leading ground-gainer with 6,082 yards, before winning the Heisman Trophy and leading the Panthers to the national title. The record stood until Ricky Williams of Texas *(see Oct. 24)* finished with 6,279 yards in 1998.

A Record 600 Goals and Counting

[Unsigned, *The New York Times*]

MONTREAL—"Gordie Howe can do more things better than anyone else. That's all there is to it." The referee who said that has seen and marveled at Howe for years. Tonight, Howe outdid even himself with the 600th goal of his career, albeit in a losing effort as the Montreal Canadiens defeated the Detroit Red Wings, 3–2.

The knowledgeable Montreal Forum crowd of 14,956 marked the moment when Howe sent a short flip shot past Gump Worsley of the Canadiens at 16:10 of the final period. With the game still fairly safely in hand, newspapers and programs were thrown onto the ice amid a round of applause. To appreciate the significance of the 600 figure, it must be realized that in the 48-year history of the league only one other player has reached 500 goals—Maurice Richard of the Canadiens. Howe passed Richard's 544-goal record two years ago *(see Nov. 10)*.

Howe was born in Floral, Sask., on March 31, 1928. He played one minor league season at Omaha, Neb. A visitor now at the Ak-sar-ben Arena, where Howe played that one season, is greeted by a huge picture of Howe in the lobby.

He joined the Detroit Red Wings in 1946, and in his 20 seasons has:

• Led the league in scoring six times.

• Been named the most valuable player six times.

• Played in 17 All-Star games

Gordie Howe of the Red Wings posing on the ice in 1966. Howe played 26 seasons in the N.H.L. He was deceptively fast and, for a goal scorer, deceivingly tough. "He can hurt a guy just by flicking his wrists," a referee said. (Associated Press)

and been named to the first team eight times.

Howe is 6 feet tall, weighs 200 pounds and has rugged good looks and an exceedingly muscular physique. He is probably the strongest player, smoothest skater and best stick-handler in the league. He can knock the puck out of the air as if it were a baseball, he helps kill penalties, he is in on all the power plays. And because Howe is so strong and so smooth at the same time, he is able to bedevil opponents and officials. "He can hurt a guy by just flicking his wrists," says a referee. "Now can you call it a foul? Is it flagrant? With Howe, you just can't tell."

Often, Howe looks as if he's loafing on the ice. But he is so deceptively fast, and knows when to relax, that he never misses the key play. He is a player who never loses his head, even in a fight. Several years ago Louis Fontinato of the Rangers, one of the game's bad boys, was giving Howe a rough time at Madison Square Garden. As Howe tells the story, he was talking to one of his teammates on the ice when he saw Fontinato coming at him.

"Excuse me," said Howe, "I've got some business to attend to." Then he punched Fontinato in the face and broke his nose.

Runners-up

1947: Ted Williams of the Boston Red Sox *(see July 14)*, disliked by baseball writers who conducted the most valuable player voting, was snubbed in favor of a Yankee for the second time after winning the triple crown for highest average and most home runs and runs batted in. This year the winner was Joe DiMaggio, 202 votes to 201; in 1942, when Williams won his first triple crown, Joe Gordon won by 270 to 249.

1956: Bobby Morrow, a 21-year-old student from Abilene Christian College in Texas, won the gold medal in the 200 meters before a crowd of 110,000 at the

Melbourne Olympics in Australia. Three days before, he had won the 100-meter gold. The first Olympian to win both sprints since Jesse Owens in 1936, Morrow was immediately called the world's fastest human.

1949: Steve Van Buren of the Philadelphia Eagles became the second player in N.F.L. history to run for 200 or more yards in a game when he piled up 205 in a 34–17 victory over the Pittsburgh Steelers at Franklin Field. The Emmitt Smith of his day, he had two 1,000-yard seasons under shorter schedules and led the Eagles to N.F.L. titles in 1948 and '49.

November 28, 1981
The Man in the Houndstooth Hat

By MALCOLM MORAN

BIRMINGHAM, Ala.—Paul Bryant of the University of Alabama, who once wrestled a bear to earn his nickname and long ago achieved immortality in these parts, today coached his 315th victory, more than any other college football coach ever. Despite the absence of two players who were dismissed from the team two days ago and the problem of two fumbled punts that led to scores and put his team behind in the fourth quarter, Alabama defeated Auburn, 28–17, before a national television audience and a frenzied crowd of 78,170 at Legion Field that included Joe Namath and other former Bryant players, assistants and friends.

Bryant, who passed Glenn (Pop) Warner with a victory two weeks ago at Penn State, today went one ahead of Amos Alonzo Stragg, who won 314 games in 57 seasons. Bryant, in 37 years at Maryland, Kentucky, Texas A&M and Alabama, has a record of 315-80-17. His players, following instructions, surrounded him at the end of the game. Bryant's houndstooth hat, his trademark, disappeared from view and was taken to a safe place. He received the game ball from Bart Krout, a senior tight end from Birmingham who was born in October 1959, one year after Bryant came to Alabama.

It was nearly an hour after the game before someone wanted to know about the next game, the Cotton Bowl against Texas on Jan. 1. "How can I have plans for the Cotton Bowl when I haven't quit shaking from the end of this game," Bryant replied.

Several years ago rival schools were telling recruits that Bryant, now 68, would soon retire. To answer the opposition and reassure recruits, Bryant said he intended

Alabama's Paul (Bear) Bryant in 1972. Outwardly remote and a disciplinarian if there ever was one, he mentored numerous star quarterbacks, trained 40 future college coaches and integrated 'Bama football in 1971. (Associated Press)

to break Stagg's record. "If someone has to be the winningest coach," he said then, "it might as well be me."

But Auburn (5–6), which has been recovering from the effects of a two-year probation, was ahead by 17–14 at the start of the fourth quarter, and all of that seemed to be slipping away. Then suddenly it all turned around. Walter Lewis, the second of three Alabama quarterbacks, threw a 38-yard touchdown pass to Jesse Bendross to regain the lead. And after three Auburn plays and a punt, Linnie Patrick, a sophomore halfback, gained 47 yards in two carries. His 15-yard touchdown, with 7:07 to go, gave the Tide an 11-point lead and secured the record.

After the record was set, the coach made certain to thank the players, coaches and friends who could not be here. He thanked President Reagan and former President Jimmy Carter, who called the locker room.

"Did the President call you?" Auburn Coach Pat Dye said, excited. "Sure he called me," Bryant said, trying to sound matter of fact. Bryant smiled. He hoped the day his team won No. 315 would end like so many others. "I want to go home and get the TV on and hold my granddaughters," he said.

Paul (Bear) Bryant, who won six national titles and 15 bowl games, retired as Alabama's coach in December 1982 with 323 victories. He died of a heart attack a month later (see Jan. 26).

Runners-up

1929: Ernie Nevers of the Chicago Cardinals, the former all-American from Stanford, scored all of his team's points, running for six touchdowns and kicking four extra points in a 40–6 victory over the Bears at Comiskey Park. The total is the longest-standing record in the N.F.L.

1956: Don Newcombe, coming off a 27-7 record for the pennant-winning Brooklyn Dodgers, was voted the winner of the first Cy Young Award as baseball's outstanding pitcher. Two awards, one for each league, were made after 1966.

Newcombe also won the National League most valuable player award in '56.

1925: Georges Vezina, the diminutive goalie of the Canadiens who led them to Stanley Cup titles in 1916 and '24, collapsed in the net during an N.H.L. game against the Pittsburgh Pirates at Mount Royal Arena in Montreal. Tuberculosis was diagnosed, and he died four months later. Each year, the league's top goalie receives the Vezina Trophy.

November 29, 1980
This Bulldog Ran Wild

By GORDON S. WHITE Jr.

ATHENS, Ga.—Georgia finished its 87th college football season today as the only undefeated and untied major team in the nation, rolling to a 38–20 victory over Georgia Tech, its archrival. And Herschel Walker completed his first college season by setting a national freshman rushing record of 1,616 yards. The Bulldog tailback, 6 feet 1 inch and 218 pounds, who was a state high school sprint champion at Wrightsville, rushed for 205 yards and scored three touchdowns. He snapped the previous record of 1,586 set by Tony Dorsett of Pitt in 1973.

The record-breaker was a 65-yard touchdown run in the fourth quarter. Walker was 44 yards short of the mark when he took off around right end and did his usual thing by outrunning everyone on defense. His other touchdowns were on runs of 1 and 23 yards.

Georgia's 11th victory, before 67,504 fans at Sanford Stadium, gave the Bulldogs their second perfect season since a 4–0 record in 1896. The first was in nine games in 1946, after which they went on to beat North Carolina, 20–10, in the Sugar Bowl. This year's team, ranked No. 1 by the two wire service polls, will again play in the Sugar Bowl. It will meet Notre Dame, which is ranked No. 2 and is the only other major undefeated team. However, the Irish have had one tie, 3–3, against Georgia Tech, a team that finished with a 1–9–1 record.

Walker stirred the fans, recalling the exploits of the 1946 team led by Charlie Trippi, a triple-threat star. Trippi and Frankie Sinkwich, a flatfooted halfback who was also a triple threat, were considered Georgia's best backs until Walker came along. Trippi and Sinkwich played on offense and defense. Trippi played all 60 minutes in the victory over North Carolina in the Sugar Bowl. He threw a touchdown pass and returned a kick 68 yards for a touchdown.

But although he neither passes nor plays defense, Walker is making his indelible mark. For the fourth time, he rushed for more than 200 yards. He has rushed for more than 100 in three other games. He is also a good receiver, picking up 31 yards today on a pass from quarterback Buck Belue.

Dorsett went on to win the Heisman Trophy as the best college football player in the nation in his senior season of 1976. He now is a star with the Dallas Cowboys in the National Football League. "I didn't know about Dorsett's record until two weeks ago," Walker said. "When I went into the game, it was the farthest thing from my mind. But our offensive line and most of the team seemed determined to help me break it."

Indeed, his mates were. "We got together before he went out there when he was 44 yards short," Belue reported, "and said we were going to try and get it for him. Then he went out and busted it on the first play."

Led by Herschel Walker's two touchdowns, Coach Vince Dooley's Georgia laid claim to the national title by defeating Notre Dame in the Sugar Bowl, 17–10. Walker, winner of the Heisman Trophy as a junior two years later, then left college to join the new United States Football League (see Feb. 23). He later played with Tony Dorsett on the Dallas Cowboys but never enjoyed quite the success he had as a collegian.

Georgia tailback Herschel Walker in a blowout over Memphis State in 1982. A former state high school sprint champion, he was uncontainable as a freshman in 1980 while leading the Bulldogs to the national title. (Associated Press)

Runners-up

1890: The first Army–Navy football game was played at West Point, N.Y. The Midshipmen won, 24–0, as Charles (Red) Emerich scored four touchdowns when they were worth 4 points each. The annual game (see Dec. 1) was moved to Philadelphia in 1899 and to the New Jersey Meadowlands in 2002. Army leads the time-honored series, 49–47–7.

1976: The Yankees signed the six-time Oakland A's All-Star Reggie Jackson, who had played the previous season with the Baltimore Orioles, to a five-year $2.9 million contract. He helped lead them to three pennants and two world championships in the next five years (see Oct. 18).

1934: The Detroit Lions began an annual N.F.L. tradition by playing at home on Thanksgiving Day, losing to the Chicago Bears, 19–16, before 26,000 fans at the University of Detroit Stadium. The game also was noteworthy in that the NBC Radio Network with Graham McNamee made it the first in the N.F.L. to be broadcast nationally.

November 30, 1941
Don Hutson: Great Hands, Big Toe

WASHINGTON (AP)—The Green Bay Packers struck through the air for three touchdowns in the second half to trounce Washington, 22 to 17, today as Don Hutson, the old Alabama flash, shattered three National Football League scoring records. Trailing by 17 points at the half, the Packers swept the Redskins off their feet in the third and fourth periods as Cecil Isbell, the veteran from Purdue, filled the air with passes which Hutson snared time and again with almost uncanny skill.

A crowd of 35,594, largest of the year in the capital, saw the Packers achieve their tenth victory in eleven contests to clinch at least a tie for the Western Division championship. Hutson scored three touchdowns and place-kicked two conversions to account for 20 of his team's 22 points. He ran his season's total to 95 points, bettering the old record of 79 established several years back by Automatic Jack Manders of the Bears.

Hutson stretched his life-time mark to 395 points in seven seasons of pro football, cracking Manders's record of 385. Don's three touchdowns gave him twelve for the year, or one more than the mark Washington's Andy Farkas set up in 1939. Another record went into the discard when Isbell completed fourteen passes, most of them to Hutson, for 167 yards, sending his 1941 aerial yardage to 1,488. Washington's Sammy Baugh, who also played a great game today, set the old mark of 1,367 last year.

Green Bay's ground game was smashed effectively when Washington forwards rushed throughout the first half and Isbell was hurried in getting his aerials off. When the Isbell-Hutson combination started to click in the third period, however, the complexion of the contest changed. Early in that period, the Packers took over on their 35. Isbell pitched to Hutson three times for 35 yards. The same pair teamed up 15 yards more on another aerial before Hutson snared an Isbell toss over his shoulder for Green Bay's first counter. A few minutes later, big George Svendsen, Packer center, intercepted a Baugh pass and dashed 20 yards to the Washington 15. Clarke Hinkle, a superb back now in his ninth season with the pros, cracked center for 8 yards, then Isbell flipped to Hutson for the touchdown.

At the start of the final period, with the Packers still trailing by 4 points, Isbell fired three straight passes to move from his 35 to the Redskins' 46. He faded back on the following play and rifled the ball to Hutson, who evaded two tacklers to score. Green Bay added two points immediately when Washington's Ray Hare picked up the kick-off on his 3 and stepped back over the goal line for an automatic safety. He was not tackled, but menacing Packers were on hand to take charge had he elected to run.

Don Hutson's remarkable game occurred at Griffith Stadium the week before the Japanese attack on Pearl Harbor. The Redskins were playing the Philadelphia Eagles there on Dec. 7 when news of the disaster began circulating in Washington. No public announcement was made at the stadium except that all military personnel should leave the park to report to their duty offices.

Don Hutson of the Packers in a 57-21 victory over the Lions in Milwaukee in 1945. Lanky, with huge hands, and playing in an era when the running game was king, he caught four touchdown passes and kicked five extra points in the second quarter. (Associated Press)

Runners-up

1974: The University of Southern California, led by running back Anthony Davis, scored 49 unanswered points in the second half to stun Notre Dame, the top-ranked defensive team in the nation, 55–24, at the Los Angeles Coliseum. It turned out to be the last season for Notre Dame Coach Ara Parseghian, who retired "for health reasons."

1987: Bo Jackson (see July 11), having hit 22 home runs with the Kansas City Royals a few months before, set the Raiders' single-game rushing record of 221 yards—including a 91-yard run past Brian Bosworth among his three touchdowns—as Los Angeles defeated the Seattle Seahawks, 37–14. It was Jackson's greatest day in the N.F.L.

1956: Floyd Patterson, 21, of Rockville Centre, N.Y. (see June 20), the 1952 Olympic middleweight gold medalist, became the youngest heavyweight champion in history when he knocked out Archie Moore, 42, in the fifth round at Chicago Stadium. Mike Tyson was six months younger than Patterson when he won the title in 1986 (see Nov. 22).

DECEMBER

December 1, 1945
Mr. Inside and Mr. Outside

By ALLISON DANZIG

PHILADELPHIA—Army closed the book on one of the unforgettable chapters in football history today as the West Point cadets defeated Navy, 32–13, for their eighteenth victory in succession, marking the first time they have ever gone through two perfect seasons in a row. The most distinguished gathering that has attended a sports event in this country in many years assembled in the Philadelphia Municipal Stadium, filled to its capacity of 100,000 for the forty-sixth meeting between the service academy rivals.

This was the first time since the 1941 contest, played a week before the attack on Pearl Harbor, that the climactic spectacle of intercollegiate football returned to its prewar setting, invested with all of its old glamour and glitter and the huge crowd able to enjoy the show unreservedly in the return to peacetime pursuits of pleasure. In honor of the happy occasion, President Truman furnished an official note with his attendance as Commander in Chief of the Army and Navy, and a host of war leaders from both branches of the military whose names have become world-wide by-words during the past four years, as well as the members of the President's Cabinet, were present.

Such glamorous figures as Generals George C. Marshall, Omar Bradley, Henry H. (Hap) Arnold, James Doolittle, Jacob L. Devers and Carl Spaatz, Admirals Chester W. Nimitz, William F. (Bull) Halsey and Ernest J. King and British Air Chief Marshal Sir Arthur Tedder and Fleet Admiral Sir James F. Somerville, all of them famous artisans in the winning of the second World War, vied with the play on the field for the crowd's interest.

As a matter of fact, the outcome of the game was decided before the President changed his seat from the Army to the Navy side during the intermission between the halves. Indeed, the result was foregone by the time that the renowned Doc Blanchard and Glenn Davis, who scored all five Army touchdowns, had gone across three times for a 20–0 lead in the opening quarter. Every one knew that the midshipmen were a hopelessly beaten team, that their line was not quite good enough to match the powerful forwards of Colonel Earl Blaik and, above all, that they had no lasting, consistent answer to the depredations of the twin football scourges of modern times, Blanchard and Davis, who raced forty-six and forty-eight yards, respectively, for two of the cadets' touchdowns.

Navy did things to Blanchard and Davis today that no other team had done. Time and again it stopped the two terrors of the gridiron or threw them for losses. But Blanchard and Davis might be checked again and again and still it was not enough. They had to be stopped every time. To miss them once was to invite disaster, for, with their power, speed and elusiveness, they are backs who are likely to go all the way if given the chance to get started or allowed the slightest loophole.

It was beyond Navy's strength and capacity to meet so exacting a require-

Halfback Glenn Davis, left, and fullback Doc Blanchard in an undated photo at West Point. Blanchard, Mr. Inside, won the Heisman Trophy in 1945 and Davis, Mr. Outside, followed in '46. (Associated Press)

ment. The Middies used few reserves, as did Army, and they made mistakes for which Blanchard and Davis made them pay dearly. The crowd would rub its eyes at the sight of the twin engines of destruction being manhandled like ordinary flesh-and-blood backs. It would rub them again and again, and then, suddenly, there was Doc or Junior streaking across the goal line.

In the dressing room Colonel Blaik finally broke down and admitted that Army is the greatest West Point team of all time—at least of all he has seen. He hasn't seen them all, but no one will probably challenge his statement.

Runners-up

2002: Michael Vick of the Atlanta Falcons set an N.F.L. single-game record for quarterbacks when he rushed for 173 yards—including a game-winning 46-yard touchdown run in overtime—in a 30–24 victory in Minnesota. Afterward, the Pro Football Hall of Fame asked for his shoes. Vick topped Tobin Rote's mark of 150 yards for the Green Bay Packers in 1951.

1924: The first pro hockey game in the United States was played as the Boston Bruins defeated the Montreal Maroons, 2–1, at Boston Arena. The two teams had just become members of the seven-year-old N.H.L., which previously consisted of just four teams, all of them in Canada (see Nov. 22).

1988: Sharply escalating television rights payments to the Olympics, a trend that led to ever more lavish Games and television coverage of them virtually round-the-clock, NBC agreed to pay $401 million for the 1992 Olympics in Barcelona, Spain. Just seven years later, NBC dwarfed this sum in another five-ring deal (see Dec. 12).

December 2, 1956
Bill Russell's One-Man Show

MELBOURNE, Australia (UP)—America's all-victorious basketball heroes, reaching Olympian heights with one of the finest team efforts ever displayed in the games, drew a citation from their coach, Gerald Tucker, today as "the best in the world."

"This team is as good as any ever assembled," said the former University of Oklahoma All-America player, after his stars swept past Russia, 89–55, to gain a gold medal. Bill Russell, the 6-foot-10-inch player from San Francisco University, who paced the gold-medal effort, declared this "my proudest moment" and hastened to dispel any suggestions that he might now turn professional. "I have no plans at this time for a professional career," said Russell. "All I can think about right now is that we won."

The tall star, filled with emotion, was near tears as fellow Americans descended to congratulate him and his teammates. "You coached a mighty good team," Russell said to Tucker, grasping his coach with both hands. Russell, who has been drafted by the Boston Celtics of the National Basketball Association, and who also has been scouted by the Harlem Globetrotters, said he was getting married in California on Dec. 9 and "I haven't got time to go thinking about anything else."

The repeat meeting of the finalists of the 1952 tournament was "no contest." Paced by Russell, who scored 13 points for a total of 113 for the tournament, and his San Francisco teammate, K.C. Jones, who scored 15 points, the Americans completely dominated the play. Russell directed the ball-control strategy with his rebounds and brilliant all-around play. Tucker indicated he was a little disturbed over the tendency to demean the efforts of the Americans because they had not faced top-flight competition in the Olympics. "Everybody down there has tried to figure out that these kids are not as good as they really are," he said. "But what more do they have to prove? They would be equal to any team in any league anywhere."

The sluggish Soviet team was not even helped by Jan Kruminsh, their 7-foot-4-inch Goliath who was cut down by the American "Davids." Despite his overwhelming height, he was outmaneuvered for rebounds and was consistently left at the far end of the court when the Americans employed their fast break. He scored only four free throws and got no field goals. Meanwhile Russell, with his whirling arms and his remarkable jumping ability, made it almost impossible for the Russians to drive in for close-range shots. As a result, the Soviet players were forced into a weaving pattern which sought to set up goals from outside. The Russian shooters were only fair, and although most of their goals were scored on outside shots they never hit often enough to harass the victors.

This was the fourth gold medal in four

Bill Russell of the University of San Francisco going up for a dunk years before it became fashionable as the U.S. dismantled the Soviet Union, 89-55, in the gold-medal game at the Melbourne Olympics. (Associated Press)

tries for the United States in basketball, which was added to the Olympics in 1936. Bill Russell and K.C. Jones, Hall of Fame teammates later on the Boston Celtics, led the United States to an average victory margin of 53 points throughout the Games.

Runners-up

1975: Archie Griffin, the unstoppable Ohio State running back, won the Heisman Trophy for the second straight year, becoming the only player to win it twice. He finished his collegiate career with an N.C.A.A. record of 31 straight games in which he ran for 100 yards or more.

1985: Dan Marino of the Miami Dolphins *(see March 13)* defended his team's 1972 record of being the only N.F.L. team to go undefeated for an entire season by shredding the Chicago Bear's vaunted defense, 38–24, at the Orange Bowl in one of the greatest Monday night games played. The Bears finished 18–1 after beating the New England Patriots in the Super Bowl.

1993: The Houston Rockets, led by center Hakeem Olajuwon, defeated the Knicks, 94–85, at Madison Square Garden for their season-opening 15th straight victory, tying the record for best N.B.A. start set by the Washington Capitols in 1948. The Rockets beat the Knicks for the first of two straight league titles the following June.

December 3, 1999
True Grit and Two Oars

By WILLIAM TAAFFE

NEW YORK—She had tried it the year before, alone, pushing her 23-foot boat, American Pearl, into the waters off Nag's Head on the North Carolina coast in hopes of reaching Brest, France, some three months later. That venture to become the first woman and the first American to row solo across the Atlantic had ended in failure, the plywood and fiberglass vessel capsizing 15 times in a hurricane that pushed the seas into waves that were 70 feet high and nearly took her life.

But today, Tori Murden, a 36-year-old adventuress from Louisville, Ky., rowed American Pearl through tranquil waters to Fort-du-Bas on the southeast coast of the Caribbean island of Guadeloupe, 81 days, 2,961 miles and one punishing tropical storm after leaving Los Gigantes on Tenirife, the largest island in the Azores off the coast of Africa. Having tried again from the opposite direction, armed with the same grit and determination and willingness to face the unknown, she had succeeded. It was approximately the same route Columbus sailed on his second western voyage in 1493—but without the manpower and companionship he enjoyed.

Though small boats ventured out to greet her, Murden insisted on rowing her 23-foot Kevlar-and-plywood vessel to dockside. There were some 50 friends, spectators and French tourists to greet her, some waving small American flags. Interviewed within a few hours of her arrival by CNN, Murden said:

"There are times that are incredibly sublime, and you feel like you're at once that puny speck of nothing and part of a

Tori Murden arriving in Fort-du-Bas harbor in Guadeloupe aboard American Pearl after she became the first woman, and first American, to row across the Atlantic alone. It took her 81 days, 2,961 miles and one tropical storm. (Associated Press)

grand universe. There are other times when it's frightening and just lonely. And so along the roller coaster there are grand moments and sad moments, but I wouldn't trade them for anything."

Murden, a lawyer and former hospital chaplain who has a divinity degree from Harvard, raises funds for the nonprofit Muhammad Ali Center, which assists underprivileged children in Louisville. She left the oceanic money-raising chores—the trip cost $100,000—to others, but during the entire voyage she wore a trademark string of pearls, one for each person who had helped her.

Murden, who on an expedition to Antarctica in late 1988 and early 1989 had been one of the first women to journey overland (on skis) to the geographic South Pole, decided to attempt a solo Atlantic crossing for the philosophical lessons the experience might teach. A strong rower—she learned at Smith College in Massachusetts and has been a flat-water sculls racer for years—she was hardly ready for the terror of Hurricane Danielle, which thrashed her on the 1998 voyage while she was two-thirds of the

way across the ocean. Because she had an EPIRB (emergency-position-indicating radio beacon) aboard, she was pulled from the water by the appropriately named Independent Spirit, a container ship 950 miles from Brest, but the boat was lost.

On her latest voyage, Murden sailed into trouble only slightly less severe. Still hoping to break the Atlantic solo crossing record of 73 days 8 hours set by Sidney Genders of Britain in 1970, she encountered a torrential storm, the remnants of Hurricane Lenny, two weeks ago. She fastened her 11-foot oars to the hull, climbed into the hull, secured the watertight hatch and barricaded herself in the coffinlike cabin, which measured 4 feet wide, 7 feet long and 3 feet high. One night the boat capsized, then righted itself, while she loudly sang hymns to keep her composure. Can songs be heard in the deep? Several hours later came the dawn and the calm.

Tori Murden later wrote of the "simple truths" she learned: "As a speck of nature, I am utterly insignificant. As an individual, I am unique and special. Though I am but a single thread, I help weave the fabric of a community. Though we stand by ourselves, we are not alone."

The Ocean Rowing Society of London, which keeps records on crossings, later calculated on the basis of satellite tracking that she had sailed 3,333 miles, not the shorter straight-line distance, because she had been blown backward by wind on some days and had to make up miles again. Her official time was recorded as 81 days 7 hours 46 minutes.

Runners-up

1949: Notre Dame stretched its unbeaten streak to four seasons and 38 games, but not before Southern Methodist University, behind the brilliant passing and running of Kyle Rote, later to star with the N.F.L. Giants, nearly pulled off an upset before 75,000 fans at the Cotton Bowl. The Irish won, 27–20, for their seventh national championship.

1956: Wilt Chamberlain made his debut with the University of Kansas by scoring a school-record 52 points in an 87–69 victory over Northwestern at Lawrence,

Kan. Ten years later to the day, Lew Alcindor (see May 4) played his first game for U.C.L.A., scoring a school-record 56 points in a 105–90 triumph over U.S.C. at Pauley Pavilion.

1994: Greg LeMond of Medina, Minn. (see May 4), the three-time winner of the Tour de France, announced his retirement from racing at age 33 because of mitochondrial myopathy, a rare (see July 23) muscular disorder brought about in his case by lead pellets remaining in his chest from a 1987 hunting accident.

Sprewell Suspended. Choked His Coach

By MIKE WISE

Coach P.J. Carlesimo, at left, and Latrell Sprewell of the Golden State Warriors in 1997. Sprewell choked Carlesimo at a practice until other players pulled him away, then returned a short time later and assaulted him again. (Photographs by Getty Images)

NEW YORK [Thursday]—The National Basketball Association suspended Latrell Sprewell of the Golden State Warriors for one year without pay today, three days after the 27-year-old All-Star guard physically assaulted his coach, P.J. Carlesimo. The penalty was swift and the most severe ever assessed against a professional player for what the league classified as insubordination. It signaled the league's determination to deal with behavior problems that have tarnished its image. And it was justified, the league said, because of the seriousness of the attack, in which Sprewell choked the coach, threatened to kill him and hit him at a practice session on Monday.

"A sports league does not have to accept or condone behavior that would not be tolerated in any other segment of society," Commissioner David Stern said in a statement. The commissioner's action followed the Warriors' decision last night to terminate the remainder of Sprewell's $32 million contract. The executive director of the National Basketball Players Association, Billy Hunter, said today that he planned to file separate grievances contesting both the termination of the contract and the league's suspension. The dispute is almost certain to go before an arbitrator. "To strip a player of his ability to pursue his livelihood for a full year based on one incident is excessive and unreasonable punishment," Hunter said in a statement. "A $25 million forfeiture of salary and one-year expulsion is staggering."

Sprewell, in his fifth season out of the University of Alabama, had earned $9.95 million entering this season—$2.95 million on his original four-year deal, and another $7 million last season in the first year of his four-year, $32 million contract. In terminating his contract, the Warriors cited the Uniform Player Contract, which states that players must "conform to standards of good citizenship and good moral character."

The incident comes at a time when the league has been beset by problems ranging from criminal actions to insubordination and disrespect for authority. In the last year, Dennis Rodman, the Chicago Bulls forward, was suspended and fined for kicking a courtside cameraman in the groin; Allen Iverson of Philadelphia, the rookie of the year in 1997, pleaded no contest to a weapons charge and Charles Barkley of Houston was recently charged in an incident in which witnesses said he threw a man through a plate-glass window after a bar disturbance in Orlando, Fla.

Stern explained his ruling by characterizing Sprewell as a player who had not only lost control during a dispute at a team practice on Monday but also one who had time to calm down before returning for a second attack.

"Latrell Sprewell assaulted Coach P.J. Carlesimo twice at Monday's practice," Stern said. "First, he choked him until forcibly pulled away. Then, after leaving practice, Mr. Sprewell returned and fought his way through others in order to commit a second, and this time clearly premeditated, assault."

Sprewell could not be reached for comment tonight. In a television interview with a San Francisco station at his home night before last, he apologized in his first public statement on the attack and admitted he had made a mistake. But he did not apologize to Carlesimo, instead portraying the coach as someone whose pattern of verbal abuse over the course of two months he could no longer tolerate.

Three months later an arbiter reinstated Latrell Sprewell's contract and reduced his suspension to seven months without pay. Sprewell was traded to the Knicks in January 1999. P.J. Carlesimo coached for two more seasons at Golden State before he was fired.

Runners-up

1960: Johnny Unitas of the Colts threw for two touchdowns in a 20–15 loss to the Detroit Lions at Baltimore, extending to 47 the record number of consecutive games in which he had passed for a touchdown. The man with the golden arm was arguably the greatest quarterback ever. The streak ended the following week in a loss to the Los Angeles Rams.

1960: Paul Hornung, the do-it-all back of the Green Bay Packers *(see Dec. 12),* scored two touchdowns and kicked two field goals and five extra points in a 41–13 victory over the Chicago Bears at Wrigley Field. That gave Hornung 152 points for the season, breaking the N.F.L. mark of 138 set by the Green Bay Packers' Don Hutson *(see Nov. 30)* in 1942.

1980: Stella Walsh, who as a member of the Polish women's track team won gold and silver medals in the 100 meters at the 1932 and '36 Olympics, respectively, was shot to death during a robbery attempt at a discount store in Cleveland. An autopsy determined that while she was setting 11 world records she had both male and female chromosomes but was in fact a man.

December 5, 1942
Magician With a Cue

DETROIT (AP) [Saturday] —Dapper Willie Mosconi returned today to the world pocket billiard championship after a year's absence, and Monday morning, bright and early, he'll return to his war job at Jackson, Mich. Helped immensely by the defending champion, Irving Crane of Livonia, N.Y., Mosconi clinched the title this afternoon on the combination of his 125-to-32 victory over Edwin Rudolph of Chardon, Ohio, and Crane's dramatic 125-to-98 triumph over second-place Andrew Ponzi of Philadelphia. Both matches went 15 innings.

The victory was Mosconi's eighth in nine matches, while the defeat left Ponzi with six victories and three setbacks. The other four contenders had been eliminated in the previous five days of the tournament. By winning, Mosconi pocketed $1,500 in war bonds and hauled off the championship trophy to show the boys on the job.

Mosconi, the 29-year-old former Philadelphian who contributed most of the long runs of the tournament, beat Ponzi, 125 to 0, in his opening match Monday, then clustered five victories before Jimmy Caras of Philadelphia beat him. But the champion came back to beat Crane, the veteran Ralph Greenleaf of New York and Rudolph in order. Mosconi rolled up an unfinished run of 71 to whip Rudolph and clinch at least a tie for the title and then sat back to watch Ponzi lose. Crane seized an early lead, but in his final

Willie Mosconi, the most accomplished pool player in history, in a practice round at the national Pocket Billiards Championship in 1933. The son of a Philadelphia pool hall owner, he didn't always wear black tie. (Associated Press)

turn at the table Ponzi clustered 43 shots before Crane closed out the match.

Mosconi made his tournament record nine out of ten by defeating Ponzi, 125 to 17, in seven innings, in his final match tonight. In another match, Caras gained his fourth victory in ten starts by downing Rudolph, 125 to 76, in eight frames. In the final match of the tournament, Crane defeated Greenleaf, 125 to 17, in four innings. The victory lifted Crane into third

place in the final standing, while Greenleaf, by virtue of having scored more points than Rudolph, took fifth.

Willie Mosconi dominated pocket billiards, or pool, through the 1950's, winning 15 world championships between 1941 and '57. He learned the game as a teenager on the cusp of the Great Depression. In a 1954 exhibition match he sank 526 straight balls—a record that still stands.

Runners-up

1947: Joe Louis of Detroit *(see June 22),* aged 33, survived a first-round knockdown and went on to win a disputed 15-round decision over Jersey Joe Walcott of Camden, N.J., at Madison Square Garden to retain his world heavyweight championship. Louis's last fight was in 1948 *(see June 25);* he retired in March 1949.

1992: Antonio Langham's 26-yard interception return for a touchdown with 3 minutes 25 seconds left gave the University of Alabama a 28–21 victory over Florida

for the Southeastern Conference title and a 12–0 record. The Tide beat Miami in the Sugar Bowl for its 12th national title but first since 1979.

1981: Marcus Allen, the smooth Southern California running back who was the first collegian to gain more than 2,000 yards, won the Heisman Trophy, outpolling Herschel Walker *(see Nov. 29)* of Georgia. Allen became the fourth U.S.C. running back in 16 years to win the award, joining Mike Garrett, O.J. Simpson and Charles White.

December 6, 1984
Upset Snaps Navratilova's Streak

MELBOURNE, Australia (AP) [Thursday]—Helena Sukova, a teenager from Czechoslovakia, ended Martina Navratilova's hopes of winning a record seventh consecutive Grand Slam tournament today when she defeated the world's top-ranked player, 1–6, 6–3, 7–5, in the semifinals of the $1.28 million Australian Open championship at suburban Kooyong. Miss Sukova, 19, the daughter of a former Wimbledon finalist, Vera Sukova, served superbly as she became only the second player to defeat Miss Navratilova this year.

Since a loss to Hana Mandlikova last January, Miss Navratilova had won a record 74 consecutive matches. She had been bidding to complete the calendar year Grand Slam—victories at Wimbledon and at the French, United States and Australian opens—and win the 100th title of her career, but was outplayed in the final set by the ninth-seeded Miss Sukova. In Saturday's final, Miss Sukova will meet Chris Evert Lloyd, who defeated Wendy Turnbull, 6–3, 6–3. Mrs. Lloyd, whose 10-year-old record of 55 straight victories was shattered by Miss Navratilova this year, is aiming to maintain a record of having won at least one Grand Slam tournament every year since 1973.

Miss Navratilova was gracious in defeat. "How important is anything?" she asked. "It hurts, but I'll get over it. I still have two arms, two legs and a heart." The 28-year-old left-hander said that she now feared a letdown. "If I'd have won, I'd have done it all," she said. "If I lost I had to start from scratch. Both are hard to cope with."

Miss Navratilova breezed through the first set and appeared in command. But Miss Sukova then began to return and pass brilliantly and put the left-hander under tremendous pressure. The teenager took the second set and then raced to a 3–0 lead in the third. Miss Navratilova fought back to 4–4, but Miss Sukova broke her serve again in the 11th game. Miss Navratilova saved 5 match points in the 12th game before Miss Sukova prevailed.

Miss Navratilova said she had given the contest her best effort. "I certainly didn't play my best, but I did my best on the day," she said. "I know I'm the better player, but today she was the better player." Entering the semifinal, Miss Navratilova held a 3–0 advantage over Miss Sukova from previous matches, two of them this year. But they had not played on grass. The world's No. 1 player said that she expected Miss Sukova to provide her a strong challenge.

Martina Navratilova won 78 of the 80 matches she played this year. From her loss to Hana Mandlikova in the finals of the Virginia Slims of California in January to her defeat by Helena Sukova here, she won 74 consecutive matches. It was by far the longest winning streak, male or female, in tennis history.

Martina Navratilova just after connecting on a forehand volley against Helena Sukova in a Virginia Slims tournament in California in 1986. Sukova had broken Navratilova's 74-match winning streak two years before. (Associated Press)

Runners-up

1925: A crowd of 70,000, the largest to date for the fledgling N.F.L., came to the Polo Grounds in New York to glimpse the heralded Red Grange as the Chicago Bears, almost a sidelight, defeated the Giants, 19–7. Grange, finishing his first pro season after a remarkable collegiate career at Illinois *(see Oct. 18),* ran for a fourth-quarter touchdown.

1998: On a play that contributed to the return of instant replay as an N.F.L. officiating tool, the Jets' Vinny Testaverde was ruled to have scored on a five-yard sneak with 20 seconds left against the Seattle Seahawks even though he never got into the end zone. The Jets won, 32–31, as time ran out. Jets Coach Bill Parcells said, "God's playing in some of these games, and he was on our side today."

1995: Patrick Roy, the two-time Stanley Cup–winning goalie for the Montreal Canadiens, was traded to the Colorado Avalanche for five players in one of the most stunning deals in N.H.L. history. Roy had been feuding with the Canadiens' new coach, Mario Tremblay. After arriving in Denver, he led the Avalanche to league titles in 1996 and 2001.

Downhill Straight to Victory

[Unsigned, *The New York Times*]

VAL D'ISÈRE, France—A.J. Kitt from Rochester outskied every European on the slate today to win the first men's downhill of the 1991–92 World Cup season at the site of February's Olympic race. Kitt, the first American to win a world-class men's downhill since Bill Johnson took the gold medal at the 1984 Olympics, covered the Oreiller-Killy course in 1 minute 55.69 seconds, .49 seconds faster than Leonhard Stock, an Austrian who won this race last year. Finishing third was Franz Heinzer of Switzerland, the World Cup downhill champion and the man who has been most touted to win the Olympic gold medal here.

When the United States ski team started making waves on the World Cup circuit last year by insisting on prize money for the racers and more publicity, some people scoffed at the arrogance of it all. Who were these Americans, many asked, to tell the Europeans how to run their sport? Some of those scoffers were probably blushing today. The 23-year-old Kitt, in his fourth World Cup season, regarded the victory as a demonstration of growing American influence at the top level of ski racing.

"It's been a long time since we've had a good downhiller," he said. "As a team, we've been together for five years now. Training together. Racing together. So we kind of know now that if one can do it then the rest can do it. It's just a matter of time before the other guys get in there." One of the other guys is Tommy Moe, a 21-year-old Alaskan who finished 13th. "A.J. won today and that's a major step for America," Moe said. "It lets some of the Europeans know we're not here to mess around. We're here to play ball."

Because of new incentives, Kitt will

A.J. Kitt during a practice run in the downhill at the 1992 Olympics in Albertville, France. Kitt's breakthrough in the World Cup two months before ended a seven-year eclipse for U.S. men in international skiing. (Getty Images)

receive $15,000 in prize money. Although he had not been among those threatening to boycott the race in the absence of cash awards, Kitt was not refusing the money. "I look forward to the day when we're racing for a $40,000 first prize in World Cup," he said. "It would reflect the caliber of the sport. It's a fun sport to watch. I don't think Alpine skiers are any different from football or basketball players in the U.S. We work just as hard as anyone else, and our sport is just as exciting as theirs."

Kitt's victory was the first World Cup victory for an American man since Johnson won the last downhill race of 1984. Julie Parisen won a women's World Cup giant slalom early this year at Waterville Valley, N.H. Kitt won the United States downhill and super-G titles last sea-

son and has been racing since 1988 on the World Cup circuit. He was 26th in the 1988 Olympic downhill as a 19-year-old.

Alberto Tomba of Italy and Paul Accola of Switzerland—neither of whom competed today—remained on top of the overall World Cup standings with 360 points. Kitt's victory moved him into seventh place in the overall standings and, of course, on top of the season standings in the downhill.

A.J. Kitt competed in four Olympics and four World Alpine Ski Championships between 1988 and '97, winning only a bronze medal in the downhill at the '93 championships in Japan. Tommy Moe, however, won the gold medal in the downhill at the 1994 Lillehammer Olympics, cementing his place in history.

Runners-up

1963: The instant replay, which changed the way viewers watched sports, was used for the first time by the CBS director Tony Verna. It caught Army quarterback Rollie Stichweh faking a handoff and running for a touchdown in the Army-Navy game. So strange did the replay seem that the announcer Lindsay Nelson said: "This is not live! Ladies and gentlemen, Army did not score again!

1963: Kansas, coached by Dick Tarp and led by George Unseld and Walt Wesley, snapped the University of Cincinnati's 90-game basketball home winning streak, 51-47, at Armory Fieldhouse. The streak, attributable mostly to the

brilliance of Oscar Robertson, Paul Hogue and Coach Ed Jucker, dated to March 1957.

1985: In the closest balloting in the history of the Heisman Trophy awards, Bo Jackson of Auburn edged Iowa quarterback Chuck Long by 45 votes of the 2,973 cast. Jackson went on to play major league baseball and pro football *(see July 11)*. One other Heisman winner did so: Vic Janowicz of Ohio State (1952).

Monsters of Midway Indeed

By ARTHUR J. DALEY

WASHINGTON—The weather was perfect. So were the Bears. In the most fearsome display of power ever seen on any gridiron, the Monsters of the Midway won the Ed Thorpe Memorial Trophy, which is symbolic of the world football championship, before 36,034 stunned and deriding fans in Griffith Stadium today on this balmy afternoon.

It being a Sunday, the Washington Humane Society had the day off. So the Bears had nothing else to combat in the play-off except the Redskins, who were pretty feeble opposition indeed. Hence it was that the Chicago Bears scalped the Capital Indians, 73 to 0, the highest score in the history of the National Football League. The only question before the house was whether the Bears could score more points when they were on the offensive or when Washington was on the offensive. It was fairly close competition, Chicago with the ball outscoring the Redskins with the ball, seven touchdowns to four.

Three weeks ago, the Redskins edged the Bears, 7 to 3. Today it was something else again. The Bears registered three touchdowns in the first period, one in the second, four in the third and three in the last. George Halas used every eligible man on his squad, thirty-three of them, and fifteen had a share of the scoring. It even reached such a stage that the Bears passed for one point after touchdown by way of variety and by way of adding to Washington's humiliation.

Halas used Sid Luckman, an Old Blue from Columbia, as his first-half quarterback, and no field general ever called plays more artistically or engineered a touchdown parade in more letter-perfect fashion. But the Lion sat out the second half and still the mastodons from the Midwest

rolled. Ray Flaherty's young men were physically in the game, but that was all. After Bill Osmanski had romped 68 yards for the first touchdown, the 'Skins reached the Bear 26, only to have Bob Masterson's field-goal effort fail. That was a blow from which George Preston Marshall's lads never recovered. Had they scored, it might have been different.

But when they missed they wound up with a minus 10 yards for their first seven passes and went speedily downhill the rest of the way. Redskins fans who had watched their heroes win their first seven games of the league season could not

believe their eyes.

At the end the Redskins band played "Should Auld Acquaintance Be Forgot?" If said acquaintance is the Chicago Bears, it should be forgot immediately. At the moment the Bears are the greatest football team of all time.

This was the first major test for George Halas's new T formation, operated by Sid Luckman, in which the quarterback lines up directly behind the center, with the fullback directly behind him and a halfback on either side of the fullback. The Bears' 73–0 whitewash remains the worst championship rout ever

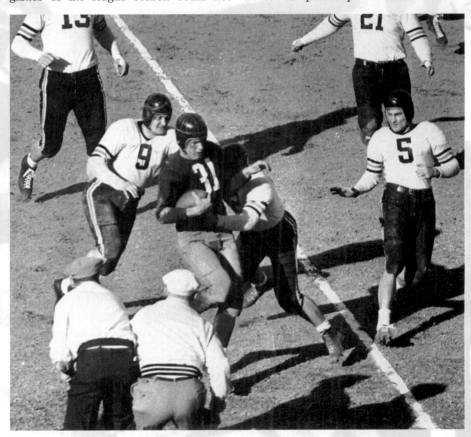

Jimmy Johnstone (31) being tackled by Sid Luckman in the Bears' 73-0 decimation of the Redskins. Washington's owner, George Preston Marshall, was angry afterward: "Our defense looked like a roomful of maidens going after a mouse. Helpless, hopeless, hapless." (Associated Press)

Runners-up

1966: Roger Maris, who broke Babe Ruth's record of 60 home runs five years before *(see Oct. 1),* was traded by the Yankees to the St. Louis Cardinals for Charlie Smith, a journeyman third baseman. Maris, a superb right-fielder as well as hitter, helped lead St. Louis to the 1967 and '68 National League pennants.

1961: In one of the classic matchups between future Hall of Famers, Wilt Chamberlain of the Philadelphia Warriors *(see March 2)* scored 78 points and Elgin Baylor of the Los Angeles Lakers hit for 63 as Philadelphia won in triple

overtime at home, 151–147. Chamberlain broke Baylor's N.B.A. mark of 71 points set the previous year *(see Nov. 15).*

1948: Doak Walker of Southern Methodist University, one of the greatest open-field runners in football history, won the Heisman Trophy, outpolling Charlie Justice of North Carolina. In a short but spectacular pro career—just six seasons—Walker combined with fiery quarterback Bobby Layne to lead the Detroit Lions to two N.F.L. titles in 1952 and '53.

December 9, 1934
The Sneakers Have It!

By ROBERT F. KELLEY and WALTER FLEISHER

NEW YORK—In one of the most wildly exciting periods that any football game has ever seen, the New York Giants scored 27 points in the final session of play at the Polo Grounds today to come from behind and defeat the Chicago Bears, 30 to 13. Trailing on the short end of a 13-to-3 score when the last quarter opened, the Giants roared through to an amazing victory while 37,000 fans who braved the freezing weather went wild with excitement and for a time threatened to interrupt play as they stormed out on the field.

Four times the Giants crossed the Bears' goal line for touchdowns in that final period as they captured the national professional championship and toppled the Bears from the throne they have occupied since 1932.

To the amazement of every one, the Giants, behind by a score of 10 to 3 at half-time, returned to the field for the third quarter wearing basketball shoes—rubber-soled sneakers they had borrowed from Manhattan College—replacing the cleated football shoes. The solidly frozen ground made cleats useless, and the basketball shoes made all the difference in the world. How effective they proved was summed up by Bronko Nagurski, star back of the Bears, who said, "I think the sneakers gave them an edge in that last half, for they were able to cut back when they were running with the ball and we couldn't cut with them."

During most of the first half, after the Bears had overcome a first-period lead that Ken Strong gave the Giants with a 38-yard placement goal, the Westerners, undefeated in thirteen National Football League games this year, seemed the certain winners. The Bears had come back in the second period with a touchdown when

Bronko Nagurski, right, of the Bears being smothered by the Giants, in white helmets, at the Polo Grounds. Behind at the half on a frozen field, the Giants switched to borrowed sneakers and gained enough traction to win. (Bettmann/Corbis)

Nagurski bulled his way across from the one-yard mark. A pass paved the way to this score. Then Jack Manders, the great kicker, put across a rifle shot from the 17-yard mark.

When Manders shot across a 23-yard field goal late in the third period it was apparently all over but the shouting. But that second score by Manders wasn't the final act in the successful defense of the title by Chicago. Instead it was the final setting of the stage for the frozen drama of the comeback by the Giants. With Lou Little, Columbia's coach, sitting up in the stands and phoning to the bench, Steve Owen directing down there and Strong playing one of the greatest games any back has ever turned in, the Giants came back to win.

The quest for the Giants' novel footwear, a brand new sight for the fans, began at 11 o'clock in the morning when John Mara, treasurer of the club, telephoned Coach Steve Owen and Captain Ray Flaherty and informed them that the field was frozen. Flaherty immediately sug-gested obtaining basketball shoes, declaring they were much more effective on a field of that sort than the cleated football boot. The Giants' leader, while at Gonzaga in 1925, had worn sneakers in a game against the University of Montana. The turf was frozen and the shoes had proved highly effective. They were also used last year by the University of Washington in a charity game against the Seattle All-Stars, the former rolling up a count of 69 to 0 in the first half. In the last half Washington loaned the Seattle team basketball shoes, with the result that there was no further scoring. This contest also was played on a frozen field and it was witnessed by Bill Morgan, former Oregon star, now playing with the Giants.

The Giants again resorted to basketball shoes against the Chicago Bears in the 1956 N.F.L. title game at Yankee Stadium (see Dec. 30). The Bears, wearing cleats, got behind by 27 points early, then switched to sneakers for the second half. It was too late, though, as the Giants won their third league title.

Runners-up

1984: Eric Dickerson of the Los Angeles Rams broke O.J. Simpson's N.F.L. single-season rushing record *(see Dec. 16)* by gaining 215 yards in a 27–16 victory over the Houston Oilers at Anaheim Stadium. Dickerson wound up with 2,105 yards for the year, compared with Simpson's 1973 mark of 2,003

1941: Two days after the Japanese attack on Pearl Harbor, 23-year-old Bob Feller *(see April 16)*, the 25-game winner and league strikeout king for the Cleveland Indians, became the first major league player to volunteer for active duty.

Feller, the greatest pitcher of his era, lost four of his prime playing years but still made the Hall of Fame.

1977: Rudy Tomjanovich of the Houston Rockets was punched in the face by Kermit Washington of the Los Angeles Lakers in the most serious brawl in N.B.A. history. Tomjanovich needed facial reconstruction and collected $2 million from the Lakers in a settlement. Washington was fined $10,000 and sus-pended for 60 days.

December 10, 1971
Mets Trade Ryan. No Kidding!

By JOSEPH DURSO

NEW YORK—The Mets finally gave up on Nolan Ryan's wandering fastball today. They traded the 24-year-old pitcher and three prospects to the California Angels for Jim Fregosi, six times the American League's all-star shortstop. Manager Gil Hodges immediately said he would move Fregosi to third base, where 45 men have come and gone during the Mets' 10 seasons in business.

"You always hate to give up on an arm like Ryan's," Hodges said today. "He could put things together overnight, but he hasn't done it for us and the Angels wanted him. I would not hesitate making a trade for somebody who might help us right now, and Fregosi is such a guy."

In order to get the 29-year-old infielder, the Mets sent California the outfielder Leroy Stanton, pitcher Don Rose and catcher Francisco Estrada in addition to Ryan. Harry Dalton, who left the Baltimore Orioles in October to become general manager of the California team, praised Fregosi for his 11 seasons with the Angels but said: "We picked up one of baseball's best arms in Ryan. We know of his control problems, but he had the best arm in the National League and, at 24, he is just coming into his own. Stanton figures to give us some of the right-handed power we need, and Rose and Estrada both have a chance to make our club."

"Only one of the four would have been with the Mets next season, and that was Ryan," said Bob Scheffing, the general manager of the Mets. "I don't think Stanton could have beaten out our other outfielders, and we have run out of options on him. As for Ryan, I really can't say I quit on him. But we've had him three full years and, although he's a hell of a prospect, he hasn't done it for us. How

long can you wait? I can't rate him in the same category with Tom Seaver, Jerry Koosman or Gary Gentry."

Ryan has been striking out one batter every inning since he signed with the Mets out of Alvin, Tex., in 1965. In three more or less full seasons with the varsity, he struck out 493 batters in 510 innings. Last season, he fanned 137 in 152, including 16 San Diego Padres on May 29, the most all year for any National League pitcher. Going into July, in fact, he had eight victories and four defeats and appeared to have found himself as well as home plate. But then he became as wild as a March hare, lost 10 of the next 12, walked nine St. Louis Cardinals in one game and 116 batters in all 30 games—both club records for wildness.

Fregosi, the last of the original Angels of 1961, was having his own problems meanwhile. He suffered from the flu, a sore arm, a strained muscle in his side and a tumor on his foot. He hit only .233 with five home runs, a marked comedown from 1970, when he hit .278 with 22 home runs.

The Mets' trade of Nolan Ryan for the California Angels' Jim Fregosi was

Nolan Ryan, aged 21, in the spring of 1968. He won 29 games over the next four seasons and showed a world of potential, but the Mets weren't patient enough, shipping him to the Angels for Jim Fregosi. (Associated Press)

unquestionably the worst in baseball history. Ryan went on to throw seven no-hitters (see May 1) and become the greatest strikeout pitcher of all time. Fregosi, on the downside of his career, batted .232.

Runners-up

1999: Laffit Pincay Jr., 52, broke Bill Shoemaker's career record for victories when he rode Irish Nip to a first-place finish at Hollywood Park in California. It was the Panamanian-born Pincay's 8,834th victory on 44,647 mounts over his 35-year career.

1989: Steve Largent of the Seattle Seahawks caught the 100th touchdown pass of his career in a victory over the Cincinnati Bengals in the Kingdome, passing Don Hutson on the N.F.L.'s all-time list. Largent retired and served three terms

in Congress; Jerry Rice broke the mark with the San Francisco 49ers in 1992 and had a record 192 regular-season touchdown catches through 2002.

1993: Ty Murray won his fifth consecutive all-around championship at the National Finals Rodeo at Las Vegas. The most accomplished rider in history, Murray competed in three of the roughest and most dangerous events—bareback, saddle bronc and bull riding—while most performers specialized in just one. He won seven all-around titles through 1998.

December 11, 1982
Showdown in the Pivot

By GORDON S. WHITE Jr.

LANDOVER, Md. [Saturday]—The $1.25 million production of the Ralph Sampson–Patrick Ewing show had an excellent one-night stand this evening in the Capital Centre. Sampson led top-ranked Virginia to a 68–63 victory over Ewing's Georgetown in a game that many agreed came close to living up to its billing as a unique attraction for the crowd of 19,035 and the millions watching on television.

The play within the play also went to the 7-foot-4-inch Sampson, who had 23 points, 16 rebounds and seven blocked shots; the 7–0 Ewing had 16 points, eight rebounds and five blocked shots. Sampson, a senior, won the battle because he had the moves to beat Ewing, a sophomore, more often than Ewing was able to use his strength. Sampson also had the better supporting players, though Ewing's sophomore and freshman teammates grew up in a hurry and made a magnificent charge at the end. Georgetown eliminated Virginia's 14-point lead in the second half and tied with 3:48 to go, and again with 3:19 left. But Virginia held on for the victory.

Following the game, Sampson said he had played while suffering from flu, which he had had for the last few days. He also said that he injured his left knee in practice on Thursday, and had had fluid drained from a deep bruise on the knee last night. Sampson was clearly exhausted after the game and said he would take an intravenous feeding of glucose for quick energy absorption. Both he and Ewing had given as much as could be asked of them. Sampson downplayed his performance while praising Ewing. "I don't think I played well," Sampson said. "Pat is an excellent player. There aren't enough

words to describe the guy. He's great. He was tough on defense, and when he tried to front me, I tried to fight him and get inside."

Terry Holland, Virginia's coach, said, "I thought Ralph had a really good night. But as the game went on he got weaker, and by the end he had difficulty maintaining his position offensively or defensively. He got to the point where he was not sweating. That's bad."

Ewing is likely to remember his first and last baskets of the game. The first one came at 2:29 of the first half when Ewing faked a leap and induced Sampson into jumping high to try to block the shot. Ewing waited, then went up and shot the ball underhanded into the basket, putting the ball below Sampson's arms. The last Ewing basket was simply a hard stuff over Sampson—a strength-against-strength victory for Ewing that cut Virginia's lead to 57–53.

"I wouldn't trade Patrick," said John Thompson, the Georgetown coach.

The matchup between Ralph Sampson and Patrick Ewing was a unique made-for-television game and helped put Ted Turner's WTBS cable superstation, which carried it, on the map. Sampson was selected first over all by the Houston Rockets in the 1983 N.B.A. draft but had an indifferent eight-year pro career with four teams. John Thompson was prescient in his comment about not trading Ewing, who led Georgetown to the N.C.A.A. title game in each of the next two seasons. Ewing was drafted first over all in 1985 (see May 12) and played brilliantly for the Knicks over 15 seasons.

Patrick Ewing of Georgetown and Ralph Sampson of Virginia, behind him, positioning themselves for a rebound in their storied matchup at Landover, Md. Sampson reigned for the night but Ewing was king for the decade. (Associated Press)

Runners-up

1981: Overweight, flat-footed and weary at age 39, Muhammad Ali lost a 10-round decision to 27-year-old Trevor Berbick at Nassau, the Bahamas. "You can't beat Father Time," Ali said afterward in his dressing room. It was the last fight of his storied career.

1959: Don Carter, the master of the light touch on the lanes and the pre-eminent bowler of his day, won his second world invitation tournament at the Chicago Coliseum. Carter, 33, rolled clutch double strikes in the tenth frame of the

third game to overtake Billy Golembiewski of Detroit for the tournament title.

2000: Shortstop Alex Rodriguez signed the largest contract in sports history, a 10-year deal with the Texas Rangers for $252 million. Television money fueled the turn-of-the-century rise in sports salaries. A year before signing Rodriguez, Rangers owner Tom Hicks had been paid $250 million by Fox Sports for the right to carry the team's games for the coming decade.

December 12, 1965
Eleven Touchdowns Divided by Two

By WILLIAM N. WALLACE

BALTIMORE—Paul Hornung, the Green Bay Golden Boy who had been returned to the starting lineup for the big game today against the Baltimore Colts, scored five touchdowns as the Packers defeated the Colts, 42–27. In the first period, a pass play of 50 yards—Bart Starr to Hornung—gave Green Bay a 14–3 lead. Hornung later scored on runs of 2, 9 and 3 yards, all off-tackle cutbacks in the typical Green Bay power style. And with six minutes left to play, Starr threw a 65-yard touchdown pass to Hornung.

Before Hornung took almost complete control of the second half, Baltimore seemed to have a strong chance to win. The turning point today came in the fog at Baltimore Stadium when the Colts' Gary Cuozzo, young and impetuous with the score 14–13 in the Packers' favor, tried to fool the Green Bay defense, mature and disciplined, but failed. With the ball on the Green Bay 2-yard-line, Cuozzo tried to loft a pass over the right side to Jerry Hill, the fullback, to put Baltimore ahead.

Dave Robinson, the big Packer linebacker, diagnosed the play, intercepted the pass and returned it 88 yards. The return set up a touchdown pass from Bart Starr to Boyd Dowler that sent the Packers to their locker room ahead by 21–13. The rest of the game was Hornung, Hornung and Hornung.

Quicksilver Gale Sayers of the Bears on a broken-field run against the 49ers in 1970. (Associated Press)

CHICAGO (UPI)—Gale Sayers, who set all kinds of records in the Chicago Bears' 61–20 rout of the San Francisco 49ers today, broke another in the dressing room after the game. For the first time, a Chicago Bear was awarded the game ball twice in one season, breaking a team tradition. But the Bears' rookie scored six touchdowns today and his teammates just had to give him the ball again.

George Halas, the Bears' owner and coach, said: "This was the greatest football exhibition I have ever seen by one man in one game."

Sayers, a high school star in Omaha, Neb., and an all-America at the University of Kansas, is 22 years old, 6 feet tall and weighs 200 pounds. He is described as an "instinctive" runner, relying more on his speed and shiftiness than sheer power.

He is also a fine pass receiver. In today's game, he gained a total of 336 yards—113 rushing, 89 on receptions and 134 on punt returns. Halas said he didn't make up his mind to take Sayers as one of his first-round draft choices until a few weeks before the N.F.L. draft. "We thought perhaps some of his performance was just luck," Halas said. "Then I saw a highlight film on him where he made two moves in one stride and ran 95 yards and that was it."

Runners-up

1951: Joe DiMaggio (see July 17), the Yankees' center-fielder since 1936 and perhaps the most graceful player ever to play the game, retired at 37 after being hobbled the previous season by a heel injury. He finished with a lifetime batting average of .325 and what amounted to automatic election four years later to the Hall of Fame.

1937: George Preston Marshall's Washington Redskins won the N.F.L. championship game less than a year after they left Boston, where they were originally called the Braves, and reinvented themselves in the nation's capital. The rookie Sammy Baugh passed for 335 yards and three touchdowns in defeating George Halas's Chicago Bears, 28–21, at Wrigley Field.

1995: NBC paid the largest sum in history for the television rights to a series of sporting events: $2.3 billion for the United States rights to the 2004, 2006 and 2008 Olympics even before the sites of those games (Athens; Turin, Italy; and Beijing) had been determined. The figure was trumped by the $2.5 billion the Fox Network paid for major-league baseball rights from 2001 to '06.

The Great Denver Shootout

By ROY S. JOHNSON

The Denver Nuggets and Detroit Pistons took the floor for a routine game at McNichols Sports Arena on this date and scored the most points in pro basketball history. The following article appeared in The Times *two days later.*

NEW YORK—There was no defense in Denver Tuesday night. The game was pure run-and-gun, highlight-film basketball. Put away those zone traps, and sit back. Doug Moe loved it. Hubie Brown would have cringed. Actually, Moe would have liked it even more had his Nuggets won the record-setting, triple-overtime game against the Detroit Pistons. But to him, a noted proponent of offensive basketball, the game was the thing. Even though his team lost, 186–184, Moe said: "It was a great game. I really got into watching it. It was exhausting for both teams but there were still so many outstanding plays that it was worth it."

First, the records: The game, which lasted 3 hours 11 minutes, established three straight single-team marks. The Pistons' point total surpassed the 173 the Boston Celtics scored against the Minneapolis Lakers on Feb. 27, 1959. Detroit made 74 field goals, surpassing the previous mark of 72 set by Boston in the 1959 game. The Nuggets established a record for points by a losing team, the previous standard having been 166 by the Milwaukee Bucks in a game against the San Antonio Spurs on March 6, 1982.

There were also three two-team records. The combined total of 370 points eclipsed the mark of 337 set in the Bucks-Spurs game. The teams hit 136 field goals, beating the mark also set in that game. The total of 93 assists broke the previous record of 89 set in a game between Detroit

and the Cleveland Cavaliers on March 28, 1973. Dozens of other club records were set, and three players scored career highs. Denver's Kiki Vandeweghe and Alex English had 51 and 47, respectively. Isiah Thomas of Detroit set his new high with 47. And his teammate, John Long, equaled his high of 41. "Everybody shot the lights out," said Moe.

For a time, it did not seem as if it would be an unusual night. In the final seconds of regulation time, the Nuggets appeared to have the game won. They led, 145–143, with 6 seconds left, and Bill Laimbeer, the Piston center, had missed the first of two free throws. After a timeout, Laimbeer missed the second shot intentionally and the rebound was grabbed by Thomas, who hit a lay-in to bring on the overtime.

Denver also seemed to be the winner in the first overtime period, leading by 157–152 with 1:24 left. But Kelly Tripucka of Detroit hit a 16-footer with 32 seconds remaining to tie the score at 159-all and force a second overtime. This one was relatively uneventful. Neither team led by more than 2, and the Nugget guard Bill Hanzlik tied the score at 171–171 by hitting 2 free throws with 17 seconds left. In the third overtime, they went to 179–179 with 1:30 remaining. Long then scored on a pass by Laimbeer. As the

Kiki Vandeweghe of the Nuggets shooting over Isiah Thomas of the Pistons at Denver in the highest-scoring game in N.B.A. history. Vandeweghe scored 51 of his team's 184 points – in a losing effort. (The Denver Post)

Nuggets set up their play, Thomas stole the ball from Hanzlik and scored an easy lay-in. Thomas then hit two free throws to put his team ahead, 185–179, with seconds remaining. That was it.

Ironically, no record was set for turnovers. The Pistons' 13 and the Nuggets' 24 were normal for regulation games. "But that was the only normal thing about it," said Moe.

Runners-up

1977: Thirty people, including the entire University of Evansville basketball team and its coaches, trainers and sportscaster, were killed when a plane the school had chartered crashed and burned soon after it took off in dense fog from the Evansville airport in southwestern Indiana.

1956: The Brooklyn Dodgers traded Jackie Robinson, 36, to the New York Giants for Dick Littlefield, a journeyman pitcher, and $30,000. Robinson *(see April 10)*

retired rather than play for the hated rivals, although the Giants had offered him $60,000 to suit up in the black and gold in 1957.

1997: Charles Woodson of the University of Michigan became the first predominantly defensive player to win the Heisman Trophy, surpassing Peyton Manning, the Tennessee quarterback, in the voting. Notre Dame end Leon Hart, a pure two-way player, was the last lineman to win the award, in 1949.

December 14, 1987
Jerry Rice, a Halo for His Helmet

By ROY S. JOHNSON and WILLIAM C. RHODEN

SAN FRANCISCO—You can't help but notice the hands. Long, dark, strong and boldly decorated with rings of gold and diamonds, they command the room when Jerry Rice talks, whether he's using one finger to tickle his temple as he ponders a thought, or waving both hands to emphasize a point. When he plays football, they command the entire field. "If I wasn't playing football, I'd be doing something with my hands," Rice said one afternoon last week at the practice facility of the 49ers, situated just south of here in Redwood City, Calif. "Electronics, or maybe something with cars. It doesn't matter. I've always liked working with my hands."

During this strike-tainted season, Rice, and his hands, have boldly commanded the attention of the entire National Football League. In just his third year out of Mississippi Valley State—one of the many predominantly black universities in the South—the 25-year-old receiver has emerged as the most dangerous scoring threat in professional football. And tonight, giving the Chicago Bears a little more than they bargained for, he caught three touchdown passes, tying two National Football League records, as the 49ers trounced the Bears, 41–0.

Rice's three receptions were thrown by Steve Young, who was acquired from Tampa Bay last spring and replaced Joe Montana early in the first quarter after Montana suffered a pulled hamstring. Rice equaled the record of consecutive games with a touchdown, making it 11 in a row with a 1-yard, first-quarter reception when he lined up left, went in motion right, ran a quick out and beat the safety, Dave Duerson, for the touchdown. He is now tied in the N.F.L. record book in the con-

Jerry Rice of the 49ers grabbing a pass against the Broncos in 1994 while already preparing for a lightning sprint downfield. He was the full package in his prime: hands, eyes, speed, sinewy strength, impeccable conditioning. (Getty Images)

secutive games-with-touchdown category with Elroy Hirsch of the Los Angeles Rams and Buddy Dial of the Pittsburgh Steelers.

But what's all the more incredible is that Rice, despite missing three games during the strike, has equaled the N.F.L. record of 18 touchdown catches in one season set by Mark Clayton of the Miami Dolphins in 1984. Rice did it with his second and third touchdown receptions in the second half, for 16 yards and 2 yards. Bill Walsh, the 49ers' head coach, has worked with an arsenal of deep-threat receivers,

including Isaac Curtis, James Lofton and Charlie Joiner. "I haven't ever worked with anyone who has the great capacity or capability of Jerry Rice," said Walsh. "He's a great blocker, studies the game, he's tough, he concentrates and has tremendous athletic ability."

A breakdown of Rice's talents reveals a mosaic of skills. With his 6-foot-2-inch, 200-pound frame coiled at the line of scrimmage, Rice presents an unnerving presence. As the play begins, Rice has the deftness to clear himself of the defender. And his upper-body strength can be likened to that of Lofton, who has been noted for wresting passes from defenders. And as for breakaway speed, there isn't a more threatening receiver in the game. With defenders forced to respect his ability to carry any reception the length of the field, it's little wonder that Rice has averaged 17.1 yards with his 50 catches.

All of this sure-handed success comes two years after Rice, the 49ers' first-round draft choice in 1985, created a host of skeptics by dropping several passes during his rookie season—15, by his estimation—after tooling into training camp with a license plate that read WORLD. "That's because I caught everything in the world in college," Rice said. "But that year, I didn't know what was happening. Now, it's almost unreal. Once the ball's thrown to me, I don't hear anything. No footsteps, no crowd. And I don't see anything except the ball."

Jerry Rice finished the 1987 season with an N.F.L. record of 22 touchdown catches and extended to 13 his mark of consecutive games with at least one touchdown catch. Even early in his career, he was serving notice that he would change the way the game is played.

Runners-up

1988: CBS won an auction to televise major league baseball with a bid that paid the 26 teams nearly $1.1 billion through 1993. The agreement resulted in a wholesale rise in player salaries and led, at least indirectly, to the labor dispute that caused the cancellation of the 1994 World Series.

1969: San Diego Chargers receiver Lance Alworth, thriving under Coach Sid Gillman's West Coast offense, set a pro record by catching a pass in his 96th consecutive pro game as the A.F.L. Chargers beat the Buffalo Bills, 45–6. Alworth, dubbed "Bambi" because of his balletic grace, broke the 1945 mark of the Green Bay Packers' Don Hutson *(see Nov. 30).*

1960: Choosing No. 1 in the first expansion-team draft in baseball history, the newly created Los Angeles Angels selected right-handed pitcher Eli Grba of the Yankees. He compiled a record of 20-24 in three years with Gene Autry's club.

December 15, 1974
A Superstar Goes Free

By LEONARD KOPPETT

Jim (Catfish) Hunter wearing his Yankees uniform for the first time in January 1975. Arm trouble ended his career at age 33, but he still went to Cooperstown. His plaque reads: "The bigger the game, the better he pitched." (Associated Press)

NEW YORK—Jim (Catfish) Hunter, baseball's most successful pitcher in recent seasons, is now free to offer his services to any of the 24 major league clubs, including the Oakland A's, who failed to live up to the terms of his existing contract. As a free agent, Hunter, 28, may well command the largest bonus-and-salary arrangement in baseball history. He has been a 20-game winner four straight years and is the current American League Cy Young Award winner, coming off a 25–12 won-lost record last season.

No player with Hunter's credentials has ever been on the open market. He has won 106 games in the last five seasons, has pitched a perfect game and led the American League in earned-run averages this year. He has pitched 10 major league seasons and not one inning in the minors. But his case has no general implication for other players, or the reserve clause in general. The issue is simply the failure of Charles O. Finley, owner and operator of the A's, to carry out payments to Hunter in the way his contract required.

Last winter, they agreed on a two-year contract for $100,000 a year, but each year only $50,000 was to be paid to Hunter as straight salary; the remaining $50,000 was to be paid to some deferment plan of Hunter's choosing. The straight-salary part was paid routinely, but the deferred payments were not made because Finley disapproved of the method Hunter chose (since this seemed to involve unfavorable tax consequences for Finley). By the time the regular season ended, requests by Hunter to have the deferred payments made were still not honored, and he argued that his contract had thus been broken by Finley. If he had no contract, Hunter said, he was then a free agent.

Finley, backed by Lee MacPhail, president of the American League, insisted that no free-agent question was involved; that the only dispute was about the method of payment and that there had not been a violation of the contract but merely a difference of interpretation. He offered Hunter the other $50,000 as direct payment. Hunter, pressing his right to take the case to arbitration, was represented in a hearing by the Major League Players Association. The case was heard by Peter Seitz last month, and Seitz reached his decision late last week.

Untried high school and college players have been given bonuses as large as $100,000 just for signing, so Hunter, physically at his peak and only 28 years old, might command a deal far above $200,000.

Jim (Catfish) Hunter signed with the Yankees a few weeks later on New Year's Eve for $3.75 million over five years— triple any other player's salary. He won 23 games for them in 1975 and was a World Series starter in each of the next three seasons.

Runners-up

1946: The Chicago Bears won their fifth N.F.L. title by beating the Giants, 24–14, at the Polo Grounds as a scandal spread behind the scenes. Phone taps showed that a gambler had tried to bribe Giants fullback Merle Hapes to fix the game; Hapes rejected the offer but did mention the contact to his teammate Frank Filchock, who threw two touchdown passes before the Bears pulled away. Both players were banned for life for not informing team officials, though Filchock's suspension was later lifted.

1982: Paul (Bear) Bryant (see Nov. 28), the winningest coach in college football his-

tory at the time with 323 victories in 38 years and the shaper of stars such as Joe Namath, Ken Stabler and Babe Parilli, announced his retirement from the University of Alabama. He died of a heart attack at age 69 a month after he was succeeded by Ray Perkins, another of his former players.

1925: The third Madison Square Garden opened at Eighth Avenue and 50th Street in Manhattan as the Montreal Canadiens defeated the New York Americans, 3–1, in an N.H.L. game. The "old" Garden lasted until 1968, when it was razed and replaced by the current one at Seventh Avenue and 33rd Street.

December 16, 1973
O.J. Writes History in the Snow

By MURRAY CHASS

NEW YORK—On a day that combined the happiest moments of O.J. Simpson's career and the most emotional of Weeb Ewbank's, the Buffalo Bills defeated the Jets today, 34–14, at Shea Stadium. Simpson was happy because he had shattered Jim Brown's rushing record and become the first runner in the National Football League to gain over 2,000 yards in a season. Ewbank was emotional because he retired after 20 years of coaching pro football.

In gaining 200 yards on a snow-covered field and leading the Bills to their ninth victory against five defeats (the Jets finished with a 4–10 record), Simpson reached that lofty yardage level for a record third time this season (Brown did it twice in 1963). With the rest of the Buffalo offensive unit geared to make sure O.J. got the record—he needed 61 yards—Simpson ran for 200 on 34 carries He wound up the season with 2,003, well ahead of the 1,863 Brown amassed in 1963.

After he ran for 57 of the Bills' 71 yards on their first touchdown drive, Simpson gained the record on the first play of their next possession. With Joe DeLamielleure, the rookie right guard, knocking Mark Lomas, the right end, out of the way, Simpson broke through the left side and gained 6 yards before John Little tackled him from behind with 10:34 gone in the first quarter. The game was stopped, the other offensive players pounded Simpson on the back and hugged him. An official handed the ball to Simpson, who took it to the Bills' bench, where he was mobbed. "We were saying let's get it in the first quarter," Simpson said of the record. "But after we got it, we relaxed and I fumbled."

After the record was broken, the Bills spent the second half focusing on the attempt to raise O.J. to the unheard-of plateau of 2,000 yards. At one point early in the fourth quarter, Simpson related, "Joe Ferguson [the rookie quarterback] came in and said I needed 50 yards for 2,000. We broke 20 off right away and we were going after it then." With 6:28 left in the game, Simpson reached the mark on a 7-yard smash through left guard to the Jet 13. This time he went to the sideline and was lifted to the shoulders of his excited teammates. He did not return to the game.

"I'm really disappointed," Ewbank said after the game, his eyes red and moist from the goodbyes associated with his retirement. "I'm sorry that we didn't do better. But the kids tried. We just have to take our hats off to a great halfback."

O.J. Simpson played nine seasons with the Bills, finishing his career in 1980 after two years with the San Francisco 49ers. He worked as a television sports commentator and as an actor in movies and commercials. He became the most widely known American ever to go on trial for murder, for the killings of his wife and a male acquaintance of hers in 1995.

O.J. Simpson of the Bills dancing through the Jets' line at Shea Stadium a few quarters before becoming the first player in N.F.L. history to gain 2,000 yards in a season. It was Joe Ferguson (12) who later told him how close he was. (Associated Press)

Runners-up

1961: Wilt Chamberlain of the Philadelphia Warriors *(see March 2)* scored 50 points in a game against the Chicago Packers (currently the Washington Wizards), starting a streak of seven games in which he totaled 50 or more. Chamberlain scored at least 50 points 118 times in his career; by comparison, Michael Jordan *(see March 28)* hit for 50 points 31 times.

1945: The Cleveland Rams, who had disbanded for a year in 1943 because of World War II manpower shortages, defeated the visiting Washington Redskins, 15–14, behind the rookie quarterback Bob Waterfield for the N.F.L. title. It was the last home game the Rams ever played in Cleveland. Their owner, Dan Reeves, moved them to Los Angeles for 1946.

1930: Bobby Jones, winner of the golf Grand Slam *(see Sept. 27)*, received the first annual Sullivan Award as the amateur player who "by performance, example and influence" did the most to "advance the cause of sportsmanship." Other notable winners of the award, named after a longtime A.A.U. secretary-treasurer, are the divers Sammy Lee (1953) and Pat McCormick ('56) and the runner Jim Beatty ('62).

December 17, 1933
When the Bears Were Young Lions

CHICAGO (AP)—In a sensational forward passing battle the Chicago Bears won the national professional football championship today by beating the New York Giants, 23 to 21. The game was witnessed by 30,000 at Wrigley Field. George Halas's Bears, trailing by 21 to 16, seized victory out of the air in the dramatic closing minutes of the game. Billy Karr, right end, who learned his football at West Virginia, plucked a long lateral pass and, eluding two Giant tacklers who chased him desperately, galloped 25 yards for the deciding score.

The game was a thrilling combat of forward passing skill, desperate line plunging and gridiron strategy that kept the chilled spectators on their feet in constant excitement. The lead changed hands six times during the furious sixty minutes of play, with first the Bears holding command and then the Giants taking it away from them. The struggle was a revelation to college coaches who advocate no changes in the rules. It was strictly an offensive battle and the professional rule of allowing passes to be thrown from any point behind the line of scrimmage was responsible for most of the thrills.

The Bears' attack was led by Bronko Nagurski, former University of Minnesota plunging fullback, who individually gained 65 yards in fourteen attempts and started the forward-lateral pass that was responsible for the winning touchdown. A notable performance was turned in also by Jack Manders. The former Gopher kicked three goals from placement, one for 40 yards in four attempts, and added a goal after touchdown for a total of ten points. Harry Newman, Michigan's all-American quarterback in 1932, was the outstanding star in the Giants' attack. He tossed seventeen

passes, completing twelve for a total of 201 yards.

Hailed as the greatest offensive teams in professional football, the rivals did not waste any time in proving it, although the gridiron was slippery, particularly the grassy spots, because of mist and fog that hung over the field as the game started. No sooner did the Bears get the ball than they went right down the field. Two field goals by Manders, from the 16- and 29-yard lines, and a touchdown by the Giants' Badgro on a 29-yard pass from Newman put New York ahead by 7 to 6 at the half.

The third quarter ended with the Bears taking the lead, 16 to 14, having chalked up a touchdown with amazing speed in six plays. The Giants, however, struck back on the kickoff. They took the ball on the 26-yard line, and with a passing attack carried to the 8-yard line. There Newman wound up the spectacular display by tossing a pass to Ken Strong in the end zone for a touchdown. Strong added the extra point, and the Giants led, 21 to 16.

Then came the thrilling climax. The Bears, apparently beaten, took to the air. The first pass, Molesworth to Brumbaugh, brought the ball to the 32-yard line. The next one, hurled from the line of scrimmage, Nagurski to Hewitt, was followed by a long lateral to Karr. He caught it out

George Halas, founder and coach of the Bears, at age 38 a few months before they won the initial N.F.L. title game. A master strategist as well as an entrepreneur, he unleashed a lateral-passing offense that set the football world abuzz. (Associated Press)

in the open and started for the Giants' goal. Ken Strong and another Giant tore after him, but Ronzani, formerly of Marquette University, knocked Strong out of the way and Karr raced across the goal with the winning points.

George Halas coached the Bears for 40 years, retiring in 1967 with six N.F.L. titles.

Runners-up

1984: Dan Marino of the Miami Dolphins *(see March 13)* capped the most spectacular single-season passing display in history when he threw four touchdown passes in a 28–21 victory over the Dallas Cowboys at the Orange Bowl. Marino, in his second year as a pro, finished the regular season with a record 48 touchdown passes and 5,084 yards in the air.

1960: Charles O. Finley, an insurance man from Gary, Ind., received American League permission to buy the hapless Kansas City A's. He moved them to Oakland in 1968 and continued his P.T. Barnum–like changes, experimenting

with orange baseballs and dressing the team in yellow and green. His players won three world championships (1972–74) after he paid them to grow mustaches *(see Oct. 17)*.

1964: Six weeks after CBS-TV bought controlling interest in the Yankees, attesting to the increasing influence of television networks in sports, Mel Allen, the long time radio and television voice of the team, was fired by his new masters. The man who made "How about that!" and the home run call of "Going, going gone!" familiar to listeners had called Yankee games since 1940.

December 18, 1971
Bobby Jones, R.I.P.

[Unsigned, *The New York Times*]

Bobby Jones, the master golfer who scored an unparalleled grand slam by winning the United States and British Open and Amateur tournaments in 1930, died today at his home in Atlanta. He was 69. Mr. Jones, a lawyer by profession, who competed only as an amateur, had suffered from a progressive disease of the spinal cord since 1948. By the middle of last December he was no longer able to go to the offices of his firm, Jones, Bird & Howell, although he tried to continue working from home. Death came from an aneurysm in his chest.

NEW YORK—In the decade following World War I, America luxuriated in the Golden Era of Sports and its greatest collection of super-athletes: Babe Ruth and Ty Cobb in baseball, Jack Dempsey and Gene Tunney in boxing, Bill Tilden in tennis, Red Grange in football and Bobby Jones in golf. Many of their records have been broken now, and others are destined to be broken. But one, sports experts agree, may outlast them— Bobby Jones's grand slam of 1930.

Jones, an intense, unspoiled young man, started early on the road to success. At the age of 10, he shot a 90 for 18 holes. At 11 he was down to 80, and at 12 he shot a 70. At 9 he played against men, at 14 he won a major men's tournament and at 21 he was United States Open champion. At 28 he achieved the grand slam—victories in one year in the United States Open, British Open, United States Amateur and British Amateur championships (*see Sept. 27*). At that point, he retired from tournament golf. A nation that idolized him for his success grew to respect him even more for his decision to treat golf as a game rather than a way of life. This respect grew

with the years. "First come my wife and children," he once explained. "Next comes my profession—the law. Finally, and never as a life in itself, comes golf."

His record, aside from the grand slam, was magnificent. He won the United States Open championship four times (1923, 1926, 1929 and 1930), the British Open three times (1926, 1927 and 1930), and the United States Amateur five times (1924, 1925, 1927, 1928 and 1930). "Jones is as truly the supreme artist of golf as Paderewski is the supreme artist of the piano," George H. Greenfield wrote in The New York Times in 1930.

Success did not come easily. Though Jones was cool and calculating outwardly, he seethed inside. He could never eat properly during a major tournament. The best his stomach would hold was dry toast and tea. The pressure of tournament competition manifested itself in other ways, too. Everyone expected Jones to win every time he played, including Atlanta friends who often bet heavily on him. He escaped the unending pressure by retiring from competition.

"Why should I punish myself like this over a golf tournament," he once asked. "Sometimes I'd pass my mother and dad on the course, look at them and not even see them because I was so concentrated on the game. Afterward, it made a fellow feel a little silly."

The quality of the man projected itself, too. He was worshiped as a national hero in Scotland, the birthplace of golf. Scots would come for miles around to watch him play. In 1936, on a visit, he made an unannounced trip to the Royal and Ancient Golf Club at St. Andrews for a quiet morning round with friends. There were 5,000 spectators at the first tee and

Bobby Jones teeing off in a 1937 practice round before—as he called it—the Augusta National Invitation Tournament. Jones, co-creator of the event, accepted popular opinion the next year and renamed it the Masters. (Associated Press)

7,000 at the 18th. Businesses closed as word spread that "Our Bobby is back." In 1927, when he tapped in his final putt to win the British Open there, an old Scot stood by the green and muttered: "The man canna be human."

Off the course, Jones was convivial in a quiet way. He was a good friend and always the gentleman, though he had full command of strong language when desired. He had a fine sense of humor, and he laughed easily. He smoked cigarettes and drank bourbon.

His putting was famous. So was his putter, a rusty, goose-necked club known as Calamity Jane. His strength was driving, putting and an ability to get out of trouble. He was an imaginative player, and he never hesitated to take a chance. In fact, he seldom hesitated on any shot, and he earned an unfair reputation as a mechanical golfer. The game often baffled him. "There are times," he once said, "when I feel that I know less about what I'm doing on a golf course than anyone else in the world."

Runners-up

1932: The Chicago Bears defeated the visiting Portsmouth (Ohio) Spartans, 9–0, to decide the N.F.L.'s regular season. The contest, played one year before the first formal league championship game, was contested on an 80-yard dirt field inside Chicago Stadium because Wrigley Field was snowbound. Bronko Nagurski threw a 1-yard pass to Red Grange for the lone touchdown.

1965: Reading plays off his wristband, running back Tom Matte, inserted at quarterback by Coach Don Shula after Johnny Unitas and Gary Cuozzo had been injured, led the Baltimore Colts to a stunning 20–17 upset over the Los

Angeles Rams and a share of the Western Conference title. The Colts went no further, but Matte's feat lives on in N.F.L. lore.

1995: In a power struggle with Indianapolis Motor Speedway, car owners who hired the drivers to race there announced they would stage the United States 500 in Michigan opposite the Indy 500 the following May. The upstart race, which initially threatened the viability of Indy, lasted five years until Roger Penske, the leading car owner, capitulated, and all others returned.

December 19, 1984
Scotty Bowman's Climb

By DAVE ANDERSON

Scotty Bowman became the N.H.L.'s career leader in victories with 691 on this date when he coached the Buffalo Sabres to a 6–3 victory over the Blackhawks in Chicago. The following column appeared in The Times on Nov. 22, when he was approaching Dick Irvin's record.

NEW YORK—He stands behind the Buffalo Sabre bench with his head tilted up, his eyes darting from side to side. During a game, Scotty Bowman never smiles, never scowls. And during his career, he has never had the recognition he deserves. Not only is he about to set a record for more regular-season victories than any other coach in N.H.L. history, but his winning percentage is also an N.H.L. record and is higher than that of Red Auerbach as a basketball coach or Joe McCarthy as a baseball manager. "I just never thought," Scotty Bowman says, "I'd be behind the bench this long."

After last night's 3–2 loss to the Rangers, the 51-year-old coach still needed a victory to equal Dick Irvin's N.H.L. record of 690 in regular-season competition. Scotty Bowman, who guided the Montreal Canadiens to five Stanley Cup titles before moving to the Sabres, already holds the record for most playoff victories: 112, compared with 109 for the Islanders' Al Arbour and 100 for Dick Irvin.

Youngsters will wonder, "Who's Dick Irvin?" But old-timers remember him. So does Scotty Bowman, who was growing up in Montreal when white-haired Dick Irvin was the Canadiens' coach. "I was working for a paint company and coaching a Midget team," recalls Scotty Bowman, whose career as a left wing ended at age 17 with a skull fracture that hospitalized him for six weeks. "I took long lunch hours to go to the Forum and watch the Canadiens practice when Dick Irvin was the coach."

Three decades later, the record that Dick Irvin would set is about to be surpassed by that young man who sat there in the chill of the empty Forum. Coincidentally, a skull fracture he suffered while playing with the Chicago Black Hawks had helped persuade Dick Irvin to end his career and start coaching. "Mine happened when I was playing for the Junior Canadiens in a 1951 playoff game," Scotty Bowman recalls. "I was on a break-away when Jean-Guy Talbot hit me over the head with his stick. It was just one of those things. He came to visit me in the hospital. He was a defenseman for me when I coached in St. Louis later on."

With the Blues, the Canadiens and the Sabres over 17 years, Scotty Bowman has an N.H.L.-record .675 regular-season percentage. In the National Basketball Association, Red Auerbach's .662, compiled mostly with the Boston Celtics, is the record for coaches who have at least 500 victories. And in major league baseball, Joe McCarthy set the record among managers who have won at least 1,000 games, compiling a .609, mostly with the Yankees. Among National Football League coaches with 200 or more regular-season victories, Don Shula of the Miami Dolphins has the highest percentage: .729.

"To me, the most important element in coaching is discipline," Scotty Bowman says. Scotty Bowman has yet to lead the Sabres to the Stanley Cup final. But he recently made a typically bold move, demoting 19-year-old Tom Barrasso, the goaltender who won the Vezina Trophy

Scotty Bowman, the never-smiling coach of the Sabres, behind the bench during a victory over the Bruins in December 1984. A week and a half later he set the record for most victories in N.H.L. history. (Associated Press)

last season and was named rookie of the year, to the minor league Rochester Americans for a week. "He was having a tough time, and he was tired from the Canada Cup series," Scotty Bowman said. "I had to get him out of the net for a while." Scotty Bowman boldly demoted an all-star goaltender, and he boldly walked away from the Montreal Canadiens after four consecutive Stanley Cup titles. Maybe that's all anybody has to know as to why he is about to set a record for winning more games than any other coach in N.H.L. history.

Scotty Bowman began his N.H.L. coaching career in 1967 and retired after his ninth Stanley Cup in 2002. His regular-season career record was 1,244–583–88 with the Montreal Canadiens, Buffalo Sabres, Pittsburgh Penguins and Detroit Red Wings.

Runners-up

1965: The great Jim Brown scored his 126th and final N.F.L. touchdown and won his eighth rushing title in nine years as the visiting Cleveland Browns ended the regular season with a 27–24 victory over the St. Louis Cardinals. Brown gained 50 yards in the Lambeau Field mud in losing to the Green Bay Packers in the league's title game and never played again *(see July 13).*

1990: Bo Jackson of the Los Angeles Raiders, who had played in the major-league baseball All-Star Game in July as a member of the Kansas City Royals *(see July 11),* reached the apex of his two-sport career when was selected to play in the N.F.L. Pro Bowl game in January. But he suffered an injury in the football playoffs a few weeks before it *(see Jan. 13),* ultimately ending his twin careers.

1998: Kelly Slater of Cocoa Beach, Fla., the brightest star in surfboarding history, clinched his sixth Association of Surfing Professionals world championship in a Pipe Masters contest at the Banzai Pipeline in Oahu, Hawaii. Surfing gained popularity when Duke Kahanamoku rode longboards off Waikiki Beach around 1910.

The Deal That Stunned Baseball

By JAMES R. HARRISON

NEW YORK—In the biggest deal of modern baseball history, Rogers Hornsby, greatest batsman of the game, and manager of the world's champion St. Louis Cardinals, was traded to the Giants tonight for Frank Frisch and Pitcher Jimmy Ring. The transaction, completed over the long-distance telephone between St. Louis and New York, involves players valued at more than half a million dollars and brings to this city the second of the two outstanding figures of the sport— Babe Ruth, king of the long distance hitters, and Hornsby, six-time batting champion of the National League.

Although President Charles A. Stoneham of the Giants declared that no money was paid to the Cardinals, baseball men were unanimous in insisting that the New York club must have handed over at least $100,000, in addition to its star second baseman and a veteran pitcher who is almost at the end of his career. Hornsby, it was pointed out, is worth much more than $300,00 at present baseball prices. Several years ago John McGraw, manager of the Giants, offered $250,000 and five players for him. Not long afterward the Brooklyn club raised this figure to a straight $275,000.

Since that time Hornsby's value has increased greatly. He went on to win his sixth successive hitting championship of the league, was universally recognized as the finest right-handed batter of them all and climaxed his career last season by leading the Cardinals to the first pennant ever won by a modern St. Louis team and later to the world's championship. The rival second baseman greeted the news with a marked lack of enthusiasm. Hornsby was quoted in St. Louis as saying that "it doesn't look right that I should be traded from a club that I just managed to a world's championship."

At his home in this city Frisch, born and brought up in New York, seemed stunned by the tidings. "It's pretty hot out there, but I suppose I'll play," he said in a listless tone.

Among other things, this is the first time in baseball history that a manager has been traded within a year of his having won the world's championship. From that angle alone the trade was enough to set the baseball tongues wagging. Not since the sale of Ruth to the Yankees in 1920 has there been a baseball trade which might be compared with the trading of a world's championship manager and possibly the flashiest second baseman of any day. Last year was Hornsby's eleventh full season with the Cardinals. His first big year was 1920, when he batted .370. After reaching .397 the next year, he went over the .400 mark in 1922, 1924 and 1925. His .424 in 1924 established a new modern major league batting mark. In 1922 he hit forty-two homers, the National League record. His batting feats eclipsed even those of Delahanty and Honus Wagner. Last year he was voted the most valuable player in his league.

With Frank Frisch at second base, the Cardinals won pennants in 1928 and 1931, when he was the National League's most valuable player. In 1933 he became player-manager, and his 1934 "Gas House Gang" won the World Series. Rogers Hornsby managed the Giants for part of 1927 but was traded to the Boston Braves after one season.

Rogers Hornsby, Bob O'Farrell and Frank Frisch, from left, in 1927. Hornsby, the player-manager of the Cardinals, was traded to the Giants for Frisch, a star second-baseman, after the '26 season. O'Farrell, a catcher, became St. Louis's manager. (Bettmann/Corbis)

Runners-up

1985: Assisting on a Mike Bossy goal in a 2–2 tie with the Rangers, Denis Potvin of the Islanders picked up his 916th career point, breaking the N.H.L. record for defensemen set by Bobby Orr, then with the Chicago Blackhawks, in 1979. Potvin was perhaps the league's greatest all-around defenseman, playing on four Stanley Cup title teams.

1980: The Jets defeated the Miami Dolphins, 24–17, in a regular-season game at the Orange Bowl that was noteworthy only for the fact that it was televised by NBC with no announcers or inane sideline interviews. Executive producer Don Ohlmeyer tried the "experiment" as much to boost ratings on a lackluster game as to improve television techniques.

1983: Guy Lafleur, the great right wing who played on five Montreal Canadiens Stanley Cup teams, scored his 500th career goal in a 6–0 victory over the New Jersey Devils at the Meadowlands. He retired with 560 goals in 1991 and stood 16th on the all-time list as of the 2002–3 season.

The Snake Strikes Again

By WILLIAM N. WALLACE

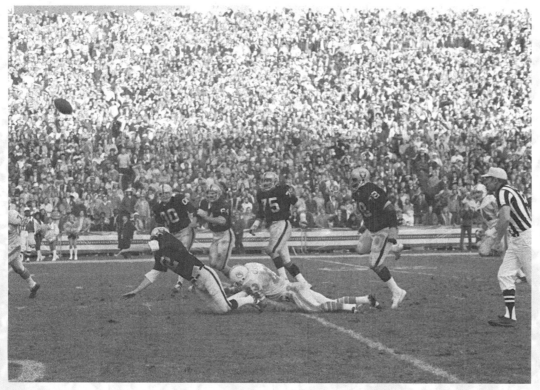

Ken Stabler of the Raiders on his knees, touchdown pass in the air, with 26 seconds left against the Dolphins in their playoff semifinal in Oakland. The play broke Miami's back, 28-26, and cemented Stabler's reputation as the Snake. (Associated Press)

OAKLAND, Calif.—The Miami Dolphins' dominance of the National Football League ended today. The Oakland Raiders beat the league's two-time defending champions, 28–26, with one of those big plays that always becomes so much a part of crucial football games. It was an 8-yard touchdown pass with 26 seconds remaining in the American Football Conference playoff contest. Ken Stabler threw the pass and Clarence Davis caught the ball in a hostile crowd five yards into the Miami end zone. The Dolphins, a remarkable team, did not go down easily.

"It was a dumb play," said Stabler afterward in recounting the event that won the game and enabled the Raiders to take a giant step toward the Super Bowl. "I never should have thrown the ball to Clarence. Or maybe I should have thrown it out of the end zone. Sometimes you get away with a dumb play and sometimes you don't."

Why was it a dumb play? "It was first down," continued Stabler, a big left-handed blond from the University of Alabama who stood waiting for an elevator with his silver and black uniform still on and beads of perspiration on his brow. The elevator would take him away from the post-game television studio back to his jubilant locker room. "It was the first down and we had plenty of time, 35 seconds left and two timeouts. Every play was going to go into the end zone anyway.

So we had three more chances coming up and things were probably going to set up better than this time. I saw Clarence. He had come back. But there were an awful lot of people around him and it didn't look like he was going to be able to catch the ball. He did. It was a great catch, but a dumb play."

Of the 60 minutes of playing time, Miami was either ahead or tied (at 7–7) to 55 minutes 58 seconds. The Dolphin lead varied from 7 points to 2 and then 5 twice. The Dolphins scored to go ahead for the final time with two minutes remaining. Finally came the last strike, the 68-yard drive in eight plays, six of them complete passes by Stabler to five different receivers.

The Snake, as Stabler is called, was the hero. On the winning play, Vern Den Herder, the Miami defensive end, had his arms around Stabler's ankles as the pass went off and the Oakland quarterback then fell to the grass. "I felt him," said Stabler. All Den Herder needed was another split second to dump Stabler and save a game that Miami had controlled during most of the afternoon. Yes, football is indeed a game of inches and tenths-of-seconds.

Ken Stabler and the Raiders lost to the Pittsburgh Steelers, 24–13, the following week in the A.F.C. championship game, but his reputation for last-second theatrics was forever established.

Runners-up

1997: Barry Sanders of the Detroit Lions ran for 184 yards in a season-ending 13–10 victory over the Jets at the Silverdome, becoming the third back in N.F.L. history—after O.J. Simpson of the Buffalo Bills in 1973 *(see Dec. 16)* and Eric Dickerson of the Los Angeles Rams in 1984 *(see Dec. 9)*—to rush for 2,000 yards in a season. Sanders abruptly quit after the next season *(see July 28)*.

1960: Philip K. Wrigley, owner of the Chicago Cubs, announced that his team would no longer use a manager in 1961 but rather a college of coaches: Charlie Grimm, Lou Boudreau, Harry Craft, Bob Kennedy and Charlie Metro. The experiment in shared wisdom ended five years later when Leo Durocher was named the skipper.

1984: Capping the evolution of women's basketball, Georgeann Wells of West Virginia University became the first woman to dunk the ball during competition in a game at Elkins, W. Va. The women's game was once a half-court affair, three players to a side. Unlimited dribbling was not introduced until 1966, and full-court play with five players to a side was not the rule until '71.

All's Well That Ended Well, 88 Years Ago

[Unsigned, *The New York Times*]

CINCINNATI—The most disastrous war that the baseball game has ever experienced came to a close here tonight when a treaty of peace between the Federal League and both parties to the national baseball agreement, known as Organized Baseball, was signed. The war has lasted about two years. The agreement gives immunity to all men who have jumped their contracts from both the major and minor leagues of Organized Baseball, as well as all other Federal League players. All of them have been reinstated or made eligible to Organized Baseball.

That there will be a wild scramble for some of the best Federal League players was clearly indicated by a provision in the treaty that the Federal League, as a league, and which, in so far as actual baseball playing is concerned, ceases to exist. The agreement does not go into the distribution of any players, and it was announced that the bars have been thrown down, and that inasmuch as all are eligible, those who are for sale will probably go to the highest bidder.

In this connection rumors flew thick and fast here tonight regarding the future status of a number of Federal League players. One of these, despite the lack of confirmation, was that Benny Kauff of the Brooklyn Tip-Tops of the Federal League would be seen next season in a Giant uniform. Semi-officially it became known that several former Federal players will be seen on the New York American League club.

Two Federal League owners were allowed to purchase existing major league teams. Charles Weeghman, who has been President of the Chicago Whales, will take controlling interest of the Chicago Cubs of the National League from Charles P. Taft of

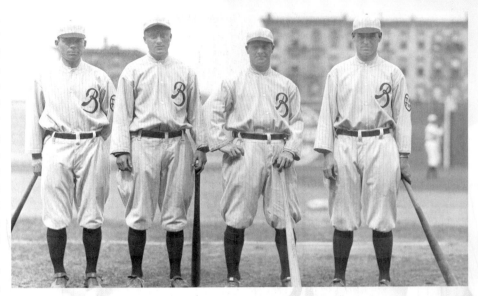

Members of the Federal League Brooklyn Tip-Tops at their Washington Park grounds in 1915. Outfielder Benny Kauff, second from right, was much in demand when the circuit folded after two seasons. (Corbis)

Cincinnati. Philip Hall and his associates, who were connected with the St. Louis Terriers, will gain control of the St. Louis Browns of the American League from Robert Hedges, John E. Bruce, and others. It was announced late tonight that all suits pertaining to baseball pending in any court would be withdrawn in the next day or two.

These other conditions of the agreement became clear: Players from the Federal League clubs in Chicago and St. Louis will join the respective clubs Mr. Weeghman and Mr. Hall and his associates will operate in the National and American Leagues, although the contracts of all other Federal League players will be sold to the highest bidders. And the National and American League will reimburse the Ward interests in the Brooklyn Federal League club, authoritatively stated to be $400,000.

When asked tonight as to the future status of Roger Bresnahan, Charles H. Weeghman, who will purchase the Cubs, said: "I don't know what disposition will be made of Bresnahan. Tinker, of course, will be our manager, and that is as far as I have taken up the question of players." When asked what disposition would be made of the suit of the Federal League against organized baseball charging violation of the anti-trust law, now pending before Judge Landis in Chicago, President John K. Tener of the National League, acting as spokesman, said: "The suit will be withdrawn."

The Federal League's capitulation ended a major threat to baseball, but all was not over. Its Baltimore franchise opted to pursue the antitrust suit all the way to the United States Supreme Court. The result was the famous 1922 decision by Justice Oliver Wendell Holmes that gave major-league baseball exemption to operate in restraint of competition. No rival circuit has since competed against the American and National Leagues.

Runners-up

1957: After hearing the San Francisco 49ers celebrating their 27–7 halftime lead through the thin walls of Kezar Stadium, the Detroit Lions scored 24 unanswered points behind the passing of Tobin Rote and the running of Tom Tracy to win the Western Conference title game, 31–27. The Lions defeated the Cleveland Browns for the N.F.L. championship, their last, one week later.

1894: The United States Golf Association, which sets the rules for the game in addition to administering the United States Open, was founded in New York City at a meeting of delegates from five clubs: Newport (R.I.) Golf Club; St. Andrew's Golf Club in Yonkers, N.Y.; The Country Club in Brookline, Mass.; Shinnecock Hills Golf Club in Southampton, N.Y.; and the Chicago Golf Club.

1985: Roger Craig of the San Francisco 49ers, an equally superb runner and pass catcher, became the first N.F.L. player to gain 1,000 yards both rushing and receiving in a single season in a 31–16 victory over the Dallas Cowboys at Candlestick Park. Marshall Faulk accomplished the feat in 1999 with the St. Louis Rams.

December 23, 1972
The 'Immaculate Reception'

By WILLIAM N. WALLACE

Franco Harris (32) of the Steelers scoring the winning touchdown after his "Immaculate Reception" playoff catch. The N.F.L.'s first use of TV replays showed that Terry Bradshaw's desperation pass bounced seven yards in a huge arc off the Raiders' Jack Tatum — right into Harris's mitts. (Associated Press)

PITTSBURGH—Television helped decide a pro football game today, the cameras re-enforcing a decision made on the field by the referee about a 60-yard touchdown play that won the game for the Pittsburgh Steelers over the Oakland Raiders, 13–7, with five seconds left. The touchdown was scored by Franco Harris, who caught a deflected pass. The football bounced off the body of Jack Tatum, the Raider safety man, went back seven yards in a big arc, Harris caught it, and then ran 42 yards for the winning touchdown.

What had to be decided by Fred Swearingen, the referee, was that the ball indeed touched Tatum, who had collided with Harris's teammate, Frenchy Fuqua, at the Oakland 35-yard line. The rule is that no two receivers can touch the ball con-secutively on the same play. The play could not legally have gone from Terry Bradshaw, the Steeler quarterback, to Fuqua to Harris without Tatum in between. Swearingen ruled that the ball touched Tatum, which made legal the ricochet to Harris. He was summoned to a field telephone by Art McNally, the National Football League's supervisor of officials, who was in the press box. McNally had access to the instant replay on television. "How do you rule?" McNally asked. "Touchdown," replied Swearingen. "That's right," said McNally. Score one for man's technology, in this case camera and film.

The play was probably a first for football because of the confirmation by television. "I've been playing football ever since the second grade and I haven't ever seen anything like this," said Bradshaw, who had no idea how the ball wound up in the hands of Harris in the end zone. As far as Tatum is concerned, the play was illegal and the touchdown fraudulent. He said that he and Fuqua got to the ball at the same time. "All I was trying to do was knock the ball loose," he said. "I touched the man [Fuqua], but not the ball." The Raiders, however, were not going to make a big issue out of the result. John Madden, the Oakland coach, in his post-game comments indicated from his view the football had indeed touched Tatum.

The situation was dramatic, too. Oakland, stymied all afternoon by the great Steeler defense, had mounted a last-minute touchdown drive and had suddenly gone ahead, 7–6. Ken Stabler, the quarterback who had replaced Daryle Lamonica at the start of the final quarter, had run 30 yards down the sideline for the Raider touchdown with only 1 minute 13 seconds left to play. All the Oakland team had to do was hold the Steelers one more time and not let them get past midfield so Roy Gerala might have a try at a long field goal.

Starting from his 20-yard line, Bradshaw threw five straight passes, two broken up by the ubiquitous Tatum, one of many defensive stars in this playoff contest. The fifth pass, blindly thrown downfield in the general direction of Fuqua, was the play that won the game. The football whistled over the head of Harris and then took its big bounce backward. "Sure, I was damn lucky," said Harris. Chuck Noll, the Steeler coach, never saw the touchdown. "But I could tell from the crowd noise. We never gave up and that was the story of our year. The pass defense was getting tired and that is how Stabler broke out and scored," he said.

Al Davis, the managing general partner of the Raiders, was all but speechless. "It's hard to believe," he said as the touchdown play slowly sunk in. Madden, his coach, said with disgust, "To lose like that!" But there was no defense against a bizarre play, a game-winning carom shot that had to be seen over and over again on television film to be believed and confirmed.

The Pittsburgh Steelers lost to the Miami Dolphins in the A.F.C. championship game at home the following week. The once moribund franchise was on the rise, however, and had won four Super Bowl titles by 1980.

Runners-up

1975: In a landmark decision, Peter Seitz, a labor arbitrator hearing baseball's case against pitchers Andy Messersmith and Dave McNally, ruled that they were no longer bound to their contracts with the Los Angeles Dodgers and the Baltimore Orioles and therefore could sell their services to the highest bidder. The ruling quickly had a marked effect on the movement of players between teams and the salaries they were paid.

1944: James F. Byrnes, the United States director of war mobilization, ordered that all horse racing operations cease within two weeks because of the sport's drain on manpower, tires and gasoline that could better be used in the war effort. An announcement on V-E Day (May 8, 1945) lifted the ban, and the Kentucky Derby was held on June 9.

1982: Chaminade College, which had a student body of 850 and whose program was only seven years old, upset top-ranked Virginia and the imposing Ralph Sampson, 77–72, in Honolulu. Referring to the famous Sampson–Patrick Ewing meeting earlier (see Dec. 11), the Cavaliers' Jim Miller said, "In less than two weeks we won the game of the century and lost the upset of the century."

December 24, 1950
'The Toe' Boots the Rams

By LOUIS EFFRAT

Quarterback Otto Graham on a scamper against the Rams in the Browns' 30-28 victory in the 1950 N.F.L. title game in Cleveland. The Browns, 49ers and Baltimore Colts had entered the league the previous December. (Associated Press)

CLEVELAND—It was the day before Christmas and all through the house 29,751 rabid rooters hoping for a miracle, while gazing gloomily at the clock, all but gave up on the Cleveland Browns in their National Football League championship play-off against the Los Angeles Rams today. But the Browns, who never have lost a play-off, did not give up on themselves and with a successful last-gasp effort became monarchs of all they survey in the gridiron world.

The seemingly impossible—impossible because of the time element—came to pass when, with only twenty seconds remaining in a spectacularly fought contest over Municipal Stadium's frozen turf, Lou Groza booted a perfect 16-yard field goal. Groza's specialty—he did it twice against the Giants last week—turned an almost certain 28–27 setback into a glorious 30–28 victory for the Browns. All of a sudden it was a "joyeux noel" for Paul Brown's charges, who, despite the herculean efforts of Otto Graham, spent most of the cold afternoon trailing Joe Stydahar's Pacific Coast representatives. In the end, it was somewhat ironic that so flashy an aerial duel between Graham and Bob Waterfield should be decided by a placement kick from the very same distance at which Waterfield had barely missed a 3-pointer in the second period.

Between intermittent snow flurries, a 28-mile-an-hour wind that blew in from Lake Erie and the 29-degree temperature, Graham completed 22 of 32 passes, four for touchdowns and an over-all 298 yards. Waterfield fired only one 6-pointer, but his 18 completions in 31 attempts gained 312 yards. Four of Waterfield's thrusts were intercepted by the victors.

It will be recalled that before peace came to professional football, the Browns, under the guidance of their canny coach, annexed every All-American Conference crown. There were some who attempted to discredit Brown's accomplishments on the basis of a weak league. "Just wait until he gets into the National League," they said. And after four years of monotonous winning in the A.A.C., Brown and his Browns joined the National. This, the first season, was a rough one, but aside from two defeats by Steve Owen's Giants, whom they conquered, 8–3, in the American Conference play-off a week ago, it was not rough enough to make a difference. Nor was it tough enough to stymie them today.

With a first down at the Rams' 11 on the final series, Graham looked up, saw 40 seconds remaining and tried a quarterback sneak. Unmindful of gaining, Otto's plan was to run diagonally in order to put the ball nearer to the center. He gained only a yard, but his principal purpose had been served. It was only second down, but Graham was confident that Groza's talented toe, which had kicked fifteen field goals this year, would do it again. A hush fell over the stadium as the teams lined up for the most important play of the game. Earlier, Tom James, the holder for Groza's placements, had been unable to handle a low pass from center following the second Cleveland touchdown. A similar occurrence would be ruinous. This time, however, everything went smoothly. James took the perfect pass from center, spotted it perfectly on the 16 and Groza booted it perfectly through the uprights.

Runners-up

1969: Outfielder Curt Flood (see Jan. 16) fired a warning shot across the bow of baseball when he said in a letter to Commissioner Bowie Kuhn that his trade from the St. Louis Cardinals to the Philadelphia Phillies should be voided and that he should be made a free agent. "After 12 years in the major leagues," he said, "I do not feel I am a piece of property to be bought and sold irrespective of my wishes."

1961: The Houston Oilers won the American Football League championship for the second straight season, defeating the host San Diego Chargers, 10–3. George Blanda threw a 35-yard touchdown pass to Billy Cannon and kicked a 46-yard field goal. The Oilers never won another A.F.L. or N.F.L. title, moving to Tennessee as the Titans in 1997.

1977: In one of the most memorable playoff games in N.F.L. history, the Oakland Raiders defeated the Baltimore Colts, 37–31, at Memorial Stadium. Ken Stabler (see Dec. 21) threw a 10-yard pass to tight end Dave Casper for the victory 58 seconds into the second overtime. The Raiders then lost to the Denver Broncos in the A.F.C. title game.

December 25, 1971
The Longest Game

By MURRAY CHASS

KANSAS CITY—Garo Yepremian, a baldish, left-footed Cypriot who makes neckties in the offseason, kicked a 37-yard field goal in the second quarter of sudden-death overtime today, giving the Miami Dolphins a 27–24 victory over the Kansas City Chiefs in the longest pro football game ever played. The immediate result, which left the Chiefs and most of the 50,374 partisan fans stunned and numbed, sends the Dolphins into the American Conference championship game next Sunday. But long after this season's playoffs are forgotten, this game will remain embedded in the memories of those who saw it in person or on television as a historical event— one that took 82 minutes 40 seconds to complete.

Ironically, it was the Chiefs, who, as the Dallas Texans, won the previously longest game— the 1962 American League championship affair at Houston that ended after 77 minutes 54 seconds with the Texans beating the Oilers, 20–17, on Tommy Brooker's 25-yard field goal. The Chiefs, the A.F.C.'s Western champion, had two distinct chances to win the game before Yepremian swung his left foot in his soccer-style manner and put the Eastern champion Dolphins into a championship game for the first time in their six-year existence.

The man who had, and missed, both chances was Jan Stenerud, the Norwegian soccer-style kicker who beat out Yepremian on the A.F.C. team for the N.F.L. All-Star game next month, despite having

scored 7 fewer points than Garo's league-leading total of 117. ("I came to Kansas City determined to show them I'm a good kicker," Yepremian said.) With 31 seconds remaining in regulation time and the game tied, 24–24, Stenerud sent a 31-yard field-goal try wide to the right. Then, after Len Dawson won the coin toss and the Chiefs

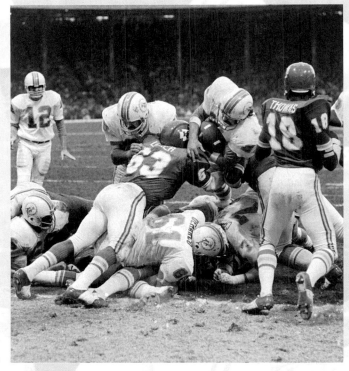

The Dolphins' Jim Kiick, with ball, is stopped at the goal line by Willie Lanier (63) of the Chiefs as Larry Csonka attempts to block Lanier and Bob Griese (12) looks on. Miami won after 22 minutes 40 seconds of overtime. (Associated Press)

received the kickoff in the first overtime period, Kansas City marched to the Miami 35. This time Stenerud tried a field goal from the 42, but the snap from center was a little high and Nick Buoniconti, the man who lost the coin toss, smashed through and blocked the kick.

Finally, with 3 minutes gone in the second overtime period, the Dolphins got the ball at their 30. For the next five plays, Jim

Kiick and Larry Csonka, the team's high-powered running duo who hadn't had too much success in the game, took turns carrying the ball. Kiick ran for 5 on the first play and then Csonka, the Sundance Kid to Kiick's Butch Cassidy, darted through a tremendous hole in the left side of the line and charged 29 yards to the Kansas City 36, a play that turned out to be the most significant run of the long, unusually warm (63 degrees) day.

Three plays later, with the ball on the 30, the 5-foot-7-inch Yepremian came onto the field and the Kansas City fans tensed. Mike Kolen snapped the ball, Karl Noonan placed it down at the 37 and Yepremian kicked. The ball shot above the outstretched, yearning hands of the Kansas City linemen and floated steadily toward the goal posts. It went between the uprights, the official in the end zone raised his arms and the Dolphins, almost as one, leaped into the air with their arms raised in triumph. The Chiefs stood disbelievingly for a moment, then slowly started trudging off the Municipal Stadium field for the last time.

Don Shula's Miami Dolphins shut out the Baltimore Colts, 21–0, the following week in the A.F.C. championship game, though they fell to the Dallas Cowboys, 24–3, in the Super Bowl as Tom Landry won his first league title. The following year the Dolphins went 17–0 in the regular and postseason (see Jan. 14), becoming the only undefeated team in N.F.L. history.

Runners-up

1984: In the midst of another hot streak (*see Feb. 1*), Bernard King, the Knicks' one-man team of the 80's, scored a team-record 60 points in a 120–114 loss to the New Jersey Nets at Madison Square Garden. The display came in the N.B.A.'s traditional Christmas Day game, patterned after the N.F.L. holiday game that years earlier had co-opted Thanksgiving.

1995: Emmitt Smith (*see Oct. 27*) of the Dallas Cowboys ran for his 25th touchdown of the season, breaking the N.F.L. record set by John Riggins of the

Washington Redskins in 1983, as the Cowboys defeated the Arizona Cardinals, 37–13, at Sun Devil Stadium in Tempe.

2001: Hideki Matsui became the highest-paid player in Japanese baseball when he signed a $4.7 million contract with the Yomiuri Giants. The next December he signed a three-year $21 million contract with the New York Yankees, following the Seattle Mariners' Ichiro Suzuki to the United States and helping globalize the national pastime.

December 26, 1960
The Dutchman's Golden Game

By ARTHUR DALEY

PHILADELPHIA—This was the Dutchman's day. Norm Van Brocklin didn't score a point as the Philadelphia Eagles outfinessed the Green Bay Packers for the National Football League championship at Franklin Field on this surprisingly warm and pleasant afternoon. But Van was a towering figure who dominated the proceedings. He threw passes with exquisite mastery. He probed Packer defenses with the delicacy of a surgeon and constantly made the bold strokes that assured success. But he contributed far more than brain and brawn. He communicated his own unconquerable spirit to the Eagles and kept their desire at a fever pitch.

Before the game the Dutchman was perched on a trunk at the entrance to the clubhouse, a benign Buddha with legs crossed and a smile lighting his features. He has a cheery word for everyone, a psychological mass hypnosis of sorts. "The field will be all right," he said. "Everything's gonna be all right." Across the field the Packers climbed into battle garb amid funereal silence. But the Dutchman had the Eagles laughing and joking. He is a compulsive laugher. He had tension broken even before it could develop.

And the Eagles played that way—loose and carefree. They looked disaster in the eye in the opening minute when a lateral by Van Brocklin was plucked out of the air by Bill Quinlan of the Packers for a first down on the Eagle 14. But the Philadelphians checked an apparently certain Green Bay score and then twice rallied to win, 17–13, just as the Dutchman had been telling them they would all along.

Van is such a cool and confident operative. In the second quarter he waited for Tommy McDonald to break clear in a cross-over pass pattern and hit him for 22 yards. Then he meandered toward the sideline and practically yawned in another lazy wait for the swift McDonald. The speed boy broke free in the corner and Van hit him for 35 yards and a touchdown. It had to be a jolt to Green Bay morale. A few moments later Van changed gears slightly and pitched to Pete Retzlaff for 41 yards to set up a field goal by Bobby Walston. Later he boomed one to McDonald for 33 yards. And as soon as he had the Packers as overhead-conscious as air raid wardens, he'd strike along the ground. This was all Van Brocklin. There was no other way to measure it.

If there was to be a secondary hero to Van Brocklin, he had to be Chuck Bednarik, a 35-year-old iron man who played on both offensive and defensive platoons for every scrimmage play. He knocked Paul Hornung, the league scoring leader, out of action with a rib-rattling tackle early in the third period. He recovered a fumble that stopped a promising Packer march in the fourth. Time was running out on Green Bay as the Packers mounted their last threat. With Bart Starr doing the pitching, they moved 55 yards to the Eagle 10. There, Bednarik made a bull-dogging dive onto Jim Taylor, the great Packer fullback, and wrestled him to earth. The gun boomed to signal the end of the game. It almost looked as if Bednarik had been shot in the britches. He leaped high in the air but came down dancing. Other green shirts joined him in impromptu jigs of joy. The Eagles had won.

Norm Van Brocklin (11) working on the Packers as if with a scalpel in the Eagles' N.F.L. title game victory in Philadelphia. Intimidating Chuck Bednarik (60), far right, lined up for the Eagles on every offensive and defensive play. (Bettmann/Corbis)

Runners-up

1908: Jack Johnson of Galveston, Tex., aged 30, became the first black heavyweight champion when he knocked out Tommy Burns of Canada in the 14th round of their bout in Sydney, Australia. Johnson reigned for more than six years until being dethroned by Jess Willard in 1915 (see April 5).

1954: Otto Graham passed for three touchdowns and ran for three more in leading the Cleveland Browns to a 56–10 rout of the visiting Detroit Lions in the N.F.L. championship game. The Lions had won two titles in a row (see Dec. 27) under quarterback Bobby Layne and halfback Doak Walker; the Browns again won the championship the following year in Graham's final season.

1964: Led by quarterback Jack Kemp and running back Cookie Gilchrist, the Buffalo Bills defeated the San Diego Chargers, 20–7, to win their first of two A.F.L. championships. Kemp, who retired in 1970 after 13 years with the Los Angeles Chargers and the Bills, became a United States congressman and a Republican presidential contender in the 80's.

The Owner Who Scores

By CHUCK FINDER

PITTSBURGH—After a 45-month hiatus, the puck still danced on his blade, the stick still shook down magic, the goal-light still glowed red around him and the atmosphere still crackled. It almost did not seem to matter that, for so long, he had traded hockey immortality for retiree golf and then for the board-room, playing with a puck on ice only twice in nearly three and a half years. Mario Lemieux made a historic return to hockey tonight, descending from the Mellon Arena's owner's box to score a goal and add two assists in a 5–0 Penguins victory over Toronto.

Perhaps hockey watchers should expect nothing less from a player who scored a goal on his first National Hockey League shift and first N.H.L. shot, scored the first time he skated on Penguins home ice, scored in his first game upon his return from cancer radiation therapy. Perhaps it was only fitting that the only player in pro hockey annals to average 2-plus points a game made this triumphant return with 3 points. And perhaps the fairy tale was supposed to read this way: First shift, first point.

It took only 1,340 days for Lemieux to register assist No. 882 of a career in which the Hall of Fame waiting period was waived for his post-retirement induction in late 1997. It only took 33 seconds of this comeback—unofficially the fourth in his 13-year, fits-and-spurts career—for Lemieux to notch that assist. He skated behind the Maple Leafs' Curtis Joseph and feathered a pass directly in front of the sprawling goaltender. Linemate Jan Hrdina missed the setup, but Jaromir Jagr did not. Jagr scored a nanosecond before Toronto's Dmitry Yuskevich shoved Jagr into the goal, dislodging it from its moor-ings. The standing-room-only crowd of 17,148 rejoiced loud-er than it had when Lemieux entered the Arena for warm-ups and pregame intro-ductions, louder than it had when his retired No. 66 was lowered from the rafters.

Lemieux logged nearly nine minutes of ice time in that first period, about half of what he intended to play over all to jump-start a comeback that he considered far easier than his returns from back surgery (three months off in 1991), Hodgkin's radiation treatments (one month off in 1993) and a year's rest (1995). Then, in the second period, he scored his first goal since Game 5 of the 1997 playoffs against Philadelphia. No. 614 of his career came at 10 minutes 33 sec-onds as Jagr made a splendid, swooping play around the right circle, then passed to a new linemate who yelled simply "Yags!" Lemieux swatted the resulting pass between Joseph's legs for a 3–0 Pittsburgh lead.

Mario Lemieux acknowledging fans in 2002 after scoring his 1,600th point. He returned to the ice in 2000 as the first player-owner in N.H.L. history after a four-year layoff. (Reuters)

"It was a great experience," said Lemieux, who holds the titles of owner, chairman, president, chief executive officer and center. "It was a moment I will cherish."

Runners-up

1967: William (Red) Holzman was named head coach of the Knicks to succeed Dick McGuire. Shaping a young team with the likes of Willis Reed (see May 8), Walt Frazier, Bill Bradley and Dave DeBusschere, Holzman turned the franchise around and won two N.B.A. titles and three conference championships before retiring in 1982.

1953: Bobby Layne, the former University of Texas All-American, hit Jim Doran with a 33-yard touchdown pass with 2:08 left in the game at Briggs Stadium and Doak Walker kicked the extra point to give the Detroit Lions a 17–16 victory over the Cleveland Browns and their second straight N.F.L. championship. Their third and last title was in 1957.

1992: Sterling Sharpe of the Green Bay Packers made six catches against the Minnesota Vikings, giving him an N.F.L.-record 108 receptions for the season. As rule changes aggressively favored passing, Sharpe raised the mark to 112 in 1993. Herman Moore of the Detroit Lions broke it with 123 in '95 and Marvin Harrison of the Indianapolis Colts took it to 143 in 2002.

December 28, 1958
Pro Football's Defining Moment

By LOUIS EFFRAT

NEW YORK—Time and fortune finally ran out on professional football's Cinderella team, the Giants, yesterday at Yankee Stadium. And so it was that the Baltimore Colts, with a 23–17 victory, won the championship of the National Football League. With a couple of minutes to go in the fourth period, the Giants seemed to have the triumph in their grasp. But with seven seconds to go, Baltimore tied the score at 17–17 on a field goal. Then, in a sudden-death overtime period, the Baltimore team coached by Weeb Ewbank fashioned the winning touchdown after 8 minutes 15 seconds. The excitement generated by football's longest game left most of the 64,185 spectators limp. Aside from an experimental exhibition contest, it was the first sudden-death game (with victory going instantly to the first team to score) in the league.

Alan (The Horse) Ameche, who had plunged for a 2-yard touchdown in the second quarter, drove over from the 1 for the tally that crushed the New Yorkers. Ameche was a hero, but he was not *the* hero. The 15,000 fans who had made the trip from Baltimore could have pointed to any one of a number of outstanding Colts. Johnny Unitas was the man who engineered the dynamic offensive that moved the visitors from the shadow of defeat to the glory of their ultimate success. Then there was Steve Myrha, who kicked a 20-yard field goal at 14:53 of the fourth quarter. Not to be ignored was the spectacular pass-catching of Ray Berry, the end, who captured twelve of

Unitas' aerials for a gain of 178 yards. The receptions and yardage were championship play-off records.

The Giants, too, had their share of standouts in what was easily the most dramatic, most exciting encounter witnessed on the pro circuit in many a season. Some voiced the opinion that it was the "great-

Alan Ameche of the Baltimore Colts scores the winning touchdown in the N.F.L. championship game against the Giants 8 minutes 15 seconds into overtime. Lenny Moore (24) makes a pivotal block on Emlen Tunnell, left, as Johnny Unitas (19), rear, looks on. (Associated Press)

est game I've ever seen." Among those who expressed that sentiment was Bert Bell, the commissioner of the N.F.L.

The Giants, after it appeared that they had fumbled away their chance for the championship, stormed back from a 14–3 deficit at the half. With the 37-year-old Charley Conerly turning in a magnificent job of passing and quarterbacking, the New Yorkers made an almost incredible comeback. Mel Triplett scored on a dive from the 1 for the Giants' third-period touchdown. A 15-yard aerial from Conerly

to Frank Gifford accounted for the touchdown that moved the Giants ahead early in the fourth quarter. It was fitting that Gifford, who carried Baltimore's Milt Davis over the goal line on his back, recorded the 6-pointer. Two fumbles by Gifford were recovered by the Colts and led to two Baltimore touchdowns earlier in the game.

When the visitors put the ball in play on their final drive in regulation time, they were 86 yards from the goal. Behind by 17–14, they had 1 minute 56 seconds to go the distance. Unitas missed with a toss to L.G. Dupre, losing four seconds. Then he hit Lenny Moore with an 11-yarder at the cost of 22 seconds. Another aerial failed, but the next, to Berry, was good for 25 yards. Then, twice in succession, it was Unitas to Berry for 16 and 21 yards. Suddenly the Colts were on the 13 yard-line. The seconds continued to tick away. When Myrha put his toe to the ball on the 20 and sent the ball through the uprights, only seven seconds remained. Then the first official overtime period in N.F.L. history began, and little more than eight minutes later it was over on Ameche's final plunge.

The 1958 championship, which came to be called the Greatest Game Ever Played, was a watershed for the N.F.L. Though by no means a minor sport before, pro football lacked baseball's mass appeal. Now, with network television coming of age, football's popularity and fortunes soared. In the end it was one game and one touchdown that changed everything.

Runners-up

1975: In one of his heroic moments as Dallas's quarterback, Roger Staubach threw a 50-yard "Hail Mary" touchdown pass to Drew Pearson with 24 seconds left to give the visiting Cowboys a 17–14 victory over the Minnesota Vikings in a divisional playoff game. The Cowboys lost in the '76 Super Bowl to the Pittsburgh Steelers.

1968: Arthur Ashe, a 25-year-old Army lieutenant fresh from winning the United States Open *(see Sept. 9)*, played a key role in the United States Davis Cup team's 4–1 victory over Australia that returned the Cup to the United States

for the first time since 1963. Ashe *(see Feb. 6)* also helped lead American triumphs in the Davis Cup in 1969 and '70.

1947: Elmer Angsman, who raced for two 70-yard scores, and Charlie Trippi, who ran for a 44-yard touchdown, led the Chicago Cardinals over the Philadelphia Eagles, 28–21, for the N.F.L. title at Comiskey Park. This is the only championship that the Cardinals, a founding member of the N.F.L., have won in their 72 years.

December 29, 1978
The Punch Heard 'Round the Gator Bowl

JACKSONVILLE, Fla. (AP)—Coach Woody Hayes, irate after Charlie Bauman, Clemson's middle guard, intercepted an Ohio State pass tonight in the final two minutes of Clemson's 17–15 Gator Bowl victory, went after Bauman after he was run out of bounds on the Ohio State sideline. Hayes grabbed Bauman and touched off a brief bench-emptying melee.

It was not clear whether Hayes had landed any punches, but Bauman said after the game, "I was hit, I don't know by who." When asked again a few minutes later, Bauman said, "I'm not saying anything." Jonathan Brooks, a Clemson defensive end, said: "A lot of players said Woody hit him. It looked like he did. I was in the middle of a whole bunch of people trying to get out of there." It took officials several minutes to clear the field. Hayes received an unsportsmanlike conduct penalty. The Buckeye coach did not appear at a press conference after the game, sending George Hill, his defensive coordinator, in his place. Hill said: "I didn't see it. I was there, but still couldn't see. Whatever it was was certainly unfortunate."

Bauman's interception spoiled a dazzling performance by Ohio State's freshman quarterback, Art Schlichter, who completed 16 of 20 passes for 205 yards. The triumph by Clemson made Danny Ford, who took over when Coach Charley

Pell accepted the head coaching job at the University of Florida after the regular season, a success in his first game as head coach. The loss was the fourth Bowl defeat in the last five years for the Buckeyes. Ford refused to criticize Hayes. "I've got an idea what happened," he said, "but I'm not saying. I think my players conducted themselves on the field with class."

Obed Ariri's 47-yard field goal and Cliff Austin's 1-yard touchdown plunge had given Clemson a 17–9 third-quarter lead, and Schlichter had scored on a 2-yard run to cut Clemson's lead to 17–15. But Clemson's Jim Stuckey and Eddie Geathers dropped Schlichter on a 2-point conversion try with 8:11 left in the game, and the Tigers' defense later held off an Ohio State rally and finally ignited Hayes's temper. Steve Fuller completed 9 of 20 passes for Clemson, although he fumbled three times—the last one setting up Ohio State's ill-fated final drive at midfield.

Woody Hayes's punch was the most shocking episode of a coach or manager attacking a player in American sports history. He was dismissed the next day after 28 years as the Ohio State coach. Hayes, 65, led the Buckeyes to three national championships (1954, '57 and '68) and four undefeated seasons.

Buckeye Coach, Woody Hayes, who had to be restrained by one of his players after he apparently punched Clemson's Charlie Bauman along the sideline at The Gator Bowl. Bauman had made a key interception at the end of the game. (Bettmann/Corbis)

Runners-up

1963: George Halas (*see Dec. 17*) won his sixth and final N.F.L. championship game as coach of the Chicago Bears as they defeated the Giants, 14–10, on the frozen turf at Wrigley Field. The Papa Bear retired in 1967 after serving the team as owner, player, coach, promoter, general manager, and traveling secretary—virtually every job available.

1963: Chuck McKinley and Dennis Ralston returned the Davis Cup to the United States for the first time in five years by defeating Australia, three matches to two, in Adelaide, Australia. McKinley outlasted John Newcombe in four sets for

the decisive victory. As of 2002 the United States had won 31 Davis Cup titles since annual competition began in 1900; Australia was second with 20 championships.

1934: The first college basketball doubleheader was held at Madison Square Garden in New York by the promoter Ned Irish, who popularized the game. He rented the Garden for $4,000 and watched 16,000 fans show up. N.Y.U. defeated Notre Dame, 25–18, in the opener, and Westminster (Pa.) upended St. John's, 37–33, in the nightcap.

December 30, 1936
A Sophomore's Great Leap Forward

By FRANCIS J. O'RILEY

A revolution occurred in college basketball when Hank Luisetti, a Stanford University sophomore, began shooting running one-handed shots in 1936. Until his prototype "jumper," players attempted either the layup or the two-handed set shot, in which their feet stayed planted on the floor.

NEW YORK—Stanford University's fine basketball team finally put an end to Long Island University's long string of victories tonight with a 45-to-31 triumph in the second game of the doubleheader at Madison Square Garden. In the opening contest Georgetown made it a clean sweep for the visiting teams by scoring over New York University, 46 to 40.

A record crowd for the season in New York, 17,623, attended the twin bill. New York spectators, who had heard, with considerable skepticism, of the prowess of the [Stanford] Indians after their fine performance against Temple, were unanimous in their opinion that, if anything, the visitors were under-estimated. They combined shooting which was as good as any ever seen in New York with a defense so effective that the vaunted power of the Blackbirds, who had been averaging better than a point a minute for the last two seasons, was not in evidence at any time.

The defeat was the first in forty-four starts for Long Island and marked the termination of the longest winning streak in the country for a major team. The Blackbirds had not been upset since the game with Duquesne on the Garden court in 1935. It was the sixth victory in a row for Stanford this season and was in the nature of a personal triumph for Hank Luisetti, who has been hailed as one of the best players ever to perform in the East.

The Coast sensation surpassed everything that had been said about him. In addition to showing the way to the scorers of both teams with 15 points, he was the best play-maker of the night. [Luisetti left his mark on the game by making a number of running one-handed shots, released from aside his right ear. This unusual method of shooting while in full motion had heretofore not been seen in the East.] It seemed that Luisetti could do nothing wrong. Some of his shots would have been deemed foolhardy if attempted by any other player, but with Luisetti doing the heaving, these were accepted by the crowd as a matter of course. He took the ball on almost every out-of-bound play.

The Coast outfit did not seem to have any set style of offense or defense. Its plays were set up on the spur of the moment. Long Island, in reaching the end of its string, fought hard, but was powerless against the team from the Pacific Coast, which gave one of the finest demonstrations seen in this section in many years.

Nat Holman, the City College of New York basketball coach, said afterward: "That's not basketball. If my boys ever shot one-handed, I'd quit coaching." Soon hundreds of players were shooting one-handers while on the move. By the 1950's virtually all players were shooting an elevated jumper—and they owed it all to Hank Luisetti, the man on the move.

Hank Luisetti posing on a court with Stanford, circa 1938. A three-time all-America, Luisetti caused a sensation not with his dribbling but with his running one-hander, which radically changed basketball. (Associated Press)

Runners-up

1956: Led by Alex Webster, who rushed for two touchdowns and caught five Chuck Conerly passes for 76 yards, the Giants trampled the Chicago Bears, 47–7, before 56,836 freezing fans at Yankee Stadium for their third N.F.L. championship and first since 1938. The Giants wore sneakers as they did in another title game (see Dec. 9).

1978: The N.H.L. agreed to expand from 17 to 21 teams by absorbing the Edmonton Oilers, the Hartford Whalers, the Quebec Nordiques and the Winnipeg Jets from the disbanding World Hockey Association for the 1979–80 season. More important than the teams was one player the N.H.L. got in the deal: a skinny 17-year-old with Edmonton named Wayne Gretzky.

1981: Wayne Gretzky (see Feb. 24) blossomed into the Great One in his second N.H.L. season, scoring five goals to lead the Edmonton Oilers to a 7–5 victory over the Philadelphia Flyers. Playing on a different level than his peers, he brought his season total to 50 goals in his 39th game of the season—the most explosive offensive stretch in league history.

December 31, 1967
Freezing (and Winning) in the 'Ice Bowl'

By WILLIAM N. WALLACE

The Dallas Cowboys and Green Bay Packers played for the N.F.L. championship on this date under painful conditions: temperatures so cold that some fans retreated to their cars in the parking lots to warm themselves. Players risked frostbite, and a thin layer of ice covered the frozen ground on the Cowboys' last stand.

GREEN BAY, Wis.—There had never been a football game like this one. Everyone agreed—Vince Lombardi, the winning coach; Tom Landry, the losing coach; Chuck Howley, the Dallas linebacker who symbolized the losers; Bart Starr, the quarterback who scored the winning touchdown with 13 seconds to play. The Green Bay Packers, frustrated and punished for 40 of the 60 minutes it takes to play these games, won their third straight championship of the National Football League today by defeating the Dallas Cowboys, 21–17, before a capacity crowd of 50,861 at Lambeau Field.

The temperature was 14 degrees below zero at the start of the game and 12 degrees below at the end. And on top of that there was a 14-knot northwest breeze blowing down from the Yukon. "It was terrible out there," said Landry, "terrible for both sides. That in itself made this game distinctive from any other."

The fact that the teams, champions of the Western and Eastern conferences of the N.F.L., were able to play such capable football was remarkable. It was remarkable too that the stadium was filled and nobody went home before the outcome was decided. No team in the 47-year history of the N.F.L. has ever before won three straight championships. But the Packers came within 13 seconds of miss-

Boyd Dowler of the Packers grabbing a touchdown pass from Bart Starr in the N.F.L. championship game. The outcome was decided in the final seconds, when the temperature at Lambeau Field was 12 degrees below zero. (Associated Press)

ing this achievement. On third down from the 1-yard line Starr drove over right guard behind Jerry Kramer's block to score the winning touchdown.

This touchdown came at the end of an exciting 68-yard drive against the gallant Cowboys and the clock. Football players are mortal like the rest of us and they have fear. "I was scared we had thrown it all away," said Henry Jordan, the Packers' defensive tackle who played a magnificent game. Jordan and his mates on the defensive unit kept the Packers in the game by holding the rampant Cowboys numerous times in the second half. They made victory possible. The Green Bay offense was in trouble most of the time and had ground to a halt after opening a 14–0 lead in the first 18 minutes.

Starr, pressured relentlessly by the Cowboy front four, was thrown eight times while attempting to pass, for losses totaling 76 yards. But Bart and all the Packers have come back so many times from the depths of adversity. They did so again by mustering their last scoring drive with five minutes left and Cowboys in the lead, 17–14. The temperature was too cold for the "electric blanket"—the heating system under the turf—to work and the field became progressively harder and harder. This was to the Packers' advantage.

Starr began to throw short wide passes to his backs, Donnie Anderson and Chuck Mercein. The linebackers covering them, Dave Edward and Howley, who is an All-Pro performer, could not react swiftly enough to tackle the attackers in the open field. "There was no traction," said Howley. "The advantage had gone to the offense."

Starr passed to Anderson for 6 yards, to Anderson again for 12 to the Dallas 39 and then a big one to Mercein for 19 to the Cowboy 11. Mercein stormed to the 3. Anderson was stopped twice and then Starr tried the quarterback sneak to score. If he had failed would the Packers have had time to kick a field goal on fourth down to tie the score and send the game into a sudden-death overtime? Their timeouts were used up. "It would have been close," said Lombardi. "We didn't want a tie. We had compassion for those spectators. We wanted to send them home right then."

The Packers defeated the Oakland Raiders, 33–14, in Super Bowl II two weeks later in Miami in Vince Lombardi's swan song as coach. It was Green Bay's third straight N.F.L. title and fifth in six years, a record to this day.

Runners-up

1972: Roberto Clemente, 38, the peerless right-fielder for the Pittsburgh Pirates, was killed on a mission of mercy he arranged to help victims of a Nicaraguan earthquake when the cargo plane he had chartered crashed into the Caribbean shortly after takeoff from San Juan, Puerto Rico. He was inducted into the Hall of Fame in a special election the following spring (*see March 20*).

1988: In an 8–6 victory over the New Jersey Devils at the Pittsburgh Civic Arena, Mario Lemieux, the 23-year-old do-everything star of the Pittsburgh Penguins,

scored one goal in each of the five possible ways: even strength, by power play, shorthanded, by penalty shot and into an empty net.

1999: Brett Hull of the Dallas Stars became the 12th player in N.H.L. history to score 600 goals when he netted two shots in a 5–4 victory over the Anaheim Mighty Ducks in Texas. He reached the milestone in his 900th game; only Wayne Gretzky (718th game) and Mario Lemieux (719th) got there faster.

Index